Wilderness Alps

NORTH CASCADES CONSERVATION COUNCIL
Seattle, Washington
founded March 23, 1957

www.northcascades.org

Wilderness Alps

Conservation and Conflict in Washington's North Cascades

Harvey Manning
with the
NORTH CASCADES CONSERVATION COUNCIL

Edited by
Ken Wilcox

NORTHWEST WILD BOOKS
Bellingham, Washington

2007

Wilderness Alps: Conservation and Conflict in Washington's North Cascades
By Harvey Manning, with the NORTH CASCADES CONSERVATION COUNCIL
Edited by Ken Wilcox

Published by NORTHWEST WILD BOOKS, Bellingham WA.
Book and cover design by Ken Wilcox.
Text printed on 100% post-consumer fiber, processed chlorine free.
Printed in Canada.

ISBN-13: 978-0-9793333-0-9
ISBN-10: 0-9793333-0-X

Front cover: Mount Shuksan above the North Fork Nooksack River, by Pat O'hara.
Spine: Western larch turning golden in the fall, by Dave Schiefelbein.
Back cover: Senator Henry M. Jackson (left) conferring with Secretary of Agriculture
Orville L. Freeman (center) and Secretary of Interior Stewart L. Udall (right) at the
January 1966 Seattle press conference on the North Cascades Study Team Report.
Congressman Tom Foley observes from behind. Photo by Howard Gray,
courtesy of North Cascades National Park Complex.
Back cover flap: Harvey Manning in the North Cascades, courtesy of Betty Manning.
Background image: The North Cascades from Mount Custer, by Ken Wilcox.

Wood engravings at chapter headings by Gretchen Daiber.

Inquiries, corrections, kudos, and criticisms welcome.
For contact information, visit www.northcascades.org.

THE NORTH CASCADES CONSERVATION COUNCIL, founded in 1957, led the fight to protect America's "Wilderness Alps," also known as the "American Alps," terms that were widely employed by the media in the 1950s and 1960s. That effort bore fruit in 1968 when Congress created what many regard as the most magnificent wilderness park in the nation. Yet even before the Council was created, its founders and members-to-be were in the forefront of the campaign to create the Glacier Peak Wilderness—one of the nation's first major wilderness areas.

Through five decades, the North Cascades Conservation Council has been centrally involved in a host of successful park and wilderness campaigns in Washington State. It has also served as a very effective watchdog over park and wilderness management in the region—work that may be less glamorous than creating a new park, but no less important to protecting, for its own sake and for coming generations, America's legacy of wilderness.

You can support the efforts of the NCCC, learn more about its activities, or subscribe to the quarterly journal *The Wild Cascades* by visiting www.northcascades.org.

Looking east into the North Cascades from Custer Ridge.

A landscape is a complex entity of physical and cultural dimensions. This piece of Earth has a reality entirely separate from us, preceding our human experience and definition of it by billions of years.

—John Miles
Impressions of the North Cascades (1996)

CONTENTS

The original manuscript for this conservation history of Washington's North Cascades was written by Harvey Manning and was first published in 1992 for limited distribution to members of the North Cascades Conservation Council (NCCC), the National Park Service, and other interested parties. Manning credits the NCCC's Grant McConnell with the concise title of that early edition: *Conservation and Conflict: The U.S. Forest Service and National Park Service in the North Cascades, 1892-1992*. The book, said Manning, was intended to be tossed "through a hundred plate-glass windows" (figuratively speaking, of course) in order to "shake up a nation." That's how badly the story needed to be told. Unfortunately, he said, "I didn't hear so much as a tinkle of broken glass."

The work was updated in 1996 and 2000. David Brower, a long-time member of the NCCC board of directors, suggested a large, full-color exhibit format for the book and prepared a *Foreword* prior to his death in November 2000. In 2004, the NCCC decided to publish *Wilderness Alps* in its present format and won the generous support of many of its members, as well as the North Cascades Foundation, to complete the project. As editor, I substantially updated and expanded Manning's outstanding work to bring the story current and hopefully make it more accessible to a broader readership. Manning did not directly participate in the current edition, he said, "because the book was and is the property, physically, spiritually and intellectually, of the NCCC." Manning also asked that he not be regarded as the sole author because, he said, he was "magnificently assisted by other unpaid volunteers of the NCCC." If we did our jobs well, that elusive tinkle of broken glass may yet become a happy indicator of the book's success.

We were devastated to learn of Harvey Manning's sudden passing on November 12, 2006, and are saddened that he was not able to see the final outcome of a project that was dear to many. His immense passion for the North Cascades will certainly live on in these pages and elsewhere. And though it is difficult to sum up Harvey's crucial role with the NCCC in protecting these splendid wilderness alps, it is no exaggeration to say that the multiple victories for park and wilderness protection in the North Cascades might not have been won without him.

Harvey will be remembered as a pioneer of conservation in the Pacific Northwest. He once wrote, "In my immediate circle of mountain companions, 'conservationists' were so notably rare as to be objects of curiosity, and I used to consider their sermons on the mount as eccentricities to be tolerated and enjoyed as one enjoys a friend's odd devotion to yodeling or smoked oysters." But as his boots carried him across the landscape, he experienced first-hand the damage that was being done to wilderness. "They've logged my memories," he wrote, "they've cut me adrift from my human youth, they've left me no changeless wilderness to connect the 'Whatever-I-was-then' to the 'Whatever-I-am-now.' They made me what I am today, those Devils, and I hope they're satisfied. Because now they're going to get it." And with great passion, great humor, and great devotion, Harvey Manning kept to his word.

—*Ken Wilcox, Ed.*

ACKNOWLEDGMENTS

Accolades are due to the scores of wilderness advocates and conservationists who, for more than a century, promoted park and wilderness protection for the North Cascades; without them there would not be much of a story to tell. We are especially grateful to Carolyn McConnell for excellent and meticulous copy-editing of early and final versions of the manuscript. Her intimate knowledge of wilderness and national park issues, particularly in the Stehekin Valley, were essential to completing the chapters on Lake Chelan and Stehekin. Kristin Carroccino's superb editing of earlier drafts of this work, especially in terms of overall readability, was equally important to the outcome.

We owe special thanks to photographers Dave Schiefelbein, Pat O'Hara, and Tom Hammond for their outstanding contributions to the book's North Cascades image collection, as well as Dave Fluharty, Karl Forsgaard, Peter McBride, Tom Miller, Ken Wilcox, and Phil Zalesky. Gretchen Daiber offered her very fine wood engravings to begin each chapter. Historic photos and other documents were obtained from various regional archives, and we were generously assisted by Nicole L. Bouché and Nicolette Bromberg and staff at the University of Washington Libraries Special Collections Division; Kelly Cahill, curator of the North Cascades National Park's Marblemount Curation Facility; Jeff Jewell at the Whatcom Museum of History and Art; Janet Collins, Director of the Huxley Map Library at Western Washington University; as well as the staff of the National Archives in Seattle and the Center for Pacific Northwest Studies in Bellingham. Superb mapping assistance was provided by Peter Morrison and Hans Smith of the Pacific Biodiversity Institute and by Richard Edwards of Seattle.

Several NCCC board members reviewed one or more drafts of the manuscript or otherwise contributed. We are grateful to Polly Dyer, John S. Edwards, Dave Fluharty, Patrick Goldsworthy, Tom Hammond, and Phil Zalesky for critical observations on the manuscript, and to Kris Berger for rescuing the editor in those final, frantic days. Kevin Herrick, before his death in 2006, also offered valuable input. Kevin and Carolyn both contributed essays (in Chapter 10) which were previously published in *The Wild Cascades*, NCCC's journal of record. We also express sincere appreciation to Betty Manning, and to our pre-publication book reviewers, Joann Byrd, Brock Evans, Michael Frome, Estella Leopold, and Mike McCloskey, whose excellent feedback improved the work significantly.

Foreword

By David R. Brower

HARVEY MANNING IS JUST THE MAN to explain the opportunity that awaits the world in northern Washington and southern British Columbia. He has spent much of his life becoming as well-informed about the region as anyone is likely to be. More than that, he has been watching how people respond to such opportunities, subject as they are to human frailty now and then. We have augmented his words with what several very sensitive beholders have beheld with their lenses in this special part of the Earth's splendor, with counterpoint in words with some magic in them, and some maps to point out where we have been, are now, and need to be.

Harvey is a loving person, but he doesn't let love get in the way when people don't love a magnificent piece of land as much as he thinks they ought to. It's not that he likes landscape more than people, but that he likes people who like landscape—especially if that landscape happens to be the North Cascades.

I can understand this. Thanks to Grant McConnell, who introduced me to the "Wilderness Alps of Stehekin" that had become part of him—and he part of them—I became an early member of the board of the North Cascades Conservation Council in 1957 and never wanted to break free. I had a hand in making a film about the place, fell in love with it in the process, found with delight that my family shared that love, and inevitably encountered Harvey.

Both of us like Glacier Peak and its surroundings, were pleased that Lake Chelan occupied the deepest canyon in America in a very imaginative way, grateful that any place in the lower forty-nine had so many glaciers, and despaired of the Forest Service's determination to trade the splendor of its primeval forests for a far less splendid sea of stumps. Early on, a lot of us shared the dream of early explorers that this should be a national park.

As often happens, there were people who didn't share that idea—and not just people in the U.S. Forest Service. When Stewart Udall became President Kennedy's Secretary of Interior, Park Service Director Connie Wirth gave him a list of new national parks he hoped to see added to the National Park System. What we thought should top the list wasn't on it at all. We were soon led to suspect that, as in Olympic National Park, the Park Service didn't quite like trees. They were to be left to Manifest Destiny as defined by the timber barons.

That was one of many frustrations. One thing about frustrated people is that they sometimes have difficulty in being jolly. At such times it is nice to have someone around who knows what to do, in print, with people who interfere with joy.

Harvey Manning knows exactly what to do. Get irate. Get good and irate. And writing as Irate Birdwatcher, he began teaching people that it was a good idea not to frustrate other people. Diplomacy is nice to have around, but the jury is still out on whether diplomats have prevented wars or just made too many of them inevitable. A barometer is of little help if it is not allowed to reveal pressure. A weathervane can often be less useful than an anemometer; knowing where the wind is coming from may be less helpful than knowing how strong it is.

Knowing when not to be a mere zephyr is something Harvey is good at. And thanks to him, and what he says here, land managers of the future may see how best to spare themselves from a full gale.

Father Thomas Berry has said that we should put the Bible on a shelf for twenty years and learn to read the Earth. Thoreau didn't want the finest pages worn out before he had a chance to read them, and those he had read he didn't want torn out either. Jamie Sayen doesn't want us to ask what we want to save next, but what we want to trash next. Looking back at our humanity's tracks, wouldn't it be nice to insist that the trash list be extremely short?

We might also apply what Howard Zahniser described to me as "reciprocal irrevocability." If you build a dam, it is there, irrevocably. If you designate a wilderness, it ought to be equally irrevocable. And the more you designate, the greater the freedom of choice down the line. If it's wilderness, it can only be revoked once. When you sever the lines of the lives that are the essence and the institutional memory of wilderness, you've fixed what you can't unfix. Nature may help you get part of it back, but never the whole thing.

As Robinson Jeffers has reminded us, a severed hand is an ugly thing. The greatest beauty is organic wholeness, the wholeness of life and things, the divine beauty of the universe. Love that, not man apart from that. (Jeffers was talking deep ecology before they named it.)

We'll do well to remember this as we think of what the North Cascades and environs should look like when our great grandchildren contemplate what their great grandchildren would like them to be for their children. That adds up to the seven generations the first Americans were considerate of. Not a very long time, in the last analysis, when you consider how long it took the North Cascades to become.

Dream a bit about what will happen if instead of trashing still more, we determine that it's healing time on Earth, and we're not going to make birdwatchers irate anymore.

—*David R. Brower*

For Grant and Jane McConnell
and for David R. Brower

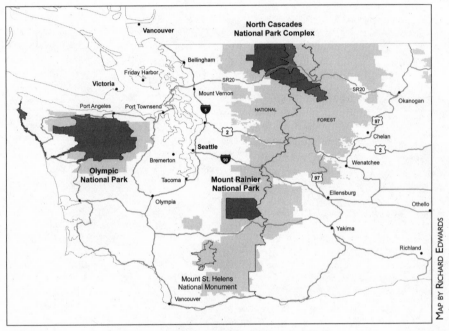

Washington's Golden Triangle of National Parks

Prologue

Be it enacted by the Senate and House of Representatives of the United States of America in Congress assembled, That there is hereby created in the Department of the Interior a service to be called the National Park Service, which shall be under the charge of a director, who shall be appointed by the Secretary. . . . The service thus established shall promote and regulate the use of the Federal areas known as national parks, monuments, and reservations . . . which purpose is to conserve the scenery and the natural and historic objects and the wildlife therein and to provide for the enjoyment of the same in such manner and by such means as will leave them unimpaired for the enjoyment of future generations.

—The National Park Service Organic Act,
Signed by President Woodrow Wilson, August 25, 1916

BEYOND THE GOLDEN TRIANGLE

IN THEIR JOURNEY WESTWARD from the Great Lakes across the Great Plains and the Great American Desert, over the Big Muddy and under the Big Sky, passing side trails to the Grand Teton and Big Hole and Gros Ventre, and to the Great Salt Lake and the Great Central Valley, to the Grand Canyon and the Rio Grande, the pioneers of the American Frontier gazed upon and heard about a goodly amount of sizable geography. Then, approaching Puget Sound they were struck dumb, or as near to it as a pioneer could be, by the hugest lump of free-standing American earth ever in view of a prairie schooner, so almighty high that the upper reaches were winter-white the whole summer long. Had they felt the need for an outside opinion, they (or their children, anyhow) could have quoted John Muir, who after completing the eighth (or thereabouts) ascent in 1888, proclaimed that "Of all the fire mountains which, like beacons, once blazed along the Pacific Coast, Mount Rainier is the noblest." His imprimatur helped establish "The Mountain," in 1899, as

Washington's first national park.

Mount Rainier was only the fifth such park in America, following Yellowstone, Yosemite, Sequoia, and General Grant (later absorbed into Kings Canyon). Crucial support for Rainier also happened to come from Northern Pacific Railroad baron James J. Hill whose trains might carry carloads of tourists there—that is, once he had swapped some treeless land-grant holdings on the flanks of the volcano for thousands of acres of the public's best timber elsewhere, which he did before selling much of it to Weyerhauser. When the government objected to trading glaciers for prime timber, Hill threatened to go into the ice business, but the public called his bluff. And thus Mount Rainier became the first vertex of what conservationists would later call the "Golden Triangle" of national parks in Washington.

The second vertex came slower, despite the oratory of the state's first elected governor who in 1889 announced, "Washington has her great unknown land like the interior of Africa." Governor Elisha P. Ferry challenged adventurers "to acquire fame by unveiling the mystery which wraps the land encircled by the snow capped Olympic Range." In Washington, as elsewhere, the frontiersman's fondness for scenery had two sides, the one an ebullient proprietary pride, the other a shameless proprietary greed. The great rainforest of the Olympics could not be seen by the timber barons, blinded as they were by so many board feet. Its fringes were homesteaded by the great-granddaddies of today's communities of Forks, Port Angeles and Hoquiam, and tens of thousands of acres of prime forest were quickly logged off. In the same period, a half-million acres of the Olympic Forest Reserve, according to historian Carsten Lien, were fraudulently acquired by timber companies colluding with the McKinley administration. For a time, the best cash crop of Olympic Peninsula Dan'l Boones was the Roosevelt elk, killed not for meat but for teeth, wanted for watch chains by the fraternal society founded in 1868 and at century's end burgeoning nationwide—the Brotherly and Protective Order of Elks. But Teddy Roosevelt's Boone and Crockett Club wanted the elk protected, as well as the forest, and they took their case to Congress in 1904, pleading unsuccessfully for the creation of Elk National Park. The elk slaughter continued into 1905 when public pressure forced the state legislature to impose a hunting ban. Then as Roosevelt's second term came to a close in 1909, he designated the last of his eighteen national monuments in the wild heart of the Olympics.

From front porches of Seattle in wintertime, folks watched the sun sink into the horizon south of South Mountain, in summertime, north of Mount Zion, and midway through the seasons, directly into the crags of Mount Constance, highest point of the skyline. It seemed apparent that parkhood for the Olympic Mountains had to come. By the late 1930s, four decades after Mount Rainier, there had been too many sunsets to be denied. In September 1937,

President Franklin Roosevelt paid a visit to Port Angeles and promised a park. Olympic National Park was so designated the following summer, assuring permanent celebration of the sunsets, the rainforest, and the elk.

The campaign for the North Cascades National Park would have been the lengthiest of the three had it truly begun, as the chronicles usually repeat, at the turn of the twentieth century. In reality, the gestation did not commence for certain until the mid-1950s and came to full term in 1968—stunningly swift for a campaign of such large dimensions, geographically and philosophically. In the wake of victory, the words and deeds of prophets and harbingers suitable for holy writ were sought out, but really, the first fifty years of intermittent calls to action never came to anything, nor led to anything beyond good memories of a worthy cause. For the generation arriving on the scene in the 1950s, everything remained to be done.

The most prominent failing of the North Cascades was that they did not stare much of anybody in the face, as the Olympics and Rainier did. Foothill and coastal hamlets might brag up their backyards but the newspapers of Wenatchee and Bellingham were not read in Washington, D.C., nor in Seattle. Nor did the hamleteers in those days solicit or encourage or desire or tolerate outside interest that might inhibit the orderly looting of said backyards. The railroad barons found no financially practical routes through the ramparts to scenery suitable for marketing in Chicago and Boston, and therefore didn't push their well-worn buttons in Congress, as they did for Yellowstone, Mount Rainier, and Glacier National Parks and other surefire ticket-sellers.

Though automobiles probed the range in the 1920s, for many years thereafter, the flower fields and glaciers of Mount Rainier, and even Yellowstone's geysers, the Southwest's canyons, and Oregon's Crater Lake drew immensely more Washington State tourists, to say nothing of those from Ohio and New Jersey. Few people knew much of anything about the North Cascades, presumably due to a lack of much of anything worth knowing. No roads traversed the North Cascades, and for the America that had recently gained the freedom of the wheels, what could not be seen from an automobile window did not exist.

A second major fault of the North Cascades was being too big to fit handily into an urban imagination. A Puget Sounder of the genteel class, which invented and fostered the notion of national parks, could wrap his mind around the compact uplift of the Olympic Mountains and the grand unity of Mount Rainier, but not until far into the twentieth century did the genteel mind expand sufficiently to embrace the thirteen thousand-odd square miles of America's "wilderness alps," extending north from Stevens Pass to Canada, and nearly from saltwater to sagebrush.

Third and finally, if the North Cascades were to be condensed into a single Rainier-like or Olympic-like symbol of essence, what would it be? Mount

TOM HAMMOND

Lake Ann from near Heather Pass, an unprotected area adjacent to North Cascades National Park.

Baker? Glacier Peak? Lake Chelan? The Cascade Crest from Park Creek Pass to Cascade Pass to Suiattle Pass? The Picket Range? All of the above? Was there such a central defining feature or was it just one big jumble of beauteousness?

To keep the record straight, there were prophets and harbingers. Henry Custer in 1859 and Edmund Coleman in 1866–68 eloquently described their explorations in the North Cascades, and as veterans of the true Alps spoke from the authority of an international perspective. In the 1890s a few of the hardier urban tourists began hiking prospector-built trails and dispatching prose po-ems to local newspapers and national magazines and journals. In 1917 Mary Rinehart's story of her epic journey across Cascade Pass appeared in *Cosmopoli-tan*. By the late 1930s, a young Bob Marshall, a leading proponent of wilderness preservation and founder of the Wilderness Society, had explored the Glacier Peak area at length and proposed a 794,440-acre wilderness area—then sud-denly died before anything could come of it. Nevertheless, these decades of now-and-then, here-and-there praise that flickered, faded, and flickered again, very gradually exposed to the world a sublime mountain wilderness worth saving. The knowledge stimulated a campaign that would culminate in the completion, on October 2, 1968, of Washington's Golden Triangle of National Parks.

Completion? Perhaps that's a good bit too strong. Indeed, a central moti-vation for this historical work is precisely the lack of completion. In 1967, testi-fying before the United States Senate Committee on Interior Affairs, a director of the North Cascades Conservation Council, who a quarter century later was to write this history, offered the following statement:

> If the Congress were to preserve in national parks and wilderness areas the maxi-mum amount of land that has been asked to date by any single proposal or by a combination of all proposals, the people of the year 2000 would say, "It is not enough. You should have saved us more." In 2000 they will say of the North Cascades Conservation Council, "You were too timid. You compromised too much. You should have been more far-sighted, more daring." . . . I hereby place on record my personal apologies to the year 2000. In our defense we will then only be able to say, "We did not ask protection for all the land we knew needed and deserved protection. We did, for a fact, compromise in the name of political practicality. We tried to save you as much as we thought possible." [H. Manning]

That was 1967. Now, in the first decade of a new century, the North Cas-cades Conservation Council calls upon Americans to come together to finish the job started in the 1950s—to help protect what remains of this vast and vul-nerable wilderness.

★ ★ ★

A reader may ask, "Why a book ? Why such a narrative of the veritable and verifiable facts? Hasn't the story been published over and over again in newspapers and magazines? Aren't they familiar to thousands upon thousands of Americans in the vicinity and across the nation? Don't government officials of the cities, the counties, the state, the federal Department of the Interior, the Congress have them in a firm grasp? The National Park Service's fine administrative history of the North Cascades, *Contested Terrain* (1998), ought to be adequate, no? The Park Service has been on the ground there going on four decades; surely they know the story well by now? Cannot a citizen simply query a ranger and get ready answers?"

The answers are no, no, no, no, and no.

The tenure of a public servant averages three or four years. Those on hand at the start of the campaign for a North Cascades National Park are long gone. Most of those now on the scene missed at least the first two or three decades. Only the North Cascades Conservation Council, commonly known as the NCCC, was there at the beginning and is still there, in the trenches, intimately familiar with the unfolding (both then and now).

Journalists work under the pressure of deadlines that rarely give them leisure to probe beneath the surface. An innocent reporter doing so in the North Cascades risks being scolded by his editor for raking muck; the Sunday supplements and travel sections don't want dirt. They want tidy little idylls of the colorful "Sons and Daughters of the Pioneers" who live, ostensibly, on the wilderness edge. Readers in cities of the North Cascades hinterland and from sea to sea are charmed by the idylls; the mythology they embody is accepted as gospel, its veracity assumed to be confirmed by its durability. Government officials at every level from Chelan County to Washington City (also known as D.C.) swallow the myth whole, most from ignorance, some for darker reasons. As for the National Park Service, the best of the rangers—and there have been superb ones—eventually have glimmerings that the official record is incomplete, but since they typically occupy posts in the North Cascades a mere several years before transferring elsewhere, they carry their newfound wisdom a thousand or two miles away. The less-than-the-best rangers (and there have been a few too many of those) scrupulously avoid such glimmerings, or at least acting upon them.

To be sure, our history is not written from the heights of Olympian indifference. We make no secret that we are in the field of battle and have a point of view, and we give due warning that there exists a strenuously opposed point of view. Our bias is up front, unhidden: we are committed to the national public interest in preserving the remaining vestiges of these Wilderness Alps. Hundreds of thousands of acres of relatively pristine, unlogged, undeveloped, unprotected wildlands lie adjacent to current park and wilderness boundaries, left out of earlier acts of Congress for no good reason, other than expediency perhaps.

Another thing our history is not is the self-pleasuring of the hermit anti-quarian. We mean to enlighten, if possible, and among the students we seek are those within the National Park Service and the U.S. Forest Service who might not have heard the whole story. We are confident that in their ranks are many of "the best" who when supplied those verified, verifiable facts will, from their first day in the North Cascades, recognize the myths surrounding park history for what they are. We would also hope to inform officials of the cities, counties, state, the Departments of the Interior and Agriculture, Congress, the general public, and, wherever possible, journalists.

Academic historians may find our work invaluable as a source, though they may deplore the absence of an apparatus. We have provided a bibliography and we invite scholars to contact the organization for further background or explanation, but in the revered interests of space and time, we have omitted the lengthy annotations that would be required to source every nuance of the story (if we have erred significantly, please tell us). The people of the NCCC were on the scene from, and before, the start. They mostly wrought the North Cascades Act of 1968, and what they did not do, many of them personally wit-nessed.

The fundamental theme of this book (and of several others recently pub-lished) is that the National Park Service and the U.S. Forest Service, by and large, have not always been satisfactory custodians of national-interest lands. As cockiness contributed to the strength of the U.S. Forest Service, meekness has been the Park Service's abiding weakness, causing it to pander to pork-barrel politicians, chambers of commerce, and others. One could argue, even today, that if the existing agencies cannot be drastically improved, perhaps it would be better to scrap them and start over. Recognizing, however, certain political ramifications and the fact that who's minding the helm matters considerably, we are not yet advocating such a radical move. But clearly, a more inspired leadership is needed—one that's seriously committed to the purpose and intent of both the Wilderness Act and the National Park Service Organic Act.

Our focus on a specific area of the nation may tend to obscure some larger issues of importance to America as a whole. For example, historians, academic and journalistic, have generally failed to digest or even nibble at the following huge chunks of red meat:

1. The 1968 North Cascades Act established the first new super-park in the American West since Olympic in 1938 and Kings Canyon in 1940 (Canyonlands in 1964 was much smaller than it should have been). After a lapse of twenty-eight years, this was the dramatic event that may have preserved the National Park Ser-vice from the fate, then impending, of becoming as significant to protection of

the American Earth as the Beefeaters are to defending the Tower of London from foreign armies. Without the 1968 Act, there might not have been a 1980 Alaska Lands Act, and there might have been little reason *not* to dissolve the National Park Service.

2. The 1968 Act gave the Stehekin Valley due, if belated, recognition as "the Yosemite of the North," recognition which still escapes the vision of too many government officials from Chelan County to Washington D.C. (Lake Chelan lies within the deepest glacier-carved gorge in the contiguous U.S. and one of the deepest in North America.)

3. The jurisdictional argument put forth by the NCCC since 1968 and elaborated upon in the 1980s by the Sierra Club Legal Defense Fund (now Earthjustice) was at long last, in 1991, accepted by the National Park Service. Officially, the Park Service clarified that it has the same powers in a National Recreation Area as in a National Park, perhaps the most important stiffening of agency spine since the administration of Franklin D. Roosevelt.

4. A lawsuit filed in 1989 by the Sierra Club Legal Defense Fund on behalf of the NCCC reverberated throughout the National Park System. Henceforth, to undertake significant planning action without subjecting it to a rigorous environmental review may entail serious career risks. In the past, to demand such a review was the riskier path. Early retirement became an alternative for rangers who could no longer endure the shame of submitting to decisions of superiors that besmirched the honor of the Park Service and Forest Service.

The community of Marblemount lies at the confluence of the Skagit and Cascade Rivers west of the National Park.

5. When the NCCC objected in 1968 to the raising of Ross Dam on the Skagit River by Seattle City Light, no opposition of the sort had ever been given more than a dismissive sneer by the Federal Power Commission (FPC). However, in 1991 a chastened Seattle City Light joined the NCCC and other intervenors in submitting to the Federal Energy Regulatory Commission (successor to the FPC) a proposal for mitigating the effects of Ross Dam and the Skagit River Hydroelectric Project as a condition of being granted a thirty-year renewal of its license to exploit the public waters. No such accord between power interests and the public interest had ever been placed before the federals. The precedent has and likely will continue to affect similar projects and decision-making across the nation.

6. The defeat of High Ross Dam was accomplished by a close alliance of conservationists in two nations. The American spearhead group, the NCCC, could not have won alone, though it expertly exploited administrative and legal recourses to buy time. Lacking this time, the British Columbia spearhead group, Run Out Skagit Spoilers (ROSS), might not have been able to mobilize its decisive forces.

7. These years of intimate cooperation between U.S. and Canadian conservationists promise a bright future for the Greater North Cascades Ecosystem that spans the international boundary. The defenders of the North Cascades are not localists or regionalists nor even nationalists, but internationalists, if not globalists. Geographical circumstances have given the North Cascades a historical importance for the peoples of two nations, from sea to sea. One intent of this book is to inform citizens of both nations what has been done here and of the opportunities that have been preserved and enhanced for those who come after us.

★ ★ ★

Before his passing, David Brower, a long-time board member of NCCC, made this request while commenting on an early draft of this book's manuscript:

Spread this book around. Add to its ideas and images. Celebrate the International Natural Festival you and your friends can introduce to perpetuity. There is nothing between Snoqualmie Pass and Allison Pass Highways the world can any longer afford to trash. Its wildness belongs to the future and knowing this you can enjoy it with deeper satisfaction, even with jubilation. Pass the word!

We dedicate this work to David and to the memory of Grant and Jane McConnell, whose inspired work helped bring a national park to Washington State's North Cascades—America's Wilderness Alps.

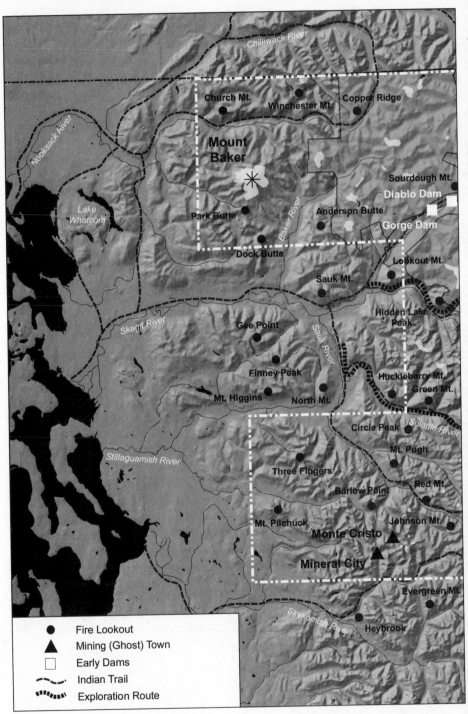

Historic features in the North Cascades.

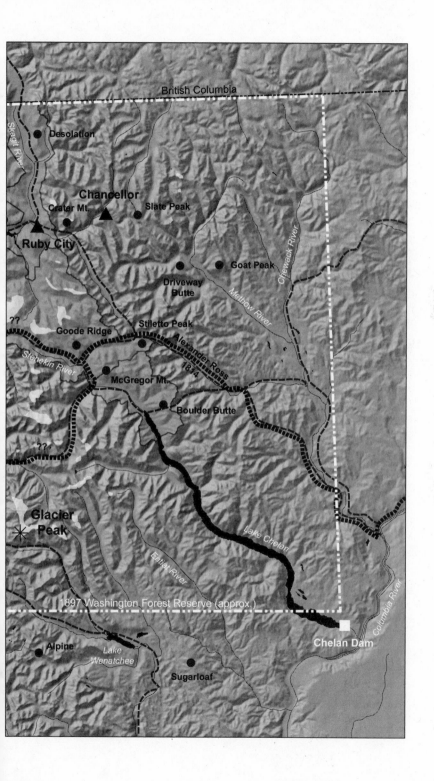

British Columbia

Desolation

Chancellor

Crater Mt.   Slate Peak

Ruby City

Goat Peak

Driveway
Butte

??

Goode Ridge   Stiletto Peak

Alexander Ross
1814

McGregor Mt.

Boulder Butte

Stehekin River

Skagit River

Chewack River

Methow River

??

Glacier
Peak

Lake Chelan

Entiat River

1897 Washington Forest Reserve (approx.)

Columbia River

Alpine   Lake
Wenatchee

Chelan Dam

Sugarloaf

THE SCENE LIES IN THE UNITED STATES ten leagues from the shores of the Pacific. The district is mountainous, its northern limits as yet barely defined by the two neighboring powers. A merely superficial spectator might call it the *American Switzerland*, with its abrupt peaks rising above the clouds, its deep valleys dividing the heights, its aspect at once grand and wild.

—Jules Verne
Begum's Fortune, 1879

1

Ice Age to World War II

So as we sit on a high ridge looking over the magnificent vista of
the North Cascades, [we] can count ourselves fortunate to have
been here when a unique combination of tectonic forces and geo-
morphic agents created a mountain range of incredible beauty and
diversity for us to appreciate and seek to understand.

—Scott Babcock, geologist
Impressions of the North Cascades (1996)

MANIFESTING A DESTINY

THE NORTH CASCADES RANGE is the product of a restless Earth, of tectonic collisions—a land uplifted high by the relentless eastward creep of
the Pacific Ocean floor, then carved into subtle and fantastic forms by
the forces of gravity, water, and temperature. In its midst, exploding cauldrons
and lava domes added their own chapters to the region's convoluted history.
Fossil evidence in sandstone, in the form of shorebird tracks and palm frond
impressions, suggests that a tropical climate persisted here some tens of millions of years ago. Yet the final two or three million years of wilderness purity in
the range—partly defined by the total absence of the genus *Homo*—were quite
chilly, except, of course, in the immediate neighborhoods of active volcanoes.
In the colder climate, snows piled deep in the highlands and flowed as valley
glaciers to the lowlands. Icecaps heaped to awesome depths in Canada and
flowed as continental sheets southward through mountain passes where peaks
as high as eight thousand feet towered above the ice as *nunataks*. Valley glaciers
and ice sheets melted back, perhaps disappeared altogether. Grew again. Re-

treated again. The North Cascades was sculpted into troughs and cirques, cliffs and arêtes and horns, defining the young character of the range. In time, a great forest alive with badgers, martens, lynx, bears, wolves, marmots, toads, newts, snails, owls, and goshawks spread into the valleys and up the mountain slopes. An ocean of temperate forest and rainforest was capped by a tumultuous sea of high meadows and wildflowers lapping at the barren talus and terminal moraines of hundreds of alpine glaciers ever-deepening their footings.

The ice was still at it (and to a lesser extent, still is) when the first pioneers arrived from afar, probably Asia. Recent archaeological work has revealed hundreds of sites of use or habitation by these pioneers in the North Cascades, located as high as seven thousand feet above sea level and as old as nine thousand years, based on carbon dating of artifacts in the vicinity of Cascade Pass. Native American presence in the North Cascades, according to archaeologists, could exceed ten thousand years. These millennia of humanity's presence made almost no real impact, at least nothing that could not be repaired by a few decades of storming, avalanching, and vegetating. Even the forest and steppe fires set by the Original Inhabitants to manage berry slopes and game animals had no lasting, discernible adverse effects either before or after the Originals had been decimated by the New Arrivals. Neither were significant marks on the land left by early European intruders, come to gather sea otter pelts to robe the mandarins of China and beaver hats to top the toffs of London and Boston.

Captain George Vancouver, in 1792, sailed the waters of the Gulf of Georgia (one of whose arms was Puget Sound) and named dozens of islands and waterways and then Mount Baker for the ship's officer who was first to spot the snowy volcano. At 10,781 feet, its summit is the highest in the North Cascades. But two years earlier, a Spanish pilot, López de Haro, had already sketched a chart showing the mountain during an expedition with Manuel Quimper. Haro's map called it "La Gran Montaña del Carmelo." The North Cascades were labeled "Sierra Nevadas de S. Antonio." But Haro wasn't first either. Local historian John Miles wrote that native tribes in the region knew Mount Baker by several names: *t'kuba* (Upper Skagit), meaning "snow all around"; *kwéq smáenit* (Nooksack), suggesting simply a "white mountain"; and words similar to *koma kulshan* (Lummi), which may suggest going "up high or way back in the mountains shooting"—a fitting description of the sporadically active volcano.

Barely twenty years after Vancouver's famous voyage, the notes and journals of early adventurers would be among the first written references to a place that would soon become known as the North Cascades. The name "Cascades" dates to 1826 and is credited to British botanist David Douglas, possibly referring to all the cascading streams and waterfalls found throughout the range, or as some prefer, in reference to the mighty Cascades of the Columbia River noted in the journals of Lewis and Clark and later inundated by Bonneville

Dam in 1937. East of the yet nameless Cascades Range, the famed trapper-geographer David Thompson completed a descent of the entire Columbia River in 1811, encountering natives near Wenatchee who had never seen a white man. His journal includes a hearsay description of Lake Chelan. Fur-trader Alexander Ross and his "Project of Discovery" crossed the northern Cascades from Fort Okanogan to the Skagit River (and back) in 1814—the first recorded crossing of the range. Though Ross kept copious notes, he failed to say much about where he was and thus his route remains debatable. It's probable he went west from Twisp Pass to Bridge Creek, descending to the Stehekin River, then up the latter to Cascade Pass. Soon, others would follow.

With the New Arrivals came the microbes and diseases that over centuries had established a symbiosis with European bodies, killing many but sparing a sufficient number to preserve hosts for the germ communities. Loosed on the unsuspecting Original Inhabitants of the Northwest, restraint was cast off, and the childhood diseases of London and Boston took whole families at once, even entire villages, so that by the middle of the nineteenth century the indigenous population was reduced to an estimated half or one-third of what it had been prior to contact. The social fabric might have knitted back together, as did that of Europe after comparable devastation in the fourteenth century by the Great Pestilence, had not the germ-carriers proliferated almost as rapidly and destructively as a measles colony. Moreover, a series of treaties having precipitated a series of wars, the U.S. Army got on its horse and galloped off in all directions. Uprisings and downputtings scarcely disturbed the peace of the North Cascades, though the name "War Creek" memorializes the military's hounding of a handful of treaty critics up from the Methow Valley to near the Chelan Summit.

In 1853, before serious trouble between the Original Inhabitants and the New Arrivals began, Captain George McClellan led a detachment of the Northern Pacific Survey on an errand of peace, seeking a railway route through the Cascades. Encountering native villages, these surveyors witnessed the smallpox epidemic first-hand. At the behest of Isaac Stevens, the new governor of Washington Territory, McClellan was to explore the mountain passes from the Columbia River north to Canada in order to pinpoint the best crossing for a railroad. From high ground near Mount Rainier, he found a good view north, seeing only a "vast sea of bare, jagged, snow-crowned ranges extending as far as the eye can reach." As the expedition pushed northward and eastward, the mountains remained "rugged and impassable." Generally avoiding the west slopes of the range, he passed instead along the south shore of Lake Chelan and its steep, towering mountainsides. Mountaineering legend and historian Fred Beckey observed in *Range of Glaciers* that McClellan was "the first to describe for the public much of the east flank of the range. . . . No one—least of all Stevens—had had a clear notion of how formidable a barrier the Cascades would be."

After the troubles between the Euro-Americans and the country's indigenous occupants were pretty much over (except at Wounded Knee in 1890), but not so certainly over that the Army didn't wish to know where to march should it have to march, several military parties penetrated the mountains. In 1879, Lieutenant Thomas W. Symons and Lieutenant Colonel Henry Clay Merriam canoed twenty-four miles up Lake Chelan to Stehekin, the latter coming by canoe again in 1880, this time in the company of an Indian chief. Symons was particularly impressed by the lake's "diamond-like clearness." In 1882 Lieutenant Henry H. Pierce traversed Cascade Pass, and in 1883 came Lieutenant Samuel Rodman, though neither he nor his predecessors to any particularly useful purpose. Rodman's party killed a few mountain goats, quite amused by their antics among the cliffs of Goat Mountain.

The surveys continued. The railroads were more substantial enterprises than the Army; their surveyors, unlike soldier boys off on a lark, were all business. D.C. Linsley, exploring for the Northern Pacific, ascended the Suiattle River and Sulphur Creek near Glacier Peak to the Cascade Crest. On July 14, 1870, he and John A. Tennant were the first Europeans to reach the head of Lake Chelan from the west, whence they proceeded up Agnes Creek to a connection with their earlier trip. (Alexander Ross of the Hudson's Bay Company had come near the lake in 1814, crossing the ridges from the east, but at the Stehekin River made a right turn up to Cascade Pass rather than a left down to the outlet.) Linsley corrected the Northern Pacific guesswork map of 1867, which erroneously placed the Skagit River north of Mount Baker and blithely proposed it as a rail route eastward. In 1872 the Northern Pacific party traced Skagit River tributaries to Harts Pass at the crest of the range. In 1887 and 1891, the railroad surveyors poked about Stehekin. In 1890 the Great Northern's man, John Stevens, took a look at Cascade Pass. Another Great Northern operative scouted Lake Chelan. Separately and collectively they concluded this was *not* the easy way to or from Chicago.

In 1846, after Great Britain and the United States split the difference between the Columbia River and "Fifty-four Forty or Fight," the boundary needed to be precisely marked at the forty-ninth parallel, not because a few yards or miles this way or that mattered much to London or Washington City, but because prospectors had to know which nation's laws governed their imagined lodes of gold, silver, and precious stones. From 1858 to 1862, two field teams, one American and the other Canadian, engaged in the Northwest Boundary Survey, erecting monuments on the line and exploring adjacent peaks and valleys. From 1901 through 1908, the survey was repeated.

From 1897 to 1899, fieldmen of the U.S. Geological Survey were in the

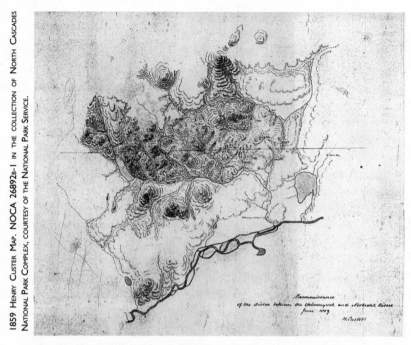

Oriented south, Henry Custer's 1859 Boundary Survey map shows the Fraser River entering from below, the Chilliwack River draining Chilliwack Lake, and the North and Middle Forks of the Nooksack draining Mount Shuksan and Mount Baker.

North Cascades going "almost everywhere, without making much ado about it." They seem to have done little journalizing, except for noting distances, compass bearings, and triangulations. However, the quadrangle they published for Glacier Peak in 1899 speaks volumes to historians experienced in map reading about what little was yet known about the region.

Explorers, surveyors, soldiers, and animal-scalpers comprised, in sum, the handful of European visitors in the North Cascades. The prospectors—would-be miners—comprised the main bulk of the invasion. A few, having got their noses gilded in California in 1849, transmitted the gold fever to a generation of dreamers, wastrels, loonies, and scoundrels. In 1858 they rushed to British Columbia's Fraser River, a few perhaps seeking a shortcut via Lake Chelan and the Skagit River. In succeeding summers, prospectors rushed again to the Cariboo and the Similkameen. It is reasonable to assume that a few strayed to one side or the other from stampede-beaten arterials, such as the lonelier boot track from the Methow River to the Pasayten River, and thence northward. However, the sought-after color in the North Cascades seems to have escaped substantial notice for two decades. Crossing Cascade Pass in 1877, perhaps the first prospector to do so, Otto Klement failed to report the rust-colored out-crops that later stirred so much excitement.

The next two decades, through the turn of the century, brought thousands of believing eyes to exult over every exposure of iron stain, the typical evidence of underlying iron sulfide, or pyrite. Though pyrite itself was "fool's gold," it sometimes contained genuine gold and was associated with lead sulfide, or galena, which often contained silver. If in quantity, the lead was valuable, then so was the copper in copper-iron pyrite (chalcopyrite) and the zinc in zinc pyrite (sphalerite); a later generation would value the molybdenum commonly mingled with the other metals. While scanning mountains for streaks of rust, hungry eyes did not overlook stream gravels. Gold was panned on Ruby Creek in 1878 and Slate Creek in 1879. Lode (hard rock) and placer (alluvial) mining spread from Index on the Skykomish River in 1882 over the ridge north to Monte Cristo on the Sauk River, where the railroad from Everett reached its terminus in 1893. Settlement meanwhile was spreading along placer gravels from the Skagit up the Sauk. Spillover into the northern tributaries of the Skagit had brought Jack Rowley and Karl von Pressentin to Canyon and Ruby Creeks where in 1879 "a hidden hand," said Rowley, led him to gold and the start of the Ruby gold rush. He left his name on a very big peak, Jack Mountain being one of the highest non-volcanic summits in the range. At 9,066 feet, it was known to natives as *Nahokameen*. George and John Rouse took up their Quien Sabe claim in 1885. A frenzy of panners returned to Ruby Creek in 1887, and in 1889 the Rouses and Gilbert Landre staked out Horseshoe Basin and Doubtful Lake. That same year, the *Belle of Chelan* began passenger steam-boat service on Lake Chelan to Stehekin, later joined by the *City of Omaha*, and in 1900, the *Lady of the Lake*. In a few short decades, overland (and overwater) access to the mountains had eased considerably. On the Stehekin River just west of Basin Creek, Pershall was thriving as a way station on the State Trail, a recently blazed path that had been improved so that horses could cross Cascade Pass, thus providing an efficient link between the Methow and Skagit districts.

The 1890s saw flurries of activity at Barron and elsewhere in the vicinity of Slate (Harts) Pass, North Creek, Railroad Creek, Thunder Creek, Miners Ridge, Trinity, the Cascade River, Park Creek, Bridge Creek, and a hundred or two other spots; from 1890 to 1937 more than five thousand claims were staked in the Mount Baker Mining District alone. No one will ever know how many rushers and drifters flowed south from the Fraser, west from the Methow, and east from the Skagit into the white space on the map. Journalists, who during and after the Panic of 1890 (and a worse one in 1893) urged unemployed read-ers to go out on the trail and get wealthy, inflated the statistics to make a better story. Monte Cristo was said to have a population of two thousand. Ruby Creek, which gained its name from a garnet that was transmuted by a miner's

L.D. LINDSLEY, UNIVERISTY OF WASHINGTON LIBRARIES
SPECIAL COLLECTIONS, LINDSLEY 937

Monte Cristo townsite, 1890s

alchemical eye, reportedly had three thousand to five thousand happy campers. The vicinity of Eldorado, located at Mineral Park on the Cascade River, was home, in summer, to hundreds. Stehekin, which in 1896 became the head-quarters of a separate Stehekin Mining District split from those on the Skagit and Slate Creek, was thronged to varying degrees, depending on whose report is believed. One census at the time put the Stehekin District population at five thousand. Naturalist-photographer L.D. Lindsley first visited Stehekin before the turn of the century. "There was newspaper talk about a thousand or more prospectors," he was once quoted. "Doubt there were more than 150, if that. Most were outside men brought in by newspaper stories."

Nevertheless, the decade of the 1890s was Stehekin's biggest for the better part of a century. Major John Horton, who arrived by rowboat in 1885 and commenced prospecting, logging, and shingle-weaving, earned status as the first white settler of economic substance. In 1892 Major George Hall began building the hotel he first leased and later sold to Merritt Field. The *Belle of Chelan* was steaming up and down the lake, carrying freight and passengers. In the late 1880s, the valley had just two miners and families as "permanent" residents. An 1892 issue of the *Chelan Leader* commented, "A year ago there was one garden in the whole valley. Now there are twelve on the north side of the river. A year ago there were four settlers on the north side and now there are thirteen, eight with families." The historian Robert Byrd wrote in 1972 that in the summer of 1892 there were more people on upper Lake Chelan and in Stehekin than at any time before or since. "Not only did Stehekin get a post office then, but one was established at Moore's Point and another at Bridge Creek." The handsome hotel built by J. Robert Moore on the alluvial fan of Fish Creek in 1890 became a favored haunt of affluent tourists. Across the lake on the alluvial fan of Railroad Creek was a less genteel settlement, Lucerne, which catered to the ruder appetites of a group described in one of their folk songs as "dirty miners in search of shining gold."

The mining never progressed past prospecting and stock-selling, the participants forming a very mixed bag of curiosities. George Logan stands as the quintessential postbellum prospector-cum-miner. From his camp near Park Creek Pass, he spent twenty-six summers poking about the headwaters of Thunder Creek, filling never so much as a packsaddle with ore; for his likes, the game was not in the finding but the seeking. Logan began his digging in 1896, the year Lawrence K. Hodges, a reporter for the *Seattle Post-Intelligencer*, systematically toured the mineral resources of Washington and British Columbia. His articles were gathered together early the next year in a book, *Mining in the Pacific Northwest*. So thorough was his work that to this day it remains a basic resource document for the geologist, not to mention the collector of old bottles and rusted-out frying pans. Hodges repeated the prediction he heard

Guests (loggers) enjoying a few creature comforts at the Skagit River Hotel near Barron in the North Cascades.

PHOTO BY DARIUS KINSEY #10264(B), WHATCOM MUSEUM OF HISTORY AND ART, BELLINGHAM WA on every hand, that the mineral district of the North Cascades was fated to rival South Africa. Over and above riches beyond counting, he pronounced, "The climate [is] peculiarly agreeable for travel and outdoor work. . . . No rain falls from June until late in September [and] snow has usually disappeared from the mountains by the middle of May." Thus, in 1896, did Hodges provide stage directions for an epic echoing that of California half a century earlier. The actors were ready, and the population of the interior North Cascades was greater than ever before, or ever after. But in 1897, the big news came from the Klondike, where the gold was in the ground, not just in dreams. Even dirty miners knew the difference. Most hitched up their galluses and got their boots in high gear for the North. Not Logan, of course.

THE GREAT BARBECUE—AND THE LESSER

Since Jamestown and Plymouth Rock the American policy on land had been to grab it away from the Original Inhabitants, or the Spaniards, or French, or whomever, and then to hasten it from the public domain to the private. In 1846 Great Britain and the United States carved up the Northwest between them. In 1854–55, tribes who had survived the onslaught of foreign diseases were swindled by foreign peacemakers, many of them manufactured by Colt and capable of firing six shots without reloading. These preliminaries over, the scene was set for "The Great Barbecue," the term applied by Bernard DeVoto, eminent historian of American expansion, to the period when some forty million acres—all but seven percent—of the State of Washington-to-be were transferred from the Original Inhabitants to the federal government and thence, for the major part, quickly into the clutch of New Arrivals. DeVoto and his friend and fellow Utahan, Wallace Stegner, became heroic voices in the call to protect the spacious beauty and wildness of the American West.

A parenthetical note may be in order about the fate of the Original Inhabitants in the Lake Chelan region. During a threatened hostility in 1879, it was reported that the Chelans could muster fifty to one hundred warriors, only a small fraction of their strength earlier in the century. Executive orders of April 19, 1879, and March 6, 1880, set aside the Columbia Reservation, better known as the Moses Reservation, bounded on the north by Canada; on the west by 121.01 degrees west longitude, rudely approximating the Cascade Crest; on the east by the Okanogan and Columbia Rivers; and on the south by Lake Chelan and the Stehekin River. In 1880 the U.S. Army built Camp Chelan at the lower end of the lake to oversee the reservation. The terms stated that "Chief Moses does hereby agree that he and his people will immediately remove to the reservation. . . ." Fat chance; in 1883–84 the reservation was abolished. One explanation is that the Chelans refused to move there. They could have had two valid reasons: first, most of the area was more mountainous than suited their traditional way of life; secondly, in that day and place, shooting Originals was viewed not as a crime but as more akin to varmint-plinking. Moving to the Colville Reservation offered a much more comfortable alternative, providing whatever safety there might be in numbers. Another explanation is that the land considered in 1880 to be useless to New Arrivals and thus suitable for Originals was very shortly coveted by the sudden influx of prospectors. However, under the terms of the Chief Moses Agreement of July 7, 1883, approved July 4, 1884, by the authorities in Washington D.C., several Chelans took up allotments around the lake and at other places on the southern end of the Moses Reservation. Under the leadership of Long Jim, about fifty Chelans who had been living on the northern shore of the lake and its outlet refused allotments, insisting they were a people separate from those of Chief Moses. White homesteaders, supported by courts and the U.S. Army, won the argument and the band of Chelans went away. An exception was the Wapato family, who accepted and retained an allotment on Wapato Point, now a swanky vacation resort.

During the same era, nearly a quarter of the state-to-be was virtually given to the railroads, starting with the Northern Pacific Land Grant of 1864. In proportion to its size, Washington suffered the most of any state—and suffers still—from these egregious handouts to the wealthy. Even today, the commonwealth agonizes over rationalizing the timber industry in order to preserve this foundation of the economy, while also rationalizing urban expansion to preserve open space in and around the cities. It is clear that we cannot achieve either goal so long as enormous acreages of the state are managed for the profit of heirs or purchasers of the land grant. In the 1890s the Populists raised the cry, "Revest the Northern Pacific Land Grant!" The demand has been repeated over the decades and still echoes loudly more than a century later.

The Homestead Act of 1862 provided that an adult citizen or first-papers immigrant could stake out 160 acres, a quarter-section, and gain clear title after he had "resided upon or cultivated the same for five years." The intent was to free industrious Americans from the iron grip of a tight-fisted Eastern squirearchy, thus populating the frontier with Jeffersonian yeomen. The result was otherwise. In the words of historian Ray Allen Billington,

> The story of settlement under the Homestead Act was not one of downtrodden laborers rising to affluence through governmental beneficence, but a tale of fraud and monopoly which only ended with seven-eighths of the public domain in the hands of a favored few.

He estimated that for every acre that passed into ownership of the "little man" under the Homestead Act and companion measures, at least eight were stolen, principally by "moneyed interests."

The Timber and Stone Act of 1878 was especially outrageous. Lands in California, Nevada, Oregon, and Washington deemed by federal agents (who were almost uniformly corrupt) to be "unfit for cultivation" and "valuable chiefly for timber," or stone, could be purchased in lots of one-hundred-sixty acres for two dollars and fifty cents an acre. Through 1945 (the law was not repealed until 1955), 2.2 million acres were taken by individuals and companies in Washington, roughly equivalent to a fifteen-mile-wide strip of forest stretching two hundred fifty miles from Canada to Oregon.

If the purview of this history were broader, vastly more spleen would have to be vented on The Great Barbecue of the Gilded Age, a period of private greed and public corruption not surpassed until the 1980s. But the heartland of the North Cascades, relatively speaking, was barely touched. The Barbecue there in the latter half of the nineteenth century was more on the order of a picnic.

The presence of the railroad entrepreneurs and their confederates, the timber barons, to whom they transferred much of their booty, in the North Cascades was not by virtue of the "checkerboard" blight that still afflicts the more southerly Cascades. A checkerboard pattern of ownership resulted when alternate sections of public land along a rail right-of-way were granted to the promoters through a lesser-known provision exercised by the Barbecuers. Under the so-called "Scripper Act," when prior preemptions in the designated railway swath left insufficient lands to satisfy terms of the grant, it would be acceptable to select lands anywhere else in the public domain. As far up the Skagit River as Marblemount the railroad exercised "scrip" rights: a timber company agent would scout out a stand of fat trees, the railroad would make the selection and sell the timber and perhaps the land to Weyerhaeuser or whomever.

The yeomen-homesteaders who had been squatting amid such stands were aggrieved that the "moneyed interests" could snatch the bacon right out of their frying pans, yet their own pretenses to Jeffersonian virtue were dubious. The homesteading typical of the upper Skagit River valley consisted of choosing one-hundred-sixty acres of forest, building a crude cabin that would be hastily occupied when the alarm was sounded that a government agent was in the vicinity, hoeing a potato patch five years, receiving clear title, then selling out to a timber lord and going to another forest to locate another homestead, or to a town to set up in business as a saloon-keeper.

Chronicles of the period lump all pre-emptions together as "claims"; research would be needed to establish how many were taken as homesteads and how many for "timber and stone." However, the latter required payment of two dollars and fifty cents an acre, and few yeomen ever accumulated that sort of capital. Swindles under the 1878 Act were typically grandiose and possible only for full-blown capitalists. Virtually the entire northwest Olympic Peninsula was taken by several timber companies and syndicates, the largest being the Milwaukee Railroad, Weyerhaeuser, Simpson Timber, Polson Logging, and smaller accomplices—a cabal boasting good connections to the McKinley administration. More notorious nationally was the corrupt acquisition of all but the entirety of California's redwood forest, a veritable theft completed by the turn of the twentieth century.

The bulk of the homesteading in the North Cascades region was done under the Forest Homestead Act (or "June Act") of 1906. Congress, in originally setting aside Forest Reserves, had closed them to every manner of entry, including homesteading. However, for many years frontiersmen had been chasing away the Original Inhabitants with gunpowder and germs, squatting on the emptied land illegally, trusting the government ultimately would accommodate them by changing its legal mind. In 1906 the Reserves (our future National Forests) were indeed reopened to homesteading, but under strict controls to halt indiscriminate settlement and the old-style timber-claiming. The newly established U.S. Forest Service embarked on a program to determine which homesteads were to be considered valid. The rule that was adopted allowed a squatter who had been on his chosen plot five years prior to the June Act to stay—but only for agricultural purposes and only if the claim held no valuable timber. Few of the squatters' claims qualified; of sixty-three applications filed in the Washington Forest Reserve by 1909, only five were accepted for patent. In some cases the Forest Service granted limited-term permits; in others it just let the squatters remain until they died.

In fairness to the squatter-homesteaders of the interior North Cascades, they tended to be a breed apart from the opportunists, speculators, and professional entrymen who so disappointed the shade of Thomas Jefferson and the upright Progressives of Gifford Pinchot's time. Largely, this was because they were too improvident to be successfully greedy, but also because, in the main, they were the odd men out, the sort who in an earlier age would have perched on pillars in deserts of the Middle East and communed with God. Their faults of diction and hygiene having been sanitized by time, they strike the modern eye as colorful characters, exemplary of the time. John McMillan, born in 1854, who rushed to the Fraser, then drifted south along the Skagit in 1884, set up shop at the foot of Jack Mountain, later exchanged his claim for that of Tommy Rowland on the Big Beaver, and for years earned his beans as a packer for prospectors. Later he worked several years as a Forest Guard; on July 29, 1922, he was buried beside the Big Beaver. Tommy Rowland, who arrived in 1895, dug a few potatoes, panned a little gold, ate a few bear, and at length revealed himself to be the prophet Elijah, was removed to the Northern State Hospital in Sedro Woolley in the lower Skagit Valley. "Old Jack" MacIntyre, a North Carolina Tarheel, trapped beaver and marten. William "Skagit Bill"

Pressentin was born on the river and was friend to the whole river community. Glee Davis' mother squatted on Cedar Bar in 1894 and ran a roadhouse, later legalized by a claim under the June Act; Glee joined the Forest Service. Bacon Creek and Goodell Creek took their names from 1880s squatters who garnered a few potatoes, a few pelts, and lots of fish.

Government maps of 1899 show a number of cabins on the Skagit, mostly unoccupied; four claims were judged "actually agricultural", only two "improved." The General Land Office tabulation in 1905 showed twelve cabins upstream from Marblemount on the Skagit, ten on the Cascade River in the vicinity of Sibley Creek, and five farther upstream—prospectors lacking the initiative to join another rush. Nascent Elijahs, perhaps.

The land that would eventually become the North Cascades National Park Complex bears the imprint of the Age of the (Genuine) Frontiersmen. In the western sector—the Skagit—the traces were all but obliterated by the dams of Seattle City Light. In the eastern sector—upper Lake Chelan and the Stehekin Valley—the very earliest Stehekinites were short-term squatters, a summer or two or three, then off to the diggings in the Yukon or to the shingle mills in Everett. A. M. Pershall, who catered to passing miners starting in 1889, received full patent on about one hundred acres in 1919, after his earlier applications had been rejected. William Purple homesteaded on the creek of his name in the 1890s. Keller received his patent about 1907, and Weaver in 1921, having filed in 1913. William Buzzard staked out his one hundred sixty acres the farthest up the Stehekin Valley of any of his contemporaries, and from 1889 cut cordwood for sale to the steamer and others and hoed potatoes for himself. In 1903 he gained clear title, apparently by purchase, which in certain circumstances was permitted under the Homestead Act. Later controversies of the 1970s–onward, mostly concerning land development, arose directly from these privatizations by early settlers.

There were other settlers of note at upper Chelan, such as Dan Devore, who after years of discouragement and unhappiness wandering the West came to Stehekin in 1889 at the age of forty and became the first horse-packer and furnisher of saddle horses. Merritt Field was one of the few to file for homestead entry, which he did in 1903, a decade after his arrival in Stehekin. Among the feats of Field in Stehekin was packing an entire sawmill to the head of Thunder Creek in the single summer of 1907; charging two cents a pound, he cleared $2,500, a fabulous sum for the times. This mill, never actually installed, with all of its parts remaining in packing crates, was the one fondly referred to from the 1930s to 1950s as the "Stehekin Hardware Store." Nothing was ever let go to waste on the frontier; scavenging was as socially respectable then as recycling is now. In 1902 the General Land Office inventoried Stehekin and found a community that was firmly established: a hotel (Field's), a post office, a schoolhouse, three residences, and two barns. A companion boom-town, Barron, located below Harts Pass, was a ghost town by 1910. Stehekin persisted.

The little mountain village at the head of the lake may be said to have had three historical epochs: the turn of the twentieth century witnessed the transition from "Early Stehekin" to "Old Stehekin" which lasted until World War II and a decade or so more, when "New Stehekin" began to emerge. This brief history of upper Lake Chelan and Stehekin, and the transition from Old to New, is important background for a community that remains entirely unique in America.

The most solid link connecting the three epochs, "Early Stehekin," "Old Stehekin," and "New Stehekin," was the Buckner family. Henry F. arrived on the lake in the late 1890s, and until his death in December of 1910, was manager for the mining company in Upper Horseshoe Basin. He and a thirty-man crew and their cook, Miss Lydia George, wintered in the basin 1909–10. Miss George is a mysterious and intriguing figure. Legend has it that it was she who skied the twenty-some miles through waist-deep snow down to Lake Chelan each week to collect and deliver the mail—wearing the long skirts of the day. A woman who would do that and winter alone in the mountains with thirty miners surely must have been quite a character. But when she lived in the

The historic Buckner Orchard in the Stehekin Valley

DAVE SCHIEFELBEIN

Stehekin Valley later as an old woman she kept silent about her life. Henry F.'s brother, William Van, bought the Buzzard place and planted a sizable orchard that still thrives today. In May of 1911 the Buckner brothers' nephew, Harry, emigrated from California, began wintering over in 1916, and through the establishment of the national park in 1968 and beyond, remained the backbone of the community—not that there was a whole lot of community left once the prospecting phased out and the economic base dwindled to a little subsistence farming, a little logging, trapping and hunting, quite a bit of tourism in the brief summer, and roaming outside in the long winter to earn cash money. The map of 1902–03 shows fifteen structures in the valley, including a school and barns. New homesteads were filed as late as the 1930s; old homesteads were abandoned or sold. The government count in 1935 found fourteen families in the valley, only two making a living from their land, one of them the Buckners.

A worthy research task (beyond the scope of this book) would be to trace the ownership of each and every parcel of privatized land along the shores of Lake Chelan upward from Twenty-Five Mile Creek and through the entirety of the Stehekin Valley. Which homesteads were legal? Which were approved by Forest Service rangers too tender-hearted to deny neighbors whose hearts were pure and whose backs were strong? How many claims, and which ones, were taken up not by impoverished yeomen but wealthy entrepreneurs who could afford the two dollars and fifty cents an acre required by the Timber and Stone Act? These questions should be answered to satisfy historical curiosity, but the research results would evoke little moral outrage. The Old Stehekinites were genuine frontiersmen, which is to say they were sly enough to bend the law, dodge around corners, and sneak through holes, yet did little lasting damage. That came later.

DeVoto's Great Barbecue would not have been half as much fun for the more ruthless exploiters had it not been for The General Mining Law of 1872, more or less the equivalent of the "letters of marque" by which pirates used to be authorized by various nations as privateers to continue their accustomed looting. Superseding earlier measures, Congress swallowed whole a body of law hammered out in the rough and rude and heavily-armed democracies of the camps. Mining areas were organized into districts, geographically cohesive units whose populations agreed to support a very specialized government. The law varied from one district to another in accordance with "local customs or rules." In general it permitted a person to claim up to fifteen hundred feet along a hard-rock lode and three hundred feet on each side by staking corners and registering at a government office. Placer claims, the basis for most patenting along river valleys and in such townsites as Silverton and Monte Cristo, had different but similar specifications. To hold a claim in perpetuity, the lode prospector was required to perform $10 worth of labor or improvements annually for each one hundred feet along the vein. By publishing notice that $500 of labor or improvements had been done and by paying $5 an acre, a claim could be patented, a process that gave clear title to the minerals, the trees, and the summer-home sites. Until the establishment of the U.S. Forest Service, patents were granted automatically with no fuss about proving the expenditure of the $500 or the existence of minerals, if any. Patenting became more difficult when Forest Service rangers began to reject fraudulent applications. But with only minor modifications in the 1950s—mainly denying title to trees on unpatented claims—the 1872 Law continues in force today. The law remains absurdly outdated, despite occasional scrutiny by some in the nation's capital.

The North Cascades Act of 1968 removed the park from mineral entry; the Washington Parks Wilderness Act of 1988 removed the national recreation areas from both mineral and hydro power entry. The Wilderness Act of 1964 allowed miners twenty years to do their darndest in national wilderness but banned new entries and new patents after that. However, patented claims in national park, national recreation area, and national wilderness lands remain fully private. For half a century and more, these ancient and often fraudulent patents were out of sight and therefore out of the government's mind and even out of the owners', who by the end of the twentieth century typically were two or three generations removed from memory of the claims. Then, as the nation's supply of land dwindled, descendants of horse-traders and road agents began roving the cities, the suburbs, the farmlands, and the wildlands, eyes peeled for privateering opportunities technically within the law, even if on the dark side of the moral line. The strategy of the privateer: espy ancient trees rooted in a cliff, trace the heir of the prospector who staked out the cliff, buy the piece of paper, and sell it to helicopter loggers. Then, note the traffic to mountain campgrounds, identify patented tracts suitable for summer homes, and away they go. This model has been used throughout the West.

The richest lode of all is the public pocketbook. Properties situated amid fine scenery have been acquired and ultimatums delivered to the National Park Service or U.S. Forest Service (with copies to the press to frighten environmentalists into agonized yelping) threatening to log, mine, or otherwise vandalize a national treasure.

The profits accruing through the General Mining Law in the North Cascades have been vastly greater in modern times than they were in that faraway past, when for every dollar's worth of mineral taken out of the range an estimated $10,000 (some put it at $100,000) was invested via grubstakes and grueling manual labor. A few miners emerged from the wilds bearing burdens of gold—in coin and greenbacks—bonanzas obtained by flimflamming greenhorns into buying their prospects. Others did quite well working the cities, in the manner of Wall Steet then and now.

The single instance of a producing mine in the heart of the North Cascades wilderness requires more than a mention, if only because of its singularity. An article in the March 1994 issue of *Washington Geology*, by Joe D. Dragovich, summarizes the history of the Holden Mine:

> In 1887 a rusty gossan, or area of weathered and oxidized metallic minerals, was observed by Major Rogers while searching the area west of Lake Chelan for a route for the Great Northern Railway. Rogers described the gossan to Mr. Denny of Seattle, who in 1892 outfitted J.H. Holden to evaluate the site. Holden staked claims in July 1892. . . . In 1928, Britannia Mining and Smelting Co., a subsidiary of Howe Sound Co., took control of the property which was explored and developed by another subsidiary, the Chelan Copper Mining Co. The subsidiary relationship was dissolved in 1937 and the Howe Sound Co. began production in 1938. The Holden mine . . . produced 10 million tons of ore, from which 212 million pounds of copper, 40 million pounds of zinc, 2 million ounces of silver, and 600,000 ounces of gold were extracted. . . . The mine was closed in 1957 when costs of operation exceeded the value of minerals recovered. The property was donated to a Lutheran church group in the early 1960s, and the town of Holden is now a church retreat. . . .

Holden Village in July 2006, dining hall on the left.

KEN WILCOX

J.H. Holden rates a moment in the spotlight of history. In 1893, Holden performed mineral surveys of Lake Chelan for the Great Northern Railroad and the Denny family, the founders of Seattle and chasers of rainbow's end. Compensating for a basic shiftlessness with industrious dishonesty, he gained that *sine qua non* of a professional prospector and confidence man—the dependably gullible grubstaker—as he poked his pick in the ground at Meadow Creek, Railroad Creek, and elsewhere. He located claims on Railroad Creek, and in 1899 incorporated the Holden Gold and Copper Mining Company, peddling enough paper to keep himself in some prosperity until 1918, when by popular request he drifted out of the spotlight of history.

That actual mining took place there at all caused general amazement. Several factors led to the mine's abrupt closure on July 1, 1957: (1) the safety record was hideous—the largest mine in the state was permitted to continue only through the bend-over backwards tolerance of state inspectors who were eventually compelled by a serious accident to bend over less; (2) the mine-workers union demanded better working conditions and higher pay; and (3) the paydirt was allegedly running out. It is suspected that a tidy tax credit was obtained by a charitable donation of the mine property to the Lutheran Church in 1960, after a failed proposal by a developer to turn the place into a resort. The church has made good use of the ancient law, operating a thriving, eco-minded tourist enterprise in a valley that, absent the short-lived mine, would otherwise be inside the Glacier Peak Wilderness. The Intalco Company inherited liability for the multi-million dollar mess that was left behind by Howe Sound, and studies and negotiations are underway to develop plans for clean-up and revegetation.

Another banquet site of the Great Barbecue of the North Cascades is of particular interest. Frontier-era law did for water what it did for minerals, putting every river and lake up for grabs by the first grabber. Decades of legislation that culminated in the Federal Power Act of 1920 permitted entrepreneurs to begin tinkering with Lake Chelan in 1892. In 1925–27, construction of a dam raised the lake twenty-one feet, converting it into a fluctuating reservoir. The elegant Field Hotel (among other things) had to be dismantled; its lumber was recycled into the Golden West Lodge that stands today. At low water, five hundred acres of mud-gray reservoir bottom—formerly primeval forest and marsh—are exposed at Stehekin. Prominent conservationists of the time, who might have prevented the desecration, may have carried on their consciences the failure to mount a protest. The crime against Lake Chelan pales to naught beside Seattle City Light's preemption of the Skagit River described later in these pages, a Barbecue ranking with those of the Colorado and Columbia Rivers. The city's main competitor for rights to exploit the Skagit was Puget Power, which was forced in the 1920s and 1950s to make do with dams on a major tributary, the Baker River—drowning the original and much smaller Baker Lake and most of the river and valley forests from the base of Mount Baker to the foot of Mount Shuksan.

It may seem petty to cite the Small Hydro Act of 1978 against a backdrop of big dams, but by guaranteeing a market and a profit to any entrepreneur of modest capital, this Public Utility Regulatory Policies Act loosed upon wildlands a legion of modern Barbecuers. Scores of North Cascades sites have been claimed. Hikers stepping into the bushes to relieve themselves are warned to beware of watching hydro developers, lest they find themselves hooked up willy-nilly to the Northwest Power Grid.

A GREAT NOTION ARISES

A rather scurrilous revisionist restatement of Frederick Jackson Turner's famous thesis on the American Frontier would hold that the manner in which the frontier shaped the American character was this: the empty lands served as a *de facto* penal colony to which the unruly and vicious voluntarily deported themselves, thereby permitting stay-at-homes to become civilized. Thus, the dregs of European society settled the American colonies, the dregs of the Eastern Seaboard settled the Midwest, whose dregs settled the Far West, whose dregs proceeded to Hawaii, where they now surf and hula, and to Alaska, where they racket about in snowmobiles shooting caribou, in helicopters shooting wolves, and in bulldozers carving their initials in the tundra. Needless to say, this libel is better accepted in Boston than Los Angeles and better yet in London, but hardly at all in Anchorage.

Whether or not it is true that the West brought out the best in the East, the West surely provided the East its favorite temples for the worship of Nature. Further, every city of the West (if not every mining camp and logging town) soon evidenced sporadic symptoms of Eastern civility, and even as the Great Barbecue was just barely passing beyond petty theft toward continental rascality, a reaction of holy disgust was setting in along the New England–San Francisco axis. In that light, the national park idea gained traction.

In 1864 Congress established Yosemite Park, transferring Yosemite Valley and the Mariposa Grove of Big Trees—the giant sequoias—to the state of California "for public use, resort, and recreation." Yosemite Valley, thereby, was not preempted by homesteaders, as happened to Stehekin Valley, but it was a very near thing. Soon after, in 1870, citizens of Montana Territory, the Washburn–Doane Expedition, explored the wonders of Wyoming's Yellowstone region. Whether through their impulse (as legend has it) or that of Northern Pacific wheeler-dealer Jay Cooke and his Tourist Department, Congress established

Yellowstone National Park in 1872 as a "public park or pleasuring ground for the benefit and enjoyment of the people." Ignoring, as is just, the claims of the earlier Hot Springs National Reserve in Arkansas, and neglecting, as is not, those of Yosemite, Yellowstone technically was America's first national park. In 1890 the small, state-managed Yosemite Park was enlarged into Yosemite *National* Park, one of three created that year in California; Sequoia and General Grant were the others, the latter incorporated in 1940 into a new Kings Canyon National Park.

Recognition of Mount Rainier was urged in a July 16, 1894, memorial to Congress by five outdoor organizations, led by the two-year-old Sierra Club. The club's founder and president, John Muir, was a member of the 1896 Forest Commission which, as one of its other recommendations, seconded the motion for Rainier. However, the creation of Mount Rainier National Park cannot be credited to poets and philosophers of San Francisco and Boston, or even Seattle and Tacoma. The checkerboard of the Northern Pacific Land Grant chanced to contain Rainier's glaciers, lava cleavers, and alpine flowers and the railroad was delighted to exchange this scenery for ancient forests elsewhere in Washington and Oregon. The park-generated tourist traffic also fed the coffers of the railroad, as well as those of hotel-keepers, restaurateurs, and the general merchantry, and thus the park was cheered along by chambers of commerce, newspapers, and the state's Congressional delegation. (The summit of Mount Saint Helens, it might be added, was also privately owned in those days, ultimately exchanged post-eruption by Georgia Pacific for a nice parcel of coastal forest.)

The Olympic Mountains, on the other hand, were handicapped by the lack of a transcontinental railroad. An 1890 proposal reached Congress in 1904, but the hour had not come for "Elk National Park." Events were unfolding nonetheless. In June 1906 Congress passed the Antiquities Act, which allowed the U.S. President to proclaim

> objects of historic and scientific interest that are situated upon the lands owned or controlled by the government of the United States to be national monuments . . . the limits of which in all cases shall be confined to the smallest area compatible with proper care and management of the objects to be protected. . . .

Three months later, President Theodore Roosevelt proclaimed Devils Tower in Wyoming as the nation's first national monument. Devils Tower was soon followed by the Petrified Forest and Montezuma Castle in Arizona, and El Morro's historic watering hole in New Mexico. The *High Country News* observed in November 1999 that while "backers of the Antiquities Act had envisioned it as a way to protect relatively small archaeological sites, Roosevelt deep-sixes that assumption [in 1908] with the designation of eight hundred thousand acres of the Grand Canyon as a national monument." (The Canyon was declared a national park in 1919.)

In 1909 a succession of game-preserve bills having failed to move, Washington Congressman Will Humphrey waited upon Theodore Roosevelt saying, "Mr. President, I want you to set aside as a national monument, 750,000 acres in the heart of the Olympic mountains; the main purpose of this is to preserve the elk of the Olympics."

Replied Roosevelt, "I will do it! Prepare your order and I will sign it!"

On March 2nd, 1909, two days before the end of his term, employing powers of the Antiquities Act of 1906, T.R. proclaimed 615,000 acres of the wet mountains as Mount Olympus National Monument. FDR made it Olympic National Park in June 1938. The thirty-year struggle to convert these lands from monument to park is fully treated in Carsten Lien's masterful *Olympic Battleground*, which in addition to documenting the history of a large tract of the American wildland also amounts to a psychohistory of the U.S. Forest Service and the National Park Service. (A reader of his book and this may find illuminating parallels.)

The preservation spark so ignited America's imagination that, by 1914 (two years before the National Park Service was created), the national parks already numbered thirteen. However, as the theory of preservation flourished, the practice languished. The parks were designated by Congress, not the President, and were miscellaneously administered by miscellaneous part-time employees of the Department of Interior. Central leadership, such as it was, was by one brilliant attorney, W.B. Acker, in the Chief Clerk's office. The U.S. Army assisted by expelling cows, sheep, loggers, and squatters. As perhaps the period's most respected and least corrupt government agency, the Army patrolled the people's parks and protected them from much of the rampant barbecuing of the 1880s–1890s. The First U.S. Cavalry was posted to Yellowstone in 1886; trails built in Yosemite for Army patrols are still hiked today. The last troops were withdrawn from the parks in 1918.

In 1908 a White House Conference on Conservation convened by President Roosevelt noted the sorry conditions of the parks. Secretary of the Interior Walter L. Fisher, deeply interested in parks, organized additional White House Conferences in Yellowstone in 1911 and Yosemite in 1912 to consider park policies. The American Civic Association recommended reforms.

Increasingly, the public was made aware of some of the looming concerns plaguing America's wild places. John Muir's passionate appeals for preservation reached all the major periodicals of the day and for many years enlightened the cause to those who might make a difference. Muir marveled at Mount Rainier, ascended the volcano in 1888, and advocated for its protection as a park. He formed the Sierra Club in 1892 "to make the mountains glad." In 1902 Muir, as poet, described a sunset at the yet unprotected Grand Canyon, "as if all the life and light of centuries of sunshine stored up and condensed in the rocks was now being poured forth as from one glorious fountain, flooding both earth and sky."

In *Our National Parks* (1901), Muir, as citizen activist, complained,

> our government has done nothing effective with its forests, though the best in the world . . . like a rich and foolish spendthrift who has inherited a magnificent estate in perfect order, and then has left his fields and meadows, forests and parks, to be sold and plundered and wasted at will. . . .

A decade later, in *The Yosemite* (1912), he blistered famously at the proposal for a dam that would inundate the Hetch Hetchy Valley in Yosemite National Park, "These temple destroyers, devotees of ravaging commercialism, seem to have a perfect contempt for Nature, and, instead of lifting their eyes to the God of the mountains, lift them to the Almighty Dollar. . . ." Muir continued to speak out loudly until the 1913 passage of the bill authorizing the flooding of Hetch Hetchy, a catastrophe that broke his heart—and, so his friends believed, killed him.

In 1914 Secretary of the Interior Franklin K. Lane received an irate letter from University of California classmate Stephen T. Mather, whose twenty-mule teams hauling borax out of Death Valley had made him a millionaire, and who now, at the age of forty-seven, was restless for new challenges. In 1905 Mather climbed Mount Rainier with a Sierra Club party. In 1912 he met Muir and shared his outrage at the violence impending for Hetch Hetchy. In 1914, touring Sequoia and Yosemite, he was appalled by illegal logging, cattle-grazing, and summer-cabin squatting. Thus his letter.

Lane's answer: "Dear Steve, If you don't like the way the national parks are being run, come down to Washington and run them yourself."

In January of 1915, Mather was sworn in as Assistant to the Secretary of the Interior. At Lane's suggestion he took on as his own assistant Horace Albright, a twenty-four-year-old attorney from California, and the partnership of these two men inaugurated the modern era of America's national parks.

On August 25, 1916, Congress passed the National Park Act, creating the National Park Service and directing it to "promote and regulate" the public use of the parks and to "conserve the scenery and the natural and historic objects and the wildlife therein and to provide for the enjoyment of the same in such manner and by such means as will leave them unimpaired for the enjoyment of future generations." Mather was named director.

That action by Congress riled a holy terror of a wildcat, namely the U.S. Forest Service, whose idealism and sense of mission were equal to those of the Park Service, but different. The Forest Service opposed creation of new national parks because nearly every one would have to be carved from the national forests. It successfully lobbied to defeat the initial proposal for a "Bureau" of National Parks, feeling that this term implied more power than a "Service." For his part, Mather was not what now would be called a "tree-hugger." In fact, he didn't want commercially valuable forests in his national parks and supported legislation to remove them from parks he had inherited, giving them to the Forest Service.

Why, then, was there an interagency feud, and why did it grow so bitter? Because, though the term was not yet invented, "multiple-use" was the watchword of the Forest Service, which felt just as capable of managing meadows and glaciers as forests, and fully able to manage forests simultaneously for board feet and hikers' feet. And because the Park Service felt timber-cruisers were not fit by training or spirit to serve as museum conservators. A National Conference on Outdoor Recreation led to a Coordinating Committee on National Forests and National Parks which achieved small compromises, but dodged the big issues. The Forest Service controlled the committee and dictated its recommendations.

Mather, however, belonged to a socioeconomic class not accustomed to being bullied. Using his personal wealth to pay Park Service employees whom Congress refused to fund, he recruited an admirable ranger corps and instituted an outstanding interpretive program. He hired a newspaperman friend as publicity chief, paying his salary from the borax fortune, which also plied editors and politicians with mountains of rich food and seas of fine wine. He took the parks cause out of the corridors of Washington, D.C., and into the main streets of America, staging a series of conferences and publishing a stream of leaflets. Exploiting literary friendships and publishing connections, in a single two-year period Mather instigated an astounding one thousand fifty articles on parks.

Another of Mather's sales strategies exploited the darling of the age, the automobile, which by giving America the "freedom of the wheels" permitted Nature-worshippers of moderate means to expand horizons from city parks to national parks. The dream of the urban middle class, which read the monthly *National Geographic* from cover to cover, was the Grand Tour of the National Parks, from Grand Canyon, Sequoia, and Yosemite, to Lassen, Crater Lake, Mount Rainier, Glacier, and Yellowstone. At each there was a decal for the car, a souvenir pillow for the sofa at home, and postcards for friends across the nation: "Having a wonderful time. Wish you were here." Soon, they all were.

The importance of automobiles to the development of the national park system cannot easily be overstated. The image of cars in parks spread rapidly as the narrow, paved, and unpaved roads slithered up the scenic slopes of mountain paradise, spinning the wheels of those who attempted them. In August 1911 (before Mather's appointment), President Taft made headlines in Seattle when his touring car stalled at Narada Falls during a visit to Mount Rainier

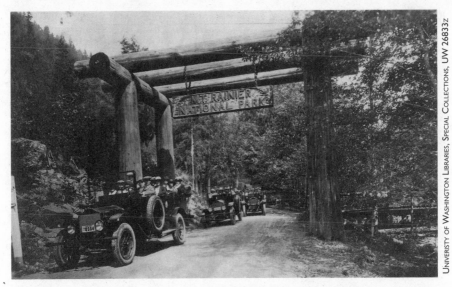

Auto stages wheeling tourists through Mount Rainier National Park (ca 1923).

National Park. The car had to be towed by mules. But the mud, the ruts, the rocks, the washouts, and the mules were all just part of the adventure.

Before Mather died in January 1930, he fought off a host of foes in government and industry and added twelve units to the National Park System for a total of twenty-one national parks and thirty-three national monuments. On Mather's watch, many of the classics were established (either as park or monument), including Grand Canyon, Bryce, Zion, Acadia, Hawaii, Lassen, and Denali. The tribute on memorials throughout the National Park System states: "There will never come an end to the good that he has done." Revisionist judgment in the new century demands that we also acknowledge the harm that was done through excessive development and a general disregard for what we now call ecosystems. Horace Albright succeeded his friend as director of the Park Service and briefly carried on Mather's work for a four-year term. Years later, Albright remained an active voice in the affairs of the nation's parks and reserves and was ultimately handed the Presidential Medal of Freedom by Jimmy Carter in 1980, as well as awards from Audubon and the Sierra Club.

VISIONS GROW: ICE PEAKS NATIONAL PARK

Whoever wishes to see Nature in all its primitive glory & grandeur, in its almost ferocious wildness, must go & visit these Mountain regions.

So wrote Heinrick Küster, who was born in the Alps of Switzerland. As "Henry Custer," group leader for the U.S. Boundary Survey, he was the first European to travel the interior of the North Cascades. His journals for July and August of 1859 were not excavated from government archives until a century later, retroactively to "begin the literary history" of the range, as mountain historian Harry Majors put it, recording its "aesthetic discovery." Old-country Alpine skills and New World bushwhacking experience took him to the first ascents of twenty peaks. If not the world's first wilderness mountaineer, he surely was among the earliest to know what he was doing, and why, and to be able to write about it. Penned Custer, "Nowhere do the Mountain masses and Peaks, present such strange, fantastic, dauntless, & startling outlines as here." Unfortunately, he was very long in finding readers.

One other early traveler combined a deep appreciation of natural beauty, a high degree of literacy, and sufficient mountaineering experience to have gained membership in The Alpine Club of his native England. In 1870, Edmund T. Coleman set out for Mount Rainier, mistakenly presumed to be unclimbed at the time. He assuredly would have reached the summit had he not fallen in with a pair of younger ruffians, true scions of frontier aristocracy; by stealing his equipment they kept him from the summit. But Coleman's place in North Cascades exploration, and in the mountaineering history of America, already was assured by his expeditions to Mount Baker in 1866 and 1868, culminating in the first recorded ascent, and by his writings, published in national magazines and in England's *The Alpine Journal*. Mount Baker, the highest mountain in the North Cascades, he characterized as "remarkable . . . for its beauty of outline bears a considerable resemblance in this respect to the Jungfrau, the queen of the Bernese range of the Alps."

Inevitably, people would find these mountains worthy of protection. The first recorded proposal for a national park in the North Cascades was traced by Robert Byrd in *Lake Chelan in the 1890s*, where he cited the *Chelan Falls Leader* for February 4, 10 and 25, and September 3, 1892; May 18, 1893; and June 7, 1894; and summarized in a footnote:

> It was primarily the early wanton slaughter of the abundant game along Lake Chelan that brought about in 1892 the first proposal for a Lake Chelan National Park whose proposed boundaries were roughly a large rectangle from the Chiwawa Valley on the west to the Methow Valley on the east, and from Twenty-Five Mile Creek on the south to Stehekin on the north. This early proposal was quickly quashed in favor of mining, railroad, and navigation interests which were rampant at the time but which never materialized.

In 1899 The Mazamas, a Portland-based outing club founded in 1894 in emulation of the Sierra Club, visited Stehekin. On March 10, 1906, its directors assembled at the town of Chelan to adopt a resolution calling for "a national park and perpetual game preserve" in the region, described as

> marvelously rich in natural beauty and grandeur, possessing hundreds of un-named snow-capped peaks and thousands of glaciers . . . the lake itself is a result of remarkable glacial work, being sixty miles in length . . . the white mountain goat, or Mazama, and other noble game are found here in abundance.

The descriptions in the club's journal must surely have introduced hundreds of interested readers to the splendors long since visible to, if not seen by, thousands of prospectors. A group of the latter and their townsfolk allies assembled at Lakeside on March 15, 1906, to adopt their own resolution condemning the park proposal. The Mazama resolution, they countered,

> does not represent the views of the people of the towns of Chelan and Lakeside, and the country adjacent. . . . we believe it is impossible to secure adequate protection to the mineral interests of our section with a National Park; therefore . . . we are first, last, and all the time opposed to the proposition to establish a National Park to take in any portion of Lake Chelan or the country adjacent thereto.

Also in 1906 Julian Itter, an adventurous young Canadian artist who had come to Seattle in 1904 and in 1905 had made his way up Lake Chelan to the Cascade Crest, opened an exhibition in January (in Seattle) of his wilderness paintings that caused something of a sensation. Supported by enthusiasts in the community, including the Seattle Chamber of Commerce, he set out for Washington City, the nation's capital, to propose to President Roosevelt a national park including Lake Chelan, Glacier Peak, and the area between Cascade Pass and the Skagit. He received such acclaim in Spokane and elsewhere that he decided to remain in the state and enlist grassroots support. He did so, but stirred such a bitter, slanderous attack by mining interests that he faltered and gave it up.

In following years the *Wenatchee Daily World* for a time declared on its masthead: "A few miles to the west and northwest, fifty miles wide and one hundred miles long, extends the premier scenic wonderland of western America, challenging in grandeur any and all national parks in the United States."

In 1916, or thereabouts, Stephen Mather thought about studying the area and went so far as to plan a trip to Glacier Peak, entering the wilderness via Lake Chelan, but the plans were cancelled and, as noted below, the result of his non-study was negative.

In 1917 Mary Roberts Rinehart wrote up for *Cosmopolitan Magazine* her packtrain journey through Cascade Pass—thirty-one horses and nineteen people, including L.D. Lindsley who she described as a "lover of all that is wild, a young man who has spent years wandering through the mountains around Chelan, camera and gun at hand, the gun never raised against the wild creatures but used to shoot away tree branches that interfere with pictures." Dan Devore was "our chief guide and outfitter . . . all soul and courage." They packed enough guns to "to meet the whole German Army." The trip was sponsored by the Great Northern Railway to drum up tourist traffic. "When the news that we had got over the pass penetrated to the settlements," she wrote, "a pack-outfit started over Cascade Pass in our footsteps to take supplies to a miner. They killed three horses on that same trail, and I believe gave it up in the end." She expected that by the next year there would be "a passable trail" to Doubtful Lake and "up that eight-hundred-foot mountain wall" to the pass. She also predicted that "perhaps before this is published, the Chelan National Forest will have been made a national park. It ought to be. It is superb." But the railroads apparently had already lost their omnipotent influence in Congress.

In 1919 the hotel and restaurant industry of Spokane, through the Chamber of Commerce, supported a park. From 1919 to 1921, three bills were introduced in Congress for a Yakima National Park farther south in the range. In the early 1920s, the Mount Baker Club in Bellingham predicted early passage of their bill, beached in Congress since 1915, for a park centered on Mount Baker. The Mazamas pursued the same goal earlier, from 1909 to final frustration in 1917, when the nation's attention turned to war.

In his landmark 1929 book, *Our Vanishing Forest Reserves*, Willard Van Name strongly recommended a park. Van Name was curator of marine invertebrates at the American Museum of Natural History in New York. He was a strong advocate for wildlife protection and frequent visitor to the Pacific Northwest.

In the late 1920s and early 1930s, the Board of Trustees of The Mountaineers, a prominent outdoor club founded in Seattle in 1906, passed several motions concerning a park in the Glacier Peak area, but that was as far as the club went. After its initial fervor for preserving natural beauty, the organization was for many decades content to encourage climbing and to enjoy a comfortable pleasuring in the natural scene. Independently of the club as a whole, its Everett Branch was notably vigilant in defending the White Chuck River from logging. In 1927 the Everett folk formed the Glacier Peak Association, led by Stuart Herz. In 1932 they sent John Lehman to the annual convention of the Federation of Western Outdoor Clubs to proselytize for a park in the White Chuck Valley and on Glacier Peak.

The National Park Service, however, was not a friend of new parks in the Northwest. As a businessman, Mather opposed expansion of the park system where it would lock up valuable resources. In 1923 he flatly opposed parks centered on Mount Baker, Mount Adams, and Mount Olympus. Albright was quoted as asking why his people would want to bother with the likes of Glacier Peak and Mount Baker when they already had Mount Rainier?

An explanation, if not a defense, of Park Service skepticism is that the boosters for local prides and joys and constituent-flattering Congressmen poured

108 bills for new parks into the hopper between 1919 and 1970. Thirteen bills were introduced in 1916 alone, some described by Mather as "fairly dreadful." Opposing such frights was described in the Park Service as "keeping out the dead cats." Albert Fall, Secretary of the Interior, promoted an "All Year National Park," an apparent precursor to Disneyland. Fortunately, by handing over Wyoming's Teapot Dome to his cronies in the oil business, Fall removed himself from office. The worst of the dead cats was Hot Springs National Park, a 1921 redesignation of the 1855 Reserve, which consisted solely of a bit of Arkansas hot water, itself protected from privatization, but entirely surrounded by eateries, sleeperies, and knickknackeries with nothing "national" or "park" about them. That astonishing action was reportedly instigated by Mather.

For chartering and nurturing the National Park System, Mather and Albright cannot be too much thanked and honored, but they also must be called to account for some failures of vision. They fashioned a collection of "America's crown jewels," parks kept small to permit the economical production of tourist-hours that were essential to winning the popularity war with the Forest Service. In so doing they did not provide for or foresee an American population that would double in a half-century. In plumping for the automobile as their transport of choice, they seemed to turn a deaf ear to contemporary predictions that the freedom of the wheels inevitably would degrade into an iron tyranny on

Camp Serene near Index, Washington (ca. 1926).

LEE PICKETT, UNIVERSITY OF WASHINGTON LIBRARIES, SPECIAL COLLECTIONS, PICKETT 3219

wheels. Even Muir had warned against the motor car in *The Yosemite* (1912):

> Doubtless, under certain precautionary restrictions, these useful, progressive, blunt-nosed mechanical beetles will hereafter be allowed to puff their way into all the parks and mingle their gas-breath with the breath of pines and waterfalls. . . .

Finally, the Mather–Albright emphasis on roadside interpretation—and more roads—tilted the internal balance of the Park Service toward frontcountry people-pleasing and away from backcountry wilderness protection.

Mount Rainier National Park was enlarged several times in the Mather–Albright era, including the 1931 transfer of national forest lands eastward to the Cascade Crest. The increments were not sought for the sake of a Greater Mount Rainier Ecosystem, but to accommodate a highway circling The Mountain within park boundaries—a scheme eventually defeated by geography and economics, though not before the Stevens Canyon Road had been bulldozed through the park's largest wilderness. The Mather–Albright park boasted the largest single-peak glacier system in the lower forty-eight states, ringed nearly around by millions of stumps. An ecosystem was, to that Park Service generation, just another dead cat.

Documents excavated from federal archives by Carsten Lien established conclusively that the superbly large Olympic National Park created in 1938 was the handiwork of President Franklin D. Roosevelt, Secretary of the Interior Harold L. Ickes, the Eastern-based Emergency Conservation Committee (Rosalie Edge, Willard Van Name, and Irving Brant), a handful of Washington state citizens, notably the Seattle conservationist, Irving Clark, Sr., and the Washington Congressmen influenced by Clark. It was *not* the work of the Park Service. That agency had just arrived on the Olympic scene in 1933, when President Roosevelt transferred to it the national monuments, including Mount Olympus, previously administered by the Forest Service. Thereafter, from Port Angeles headquarters to the national office in Washington, D.C., the Park Service labored assiduously, yoked up with the Forest Service and the timber industry, to exclude the rainforests that were soon to become the park's chief and unique international boast. In the regional offices at San Francisco, however, George Collins and regional biologist Lowell Sumner sounded this alarm to the Sierra Club. David Brower produced a special issue of the *Sierra Club Bulletin*, illustrated with telling Sumner photographs that shot down the Park Service plan to eliminate those forests from the park's boundaries.

Under Franklin D. Roosevelt, the most preservation-minded of presidents, and Harold Ickes, one of the very few Interior Secretaries who have served as other than chief chef of the Great Barbecue, the North Cascades was about to receive a careful and caring look. After years of active interest in protecting various bits of the North Cascades, came a hint of a payoff. As part of a study

1937 CASCADES ICE PEAKS NATIONAL PARK PROPOSAL

NORTH CASCADES CONSERVATION COUNCIL

Ice Peaks National Park, proposed by the NPS in 1937. The NCCC's later proposals for a North Cascades National Park (encompassing Glacier Peak and the Stehekin River) and Chelan National Mountain Recreation Area are also shown.

of public lands by FDR's National Resources Planning Board, which picked up where the first Roosevelt's Conservation Commission had left off, the Park Service was ordered to survey possible additions to the National Park System. Arno Cammerer, director of the National Park Service, appointed a special committee headed by O.A. Tomlinson, superintendent of Mount Rainier National Park, to investigate the Cascades. From August 18 to September 11, 1937, field teams scouted two hundred fifty miles along Washington's Cascade Crest, from Mount Saint Helens to the Canadian border. The report of November 1937, having delineated a preliminary proposal, declared

> Such a Cascade park will outrank in its scenic, recreational and wildlife values, any existing national park and any other possibility for such a park within the United States. Establishment of this area as one superb park is an inspiring project to fire the imagination, worthy of the nation's effort. . . .

Indeed. Further boundary studies took place the next year, culminating in the Ice Peaks National Park proposal of 1940. Spanning the breadth of the range on the north—a hundred miles wide at the boundary with British Columbia—the protected area would have quickly narrowed to thirty miles, then twenty, then ten or less to a wider bulge at Mount Rainier, then wider still to encompass Mount Saint Helens and Mount Adams, stopping just twenty-five miles short of the Columbia River. This was to be no Mather–Albright jewel park, but one in a new Roosevelt–Ickes generation of super-parks on the Olympic model. However, before the park proposal was made public, the Washington State Planning Council, an inflated fraternity of mining, lumbering, and other exploiter interests who fought hard and failed to stop the creation of Olympic National Park, hastily organized a formidable opposition to Ice Peaks in the summer of 1940. The Council conducted its own "study," then staged rallies, misrepresented as public hearings. Audiences of curious citizens who attended to learn what was going on were shown a map of the state's national forests and left to infer that *that* was the proposed park.

Prior to public exposition and supposed discussion of the Planning Council's "Cascade Mountains Study," five thousand leaflets were already printed, and radio scripts prepared for all the larger stations of the state reporting the Council's decision—already made in a closed meeting—"that no additional lands of the Cascade Mountains be converted into use as a national park." The full report, a fifty-six-page book, was a masterful exercise in the now familiar Big Lie technique.

The National Park Service Director ironically answered the Planning Council, "I note your statement that the data supplied by our field representatives was of great value to you in compiling this report. At the same time, I am aware of the fact that you included in your report none of that valuable data. . . ."

Ickes, in his response to an article in the July 1940 issue of *Mining World*, was more blunt, "I suggest that before you printed this obviously biased attack on the Department of the Interior you might have attempted to ascertain the facts from any authorized representative of the Department. . . ."

As it happened, history was stacked against the Ice Peaks proposal. Roosevelt was preoccupied with preparing America for its inevitable entry into another World War. Olympic National Park was already under counterattack by the reducers; the forest exploiters who had suffered a stunning defeat there weren't about to stand still for a one-two punch. The citizen defenders of the land did not distinguish themselves as a group. The Sierra Club did not advocate for the proposal and The Mountaineers generally sat out the battle, except for its noble little Everett Branch, which vocally supported the grand park proposal.

As World War II swallowed up the idealism and energy of America, there was nothing to show in the North Cascades for all the talk about a national park. Zero, naught, a nullity. Nothing solid and lasting had been accomplished. In effect, everything remained to be done.

Still, the specter of the Park Service had hovered over the North Cascades for half a century. If it never had touched down, it certainly gave the Forest Service something to worry about when it awoke at night in a sweat and couldn't get back to sleep.

THE GREATEST GOOD OF THE GREATEST NUMBER

Twice in the history of the nation the forests of the West have been of deep concern to the East and its colonies of civility scattered through the heartland of Barbecueism. The second occasion began in the final years of the twentieth century and continues now; the first was in the latter decades of the nineteenth for which some further elaboration is in order.

During the administration of President Ulysses S. Grant from 1869 to 1877, investigators later estimated that $40 million in timber was stolen from public lands in the Territory of Washington. In 1875 the American Forestry Association was formed to spur action, and under its stimulus colleges began to offer courses about trees, mainly their identification. In 1879 Carl Schurz, an anomaly among Secretaries of the Interior since he was not a co-conspirator but a sworn enemy of the Barbecuers, warned that even greater crimes were being plotted. The public conscience stirred by Schurz and fellow reformers met fierce opposition from the entrenched corruption of the West. In 1891 these public-minded reformers sneakily attached to another bill a rider later referred to as the "Forest Reserve Act." Once it was law, the president was authorized to set aside by proclamation—no Congressional consultation or approval required—forest land in the public domain that was "wholly or in part covered with timber or undergrowth, whether of commercial value or not, as public reservations." President Benjamin Harrison instantly proclaimed the first reserve and others in the next years. In 1893 President Grover Cleveland set aside the Pacific Forest Reserve centered on Mount Rainier.

The hastily contrived rider had two serious flaws that antagonized two separate groups who were themselves antagonists. Western pioneers complained that the act made no provision for any use whatsoever of a reserve. Just sitting there growing plants and animals it was obviously useless. Eastern reformers, on the other hand, were outraged that the act made no provision for enforcement or administration. The Westerners just kept on using and abusing the public domain as before. When William Andrew Jackson Sparks, possibly the only honest man ever to hold the post of U.S. Public Lands Commissioner, went after the crooks and revested eighty million acres fraudulently preempted, Congress got him fired.

At the urging of the American Forestry Association, the Secretary of Interior asked the National Academy of Science to sponsor a commission to study the situation. Seven men were appointed, including Gifford Pinchot, a wealthy and well-connected youth, and John Muir, then in his late fifties. In the summer of 1896, the commission toured the West, recommending in its report the creation of two national parks—Rainier and Grand Canyon—and thirteen forest reserves. In February of 1897, his administration ten days from ending, President Cleveland proclaimed reserves in seven states totaling 21.2 million acres, the largest single set-aside in the history of the nation. Washington got three of these creations: the Olympic, the Rainier (encompassing the former Pacific Reserve), and the Washington Forest Reserve in the North Cascades.

The howl from the West rose to such a fury that on June 4, 1897, Congress passed the Sundry Civil Service Act, to which had been tacked on the Pettigrew Amendment, later dignified by referring to it as the "Organic Act" and hailing it as "the Magna Carta of American forestry." The presidential authority to make reserves was affirmed, a provision that pleased Eastern reformers but didn't frighten Westerners so long as the White House was occupied by William McKinley, who in his term added only seven million acres of reserves, but also removed 750,000 acres from the Olympic Reserve to allow their preemption for logging. The act further gratified land-grabbers by suspending the existing reserves for one year, except in Muir's California, and returning them to the public domain, up for grabs. Additionally, the Act contained a "lieu-land clause" which entitled any person owning land within a federal reserve to trade for an equal acreage elsewhere in the public domain outside the reserves. Ostensibly intended to succor the lonesome homesteader cut off from fellow yeomen, the clause was almost exclusively exploited to exchange rock, ice, worthless mining claims, and clearcuts for fat forests. The Northern Pacific Railroad took one hundred thousand acres in Washington alone, not counting the later "scripping" for Mount Rainier, which accounts for much of the Northern Pacific/Weyerhaeuser presence beyond the limits of the checkerboard, including privatized forest land in the Skagit River watershed.

The act failed to resolve the problem of administration. Management of the reserves was left in the Department of the Interior under its General Land Office, the hot kitchen of the Barbecuers. The U.S. Geological Survey was charged with mapping the reserves, a task it set about efficiently, nobly, and often heroically, if quietly. The Division of Forestry in the Department of Agriculture was assigned to provide technical advice. The arrangement was unsatisfactory, even granting that many Land Office employees were as upright as circumstances permitted and as a group seem to have done a fairly decent job of halting illegal logging and grazing, frustrating fraud, and expelling squatters. They worked primarily in near-urban areas, where the thieves were thickly settled. The interiors of the reserves were largely as unknown to the Land Office as to the thieves, prospectors not then being considered members of the criminal class. Still, the forests remained in trouble. But help was on the way.

Gifford Pinchot, a patrician Progressive and, to be redundant, sublimely self-righteous, graduated from Yale in 1889. A lover of the great outdoors, he was determined to live and work in the trees, and on the advice of Dr. Detrich Brandis, Germany's foremost authority on silviculture, enrolled in the French Forest School at Nancy. Shocked by the immorality of fellow students and impatient to employ his new wisdom as the first native-born American to take graduate training in forestry, Pinchot did not stay to obtain a doctorate but after little more than a year returned home to serve as "America's first scientific forester" (his own description). He found work preparing a forest plan for George Vanderbilt's Biltmore Estate in North Carolina. In 1895 at the age of thirty-three he was employed as a special forest agent to survey the reserves. In 1896 he toured with the Forest Commission, adding new associations to his inherited familiarity among the wealthy and mighty. In 1897 Pinchot visited the North Cascades, among other tours, becoming one of the first to attain the summit of Columbia Peak near the mining town of Monte Cristo. In 1898 he gained lodgment in the niche he had selected as a power base, the Division of Forestry, which had all of a dozen employees. That year, America's first four-year course in forestry commenced at Cornell University, under the aegis of Dr. Bernhard Eduard Fernow, a German, as were all foresters except those who were French or who were named Pinchot. In 1900, the year he became Secretary of the American Forestry Association, Pinchot succeeded in instigating a program at Yale, thus escaping the domineering German.

A most dramatic and influential role in American forest history was played by the young anarchist who in 1901 shot President William McKinley dead, thus transferring the presidency to a maverick thought to have been safely isolated in the vice-presidency. Among other serendipities, Theodore Roosevelt was a devoted friend of Pinchot. However, the latter did not depend on assassins, or even presidents, to make his luck for him, but indefatigably worked both sides of the street and the alleys as well. In 1905 the American Forestry Association, which he had made his own, Pinchot summoned more than two thousand attendees to the Second American Forest Congress. On February 1 that year, the U.S. Congress, thoroughly softened up by his lobbying East and West, high and low, transferred the forest reserves from the Interior Department to Pinchot's snug stronghold in the Agriculture Department. On July 1, he renamed his agency the United States Forest Service and changed his title to Chief Forester.

Upon completion of the transfer, Pinchot sat down and wrote himself a letter, signed by the Secretary of Agriculture, which is regarded as the "fount of administrative doctrine in the Forest Service." In the letter he instructed himself that

> all land is to be devoted to its most productive use for the permanent good of the whole people. . . . [Where] conflicting interests must be reconciled the question will always be decided from the standpoint of the greatest good of the greatest number in the long run.

Decades later, Grant McConnell, a professor of political science whose academic interests focused on public land policy (and a champion for the North Cascades), commented:

> This language, more widely quoted within the Service than any other, became its high doctrine in subsequent years. 'The permanent good of the whole people' and 'the greatest good of the greatest number in the long run' are phrases it is tempting to regard as decorative cliches, but they are the terms on which a structure of administration has been built. Out of this language evolved justification for what has come to be known as 'the multiple-use policy.' The 'greatest good' formula, in particular, is to be heard from even the most humble of the Service's officers. . . .

That this slogan was a very slightly amended bit of plagiarism seems never to have been appreciated by Pinchot. He was not an intellectually sophisticated man, and all the evidence indicates that he thought he had invented a scientific formula that would lead inevitably to certain and unquestionable results. The fact, of course, was that this formula, minus the bit about the long run, was the invention of an eighteenth-century English philosopher, Jeremy Bentham, and that it was riddled with ambiguity. Specifically, what kind of good, and for which people? Are all "goods" equal in nature? And are all desires to be placed on the same plane? Such questions never entered into Pinchot's reflection, at least insofar as we are able to determine from his autobiography, his speeches, or his teachings to his agency.

Pinchot's imperial rescript is by no means as self-evident as the Golden Rule. However, other statements elucidate his thinking:

> The object of our forest policy is not to preserve the forests because they are beautiful . . . or because they are refuges for the wild creatures of the wilderness . . . but for the making of prosperous homes. . . . Every other consideration comes as secondary.

"Forestry," announced America's first scientific forester, "is tree-farming." Useful as sermons and slogans were, Pinchot needed a word, a new word, that expressed his stern rejection both of free-enterprise looting and the halting of it by simple lock-ups. Hearing that certain lands in British India had been designated "forest conservancies," he found exactly the lack of denotation and richness of connotation he wanted and proceeded to give "conservation" the meaning it now has in America. Or perhaps one should say, *lack* of meaning.

The term "conservation" proved flexible enough to take whatever shape was wanted by whatsoever hand took it up. It could embrace whatever it was Pinchot and his Forest Service had in mind, could be artfully employed to mask the same old intentions of the same old looters Pinchot sought to shackle, and could win such general social acceptance as to drive from the public forum formulations more precise. David Brower aptly noted that *conservation* takes care in the spending of the golden eggs; *preservation* takes care to save the goose. An example of how Pinchot influenced the vocabulary to serve his ends is found in the 1906 purposes of The Mountaineers: "to preserve the natural beauty of Northwest America." Half a century later when the organization began to aggressively pursue that purpose, it did so under the leadership of its "*Conservation* Committee," and the spearhead group formed in 1957 to pursue a preservation agenda in the North Cascades took the name "North Cascades *Conservation* Council," or "NCCC," as the organization is generally referred to throughout this text (occasionally scribed as "N3C" by others).

Pinchot's undiluted utilitarianism—a heritage from the Bentham-Mill definition of utility as a benefit to the population at large, as distinguished from the purely selfish greed of the Industrial Revolution—is exemplified by the Hetch Hetchy controversy. He vigorously promoted the reservoirization of the valley that was just "another Yosemite" because only when the water was piped and its hydropower wired to the people of San Francisco could it become useful. After all, the nation already had *one* Yosemite. A possible epitaph for Pinchot: "He understood greed; could not understand Muir."

Michael Frome, author of *The Forest Service, Whose Woods These Are, Battle for the Wilderness*, and many other books, has commented on the Forest Service psyche:

> Pinchot stimulated organizational esprit and individual imagination, a get-up-and-go attitude hard to match in government during any period in history. In its early years the Forest Service fought on many fronts for the protection of natural resources . . . pioneered in bringing order out of chaos in the public domain . . . unusual in government for its fearlessness, stimulated a sense of belonging and spirit of loyalty derived essentially from Pinchot's crusade.

Pinchot has even been likened to the saints who preached up the crusades, inspiring young knights to take the Cross and save the Holy Land. His early Forest Service fought the infidel, saved the maidens, and brought order out of chaos. Its spirit of one for all, all for one, made it the closest thing America has known to a whole army of Lone Rangers.

Grant McConnell touched up the glamorous portrait of a band of Sir Galahads by adding a bit of Don Quixote: "men in office unlearned in reading the signs upon the land itself and ungifted with the sense of moral direction wandered before the pressures of all the winds that blew." Combining the characterizations, one could also say that Pinchot's Forest Service didn't know exactly where it was going but was determined to go there like a bat out of hell.

Of course, not everybody loves a policeman. Giants of industry and Populist squatters alike hated the holier-than-thou friars from Washington D.C. Congress vented the hatred. President Theodore Roosevelt, who from the moment he took office was the firm ally of his friend, later remarked, "Every year the Forest Service had to fight for its life. . . . [More] time appeared to be spent on it during the passage of the appropriations bill than on all other government bureaus put together."

Seeing that history was against them, corporations accelerated the pace of their lumber stealing. Timber cruisers for the Northern Pacific and the barons (Weyerhaeuser foremost among them) ranged the state of Washington marking the lushest forests for fraudulent entry or "scripper" exchange. However, Pinchot's boundary men also were in the field, and they moved like the wind. Their surveys were far from perfect, but as Pinchot said, they were competing with "as competent a body of land thieves as ever the sun shone on."

By 1906 the reserves were increased to 107 million acres. In 1907 a cabal of Western senators, led by Charles Fulton of Oregon, attached this rider to an appropriations bill: "Hereafter no forest reserve shall be created, nor any addition made to one heretofore created, within the limits of Oregon, Washington, Idaho, Montana, Colorado, or Wyoming except by act of Congress." On February 25th the bill passed. A few years later California, Arizona, and New Mexico were added to the list.

An appropriations bill generally being veto-proof, Roosevelt and Pinchot had to get cracking. In less than ten days of feverish drafting, thirty-three proclamations were brought to Roosevelt. He signed them, the last only days before his presidency expired. He kept the documents secret for a time that they might explode into the general view at once. To the consternation of the Western crooks and the delight of the Eastern Progressives ("A bully show! Just bully!"), the 15.6 million acres of that final act of Barbecue snuffing brought Roosevelt's total between September 1901 and March 1907 to perhaps 148 million acres. One source says that as of June 30, 1917, one hundred forty-seven national forests had 176.3 million acres, of which 21.1 million were privately owned "in-holdings"—patented claims and grant lands. At the end of 1933, there were, according to another source, "141 national forests embracing 182,097,802 acres of which a little over 86 percent is public land." To this day the problem in sizing the National Forests continues to be who is counting what and for what purpose. Boundaries shift, records are confused, some Forests are merged or split or renamed, as in the Cascades.

In 1907 the "forest reserves" were renamed "national forests" to correct the impression that the land still was withdrawn from use, as initially it had been. The North Cascades were originally within the bounds of the 3.5 million-acre Washington Forest Reserve. As of 1917, the North Cascades north of Stevens Pass had been apportioned among four national forests, including the Chelan National Forest of 724,110 acres (inholdings, 46,681 acres); the Okanogan of 1,541,000 acres (inholdings, 54,675 acres); the Wenatchee of 1,157,000 acres (inholdings, 491,724 acres); and the Washington National Forest of 1,490,000 acres (inholdings, 35,786 acres). The latter was renamed Mount Baker in 1924 and ultimately merged a half-century later into the Mount Baker–Snoqualmie National Forest. The Chelan was shuffled about over the years and eventually split between the Okanogan and Wenatchee National Forests. Today, the Okanogan, Wenatchee, and Mount Baker-Snoqualmie National Forests all lie within Region Six of the Forest Service, headquartered in Portland, Oregon, under a Regional Forester who reports directly to the Chief (formerly, Chief Forester) in Washington D.C. The Chief has considerable autonomy, but serves under the Secretary of the U.S. Department of Agriculture. (The National Park Service is within the Department of the Interior.) The various national forests are organized into a dozen districts and are run with a degree of latitude by Forest Supervisors whose offices are located near Seattle and in Wenatchee and Okanogan. Like parish priests under the bishops, the District Rangers are the hands-on managers. It should be, but is not, needless to say that all these functionaries are subject to the Word of a Higher Authority, including the U.S. Congress. But as with the Bible, the laws written by Congress have been, over the years, variously interpreted and selectively obeyed.

The crusade preached by Pinchot quickly recruited an able, willing, dedicated, and high-spirited corps of youths who would, in years ahead, give the
"forest ranger" a national reputation compounded of the better parts of mountain man, cowboy, Paul Bunyan, Nattie Bumppo (from *Last of the Mohicans*),
and the more practical aspects of missionary priest and college professor, not to
mention the kind-hearted yet strict Irish cop on the beat. The more clean-cut
of the Land Office precursor-rangers came over, joined by folks who had grown
up in the forests, as well as city-dwellers who had fallen in love with wildlands
while hiking, hunting, or fishing and aspired to gain proficiency in use of the
grubber's Pulaski, McLeod, double-bitted axe, and misery whip, and to learn
all the verses of "The Preacher's Daughter" and "The One-Ball Reilly." From
laboring on a trail crew a recruit might progress to Forest Guard, usually only
for the fire season (summer through early fall). At one time or another there
were, in the Stehekin area, guard stations at McGregor Flats, Bullion Flats,
Bridge Creek, and High Bridge. The Skagit area once had a dozen: at Mineral
Park and Marble Creek on the Cascade, Koma Kulshan at Baker Lake, and on
the main river at Reflector Bar, Ruby, Roland, Lightning Creek, and Boundary,
among others. To advance to Forest Ranger required passing a three-day test:
identifying tree species, using axe and saw to fell a tree precisely in the desired
direction, setting and following a compass course, building a campfire, packing a horse, and baking biscuits. Promotion to District Ranger came only after
lengthy demonstration of heroic physical performance, plus a certain amount
of higher education, which might be obtained on leave after joining up. The
leap to Forest Supervisor ordinarily demanded lengthy field experience, a college degree, and a degree of political savvy that was also the first essential for the
next step up to Regional Forester.

A complete legendry of rangers would fill many more pages than the epics
of Homer, the sagas of the Norse, and the novels of James Fenimore Cooper.
J.R. Bruckart was District Ranger at Darrington from 1910 to 1927, succeeded
in that year by Harold Engles, nine years after he, as a squatter in the backwoods
of Oregon, had "joined the Forest Service out of hunger, literally." A companion of the trails said, "The twenty-five-year-old Engles was the perfect hiking
machine. He stood well over six feet, carried not an ounce of fat on his lean,
muscular frame and had the constitution to match." Equally remarkable was
his choice of books for campfire reading; while out on the trails he carried such
matter as Voltaire's *Letters on the English*. He submitted an essay on the book to
the official journal of the regional office, but it wasn't published. Engles retired
in Darrington at the foot of Whitehorse Mountain, and continued climbing
nearby peaks well into his eighties. In 1985, at age eighty-three, he climbed
Three Fingers Mountain, to the lookout cabin he originally envisioned on his
first visit (of many, many) to the summit in 1929. Engles does not stand alone

Early truck logging in western Washington.

PHOTO BY DARIUS KINSEY #10096 (B), WHATCOM MUSEUM OF HISTORY AND ART, BELLINGHAM WA

in the pantheon of the west-of-Glacier Peak demigods. Nels Bruseth, smiling and spirited, was ever at his right hand. Harry Bedal, born on Sauk Prairie in 1890, was long since a legend when Engles arrived, as were his daughters, Jean and Edith; their mother was the daughter of the Sauk-Suiattle chief who guided the Northern Pacific survey over the Cascades in 1870. Engles was famous among wilderness mountaineers until his death in 1993. Not so his predecessors, many of whom flocked to follow Pinchot.

In 1898, shortly after creation of the Washington Forest Reserve, but before there was a Forest Service, Arthur Moll, a homesteader on the Sauk, was named Ranger of the Darrington District, though he perhaps suffered from the prejudice against former Land Office employees. George Sawyer, on the Silverton District starting in 1908, ran the pioneering Silverton Nursery to replant burns on Long Mountain and Buck Creek. Armstrong, Atkins, and Bradner are early Forest Service names. In 1911 C.C. McGuire transferred to Darrington, basing himself at the Blue Bird Ranger Station before moving to the town of Glacier near Mount Baker to serve as District Ranger there in 1913. McGuire calculated the immense amount of timber in the district by running long transects, from ridge to ridge, across Canyon Creek and the Nooksack and Chilliwack

Rivers. "It was interesting work," he said in an interview later in life. "I might have covered more territory if I had refrained [from] climbing every high peak en route just to see what was on the other side." McGuire's neighbor at Texas Pond, north of Darrington, was Thomas "Tommy" Thompson, a "charter member of the Forest Service" who succeeded Al Conrad, the Skagit District Ranger from 1909 to 1915, and carried on in famous style to his retirement in 1943. Most storied of the Stehekin District Rangers was E.O. "Jack" Blankenship, who in 1906 came to Stehekin, where "The House That Jack Built" is still in use as a store selling local crafts. He filled the post of District Ranger until 1920 and then resigned to pursue other activities in the valley. The isolation of Stehekin made the relationship between the Forest Service and that community particularly close. From the beginning in 1905, the seasonal Forest Service jobs were, with tourist revenues in summer and downlake employment in winter, virtually the sole sources of Stehekin cash—and remained so into the 1950s. By 1910 "seasonals" were staying the year around, or at least trying to, a pattern that continues today.

The duties of the district staffs were varied. Timber sales were held starting in 1908, less by national or regional plan than to accommodate local requests. The more usual sales were for fence posts and shake and shingle bolts. In the era of World War I, the ancient cedars on the banks of the Cascade and lower Skagit were felled, sliced into chunks, and floated downstream on spring floods. Then in 1922, a twenty-year contract on fifty-eight hundred acres of the Sauk and White Chuck valleys was awarded to the Sauk River Lumber Company. With four hundred million board feet of Douglas fir, red cedar, western hemlock and silver fir approved for "harvest," railroad logging quickly commenced. Steam locomotives and logging crews (housed on flatcars) rolled ever deeper into these wilderness valleys, occasionally stopped by the ranger during periods of high fire danger. On the North Fork of the Sauk, the Harold J. Engles Memorial Cedar Grove is a mere remnant of what was taken from the Sauk and White Chuck and from a thousand riparian forests up and down the Cascades.

The rangers also examined mining claims submitted for patent, which, more often than not, were rejected. Homestead claims were examined and, if they wouldn't grow potatoes, denied, making the rangers unpopular among squatters. However, these ancient fixtures of the landscape and newer arrivals able to present a reasonable justification might be issued special-use permits, which carried no long-term or ownership rights but allowed temporary squatting. The Geological Survey, having done as much mapping as its funds permitted, left the area, not to return until after World War II. The rangers set about preparing such maps as were needed for administration, including boundary-marking. Albert H. Sylvester, who began with the Geological Survey in 1897 and proceeded upward in the Forest Service to Forest Supervisor, placed thousands of names on maps of the West, prior to his retirement in the 1930s. In the 1920s Lage Wernstedt mapped the North Cascades indefatigably, climbing every mountain necessary to his purpose and a good many that were not. Regrettably, a clean-files fanatic at Wenatchee National Forest apparently threw out most of his priceless journals and negatives.

Through the 1930s, "forestry was 90 percent fire protection." Getting crews to the blazes required a system of trails that gave quick access to all parts of the forest, whether or not they interested prospectors, trappers, or fishermen. Trails were kept passable after the dreams of gold played out. In a single summer, Harold Engles and his crew built or rebuilt seventy-nine miles in his district. Trail shelters were spotted about the country so that patrols could find comfort in a storm; each served as a telephone booth, the lines powered for message transmission by a hand-crank electricity generator. Hundreds of miles of telephone line were strung; the wire has mostly been recycled and the porcelain insulators became treasured collectables. In 1907 a line was laid from Chelan along the lake to Stehekin and on up to Horseshoe Basin, presumably for the convenience of the miners. In 1917 a fire-lookout cabin replacing the tent used since 1915 was built atop Sourdough Mountain. It was said to be the first lookout cabin in the nation. In the 1930s Mount Baker National Forest had forty-three lookouts, including those on Easy Ridge and Copper Ridge, grandly viewing the Pickets, and on Hidden Lake Peak on the far end

Sourdough Mountain Lookout, north of the Skagit River (1921).

SOURDOUGH MOUNTAIN LOOKOUT, NOCA 11265 IN THE COLLECTION OF NORTH CASCADES NATIONAL PARK COMPLEX, COURTESY OF THE NATIONAL PARK SERVICE.

of the ridge culminating in Eldorado Peak. In Stehekin country, McGregor Mountain's lookout was built in 1926, and in the next dozen years, others on Stiletto, Goode Ridge, and Boulder Butte. The lookouts atop Sauk and Crater are long gone. A 1965 act of Congress made the Forest Service liable for attractive nuisances, leading it to demolish and burn all but a handful of these historic cabins.

In his tenure, Gifford Pinchot enjoyed a series of triumphs, but in his lofty arena you certainly can't win 'em all. In the end, a single defeat outbalanced all his victories. Wisely, he insisted that a rational policy for the totality of the nation's forests demanded strict government inspection and supervision of private holdings, the millions of mostly stolen acres that on the average were (and are) at least three to ten times more productive (of timber) than National Forest lands. But his proposal was soundly rejected by the Society of American Foresters, which had become so dominated by industry hacks that it had discredited the name "forester" and was better known as the Society of American Loggers.

Pinchot's vision encompassed all the federal lands, and he likely would have succeeded in absorbing the under-administered national parks (in the pre-National Park Service era) had he not, in 1910, over-reached himself in a quarrel with Secretary of Interior Ballinger and been fired (as was Ballinger, too) by President Taft. Taft was rebuked in his bid for a second term when Roosevelt mounted a third-party Progressive candidacy that elected Woodrow Wilson. The martyred Pinchot was prominent in the hustings. Thereafter he pursued an independent career as prophet, was elected governor of Pennsylvania in 1922, and at one point was talked up as a presidential candidate. In 1946 Pinchot died of leukemia at the age of 81.

Long before his death, he was, to the Forest Service, a memory the more cherished for his absence. Very early on, the ranks of the crusaders were split between the Faithful and the Compromisers. Pinchot's successor, Henry S. Graves (1910–1920), spent his term in the trenches defending the very existence of the Forest Service. William B. Greeley, Chief from 1920 to 1928, maintained a policy of Greeleyism, characterized as the cooperation of the Forest Service and the timber industry, or "the lumbermen leading the Forest Service by the hand." Greeley finally resigned to become secretary-manager of the West Coast Lumberman's Association. R.Y. Stuart, a career forester under Pinchot's tutelage, was appointed chief and served five quiet years during the Depression era. Stuart helped shape natural resource job programs for the unemployed and dutifully prepared an inventory of projects for the Civilian Conservation Corps that would quickly emerge under Roosevelt's New Deal. In 1933 Stuart mysteriously fell to his death from the window of his seventh-floor office. Next appointed was Ferdinand A. Silcox, who had served under Greeley, and Pinchot was pleased with the choice. Silcox, he said, would restore the agency's roots as an "advocate of the public good and not the humble little brother of the lumbermen." Chief from 1933 to 1939, Silcox revived the call for government regulation of private lands but was unable to enlist the support even of his staff; the bureau's oft-praised decentralization meant that the regional offices were virtually independent, and still firmly in the hands of the Greeleyites. Silcox found friendlier ears when he promised a much more aggressive policy of fire suppression. The threat of human-caused and natural wildfire was a concern that Silcox took very seriously. Writing for *Sierra* in 1995, Ted Williams noted that under Silcox, "The Forest Service even hired an anti-fire preacher who mixed Biblical and government gospel in wailing, ranting sermons. . . . To tolerate fire in the forest was to support tyranny in the world." Silcox's dedicated efforts would help set the stage for Smokey Bear's illustrious debut a decade later. While the folly of a broad policy of fire suppression is apparent today, Silcox certainly exhibited a kind of integrity that would become increasingly scarce as the agency carved its path through history.

The Forest Service of Pinchot's bright dawn was a different institution from what it became under his successors, but perhaps the fault lies in Pinchot's Dogma of Forester Infallibility, wherein, as Grant McConnell summarized, "virtual autonomy was achieved within a departmental structure and the demand for extreme administrative discretion was clothed in an appeal to science and a policy without standards—the so-called 'multiple-use' policy."

GOOD COLLIDES WITH GOOD

The U.S. Forest Service has been likened to the Roman Catholic Church as an ideological monolith; in reality, both institutions tolerate and even encourage limited diversity. Hikers who have traveled the backcountry over the years tend to sentimentalize the Old Ranger, viewing him as a species distinct from his modern successor, and in a number of respects this is true. However, the fundamental dichotomy, dating from the very start, is between the bureaucrat of Washington D.C. and the ranger in the field. The latter, the Old Ranger who finally faded away after World War II, was wholeheartedly devoted to "the greatest good" but tended not to pursue the principle beyond taking good care of his beloved forests. Never having studied in France nor read the operations manual of the Prussian Forest Service, he didn't understand that Pinchot intended him to be a tree-farmer. A just complaint against the Old Ranger is that he was such a nice guy that he deluded wilderness travelers into mistaking the intentions of the Forest Service—which was, after all, headquartered far, far away in a city where forests were not trees but statistics in a ledger.

While internal contradictions eventually were to strain the fabric of the bureau, throughout the early period the Old Ranger and the city bureaucrats were united by two convictions: the National Park Service was a bunch of smart-aleck summer soldiers in fancy hats who didn't know beans, and anything the Park Service could do the Forest Service could do better. The National Park Act of 1916, Stephen Mather's 1,050 park-plugging publications in two years, and his training-up of a corps of Park Rangers who competed with Forest Rangers for public favor, demanded massive retaliation.

Even before World War I, city adventurers in tin lizzies and merry Oldsmobiles were probing wagon roads into the forests. Whether by calculated strategy of the general staff in the war room in Washington, D.C., or simply because Old Ranger liked the people who came to admire his trees, the Forest Service began improving roads and extending them and providing roadside camps, in order not to let Mather hog all the freedom wheels of America. Though trails and trail shelters were built for maintenance and administration of the forest, hikers were welcomed and were provided free maps when they stopped at ranger stations to obtain the required campfire permits. By 1917 six shelter cabins were strung along the Stehekin River and Bridge Creek—several more than the Forest Service required for its own people. Rangers commenced the task, later assumed by the state, of packing cans of little fishes to rivers and high lakes, entirely barren of fish in their natural state, to provide sport, though few survived.

The Forest Service cooperated with the State Highway Department in the 1920s construction of the Mount Baker Highway to Heather Meadows, doing so as a rejoinder to the Park Service highway to Mount Rainier's Paradise meadows. It also sponsored a campaign, not abandoned until the mid-1960s, to build an Around-Mount-Baker Highway, a rejoinder to the projected Around-Mount-Rainier Highway.

In 1918, the year after Mary Roberts Rinehart published the tale of her Cascade Pass trip, an August 5th Forest Service memo identified the bugaboo that may have been keeping a few mucky-mucks in Washington, D.C., awake at night:

> A large portion of Chelan National Forest at the northern end of the lake, extending to the summit [Cascade Pass], should always be reserved for the use of campers. . . . [Any] effort on the part of the Forest Service to place sheep on areas which are the frequent camping grounds of the tourists would certainly lead to a revival of the agitation to have the whole Forest thrown into a national park with sheep grazing excluded.

Agitation? The Mazama manifesto of 1906 and the Rinehart article of 1917 scarcely add up to that. Obviously, though, a nerve had been struck. The less-than-glowing remarks about the North Cascades by Mather–Albright were soothing to some ears, yet in the early 1920s, the Mount Baker Club was still crying "Park! Park!" In the fall of 1927, the Glacier Peak Association was formed. In 1929 Willard Van Name was heard nationally, and, as the creation of Olympic National Park was to testify, his voice had to be reckoned with. In 1926 Secretary of Agriculture William M. Jardine designated 74,859 acres around Mount Baker to be used for recreation (resource extraction was also allowed), and the tourist-serving Mount Baker Lodge was dedicated at Heather Meadows. In an interesting twist of terminology, the area was designated the Mount Baker Park Division (Columbia Gorge was another example). The name was later changed to Mount Baker Recreation Area, and as such enticed tourists to Heather Meadows, which was, and is, along with Paradise Valley at Mount Rainier, one of the two most outstanding car-accessible alpine parklands in the Cascades, its splendid vistas of Mount Baker and Mount Shuksan right up there with Mount Rainier.

Responding to concerns for wildlife, the Forest Service in 1926 set aside a Mount Baker Game Preserve of 188,000 acres and an Upper Skagit Game Preserve of seventy-four thousand acres. Then responding to concerns about another locality, in 1931 it established a Glacier Peak–Cascades Recreation Unit of 233,600 acres, or 360 square miles—a handsome preserve indeed, except that it was not actually preserved from logging, mining, or grazing.

Tourists enjoying miniature golf at the Mount Baker Lodge.

PHOTO BY BERT HUNTOON #1995.99.1310, WHATCOM MUSEUM OF HISTORY AND ART, BELLINGHAM WA

Far more influential nationally was the wise and admirable, yet maybe sly and devious, Forest Service initiative in wilderness preservation. Heirs of Muir complained about the Mather–Albright program and its emphasis on roads to everywhere, resorts operated by private enterprisers, and the reluctance to set aside road-free enclaves. The birth year of the wilderness concept in the Forest Service is, arguably, 1919, when the agency hired Arthur Carhart, its first full-time landscape architect. Aside from spreading the gospel under his informal title of "the beauty engineer," his efforts led, in 1926, to a Superior Primitive Area in Minnesota in which "no roads will be built as far as the Forest Service can control." In 1930 it became the first area in the nation's history to be formally protected by Congress as wilderness. By 1964 the Primitive Area had evolved into the Boundary Waters Canoe Area and in that year was given permanent protection by the Wilderness Act.

Aldo Leopold, fresh out of Yale, joined the Forest Service in 1909 at the height of its heroic age, and was posted to Arizona. Beginning as an orthodox Pinchot utilitarian, he learned from the land, slowly but deeply. In 1924 he warned, "The existence of a wilderness-recreation famine has emerged as an incontrovertible fact." Encouraged by Carhart, he succeeded in convincing his Regional Forester to set aside the Gila Wilderness Reserve in New Mexico in 1924—the nation's first formal wilderness area (designated by the agency, not Congress).

In 1929 officials in Washington, D.C., took to heart the several and varied aesthetic, biological, and political merits of wilderness protection and at the urging of Leopold and company issued Regulation L-20, providing for the setting aside of "primitive areas" that were "to be kept in as near a natural and primitive condition as is physically and economically possible, in the interests of public education, research, and public recreation. . . . No roads. . . ." The same year the Secretary of Agriculture announced that "national forest administration . . . aims at the coordinated development and use of all the forest resources, including recreational and wildlife resources." Since these two uses, recreational and ecological, had been subordinated under the 1897 Magna Carta, the announcement represented a significant policy revision, a major step toward "multiple-use," a term that first publicly appeared in the 1936 Annual Report of the Secretary of Agriculture.

The appearance of Irving Clark, Sr., on the wildland scene may well have snapped the Forest Service to attention. Clark was an enthusiastic participant in the exploration by The Mountaineers of "the natural beauty of Northwest America." He was less pleased by the club's neglect in the 1920s of the founders' mandate to preserve that natural beauty. (Why and how the departure from Muirism came about has never been addressed by historians.) The revered president of the club, Professor Edmond Meany, must have played a large role

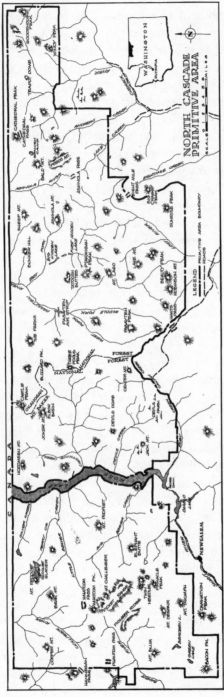

North Cascades Primitive Area established by Ferdinand Silcox in 1935.

MAP COURTESY OF THE WILDERNESS SOCIETY

in the club's apparent shift in priorities. His focus was on climbing and his historical writings are exceedingly respectful of the economically powerful. At the University of Washington he initiated a curriculum in forestry, which is to say Pinchotism, tailored to the wishes of the timber industry by Greeleyism. Clark decided that rather than try to stir up a sluggish club, he could use his energy better in the Democratic Party and, after its founding in 1935, The Wilderness Society, of which he became a council member. In 1926 Clark queried the Forest Service about its wilderness intentions in the North Cascades. Presumably dissatisfied with the answer, he asked again in 1929 about set-asides and was solemnly informed:

> We are making quite detailed examinations previous to setting aside such areas permanently. In Washington there may be such areas set aside in the vicinity of the head of Lake Chelan, Glacier Peak. . . . It is safe to say that the next many generations will in no way suffer from a lack of wilderness resources.

Was this the honest vow or devout hope of a pure-hearted Old Ranger, or the deliberate fraud of a bureaucracy that was growing ever more duplicitous? Possibly the spokesman simply misspoke in referring to Lake Chelan and Glacier Peak, and meant to refer to wilderness resources elsewhere in the North Cascades. In 1931 the Whatcom Primitive Area of 172,800 acres was established, the eighth such tract in the national forests. In 1935 it was enlarged to the 801,000-acre North Cascades Primitive Area. Both Lake Chelan and Glacier Peak were excluded.

In that period, it should be said, the administration of Franklin D. Roosevelt ranks with that of Theodore Roosevelt in terms of the care of natural resources. Much of FDR's achievement was through his Secretary of the Interior, Harold Ickes, the "Old Curmudgeon," who rampaged through the nation's capital as the last of the fire-snorting Progressives. Ickes got the national monuments, which had been administered by the Forest Service, transferred to his Park Service, frightened the Forest Service by agitating to move it back to Interior, and in his Civilian Conservation Corps gave the nation an idealism equal to that of the Forest Ranger and Park Ranger, and one that remains vividly alive six decades after the CCC's wartime demise.

Simultaneously, Roosevelt buttressed the Forest Service against the Ickes assault, accidentally or otherwise, by appointing as Chief, in 1933, his personal choice, Ferdinand Silcox. The new Chief could not be classified as a Muirite yet he at least, unlike Pinchot, understood Muir. Certainly he was no Greeleyite and, had he been granted another few years, might have rooted out that breed from strongholds in the regional offices and Washington headquarters.

In that era, citizen activism was not the force it was to become when well-drilled legions of the middle-class and even the plebes formed ranks across the nation in the 1950s and 1960s. Preservationism became—in the same way as attending to the deserving poor—the worthy cause of a small group of patricians tightly bound by family, education, and money, who maintained as retainers, in the same way they did their gardeners and ministers, such holy men as Muir. Even in the Sierra Club, which was to become the New Model Army of the citizen rankers of the future, the flame of Muirism burned lower than before, though by the end of the 1930s it leapt higher.

Most significant of new ventures of the decade was the 1935 founding of The Wilderness Society. The names of all the founders were—or would become—illustrious, among them Aldo Leopold and Robert Marshall. Leopold had left Arizona in 1924, moving to Madison, Wisconsin, to do research in the U.S. Forest Products Laboratory. In 1928 he quit in disillusion and in 1933 joined the faculty of the University of Wisconsin. These were the steps in his life trajectory from tree-farmer fundamentalism ("every word in the Pinchot Book is true") to the holism expressed in his posthumous and profoundly influential *Sand County Almanac*.

Robert Marshall, a young man of good family and comfortable wealth and thus qualified to be a Progressive preservationist, attended the New York State College of Forestry, the Harvard Forestry School, and John Hopkins University, where he earned a Ph.D. in forestry. He joined the Forest Service in 1925. Tours of duty in several regions for several government bureaus elevated him to the status—well deserved—of "golden boy." In 1930 Marshall wrote, "There is just one hope of repulsing the tyrannical ambition of Civilization to conquer every niche on the whole earth. That hope is the organization of spirited people who will fight for the freedom of the wilderness."

Epic adventures in New York's Adirondacks and Alaska's Brooks Range added to the reputation he made as a silviculturist in Montana and augmented his connections, which by 1935 had extended to fellow founders of The Wilderness Society—Benton MacKaye; Robert Sterling Yard, who managed the group's day-to-day affairs; Aldo Leopold; and four others. Marshall has long been recognized as the Society's principal inspiration. At the suggestion of President Roosevelt, in May of 1937 Silcox appointed Marshall to head the Forest Service Recreation and Lands Division.

The forest lands hadn't seen his sort of frenetic energy since the high prime of Pinchot. Over three summers, Marshall ranged the trails of the West, inventorying wildlands, drawing up proposals. He was known to cover thirty to fifty miles in a day—on foot. After a summer visit to the Glacier Peak Limited Area, Marshall wrote,

> The man who climbs the trail up Agnes Creek [near Stehekin] to the crest of the Cascade Mountains may not see any more jagged peaks than along the Stevens Pass Highway, but the environment from which he sees them exhibits no sign of

civilization save the dead ashes of a few old campfires and the simple trail which has changed but little since it was tramped out centuries before by the feet of Indians.

Simultaneous to his marathon outings, Marshall so vigorously lobbied the Forest Service that eventually he had won to the wilderness idea all but two or three of the Regional Directors. Most of Marshall's wilderness proposals were fated to die with him, however. Not so his "U" Regulations, adopted by the Forest Service in 1939. Under these, the Secretary of Agriculture would designate unbroken tracts of one hundred thousand or more acres as "wilderness areas" (U-l) and others of five thousand to one hundred thousand acres as "wild areas" (U-2). In both, commercial timber-cutting, roads, hotels, resorts, summer homes, motorboats, and airplane landings were prohibited. Provision also was made for "recreation areas" (U-3) of any size. The Regulation L-20 of 1929 was superseded and revoked, but primitive areas were to remain protected as "wilderness" until the time came, as it did in the 1950s, for them to be re-studied. The U Regulations ended with passage of the Wilderness Act in 1964. Today, wilderness areas are exclusively designated by Congress.

Bob Marshall was the single most important figure in the pre-World War II history of North Cascades preservation, though not for accomplishments he lived to see. His 1939 proposal for a 795,000-acre (1,240 square-mile) Glacier Peak Wilderness Area reaching from Lake Wenatchee to Ruby Creek was approved by Silcox and was therefore certain to become official. However, during a final furious-paced hike through the North Cascades in September 1939, Marshall was already dying. For years his death, at age 38, was attributed to a heart attack caused by strenuous exercise, leukemia not then being a socially respectable disease. Still, all would not have been lost had Ferdinand Silcox not suffered a heart attack and died three months later.

Having supported in the central Sierra Nevada the Kings Canyon National Park proposal, which he signed into law in 1940, Roosevelt's gaze was drawn eastward to the war, leaving Ickes on his own; his Ice Peaks Park took multiple torpedoes and sank without a trace, the very memory of it buried in the archives until exhumed two decades later by the NCCC. Within the Forest Service, the wilderness chapel was devastated by the sudden double loss of Marshall and Silcox. In 1940 a perfunctory nod to their preservation goals was made by designation of a Glacier Peak Limited Area of 352,000 acres, of which 233,600 acres had constituted the old Glacier Peak–Cascades Recreation Unit.

The "limited area" classification, employed nowhere in the national forests except Region Six (Washington and Oregon), was explained as signifying that further study was in progress and that meanwhile there would be no development. Some rangers pretended that "limited" entailed guaranteed status as Wilderness. Others were frank to admit it simply meant "We haven't yet figured out where to put the logging roads." The public was encouraged by lines and words on maps to suppose "limited" was a protected status, not knowing it represented nothing more than a stroke of the Forest Service pencil, as quickly eliminated by its eraser, without public hearings or notice. Indeed, a time came when citizens protesting a timber sale in a limited area were blandly informed there was really no such thing as a limited area and never had been.

Plainly, the Forest Service intent was to divert public attention from the scuttling of the Marshall–Silcox wilderness plans. But the ploy backfired. Attention was directed to, not from, the possibility of wilderness designation. The Mountaineers conservationist Richard J. Brooks and others exploited the existence, however slippery, of the limited area designation in order to hold the rangers' feet to the fire.

And thus the wilderness idea was kept alive.

Glacier Peak from Image Lake.

Phil Zalesky

2

To the Glacier Peak Wilderness

If the dozen greatest Cascades Peaks were to be identified with the
ruling deities of classical antiquity, lonely Glacier Peak would undoubtedly be the mountain to typify Artemis. . . . [T]his virgin
goddess shunned civilized life and withdrew into the wilderness to
roam with the wild creatures who inhabit it. Given her choice of a
Cascade dwelling place today, she would find Glacier Peak ideal, for
it is the most remote and inaccessible volcano in the range.

—Stephen L. Harris
Fire & Ice: The Cascade Volcanoes (1976)

THE OTHER SIDE OF THE MOUNTAIN

THE DEATHS OF ROBERT MARSHALL AND Ferdinand Silcox in 1939 marked
a sharp, almost complete, and years-long discontinuity in the conservation history of the North Cascades. Postwar stewards of the American
Earth could not simply pick up the reins and "Giddy-ap!" the horses to get the
wagon rolling again. Brush had overgrown the track, the wagon was dry-rot-
ting in the barn, the horses were scattered, and the reins that had been dropped
in the 1940s were, by the 1950s, golly knew where.

Grant McConnell, who studied both sides of the great lacuna of World
War II, wrote in 1969 of the "Old Conservation" that dawned so brightly in the
Progressivism of Pinchot and Theodore Roosevelt and faded in melancholy
twilight at the end of the New Deal of Harold Ickes and Franklin D. Roosevelt.
It was, he said, "hardly a popular movement. The achievements were made by
the fortunate influence of a handful of thoughtful men upon a few receptive

presidents . . . the work of an elite." Of the "New Conservation" (environmentalism, ecologyism) he said, "What we see today, what goes by the old tag of *conservation movement*, is a different kind of animal. We now behold a movement with a strong popular base . . . a body of belief firmly grounded on a set of principles cherished by a substantial and growing segment of the public."

This "different kind of animal" evolved simultaneously in a number of provinces of the American Earth. The subspecies that leapt from the North Cascades wilderness in the 1950s was perhaps as indefatigable and passionate as any of its kin, as smart when brains were needed, and just as fierce when the situation called for teeth and claws. Certainly it proved to be among the most successful in the country. In hindsight, and in view of the formidable difficulties of the time, the success of the New Conservationist came so remarkably swiftly that it had the appearance of a single giant leap forward. In the era of the hero elite, that's just what had occurred. However, the campaign for the Glacier Peak Wilderness of 1960 was won not by a squadron of galloping cavalry, sabers on high, but by regiments of infantry trudging from trench to trench, inch by inch, their typewriters maintaining a withering fire of letters, supported by a cannonade of pamphlets, magazines, books, and films.

The acrobatic peculiarity of this particular leap forward was a midflight, midair change of direction. The campaign sought to save the heart and soul of the U.S. Forest Service, but by the time its initial objective—a Glacier Peak Wilderness within the National Forest System—was attained, the leapers, despite some anguish and quarreling, turned away from the Forest Service and took aim on a North Cascades National Park. Not wilderness, but park, despite considerable doubts in some quarters that the National Park Service had enough heart and soul worth saving.

THE LONG RUN SHORTENS UP

At the conclusion of World War II, Pinchot's "long run" appeared to extend far beyond the horizon. Despite nearly a century of thought-free looting, the empire of the lowlands and foothills that were privatized by the Great Barbecue was still a Fort Knox of green gold sufficient to keep the big mills of the timber barons highballing for decades. Enough of nature's bounty was left to continue feeding, as had been customary, the rabble of small mills. However, unlike their snaggle-toothed granddaddies, the new barons were a college-educated gentry ringed by retinues of degrees in business administration with majors in bottom-line accounting. These students of corporate greed took principled offense at opportunistic price-cutting by the rabble, and in the name of free enterprise conspired (ever so discreetly and illegally) to stifle the small mills by denying them a supply of Barbecue timber.

For half a century the national forests had been dedicated to preserving forests, a labor of love for the Old Ranger who thought that was the definition of forestry. But simply preserving the forest brought a nagging frustration to the administrators of the Department of Agriculture who wanted the forests to behave more like cornfields. Tearful petitions by the starveling mills for access to non-Barbecue timber—the National Forests—brought joy to the Utilitarians, who felt compelled to unlimber their ploughs and manure-spreaders and reapers, and begin some serious farming. In Washington D.C., Chief Richard McArdle (1952–1962) exulted, "The Forest Service has moved from the era of *custodial* management into the era of *intensive* management." The idea that man should not try to manage wilderness, because in the attempt he surely would manage it out of existence, was apparently beyond his grasp. McArdle's sense of wilderness was worthy of Mrs. Malaprop, "a place where the hand of man has not set foot."

A paradox took shape. The Barbecuers generally didn't give a hang about forestry. They exercised their constitutional freedom by advancing tree by tree outward and upward from their mills to the horizons, leaving nothing but stumps, fireweed, and huckleberry bushes in their wake. Because of the obvious messes left behind, conservationists, Old or New, could not but condemn them as devils. By contrast, the Forest Service was seen as a choir of angels, or at least the hope and trust of the Long Run.

Yet the abrupt appearance of "intensive management" shocked wilderness travelers right down to the holes in their wool socks. Step by step, the Barbecuers would advance up a valley from the mountain edge to the deep interior. They were perhaps a dozen years or more getting there, so that hikers lost a mile or two of wilderness trail a year. An intensified Forest Service would then initiate a new cutting circle by basically ramming a road the full length of the valley and locating the very first clearcut, quite purposefully, deep in the mountain interior; in a year or two they removed the entire valley from wilderness and any possibility of protected status, as happened with the Middle and South Forks of the Nooksack River, for example, or the White Chuck River, or the Sauk, Stilliguamish, Skykomish Rivers, and countless others. The hikers of the 1950s found themselves driving long distances through virgin forest to a trailhead in a road-end clearcut, formerly the location of the camp at the end of a backpack of two or three days.

Chief McArdle had a nifty way of shrugging off the concerns. Writing for the *Journal of Forestry* in 1953, he excused the appalling destruction of wild and remote river valleys this way:

> I believe that our inability to satisfy completely each and every group of national-forest users is a definite sign of success in doing the job assigned to us. When each

group is somewhat dissatisfied, it is a sign that no one group is getting more than its fair share. The guiding principle laid down for us nearly fifty years ago still hits the mark. . . . 'the greatest good of the greatest number in the long run'. . . . That is still the guiding policy of the Forest Service, and I hope it always will be.

The paradox was this: what was supposed to be *good* forestry by the intensive managers turned out to be far more rapidly destructive of wilderness than the *evil* non-forestry of the barons. In either instance, the destruction of old-growth forests is much more akin to mining than farming, since trees that are hundreds or thousands of years old are not in any practical sense a renewable resource. However, had the Forest Service advanced up the valleys a mile or two a year, hikers would have sighed and grumbled but stoically swallowed the future as they had the past. But here were vaulting, preemptive clearcuts, the abrupt obliteration of miles of trails, and gross, unnecessary intrusions into untrammeled wilderness. Had Bob Marshall gazed down from the wilderness of the sky and sought a way to arouse legions of successors to carry on where he left off, he could not have found a better means to do it. Like nothing else could, the intensive management of the public's forests inspired the New Conservation.

THE NATIVES GROW RESTLESS

Though the Old Conservation was ended as an organized movement by World War II, certain of its paladins crossed to the New side of the mountain. A few deserve mention here. In the prewar Pacific Northwest, Irving Clark, Sr., of Seattle pushed for major expansion of Alaska's Glacier Bay National Monument, established by President Coolidge in 1925. (In 1939, the monument was doubled in size by FDR to nearly 3,600 square miles, eventually to become, in 1980, the nation's largest national park.) Clark was also a leader in the postwar defense of Olympic National Park, as he had been in its prewar creation, and at several junctures from the 1920s to the 1950s spoke effectively for the North Cascades. In 1954 he was made honorary vice president of the Wilderness Society. The NCCC presented its first Northwest conservation award to Clark at the Northwest Wilderness Conference in Seattle in March 1958.

Leo Gallagher, a conservation leader with The Mountaineers (Tacoma branch), cherished memories of a 1920s packtrain journey up the White Chuck River to Glacier Peak, and for three decades afterward was a strong vocal and financial supporter of wilderness. Bridging, on her own, the New and the Old, was Pam Olmsted Bobroff, a 1950s activist whose father was of the family whose accomplishments included New York's Central Park and the drafting of the National Parks Act. Her mother, Virginia, was a family friend of Bob Marshall and a companion on his final pack trip in the North Cascades, to Image Lake.

It has been observed that transformation of the economic base of the Puget Sound region was the necessary precondition for the emergence there of the "different kind of animal" who would sustain the battle to protect wilderness. So long as timber was king, receiving kneejerk obeisance from such dependents and allies as the shippers, bankers, merchantry, the Chambers of Commerce, the press, and the government, no more than a handful of morally heroic and financially secure Progressives could be expected to speak out against the dominant culture. The silence of the Boy Scouts of America, an organization whose very life, in the Northwest at least, was wilderness, would be mystifying were not its upper-level structure as tightly intertwined with the business establishment as the symphony orchestra and public art museums. Scouts who set out from Camp Parsons into the Olympics in 1938 heard not a whisper about that year's historic creation of a national park. The debate teams of high schools were composed of earnest, thoughtful youths in the years from 1938 to 1942 and might have been expected to be hotbeds of Progressive–New Deal agitation. For eight successive semesters the debate squads of Seattle cast ballots to choose the city-wide topic. Eight times "conservation" was nominated, and eight times lost out to such gripping questions as "What is the best form of city government?"

The regional giant, Weyerhaeuser, was not stripped of its imperial crown by World War II and the company remained powerful. But the swarms of engineers drawn to Seattle by the Boeing Company owed none of their prosperity to timber, nor did their butchers and bakers and bankers, nor the teachers who instructed their children. Further, the drudgery of the drafting board demanded intense re-creation on weekends and vacations, which often as not were spent in and around the wilderness. These new arrivals in Seattle were readily recruited to the conservation cause, and their growing numbers heartened native-born conservationists.

Richard J. Brooks may be cited as an example of a native-born New Conservationist. As a Boy Scout, he experienced not one but two wilderness epiphanies, the first hiking from Camp Parsons into the just-created Olympic National Park, the second with his home troop on Glacier Peak in the North Cascades. In 1947, learning that a Congressional committee was considering a proposal to reduce the size of Olympic Park, he hitchhiked to Lake Crescent and witnessed Irving Clark, Sr. and John Osseward doing battle with the Barbecuers—and winning. He saw that it was *not* true, as most of his Seattle contemporaries glumly assumed, that the tree-eating dragons were invincible. When, in 1948, he found the trailhead on the White Chuck River located where, a scant decade earlier, his troop had made its second night's camp, he took up the cry, "Save the White Chuck!"

Phil and Laura Zalesky joined The Mountaineers in 1953, took the club's climbing course that spring, and that same year began climbing and hiking in the Cascades. In 1954, having been elected chair of the club's Everett Branch, Phil read an essay by Bernard DeVoto in *Harper's Magazine* decrying the neglect of national parks and wrote letters of protest to Congressman Jack Westland, who at the time represented (some say *mis*represented) the North Cascades. Zalesky received scornful replies, and took them to Seattle to a meeting of The Mountaineer's conservation committee. After listening to Brooks wail about the crimes being committed against Glacier Peak, where Phil and Laura had explored the previous summer, Phil presented his case against Westland and the couple was instantly recruited to the committee.

Dozens more cases—hundreds more—could be cited. The fact was that the Barbecuers could bluster about payrolls and the New Rangers and could chant the pseudoscience they'd learned in forestry school; the different kind of animal, whether native-born or new immigrant, wasn't listening.

STEHEKIN ENTERS THE DOWNLAKE WORLD

The specter of intensive management was slow to appear on the east side of the Cascades. West-side forests began at tidewater and covered a wide belt across the lowlands and up the valleys to the cold timberline; east-side forests were confined to a narrow belt between that upper timberline and the lower, dry timberline of the sagebrush steppe. The east-side timber industry was not a Goliath clearcutting the entire visible world, mowing the richest cellulose-producing lands of the planet, but a handful of gypo loggers and peckerwood mills "high-grading" the scattered stands of valuable Ponderosa pines and Douglas firs at handy locations near existing roads.

Guarded from assault by a treeless steppe, by mile-and-a-half tall peaks, by a fifty-five-mile-long lake, Stehekin seemed a citadel so protected by economics and geography there would never be a worry about sacrilege by Barbecuers or intensive managers. When the world was too much, with people burned out by so much consuming and spending, they had only to voyage up the lake to enter Elysium, Narnia, Avalon . . . Stehekin.

Stehekin Valley, the "Yosemite of the North," and Lake Chelan, a Norway-like fjord amid Swiss-like peaks, were the dazzlement of the 1890s. To those who knew them, they seemed certain to become a national park—and soon. The area's reputation for grandeur spread in certain circles, and by the 1920s the gentility of not only the Northwest but the nation was coming to the edge of the Cascades by rail, then voyaging by boat to the heart of the range, to summer amid the wildland peace. But by the end of the 1920s, the automobile had spawned highways and byways to a glut of easy scenery. Chelan's fjord

Lake Chelan, photographed by L.D. Lindsley in 1911.

and Stehekin's valley vanished from the national imagination and became the semi-secret retreat of a few. It was, perhaps, too isolated from the national mainstream to maintain the momentum of a movement that earlier had seemed to need only Muir's voice to join America's treasurehouse as another Yosemite.

In 1937 and again in 1940, Grant McConnell, a member of the Wyeasters mountaineering club in Portland, Oregon, came uplake to climb. Memories of those trips were his spiritual support in the years his Navy destroyer bucketed around the Pacific Ocean, and never more so than on May 2, 1945, when his ship was sunk by a kamikaze off Okinawa. Home on a thirty-day survivor's leave, he and his wife, Jane, spent most of June in a cabin she had acquired for them at the foot of SiSi Ridge. In December they returned, intending to remain until his discharge pay ran out. At an expenditure rate averaging thirty-five dollars a month, they stayed three years, conceived a daughter and a son, and became full and true members of "Old Stehekin," a community that in the 1940s was very little changed since the turn of the century.

The idyll could not permanently satisfy an academic who had studied at Reed, Harvard, and, as a Rhodes Scholar, Oxford. In a mighty wrench he moved his family to Berkeley to complete his doctorate at the University of California. His thesis on agricultural policy and politics was published to such acclaim as to bring appointment to the faculty. The question then was, what to do for an encore?

"I had to pick some other topic," he wrote. "I looked around and, well, I'd been interested in the out-of-doors, and there was beginning to be quite a bit of noise . . . about [a proposed dam at] Echo Park, in Dinosaur National Monument. So I decided to examine the set of ideas that were at issue. . . ."

The resulting article appeared in the September 1954 issue of *Western Political Quarterly*, and because the research had entailed interviewing leaders of the Sierra Club, it served to hitch him to what was rapidly taking shape as the main force of New Conservation. McConnell was already acquainted with the group, as a short-term member of the Sierra Club during a brief San Francisco residence in 1941. He then met Doris and Richard Leonard (a future club president), and "a very dashing young fellow by the name of Dave Brower."

At Berkeley in the fall of 1956, McConnell taught a course on interest groups. He invited David Brower, as a "real live lobbyist," to address the class. McConnell then showed slides of Stehekin, and Brower was hooked. He demanded that McConnell rejoin the Sierra Club and when he did, promptly placed him on the Conservation Committee.

THE CALIFORNIA INVASION

During the period when the Puget Sound community was emerging from its post-frontier chrysalis, the streetside truism was, "To see what Seattle will be in the near future, take a look at the California of the recent past." Freeways, patios, smog, earthquakes, and public nudity—inventions of the south were soon adopted by the north. The formerly courteous provincials saw that the higher the level of civilization, the greater must be the brutality of the lonely crowds. With the bad came the good, notably the emigrants from the south who had no family, economic, or historic loyalties to the timber industry, and who were born-again members of John Muir's Sierra Club.

John and Polly Dyer arrived in Seattle in September 1950, and the following spring enrolled in the climbing course of The Mountaineers. John, one of the Sierra Clubbers who in the 1930s invented the Yosemite–High Sierra School of rock-climbing, was recruited into the climbing course faculty and was regarded with awe for having participated in the 1939 first ascent of Shiprock. It was one of the most famous mountaineering feats in American history, made so by an article in the *Saturday Evening Post* written by (none other than) David Brower, who led all of the pitches on the ascent that John didn't. While the couple lived in California, Polly for three years typed *The Yodeler*, bulletin of the Sierra Club's San Francisco chapter, of which Edgar Wayburn then was chair and the Leonards also prominent. The Dyers were not immediately drawn into Mountaineer conservation efforts, which in 1951 were few. However, the next year the Dyers plunged into the thick of things. Knowing shorthand, Polly agreed to a secretaryship of The Mountaineers' conservation committee.

Among other expatriates on the committee, a second couple was destined for leadership. Patrick D. Goldsworthy was introduced to the High Sierra and the Sierra Club in 1940 while serving as hired packmule for the illustrious photographer Cedric Wright. Returned from World War II, he was taken on as a staffer for the club's high trips, at first in the commissary alongside his wife Jane, affectionately known as "Miss Management." He then served as assistant trip leader under Dave Brower, succeeding to the top post when Brower's conservation work became full time. In 1952 Goldsworthy was appointed to the research faculty of the University of Washington School of Medicine, and in 1953 the couple took The Mountaineers' climbing course and the next year joined the conservation committee.

In an earlier era the New England-San Francisco axis connected Thoreau people to Muir people, raising the energy level on both ends of the line. The San Francisco-Puget Sound axis now did the same in a synergy among surviving paladins of the Old Conservation, the indigenous "different kind of animal" leaping out of the Northwest brush, and the emigrants from throughout America, most especially California. The resulting critical mass helped produce an explosion of conservationist ambition in the West.

Another kind of critical mass, also rooted in San Francisco, brought several leading poets of the Beat Generation to the North Cascades, Gary Snyder among them. Encouraged by fellow poet-mountaineer Kenneth Rexroth to visit the North Cascades, Snyder did in 1952–53 and found work there as a fire lookout first atop Crater Mountain and, later, Sourdough Mountain. He

NCCC co-founder Polly Dyer.

Phil Zalesky

quickly introduced the area to fellow poet Philip Whalen who was hired to man the cabin on the summit of Sauk Mountain in 1953, then Sourdough (1954–55). Intrigued, their friend Jack Kerouac applied and was stationed at Desolation Peak in 1956. Some of Kerouac's best writing emanated from his single summer stint high above Ross Lake, close to the Canadian border. That cabin, as well as Sourdough, remains in service today.

THE SLEEPING GIANT BLINKS AWAKE

In 1906, with Theodore Roosevelt in the White House and Gifford Pinchot's fieldmen racing the Barbecue thieves, The Mountaineers club was founded "to preserve by the encouragement of protective legislation and other means the natural beauty of Northwest America." There were other purposes, as well, that were furthered by wilderness explorations on the annual Summer Outings and, from 1935 on, by the climbing course. A Northwest School of Mountaineering was developed to help its students become as proficient on snow, ice, and rain-wet, moss-slimy, and rotten rock as the attendees at Yosemite–High Sierra School were on dry, clean, solid granite. Club members enthusiastically exploited the abundant natural beauty of the Cascades and Olympics for their recreation. The concern for preservation, however, languished. Irving Clark, Sr., Leo Gallagher, stalwarts of the conservation movement, and a scattering of others persisted in the cause for the North Cascades, but they worked as individuals, feeling their energies could be utilized more efficiently that way, rather than goading the sleeping giant.

By the end of World War II, The Mountaineers had been so long absent from conservation that few members were aware of this chartered purpose. Gallagher did what he could, serving in 1949 as president of the Federation of Western Outdoor Clubs (FWOC) and arranging for The Mountaineers to host the annual convention that year. In April 1951 he represented the club at the Sierra Club's First Biennial Wilderness Conference (a 1949 conference on the subject was not called by that name).

Art Winder, as chair of the public affairs committee of The Mountaineers, regularly reported to the board of trustees on the current state of the wild world. A leading climber of the early 1930s, he commanded the respect of the climber-dominated board, which patiently heard him out and authorized him to write such letters of club support as he recommended for the initiatives of other organizations.

Stimulated, no doubt, by the two 1949 conferences, Winder sought wider attention. The June 1950 issue of *The Mountaineer* reported of a board meeting, "Conservation in general was discussed, it being the consensus of opinion that The Mountaineers as a Club, a key member of the FWOC, did less along these lines than many smaller clubs, which condition should be remedied to help preserve our forests, trails, and wilderness areas." The annual issue of *The Mountaineer* dated December 15, 1950, carried a stirring message, in which Winder wrote,

> there is a wealth of opportunity for the true lover of the natural scene . . . but very few have come forward to assist. . . . With a larger and more vigorous Public Affairs Committee, there is no limit to the possibilities that our club can accomplish. You can help.

The February 1951 *The Mountaineer* announced a meeting of the committee and hoped for a large turnout. The Dyers responded but came away disappointed. The following year, however, under a new name, the Conservation *and* Public Affairs Committee met in April, May, and June, with Polly Dyer as secretary. That fall as The Mountaineers' delegate to the Federation of Western Outdoor Clubs meeting at Snoqualmie Lodge, she renewed her old acquaintance with Ed Wayburn, FWOC president for the year, and was appointed to the resolutions committee. The March 1953 issue of *The Mountaineer* stated that the Conservation Committee, as the re-simplified name had it, met monthly on Mondays, and in that month, three Mondays. In later reflection, Winder judged 1954 the turning point for the club's commitment.

The Washington Automobile Club, a unit of the American Automobile Association that helped drive the notion that parks were for cars, proposed a funicular tramway to or near the summit of Mount Rainier, a system of Swiss-like huts, guides and ski instructors, and a swimming pool and golf course in Paradise Valley. From a conservation standpoint, the plan was preposterous, but so was most everything proposed for the public lands by "Asphalt Al" Leland, the state's panjandrum of highways; Governor Arthur Langlie, a favorite of President "Interstate" Eisenhower; and Oregon's ex-governor become U.S. Secretary of the Interior, Douglas "Give-Away" McKay. The Chambers of Commerce cheered the proposal, the newspapers beat the drums, and most painfully, some Mountaineer skiers exulted in the prospect of glacier tours and cozy huts with hot soup, cheese sandwiches, and lots of yodeling. The National Park Service wrung its hands.

Public meetings were held, John Dyer the chief organizer. Knowledgeable Mountaineer skiers succeeded in diverting the ski lobby to areas outside the park. Better weather and better snow on the lee of The Mountain (Rainier) eventually brought about the Crystal Mountain ski area, financially backed by a number of Mountaineers, notably Leo Gallagher whose mattress factory in Tacoma was humming along nicely. More immediately, the club instigated two thousand letters opposing the desecration of Paradise Valley—ten letters against for every one in support. The Mountaineers had flexed muscles, defended Rainier, smitten the ineffable Langlie and Leland, and was proud of it.

From 1954 the monthly issue of *The Mountaineer* was packed with announcements of meetings, calls to write letters, and thoughtful analyses of a variety of conservation issues. Winder, his lonesome efforts at last rewarded, was pleased in the fall of 1954 to yield the chair of the conservation committee to Polly Dyer.

Meanwhile, in Another Part of the Forest . . .

In December 1939, while in Washington, D.C., on other business, Irving Clark, Sr. stopped by Forest Service headquarters to urge Chief Silcox that the proposed memorial to Bob Marshall be a wilderness dedication in his favorite area, the North Cascades. Silcox said that was being given first consideration. Later, Clark again looked in on Silcox. The Chief was out of the office, but an aide said he was very anxious to complete the wilderness dedication as a memorial to Marshall. However, he was delaying doing so, pending the decision of the Supreme Court in a suit challenging aspects of the Northern Pacific Land Grant. The possibility existed that vast tracts of land could be stripped from the Barbecuers and returned to the public domain, including the Forest Service domain. In 1940 the court voted four to four, one justice abstaining, and the suit died. Shortly after Clark's visit, Silcox was dead, and with him, the Marshall proposal. Marshall and Silcox were weakly honored (if that is the word, and it is not) by the Glacier Peak Limited Area—at 352,000 acres, it was less than half the size of the 795,000-acre wilderness recommended by Marshall.

A decade later, Irving Clark and Art Winder called upon the supervisor of Mount Baker National Forest to discuss the area's future. Did this meeting persuade, maybe goose, the Forest Service? In the aforementioned article published in the December 15, 1950, issue of *The Mountaineer*, Winder reported:

> Attracting a great deal of interest also is the decision of the Forest Service to convert the large Glacier Peak Limited Area of Washington State into a Wilderness Area. A limited area is land set aside from the public domain on a "stop-look-listen" basis, pending completion of studies which will determine the best use for which the region should be suited, and thus better serve the people of the vicinity. It is unquestionable that the Glacier Peak region, with its tremendously rugged mountains, beautiful mountain meadows and lakes, is admirably suited for use as a wilderness area, with its attendant recreational values, and thus is better left in its comparatively primitive state. A conference of interested groups will be held this winter for the purpose of deciding final boundaries. . . .

PHOTO BY JOHN MONTOUX, COURTESY OF THE WILDERNESS SOCIETY

Chief of the Forest Service (1933-40) Ferdinand Silcox (left) with Bob Marshall, head of the Recreation and Lands Division.

Hindsight queries the adjective "large" for the limited area, and the motivation to "better serve the people of the vicinity." But the more burning question is, whatever happened to that promised conference?

If there was a goosing, it surely didn't go far enough. The Forest Service was heard to murmur in 1951 that studies ought to begin soon. At the FWOC convention in 1953, a Forest Service representative asked Polly Dyer what subject the conservation community wished to address. Polly didn't have to fumble for an answer. Though not yet chair of the conservation committee, she had been a key member for a year and knew what folks were talking about: the cover of the July 1953 *The Mountaineer* featured the "Proposed Glacier Peak Wilderness Area." A resolution adopted by the 1954 FWOC convention added underlining. The ground was prepared for what was to be, in six big years, a great leap forward, if only inch by inch.

1955: A SERENDIPITY

The conservation committee of The Mountaineers was entering a period of vigor unmatched in the club's history. Three joint field trips with the Forest Service were held during the summer of 1955, along the White Chuck River, the Suiattle River, and the North Fork Sauk River—the major western approaches to Glacier Peak. The club was represented on these trips by Richard Brooks as chair of the subcommittee that arranged the trips, as well as Polly Dyer, Phil and Laura Zalesky, Leo Gallagher, Paul Wiseman, and Pam Olmsted. Forest Service people included Art Harrison, Supervisor of Mount Baker Forest; his recreation officer, Suiattle District Ranger Dick Woodcock; Darrington District Ranger Harold Engles; and a staffer from Region Six headquarters. Virlis Fischer, from Portland, appeared uninvited shepherding a guest, Irston Barnes of Washington, D.C. A nature columnist for the *Washington Post*, Barnes wrote glowingly about the magnificent forests and wilderness values of Glacier Peak, giving the area its first national exposure.

Each field trip had negligible value as a boundary study, but great importance as a meeting of minds—a non-meeting, rather. In fact, a confrontation. The Forest Service was startled to learn the club was dead serious in seeking a wilderness area and dismayed to find the group could not be shrugged off by a public relations exercise. The Mountaineers were stunned to hear Forest Supervisor Harrison brag up his clearcuts and praise a stand of ten-year-old

Grant McConnell (left) and Richard Brooks enjoy a rest on the Rainbow Trail overlooking Lake Chelan (post-1968).

HARVEY MANNING

second-growth as a foreground for Glacier Peak. He seemed baffled when they expressed strong preference for old growth.

Brooks did most of the talking on the trips, addressing the Forest Service in such terms as may have shocked Barnes' sensitive ears. Yet whenever Brooks paused to engulf another sandwich, Polly Dyer and Phil Zalesky broke in to convey the identical message, as adamantly—if at lower decibels—that the Forest Service's intention for a boundary at the thirty-five-hundred-foot level meant little more than "wilderness on the rocks," to use the phrase later coined by Dave Simons, a young photographer working with Brower. Most of the old-growth forest resided below that elevation; most of the rocks above. The proposed boundary, therefore, was unacceptable to this cohesive group that planned to be in the contest for as long a run as it took. Personal and business affairs subsequently diverted Brooks from the conservation committee, but his compatriots of the 1954–1955 period credit his tireless filibuster and sheer voice volume with keeping Glacier Peak ever before their eyes and upon their ears.

Key members of the conservation committee had little or no personal acquaintance with the Glacier Peak area, but Phil and Laura Zalesky knew it well and arranged "show and tell" trips—the walks-and-talks that excited the committee leadership. One of these trips concluded in a momentous serendipity. Polly Dyer and Phil and Laura Zalesky backpacked from Lucerne on Lake Chelan up Railroad Creek and down Agnes Creek to Stehekin. In the restaurant at the boat landing, they were approached by a woman who had spotted their ice axes and asked what peaks they had been climbing. Polly explained

Phil and Laura Zalesky

they indeed were climbers, yet this particular trip was to study the wilderness. The woman said, "You should meet my husband, but he's seven miles up the valley." As an up-valley Stehekinite, Grant McConnell avoided The Dock during the mob scene of boat arrivals and departures, mainly coming to pick up and post letters. Jane was doing mail duty that day—that historic day—when Puget Sound conservationists first heard of the McConnells, and the McConnells first heard that there were Puget Sound conservationists.

As it happened, Grant had been trying to learn if there really were any conservationists, and if so, who they were and where. Rick Mack from Yakima chanced to visit the McConnells, and Grant had been picking Mack's brains for possibilities. So, on this fateful day, Jane was bringing Mack to the landing to catch the boat, and as she made the acquaintance of Polly, Rick came up and said (of Polly), "This is the person I was telling Grant about." The previous year Rick and Polly had met at Snoqualmie Lodge during a meeting of the Federation of Western Outdoor Clubs. So it was that separate threads began winding together into a skein.

Later, in Berkeley, Polly Dyer stopped in to meet Grant McConnell. "Grant suggested that we should include more than Glacier Peak" in the wilderness proposal, she recalled. "Of course, he was more familiar with the east side than we were at the time." Back in Seattle, Polly Dyer arranged for Phil Zalesky to stage his slide show for the monthly meeting of The Mountaineers. So many of the club's trustees were in the audience that the evening amounted to a formal presentation by the conservation committee to the board. Leo Gallagher was so impressed that he paid Zalesky's way to the Labor Day convention of the Federation of Western Outdoor Clubs in the San Jacinto Mountains outside of Palm Springs, California. The slide show led Ed Wayburn, president of the FWOC, to assure Zalesky he had the strong support of the FWOC and the Sierra Club.

Phil's slide show also was a featured presentation at the dinner meeting of the first Northwest Wilderness Conference, in Portland in 1956. The main event of that dinner was the first-ever public reading of the wilderness bill that Howard Zahniser, Executive Secretary of the Wilderness Society, was drafting for Senator Hubert Humphrey, shortly before the bill was to be introduced in Congress. Also, David Brower received an award from Edward Graves of the National Parks Association for his efforts in the Dinosaur National Monument battle at Echo Park. Brower's tenacity and Zahniser's persistence were both instrumental in securing an act of Congress not only to stop the Bureau of Reclamation from flooding the spectacular converging canyons of the Green and Yampa Rivers in northwestern Colorado, but to ban similar projects from being constructed in *any* national park or monument. And while Zahniser and Brower may have shared the spotlight at the Portland conference, the Glacier

Peak proposal was by no means short-changed; this was its initial national exposure in the presence of national leaders.

At his typewriter alternately in Stehekin and Berkeley, McConnell kept up a rapid-fire correspondence with Wenatchee Forest Supervisor Ken Blair, politely inquiring his intentions, and Howard Zahniser, suggesting that the Wilderness Society's governing council meet in Stehekin. A December 9, 1955, letter from Ed Wayburn, chair of the Sierra Club's conservation committee, said he had read McConnell's correspondence with Dave Brower. Wayburn wrote that he was "greatly impressed by your knowledge . . . The Sierra Club is actively interested in the Glacier Peak area. We lack firsthand knowledge and would like to have you meet with us. . . ." They met in January 1956.

In December 1955, *The Mountaineer* published maps of the 1939 Marshall-Silcox proposal and the 1940 Glacier Peak Limited Area, and considering what was excluded, both maps are rather puzzling to the retrospective eye.

How could Bob Marshall, for example, have omitted all of Lake Chelan and the entirety of the Stehekin Valley below Bridge Creek? The whole of the Entiat and most of the Chiwawa? The entire Little Wenatchee except the headwaters? The White Chuck almost to Kennedy Hot Springs? The lower valleys of Sulphur, Downey, and Buck Creeks? The Cascade River upstream to Mineral Park? Did Marshall judge their exclusion to be more expedient? Did he just miss them? Was this the downside to walking thirty-plus miles a day? Some things and places cannot be seen, much less felt, without sitting still on occasion. Yet Marshall,

Howard Zahniser in 1946 on a backpacking trip with New York conservationists Paul A. Schaefer and Edmund Richard in what is now the New York State High Peaks Wilderness Area.

PHOTO BY PAUL SCHAEFER, COURTESY OF THE ZAHNISER FAMILY

we must assume, was well aware of what was at stake and was as determined as anyone to bring wilderness protection to the North Cascades. Quoting from Marshall biographer James M. Glover in *A Wilderness Original*, Marshall said, "I honestly believe that the Forest Service wilderness areas . . . are far safer than Park Service wilderness areas." It was a crucial point and something he had thought about long before his arrival in the North Cascades. After surveying the Glacier Peak area and preparing his report, Marshall said to his friend Irving Clark, "I know and you know perfectly well that if the area should be made a park, [the National Park Service] would have extended roads into its heart." For that reason, "I advocated for six years that the entire North Cascade country, down to Stevens Pass, should be created as a National Forest wilderness."

Polly Dyer, NCCC co-founder and current board member, agreed. "Some of us on the NCCC board also didn't go for NPS status initially—for exactly the same reasons Marshall had in 1938."

If Marshall, a genuine saint of the conservation movement, let slide some of the best available wildlands in his vision for the North Cascades, then what of the successors of Silcox, whose careers reeked of something other than sanctity? The view of the 1940 Limited Area was clearly that of a blind man—or an intensive manager. Marshall, in fact, had included Lyman Basin–Miners Ridge and the upper North Fork Sauk–Sloan Creek, but the Limited Area sliced them out. Most significantly, Marshall embraced the huge province from Cascade Pass north through Eldorado to the overlook of the Skagit; the upper Stehekin, Park Creek, and Bridge Creek to the headwaters of the Twisp; and from there northeast to Silver Star Mountain, Harts Pass, and Canyon Creek. The 1940 surgery by the Forest Service deleted all of that.

The failures of the Forest Service were not entirely the fault of vision. The philosophy of wilderness preservation was also fundamental. Though "wilderness" was the heart of the matter, the concept was too narrow in its focus to protect the lower Stehekin Valley or Lake Chelan itself or a score of other entryways to the North Cascades. There had to be something more, another form of wilderness protection that was not in the Forest Service manual. Marshall's vision was limited by the official vocabulary available to him in the Agriculture Department. In the Interior Department of Harold Ickes, the constraints of precious little jewels were being challenged by a new term, "super-park." The great notion of what we now refer to as a "greater ecosystem" was taking shape in the minds of many wildland travelers, but had yet to be given the phrasing and promotion needed to plant it in the public mind. The concept of a national park was well established among the citizenry: a national park was permanent; it crudely protected many spectacular landscapes, but frequently sacrificed wildness for creature comforts, pristine ecosystems for parking lots and scenic drives. Wilderness, though much less understood by the masses, was all about keeping intact ecosystems wild; yet the land designations were agency driven and vulnerable to the whims of a bureaucracy that was becoming increasingly dedicated to timber and mineral extraction—not just in the North Cascades, but all across the West.

1956: The Arena Enlarges

The earliest notice of the North Cascades taken by the Sierra Club was the 1912 publication of an illustrated article about a Mazama trip to the "Lake Chelan country," described by C.L. McFarland (of the Mazamas) as "that ever alluring, ever forbidding region of countless jagged peaks . . . vast and inaccessible." A quarter-century later, the February 1937 *Sierra Club Bulletin* carried "The Cascade Range in Northern Washington," by Hermann F. Ulrichs, a vivid portrait as evocative as any the area has known. Ulrichs managed twenty-one first ascents in his first five years in the North Cascades, considering it a perfect range for mountaineering, possibly the nation's best. Duly impressed, he wrote:

> The crowning glory of the Cascades is, for me, the unusually extensive subalpine zone, which commonly begins above 5000 feet and makes a rich green fringe between the ultimate edge of the forest and the everlasting rock and snow. . . . It would be hard to imagine a more striking and felicitous contrast than that between this idyllic, really Arcadian, country of intimate beauty and delicacy, and the almost savage ruggedness and grandeur of the big peaks, the deep valleys far below, and the magnificent panoramas of distant snowy ranges glowing in the soft light."

One may assume the article was a stimulus for the climbing parties that came north from California that year to lay hands on the rock and boots on the ice. The same year the Wyeast climbers from the Portland, Oregon, area took the voyage recommended by Ulrichs: "The most direct and beautiful approach to the heart of the range is by way of Lake Chelan, which will some day be classed as one of the unique wonders of the nation." The Sierra Club did not, let it be noted, support the Ickes concept of a Cascades super-park—but then, neither did The Mountaineers, whose climbers during the same period were exploiting much quicker access elsewhere. Nor did the Sierra Club support the Ickes proposal of a super-park on the Colorado Plateau that could have saved Glen Canyon, nor even a Kings Canyon National Park, until Secretary Ickes had dinner with club directors at the Bohemian Club and shook them up a little. The club board was composed mostly of Republicans, and editor/director Francis Farquhar would flag down a proposed resolution congratulating Ickes by saying, "We do not praise a government employee for doing his job."

After World War II a great notion stirred in the environs of San Francisco Bay—the desire for a beyond-Sierra Club structure to address the needs of beyond-California lands. An Atlantic chapter was formed, a clustering of exiles able by their location to revive the old Boston–San Francisco axis. When Polly and John Dyer moved to Seattle, Dick Leonard suggested they explore the possibility of a Northwest chapter in Seattle. In 1952 a new epoch began for the Sierra Club when David Brower was hired as its first executive director. Mike McCloskey, who succeeded Brower as executive director some years later, observed that "The Young Turks on the board decided that the organization should become a more forceful conservation voice and that it should go national, forming chapters around the country." Brower, having begun his conservation activism in 1938 working toward the Kings Canyon National Park, knew the other side of the mountain and was, himself, a prototype of the different kind of animal. The new executive director flew north, was picked up at the airport by Polly and taken to Seattle for the first meeting of the Dyers and Goldsworthys, thus uniting two strands of the Muir Connection. Brower agreed that a Pacific Northwest chapter was a great idea, and in 1954 it came to be. Patrick and Jane Goldsworthy did much of the legwork, and John Dyer prepared the bylaws and conducted diplomatic negotiations with the Sierra Club board, many of whose members were reluctant to go national. Leo Gallagher of The Mountaineers opposed the creation of the new chapter. "We already have The Mountaineers," he said. Others respectfully disagreed. John Dyer's subtle strategy defined the chapter to include Idaho, Montana, Alaska, British Columbia, and Alberta, so that the Sierra Club could have a voice even where it had no members. At the time, the club had just one member in all of Idaho and Montana, two in the Canadian provinces, and a dozen in Alaska. The Northwest chapter thus became the first international chapter of the Sierra Club. (The Pacific Northwest chapter has since evolved into the Oregon, Northern Rockies, Western Canada, Alaska, and Washington–Cascade chapters representing tens of thousands of members. By 2006, the club had grown to sixty-seven chapters and more than 750,000 members.)

Glacier Peak, of course, remained at the top of the new Sierra Club chapter's to-do list and became increasingly important to the club as a whole. On March 14, 1956, Brower wrote Forest Service Chief McArdle in Washington, D.C., inquiring about Glacier Peak. The April 14 response:

> The supervisor of the Mount Baker and Wenatchee Forests started making an analysis of the Glacier Peak Limited Area and adjacent terrain in December, 1955. . . . Since the existing limited area was established almost solely by superficial ocular examination, it is expected that the boundary based on this set of criteria may not coincide with the existing one. . . .

Thus did the prophet of intensive management give fair warning. Nothing in the limited area was secure, with the exception (one could hope) of the cold black rock and blue ice of Glacier Peak itself. The Sierra Club mobilized, moving the North Cascades up on its agenda, as well as keeping dams out of the Grand Canyon and saving the California Redwoods. Previously the club had characterized the Glacier Peak region as the "most truly Alpine of our mountains." In the summer of 1956 the club went there for a Base Camp, a Knapsack Trip, and a High Trip led by Pat Goldsworthy and attended by the entire Brower family and Howard Zahniser of the Wilderness Society.

In the following five years, with Brower at the helm, the Sierra Club scheduled thirteen outings to the North Cascades with seven hundred participants, and financed four study summers by Dave Simons, five part-summers by Sierra Club photographer Philip Hyde, one by John Warth, and one part-summer by Ansel Adams. The club also assisted Charles D. ("Chuck") Hessey, Jr., in producing films of Glacier Peak country that were particularly influential with audiences in Yakima, Wenatchee, and Chelan, and produced its own film, *Wilderness Alps of Stehekin* (noted below). Three brochures were issued, 125,000 copies in all, including one headlined, "What Is Your Stake in the Northern Cascades?" as well as 350,000 copies of sixteen wilderness postcards. The *Sierra Club Bulletin* published 108 pages of text and as many pages of photographs.

The success of the Biennial Wilderness Conferences staged since 1951 by the Sierra Club inspired Karl Onthank, as president of the Federation of Western Outdoor Clubs, to fill the alternate years with a Biennial Northwest Wilderness Conference. The first, chaired by Leo Gallagher, was held in Portland April 7–8, 1956. Howard Zahniser took the occasion to unveil his Wilderness Bill, which he and David Brower originally drafted at the Cosmos Club in Washington D.C., and which was about to be introduced in Congress by Senator Humphrey; the conference wired its endorsement to the Senator. After the conference "Zahnie," at Leo's invitation, addressed the annual banquet of the Tacoma branch of The Mountaineers. He was not unfamiliar with the Puget Sound region, having been a frequent visitor, usually on Olympic National Park matters, staying with his friend and fellow member of the council of The Wilderness Society, Irving Clark, Sr. Though very much a national figure in the wilderness movement, Zahniser tended to keep a much lower profile than Brower and others, and instead developed countless personal relationships in all the right places to help build the cause. He was appointed executive secretary of The Wilderness Society after the death of co-founder Robert Sterling Yard in 1945; Olaus Murie, an accomplished Wyoming wildlife biologist, was named president. Zahniser worked feverishly to move wilderness proposals forward, to build the national campaign, and to ensure regular publication of the Society's ground-breaking journal, *The Living Wilderness*. It was Zahniser's firm belief that "Some of the earth should be so respected as not to be dominated by man and his works." Some areas, he said, should be "so managed as to be left unmanaged [by man] . . . in every way unmodified by his civilization." By 1951 he was outlining his proposal for a national wilderness act. Later that year a heart attack demanded that he ease up on the throttle some.

Since Zahniser knew little of the North Cascades in 1951, Leo Gallagher took the opportunity to educate him, hiring a twin-engine, five-passenger airplane for a tour of inspection; Phil Zalesky and Jack Hazle, vice president of The Mountaineers, came along to steer the pilot and point out boundaries of the conservationists' proposal for a Glacier Peak Wilderness. Spring snows prevented Zahnie from viewing the high-country greenery, but that summer (1951) a Sierra Club outing to White Pass, led by Patrick Goldsworthy, made up for it. On the way to the pass, Goldsworthy recalls Zahniser exclaiming, "The Cascades is a vast sea of peaks with wave after wave of ranges as far as the eye can see." Then Phil Zalesky walked Zahnie to the ridge above the pass to show him Glacier Peak—and proceeded to explain what he would see were it not for the fog that had enveloped the two-mile-high sleeping volcano. But neither snows nor mists could bar him from the forest experience; he was particularly struck by the magnificent grove at the start of the North Fork Sauk River trail—a grove, incidentally, that still existed only because District Ranger Harold Engles, the quintessential Old Ranger, refused to hold a timber sale there. The refusal lost him a very good friend, a logger who wanted the trees. Phil Zalesky remembers a field trip with Leo Gallagher and Harold Engles, among others, where Engles said that such a timber sale "would never happen" because those big trees "had a higher purpose." Engles, we should note, knew and loved the Glacier Peak region as well as anyone, having built trails and fire lookouts in some of the wildest and most precipitous places imaginable.

Later, when Howard Zahniser was in search of just the right word to help define "wilderness" in his draft wilderness bill, Polly Dyer suggested "untrammeled." It was perfect. And thus emerged Zahniser's definition of wilderness:

> A wilderness, in contrast with those areas where man and his own works dominate the landscape, is hereby recognized as an area where the earth and its community of life are untrammeled by man, where man himself is a visitor who does not remain.

1956: STEHEKIN SPEAKS

As late as 1955 Professor Grant McConnell preserved a respectable academic objectivity about the North Cascades. He considered Ken Blair, supervisor of Wenatchee National Forest, unusually intelligent, folksy, well-spoken, and perhaps the ablest of the Region Six supervisors. Blair described a study process involving ten map overlays of the Glacier Peak area, an innovative means to inventory the land and its values. McConnell learned that there was to be a great deal more logging activity than in the past; still, it was a distant prospect.

In the spring of 1956, however, the implications of the generalities struck close to the McConnell home, in a future only as remote as a few weeks. While still in Berkeley, packing for the summer trip to Stehekin, McConnell received a call from Jack Stevens, a young orchardist in Manson near the foot of Lake Chelan. The Forest Service was rumored to have issued a call for bids on a timber sale in the Stehekin Valley. Details were obscure but alarming. To be sure logging had been done on homesteaded lands in the valley, but never on a large scale and not at all on public lands. Nevertheless, if the east slopes of the Cascades lacked an abundance of lush forests with giant trees, it was managed by the same Forest Service as the west side and its New Rangers had gone to the same schools and reported to the same politicos in Washington D.C.

This timber sale was rumored to be the first of an annual series, the introduction of intensive management. It looked as if Stehekin had been annexed to the downlake world. So it was that the professor was driven from the scholarly cloister to the activist arena.

Had the sale been intended to set off a bomb under the professor's chair, the Forest Service could not have done better. The McConnells detoured to Puget Sound to spread the alert. A call to Polly Dyer brought about a meeting at the Dyer home in Auburn attended by a dozen Mountaineers, including the club president, Chet Powell; Paul Wiseman, who was to succeed him in office; and the Goldsworthys. McConnell argued for a specialized group to confront the threat. The response: "We already have The Mountaineers."

It was a fair enough answer. Neither in Berkeley nor in Stehekin was McConnell so situated as to realize how active the club had suddenly become. For example, in June 1956 *The Mountaineer* published the map and accompanying text of the proposal submitted earlier in the spring to the Forest Service and the Federation of Western Outdoor Clubs. As the conservation committee's studies conducted in 1955 had not been carried north of Cascade Pass, the group accepted Marshall's boundary line for that area without examination. To the south, however, Marshall's boundaries had been pushed out to take in the Stehekin as far downstream as Agnes Creek, which was included in its entirety; plus the headwaters of Company, Devore, and Riddle Creeks; more of the Chiwawa, Little Wenatchee, Sulphur, Downey, Illabot, and Found Creeks; and a bit more of the south bank of the Cascade River. Though in hindsight it was a timid advance, this first effort by these fresh minds was a giant leap beyond the bounds of the Glacier Peak Limited Area and a healthy stride beyond even Bob Marshall's modest vision. More study was to engender greater boldness.

Yet speculative proposals had little or nothing to do with the immediate reality of the Stehekin timber sale; the bids were due on July 19th. The Auburn group agreed to set up an emergency committee of correspondence, a round-robin exchange of letters among leaders of the Sierra Club and The Mountaineers. McConnell proceeded from Auburn to Wenatchee to ask about the sale. Blair was not in the office, but underlings denied any such sale was in mind. However, once in Stehekin, McConnell talked to Ray Courtney, second-generation Old Stehekinite and close observer of the scene, who affirmed he had seen the sale notice.

McConnell devised a clever gambit. He wrote a letter to Chet Powell, president of The Mountaineers, to the effect: "The timber sale in Stehekin would be such a disaster, I am assured by officials of Wenatchee National Forest it is not going to happen. It was a false rumor. However, I've been advised to contact Supervisor Ken Blair, and so am sending him a copy of this letter."

The desired effect was obtained. Letters from Blair informed McConnell there was to be a small timber sale to clear an emergency landing strip, "needed for the safety of our patrol planes and other fliers," but denied the existence of plans for the other sale and assured him it would not happen. But the word transmitted orally by a local ranger was that the sale had merely been postponed. Blair, we can surmise, was on a fast track to higher office. To get there, he had to finesse McConnell. It could not be done, though Blair hardly can be blamed for trying.

The information assembled by McConnell from reading Forest Service memos that officially didn't exist, and keeping his ear to the ground and his eyes open added up to something of a horror story. The era of intensive management meant that forests so far untouched were to be sold at the rate of some five million board feet a year, in the Stehekin Valley to start, then continuing up Agnes Creek where the real timber prizes lay. The pressure for the "cutting circle" came from Chelan Lumber and Box, a small operation in Manson, of the sort known in the trade as a "jackknife mill," with a payroll of some eighty men in a community of five thousand. Though it sought orchardist support as the main supplier of apple boxes, timber abounded in much handier locations than Stehekin. In effect, if not intent, the operator, George Wall, was a stalking horse. Weyerhaeuser had sent a cruiser through the area. If Wall could open the door, the barons could follow, most likely by buying up his smallish company, a strategy that bigger companies employed when a front seemed politic. Wall had other powerful connections; his father was a state senator and leader of the Washington State Republican Party. Perhaps most important, the Forest Service needed a George Wall, a Chelan Box, as an excuse for intensive management of a new cutting circle in Lake Chelan and Stehekin.

Wall must have had oral assurances from the Forest Service, or he would not otherwise have been readying an operations base, nor driving pilings in the lake to hold logs for rafting to the mill. From aerial photographs of the Agnes valley, he "counted" eighteen billion board feet. As preparation for the big push to timberline, he was buying Stehekin properties and cutting rights, and in the summer of 1956 had eight loggers and two trucks in the valley. McConnell daily heard the whine of saws, the crash of big firs and pines. The first sale of public timber, however small, would be a foot in the door, the camel's nose under the tent, permitting Wall to claim vested interest status should the unofficial plans unravel.

Wall, however, did not have the political support enjoyed by many timbermen of the west side. Though a kneejerk reaction by the Chelan Chamber of Commerce backed him and opposed wilderness, many folks in the orchardist-dominated communities wanted to shut out ugliness from their private Shangri La. Sad to say, their motivation was to prove to be less the national interest than the local. Later, when they realized the national interest would conflict with their local rights to build, subdivide, and speculate, and otherwise do business in Stehekin, most were to swing around. As for the handful of year-around Stehekinites, they hated the prospect of large-scale logging but feared the power of George Wall. Except for Ray Courtney, Paul Bergman, and one or two others, they kept their mouths shut, believing they faced an unstoppable juggernaut. A few, certainly, looked forward to gleaning the bones of the Barbecue.

McConnell evaluated the threat as that of a headlong rush by a tiny group of exploiters whose interests were hand in glove with the ideologues of intensive management, and they were powerful in the Republican government of Chelan County, the state, and Congress. If the steamroller could not be halted, no paranoid nightmare was required to envision Wall's logging road pushing up the Agnes valley to near the then-projected Kennecott Copper Company road up the Suiattle River valley west of the crest; the gap inevitably would be closed, fully bisecting the wilderness.

McConnell's letters amounted to a week-by-week hotline around the nation. Blair complained to his staff that the professor was causing him all sorts of trouble in Washington D.C. Senator Henry Jackson (an Everett native still in his first term) asked the big question of Chief McArdle, who denied the sale (and perhaps told his aides to scratch Blair's name from the promotion list). Blair, in a letter to Congressman Don Magnuson, denied the sale ever was planned, then admitted that certain blocks of Stehekin timber were ready to be cut (that is, the trees were "over-ripe, decadent," et cetera) and would be

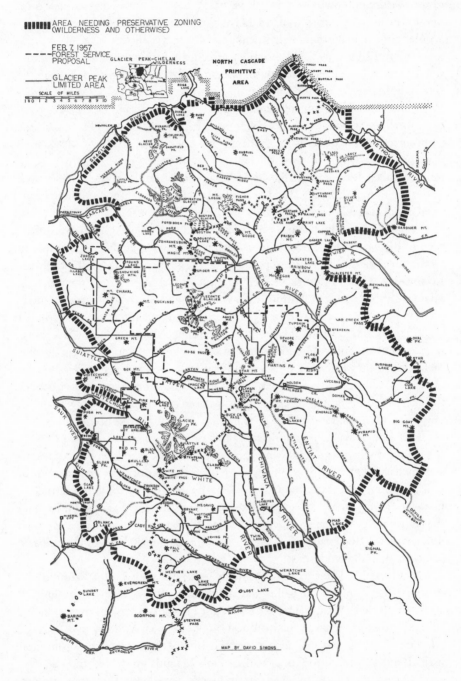

*The heavy outer line on this map would later form a
basis for NCCC's 1963 national park proposal.*

sold in the next year or so. He affirmed that sales in the Agnes Creek drainage were "under consideration."

In a July 10, 1956, round-robin letter, McConnell reported a dinner meeting in Stehekin of a few local residents and Blair, who promised that no sales would be made in Stehekin until the Glacier Peak Wilderness boundaries were settled. However, he gave firm assurance that there would be eventual logging on the Stehekin and up Bridge Creek and Park Creek; as for Agnes Creek, he acknowledged the existence of a "sensitivity." He thought to counter objections by conjuring up the specter of a national park, which never had ceased to haunt the Forest Service. McConnell failed to share Blair's abhorrence; clearly the best of wilderness areas would not save the lower Stehekin, rendered ineligible by a scattering of houses and roads, and the wilderness intended by the Forest Service would not save the upper Stehekin and its tributaries.

The round robin revolving around McConnell's letters continued to year's end, in November reaching another personage of history-book stature, Sigurd Olson, then president of the National Parks Association. Olson had also worked with Zahniser and Brower in drafting the wilderness bill and afterwards spent years in the hot seat in Minnesota deflecting rural angst and defending the legislation for Humphrey. McConnell sent a statement on the North Cascades accompanied by a hundred color slides, asking Olson to "get them to the right people" in the National Parks Association. "Very few people have seen the area," he wrote. "It is so vast that my own ignorance is enormous—and I've been going there twenty years and for three years lived in the heart."

1957: The Forest Service Acts, Conservationists React

On February 7, 1957, Region Six headquarters of the Forest Service issued a *Glacier Peak Land Management Study* embodying a preliminary proposal for a 434,310-acre Wilderness Area, nominally larger than the Limited Area. McConnell wrote Ken Blair thanking him for his labors, praising the pioneering method of analysis by use of overlay maps. The letter's sugar coat then wore thin. Since this momentous work was to serve as a model for the nation, the "job should be complete," he wrote. It should encompass a larger region; Stehekin had been omitted, together with the entire northern sector of Marshall's proposal. To provide a proper basis for rational land-use planning, McConnell argued, the study should cover such roaded areas as the lower Stehekin Valley, where roadside recreation and wilderness recreation were two sides of the same coin.

McConnell's critique was broadly distributed by the Sierra Club, whose board already had resolved that the Forest Service Chief should take steps as soon as possible, either by interagency cooperation or collaboration, to conduct a comprehensive study of the North Cascades between Stevens Pass and Canada, aiming to preserve the entire region in a primitive condition.

Fred Packard, executive secretary of the National Parks Association (later to become the National Parks Conservation Association, or NPCA), reported to McConnell that he had shown the hundred slides to Chief McArdle and Assistant Chief Cliff. McArdle vowed he would "fight to the death to preserve a region as fine as that." His staff was impressed by not only the Glacier Peak vicinity but also the classification-lacking region extending north to the boundary of the North Cascades Primitive Area. Cliff announced his intention to come out in the summer to see the country for himself. Packard concluded by informing McConnell that he was going to show the slides to Senator Jackson and the National Park Service.

While the round-robin group kept their typewriters at white heat, the heavy artillery of the printing press stepped up its bombardment. In late 1956 and early 1957, the Sierra Club issued more pamphlets and published more articles in the *Bulletin*; *The Mountaineer* carried a John Warth summary; *The Living Wilderness* by The Wilderness Society featured Glacier Peak on its cover and in an editorial; The Mountaineers published a major leaflet by its conservation committee and distributed twenty-five thousand copies; and John Oakes wrote a column in May 1956 for the *New York Times* supporting Senator Humphrey's wilderness bill. The Spokane Mountaineers, the Alpine Roamers of Wenatchee, the Cascadians of Yakima, and even the Manson Boat Club were adding their voices to the chorus calling for protection of Lake Chelan, Stehekin, and the Cascades' west-side river valleys. McConnell's knowledge of politics helped Polly Dyer lobby successfully in Olympia for a memorial to Congress through the Washington State legislature in April; Senate Joint Memorial 23, called for an "adequate Glacier Peak Wilderness Area." And in 1957, The Mountaineers Summer Outing, an annual tradition since the club's founding in 1906, returned to Glacier Peak—oddly enough, its first visit to the North Cascades since the 1930s.

The Labor Day convention of the Federation of Western Outdoor Clubs resolved that it

> Supports and recommends that the Glacier Peak Wilderness Preference Area Proposal of February 7, 1957, of the U.S. Forest Service be augmented to include all areas, except Cady Pass, that have been proposed by The Mountaineers in 1956 as part of a proposed Glacier Peak Wilderness Area.

A 1957 Sierra Club outing found Grant McConnell and Ed Wayburn in a *tête-á-tête* warily circling a controversial subject—only to discover that they were already in agreement that the Stehekin Valley belonged in the same company as Yosemite Valley and should be a national park. Wayburn said, "We've got to convince Ned Graves," western representative of the National Parks Association. They boxed him in on the Cascade Pass trail and kept quiet to let the country speak for itself. At last, Graves burst out, "This ought to be a park!"

The idea began to circulate in leadership circles. The time for a public surfacing, however, had not yet arrived. As they were later to confess, McConnell and Brower had long since agreed, confidentially, that the ultimate goal must be a park, that the Glacier Peak Wilderness was merely a preliminary. It was not politic at the time to say "park" in any but the most guarded company; circumlocutions were employed in a code by which the conspirators could recognize each other.

An amusing panel discussion took place in Seattle on December 6, 1957, at a meeting of the Society of American Foresters, Puget Sound Section (now the Washington State SAF). More than two hundred members were in the audience, the largest attendance in years. Regional Forester J. Herbert Stone sat on the panel, and conservationist Phil Zalesky debated the Reverend Riley Johnson, vicar of Saint Andrews Episcopal Church in Chelan. "Rev Riley," as he came to be almost fondly known, was a circuit-riding, outspoken foe of wilderness, tirelessly addressing Chambers of Commerce from his Chelan pulpit, praying the best for Mr. George Wall and his Chelan Box Company. Johnson and Wall were prominent faces in an increasingly vocal campaign against wilderness, with Johnson chalking up dozens of appearances hither and thither. A September news story on Glacier Peak in the Spokane *Spokesman-Review* quoted them both. If the timber is "locked up" in wilderness, said Wall, "it will be lost to our economy for all time." While Johnson predicted "an economic crisis from Oroville to Moses Lake." Oddly, both towns are farming communities and neither is located anywhere near Glacier Peak. One could surmise that the entire state faced a pending disaster. In Yakima, Rev Riley just as eloquently pulled strings with the Lord for the benefit of the new Boise-Cascade company—a major timberland owner (spun off from Weyerhauser), and an emerging Northwest powerhouse in the pulp, paper, and building materials industries.

At that December meeting in Seattle, the Rev boomed forth, "Who goes into the wilderness anyway? You wouldn't catch me carrying my wife on my back into any wilderness!" (Approving laughter from the foresters.)

When Zalesky's turn came, he responded, "Indeed, who does go into the wilderness? I have seen babies only days old being carried into the wilderness on the backs of their parents . . . I know an eighty-year-old man who climbed Mount Rainier and camped on the summit. In addition, the greatest teacher of all time went into the wilderness at Galilee to re-create body and soul." (Appreciative laughter.)

The Rev retorted, "Yes, it is true that Jesus went into the wilderness." Then, drawing out the syllables for emphasis, he added, "But I want you to know that *He was chased in there by the Devil!*"

Zalesky addressed the crowd and pointed to widening public support for wilderness around the country—in the Appalachians, at Dinosaur National Monument, and at Olympic National Park where the "most influential advocates" for preservation, he said, were "the labor unions, many of whom were involved with the forest industries." Even the U.S. Forest Service, he added, "deserves special praise for conceiving and establishing wilderness areas . . . long before there was any widespread pressure advocating such a policy." The audience seemed receptive, Zalesky later observed, though one can imagine a degree of nervous twitching in the wings.

The single most momentous action of 1957 was the production of a film. In spring, at the Sierra Club Wilderness Conference in Berkeley, the McConnells viewed the films of the Colorado River and Dinosaur National Monument that had been such potent educational devices and political weapons for conservation. Jane McConnell called her old friend and schoolmate Abigail Avery, in Massachusetts, who many years earlier had come to Stehekin to climb with the McConnells, fallen in love with the Valley, and acquired her own cabin as a base for backcountry hiking.

Asked Jane of Abby, "Wouldn't it be nice to have a film about the North Cascades?" Abby wrote a check for $5,000.

The production was quickly underway. Ray Courtney, who would soon join the NCCC board of directors (serving from 1957 to 1962), handled the packtrain. Dave Brower brought the camera and his two sons, one of whom, Ken, partnered with the McConnell's daughter, Ann, in picking huckleberries for the camera—well chaperoned by brother Jim and father Grant and sundry supporting performers. The *Wilderness Alps of Stehekin*, its sound track featuring Brower's eloquence, was edited to a length suitable for a half-hour slot on television. His rich narrative pointed to "an amazing wilderness of rugged Alps built in grand scale, unique, unsurpassed anywhere in the United States." In one scene as they hiked in the rain refreshed, he said, "we looked up to see the old contest between the crags and the mists."

For hundreds of thousands of Americans, the film offered their first view of the North Cascades. One hundred twenty-five copies were printed to be shown to outdoor clubs, service clubs, church groups, youth groups, voter groups, friends and neighbors. From the time of its premiere at the second Northwest Wilderness Conference in Seattle in March 1958 to the passage of the North Cascades Act ten years later, thousands of showings were staged across the nation; Polly Dyer estimates she personally arranged more than a hundred. The film won awards for Brower and the Sierra Club. For the nation, *Wilderness Alps of Stehekin* helped magnificently to win a wildland.

1957: The North Cascades Conservation Council

In June 1956 Grant McConnell was still proposing a new organization that would not be distracted by a thousand-and-one crises and thus be able to focus in tight on the North Cascades. The notion was met by silence in Puget Sound. He persisted, however, in a letter to Ed Wayburn where he summarized a number of Bay Area discussions, including one among David Brower, Polly Dyer, and Ned Graves. The letter was circulated through the executive committee of the Sierra Club board. Some were skeptical, but Wayburn was already convinced and argued that a new group was imperative. "[The] Northern Cascades wilderness, to me," said Wayburn, "represents the greatest series of challenges which the Sierra Club has at present." He had set up a North Cascades subcommittee of his conservation committee, appointing McConnell to the chair, inviting Al Schmitz, Polly Dyer, and Patrick Goldsworthy to serve.

Wayburn was concerned about a possible lack of coordination of the sort which had contributed to defeat in the Three Sisters wildlands of Oregon, where the Forest Service had cut fifty thousand acres from the primitive area when reclassifying those lands as wilderness. The California contingent of activists was so large and powerful that it "seemed at times to go off on a tangent," causing friction with the smaller but indispensable Northwest groups. Wayburn wrote the conservation committee of The Mountaineers pointing to the success of Olympic Park Associates, originally organized to fend off the timber industry's attempt in 1947 to reduce the size of Olympic National Park. The group further rebuffed the next such attempt in 1952. He stressed the urgent need for a "communications center" that went beyond the round-robin "committee of correspondence."

Patrick Goldsworthy lengthily argued in a January 25th response that The Mountaineers' conservation committee had become, just two years after the "turning point" defense of Mount Rainier National Park, a large and vigorous group, conducting field studies, taking slides, preparing displays, and preparing a substantial brochure. Communication, he said, was being excellently handled by the Glacier Peak subcommittee chaired by Phil Zalesky. Additionally, the Pacific Northwest chapter of the Sierra Club was coming along strong. A new organization would be "just one more group, the same people who would do the work anyway, duplicating efforts. . . ."

There arose a situation, not quite a conspiracy. Conservationists from around the area—Seattle, Ellensburg, Eugene, and Portland—were summoned to Portland, the announced reason being to meet with Region Six Forester J. Herbert Stone about boundaries for a Glacier Peak Wilderness. Many of those attending had no prior knowledge that they would be called to a later meeting at the Mazama clubroom whereupon they were startled to find The Mountaineers' representatives had come from Seattle with a name, bylaws, and a slate of officers for the new organization.

On March 23, 1957, at the clubroom of the Mazamas, the deed was formally done. McConnell, unable to attend, was surprised and overjoyed to receive a handwritten note from Phil Zalesky: "I was sorry that you were unable to make the Glacier Peak Conference in Portland on March 23," he wrote. "One of our accomplishments, at any rate, was the formation of the North Cascades Conservation Council. . . . "

Officers were appointed, including Phil Zalesky of Everett as president; Patrick Goldsworthy of Seattle, first vice president; Una Davies of Oswego, Oregon, second vice president; Neva Karrick, also from Seattle, recording secretary; Polly Dyer of Auburn, corresponding secretary; and Yvonne Prater from Ellensburg, treasurer. By year's end the directors of the NCCC were so well distributed organizationally and geographically as to be a true council: The Mountaineers and the Puget Sound region were represented by some ten members; areas and groups east of the Cascades by eleven, including two from Stehekin and three from the lower end of Lake Chelan; plus Oregon by three, and California by three. Almost a half-century later, as this book heads for the press, Phil and Laura Zalesky, Patrick Goldsworthy, and Polly Dyer are still among the most active members of the NCCC board of directors.

The meeting that day with Regional Forester J. Herbert Stone was none too heartening, and it generated a follow-up letter from President Zalesky (drafted by Goldsworthy) to Chief McArdle in Washington, D.C. The letter explained that the Council was kindly introduced, in Stone's office, to the agency's preliminary proposal for a Glacier Peak Wilderness, released a month earlier. Being diplomatic, they called it "generally adequate" despite "very serious omissions." Resource extraction, they said, "has been allowed to dominate the recreational and wilderness values." And too many important areas were simply left out. A copy of the Council's own detailed proposal was included with the letter.

And so it began. The new Council had hit the ground running.

In September 1957, the new board adopted a variety of resolutions against a growing list of major threats to the wild interior of the North Cascades, including: a proposed open-pit copper mine on Miner's Ridge near Glacier Peak; one or more trans-Cascades highways, favored by the pro-pavement crowd; a potential new dam in the wilderness valley of Thunder Creek; and a planned reduction of the Goat Rocks Wilderness for a ski area expansion—the latter being somewhat south of the group's main area of interest, but worrisome, just the same. Another resolution supported a new and substantial Alpine Lakes Wilderness south of Stevens Pass. And David Brower, Ray Courtney, and Chuck Hessey, among others, were elected to the board. With 104 paid members and an early bank balance of $123.71, the new group quickly became a leading voice for the protection of Washington's wild places. Nevertheless, the Glacier Peak cause remained front and center, NCCC director John Warth calling it "the only true wilderness volcano left in Washington."

1958: A Very Big Year Indeed

To date, newspapers in the region had not been particularly kind to the idea of wilderness. In early 1958, Zalesky wrote,

> The opponents of the [Glacier Peak] wilderness area are making tremendous gains in developing public opinion . . . not one newspaper in the Northwest has come out backing any desirable wilderness proposal. . . . Almost all the reporting on the controversy has shown a slant toward the timber industry's point of view.

The media drought, however, was about to end. On the last Sunday in February, 1958, the Spokane *Spokesman–Review* ran a story by Chuck Hessey on Glacier Peak and the North Cascades, complete with photos, winter and summer. The article had been rejected by a west-side paper for being "too controversial." In August 1958, conservation received its first front-page attention in Seattle newspapers for many years—but not for the North Cascades *per se*. The story was Olympic National Park, its Coastal Strip, and the beaches of the ocean wilderness. The tourist industry of the Olympic Peninsula comprised approximately three third-rate motels and five greasy-thumb hamburger joints, but it wanted to open up the oceanfront to tourists by building an Oregon-like beach-side highway. The National Park Service was as mutely inglorious in response to this idea as it had been four years earlier on the proposed commercialization of Mount Rainier National Park. In *Washington Motorist*, the American Automobile Association demanded a highway from Moclips to Queets, and from Ruby Beach to Neah Bay. "We're going to keep battling until we get it," they wrote.

But it was not to be. Howard Zahniser managed to recruit the ever-newsworthy Supreme Court Justice William O. Douglas to lead a multi-day, twenty-two-mile coastal hike co-sponsored by The Wilderness Society and the Federation of Western Outdoor Clubs. Justice Douglas, the son of a Minnesota clergyman, spent most of his childhood in eastern Washington, came to love the outdoors, and finished high school in Yakima in 1916. He earned a law degree in 1925, joined a large Wall Street securities firm, and taught at Yale. By 1937 he chaired the Securities and Exchange Commission (at age 39), and two years later was appointed by FDR to the U.S. Supreme Court. Despite a permanent niche inside the Beltway, Douglas maintained a summer home at Goose Prairie on the Bumping River east of Mount Rainier. He hiked the hills often and became an outspoken proponent of wilderness preservation. To save the wild Olympic beach?—now that was an easy sell. Several years prior, the

Justice had led a similar publicity hike on the Chesapeake and Ohio Canal in Washington, D.C., and Virginia to thwart plans there for a destructive highway project. Douglas accepted. Zahniser sent out the invitations and Polly Dyer did the organizing. Setting his usual mean pace for three days, Douglas was followed by the largest party that ever walked the Olympic Park beach. Seventy hikers were greeted at road ends by the non-hiking antagonists carrying signs reading, "Birdwatchers Go Home." The press loved it. The general public had never heard "birdwatcher" employed as an epithet. Justice Douglas countered, calling the Olympic coast "our last chance to save a piece of our seashore free of the noise, smell, and sight of automobiles." A new road along this 43-mile wilderness shore, he said, would be "a tragedy—a needless sacrifice."

Meanwhile, the *Seattle Times* (August 3, 1958) found room to editorialize against Zahniser's wilderness bill:

> To our mind, the scope of this measure is of such magnitude as to constitute a threat to the recreational assets and the economies of the Western states. . . . A primitive wilderness is of no value at all to the vast majority of us. Small children can't carry a pack 15 or 20 miles into a trackless forest. Neither can elderly persons. And most of the rest of us would not care to.

Howard Zahniser had already addressed these and other typical broadsides against the bill, explaining that "Wilderness is for all—for anyone who chooses to use it without destroying it." He compared wilderness areas to art galleries. "They are not just for the few who happen to be in them at any one time." In response to the negative media coverage, Patrick Goldsworthy appealed to the NCCC membership to "Limber up your writing hand as letters are badly needed." The membership, now well over three hundred, happily obliged.

The idea that wilderness preservation was bad economic policy had been floated many times before. A John Warth review of George R. Leighton's 1939 book, *Five Cities*, in the August 1958 edition of the *NCCC News* (the group's fledgling newsletter) captured this revealing quote from Richard Ballinger. Ballinger was Seattle's mayor from 1904 to 1906, and in 1909 was appointed by President Taft as his Secretary of Interior:

> You chaps who are in favor of this conservation program are all wrong. You are hindering the development of the West. . . . In my opinion, the proper course to take is to divide it up among the big corporations and the people who know how to make money out of it and let the people at large get the benefit out of the circulation of the money.

Blunt language even for the times. Halfway through his term, Ballinger was booted.

East of the Cascades, the Reverend Riley sent out twelve thousand copies of his sermon *Are You Aware?* and was anointed as president of a newly-organized National Forest Multiple Use Association. His patron, George Wall, was said to be paying the Rev's rent. More openly, Wall provided his church with "the first stained-glass window in North Central Washington." A serendipity of the conflict for Wall was the opportunity to stick it to a vocal opponent. The Maxwell homestead, far up the Stehekin Valley and well beyond the closest habitation, was the heart's desire of Ray Courtney, not only for its sublime location at the foot of the buttresses and ravines rising straight up to the summit of McGregor Mountain, but for the splendid big old Douglas firs and Ponderosa pines. Wall acquired the property. He was perfectly willing to sell to Ray, who was perfectly willing to pay the extra cost of keeping the trees. Inexplicably, Wall ripped out the mature trees and sold Ray the stumps. Ray, not a vindictive sort, might have called it spiteful barbarism, but instead, just carried on.

McConnell heard the saws and the trucks hauling some 410,000 board feet from the property. His letters commented, "The Valley just isn't big enough to stand much more of this. It all shows the early need of land purchases." But shocker upon shocker, 1957 was also the year of the Forest Service timber sale that would open the forest canopy for an airstrip. A half-century later, that scar remains an outrage to many.

For Wall and the Rev, everything didn't always go their way. Jack Stevens, the orchardist who had alerted McConnell to the impending timber sale in 1956 and who later became an NCCC board member, founded another group, Recreation Unlimited, which soon had sixty-five members, an impressive number for a community the size of Manson-Chelan. Between April 27 and June 23, Stevens' organization showed *Wilderness Alps of Stehekin* to 1,448 viewers. The secretary of the Wenatchee Chamber of Commerce was reported to have warned the Rev and Wall not to disparage the film. "It's too beautiful," he said.

Members of Washington's Congressional delegation were also observing the developments. Thomas M. Pelly, a Republican representing the First District in Seattle, was quoted in the July 1958 *NCCC News* as having read into the Congressional Record: "In our state, right now also there is much interest in preserving against the inroads of civilization in the Cascade Mountains around Glacier Peak. And here I must agree . . . that if we do not set aside such a region now, it will be too late."

Two pivotal events in the summer of 1958 would echo in the corridors of history. On June 4th, Dave Simons' thirty-six-page report, entitled "The Need For Scenic Resource Conservation in the Northern Cascades of Washington," was distributed by Dave Brower to the Sierra Club conservation committee and "special conservation cooperators." The report contained "the result of concentrated field studies made in the region in the course of the several summer months of 1956 and 1957. . . ." and concluded that "a positive program for a Northern Cascades National Park seems inescapable . . . the need is immediate."

The second event began on August 23, when twelve of the fifteen members of the council of The Wilderness Society gathered in Stehekin for their thirteenth annual meeting. The four-day conference was attended by some ninety-two representatives of the National Wildlife Federation, National Parks Association, Student Conservation Program (now Association), Federation of Western Outdoor Clubs, Sierra Club, Trustees for Conservation (the new lobbying arm of the Sierra Club), North Cascades Conservation Council, Washington State Sportsmen Council, Olympic Park Associates, Recreation Unlimited, The Mountaineers, Wenatchee Alpine Roamers, Yakima Cascadians, and others.

Grant McConnell reported on the threat of a new copper mine on the other side of the crest. Ken Blair, supervisor of Wenatchee National Forest, spoke on Glacier Peak, reporting that Regional Forester J. Herbert Stone had made his final recommendations and the proposal was on the desk of Chief McArdle awaiting the next step—public hearings come fall or winter. Blair said, "the area that would be opened into the Agnes is not proposed only for patch logging but also for the roadside recreation," which went over about as well as "even though a road is proposed up Bridge Creek . . . that doesn't necessarily mean it will be there." He further offered that "some timber can well be taken out without destroying the wilderness character."

Grant McConnell addressed the convocation. Among the heavy hitters who listened to his stirring lecture and who viewed *Wilderness Alps* and Paul Bergman's slide show were Wilderness Society President Harvey Broome and council members Stewart Brandborg, Robert Cooney, Lois Crisler, Bernard Frank, Robert Griggs, Richard Leonard, George Marshall, Olaus Murie, Sigurd Olson, Howard Zahniser, and William Zimmerman (Broome and Frank were among the eight original co-founders of The Wilderness Society).

Conrad Wirth, director of the National Park Service, was also in attendance—not wearing his ranger hat but that of a Wilderness Society member. In 1933 Horace Albright put him in charge of the Civilian Conservation Corps' state and local parks construction program. In 1951 he was named National Park Service director. Like Mather, Wirth excelled as an enthusiastic proponent of "roadside wilderness" and aggressive development of visitor facilities in the national parks: paved highways and back roads, trails, visitor centers, campgrounds, scenic viewpoints, picnic areas, and the like—hardened infrastructure that was presumed to be necessary not only to satisfy the public's rapidly growing demand for outdoor recreation and cozy accommodation, but to provide for orderly use of the parks by concentrating the impacts of heavy use to locations where it could be managed more effectively. In short, a paving of paradise was necessary to help keep the hordes from "loving the parks to death." Convenient facilities for recreational enjoyment, argued Wirth, would help win overall public and Congressional support for a national park system that had suffered from neglect and inadequate funding from Congress since before World War II. Wirth's "Mission 66," green-lighted by President Eisenhower in January 1956, promised a full decade and a billion dollars worth of major park "improvements" from Denali to the Everglades.

Conrad Wirth's presence in Stehekin in the summer of 1958, as a friend of The Wilderness Society, was serious business, and it befuddled the Forest Service. The Forest Service was further aggravated that Wirth was accompanied by the Park Service's regional director from San Francisco, Lawrence Merriam. After all, the Park Service had been denied Forest Service permission to enter the North Cascades and by its presence appeared to be breaking the law. Taking advantage, Ed Wayburn and Dave Brower cornered Wirth, filled his ear, then put him and Merriam in an airplane, with McConnell as tour guide.

"It is a most beautiful area," Wirth said of the sprawling forests, peaks, and glaciers below. "The [proposed] boundary lines aren't any too large. . . . And I will say, which perhaps I should *not* say, that I am very much interested in it. . . . [We] could go to the Department of Agriculture and suggest a study."

McConnell recalled that when Wirth saw the dramatic rock spires of the Picket Range, his jaw dropped. "I want that!" he declared emphatically. Wirth's post-flight public remark that the trip had "expanded my vision" made Blair and Stone absolutely furious. McConnell's public undressing of the Forest Service at Stehekin brought a later comment from Sig Olson, "You lit a bonfire."

The big year was not over, even then. The park spark was glowing brighter. In August the National Parks Association urged a national park, as had the

Grant and Jane McConnell with Harvey Manning in Stehekin.

PHOTO COURTESY OF BETTY MANNING

Sierra Club. The pitch was further made between the lines in a major article in the August 1958 *Sunset Magazine*, including a plug for the *Wilderness Alps* film. A note of thanks was sent to travel editor Martin Litton, who quickly responded with a note of his own: "It is especially encouraging," he wrote, "to see this kind of response from the State of Washington, where people who really care about their inspirational heritage are having such an uphill battle against the forces of greedy exploitation." (Litton was a great friend of wilderness who had worked with Brower in the fight against dams at Dinosaur. At Brower's suggestion, Litton was made travel editor at *Sunset*.)

It had been a good year, despite a few potholes on the proverbial road to success. The American Automobile Association's Washington State office made known its opinion on the wilderness bill in the September 1958 issue of *Washington Motorist*:

> We cannot agree with the conservationists that motorists are more destructive to scenery than campers and hikers. . . . Whenever the Auto Club locks horns with the wilderness groups, the fur flies. Most advocates of more primitive areas [believe they] should be preserved as jewels in a vault—preserved for some nebulous 'future generation.' . . . The Auto Club thinks it would be in the public interest to build a highway along the [Olympic] coast. . . . No one has the right to deny access to these areas to folks who have neither the ability nor the inclination to tramp through the brambles. . . . If these people simply want to be alone in the woods, they can get pretty secluded 10 miles off the Snoqualmie Pass Highway in the Cascades.

The press wasn't the only source of frustration, of course. Sometimes, the difficulties came from within. After attending The Wilderness Society Council gathering in Stehekin, Polly Dyer drove directly to Camp Meriwether in Oregon, where the Mazamas were hosting the annual convention of the Federation of Western Outdoor Clubs. Polly, as presiding officer, was accused of railroading through a resolution favoring a park in the North Cascades, but the initiative came from the Resolutions Committee chaired by Una Davies of the Trails Club of Oregon (also an NCCC board member). The debate over park versus wilderness would linger a while longer.

And to be fair, the media weren't all bad either. In October, *Holiday Magazine* published the North Cascades-inspired work of poet-novelist and one-season Desolation Peak fire lookout Jack Kerouac, who was splashing in the recent success of *On the Road* and *Dharma Bums*. Kerouac's descriptions were still fresh from a place worth fighting for:

> Sixty-three sunsets I saw revolve on that perpendicular hill . . . mad raging sunsets pouring in sea foams of cloud though unimaginable crags like the crags you grayly drew in pencil as a child, with every rose tint of hope beyond, making you feel just like them, brilliant and bleak beyond words. . . . August comes in with a blast that shakes your house and augurs little Augusticity . . . then that snowy-air

and woodsmoke feeling . . . and the wind rises and dark low clouds rush up as out of a forge. Suddenly a green-rose rainbow appears right on your ridge with steamy clouds all around and an orange sun turmoiling. . . . and you go out and suddenly your shadow is ringed by the rainbow as you walk on the hilltop, a lovely haloed mystery making you want to pray.

1959–60: To Square One

In February 1959, twenty years after the near-victory of Marshall and Silcox in establishing a protected area around Glacier Peak, the Region Six office of the Forest Service released its proposal for Glacier Peak. The agency put forward a new wilderness area encompassing just 422,925 acres—11,400 acres smaller than the preliminary proposal two years before. An obvious disappointment. Roads were still projected far up Agnes Creek, up the Suiattle to Miners Ridge and Suiattle Pass, along the Chiwawa nearly to Red Mountain, up Railroad Creek to Big Creek, along the White Chuck to Kennedy Hot Springs, and up the White River to Indian Creek. The roads, said the Forest Service, would at once "enhance travel to the wilderness," permit more people to "enjoy road-side recreation close to scenic features," and "give access to patented mineral properties"—not to mention the big old trees. But there was soothing syrup too: "Commercial timber harvesting in the Suiattle, Chiwawa, White Chuck, White, Railroad, and Agnes will be done in such a way as to protect scenic and recreational values." (The term "harvest"—as if an old-growth forest is tantamount to a cornfield—has always been troubling for conservationists.)

Public hearings were scheduled. However, in keeping with the strategy of shunning large cities and their "unfriendly" audiences in favor of smaller population centers dependent on exploitation of public lands, hearings were held not in Seattle (nor San Francisco or Boston) but in Bellingham on October 13 and Wenatchee on October 16. The box score kept by the NCCC tallied forty-three speakers in Bellingham and sixty-three at Wenatchee; sixty-three opposed the Forest Service proposal as too small, twenty-four thought it was too large, and nineteen said it was just right.

The testimony of the opposition was interesting. Virlis Fischer, incorrectly representing himself as speaking for the Mazamas, lectured that "With all due respect for the thought and hard work that was put into [the studies] by various individuals, we have found the Forest Service study to be the only one which meets our definition of scientific methodology."

George Wall complained, "We are growing tired of the folks from the East and the South who continue to view the state of Washington as a colony." The map of his own proposal showed logging up the Stehekin to timberline, similarly up Devore and Company Creeks, and more up the South Fork Agnes Creek and even into the West Fork Agnes.

The Rev Riley took another tack, reflecting the persistent hysteria of McCarthyism at the time: "I should remind you," he said, "that it was pointed out by the Communist leaders that the way they could destroy our free republican system would not be by war but by the slow economic destruction of our society."

Also speaking were John Osseward and Olaus Murie, George Marshall (brother of Bob and now editor of *The Living Wilderness*), Dave Brower, Patrick Goldsworthy (who since April 1958 was the new president of the NCCC), and a galaxy of local, regional, and national stars. The Forest Service proposal was characterized as a "starfish wilderness," tentacles of snow-and-meadow ridges extending out from Glacier Peak, leaving unprotected the ancient forests of the intervening valleys. Speaking in Bellingham for the NCCC, President Goldsworthy said the group intended to "bitterly oppose" the exclusion of the White Chuck, Agnes, and Suiattle valleys from the Forest Service's proposal. In broader terms, he argued that "The untimely death of Silcox and Marshall in 1940 marked the start of accelerated progress backward in wilderness preservation." The current proposal, he said, was clearly another step backward and it set up "a conflict that we do not mean to lose." Strong words, but indicative of the sentiments of the time. Echoing the concern, the Autumn 1959 issue of *The Living Wilderness* declared that the 1959 proposal by the Forest Service was "a mockery of the idea of wilderness as, history tells us, the Forest Service so conceived it during a past of wilderness leadership."

This is not to say that a proposal by The Mountaineers in May 1959, prior to the hearings, earned high marks either. The inadequacies are, and were, embarrassing. The Mountaineers proposal was self-described as "Logical Boundaries of a *Minimum* Glacier Peak Wilderness Area" [*emphasis added*]. The Sierra Club in 1957 had published a map by Dave Simons indicating a need for protection over a far larger area—for example, down Lake Chelan as far as Safety Harbor. The Mountaineers' defense was that politics is the "art of the possible."

Edith Wolten of Blaine also testified at Bellingham, and she countered the argument that wilderness can be enjoyed only by an elite group of hardy backpackers and the well to do:

> My husband and I are not wealthy, and this summer we took our six children to Image Lake [near Glacier Peak]. It is 13 miles. The youngest girl is four and a half. The little boy is five and a half, and he carried a pack all the way in and all the way out, and they enjoyed it and he was very proud of having carried a pack.

Dolly Connelly from Bellingham carried the idea a bit farther:

> I don't know anything more irritating than the argument that few people use the wilderness areas. . . . There is nothing but just simple laziness and indifference

that prevents people from enjoying wilderness areas. We have run across people in there who didn't even have hiking boots, who wouldn't have known an ice axe if they had seen one, who had army surplus packs on their backs that they bought for 50 cents, and they were having as good a time as a mountaineer with all his elegant gear. It doesn't take anything but the urge to put one foot in front of the other and the esthetic capacity to enjoy it.

Gerry Worthen of the Bellingham Sportsmen's Club was poignant. "It is time to get away from television and chase our children outdoors where they can grow up and become useful citizens of God." He added that wilderness is there for everyone and that abolishing it would be analogous to abolishing church just because "more people stay away than attend."

Henry Kral, an Everett plywood millworker and NCCC member, acknowledged that:

We, like any other lumber industry, are dependent on timber for our livelihood and success of our mill. At the same time many of us also depend on our forests for our recreation and relaxation. Since the volume of timber and other commercial resources involved is a very small part of the resources available in our great state, we feel it would be a tragic loss if the Suiattle, White Chuck and Agnes Creek valleys were excluded from the Glacier Peak Wilderness Area.

Virginia Simmons of Seattle was also not pleased with the Forest Service's proposed boundaries. "For those of us who dream of virgin forest with clear streams cascading at the foot of snowclad mountains, this proposal is a nightmare."

John McLeod of Chelan countered, "As far as this Mountaineer group going up and yodeling on a mountain and whatnot, I don't think that is the big portion of our population. . . . why not open this lower area so that the majority can enjoy it."

J.D. Bronson of Yakima and President of the Western Pine Association warned,

Disease, insects and overmaturity are breaking up old-growth stands. . . . Miles of hiking would face wilderness enthusiasts before the rugged backcountry could be reached. . . . Including commercial timber stands as proposed would serve no useful purpose in the wilderness area scheme.

Dave Brower called the wilderness proposal "pitiful . . . shrunken and withered to a remnant resembling a badly eroded snowbank," then added

There is no more important challenge in scenic-resource conservation before the nation today than the challenge posed in the Northern Cascades . . . [to ensure it] is not gouged for its stumpage and low-grade ores for short-term benefits and long-term deprivation. . . . Our government agencies should choose to cooperate and allow this area to be the center of a golden triangle of national parks benefit-

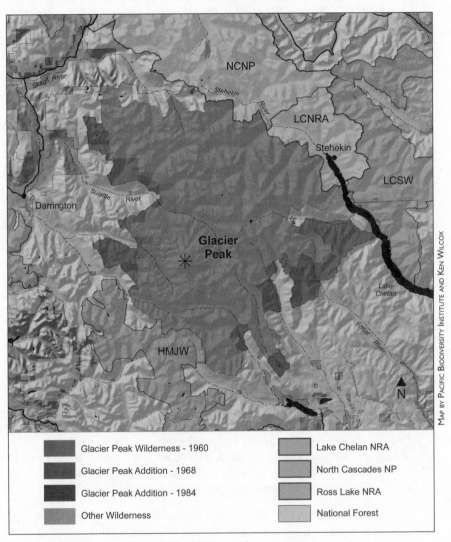

Glacier Peak Wilderness: 1960, 1968, 1984 (current).

ting all the state. . . . Washington is one of the few places, in all the world, where [wilderness] is magnificently displayed, and where by accident or design there still remains to us the opportunity to save enough of it.

The Forest Service received close to a thousand letters—an unprecedented number for any issue in the history of the agency. The NCCC membership, having doubled in a year to more than six hundred, turned up the heat considerably (the Sierra Club's membership, based in California, was also on a tear—adding two hundred new members each month). On January 3, 1960, the *New York Times* carried a column by John Oakes, editorial page editor, in support of the conservationist proposal. "Only intense public pressure," he wrote, "will induce the Forest Service to give the proposed Glacier Peak area the boundaries it must have if it is to be kept as one of the last and greatest examples of primeval American wilderness." Nevertheless, the agency remained committed to its tentacled plan.

Conservationists still had a final card to play—a direct appeal to the Secretary of Agriculture, bypassing the Forest Service. The Forest Service was to claim later that the original proposal had been amended in Portland by Region Six before being transmitted east, but this appears doubtful.

September 10, 1960. Ervin L. Peterson, Assistant Secretary of Agriculture, announced that Secretary Ezra Taft Benson had overruled the Region Six Forester and the Chief of the Forest Service. Peterson added 35,580 acres to the 1959 Forest Service proposal, designating a 458,505-acre Glacier Peak Wilderness Area. The thousand yelping letters had apparently gained protection of the Agnes, Suiattle, and Chiwawa valleys. That was the good news. The bad news, other than the pitiably small size of the preserve (the Marshall–Silcox proposal, which many considered woefully inadequate, was 795,000 acres), was the total exclusion of the entire northern sector, including Stehekin, and the omission of the White Chuck River. In addition, a car campground was planned for Kennedy Hot Springs. A logging spur on Kennedy Ridge would take cars to picnic tables an easy stroll from the glaciers. The road might have gone higher, except for the agency's one firm rule, "No logging above timberline."

A wilderness was won, but by 1960 conservationists' teetering faith in the U.S. Forest Service had tumbled to an historic low. A fraction of the wild North Cascades was now more or less secured (permanent designation by Congress of the Glacier Peak Wilderness would come later), but what of the rest? In retrospect, it is clear that 1958 was the turning point at which the fight against the Barbecuers of the North Cascades became a burgeoning stampede for a national park. It would take another ten years to pull it off.

Happily, the wagons were now circled, the horses shod and rested, as the cavalry prepared for the next long ride ahead.

Mount Formidable. August-September 1963 issue of The Wild
Cascades, *journal of the North Cascades Conservation Council.*

To the North Cascades National Park

We reached Buck Creek Pass in the twilight hours; the bright sun drifted away from us and those deep shadows of evening grew long in the valley below. . . . the coldness and freshness of the atmosphere crept into our campsite on Buck Creek. The evening noises began and the mystery of the camp fire with its warmth and light performed its ancient magic. Our sleeping bags were warm and dry; the cold air about our faces reminding us of eventual autumn and of the evening's task of cooling the earth. As we drifted into deep sleep our minds and souls received the spectacle that was ours for a few moments of our lives but that will live forever within us.

—John Swanson, Minneapolis (January 1960 *NCCC News*)

THE FOREST SERVICE: LOST IN THE WOODS

DURING ITS FIRST HALF-CENTURY in the North Cascades, the Forest Service gained the respect, admiration, and loyalty of the general citizenry, including many conservationists. Later, it would become apparent that too many good people had failed to review the agency's philosophical underpinnings, not quite grasping what its top leaders were actually saying. A surface view found the national forests a land of wilderness grandeur, the Old Ranger a rough-hewn sweetheart, his custody light-handed, loving, and light-years safe from meddling by the desk foresters of Washington, D.C. Then in the second half-century, conservationists discovered that their trusting fondness rested on a basic misunderstanding. So enchanted were they by the pristine wild country and the nobility of the wildland managers, they had neglected

124 • WILDERNESS ALPS

to analyze what The Founder, Mr. Pinchot, truly meant by his "greatest good for the greatest number in the long run."

Since the maxim required little understanding and less humility for ecology, the Forest Service set out in the 1950s on a crash program of intensive management generally based on weak theories derived from sketchy data in parodies of the scientific method. Managers laid out clearcuts in the high-elevation, slow-growing Pacific Silver Fir Forest Zone on the exact pattern used in the fast-growing, lowland Western Hemlock Zone. They planted seedlings in spring that burned out in summer; planted seedlings in fall that froze in winter. Twenty years later they began removing the little signs they had installed, "Harvested 1950. Replanted 1951." Passersby wondered why the rangers were growing fireweed plantations. They planted Douglas-fir seedlings in the Mountain Hemlock Zone and when queried by folks who knew that nature had a suitable tree for every zone and that substitutes will not do, replied, "That's all they had in the nursery." Laymen knowledgeable enough to count annual growth rings in stumps could determine that a clearcut had wiped away a stand of 350-year-old trees and that the regrowth was, after thirty years, Christmas-tree sized. Some rangers seemed incredulous that laymen knew how to count rings without taking off their caulked boots.

On the west side of the North Cascades, Supervisor Harold C. Chriswell of Mount Baker National Forest pushed timber sales farther up the White Chuck and every other entry valley. He praised potential ski lifts along the route of the to-be North Cross-State Highway (now Highway 20), and nurtured his personal pet, the Around-Mount Baker Highway. By building logging roads up Swift Creek from Baker Lake toward Austin Pass, he was preparing for a link-up with the existing Mount Baker Highway at Heather Meadows. On the east side, Supervisor Andrew Wright of Wenatchee National Forest repeated the paeans of his predecessor, Ken Blair, in praise of motoring down Bridge Creek to Stehekin and up Agnes Creek to a tree-farm picnic view of Agnes Peak. Wright planned to log Fish Creek, hauling the logs on a road to be built along Lake Chelan to Stehekin where the log rafts would be floated to George Wall at Chelan. He answered letters complaining about sheep on the Chelan Summit Trail by informing hikers that "there is no conflict between grazing and recreation." He expanded the horizons of recreation into a brave new world by welcoming a vanguard of motorized invaders; he improved trails into motorcycle roads, and replaced his rangers' horses with Yamahas.

Some Forest Service officers were troubled by what they were witnessing, including the growing discrepancy between academic dogma and the realities they perceived in their workaday lives. The Old Ranger who knew the forest as a whole was disturbed to find many of its qualities, processes, and inhabitants excluded from the official "greatest good" for no apparent reason other than to allow a theoretical increase in log output. Eventually a new breed of rangers would resurrect old intuitions, buttress them with more exact science than offered through the heritage of Pinchot, and rise up in an insurrection, raising the possibility of a full-blown revolution. But that came many years later. At the century's middle, no such hope could be seen.

In December 1960 Congress passed the Multiple-Use Sustained-Yield Act. Its provisions, essentially a restatement of the 1897 Organic Act that created the forest reserves, were sought by the Forest Service, at least in part for propaganda purposes, as well as a strategic maneuver to stall the wilderness bill, still languishing in Congress. Before this 1960 law was adopted, "multiple-use" had no explicit legal standing. Among the multiple uses enumerated by the Forest Service, wilderness was *not* included, although a corrective amendment recognizing wilderness was ultimately forced on the agency. In Washington, Chief McArdle hailed passage of the act by declaring that "sustained yield" justified the immediate task of "converting old-growth timber stands to fast-growing young forests." Doddering ancients were to be replaced by vigorous infants of chosen races, a sort of forest eugenics. It was as if the Society of American Chemists had turned to the alchemists for leadership.

The distinction between public and private ownership became one without a difference. The Old Ranger, having retired, reflected that the Forest Service of his youth had adhered, in theory at least, to Pinchot's principle of "preservation through use"—use based on the nature and needs of ecosystems, as later pointed out by Michael Frome and other Forest Service historians. He now had to ask whether the founder of the Forest Service was being ignored altogether.

Other observers of the forest scene questioned whether Pinchot, a sure accomplice in the drowning of Hetch Hetchy, deserved unquestioning reverence. Chief McArdle scarcely can be called a traitor when it was Pinchot who, in *The Use Book*, said, "All trees in the national forests for which there is a market are for sale."

A Decade of Pamphleteering

As the old forests of the North Cascades fell in greater swaths, conservationists campaigned hard to build public awareness about these troubling trends in the public's woods—and the increasing urgency of protecting a national treasure. From the mid-1950s, the publications of The Mountaineers, Sierra Club, and other groups in the West and across the nation poured out words and photos about the North Cascades. During the summer of 1957, the area received its specific journal of record, the North Cascades Conservation Council's *NCCC News*. Issued monthly, the mimeographed pages contained a wealth of natural and human history, detailed action programs, the latest news from the front, and calls to write letters. In May 1961 the name was changed to *The Wild Cascades*, as suggested by the new co-editors, Harvey and Betty Manning, recruited on a seemingly impromptu visit to Cougar Mountain by the Zaleskys and Goldsworthys. As graduates of The Mountaineers' climbing course, they determined that the 1960 publication of *Mountaineering: The Freedom of the Hills*, a new textbook for the climbing course, meant that after five years of editorial labor on that project, Harvey Manning was free of *Freedom*—and an easy mark for the press gang.

The *Wild Cascades* continued the course set by *NCCC News*. Patrick Goldsworthy was *de facto* co-editor as well as production manager. Jane Goldsworthy was general operations manager. Work parties gathered at the Goldsworthy home to staple, fold, stamp, address, and sort bundles for mailing. A new look was given by Betty, previously the editor of *The Mountaineer Bulletin*, who in laying out articles and cutting the stencils embellished odd spaces with odd drawings. A unique tone was introduced by "Moral Tales for Young Birdwatchers," a series inspired by a *Seattle Times* editorial supporting the Mount Rainier tramway and scorning the obstructionist Audubon Society and The Mountaineers as so many "birdwatchers and mountain climbers." The September 1961

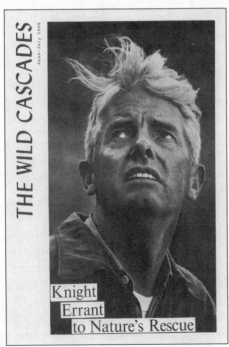

David Brower. June-July 1969 issue of The Wild Cascades.

issue of *The Wild Cascades* clarified for the *Times* that "Mountain climbing" was actually a "disease endemic to the Northwest, believed to be caused by congenital deformity which gives abnormal sensitivity to neon, hydrocarbon vapors, and the crash of bowling balls. In extreme forms leads to birdwatching." Birdwatching, according to the editor, was "symptomized by a morbid curiosity about birds and other objects lacking economic value." And so it remains.

In 1962 mimeographing yielded to the cleaner and more versatile multilithing. The year additionally was marked by the debut of a gonzo journalist, the "Irate Birdwatcher," who fulminated on the mortal sins of such Forest Service supervisors as "Logger Larry" and "Dandy Andy." Bill Nordstrom stepped forward to volunteer his printing skills as publishing advanced to offset technology. Photographs could now be used to supplement the superb maps of Noel McGarry, a professional cartographer, and the evocative line drawings of Liza Anderson. The drawback was that the production process became lengthier and costlier, reducing publication to bimonthly, then quarterly, eventually to once in a blue moon (after the park was established). Livened by the whirlings of the Irate Birdwatcher and company, notably Les Braynes, a good ol' boy who loved guns and eagerly adopted every new means of transport, from Tote-Gote to Honda to snowmobile to helicopter. With Braynes utilizing as his amanu-

Sauk River forest. November 1962 issue of The Wild Cascades.

DAVE SIMONS, NORTH CASCADES CONSERVATION COUNCIL

ensis Charles ("Chuck") Hessey, the journal of record became, in the opinion of NCCC board member David Brower, "the liveliest conservation publication in the nation."

One of Irate's livelier editorials on grazing on public lands once drew the indignation of an agency official who reportedly pondered a lawsuit for libel against the publication. "He's gone too far! Call the lawyers!" The notion of a suit was quickly dropped, however, when a friendly staff member pointed out that the newspapers could have carried the story with this headline: 'FOREST OFFICIAL DENIES UNNATURAL FONDNESS FOR SHEEP.'

Freedom of the Hills surprised The Mountaineers by turning an unexpected profit, a problem solved by Leo Gallagher and President Jesse Epstein, who respectively urged and oversaw establishment of a Literary Fund to invest the profit in furthering the purposes of the club, which by now had regained its organizational memory about preserving natural areas. In 1964, the Fund subsidized Tom Miller's *The North Cascades*, a big-page volume of photographs from a climber's perspective. Miller remarked, "Nobody ever had taken sunset pictures from the summit of [Mount] Torment. Nobody, including us, ever wanted to." The printer's bill temporarily emptied the Literary Fund. Dave Brower stepped in to complete the publicity effort, buying hundreds of copies and sending them across the nation. Thus it was that New Orleans, for ex-

Betty and Harvey Manning in the Canadian Rockies.

ample, first learned about the area that contained most of the glaciers in the Lower Forty-Eight.

In March of 1965, Brower telephoned Harvey Manning, commanding him to write an "exhibit format" book and to get to work on it *now*. David Brower's commands were always obeyed. (Brower later protested that he gave no such command, just a suggestion, and that the author was simply a push-over.) Three breathless months later, *The Wild Cascades: Forgotten Parkland* was sent to just about every member of Congress and virtually every daily newspaper in the nation. Brower called Manning's text "inspired and delightful." Contributing photographers included Dave Simons, John Warth, Bob and Ira Spring, Ed Dolan, the Courtney family in Stehekin, and Ansel Adams of Yosemite fame. It was the eleventh in the Sierra Club's exhibit-format series that Brower had inaugurated in 1960 with *This Is the American Earth*, which showcased Ansel Adams' stunning black-and-white photography. *American Earth* earned such awe that any subject so treated was automatically lodged on the nation's agenda. A review of *Forgotten Parkland* in the *Wenatchee Daily World* acknowledged the work as a "technical masterpiece . . . on the slickest of paper . . . tells the story magnificently . . . poignant, irresistible . . . propaganda ammunition." The editorial continued, "If Congress heeds the voices, we may wake up some morning to find a vast area of the North Cascades shut off from all future development," which, of course, was the general idea. Timber and grazing interests, the Chamber of Commerce, and several county commissioners met in Wenatchee to plot a response, deciding that they, too, could publish a book "stating the case *against* the park." The next issue of *The Wild Cascades* (the NCCC journal) read, "We are extremely happy [they] have decided to publish a book, and thus help us publicize the area. May they sell thousands of copies. The N3C Bookshop will assist to its utmost."

Thousands bought the Sierra Club books. Hundreds of thousands read Martin Litton's story in the June 1965 issue of *Sunset Magazine*. The cover asked, "Does Washington Get the Next National Park?" The answer was urged by a fourteen-page article entitled "Our Wilderness Alps." Wrote Litton,

> You crave the heights, grassy or icy, flat or sharp. . . . Finding yourself on Cascade Pass after an hour's slow walking is about as dreamlike as waking up on a Nepalese col, face to face with Everest. . . . [Yet] the tide of civilization continues to lap ever higher around the base of Glacier Peak.

Curiously, through the early years of the park campaign, the subject of park and wilderness protection was blacked out in Seattle, though frequently reported in the newspapers of Everett, Bellingham, and Wenatchee. The NCCC took this to mean nobody in Seattle was listening. In late spring 1965, NCCC was amazed to be approached by Walt Woodward, a journalist who had earned his niche in the hall of fame when, as owner-publisher of the Bainbridge Island newspaper, his was the sole public voice to oppose the World War II "relocation" to concentration camps of Americans of Japanese ancestry. Woodward had just been engaged by the *Seattle Times* as a roving columnist, free to choose his topics. Ross Cunningham, editorial page director, requested only, "If you've no objection, I'd appreciate your taking on the North Cascades. I've been following the situation a long time and I think a park is the answer." Walt obliged, running seventeen columns in twenty-three days, letting each participant in the controversy speak his piece to the newspaper's readership of a quarter-million. In the final installment, Woodward asked an anonymous "expert" what might come of the Study Team's work. The reply, "a bowl of mush. Agriculture and Interior still can't agree."

The *Times* broke the Seattle print media's silence. The broadcast media silence had been broken earlier by KING-TV, whose president, Stimson Bullitt, was a member of NCCC. His program director, Bob Schulman, had been on the William O. Douglas Olympic Coast hike of 1958 and conversed there with Olaus Murie. Schulman assembled footage of conservationists, rangers, and loggers (and forests, rivers, and glaciers), and assured conservationists solemnly that the production would be "completely objective—on our side." As it happened, there was no need to impose a bias—not when a Forest Service ranger was pleased as punch to stand by the White Chuck River and extol the joys of car-picnicking at Kennedy Hot Springs and running quickly to the summit of Glacier Peak. Additionally, by giving the Washington State Sportsmen Council free rein to elaborate its reasons for opposing a park, as it had opposed a wilderness, not a word of editorializing was necessary for the film to demolish the credibility of the big-game hunting lobby. At an event attended by scores of media folk, government officials, and general all-purpose Seattle dignitaries, Brower formally presented Bullitt a Sierra Club award (and a copy of hot-off-the-press *Forgotten Parklands*) in recognition of *The Wind in the Wilderness*. The half-hour program played a number of times on the three Bullitt stations in the Northwest, and a copy joined Brower's own film and those of Chuck Hessey on the national tour.

That eventful spring of 1965 witnessed an honest-to-golly publicity blitz. But that's getting a little ahead of the story.

THE PARK SERVICE SLIPS IN THE BACK DOOR

Between the World Wars and afterward, the national parks captivated many, including a large share of the nation's urban middle-class. Families of modest means, enabled by the new freedom of the wheels, were able to join upper-class

Americans in feeding the bears at Yellowstone, watching the fire fall from Glacier Point at Yosemite, and joining hands to form a ring around a giant tree in Sequoia. During the first half-century of parks in the state of Washington, visitors drove to Mount Rainier's Paradise Valley, past big trees and waterfalls to the flowery alpine meadows (and a short-lived nine-hole golf course), and later to Yakima Park to feed the bears. They drove to the rain forests and the ocean front of Olympic National Park and the meadows of Hurricane Hill and its views across valleys of ancient forest to the Alaska-like glaciers of Mount Olympus. The Mather–Albright strategy firmly allying the Park Service to the automobile was a smash Madison Avenue success. By the late-1950s, more than a million people a year were visiting the two parks.

However, if the car-tourist's loyalty to the parks was a mile wide, for many it was only an inch deep. As the 1954 confrontation at Mount Rainier between commercial recreation and natural area protection proved, the Park Service could not depend on the American Automobile Association and the Chamber of Commerce for much more than trouble. The soul of the national park idea would find its more dedicated friends in another group of park visitors altogether: those who hiked the Wonderland Trail of Rainier and the Hoh River Trail of the Olympics.

But the Park Service continued to prefer quantity of fans over quality. The true believers whom the rangers should have been courting became disenchanted, troubled by the free rein given concessionaires to profit from the nation's crown jewels by half-burying the gems in commercial rubbish. Motorboats on all but a single arm of Yellowstone Lake. A highway over Tioga Pass in Yosemite National Park. In the same period that The Mountaineers were galloping to the rescue of Paradise Valley, the Park Service was erecting there a new interpretive center apparently intended as a memorial to flying saucers which, in 1947, had first revealed themselves to Earthlings in the vicinity of The Mountain in Washington's first UFO sighting. The building was designed for a site in Hawaii. It was not used there, but was so admired by Senator Jackson that he insisted on having it built at Rainier. The fond dream inherited and promoted by Mather–Albright of an Around-Mount Rainier Highway had been defeated by geography, yet the Park Service insisted after World War II on completing a link in the discredited plan, the Stevens Canyon Road, which sliced through what had been one of the wildest sections of the park. Additionally, the road to Mowich Lake, which had been closed for years and which many believed should have been permanently eradicated to embed Spray Park deeper in wilderness, was reopened.

The record in Olympic National Park was so distressing that it was virtually erased from the memory of the Park Service until Carsten Lien, in *Olympic Battleground*, told in painful detail how certain of the most honored figures in the Park Service labored to exclude the rain forests from the park and were only thwarted by Franklin D. Roosevelt and his inner circle. Lien describes the Park Service's attempt to build a cross-Olympic highway from Hood Canal up the Dosewallips River to Anderson Pass and down the Enchanted Valley and Quinault River to the ocean, in order that tourists could "do the park" in an hour. Already having roads to meadow elevations at Deer Park and Obstruction Point, it actually placed location stakes beside the tundra trail along Grand Ridge for a high-elevation connection between the two and would have had the bulldozers gouging through had not World War II intervened. Incredibly, as late as November 16, 1965, at a dinner meeting of conservationists, Superintendent Ben Gale asked his table companions, "Would you *really* object to a highway along the Ocean Strip, if you couldn't see it from the beach?" He was dumbfounded by the way the room went abruptly silent as his query was repeated in shocked whispers from table to table. Many of the diners looking at Gale in consternation had been companions of Supreme Court Justice William O. Douglas on his famous march along the wilderness ocean beach in 1958, or his repeat march in 1964.

Inviting the Park Service into the North Cascades, therefore, was not without reservation. In the latter years of World War II, the World Series of Baseball pitted against each other two teams composed of the halt and the lame. Asked for his prediction of the outcome of the series, a veteran of the Golden Age of

Rialto Beach along the wilderness Olympic Coast.

KEN WILCOX

the sport declared, "I don't see how either one of 'em can win." Would the Forest Service's Old Ranger be resurrected in time to go to bat for the North Cascades? Most likely not. He may have considered it a losing game. Like the fellow who was losing his shirt at poker (to mix up the metaphors) said when told the house dealer was crooked, "Yeah, but it's the only game in town."

Grant McConnell made his decision to support a North Cascades National Park on two grounds: first, Wenatchee National Forest intended to log the Stehekin drainage all the way to timberline; and second, the very best wilderness obtainable could not, by definition, protect the lower Stehekin Valley. Richard Brooks similarly realized that Mount Baker National Forest was planning to log to the west-side meadows on Glacier Peak. David Brower and Ed Wayburn and their compatriots in California reached the same conclusion at virtually the same time.

In May 1958 the National Parks Association recommended that the Park Service and Forest Service enter into discussions toward a national park. On Memorial Day, the Federation of Western Outdoor Clubs resolved that the Secretary of the Interior and the Secretary of Agriculture should be directed to make a joint study of the North Cascades. On June 4, 1958, David Brower released the Dave Simons prospectus, *The Need for Scenic Resource Conservation in the Northern Cascades of Washington*, which concluded that a national park was the only real choice. Brower had floated the notion at the founding meeting of the NCCC in 1957, but the sins of the Park Service at Rainier and Olympic were then too fresh in directors' minds, while disillusion with the Forest Service was not yet terminal. On July 4 the Sierra Club directors unanimously agreed that Congress should direct the Park Service to survey for a park the region from Lake Chelan to Glacier Peak, and from Stevens Pass to Foggy Pass, following the tentative boundaries outlined in maps prepared by The Mountaineers. Three weeks later, on July 26, 1958, a motion came before the directors of the NCCC that Congress be memorialized to conduct a joint Park Service–Forest Service study to define a park between Stevens Pass and the North Cascades Primitive Area. A third of a century later, Phil Zalesky, who had been succeeded as president by Patrick Goldsworthy, recalled the period:

> It was during his first summer as president that Goldsworthy called a meeting on rather short notice. Grant McConnell and Dave Brower convinced Goldsworthy that it was time to act on the national park. I was taken completely by surprise. . . . This was not what I had worked for, nor what I wanted. Nobody had put any more time into the Glacier Peak Wilderness plan than I had. "National park" carried far more development than I cared to see in the Glacier Peak area. There was no mention of the Stehekin at this board meeting. I resisted the motion strongly. I pulled out every parliamentary trick I knew to stop the steamroller. The decision was postponed to the next month.

Before the next meeting late in August, I tried to work several board members. By the time of the meeting I knew the support was there. I remained silent. What was the use? Two of us voted against a park. At the end of the voting, someone's patience gave out and they wanted to know why I opposed. I explained. We had a break after the vote and I departed to go camping with Laura. I wasn't certain at that point whether I could continue to support the N3C. My fellow naysayer did drop out, feeling the Sierra Club muscle had taken over a Mountaineer initiative.

How I came out of the wilderness to support the national park is something I cannot recall. It was a subtle process. Once I got on the bandwagon, however, I threw myself into the thing.

Grant McConnell, writing in the exuberant aftermath of the 1968 victory, also recalled the time:

Seattle, NCCC board meeting: throw fat into fire: ought to go for a Park. Silence, then storm. Phil Zalesky, big passionate Phil, tells all about lousy behavior of NPS in Olympic Park—logging, exploitation and so on; we haven't even got the Glacier Peak Wilderness Area yet. Others demur, too: would bring in more people than the country can stand. Besides, we can't win; besides FS has the power and we have to get along with them; be reasonable—better to get along with FS, compromise where necessary, but save *something*. Awfully strong argument. But join with Brower and shout them down. Bad strain on Pat, who steps in now and then to calm things down. Won't be calmed. The end of the N3C? No matter, this is showdown. The two radicals get mean: just what would you bargain away? Cascade Pass? Thunder Creek? Lyman Lake? Really dirty . . . and Phil is hurt. The vote: divided, but it's for a Park.

It had to be. But what have we done to Phil and the others? Will N3C survive?

Region Six, USFS, announces plan for Glacier Peak Wilderness Area. A monstrosity, practically all the valleys deleted, looks like a starfish or a very nasty Rorschach blot. Just a few miles from side to side. Utter tokenism and utter defeat.

News stories: storm brewing in North Cascades. Treewatchers on warpath. *New York Times, Washington Post, Christian Science Monitor, San Francisco Chronicle*—and all sympathetic. Pieces in *National Geographic, Sunset* and still others. Even something halfway favorable in Seattle papers. More important: an issue.

Word from Seattle: Phil is shocked, has changed his mind; and anyhow he had never left us. N3C unified as never before.

Big, big-hearted Phil.

Another who agonized was Howard Zahniser, a devoted friend of the North Cascades and an "actor" in the film, *Wilderness Alps of the Stehekin*. As Dave Brower said,

Zahnie would rather not have had to encounter . . . the attempts to establish a North Cascades National Park. He was promoting wilderness in both the Forest Service and Park Service, simultaneously trying to get them to mend their ways and to cool the growing rivalry between the two. He was chagrined that so much creative energy of so many dedicated people inevitably was going to be diverted into a dogfight over who got which bones when they should be making common cause to get more bones for both.

But the stampede was on. In March of 1959, the Spokane Mountaineers voted for a park, urging inclusion of Glacier Peak and the upper Suiattle, the upper Entiat, Chiwawa, and White Rivers, upper Thunder Creek, Cascade Pass, the entire drainages of the Stehekin River and Railroad Creek, and the northwest shoreline of Lake Chelan. On June 4, 1959, The Mountaineers endorsed the park. The NCCC's Polly Dyer later recalled how the Simons study favoring a park helped settle much of the angst among those who initially resisted the park idea. In summer, the *NCCC News* noted the spontaneous establishment of grass-roots citizens committees for a North Cascades National Park. In October the Secretary of the Interior's Advisory Board on National Parks, an eleven-member non-governmental group, expressed hope that the North Cascades "be most fully and securely conserved."

The Forest Service, still not interested in shedding territory to its rival, objected to Washington Congressman Tom Pelly's request to the latter in 1959 that it conduct a study of the North Cascades for park potential. Chief McArdle further refused to allow even a joint study of the area. Since the Park Service could not legally undertake a study without Forest Service permission, the impasse shifted to Congress.

On January 6, 1960, Congressman Pelly, a Seattle Republican, introduced H.R. 9360, and Congressman Don Magnuson, a Seattle Democrat, in bipartisan fashion, introduced H.R. 9342 in the U.S. House of Representatives. Their wording identical, the bills called for the Secretary of the Interior

> to investigate and report to Congress on the advisability of establishing a national park or other unit of the national park system in the central and North Cascades. . . . [The] Secretary of the Interior, in cooperation with the Secretary of Agriculture, is hereby authorized and directed to make a comprehensive study of the scenic, scientific, recreational, educational, wildlife, and wilderness values of the central and north Cascades region . . . for the purpose of evaluating fully the potentiality for establishing therein a national park. . . .

The *NCCC News* reported growing momentum for what Brower and Goldsworthy were calling the "Golden Triangle of National Parks." More citizens committees formed and hundreds of petitions supporting a national park study were included in the mailing of the *NCCC News*. More than two thousand signatures were gathered in a single month.

"All we want is the facts," declared Patrick Goldsworthy. "We have the Forest Service facts. This bill will provide the Park Service facts." The bill called for a report to Congress on results of the study within one year.

On February 4, Senator Warren G. Magnuson introduced S. 2980, repeating the Pelly-Magnuson bills. Letters flooded Congress. The Kittitas County Democratic Convention endorsed the Magnuson and Magnuson bills (both Magnusons were Democrats). The King County Republican Convention passed a resolution to "commend and heartily support the proposal by Representative Thomas M. Pelly for a study of the Northern Cascade Mountains by the National Park Service." In the *Seattle Times*, Walt Woodward wrote that Pelly was open to "trading off some Olympic National Park land in the creation of a North Cascades park," a point that may have been aimed at those who preferred their timber horizontal rather than vertical.

Petition signatures supporting the study bills continued to pour in. A woman in Ellensburg was so inspired after attending a meeting there that she went home and canvassed her neighbors. Virtually the entire neighborhood signed the petition. From January to June, 10,440 people signed; 7,304 from the state of Washington, 834 from California, 506 from Oregon, 389 from Massachusetts, 238 from New York, 145 from Connecticut, 108 from Illinois, the remainder from the other forty-one states. The data were sent to all members of the Washington delegation and all members of the Senate and House Committees on Interior and Insular Affairs. The campaign for a national park had gone emphatically national.

But Congressman Walt Horan, whose district included the east side of the North Cascades, urged Interior Secretary Fred Seaton to postpone indefinitely any plan to investigate the park potential. At the state level, John A. Biggs, director of the Department of Game, strenuously opposed making Washington State the first in the nation with three large national parks. "We cannot afford the creation of a North Cascades National Park," he said. "In effect the park would constitute a permanent, severe and costly blow to good fishing and hunting."

For some, the new focus on the National Park Service had begun as an uncomfortable necessity. In later years, amiable debate revolved around who it was, in the 1950s, that first plumped for a park. Nobody contests Phil Zalesky's claim to be—among those who labored so long and crucially—the last. Once won over, however, he by no means dragged his feet, though in later years he gained a certain wry satisfaction from his 1958 dissent. In 1972 Zalesky magnanimously refrained from comment when Nixon's National Park Service director, George Hartzog, informed two hundred attendees at a national symposium in Yosemite Valley that if he had his way the national parks would be devoted solely to recreation, ignoring "natural area protection." In the 1980s, at a meeting of the NCCC board where loud and bitter criticisms of the Park

Service's behavior in Stehekin were being voiced around the table, Phil turned to his neighbor, smiled, and murmured, "Seems to me I've heard these things said before."

A GLANCE ASIDE: THE POLITICAL LANDSCAPE

Early in the 1960s, a big scholarly-like conference on outdoor recreation was staged at the University of Washington, attended by experts in and out of government from throughout the West. One of the academic experts, a University of Washington political scientist, argued that the national park idea was defunct; there never would be another national park established; the existing ones would be dismantled; and the land would be transferred to expert, academia-trained managers who, their hands not manacled by inexpert citizen amateurs, would be free to respond quickly and expertly to the changing needs of society. Sage nods of approval were registered by Forest Servicers, engaged at that time in fighting off the manacles proposed by the Wilderness Bill, and in barring the Park Service from crashing the gates of the North Cascades.

Prospects for a park were not particularly bright, despite the movement that was underway. One important consideration was the veritable drought that was underway in the creation of major wildland parks in the U.S. The last large new parks were Olympic in 1938, Kings Canyon in 1940, Big Bend in 1944, and the Everglades in 1947. New national parks were not much on the political menu during the war years, with the exception of Texas' Big Bend on the Rio Grande, the Florida Everglades (authorized by Congress in 1934 but not officially established until 1947), and a major addition to Grand Teton National Park that was adamantly opposed by Wyoming ranchers and the grazing-friendly Forest Service. It would be the 1950s before serious headway could be made on other prospects, including the campaign by the Sierra Club and others to create a new Redwoods National Park along California's northern coast. The Redwoods campaign, or at least the timeline, more or less paralleled preservation efforts in the North Cascades. The Park Service had been in that fray since 1919 when Director Stephen Mather proposed a national park in the redwoods, while Congress formally considered it a year later. But no park resulted. In 1931, having already acquired about three thousand acres of redwoods in smaller parcels, the League purchased from Pacific Lumber Company a spectacular 9,410-acre stand—the largest contiguous block of old-growth redwoods anywhere—and christened it Humboldt Redwoods State Park. In 1933, Save the Redwoods League's champion conservationist, Newton Drury, was offered the job of Park Service Director by Interior Secretary Harold Ickes, but Drury, preferring to stay close to the giant trees, declined. Drury and others were somewhat perturbed with the Park Service's continued emphasis on over-development of roads, hotels, and the like within many parks. The Service, he said, was becoming "a glorified playground commission." In the minds of the advocates, the preservation of wild places was of a much higher order. Yet Ickes acknowledged the critics and again, in 1939, offered the position to Drury who finally accepted, probably intending to do his best to keep the wild places wild. That was an especially serious challenge during World War II when the war profiteers insisted that the resources inside national park boundaries—such as the Olympics' giant Douglas fir, red cedar, and sitka spruce trees—were in critical need of exploitation in order to protect national security. Drury relented. His complicity in opening Olympic National Park to commercial logging in the 1940s has been harshly criticized as an unnecessary sellout to local timber politics. However, Drury did help hammer out a solution to the battle at Grand Teton in 1950. The next year, with the formidable Bureau of Reclamation pushing hard for dams inside Dinosaur National Monument, Drury resigned in protest and returned to his work with the League and became focused on expanding redwood state parks. The final push by Edgar Wayburn and others for a Redwoods National Park, as with the North Cascades, carried through the 1950s and well into the 1960s, with Mike McCloskey as chief lobbyist.

New national parks were not much on the agenda during the Eisenhower years either. The national platform of the Republican Party expressed a certain pride in Theodore Roosevelt and Gifford Pinchot, then in the same breath called for the public lands to be released to the free-enterprise Barbecuers. In the eight years of the Eisenhower administration, the two additions to the national park system were minuscule. Bernard DeVoto warned in 1954 that the administration's conservation policy, only a year and a half into its first term, had returned to one of "reckless destruction for the profit of special corporate interests." In 1959 Peter Matthiessen observed in *Wildlife in America* that former Chevy dealer and Oregon Governor Douglas McKay's appointment as Interior Secretary had "demoralized" the expert staff of the Fish and Wildlife Service. To make an impression, McKay quickly eliminated five divisions and four thousand jobs from the Interior Department. His most "inglorious achievement," said Matthiessen, was "to lease away more public land than any Secretary of the Interior in the history of his country," including hundreds of leases on refuge lands. Responding to public outrage, he backed off the proposed Echo Park Dam in 1955. McKay quit in 1956 to run for the U.S. Senate. He lost, became ill, and died in 1959. His successor, Frederick A. Seaton, a savvy, quasi-Teddy-Roosevelt Republican, immediately went to work trying to restore some credibility to Eisenhower's hammered bureaucracy. At a press conference in 1957, with his young assistant, Ted Stevens, at his side, Seaton announced his support for a new wildlife refuge in arctic Alaska. Congress dabbled, then failed to act on the proposal. Only in the final moments of his presidency would Eisenhower earn himself a legacy—thanks to Seaton (himself better remembered for bringing Alaska and Hawaii into the Union). In December 1960 the arduous campaign led by Olaus and Mardy Murie, George Collins, Lowell Sumner, and William O. Douglas to protect America's "Last Great Wilderness" realized an historic milestone in American wildland preservation when Eisenhower authorized Seaton to designate an 8.9-million-acre Arctic National Wildlife Range. Doubled in size and renamed in 1980, the Arctic National Wildlife Refuge now encompasses nearly twenty million acres. But also in 1960, Seaton opened up twenty million acres of the adjacent North Slope to commercial oil and gas development. Eight years later, a vast oil reserve was discovered at Prudhoe Bay. Senator Ted Stevens, obviously moved by the profound richness of this wild, immense place, has led the campaign for oil and gas development inside the refuge almost ever since.

In November 1960 Eisenhower's anointed heir, Richard M. Nixon, was defeated by Massachusetts Senator John F. Kennedy, and the hope for wildlands protection that had been springing eternal took on immediate substance—but not because of President Kennedy himself. Somewhat partial to his two-passenger rocking chair, Kennedy would not have competed well as an outdoor sportsman against Franklin D. Roosevelt in his wheelchair. While he had not yet demonstrated much in the way of serious public lands convictions, he did offer support for the wilderness bill in his message to Congress in February 1961. The more distinct turning point occurred when he appointed Arizona Congressman Stewart L. Udall as his Secretary of the Interior. Udall, who had been supportive in the Dinosaur National Monument and Echo Park campaigns, had earned much respect among conservationists. Though not famous for conservation consistency (he was initially wrong on the Grand Canyon dams, for example), Udall evolved because he was, according to his own statement, "convinced by David Brower." In backing the Wilderness Bill, three national seashores, and Redwoods National Park, he established himself as the greatest Interior Secretary since FDR's "Old Curmudgeon," Harold Ickes. Among his convincings by Brower, who had helped to get him appointed, was the desirability of a Park Service study of the North Cascades. Kennedy had not been in office more than a few months when, in 1961, he emulated Theodore Roosevelt by holding a series of White House conferences around the nation. During the one in Seattle, Udall invited Patrick Goldsworthy on an inspection tour of Mount Rainier National Park, and while riding together in the back seat of a limousine, assured Goldsworthy there would be a North Cascades National Park. After a speech in Tacoma, Udall was briefly accosted by NCCC's roving reporter, Eileen Ryan, who stuffed a copy of the proposal for a 125,000-acre Cougar Lakes Wilderness in his coat pocket. She later reminded her readers that Udall's "fellow tramper-along-the-Potomac" was William O. Douglas, and that the two were well enough acquainted to be "booted out of a Maryland inn for 'looking like bums.'" When Cougar Lakes, in south-central Washington, finally received protection in 1984, it was named for one of those who knew it best: William O. Douglas.

Despite White House interest in the North Cascades, obstacles in Congress were substantial. In the Democrat-controlled House, the chairman of the Interior Committee, which held the hammer on national parks, was Wayne N. Aspinall of Colorado, devoted friend of miners and herders and stern foe of the wilderness bill. The latter he had kept buried in his committee since 1956. As for the parks, his middle initial was taken by conservationists to mean "Never." The ranking Republican on the committee was John Saylor of Pennsylvania, as firm a friend of wilderness and parks, including the North Cascades, as ever sat in Congress, but a member of the minority party.

The Republican Congressional delegation from Washington State was a good news-bad news lot. Thomas Pelly of Seattle was the first member of Congress to listen to Patrick Goldsworthy and fellow activists. Pelly's minority status was not a handicap in the fraternal relationship that existed between him and the two Democratic senators, Warren G. Magnuson and Henry M. "Scoop" Jackson. Indeed, it was Pelly who brought the North Cascades to the attention of Magnuson, who then enlisted Jackson—a formidable pairing, since Magnuson as chair of the Appropriations Committee and Jackson as chair of the Interior Committee were the most powerful duo in the Senate (the Interior Committee later became the Committee on Energy and Natural Resources).

The bad Republican news was the two congressmen who represented the North Cascades. Many believed that Walt Horan, representing the east side, was mentally mired in the remote past. On the west, the Eisenhower landslide of 1952 had swept into office that year's National Amateur Golf Champion, Washington's own Jack Westland, whose campaign was largely based on newspaper photos with fellow golfer Ike. Westland, a Republican, shook hands all around with the big boys of the forest industry, and when he got his hand back he found therein handsome campaign contributions. In Congress, his attitude towards parks was epitomized by his stand on the tiny Virgin Islands National Park, a gift of the Rockefellers. The vote in both houses of Congress had been unanimous except for a solitary "nay," cast by the west-side Congressman for the Second District, Jack Westland. For his lack of support for conservation, the *NCCC News* suggested that Westland's campaign funding must have come from the Association to Bring Back the Nineteenth Century. "The Westlands of the world," the editor lamented, "will always be with us, urging us backward toward the primordial ooze (where the *laissez* was really *faire*). But for every Westland there will be a Pelly. For every Douglas McKay there will be a Stewart Udall."

The election results of 1960 were much more joyous, having placed Udall at the helm of Interior. For conservationists, the 1964 outcome was equally triumphant. President Lyndon B. Johnson's overwhelming victory was buttressed by a friendly Congress where Democrats held two-thirds majorities in both houses. Even better news was that Goldwater's landslide loss had swept away both Horan and Westland. Horan was replaced by Spokane Democrat Tom Foley, who was prudently loyal to his conservative east-side constituency, but as a protege of Senator Jackson quietly went along with him on the North Cascades. Westland's replacement was of quite another color. In 1961 Phil Zalesky had been asked to present his slide show to the Snohomish County Young Democrats. Afterward, he was queried from the audience on his opinion of Westland. Phil unloaded. He then was asked if he was planning to run for the office. He wasn't, but someone in the audience was—the Snohomish County prosecuting attorney, Lloyd Meeds. Scoop Jackson held the same post before first running for Congress, and winning, in 1940. Meeds planned on repeating history and asked Zalesky if he would help in the campaign. "Gladly," he said. He organized conservationists for Lloyd Meeds, obtained every available conservationist mailing list, and assembled work parties to fold, staple, stamp, and address mailings for the future Congressman. By this time, the NCCC membership had already reached nearly one thousand and Meeds was happy to make the acquaintance.

On viewing Phil's slides, Lloyd Meeds had pledged to support a North Cascades National Park and was more than good as his word. He obtained appointment to the House Interior Committee, where he could work with Saylor against Aspinall. He did not seek the committee assignment solely because of the park. In family lines Meeds was one-eighth Indian; in his dedication to rectifying ancient wrongs he was *all* Indian. Indeed, his support of Indian fishing rights ultimately led to his departure from Congress, but not before he made a mighty and lasting contribution to the North Cascades. Though he could not budge Aspinall, who was playing a very deep game in order to divert most of the flow of the Colorado River—and ultimately, much of the Columbia River—to deserts of the Southwest, he could lobby other members of the committee and did so effectively. Among his converts was Morris Udall, brother of Stewart. Meeds somehow hornswoggled Aspinall into holding committee hearings in Seattle. The hearings busted Wayne "Never" Aspinall's roadblock. Another key action came during the final markup of the North Cascades bill. Aspinall had balked, making the excuse that he couldn't push the measure to a vote because Washington Governor Dan Evans had proposed different park boundaries. The committee still sitting, Meeds phoned Evans, explained the urgency, and asked if he would accept the park of the final bill. Evans agreed. Aspinall had no other tricks in his bag, and the bill proceeded out of committee to the floor of the House and was passed.

Senator Henry M. Jackson at a Seattle press conference on the North Cascades in 1966.

PHOTO BY HOWARD GRAY, NOCA 19632, IN THE COLLECTION OF NORTH CASCADES NATIONAL PARK COMPLEX, COURTESY OF THE NATIONAL PARK SERVICE.

No great monuments to Lloyd Meeds have been erected in the North Cascades, or in the Alpine Lakes Wilderness, where his efforts were also heroic. His concern for native rights led him to oppose provisions of the 1980 Alaska Lands Bill, and for that he was denounced by conservationists who were unwilling to make allowance for how much the nation owed Meeds for other services. There were more of Meeds' "other services" to future generations than most people know, even in the environmental community. Phil Zalesky recalls several in particular. At one point, Mount Baker National Forest Superintendent Chriswell pressured Meeds to help keep the Stehekin drainage out of wilderness; the Congressman asked Zalesky what NCCC thought of that, and suffice it to say, *that* ended that. When Kennicott Copper Company was beating the drums to announce its open-pit mine on Miner's Ridge ("big enough to see from the moon"), Zalesky went to Meeds' office and was emphatically told, "It'll never happen." Olympic Peninsula ski buffs were crying out loud for a ski resort in Seven Lakes Basin; the proposal didn't get off Meeds' desk alive. The issue of the North Cascades National Park had helped defeat Congressman Westland and elected Lloyd Meeds. The one became permanently livid and the other never forgot.

The election of 1968 must be briefly noted, not for any good news, but because it made for a very nervous summer. The prospect loomed of eight years with a president who for two terms had been vice-president in what was arguably the worst conservation administration in more than fifty years—since the William McKinley era of corporate togetherness of the late 1890s. Richard Nixon seemed to promise something comparable, perhaps worse. Conservationists certainly lamented the lack of meaningful conservation initiatives in the Eisenhower–Nixon years, but there was another reason for distress. During the reelection campaign of 1956, a scheme was devised to turn environmentalism into a liability for the Democrats. Fortunately, the scheme was upended, thanks in part to objections from the former Park Service director—and by now senior statesman—Horace M. Albright. "I have noted with dismay and some apprehension," he wrote, "the recent efforts to inject politics into the great non-partisan cause of conservation of natural resources." Nixon's loss to Kennedy in 1960 offered some hope to those who remembered the disappointing Fifties, but Johnson's gathering messes at home and in Vietnam in 1968 were not aiding the Democrats' chances, Senator Humphrey's in particular. Ultimately, Nixon would win the electoral votes handily, though he squeaked past Humphrey in the popular vote by just six-tenths of one percent. Democrats retained control of both houses of Congress, but by much narrower margins than before. The outlook for new progress on parks and wilderness areas dimmed considerably.

The political parties within Washington State in 1968 did not correspond precisely to their national counterparts. The national Democrats were overwhelmingly pro-Wilderness Bill and, before long, pro-North Cascades National Park, save the thorny exception, Mr. Aspinall from Colorado. Also pro-park, thanks to Irving Clark, Sr., and Jr., were Washington State's Democrats, with the exception of Albert Rosellini, Washington's governor at the start of the decade. Rosellini campaigned shotgun in hand and retriever at heel, both of which were suspected of having been borrowed for the photo opportunity. He generally accepted his land policy in one gulp from the Department of Game.

State Republicans ranged across the philosophical spectrum from the Gilded Age to Bull Moose, conservative to progressive. Some kept a foot in both camps, which required a certain amount of hopping not to fall flat on their faces. Dan Evans, who replaced Rosellini in the governorship as the park battle climaxed, seemed to struggle at times with a similar split political personality. When forced to take a leap, he would often land safely on the side of the Republican power interests, whatever they might be. But Evans could also come down on both feet for the wilderness he had come to love on Boy Scout hikes into the Olympics from Camp Parsons.

Senator Jackson was, of course, the state's kingfish. Early in the 1960s he received a delegation of North Cascades activists, heard them out, and responded with a brief but pithy lecture on the workings of the system. "I can't *give* you a national park," he said. "But if you get up a big enough parade, I'll step out front and lead it on in."

Renowned photographer Darius Kinsey and his wife, Tabitha (who ran the darkroom), lived in Sedro Woolley in the lowlands west of the North Cascades. Their images of logging in the late 1800s and early 1900s are among the best records we have of the region's immense, primeval forest that quickly succumbed to the axe and saw.

Members of the 1906 Mazama outing on Mount Baker gazing into giant crevasses.

Bob Marshall (right) with Fred Cleator near Cloudy Pass, September 1939.

Hand logging giant Douglas fir trees (ca. 1909).

Commercial Logging in Olympic National Park (ca. 1950s).

1927 visit to Cascade Pass by former Governor Louis Hart and D.G. McIntyre to promote development of a North Cascades Highway over the pass.

The horseman on the left is believed to be packer Ray Courtney, leading a team to Cloudy Pass and pausing to enjoy the view of Lyman Lakes.

PHIL ZALESKY

*Near the White Chuck River on the way to Lake Byrne
(Laura Zalesky); Glacier Peak Wilderness.*

PHIL ZALESKY

The Triplets from Sahale Arm, near Cascade Pass;
North Cascades National Park.

PHIL ZALESKY

Laura Zalesky and Patrick Goldsworthy hiking in the North Cascades Primitive Area, designated and renamed the Pasayten Wilderness in 1968.

PHIL ZALESKY

Hoary marmot; Pasayten Wilderness.

PAT O'HARA

Horseshoe Basin; Pasayten Wilderness.

DAVE SCHIEFELBEIN

Western larch turning gold, late summer.

TOM HAMMOND

A view of the Northern Pickets from one of the many summits in this remote area of the North Cascades; Mount Fury to the left; North Cascades National Park.

Waterfall near the headwaters of Bacon Creek; North Cascades National Park.

KEN WILCOX

TOM HAMMOND

McMillan Creek is defined by peaks of the Southern Picket Range that tower more than 6,000 feet above the valley floor; North Cascades National Park.

The Southern Pickets rise more than a vertical mile above Goodell Creek's lush temperate rainforest; North Cascades National Park.

Photo spread by Tom Hammond

Fireweed on the trail to High Pass near Buck Creek Pass; Glacier Peak Wilderness.

Mount Rainier in alpenglow from a jetliner; Mount Rainier National Park.

Spillway Glacier tumbles off Icy Peak; Mount Blum (left), Mount Hagan (right), and Glacier Peak loom behind; North Cascades National Park.

TOM HAMMOND

The Chikamin Glacier on Dome Peak, the largest glacier feeding Lake Chelan; Glacier Peak Wilderness.

PHIL ZALESKY

Full moon over Glacier Peak; Glacier Peak Wilderness Area.

DaKobed Range and Upper Suiattle River; Glacier Peak Wilderness.

PHIL ZALESKY

DAVE SIMONS

This image of the Suiattle River's old-growth forest was taken by Dave Simons (ca. 1959) in support of NCCC's proposal for a North Cascades National Park.

Brower's Mendicant Friars

In crafting its proposal for a North Cascades National Park, the NCCC would be aided by the exemplary work of several key individuals. Early in 1956, Grant McConnell, then a professor at the University of California at Berkeley, recalled a meeting with young Dave Simons: "He was very unprepossessing personally, but I had to hope for the best, since no other students had responded to my call for help. As it turned out, he was the best."

John Warth, long-time wilderness activist, remembered hiking with Simons:

> The Sierra Club had given him a little money and he'd used most of it to buy an old-fashioned 4x5 studio camera, complete with a big heavy tripod. He lurched along the trails, camera, tripod, and accessories stowed in a huge suitcase lashed on top of his pack, bumping into trees. It took him forever to set up his antique rig. There he'd be, head and shoulders under the black hood. . . . And there I'd sit waiting, watching the sun go down.

"I never before saw so much talent cut off so short," said David Brower in the obituary. "I don't know how the Cascades of Oregon and Washington could have had a better friend."

In the fall of 1954, Dave Simons arrived in the Bay Area from the milltown of Springfield, Oregon, to enroll at the University of California, the winner of a Westinghouse award in natural science. Soon he was attending meetings of the Sierra Club conservation committee. McConnell had heard alarming rumors about the future of the Stehekin Valley and began to look for more help:

> I came back to Berkeley in a panic. . . . I managed to interest Dave Brower and got the Sierra Club Conservation Committee to put the area on its agenda, but only pretty low on the list, what with Dinosaur's fate unsettled and other big fights going on. The problem was that the North Cascades were so little known. How could we get people excited when they didn't know what we were talking about? We needed masses of data, we needed pictures and maps. In fact, we needed a new Bob Marshall to inventory the area and give us information to work with. I looked for help around the Bay Area . . . but it was discouraging. Then in early 1956 a member of the Sierra Club Conservation Committee broke the dam for me—he sent Dave Simons.

McConnell brought Simons to the attention of David Brower, who was equally impressed by the youth's intellect, excellent photography, and passion for wilderness, and agreed that a way must be devised to put him to work. In that pre-*This Is the American Earth* year, the Sierra Club had barely eight thousand members and not much money. Brower scrambled together sufficient nickels and dimes to keep Simons in summertime camera film and peanut butter. McConnell had an old beater of a car he intended to take to Stehekin to join the Valley's fleet of beaters; driving it north provided Simons transport; the

McConnell cabin served as basecamp. In Seattle he subsisted with a sleeping bag on the floor of the Dyers' living room. In 1956, and again in the summer of 1957, Simons ranged through the North Cascades—widely but slowly, because in contrast to Bob Marshall, who traveled at a fast trot, Simons gave the impression he'd gladly take root wherever he happened to stand, content to "see the world in a grain of sand, all heaven in a flower." His photography was exceptional, earning him publication in the Wilderness Society's journal, *The Living Wilderness*. And he could capture the nuances of wildness in his writing. On a hike to Waptus Lake in 1957, in what would later become part of the Alpine Lakes Wilderness, Simons wrote of his twilight arrival:

> Our weariness vanished as we broke from the forest onto the beach of the lake. The surface was calm, and miles away at the lake's end two mountains seemed nearly buoyant as their glaciers and snowfields shimmered in the first rays of the rising moon. The nocturnal expansion of scale was everywhere; moderately deep valleys became unfathomable abysses, and ridges became mountains . . . we sat on the beach for more than an hour, while the moonlight spread upon the peaks, and an owl called from far across the lake. As the faint glow of Comet Mrkos faded behind the pointed summit of Bears Breast Mountain, we knew the bounty available to those who approach the wilderness, not blatantly or with pretension, but with reverence. This is the discovery that lies within the wilderness experience—a discovery which is a simultaneous reflection of humility.

As a wilderness mountaineer, Simons was totally disorganized, absolutely requiring a companion, or keeper, on the trails. Roger Avery, Paul Tschirlie, and John Warth were the most frequent keepers. Among their memories is "learning the distinction between *getting there* and *being there*." But it was the twenty-one-year-old Simons who prepared *The Need for Scenic Resource Conservation in the Northern Cascades of Washington*, encapsulating his own two summers in the field and two years in the library, and a half-century of efforts by others to preserve portions of the North Cascades. Available means of land protection were analyzed. Past performances of Forest Service and Park Service were compared. The conclusion, in text and map, was a proposal for a North Cascades National Park.

Having made his case and thereby set the agenda for the NCCC and the alliance it spearheaded, Simons was free to return to his home hills in the Oregon Cascades. The October 1959 *Sierra Club Bulletin* published his finest single essay, "These Are the Shining Mountains," a proposal for a Cascade Volcanic National Park. The park would encompass the diverse volcanic features centered in the Three Sisters area of central Oregon, the richest museum of vulcanism in America, as well as "one of the two great wilderness climax regions of the Cascade Range." Simons nevertheless remained committed to the North Cascades and was elected to the NCCC board.

What price the rigid orthodoxies of 1960 academia? Rewarded as a National Merit Scholar by a trip to Washington, D.C., where his fellows visited the Lincoln Memorial, Simons sought out The Wilderness Society. This brilliant student who had opted to study the earth first-hand, rather than second or third, had become, by the measure of a grade sheet, a poor student. What price war? In 1960 a terrible price was paid by a young male student who failed to play the grades game. Ousted by the university, Simons was exiled to Fort Bragg, North Carolina. He did not despair. In whatever moments he could salvage from Army routine, he continued revising a second report on the North Cascades, printed his Oregon photos, and issued a flood of letters. When he could get a pass, he went to Washington, D.C., to plead his causes. The final chapter was a grueling journey in November 1960. His letters, photos, and grand plan for a park had stimulated Oregonians to form a new group to promote the volcanic cause. On a two-week furlough to attend the initial meeting of the Oregon Cascades Conservation Council, he traveled overland across the continent. He couldn't afford air fare so he took the bus—one week riding west, another week riding east, with two days in Eugene. Was it the exhausting bus trip, the frantic pace of the last year, some failure of army medical care, just bad luck? On December 19, 1960, he was hospitalized for infectious hepatitis. Though always strong and healthy, two days later he was dead.

David Brower said in elegy:

> One of the sad things is that so few people know how very much David did—including the stirring of people at least twice his age into action, and well-advised action, too. Few will know how great a loss his death means to conservation. It means that much history which should have been written, now cannot be. . . .

Decades later, the Cascade Volcanic National Park is still wishing to be born. The O3C flickered and died. But the NCCC flourished with him and after him, and the North Cascades National Park is his monument.

The later-to-be-canonized "archdruid" of America, David Brower, had urgent need for an order of Simons-like friars gladly willing to take vows of poverty and go forth preaching the love of the Earth while crying anathema on the Barbecuers. In the aftermath of *This Is the American Earth*, the Sierra Club's yearly doubling and tripling in membership served as a volcano vent of idealism that had been all but smiled to death by Likeable Ike. Under Kennedy–Udall, this passion for the planet was finding its international outlet in the Peace Corps in early 1961, a year before Rachel Carson's explosive expose on the effects of DDT, *Silent Spring*, first appeared in *The New Yorker*. The magma was rising and Brower got his friars, from coast to coast.

The Pacific Northwest provided the first of the order and also the second. Grant McConnell and Polly Dyer, among others, had been nagging Brower to establish a Northwest Conservation Office to keep all issues in view and to sup-

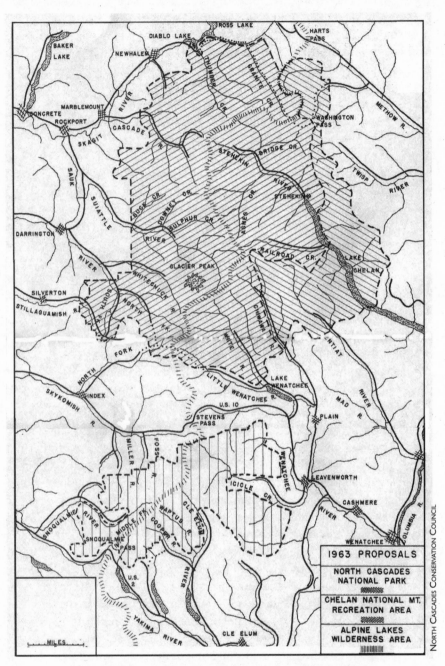

NCCC's 1963 national park proposal prepared by Mike McCloskey.

port and help organize volunteer groups to cope with them. Karl Onthank of the Obsidians of Eugene, Oregon (close to Simons' home in Springfield), had a candidate in mind—his next-door neighbor, Mike McCloskey. Just graduated in 1961 from the University of Oregon Law School, J. Michael McCloskey had little time to think about passing the bar before he was convinced by Onthank to let himself be conscripted by Brower.

McCloskey's position was partially funded by the San Francisco office, plus whatever petty cash the Pacific Northwest Chapter of the Sierra Club could spare, and to a lesser extent by the similarly lean coffers of other member organizations of the Federation of Western Outdoor Clubs, and quite considerably by individuals. Leo Gallagher initially paid about half of McCloskey's support. All the money together was barely enough to pay for gas, the rent on a backstreet, upstairs, cubbyhole office in Eugene, grandly described as the Sierra Club's Pacific Northwest Headquarters and office of the Northwest Representative of the Sierra Club and the Federation of Western Outdoor Clubs, and (separately) the NCCC. McCloskey's work benefited various groups, although the job was under the Sierra Club's organizational umbrella out of convenience. Mike was a true mendicant, occupying guest bedrooms and sitting down to family dinners and breakfasts throughout the Northwest; in Seattle, Emily Haig kept a room for his exclusive use as a "branch office."

Mike McCloskey was responsible for a huge territory and a host of issues; however, his primary initial assignment was clear. In the spring of 1963, he more than earned his keep by producing for NCCC an entirely new and painstaking *Prospectus for a North Cascades National Park*, a pivotal 130-page work based on much original research. Though recognized to be Brower's friar, his chief reporting responsibility at the time was to the board of directors of the NCCC, including Brower, who remained an active board member. At the fall meeting of the directors, the McCloskey prospectus was exhaustively discussed and applauded. McConnell spoke for the group, "I believe we've got to invest some money in this young man's education!" The board thereby voted most of its existing treasury to send McCloskey on his first lobbying trip to Washington, D.C., which, by all accounts, was a resounding success.

When Mike was summoned to the San Francisco headquarters of the Sierra Club in early 1965, attorney Rod Pegues took his place and kept the candle burning for two more years, succeeded in 1967 by a brand new lawyer from Ohio, Brock Evans. After his first year in law school, Evans worked a summer at Glacier National Park and immediately knew that he would have to do what had been done by another Midwesterner, John Muir, and go west. In June 1993, he recalled his introduction to the North Cascades thirty years earlier:

> Becoming enchanted by the magnificence of the Northwest forests right after I moved to Seattle in 1963, I seized every moment I could to explore them, both as a

part of my first ventures into the wilderness through The Mountaineers Climbing Course in 1964, and then on my own. Having joined the N3C, having read everything I could get my hands on, I traveled up into the great valleys of the Cascade, Suiattle, White Chuck, and Sauk, to see for myself. Heart pounding, full of growing anger and dismay that my government would do these things, this young lawyer ever more quickly moved towards his final break with his chosen legal career. . . .

That final break came in June of 1966, when I heard about a place called Barclay Creek, "the nearest big tree forest to Seattle." I still remember the date, June 12, when Rachel and I drove up a bright Sunday morning to see it. Stepping out of the car only a mile off the Stevens Pass Highway, we entered the great forest of Barclay Creek, for what must have been about the last time. We didn't know it at first. It was just a beautiful, magnificent cathedral that quiet Sunday morning, golden bars of light slanting through to touch the green moss on the forest floor. Squirrels chattered high up, and little streams danced across the trails, and we wandered, two children in a magic land. Only a few yards in, we saw the first yellow sign tacked to a tree: "Clearcut boundary, U.S. Forest Service" . . . and then another, and another . . . we stumbled along, and the whole first five miles of that six-mile trail to Barclay Lake all had been sold. . . .

You know the rest. It was logged off the next year, shortly after I came on as Northwest Representative. I issued a bitter press release, really a lament and a requiem. But returning home on that June day the year before, I made my vow: that I would give the rest of my life that such crimes (because they are crimes, aren't they?) would never happen again. . . . I would do everything in my power, small though it might be, to fight, to join with the others who had sounded the alarm, and fought so hard for so long to save what had now become my beloved North Cascades, my place too.

The passion of his epiphany year took him to the corridors of Congress, where his tireless, home-stretch lobbying proved crucial to the passage of the 1968 North Cascades Act. Evans later applied his talents to the campaign for an Alpine Lake Wilderness, followed by much work in the national sea of other troubles. Before leaving Seattle for duties elsewhere with the Sierra Club, and the National Audubon Society after that, he had enlarged and solidified the office of "Northwest Rep" as the basecamp for swarms of assistant friars, a prototype for other offices of the Sierra Club and other organizations throughout the nation. Many years later Evans was surprised to learn that much of his salary had been paid by Leo Gallagher. And certainly many others would be surprised to find that the Sierra Club's D.C. lobbying efforts began in the Pacific Northwest, or more specifically, the North Cascades.

As recipients of the Sierra Club's annual John Muir Award, both Evans and McCloskey joined an exclusive list of American conservationists so recognized: Olaus and Margaret Murie, Ansel Adams, Sigurd Olson, William O.

Douglas, David Brower, Wallace Stegner, and others. Evans spent fifteen years with Audubon before becoming Executive Director of the Endangered Species Coalition in 1997. In 1969 McCloskey followed Brower as second Executive Director of the Sierra Club, retiring in 1999. His memoir, *In the Thick of It: My Life in the Sierra Club*, was published in 2005.

THE BIG PUSH—OBJECTIVE: MORATORIUM

The graying eminence of conservationist-general Brower's staff, Grant McConnell, enunciated as a first principle of political strategy that the North Cascades issue had to be nationalized, the center of decision-making transferred from the Barbecuer backyard to Washington D.C., where voters of California, Illinois, Pennsylvania, Massachusetts, and Alabama would have a say in the disposition of a national treasure. The North Cascades Study Bill was intended to do just that. In the *Congressional Record* for June 7, 1961, Congressman Pelly cited the signatures of 21,669 Americans on petitions asking for the study. The signers were coast to coast, border to border. Pelly took special care to note that, in contrast to proposed parks that had been violently opposed by their close neighbors, 3,472 residents of Washington's Second District, then (mis)represented by Westland, signed in support of the North Cascades proposal.

Citizens committees were continuing to spring up on every hand. In April 1962, the *New York Times* editorially endorsed the park. The Sierra Club's North Cascades wilderness postcards went in the mail by the tens of thousands, friend to friend, along the way doubtless enlisting a legion of converts within the Postal Service.

The opposition soon rose to the challenge. On June 7, 1961, Secretary of Agriculture Orville Freeman wrote Senators Wayne Morse, Henry Jackson, Warren Magnuson, and Maurine Neuberger, otherwise known as "the Oregon–Washington four," insisting the Forest Service could manage just fine on its own:

> The high mountain areas of the National Forests in Washington . . . are attracting increased public attention. . . . Our citizens have varying . . . interests in the multiple purposes for which these lands can be used. I agree fully that we should . . . ascertain the wisest possible use of this heritage. I have, therefore, asked the Forest Service to make a careful study of these high mountain areas. . . .

Many secretaries of agriculture have seemed content to let the Forest Service write forest policy and budgets. Farmer Freeman had abundant precedent for sending the fox to study the hen house. The "fox," Regional Forester J. Herbert Stone, asked Congress to join him on tour October 2–11. Members of the House Committee on Agriculture, Subcommittee on Forests, were led by Region Six of the Forest Service through lumber mills and banquet halls, breaking bread and tilting glasses with the Chelan Chamber of Commerce, Western Pine Association, Industrial Forestry Association, and Western Forest Industries Association. Alerted by Pelly, Chuck Hessey put in an uninvited appearance at Chelan, as the skeleton at the feast. On the Chelan ferry to Stehekin, *Lady of the Lake*, he was eyed askance by Blair and Stone, who must have been aghast to see that their semi-secret councils had been infiltrated. George Wall welcomed the boat party at Stehekin with an array of spirits sufficient to stupefy half of Chelan County.

Hessey's stinging report in *The Wild Cascades* observed that these Forest Service high officials "could, many years ago, have filled their offices capably enough, but they lack in this decisive time that extra dimension of thought possessed by many of their predecessors." Such as Marshall, Silcox, and Leopold.

In June 1962 Tom Pelly blew the whistle to send the troops over the top in the second major offensive of the North Cascades national campaign: the Pelly Moratorium. In a letter to Secretary Freeman, he requested a moratorium on further logging and a suspension of long-term commitments at twenty specific sites—an action hailed in *The Wild Cascades* as "A Historic Moment for the North Cascades National Park."

From The Wild Cascades, *June-July 1965.*

The Forest Service was backed into a corner. The public could not comprehend, nor could Congress, the urgent necessity to log five-hundred-year-old forests right this minute. What difference to the economy of America would be made by a delay of a year or two, even a decade or two? Wasn't a fundamental plank of the Pinchot platform the "long run"?

A September 13, 1962, letter from John A. Baker, Assistant Secretary of Agriculture, gave Congressman Pelly his answer:

> Three of the areas you mention (#11, 12, and 13) constitute a major part of the Cascade Pass–Ruby Creek area where preservation of scenic values and development of them for enjoyment by large numbers of people was specific as the management policy in this September 6, 1960, decision . . . which established the boundaries of the Glacier Peak Wilderness Area. . . . five of the areas . . . (#1, 10, 20, and parts of 14, and 15) were given careful analysis. . . . The decision was to not include them because they were considered not predominantly desirable for wilderness. Area #19 . . . is already located within the Northern Cascade Primitive Area. . . .
>
> I requested, on June 7, 1961, that no further development be undertaken in the North Cascades Area (except the Trans-Cascades Highway) pending preparation of a statement of objectives and policies for the high mountain areas . . . On March 30, 1962, the "Management Objectives and Policies for the High Mountain Areas of National Forests of the Pacific Northwest Region" were approved. . . .
>
> There are roads (more than eighty-six miles) in ten of the areas. Approximately two hundred miles are proposed to be built . . . in eighteen of the twenty areas. . . . Eighteen of the areas contain timber stands. Five areas (#4, 7, 9, 10, and 15) have operating timber sales or sales under contract. In three areas, #2, 5 and 15, additional timber sales are proposed for the five-year period ending in 1967 . . . Insect and disease attacks . . . salvage . . . substantial and persistent unemployment. . . . adverse effect on the economy. . . .
>
> There are ten of the areas in which no developments are planned within the next five years. . . . As for the other ten, numbered 2, 4, 5, 7, 9, 10, 14, 15, 16, and 20 in your letter, I think it is necessary that the present . . . management actions proceed. . . .

The circumstantial, by-the-number detail was calculated to give the appearance of thorough, fair deliberation. However, to those who looked beyond the numbers to the ancient forests they represented, Baker's letter was not an answer but an evasion. The Federation of Western Outdoor Clubs endorsed the moratorium. Congressman Westland took his eye off the ball long enough to denounce it. On August 14, 1962, Senator Magnuson wrote Secretary Freeman analyzing and amending, but overall supporting, the Pelly request. On February 9, 1963, Pelly wrote Freeman renewing his call for a moratorium.

The Forest Service continued to stonewall, but the moratorium was imposed. A new front had opened in the nation's capital that took the initiative from the Forest Service to a higher authority: The White House—and the interagency North Cascades Study Team.

Simultaneously a bold new front opened in the West.

1963: OFFENSIVE ON THE WESTERN FRONT—THE BILL FOR A NATIONAL PARK

The NCCC and the alliance it spearheaded decided late in 1962 that commando bombardments and raids had done what they could and the time had come for a main-force attack. The McCloskey draft of a bill to create a North Cascades National Park embodied the best thinking of the best available minds and was far readier for Congressional consideration than most legislation when introduced. However, the appointment of the Study Team caused the Council to hold its fire, but only briefly. The May–June–July 1963 issue of *The Wild Cascades* explained:

> Then, suddenly, came word that the "Treaty of the Potomac" had resulted in an agreement . . . to carry out a joint study. . . . We don't know what the results will be, and we don't know whether we'll agree with the recommendations. However, we decided to postpone public release of the park proposal in order to allow the Study Team a fair chance to do its work in an objective atmosphere.

> Unfortunately, the Hon. Jack Westland, Representative from the nineteenth century, has seen fit to denounce our park proposal as a secret and sinister plot hatched in dark conspiracy with such ultraliberal fanatics as President Kennedy. Well, we will have more to say in the future about *Through the Looking Glass* with Hon. Jack.

> For now, suffice to say that though we do not wish to embarrass the Study Team, we do feel that you must know the facts of the matter . . . The following . . . outline of the North Cascades National Park proposal . . . is subject to change in the light of your comments, which are very much desired—as are those of the Study Team, and those of the Hon. Jack, too.

Furrowings of the brow greeted the Council's 1963 park proposal, but no deeper than the furrowings that went into the drafting. The park-worthiness of the entire Cascades from Snoqualmie Pass to Canada was acknowledged . . . someday, someday. But in the 1960s? Not everything could be preserved in this first action. The priority had to be the lands most immediately endangered, lands that required the protection only a park could give. Two areas were judged to be at the top of the Barbecuer hit list.

One was Glacier Peak. Since 1960 the peak itself and the adjacent meadows and some of the forests had been made temporarily safe, pending the Congressional guarantee that would come with passage of the pending Wilderness Bill. However, the 1960s Forest Service lacked the will to preserve wilderness lands having high commodity value. Further, it had no intermediate designation between U-1, U-2 (wilderness, large and small), and U-3 (recreation area, commodity extraction permitted after holy water had been sprinkled by landscape architects). The Forest Service refused to preserve the roadless forests of the Pelly Moratorium. Neither would it preserve the forests of valleys already roaded. Further, its firm strategy was to log at valley heads in order to preclude wilderness status for entire valleys. Whatever the perils in Park Service management, there at least would be no logging in a park. Forests of the Sauk and White Chuck and other streams would be safeguarded.

The other most-endangered area extended from the Stehekin Valley southward down Lake Chelan and west and north through Cascade Pass and Eldorado to the Methow and Skagit Rivers. Park status would exclude further logging from the Stehekin and Cascade valleys, where existing roads made them ineligible for wilderness designation.

The NCCC's proposed park totaled 1,038,665 acres, 458,505 in the existing Glacier Peak Wilderness and 580,160 acres to be newly protected. Accompanying the park would be a 269,521-acre Chelan National Mountain Recreation Area, bringing the total protected to 1,308,186 acres.

Not enough, to be sure. Later generations have said so, and the generation of the 1960s knew so even then. But asking for too much would have risked getting nothing. Trust had to be placed in geographical fortuities. Why was the North Cascades Primitive Area—the largest such area in the Northwest—excluded? Because the western section of this 801,000-acre de facto wilderness, the Pickets, was formidably rugged and its valleys drained north to Canada, the forests were economically available only to loggers who had no votes south of the international boundary. The eastern section had been swept by a series of 1920s fire storms that had left vast tracts of photogenic silver forests and scraggly lodgepole pine; the impending reclassification of the primitive area to a wilderness could be expected to be much easier than Glacier Peak.

But how on Earth could Mount Baker and Mount Shuksan be omitted—two of conservationists' greatest glories of the Cascades? That was just it. The park acreage had to be held to practical political limits, and these areas were so compelling that it was believed that they were virtually guaranteed high status as eventual park additions. And Lake Chelan? This fifty-five-mile-long fjord was also adjudged so magnificent a feature of the American earth that it would surely and inevitably make its own future—at no great distance in time—and with much less struggle required than to preserve ancient forests from chainsaws.

The concept of "national recreation area" was injected into the North

Cascades by the McCloskey prospectus; but the NCCC came to rue the day. Adopted by foes of the park, given different boundaries, misunderstood and exploited by citizenry and bureaucracy alike, the "national wreck area" became a proximate cause for many of NCCC's future efforts to protect what remained vulnerable—and a primary motivation to right the perceived wrongs committed in the name of the 1968 North Cascades Act.

In the minds of the conservationist inventors of the 1960s, the national recreation area they proposed was the soul of simplicity: it would "be managed in the same manner as [the park] . . . with one exception. . . . [The] hunting of deer and other game animals will be permitted within its boundaries." The managing agency would be the National Park Service, which would have all the powers there that it had in national parks.

Why would the NCCC, whose members viewed wildlife as an essence, as the "indicator" of wilderness, propose that the shores and slopes of Lake Chelan as far north as Railroad Creek, and the golden lakes highlands of the Lyall larch ("the evergreen that is not" because it sheds its needles), be conceded to the heavy cavalry, each rider-gunner potentially affecting the land as heavily as hundreds of light-stepping, peace-loving pedestrians?

The answer lay in the 1963 Leopold Report (by Aldo Leopold's son and others), *Wildlife Management in National Parks*, which recently had been submitted to Interior Secretary Udall:

> Portions of several proposed parks are so firmly established as traditional hunting grounds that impending closure of hunting may preclude public acceptance of park status. In such cases it may be necessary to designate core areas as national parks in every sense of the word, establishing protective buffer zones in the form of national recreation areas where hunting is permitted.

A closer-to-home motive was the common cause being made by pragmatists among both the non-hunting and the hunting-and-fishing conservationists. Habitat preservation was the linkage. The sportsmen fees paid to the Washington State Game Department had helped bring into public ownership wetlands, streambanks, and uplands. Game Department biologists had supplied McCloskey data on where hunters found their sport, and he had drawn boundaries of the recreation area to leave open to shooting the most productive terrain, removing from the annual kill—by placement in the park—just sixty mountain goats and eight hundred deer, the latter amounting to about seven percent of the kill in Chelan, Skagit, and Snohomish Counties, a negligible percentage in Whatcom and Okanogan Counties, and a reduction of about nine-tenths of one percent in the statewide kill. By adjusting the seasons and number of permits in adjacent lands, many of the deer might still be taken outside the park, resulting in a scarcely measurable reduction in the total kill. Reductions would be insignificant in the annual kill of elk, furbearers, and wildfowl.

Unfortunately, the strategy didn't work. The olive branch was contemptuously hurled back. In June 1963 the Washington State Sportsmen Council, never deigning to examine the proposal, rejected the national park. The dogma was that critters are given by God into the custody of man not for the benefit of sentimental gawkers but for the pleasure of them who eats 'em, skins 'em, or just plain plinks 'em for the sheer joy of it (as a few are prone to do). On July 30 the director of the Washington State Game Department, John A. Biggs, delivered what looked like a kneejerk response. His aide, J. Burton Lauckhart, chief of the Game Management Division, wrote a lobbying letter to Thomas L. Kimball, executive director of the largest outdoor organization in America, the National Wildlife Federation, which at that time might have been more accurately referred to as the National Wildlife Eaters Federation. (The Federation has since become a much stronger voice for wildlife conservation.)

Summarizing events of 1963 in *The Wild Cascades*, Patrick Goldsworthy said:

> This has been the Year of the *North Cascades National Park Prospectus*. Over five years of research, culminated by the intensive efforts of J. Michael McCloskey, has produced this impressive 120-page document. . . . We have given top priority, during the entire year, to assisting McCloskey . . . in editing this milestone of conservation literature.

The timing was close, the glue hardly dry, when the *Prospectus* was rushed from the bindery to the Study Team hearings.

1963: Offensive on the Eastern Front—The North Cascades Study Team

On a visit to the Kennedy White House arranged by Supreme Court Justice William O. Douglas, David Brower, and Grant McConnell were assured by a White House aide, "This is a *friendly* administration." The friendliness was that of Interior's Stewart Udall. Agriculture's Orville Freeman more or less read the script written for him by the tree-farmers. The scuffling of these two embarassed the Oval Office, where most eyes were fixed on the moon. Udall and Freeman were sat down at a table and, on February 1, 1963, the White House announced the "Treaty of the Potomac." The previous Monday the two secretaries, pistols to their heads, signed a letter to the president reporting, "We have closed the book on these disputes." On March 5 the Bureau of Outdoor Recreation, a new unit established in 1962 within the Interior Department, issued a press release:

SECRETARIES OF AGRICULTURE AND INTERIOR APPOINT NORTH CASCADES STUDY TEAM: The Secretaries of Agriculture and the Interior today appointed a five-man North Cascades Mountains study team to explore all the resource potentials of Federal lands in a portion of Washington State to recommend the form of management and administration for it which would best serve the public interest. . . .

The study team . . . will be headed by Edward C. Crafts, Director of the Bureau of Outdoor Recreation. . . . Serving with him will be two men from the Department of Agriculture, Dr. George A. Selke, Consultant to the Secretary of Agriculture, and Arthur Greeley, Deputy Chief of the United States Forest Service, and two from the Department of the Interior, Henry Caulfield, Assistant Director of the Resources Program Staff, and George B. Hartzog, Jr., Associate Director of the National Park Service. . . .

The Bureau of Outdoor Recreation emanated from the National Outdoor Resources Review, proposed by David Brower in the 1956 *Sierra Club Annual*, taken up by Joseph Penfold of the Izaak Walton League, and diluted by him to a form palatable to Congress. Penfold was appointed to the Review Commission. Brower was not, because as Fred Seaton, Udall's predecessor as Secretary of the Interior, explained to him at a San Francisco breakfast, he was too environmentally one-sided. Appointed in his stead was Weyerhaeuser's well-rounded Bernard Orell.

The Wild Cascades, uncharacteristically politic, refrained from remarking that, prior to moving to the Bureau of Outdoor Recreation, Edward Crafts had been twenty-nine years with the Forest Service, the last ten as Assistant Chief. The promotion he sought to Chief was successfully opposed by Brower and Justice William O. Douglas because he was such an expert proponent of the Forest Service policies they deplored. Four of the Study Team members obviously would split two against two. The transfer to Interior theoretically had cleaned Crafts' slate, but when push came to shove, was there any question how the tie would be broken?

Nevertheless, if a technical victory was ruled out before the campaign opened, the period of the Study Team was certain to provide the North Cascades their bulliest pulpit ever. The study that had been sought through a hat-in-hand Park Service request to set foot on Forest Service land (and denied), then pursued through bills in Congress (and blocked by Aspinall), was finally happening. A *de facto* moratorium on logging in the North Cascades was obtained. Secretary Udall would be in constant hover. The conservationist eyes of the nation would be trained on the stage.

Between July 15 and 24, 1963, three of the five Study Team members, Selke, Hartzog, and Greeley, toured roads of the Skagit and White Chuck Rivers, Mount Baker, Lake Chelan, Stehekin, and Mount Rainier. John Doerr, Superintendent of Olympic National Park, accompanied the team on the entire trip, as did J. Herbert Stone, regional director of the Forest Service. Various Forest Service rangers joined the group while it was in their districts, and State

Land Commissioner Bert Cole, who prior to his election was a gypo logger on the Olympic Peninsula, spent four days on the tour as the governor's representative. Public contacts were not invited and, reportedly, none was attempted. Resource sub-studies were conducted in the field most of the summer by a number of teams from state and federal agencies.

During the week of October 7, the team held public hearings in Wenatchee, Mount Vernon, and Seattle. Though the chambers of commerce and commodity industries turned out in force to chant stereotyped testimony, much of it undocumented and inaccurate, and though their ignorance was magnified by the local press, of the two hundred witnesses who spoke (from a total attendance of six hundred) 45 percent voiced support for preserving wilderness values. In addition to oral testimony, a week after the hearings the team had received three hundred statements for the record, nearly all for the park.

The Sierra Club, National Parks Association, The Wilderness Society, and Federation of Western Outdoor Clubs spoke in support of the park proposal. So did The Mountaineers, Mazamas, Cascadians, Seattle Audubon, and Washington Alpine Club. The NCCC presented to the Study Team petitions containing tens of thousands of signatures favoring a national park. The Nature Conservancy and Garden Clubs of America urged preservation of natural values. Editorial support for the park appeared in the *Seattle Argus*, the *Portland Reporter*, and the *New York Times*.

The following year, 1964, was eventful. President Kennedy had been assassinated in Dallas and President Johnson was now in the Oval Office. Secretary Udall remained; his book, *The Quiet Crisis*, published in 1963, would have pleased both Presidents Roosevelt. In 1964 *The North Cascades* was published by The Mountaineers. *The Wind in the Wilderness* was aired in Seattle, Portland, and Spokane. The Goldwater debacle replaced Congressman Westland with Lloyd Meeds. Howard Zahniser offered his final testimony to Congress in support of the sixty-sixth draft of his wilderness bill. In early May Zahniser died of a heart attack at the young age of fifty-eight—just weeks before the bill was at last set free by Wayne N. Aspinall, his price having been grudgingly paid, giving the miners, the cows, and the sheep continued run of the wilderness. But not the loggers. And not the mechanical contrivances that fundamentally alter the experience of wilderness.

On September 3, the Wilderness Act, originally unveiled by Zahniser in 1956 at the first Biennial Northwest Wilderness Conference in Portland, was signed by President Johnson in the Rose Garden. Johnson called it an "important milestone" in saving "what is best in our natural environment." Alice Zahniser and Mardy Murie, whose husband, Olaus, had died the previous October, attended the signing ceremony. Mardy returned to her cabin in the Tetons (with a pen from Johnson) and remained a wildlands activist for almost another forty years. A Seattle native, Mardy Murie was recognized for her lifelong dedication to conservation when Bill Clinton presented her with the Presidential Medal of Freedom in 1998. She died in her Wyoming cabin in October 2003 at the age of 101.

Under the Wilderness Act, all "wilderness areas" designated by the Forest Service under the U-Regulations received immediate statutory protection, including fifty-four areas in thirteen states, 9.1 million acres in all. The largest were the Bob Marshall and Selway–Bitterroot Wilderness Areas in Montana and Idaho, at around a million acres each. At less than half that size, the North Cascades' Glacier Peak was the largest of three areas in Washington, the others being Goat Rocks and Mount Adams well to the south. Among the Pacific states, all but one area, the John Muir Wilderness in the Sierra Nevada, were considerably smaller than the Glacier Peak Wilderness.

In the fall of 1964, President Johnson was elected to a full term, along with what he called his "Conservation Congress." Having concluded its work just prior to the election, the 88th Congress reshaped the American political landscape significantly. According to the *Washington Post*, they "talked longer, spent more, and passed more major legislation than any other in recent history."

Events of 1965 kept up the beat. The *Seattle Times* ran Walt Woodward's string of seventeen columns on the North Cascades. *Routes and Rocks: Hikers Guide to the North Cascades from Glacier Peak to Lake Chelan*, by Dwight Crowder and Rowland Tabor, a detailed and sensitive survey of the core of the proposed park, was published by The Mountaineers. Also in 1965, *Sunset Magazine* put the North Cascades on its cover, and the Sierra Club published *The Wild Cas-*

President Johnson signs the Wilderness Act, September 3, 1964.

NATIONAL PARK SERVICE

3: To the North Cascades National Park • 177

cades: Forgotten Parkland by Harvey Manning and Ansel Adams. President John-son was mildly encouraging with his White House Message on Natural Beauty, in which he recited some of Udall's prose. "The forgotten outdoorsmen of today are those who like to walk, hike, ride horseback or bicycle. For them we must have trails as well as highways. Nor should motor vehicles be permitted to tyrannize the more leisurely human traffic," a subtle acknowledgement that maybe parks aren't just for cars after all.

THE EMPIRE STRIKES BACK

A national park or wilderness area requires, and deserves, formal designation by Congress. Administrative designations by the Forest Service (or any other agency), such as "recreation area," "primitive area," or even "wilderness area" prior to the signing of the Wilderness Act, could be changed or undone on a whim and were therefore not nearly as secure as something that takes an act of Congress to establish. To counter increasing interest in new national parks at Mount Baker, Lake Chelan, and Glacier Peak, the Forest Service developed recreation plans for each area and went so far as to designate, in 1926, a 74,859-acre Mount Baker Recreation Area surrounding that mountain and Mount Shuksan. A 234,000-acre Glacier Peak–Cascade Recreation Unit was estab-lished in 1931. About the same time, a 173,000-acre Whatcom Primitive Area was delineated, then expanded in 1935 to eight hundred thousand acres and renamed the North Cascade Primitive Area. Logging, mining and dams were generally allowed as long as they were deemed compatible with recreational uses. In 1946, "Limited Area" status was established at Alpine Lakes, Cougar Lake, and Monte Cristo Peaks, but this was merely a holding zone while the Forest Service explored other options. Ultimately, sixteen limited areas were announced in Region Six and all were included along with wilderness areas, primitive areas, and the like on a Forest Service map titled "Dedicated Areas of Region Six." The public was led to believe they had some permanence. The boundaries of all these areas typically encompassed some of the most rugged and inaccessible portions of the range, predictably excluding the vast majority of old-growth forests.

In the 1960s, as the Study Team inched closer to a national park in the North Cascades, John Warth told a tale of "phantom recreation areas" in the April–May 1965 issue of *The Wild Cascades*:

> The favorite device of Region Six of the Forest Service.... Now you
> see it, now you don't. Or one person sees it, another doesn't....
> with some they produce confusion . . . with others the reassurance

that comes from the raising of false hopes. When these phantoms have served their purpose they quietly disappear and no one ever hears of them again.

Warth reviewed some history of the Forest Service in the shadows: Glacier Peak–Cascade, Mount Baker, and an elusive Glacier Peak "Wilderness Area" announced in 1936 by the Regional Forester, who withdrew his signature a month later, almost without notice. Glacier Peak's administrative wilderness was claimed in Forest Service publications for several more years, until the deaths of Marshall and Silcox. The primitive areas the Forest Service established in the Olympic Mountains were intended to forestall the Olympic National Park and were quietly disestablished when Congress created the park.

One other example in Oregon is worthy of mention. Early in 1961, eleven Northwest outdoor organizations formally appealed the management plan for a highland forest area in Oregon. The Forest Service refused to hear the appeal until members of Congress stirred such a fuss that the Secretary of Agriculture sent Region Six back to its drawing board. The rangers emerged with a new "High Mountain Policy" for "Landscape Management Areas," places where tourists might be expected to pull cars off the road and aim their cameras. To a degree, the policy was a reiteration of the U-3 Regulation for Scenic Areas that had been on the books since 1939, but had generally been applied to smaller areas. While this new policy was a breakthrough, some of the Landscape Management Areas so designated happened to be candidates for the scenic protection that deserved to be provided by national parks. Indeed, some were actively being proposed as national parks. The Forest Service could not (or would not) provide such protection under its "new" policy. The high-mountain forests could be logged, though less swiftly than elsewhere, on the apparent assumption that if the logging was done slowly enough nobody would notice. Architects would design the clearcuts to conceal them from roadside viewpoints, the theory being that what people couldn't see from the car they wouldn't care much about. Nevertheless, the policy was significant: it was the first time the Forest Service had backed off commercial logging across a particular landscape.

These kinds of strategies continued even as the Study Team conducted its work in the early 1960s. Officials announced that the report of the North Cascades Study Team, initially scheduled for completion by the end of 1964, was being delayed to March of 1965. Jumping the gun, in February the Forest Service deployed trumpets and snaredrums to announce designation of a 533,460-acre Eldorado Peaks High Country Recreation Area to help fill the white space on the map between the North Cascade Primitive Area and Glacier Peak Wilderness. Staff of the Region Six office in Portland and of the Wenatchee, Mount Baker, Snoqualmie, and Okanogan National Forests doorbelled the countryside, newspaper to newspaper, Chamber of Commerce to

Chamber of Commerce, logger to logger, drumming and bugling for support.

Patrick Goldsworthy complained to Senator Jackson that the Treaty of the Potomac required the Forest Service to cooperate fully with the North Cascades Study Team, and that this action outrageously circumvented the process. The Forest Service responded that it was merely obeying the Secretary of Agriculture's order that the area be used predominantly for recreation. That reasoning failed to acknowledge that by formally designating a "recreation area" the agency had disregarded the legal procedures required for such a designation. Region Six had created an entity that, by law, could be created only by the Secretary of Agriculture. Region Six sputtered back, saying the recreation area was not what it seemed, though what it seemed to everybody in the Northwest was what had been clearly delineated by the Forest Service's own maps and description.

Goldsworthy's letter was answered not by the senator but by Regional Forester Stone: "There has been no official announcement of classification of . . . Eldorado Peaks Recreation Area by the Wenatchee National Forest. I can therefore only interpret your concern as being in reference to the *Wenatchee Daily World* coverage of the Forest Service proposed management of this area. . . ." The *Daily World* story of February 23 had begun,

> Dedication of half a million acres of Forest Service land in the North Cascades as the Eldorado Peaks Recreation Area was announced today by the Wenatchee National Forest. Ken Blair, Wenatchee Forest supervisor, told the *Daily World* . . . the program has been approved by the regional forester. . . . No action was necessary by the chief of the Forest Service or the Secretary of Agriculture. . . .

Deputy Chief of the Forest Service A.W. Greeley explained to Senator Jackson that Blair, in discussing plans at a meeting of the Wenatchee Chamber of Commerce, either had misspoken or been misheard, or in any event, misunderstood. The phantom of the "Eldorado Peaks" could not be dispelled. Rangers tried to unspeak the misspeak and explain what Blair had meant to say or should have, although the journalists continued to get it wrong.

1966: Year of the Study Team Report

In the meantime, the Study Team's report was delayed and delayed again. Finally, at a pivotal Seattle press conference held January 6, 1966, Senators Jackson and Magnuson introduced Edward C. Crafts, Study Team Chairman, who summarized *The North Cascades Study Report*, dated October 1965 (though not released until January). Crafts concluded, "I have been involved in this since March 5, 1963, and I know of nothing that I have been involved in in my thirty-two years experience that has been more controversial up to this point, and I think the controversy is probably just beginning."

All five members of the Study Team were present, as were President Johnson's top officials of the Interior and Agriculture Departments, respectively, Secretaries Stewart Udall and Orville Freeman. Congressmen Lloyd Meeds and Tom Foley rounded out the field of presenters. The team had agreed on a joint recommendation for a new North Cascades National Park, an Okanogan Wilderness (the former North Cascades Primitive Area), and small wilderness areas at Alpine Lakes and Mount Stuart. Remarks suiting the occasion were delivered along with others that were not. Senator Jackson astounded the populace on hand by also inviting his friend Fred J. Overly, the former superintendent of Olympic National Park and a long-time advocate for *less* park and *more* logging. Prior to the press conference, the importance of an Olympic logging controversy to events unfolding in the North Cascades was not entirely apparent to most observers.

With Overly's assistance, stealth maneuvering by a handful of top officials in the Park Service, most surprisingly the director, Newton B. Drury, and Conrad Wirth, his Chief of Lands, managed to open up Olympic National Park to commercial "salvage" logging in the 1940s, while miraculously keeping the conservation-minded Interior Secretary, Harold Ickes, almost completely in the dark. Under the guise of preventing insect infestation and preserving scenery, logging contracts were let, at first for downed trees, then for standing timber that might be at risk of blowing down, a relatively common occurrence adjacent to cut-over

Fred Overly, Regional Director of the Bureau of Recreation, addresses Seattle press in January 1966 on proposed deletions of ancient forest from Olympic National Park.

areas. The more trees "at risk" were cut, the more other trees became threat-ened, creating a snowball effect for more and more logging. Those in the agency who opposed these maddening policies were largely disregarded.

At the January press conference, Overly, a logging engineer by trade, was invited by Jackson to present to the media his proposal that Olympic National Park be reduced by fifty-nine thousand acres, mostly in the rainforests of the Bogachiel and Quinault River valleys. These prime, timbered valleys on the west slopes of the range, it was argued, offered little to the park experience and should be open to exploitation for the benefit of nearby logging communities. It was not a new idea. Twenty years earlier, *Assistant* Superintendent Overly was telling the Park Service that it would be economically desirable to log 80 per-cent of the Hoh River valley, the symbolic centerpiece of the Olympic Rainfor-est. The Park Service "would do well," he wrote, "to endorse the elimination of these areas from the park." Wirth and the superintendent at the time, Preston Macy, agreed. The public strenuously resisted, siding with the conservation-ists, and the proposal died. Logging inside the park continued nonetheless.

Through 1948 more than ten million board feet of timber had been re-moved from the park, and the local mills and logging outfits clamored for more. That year, Wirth sent Overly to Washington, D.C., where he managed real estate deals and the Olympic National Park logging program, before return-ing to Olympic as superintendent in 1951 (Macy was sent to Mount Rainier). Overly's return coincided with a campaign by industry and the Port Angeles Chamber of Commerce to have three hundred thousand acres of ancient forest removed from the park. The campaign failed miserably, yet the annual cut from the park still climbed, reaching 14.6 million board feet in 1953, a volume rep-resenting thousands of truckloads. Overly mapped the routes for new logging roads within the park, ran logging contracts through the park-managed natural history association, and sent trail crews into the backcountry to fell trees and float them down the rivers. It was pure stealth. The activity quietly intensified, but amazingly remained under the radar of most conservationists for years.

In the mid-1950s, Olympic Park Associates (OPA), which formed in 1948 to defend the park's boundaries and to "save the park from the Park Service," was finally tipped off on the magnitude of the logging by seasonal natural-ists and non-career summer rangers, including Paul Shepard and Carsten Lien. Shepard, Lien, and other seasonal staff were appalled at the increasing destruc-tion they encountered each summer season or otherwise heard about from dis-gruntled park visitors. OPA began to get a sense of the true extent of the com-mercial logging that was taking place when they caught Superintendent Overly holding Forest Service-scale timber sales inside the park's boundaries. While Shepard approached his contacts with national conservation organizations, Lien informed the Conservation Committee of The Mountaineers in Seattle.

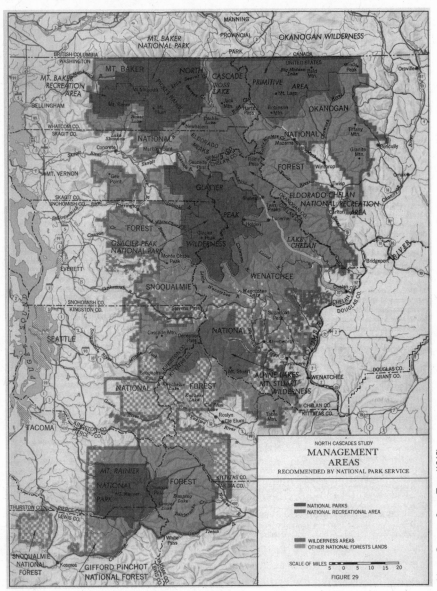

These two maps from the 1965 North Cascades Study Team Report illustrate the divergent opinions of the Departments of Agriculture and Interior on what to protect and how to get it done (or not). Note the Park Service envisioned two national parks (Mount Baker and Glacier Peak), a large national recreation area from the Skagit River almost to the Little Wenatchee

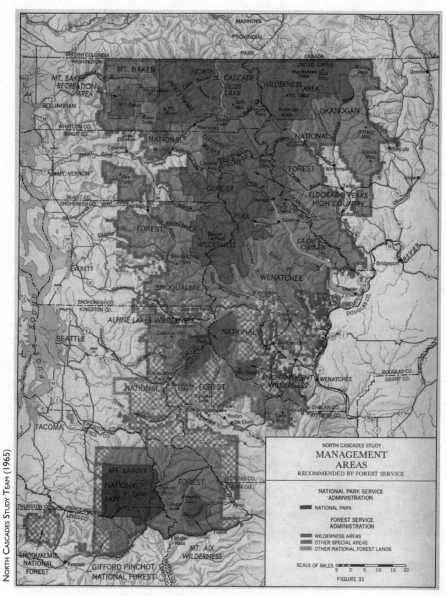

FIGURE 31

River, including a third of Lake Chelan, and a larger Alpine Lakes-Mount Stuart Wilderness. The Forest Service proposed no new park, much less wilderness, and a scenic area called Eldorado Peaks High Country. (See next page for the Study Team's joint recommendation.)

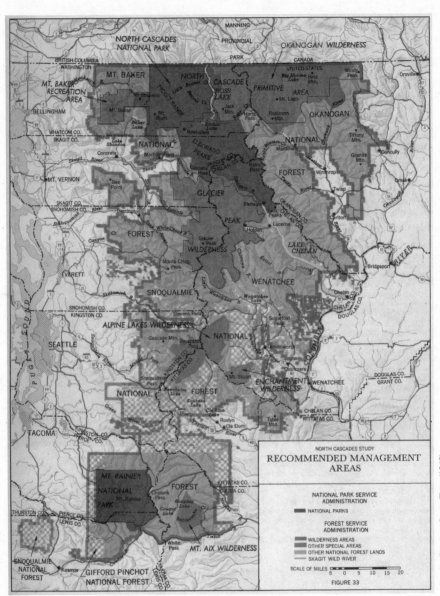

Joint recommendations of the North Cascades Study Team(1965).

An ad hoc committee representing a number of organizations was formed, and the issue exploded in the face of the National Park Service. In little more than a year, the group was able to generate enough of an outcry, both regionally and nationally, not only to put a stop to almost all logging in the park, but also to get Fred Overly shipped off to the Great Smokies. Just prior to Overly's departure, Phil Zalesky recalls a meeting at Seatac Airport arranged by The Mountaineers between conservationists and Conrad Wirth, who was now director of the National Park Service. A list of questions had been prepared and Zalesky, at the head of the table, handed it to Wirth. Wirth glanced at the list and immediately slid it back across the table saying, "Phil, this won't be necessary. We took a calculated risk and there will be no more salvage logging at Olympic National Park." The ordeal was over.

In May 1963, however, Overly was back, this time as Regional Director of the Bureau of Outdoor Recreation based in Seattle—thanks to some crucial inside help from Jackson. In a twist of irony, the Bureau owed its existence, at least in part, to the work of David Brower. The new agency was led by Director Crafts, the former assistant chief of the Forest Service. With Crafts and Overly at the helm, conservationists were not precisely optimistic about the prospects for wildland recreation or old-growth forest preservation in the Pacific Northwest. As if the logging threat wasn't enough, Crafts and Overly announced in early 1964 plans for a new highway cutting through the "Ocean Strip" of the Olympics—the largest unspoiled coastal wilderness in the contiguous U.S.

All of this was familiar background to many of the park and wilderness advocates attending Jackson's January 1966 press conference with the North Cascades Study Team. Years later, Carsten Lien would tell the story in *Olympic Battleground: The Power Politics of Timber Preservation*. "Jackson's strategy," wrote Lien, "was to tie Overly's Olympic National Park proposals so tightly to the North Cascades Park proposal that it could not move forward without the Olympic reduction." In the "carnival atmosphere" of the gathering, he said, reporters "instantly saw the reality of what was unfolding," perhaps recalling Woodward's comment in the *Seattle Times* six months earlier about Congressman Pelly's openness to "trading" Olympic for North Cascades timber. Three days after the press conference, the *Times* reported that Jackson had "refused to separate or segregate" the two proposals. The uproar that followed was shrugged off by the Senator, never an easy blusher. What was *not* supposed to seem as *quid pro quo*—a new park in the North Cascades in exchange for less park in the Olympics—appeared to many as exactly that. Irving Brant, an accomplished journalist, conservationist, and political strategist well connected to many top officials of the FDR and Truman administrations (including the presidents themselves), immediately wrote to Udall to condemn Overly's big idea. Udall responded cautiously, his own conservation instincts perhaps uncomfortably squeezed by the need for diplomacy with the Senator.

Joint hearings on the two proposals began in February and both Udall and Jackson politely allowed Overly to sit up front where he could take most of the heat. The testimony against him was substantial. Lien described the public's reaction to the Olympic proposal as "overwhelming and universal condemnation," making it "untenable for Jackson to pursue." Everything had "backfired." Even the governor, Republican Dan Evans, opposed the Olympic reduction, and at least in general terms, supported a new park in the North Cascades. Preston Macy, now retired, expressed some regret over previous pro-logging policies at Olympic National Park. In the end, Senator Jackson defended Overly and suggested that he was only doing what the Park Service had requested of him. Regardless, the Olympic Park reductions were not to be.

Subsequent protests about the fitness of Overly to hold public office anywhere within two thousand miles of the Olympics brought from his boss this defense: "Fred Overly is a career public servant of great ability. . . . He serves a public interest as he sees it and he has my strong support." Inasmuch as Overly's boss was the same Edward C. Crafts who chaired the North Cascades Study Team, questions arose about all career public servants of the Bureau of Outdoor Recreation. With Craft's boss being Udall, that raised questions which were not so easily voiced.

Keeping in mind that Forest Service enthusiasm for wilderness had been dwindling for a quarter-century, and that in the half-century of its existence, the Park Service consistently had esteemed wilderness less than highways, conservationists should not have been so surprised by the Study Team Report's recommendation that "High priority should be given to the construction of an adequate system of scenic roads." These were to include completion of the North Cross-State Highway; a road from the head of Ross Lake in British Columbia along the lake to the North Cross-State; a road from Heather Meadows tunneling under Austin Pass to Baker Lake; roads through Curry Gap, Cady Pass, and Harts Pass; and a road splitting in two the Alpine Lakes area. "A north-south Cascade scenic road was explored but was not considered feasible," said the report.

Much of the 190-page document could be dismissed as piety and boilerplate. As for substance, an Okanogan Wilderness of 495,000 acres was proposed for the residue of the North Cascades Primitive Area not disposed of otherwise. The NCCC had recommended a North Cascades Wilderness slightly larger than the primitive area, reserving its park recommendation for the area to the south. Reclassification of the primitive area substantially without change had long been accepted by all parties as a foregone conclusion. (Later, the bulk of it would be known as the Pasayten Wilderness.) Further, three small additions (39,000 acres) to the Glacier Peak Wilderness were proposed, plus a minute

(7,000-acre) enlargement of Mount Rainier National Park.

Three sections of the Washington Cascades were embroiled in major controversy when the Study Team arrived. The first was the broad swath of wildlands from Chelan to Mount Baker (discussed below). The second was at the opposite end of the study area, east of Mount Rainier National Park, where there once had been a Cougar Lakes Limited Area and where conservationists had drawn up a detailed proposal for a 125,000-acre Cougar Lakes Wilderness. Crafts went along with his old friends at the Forest Service and carried with him the entire team, whose members were frank to admit they'd barely glanced at the area. Instead of a more comprehensive Cougar Lakes Wilderness, the report proposed a 45,000-acre Mount Aix Wilderness of crags, talus, and a gorgeous array of high alpine flowers. As usual, the lowland rivers and trees were excluded.

The third controversial area was located where once had been an Alpine Lakes Limited Area in the crest region between Snoqualmie and Stevens Passes. Here, conservationists had drawn up a detailed proposal for an Alpine Lakes Wilderness of between 278,000 and 334,000 acres, depending on whether some intervening private land could be acquired between blocks of public land. That proposal was substantially endorsed by the Study Team's two Park Service representatives, Director Hartzog and Dr. Owen S. Stratton who had replaced Caulfield on the study team early in the process. Tie-breaker Crafts cast his ballot with the Forest Service representatives, Selke and Greeley, for a much-reduced Alpine Lakes Wilderness on the rocks (150,000 acres), separated by a proposed scenic logging road from a much smaller Enchantment Wilderness (30,000 acres). Again, rocks, ice, and high-meadow wildflowers were included. Most of the trees were not.

So it was that, thanks to Crafts, the Forest Service "won" two out of the three contests. In 1976 Congress overruled Crafts by uniting the two fragments into a single Alpine Lakes Wilderness. In 1984 Congress again rebuked the Study Team Chairman by passing the Washington Wilderness Act, which increased Alpine Lakes to nearly 363,000 acres and placed 166,000 acres of the Cougar Lakes country in a new William O. Douglas Wilderness.

The "tidy little man with the tidy little mind," as Chuck Hessey not-so-fondly described Crafts after their voyage together on Lake Chelan, could not throw all three games, caught as he was in the national spotlight. In the biggest game of the three, he had to be ingenious. He congratulated himself in the report for devising "a new set of recommendations that has not heretofore been proposed." It was somewhat more acrobatic than a simple exercise in tie-breaking. Crafts was looking not at two choices, but rather was surrounded by choices. The one with the longest standing and best credentials—and the one most likely to serve the interests of wilderness preservation—was the NCCC's 1963 park proposal and a companion 1960 proposal for a North Cascades Wilderness, the reclassification of the existing North Cascade Primitive Area.

The two Park Service representatives, Hartzog and Stratton, proposed a national park centered on Glacier Peak; a Mount Baker National Park north of the Skagit and west of Ross Lake and including the Picket Range, Mount Baker, and Mount Shuksan; a North Cascades (Okanogan) Wilderness east of Ross Lake; and an Eldorado-Chelan National Recreation Area north and east of Glacier Peak.

Ever-resistant to protecting more land through National Park or wilderness designations, the Forest Service pair on the Study Team proposed to "manage certain areas with special emphasis on recreation, including Eldorado Peaks High Country, the Mount Baker Recreation Area. . . ." In these recreation areas, the Forest Service's Greeley and Selke would "perform only such timber removal as public interest and the resource importance of the area clearly justifies. . . ." which was to say, multiple-use and intensive management. Unlike a Congressionally designated national park or wilderness, these recreation areas were not permanently protected and would remain vulnerable to the whims of agency policy. The Forest Service could tolerate a wilderness designation for the North Cascade Primitive Area, but little else for the largest wilderness landscape of the North Cascades. Crafts, however, was astute enough to know that some compromise would be necessary if the Study Team's work was going to enjoy any credibility with the public.

So where did the public stand? Crafts totted up 2,591 statements, oral and written, to the October 1963 hearings and found the ratio to be about four to one in favor of a park. He therefore proposed a park. His park stretched from Lake Chelan through Cascade Pass to Eldorado and Shuksan and the U.S.–Canadian border, omitting Glacier Peak and Mount Baker but including the Pickets (a useful makeweight, since the Forest Service would object only mildly, pro forma). He could not escape without giving up some genuine substance and did so, notably the head of Lake Chelan and Stehekin Valley, Bridge Creek, Granite, Panther, and Thunder Creeks—glorious, parkworthy country all, yet a relatively painless loss to the Forest Service, containing comparatively few potential logs for the mill.

Two days after the Study Team press conference, the directors of NCCC and leaders of the coalition met in extraordinary session. The attitude of the disgruntled group could be summed up as, "I don't see how either one of 'em can win." The Forest Service was unregenerate, as expected. But how could the Park Service be cheered when it advocated for "roads and overlooks such as at Buck Creek Pass" that "appear to offer excellent opportunities for scenic viewing on a grand scale"? Had the Park Service failed to note that Buck Creek Pass was *inside* the existing Glacier Peak Wilderness where roads are not allowed? The Park Service pair also lauded the "imaginative mass transit approach of European recreation managers . . . the funicular, the monorail, the tramway . . ." NCCC directors spoke to this and the laundry list of scenic roads: "The appearance in the recommendations of the Study Team at various points of demands for mass recreational facilities is alarming."

The meeting concluded that NCCC's original proposal was the best choice because it met the need to halt logging damage in the scenic heartland around Glacier Peak. The Study Team proposal did not. The group also decided that it could support the Study Team's park *only* if it were enlarged by addition of the Park Service pair's proposal for a Mount Baker National Park; *and only* if to the proposal for an enlarged Glacier Peak Wilderness was added a Cascades–Chelan National Recreation Area wrapped around the eastern, southern, and western boundaries of the Wilderness to safeguard its peripheral forests; and finally, *only* if the tramway-helicopter notions were extinguished and the Pickets and Eldorado–Chelan sectors were designated as Wilderness.

February 11–12, 1966, hearings were held in Seattle before the Senate Committee on Interior and Insular Affairs, Senator Jackson presiding. Other members of the committee were present, as well as assorted Congressmen and public officials. The published record bore the title *North Cascades–Olympic National Park*, reflecting Jackson's dogged determination to keep chewing the old Olympic bone. The 1,062 pages of published testimony could have been fewer had they omitted the Olympics, but the opportunity to settle Overly's hash once and for all by skewering him on the public record was not unwelcome. Some two hundred speakers are listed in the report and close to two thousand contributed additional comments. The report's total number of words must have approached one million.

The balance of 1966 continued in lively fashion. Secretaries Udall and Freeman personally inspected the North Cascades, attention thought to be unparalleled in the history of federal lands. A headline declared, "Udall Says North Cascades Would Make Ten Parks." Freeman expressed his opinion that one was too many. Meanwhile, conservationist effort had to be diverted to stamp out a nasty brushfire, the announced decision of Kennecott to immediately begin an open-pit mining operation at Miners Ridge (detailed in John McPhee's trail-side conversations with David Brower, *Encounters with the Archdruid*, published in 1971). In the real world of the 1960s, there was clearly no chance that the mine ever would happen, and Congressman Meeds, for one, believed the "decision" was actually an attempt to profit from the preservation push by bluffing Congress into buying the claims. But the conservationists couldn't take for granted that the real world also embraced Washington, D.C.

For much of that year, the center stage was occupied by the tactical efforts of Washington Governor Daniel J. Evans. Requested by the Treaty of the Potomac to submit a Governor's Plan for the North Cascades, he appointed a sixteen-member committee. Appointees included two editors of Eastern Washington newspapers; three loggers; two hunters; three Chamber-of-Commercers; the state's chief highwayman; the director of the state Department of Conservation, a unit whose functions were so contrary to what Pinchot had in mind that conservationists regularly attached the prefix, "Anti," to the second noun; and the Director of Washington State Parks, who a quarter of a century later, as Pacific Northwest Director of the National Park Service, would be sued by the NCCC for various management failures in Stehekin.

These thirteen appointments seemed to have stacked the deck solidly enough to content the greediest of Barbecuers. Still, three members had impeccable conservation credentials. Emily Haig, who for a decade before becoming an NCCC director had been in the frontlines with Seattle Audubon and Olympic Park Associates defending Olympic National Park. (As a young woman in San Francisco she had also met John Muir. Later in life, Emily Haig was presented with the NCCC's Irving M. Clark Award.) Also appointed to the committee were Jonathan Whetzel of the state legislature, a recent member of The Mountaineers' Conservation Division; and Dr. William R. Halliday, who had alerted David Brower and the conservation community to the danger at Glen Canyon and was now chair of the National Parks Committee of the Conservation Division of The Mountaineers, and a director of NCCC.

Governor Evans' study committee convened on March 4, deliberated for months to no result, in part because few of Evans' appointees knew the North Cascades well enough. The issue was finally handed to a three-man Subcommittee on Boundaries, composed of John Biggs, Director of the Washington State Department of Game as chair; Bernard Orell, vice-president of Weyerhaeuser; and Dr. Halliday. When the exhausted trio emerged from a sweat-filled room bearing a "no park" plan, Evans ordered them back to the room, demanding, "I must have a park."

They gave him one—the Pickets—a region of predominantly vertical terrain, virtually inaccessible to chainsaws. Mountaineering legend Fred Beckey describes this remote region well:

> the grandest scenes in the North Cascades. . . . rock walls rear abruptly from glaciers in convoluted topography. The narrow serrate ridge crests . . . sculptured by glacial ice cutting and moving along the flanks. . . . expansive alpine cirques. . . . an amazing array of steep rock peaks and pinnacles. . . . deep gorges . . . crevassed ice falls . . . brush-thick stream valleys [and] avalanche slopes.

Obviously the Pickets, spectacular as they are, were too steep and rugged to develop or exploit, and thus they became every Barbecuer's sacrifice area. As for the rest, the Evans committee plan was a mélange of wildernesses already accepted by all parties, plus areas to be given high-sounding, but meaningless, designations. The total acreage was impressive, but the actual sum of new protection was next to nil. Two of the governor's three conservationists, Whetzel and Haig, rejected the pleas of their old friend, the Governor, and dismissed the mélange. Though it was to resurface in the Congressional hearings, by then the "Dan Plan," said the critics, had gone the way of a mugwump's ideals. (The term "mugwump," used by some conservationists at the time—and with all due respect to the honorable governor—dates from 1884, when James G. Blaine was the Republican candidate for president, perceived as corrupt by liberal Republicans. Blaine's regulars excoriated these holier-than-thou types as mugwumps. Its fame comes from the famous Nast cartoon showing a critter sitting on a fence, mug on one side, wump on the other.) Governor Evans nonetheless met with NCCC President Patrick Goldsworthy urging him to support his plan, warning that there might not be any park otherwise. Goldsworthy humbly apologized but said he could not agree. In future battles, the former governor would eventually come around to taking much stronger stands on wilderness protection.

By the end of 1966, a formidable momentum had developed toward creation of the park, thanks to the good work of many, with none more dedicated to the cause than Patrick Goldsworthy. Early that year, the Sierra Club presented its first William E. Colby Award to Goldsworthy "in appreciation of the imagination, persistence, and insight with which he has brought many persons of divergent views together in a common cause to which the Club is devoted." (A friend of John Muir, Colby was a Sierra Club leader for more than six decades after joining the club in 1898.)

1967: The Park Bill Enters Congress

On January 30, 1967, President Johnson asked Congress to establish four new national parks, including the "spectacular area of unparalleled mountain masses, glaciers, meadows, and timbered valleys" in the North Cascades. The same day, the *Seattle Times* editorially endorsed a North Cascades National Park. Neither statement indicated *which* park. No word from Washington, D.C., suggested who was winning the backroom wrestling match, Tie-Breaker Crafts and the Forest Service or his nominal superior, Udall. Apparently everything came down to Senator Jackson's response to the "parade" he spoke of several years before.

Jackson indubitably had been impressed by the park and wilderness parade and had gone out front to "lead it on in." But *where* was he going with it? Patrick Goldsworthy brought an answer to a NCCC board meeting—an advance copy of S. 1321, to be "introduced in the First Session of the 90th Congress, March 20, 1967, by Mr. Jackson and Mr. Magnuson." The bill's introduction was "by request," meaning it was not sponsored by the senators but was dumped in the hopper at the request of, in this case, the White House. Lloyd Meeds could not have done other than follow his party leader; concurrently he introduced in the House the identical H.B. 8970. The NCCC directors read the Jackson bill in stunned silence. It described a park half the size of the Council's 1963 proposal. The boundaries were bizarre.

Goldsworthy met with Jackson, who explained, "If you folks veto this bill, it is dead, right now. In that case I will work with you to get the bill you want. It will take a long time." By way of a reality check, Jackson added, "In view of the drift of national politics, we might be at it for years and fail. On the other hand, if you support *this* bill, I believe I can get it for you—and soon."

The drift in national politics was real: the Cold War, escalating U.S. involvement in Vietnam, a growing anti-war movement; surging racial tension, conflict in the Middle East, repression and violence in Indonesia, and a slowing economy, amid the ongoing quest to send a man to the moon, marred by the fatal fire on the Apollo launchpad in late January. There was no choice but to swallow Jackson's bitter pill and put on a happy face.

Far from perfect, the bill offered the best opportunity yet to get something moving for the North Cascades. Already a decade had passed since the NCCC was formed to guide the campaign; it had been twenty years since the last large national park, the Everglades, was created; twenty-seven years since the Ice Peaks National Park proposal was quietly filed away; fifty years since the first big push to establish a park at Mount Baker; over sixty years since the Mazamas adopted a national park resolution at Chelan; and seventy-five years since the first park was proposed for the North Cascades, also at Chelan.

The Jackson bill called for a two-unit, 570,000-acre North Cascades National Park; a 100,000-acre Ross Lake National Recreation Area (NRA) dividing those two units; a nearly 500,000-acre Pasayten Wilderness, reclassified from the east section of the North Cascades Primitive Area; and the addition of 10,000 acres to the existing Glacier Peak Wilderness.

The NCCC recognized that "The bill has certain defects or omissions which can be remedied by amendment; and as *amended*, it deserves and must have conservationist support or it cannot pass. Already, powerful forces, within and without the State of Washington, are mobilizing to defeat the bill." Clearly, the bill needed to be "tightened up to protect the wilderness inside the Park boundaries from further encroachment by roads or tramways." Eight necessary amendments were identified: (1) Horseshoe Basin must be added to the Pasayten Wilderness; (2) the Granite Creek drainage must be added to the Park; (3) all presently roadless areas in the Park should be immediately designated as National Wilderness; (4) the Ross Lake NRA was too big (that is, the enclosing wildland was too small), and the boundaries should be drawn down closer to the reservoir to prevent development of a Ross Lake Highway; (5) the Mount

Baker region should be added to the Park; (6) the Cascade River valley must be added to the Park; (7) the Glacier Peak open-pit copper mine threat must be ended; and (8) more acreage should be added to the Glacier Peak Wilderness.

Jackson's S.1321 was not the only bill in town. On August 7th, Congressman Pelly introduced H.R. 12139, embodying the 1963 NCCC proposal, not expecting it to go head-to-head against the Jackson bill, but to complete the historical record and lay groundwork for a future enlargement of whatever park might materialize. Congresswoman Catherine Mays, a Republican, introduced on behalf of Governor Evans H.R. 16252, an official proposal by the state of Washington, drawn up by John Biggs.

And so the hearings began.

April 24–25, 1967. Room 3110 in the New Senate Office Building, Washington, D.C., Senator Jackson presiding. Udall led off, followed by Greeley of the Forest Service, and John Biggs presenting a statement on behalf of Governor Evans. Next up were John M. Nelson, superintendent of Seattle City Light, and Patrick Goldsworthy of NCCC. Additional testimony was given on all sides, and it was heartening to note how many members of the conservationist coalition managed to be there on that far side of the continent.

Three hearings were held on the mountains' end of the continent: Seattle, May 25; Mount Vernon, May 27; and Wenatchee, May 29. The published record of all the hearings measured one and a half inches thick at the spine, slightly more than the Study Team Report hearings, and with a few more pages (1,103 pages total). The result was Amended S. 1321, which on October 25 was reported by the Interior Committee to the floor of the Senate. On November 2, the bill easily passed.

Four amendments had been made. Two strengthened the bill, one by enlarging the Pasayten Wilderness eastward twenty-two thousand acres to take in Horseshoe Basin. Of the conservationists' requested amendments, this was the only one accepted, and only in part. The amended bill also extended Ross Lake NRA three miles (fifteen hundred acres) downstream to take in Seattle City Light's proposed, but later shelved, Copper Creek dam and reservoir.

Two amendments drastically weakened the bill. Four miles of Thunder Creek (3,500 acres) were transferred from the park to the Ross Lake NRA so that Seattle City Light could, if and when it wished, drown this pristine valley. Also, fifteen miles (62,000 acres) of the lower Stehekin Valley and upper Lake Chelan were removed from the Park and put into a new unit, the Lake Chelan NRA, where hunting would be permitted. This was not the Chelan National Mountain Recreation Area proposed by the NCCC. The concept was adopted, but in perverted form, excluding the Stehekin Valley from the park and a large area down Lake Chelan from any protection at all. The general impression at the time was that John Biggs and Scoop Jackson had cut a deal. Queried years later, Biggs denied it. No documentation has been found and the details remain a mystery. The August–September edition of *The Wild Cascades* observed:

> This [deal] is stated as a gesture to fishermen and hunters. Was it also not done to pacify a handful of Stehekin Valley residents? Thus possibly the Stehekinites would not emulate their Quinault Valley counterparts who constantly complain about having lost their individual identities because they are surrounded by Olympic National Park.

It was believed that Olympic National Park inholders urged Stehekin residents to hang tough in opposition to a park—a foreshadowing of the national alliance of inholders that, some years later, would consistently oppose the national interest.

The revised acreage totals in the Senate bill were as follows: North Cascades National Park, 504,500; Ross Lake NRA, 105,000; Lake Chelan NRA, 62,000; Glacier Peak Wilderness, 10,000 added to the existing 458,500; and a 520,000-acre Pasayten Wilderness.

So much for the U.S. Senate. It was now time for the U.S. House of Representatives, where the king of the congressional mountain was Wayne N. Aspinall. The committee chairman had held onto the wilderness bill for most of a decade and was on record opposing any new parks, and, for that matter, old parks, anywhere. The thickness of the published record of the three hearings on H.B. 8970 and related bills by the subcommittee on National Parks and Recreation of the Committee on Interior and Insular Affairs of the House of Representatives, held in Seattle, April 19–20, 1968; Wenatchee, July 13; and Washington, D.C., July 25–26, measures a bit under one and a half inches (985 pages), somewhat less than the Senate record. Only a selection of statements was published, a fraction of the avalanche Aspinall helped trigger.

Aspinall apparently censored the Congressional reports, but he could not suppress the press. He arrived in Seattle fuming that the issue had become a controversy "blown out of all proportion." He excoriated newsfolk to their faces and Senator Jackson in absentia. He was furious that some seven hundred to eight hundred requests to testify had been received; he "never had seen anything like it before." Muscling through the crowd that jammed the lobby of the Benjamin Franklin Hotel, he complained, "I don't know who these people are." Despite the number of requests to testify, his staff had provided a hearing room that was far too small, and though committee member Mo Udall hunted up a second room to let the hearing be held in two sections simultaneously, it still was necessary to draw lots for the right to speak.

Conservationists were as alarmed as Aspinall by the number of requests to testify. "Rev Riley" Johnson, promoted to a pulpit in Yakima, and the president of the timber industry's front group, Outdoors Unlimited, had vowed that this was *his* hearing where he would bury the birdwatchers, it was said. As it happened, God called him to other vineyards that day. However, his hired hand, attorney Bill Lenihan, promised to flood the hearing with skiers supporting the Forest Service, which had promised a string of resorts from one edge of the Cascades to the other. A quarter-century later, geographical fact and economic reality had extinguished all these fancies but one, and that on lands never proposed for the park; in 1993 this last scheme, on Sandy Butte in the Methow Valley, guttered out. Nevertheless, the Lenihan threat was directly responsible for the intimidating turnout. He delivered a legion of opponents to bulk out the thin forces of the multiple-users. But Patrick Goldsworthy and his lieutenants responded with an extraordinary showing that overwhelmed him; the final score had Goldsworthy beating Lenihan by more than three to one. The Aspinall strategy of reserving insufficient space also backfired. Many folks couldn't speak, couldn't even squeeze into the hearing rooms and had to stand in the halls, shoulder to shoulder and belly to belly. The density of sweating humanity in itself awed the Congressmen.

Commissioners of four counties of the North Cascades—Okanogan, Whatcom, Chelan, and Skagit—opposed the park, as did the councils of thirteen cities and the port commissioners of Bellingham and Skagit County. Lloyd Meeds, who represented most of these jurisdictions in Congress, asked the president of Multiple Use for the North Cascades if he by any chance had a financial interest in a mine in the area; the president conceded he did; Meeds, smiling, excused him from further questioning.

A momentous exchange took place between Congressman Mo Udall and Governor Evans. The governor, presenting his plan, was questioned at length. Mr. Udall: "This last is a tough question I would ask you. . . . When the House calls the roll I have to vote 'Yes' or 'No.' If it comes down to a question of the Senate-passed bill, a national park of that size, or no national park at all, how do you advise me to vote?

Mr. Evans: "If I were in your place and had a vote, I would vote 'Yes.'"

Mr. Udall: "I thank you, Governor."

Mo Udall thereby saved Dan Evans from himself, rescued his reputation as a good ol' Camp Parsons Boy Scout and Bull Mooser friend of the land, because at day's end when park loyalists emerged from the bad air of sardine-packed rooms to fresh air of the streets, they were unforgettably gladdened to see newspaper headlines reading "EVANS FOR PARK." Evans' "mugwumping" was forgiven. History would remember that splendid headline.

The Washington Post called the Seattle hearing on the national park "an event of national significance . . . focused on the finest mountain wilderness in the United States. . . . In our view, the national interest in saving this unspoiled alpine region in the far Northwest is enormous."

1968: THE FINISH LINE

Aspinall had arrived in Seattle as a lion roaring "Never!" He left as a lamb bleating, "I'm going to do my darndest to get a bill out of our committee before it adjourns in August." However, once beyond reach of a lynch mob he began issuing *pronunciamentos*. These were aimed not at the quite ruly Seattle mob, but at Jackson. The two high lords of the American earth, secure in their citadels, one commanding the Senate, the other the House, exchanged thinly veiled threats. Aspinall held hostage two of Jackson's darlings, national parks in the North Cascades and the Redwoods. Jackson bound and gagged Aspinall's sweetie, the Central Arizona Project, intended to fruit the cactus plains of the Southwest—with water from Washington. The two marcher earls rumbled warnings like daggers held to soft, white throats.

It was all bluff, of course, pure show-biz staged by two of the hammiest actors of the Congressional troupe. However, trembling conservationists didn't know what these two statesmen might run amok, even go berserk, and bathe Washington D.C. in blood for the sheer Elizabethan drama of it. Rumor followed rumor during the spring and summer of 1968. The bill was moving. The bill was dead. Aspinall bit his thumb at Jackson. Jackson slapped the pommel of his rapier.

Then Aspinall got his bill released by Jackson and thereupon released Jackson's bills. Catherine May, the Republican Congresswoman from Yakima who had endorsed the governor's proposal, acquiesced and agreed to support the Jackson approach. On September 16, 1968, the House voted "Yea." On September 19 the Senate passed the House's amended bill and sent it along to the White House.

In *The Mountaineer*, Grant McConnell summarized the period leading to establishment of the Park:

First perception: The Park was inevitable. Nobody who has ever seen the area, or even who has seen just a few pictures of it could believe otherwise. . . .

Second perception: The Park was an impossibility. This was Forest Service domain, and that Service never surrenders. It has the most massive political system in the United States, and the most determined leadership. It has the loggers, the grazers, the miners, the local officialdoms, the "sportsmen"—men who count among the petty and the big elites of America—all lined up to echo the official line. In July and September 1968, there were the Grangers, the cattlemen, the miners, the county commissioners of all the counties involved, the mayors of Chelan, Brewster, Pateros and all the other places known only to locals, and their congressmen, behind the Forest Service and against the Park. And Boise–Cascade, Georgia Pacific, the big mill owners, the corporations and the little mills too. And always, paid by public money, the propagandists of the fully alerted, fully politicized Forest Service constantly at work. You can't win; we're too strong, too big. . . .

Which? Either or neither, who knew? The Park won—perhaps because there was something categorical in its necessity; not to have won would have been defeat in an absolute sense; not to have won would have been the failure of a moral order. But it was all so tenuous, so much a matter of chance, hanging so on those few of the things that were tried that worked. Who would be on hand? Who would come through with those last few dollars, that last bit of energy? And at the very last stage it was in the hands of the gods and Wayne Aspinall. Would he settle for anything less than the Columbia River water dumped into the Colorado, something that Scoop Jackson could never give? And would there be time before the Ninetieth Congress adjourned? It was a cliffhanger right down to the last. But . . .

October 2, 1968. The East Room, the White House. Band playing as you walk in from the Pennsylvania Avenue portico. Military aides in dress uniforms complete down to the white gloves. Buzzing and smiles of Congressmen and Senators. "Ladies and Gentlemen, the President of the United States." A stooped, tired man with an almost apologetic smile. This was one of the few good things that had happened. A glance upward from the prepared speech and a nod to the Congressmen, "Why don't you fellows tell folks about *this*, and not some of those other things they are talking about?" (Laughter.)

And then President Johnson sat down and signed the bill.

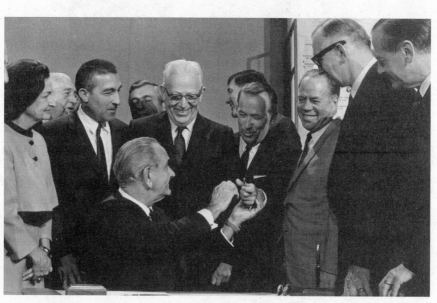

President Johnson presents a pen to Senator Jackson during the signing of the North Cascades Act of 1968. Looking on are Lady Bird Johnson (left) next to Interior Secretary Stewart Udall.

THE WILD CASCADES

August - September 1968

NORTH CASCADES CONSERVATION COUNCIL

NCCC's Patrick Goldsworthy greets President Lyndon Johnson at the signing the North Cascades Act of 1968.

4

Why It's Never Over Until It's Over

Start out in the morning on an all-day fishing trip. Fish all day and catch one about six inches long. Then about 6 p.m. get lost and wander about for an hour, in the same circle three times, and finally wet and tired find the trail and still be five miles from camp.

—William O. Douglas
As a North Yakima High School student, 1916,
Quoted in *The Wild Cascades*, January 1969

THE GOLDEN TRIANGLE, AT LAST

ON THE EVENING OF OCTOBER 26, 1968, the NCCC and the organizations it had served in the Park campaign assembled for a semi-uproarious, semi-solemn celebration. The two hundred fifty celebrants, from many units of the Federation of Western Outdoor Clubs, filled to capacity the banquet hall of Seattle's University Towers. The master of ceremonies, Irving Clark, Jr., represented in his own words and those of his late father some four decades of family devotion to the natural beauty of Northwest America. Three national park superintendents, Ben Gale of Olympic, John Townsley of Rainier, and newly appointed Roger J. Contor of North Cascades signified, by their presence, that Washington's "Golden Triangle" of parks was now a reality. David Brower was there, his efforts crucial to the two new parks of 1968, the North Cascades and Redwoods (both bills were signed by Johnson on the same day). Brower was the living connection to the last large wilderness park in the American West to be established by Congress, twenty-eight years before—Kings Canyon in 1940 (Canyonlands was made a park in 1964, but was far smaller than it should have been). Among the throng, Congressman Lloyd Meeds stood for the good that can be done by a tribune of the people. The remaining celebrants stood, perhaps, for the undying principles of John Muir. The happy crowd outnumbered the total membership of the NCCC in the darker days of the early 1960s. Few, if any, veterans of that slough of despond had expected to live to see the park. Their persistence was sustained less by hope than by the moral obligation to hold the torch aloft so that the next generation, or the next, might carry it to victory—and the stubborn determination not to let the naysayers stand in the way.

The glow of euphoria, the faces set in blissful smiles, the chuckles and chortles, head-noddings and back-clappings were inspired by a number of things: there would be no road down Bridge Creek to the Stehekin! There would be no more motorcycles at Park Creek Pass! The chainsaws *never* would be heard in the Little Beaver or the headwaters of the Chilliwack! And if, next summer, a grizzly went over Cascade Pass to see what he could see, he would not, as was reported to have happened to the one that tried it the previous summer, get shot dead and "et up."

Amid the din of the gala, many a banqueteer privately marveled, "How on earth did we manage it?" To whatever extent they could fully comprehend what they had done, they knew it was remarkable. The park of 1968 did not have its firm beginning in the 1890s or even the 1930s. Whether the campaign be dated from Dave Simons' brief of 1958, the birth of the NCCC in 1957, or the scattered murmurings of the mid-1950s, it was lightning-swift. In modern times, no park of significant size had had so brief a gestation. Accompanying the "How?" was the "Who?," asked not as a means to populate a pantheon of egos, but to perhaps provide lessons helpful in future efforts.

The White House was, of course, the beginning and the end. Few presidents have appointed anyone as politically open-minded as Stewart Udall to be Secretary of the Interior. Only two presidents since Lyndon Johnson have signed major park legislation or national monument proclamations—Jimmy Carter and Bill Clinton—both of whom left major legacies in wildland conservation, legacies befitting a Roosevelt. Johnson could well have lodged himself in the company of both Roosevelts, had he bestowed the "Christmas present to the nation" proposed by Udall, by exploiting presidential powers under the Antiquities Act to add more than 7.5 million acres to the National Park System without having to persuade Congress. By the end of Johnson's term in January 1969, U.S. presidents had proclaimed a total of eighty-seven national monuments, while Congress legislated another twenty-five of its own, plus several more that were authorized but never implemented. Johnson's prior endorsements of the Wilderness Act and Canyonlands National Park in 1964, and the signing of the Wild and Scenic Rivers Act in 1968—on the same day that new parks were created in the North Cascades and the Redwoods—offered hope that he might do more to soften his war-torn legacy. But Johnson was reportedly annoyed at Udall for naming a stadium after Robert Kennedy. Furthermore, Congressman Aspinall had promised he would introduce legislation (which he did not) for Udall's more ambitious proposals in the next session of Congress. Minutes before the Nixons arrived for the inauguration, Johnson signed Antiquities designations for a meager 384,500 acres, none of which was on the wish list hastily submitted to Udall by Patrick Goldsworthy for the North Cascades and by David Brower and Edgar Wayburn for other deserving areas. Johnson would agree only to establish Marble Canyon National Monument (26,000 acres), and expand the Arches and Capitol Reef monuments in southern Utah, as well as Katmai in Alaska. Johnson took a pass on creating Udall's 4.1 million-acre Gates of the Arctic National Monument, a 2.2 million-acre Mount McKinley National Monument, and a 911,700-acre Sonoran Desert National Monument in Arizona. Ultimately, the two Alaskan monuments would be established by President Carter a decade later, and a half-million acre Sonoran Desert National Monument would be signed into being by President Clinton a few days before his departure in January 2001. Inexplicably, every Republican president since Herbert Hoover has largely ignored the calls for new monuments under the Antiquities Act. Minor exceptions include two small historic sites established by Eisenhower and three others by George Bush (the elder). The Republicans' shift away from park and wilderness protection and environmental stewardship generally was cemented during the Reagan administration and worsened considerably under Bush II who presently holds the worst record in the entire history of the National Park system.

During the Johnson years, a strong Democratic Congress could rightly take credit for most of the environmental good that was done over that period. The key figures in Congress were named earlier in these pages. However, an additional comment must be made about Senator Jackson and his role in passing the Wilderness Act, the National Wild and Scenic Rivers Act, the Scenic Trails Act, and the National Environmental Policy Act. Historians will be a while assessing his true contributions to this impressive list of legislation. As Interior Committee chairman, he was in a position to take credit properly belonging to the originators of legislation. Furthermore, before turning his files over to the public he took pains to have them thoroughly purged. Carsten Lien was able to document Jackson's attempts to delete portions of Olympic National Park by searching other files that contain letters from Jackson and copies of letters he received. A similar effort in the North Cascades appears likely but has not been adequately researched. Undoubtedly, he sometimes treated these affairs as photo opportunities, as most politicians seem prone to do. Had he been motivated by a deeper understanding and love of the wild, surely he would not

Governor Dan Evans (ca. 1960s)

UNIVERSITY OF WASHINGTON LIBRARIES, SPECIAL COLLECTIONS, POR0032

have let the Forest Service dictate the park boundaries, nor would he have kept pumping gas in the tank of the North Cross-State Highway Association. Yet let it be said that nobody who was there can conjure up a scenario for such a speedy success in the North Cascades that did not have, as chair of the United States Senate Committee on Interior Affairs, one highly influential senator from Washington State. In fact, there probably would not be a North Cascades National Park had it not been for Jackson. In 1969 the Sierra Club recognized the Senator by presenting him with its John Muir award.

The public career of Dan Evans, legislator, governor, and senator, might also have to wait some years before receiving a fully objective and entirely dispassionate evaluation. There can be no disagreement that he was among the most powerful public figures in the state of Washington in the latter half of the twentieth century and among his peers and contemporaries perhaps the best liked. In the matter of wildland preservation, no governor—or senator—before or after comes to mind who took as much interest or more action. If some of that passion derived from his being a Camp Parsons Eagle Scout, so did much else of his spirit and integrity. He never will be forgotten for his timely "Yes" in the newspaper headlines of 1968; or his 1976 flight to the White House to rescue from veto the Alpine Lakes Wilderness; or his elder-statesman role in sheparding the Washington Wilderness Bill of 1984. Evans was also directly responsible for adding the northern strip of the Olympic beach wilderness to Olympic National Park. To be sure, a certain ambiguity caused him to even-handedly add weights to both sides of the conservation scale (some of the good governor–senator's not-so-positive contributions to wilderness will be described later). His role in the North Cascades has already been explained as something just short of glorious—yet there was that resounding "Yes."

The roster of indispensable citizens was headed by the one-and-only David R. Brower, in 1968 serving his sixteenth year at the helm of the Sierra Club, a period in which the club's membership increased from two thousand to well over seventy thousand. Wilderness protection in the U.S. also increased dramatically, with Brower having a hand in much of it. However, it must not be forgotten that other leaders of the Sierra Club were indefatigable and influential as well, prominently Edgar Wayburn, who was instrumental in the Redwoods and Alaska victories and who, in 1999, joined Mardy Murie as a recipient of the Presidential Medal of Freedom (at age 92).

But can any group of citizens and their leaders take precedence over the work of The Mountaineers? If the campaign for a park may be described as having two birthplaces, Stehekin and Glacier Peak, the latter half had its home in the conservation committee of The Mountaineers. There, too, was hatched the conspiracy which, in the "Portland Surprise," brought creation of the NCCC, and under the aegis of one organization or the other (or both), those conspirators were principal leaders. The membership of The Mountaineers made their loud voice heard as individuals, speaking at hearings, and writing letters.

Shortly after the signing ceremony in Washington, D.C., Senator Jackson sent a nice gift to Patrick Goldsworthy—a pen used by the President to sign the North Cascades Act. Phil Zalesky has said of Patrick Goldsworthy, his successor as NCCC president:

> Many people had involvement in the creation of North Cascades National Park, some major and some minor, but among those one individual deserves special recognition. Patrick Goldsworthy, backed by his wife Jane, untiringly provided the vitality keeping the endeavor organized, conhesive, and providing a driving force to it all. Mapping. Writing. Conferences with politicians. Pushing the Pelly petition. Lining up people to testify. Working on the draft of the bill. Dashing back and forth to the printer. On and on and on. All of this was done to the detriment of his professional career as a biochemist. I am extremely grateful that we had the right person in the right spot at the right time. Without him I do not believe the park would be there today.

The political scientist, Grant McConnell, presumed to know about such things, asked:

> Were there ever so many public hearings on much of anything else in the history of the nation's land policies? In 1963 the Study Team hearings in Wenatchee, Mount Vernon, and Seattle. In 1966 the Seattle hearings on the Study Team Report. In 1967 the Senate Interior Committee hearings in Washington, D.C., Seattle, Mount Vernon, and Wenatchee. In 1968 the House Interior Committee hearings in Washington, D.C., Wenatchee—and the climactic one in Seattle said

to have brought out more people than any other Congressional hearing ever. At each of these, Pat had his ducks in a row, efficiently shepherding witness after witness to the stand. He, himself, testifying from an armful of data, was persuasive and believable beyond all others.

Patrick Goldsworthy's leadership style was so patient it often seemed like followship. At board meetings he withheld the gavel to permit full expression of every opinion, to every opinion of those opinions, and when exhaustion had cooled the fires of debate would nudge disputants to a mutually agreeable accommodation—not a grudging compromise between positions, but a happy synthesis of positions. Only twice did his dogged pursuit of a consensus fail, and in both cases, just barely. The up-down park vote in 1958 lost one director, through resignation—the honorable course, maybe, for an organization whose very existence depended on undivided unity of the leadership. On the second occasion, during the park hearings, two directors (of the thirty) testified in outright opposition to the council. For this they could be excused, but by also identifying themselves as directors, the majority felt pressed to protect the organization's credibility. The two stood for reelection and were defeated.

The Northwest Conservation Representative, a post created by Karl Onthank and David Brower (and originally suggested by William O. Douglas), proved indispensable. Mike McCloskey was succeeded by Rod Pegues, and the third in the line of succession, Brock Evans, who virtually resided in the cloakrooms and offices of Congress that final year.

The citizenry: Polly Dyer, in the thick of things from the early 1950s, somehow managed to be everywhere, almost at once, from the Federation of Western Outdoor Clubs to the North Cascades. She provided in her own person the glue that welded California to Puget Sound, Puget Sound to Stehekin. Grant McConnell was the last of the genuine Old Stehekinites. Through his academic work on a general theory of interest-group roles, he was the strategist who structured the philosophical apparatus of the campaign. The "youth group," the future, included a Kenmore high-school student, David Fluharty, who made his first appearance at a Congressional hearing, then twenty years later became president of the NCCC and a principal analyst of Park Service policies and proposals. The Mannings, their long and unfettered support as the living, breathing machine behind *The Wild Cascades* and anything else worth quietly printing or uttering out loud, were vigorous participants throughout the campaign. Dozens of leaders are named herein and scores of others are left out because to be all-inclusive would fill a telephone book. We should at least recall the hundreds of good troopers who on signal leapt to typewriters to be-letter the government and the press; the scores who jumped on bicycles and pedaled to hearings; and all the others who cared.

On the evening of February 10, 1966, a woman in San Francisco telephoned the editor of *The Wild Cascades*. She and her husband had received the alert about the need for letters or testimony at the next day's Senate Interior Committee hearings on the *North Cascades Study Team Report*. They would write letters, of course, but in-person testimony would obviously be better. She asked if this hearing was truly crucial. The editor could only tell her that Senator Jackson had promised that if we gathered up a big enough parade, he'd lead it on in.

"He doesn't want to hear testimony tomorrow," said the editor. "He wants to see what sort of a parade we've got up."

"Then it's really important?" asked the stranger.

"We think this is maybe where we get a chance to keep the parade going. Or where we don't."

"All right," she said, abruptly resolute. "We've been saving up for a new dining room set, but we talked it over last night and decided we can do without *that*. But we can't do without the North Cascades."

Another recollection:

The hearing was droning on next morning, Senator Jackson growing grumpier by the minute. A commotion in the rear of the room. Jackson looks up, startled. Goldsworthy darts to the commotion, returns to the front of the room for whispered consultations, and the commotion is ushered to the microphone. She is in such a fluster that Jackson wakes all the way up and, for one of the few times ever recorded in public, smiles. He verges on laughter as she explains last night's decision about giving up the dining room furniture for an airplane ticket, the mad scramble to get husband off to work and kids off to school and herself to the airport, and the discovery on landing in Seattle that she had left her wallet home and had barely enough silver in her purse for the bus downtown, and she had no idea how she was going to get home or even to the airport, but THIS TRIP WAS REALLY NECESSARY! Jackson was charmed. He had been enduring an impressive, well-drilled parade. Here was helter-skelter, impassioned, from-the-heart Citizenry. Put her up there with Brower and Goldsworthy.

Postscript: Polly Dyer collected her after the hearing, fed her, provided a bed, and got her to the airport on time for the flight home.

What To Do For an Encore?

The national park idea has flamed brightly on many scenes for the past thirteen decades. The heroic creations, the beacon years that lighted a continuing way, are fewer. Olympic in 1938, Kings Canyon in 1940 were super-parks on a scale that were unsettling to the Mather–Albright jewel-tenders, yet inspired the Roosevelt–Ickes visionaries.

What followed? A few small beauties and important sites of interest, though not much else: Virgin Islands, in the 1950s, an adjunct of a Rockefeller resort complex. Canyonlands, at 257,640 acres, only half of what Stewart Udall had hoped for. Signed into law just days after the Wilderness Act, it was regarded by some as 1964's insult to the 1930s proposal for an Escalante super-park of 4.5 million acres. Although eighty thousand acres were added in 1971, the main mistake wasn't substantially remedied until September 1996 when President Clinton proclaimed 1.9 million acres of Bureau of Land Management (BLM) lands in southern Utah as the Grand Staircase–Escalante National Monument.

After 1940 came twenty-eight years—a full generation—lacking a brilliant new beacon of wilderness for the National Park Service in the American West, the only exception being a stripped-down Canyonlands. Down south, Texas received its first national park at Big Bend in 1944 (now 801,000 acres), and in the East, a new 460,000-acre Everglades National Park was established in 1947, expanded to 1.2 million acres in 1950 (now 1.5 million acres). The grand Arctic refuge of 1960 was administered by the Fish and Wildlife Service. Although its original champions, Collins and Sumner, had belonged to the Park Service, they were concerned enough about the agency's propensity to spoil wildlands with damaging roads and visitor comforts that they worked strategically to keep the refuge out of the National Park System.

In the gathering post-war darkness, certain pundits of academia and the Forest Service capered on the grave of the park movement from the late 1940s, through the 1950s, and into the 1960s. As sure as similar voices in American politics today would like to sell off the national parks, national forests, and other public lands, creating new parks in those years was never a simple exercise. In 1940 all state and federal parklands combined added up to 23.6 million acres, dwarfing the original 4.5 million acres that were placed under the guardianship of the National Park Service at its inception in 1916. By 1961 the sum was only 28 million. Yellowstone, Yosemite, and Rainier, of course, were gifts of the nineteenth century. In the early decades of the twentieth, the nation's emerging park system was on a roll, relatively speaking. Crater Lake was signed into law by Teddy Roosevelt. Glacier National Park emerged under Taft. Wilson authorized Rocky Mountain, Lassen, Hawaii (though it started small), McKinley, Grand Canyon (at first a large national monument set aside by Teddy Roosevelt), and Zion. The Coolidge years brought us Bryce Canyon, and Hoover signed the bill creating Great Smokey and Carlsbad Caverns National Parks in 1930. During FDR's watch, we gained Shenandoah, Olympic (also an early Teddy Roosevelt national monument), Kings Canyon, and Big Bend. We should also note seven other major national monuments that were proclaimed between 1918 and 1943, most of which would be incorporated into national parks decades later: Katmai and Glacier Bay in Alaska, Death Valley and Joshua Tree in California, Organ Pipe in Arizona, White Sands in New Mexico, and Jackson Hole (Grand Teton) in Wyoming.

The national parks parade nearly ended under Truman (Everglades), then fizzled altogether under Eisenhower. Then came 1968. Although the Redwoods could be celebrated, it too was a mere mini-park, almost too late, and costly because the Save-the-Redwoods League wanted something other than what was actually delivered, the Sierra Club wanted something more, and the private owners of the last great unprotected redwoods forest much preferred stumps. Senator Jackson and Governor Evans, acting far too cautiously, might also may have come up short for America in the North Cascades, had it not been for the grand parade. The adrenalin pump of mid-1960s set the old, tired, and withered national park idea a-blooming once again, seeding and fertilizing park proposals from coast to coast. To be sure, the Alaska Lands Act would be sabotaged by a dozen years of Barbecuer-friendly administrations, until 1980— the first beacon year after 1968. It can be argued that 1968 made 1980 possible. Had the gains of 1968 not been realized, what might have become of those 80 million acres of new parks and wilderness areas in Alaska? As it was, that battle went down to the wire, the bill signed by Carter during his final few weeks in office. In appreciation, Carter was burned in effigy in Fairbanks.

It may also be that 1968 brought the soul of the National Park Service back from the brink of a yawning pit. Distant viewers from around the nation (and

NATIONAL PARKS OF THE U.S. (LARGE AND SMALL), 1872–1968:

1872	Yellowstone (WY, MT, ID)	1921	Hot Springs (AR)
1890	Sequoia (CA)	1928	Bryce Canyon (UT)
1890	Yosemite (CA)	1929	Grand Teton (WY)
1899	Mount Rainier (WA)	1930	Carlsbad (NM)
1902	Crater Lake (OR)	1930	Great Smoky (NC, TN)
1903	Wind Cave (SD)	1935	Shenandoah (VA)
1906	Mesa Verde (CO)	1936	Mammoth Cave (KY)
1906	Platte (OK)	1938	Olympic (WA)
1910	Glacier (MT)	1940	Isle Royale (MI)
1915	Rocky Mountain (CO)	1940	Kings Canyon (CA)
1916	Lassen (CA)	1944	Big Bend (TX)
1916	Hawaii (HI)	1947	Everglades (FL)
1917	Mount McKinley (AK)	1956	Virgin Islands (VI)
1919	Acadia (ME)	1964	Canyonlands (UT)
1919	Grand Canyon (AZ)	1968	North Cascades (WA)
1919	Zion (UT)	1968	Redwoods (CA)

Seattle) saw lines on a map, read acreages in print, and gaped at the magnifi-
cence preserved in the North Cascades: nearly 1.7 million acres of two national
wilderness areas, two national recreation areas, and a national park. Distinctly
superb! The conservationists, on the other hand, saw large valleys of ancient
forests still unprotected, free-flowing streams unprotected, meadowlands unprotected, wildlife unprotected. The achievement was measured against the
opportunity and given not so much as a gentleman's passing grade. But it was
a first step that would lead to other victories.

The single most important goal had been to save the low-country ancient
forests and wild rivers that are indispensable to the larger ecosystem, and that
provide respectful entryways to the high-country meadows, glaciers, and rocks.
Prior to 1968, some of these valleys had enjoyed temporary stays of execution
through the *de facto* Pelly moratorium. The Forest Service was frank to announce
that it would respond to passage of the 1968 Act by reactivating cutting circles in
the Cascade, Suiattle, White Chuck, Sauk, White, Chiwawa, Entiat, and Methow
Rivers. In the end, the heirs of Pinchot and Greeley, and not of Marshall, would
triumph. They would grant to the nation and the future no better than a starfish
wilderness, or as Dave Simons would call it, "wilderness on the rocks."

There was in 1968 a cross-mountain highway under construction which
was sure to become a primary tourist access, yet the park legislation omitted
the entire east section of the route, including Early Winters Creek, Washington
Pass, Rainy Pass, and Granite Creek, as well as the scenic climax at Liberty Bell
and Silver Star Mountains. It also excluded the Cascade Crest trail corridor
from Rainy Pass north to Harts Pass.

All of Mount Baker, the Cascades' whitest volcano up high and greenest
volcano down low, and part of Mount Shuksan, often regarded as the most
beautiful mountain in America, and most of their enclosing Nooksack River
and Baker River valleys were left to multiple-use. Lake Chelan and its tributary
valleys and rimming highlands were almost totally omitted. Lake Chelan, of
course, is where it all began. Nor was the Glacier Peak Wilderness made safe in
1968 from Kennecott Copper, nor the Big Beaver and Thunder Creek valleys
safe from Seattle City Light. Clearly there was still much work left to do.

The opening round of the next phase was fired not from Seattle, or California, or anywhere in the West. On February 25, 1969, conservative Congressman John Saylor of Pennsylvania, who for half a dozen years had been in close
communication with Patrick Goldsworthy, introduced in Congress H.R. 7616,
a bill to add Mount Baker and Granite Creek to the park. He had sought unsuccessfully to make the additions through amendments to the 1968 Act. Now
he struck off alone, laying another plank in the legislative record, a platform for
the resumption of the cause, whenever it might occur, which he unfortunately
did not live to see. Congressman Saylor passed away in 1973, remembered as

one of those now hard-to-find T.R. Republicans, a sponsor of the Wilderness Act, a foe of Echo Canyon Dam, a friend of the North Cascades. Speaking to a grasslands symposium in North Dakota in the fall of 2003, Jim DiPeso, Policy Director for Republicans for Environmental Protection (or REP America), called Saylor "one of the most relentless, dogged advocates for wilderness conservation our nation has ever seen."

So 1968 could not be accepted as the end. It had to be a new beginning.

Still There: The Forest Service

What wasn't protected under the North Cascades Act was still managed by the Forest Service. The Act directed the Secretaries of Agriculture and Interior to complete, within two years, a mutually agreeable development plan for "administrative and public-use facilities within the Park and Recreation Areas, the adjacent National Forests, and along the North Cross-State Highway." A "joint plan" of sorts was produced, so very short and inadequate that it was obviously meant as no more than a preliminary announcement of an intent to make a plan. The National Park Service was sharpening pencils and putting on the coffee water when, in March 1969, the Forest Service struck up the pit orchestra and flung open the curtains on a "Development Plan for the North Cascades National Forests." Even the ranger-friendly *Wenatchee Daily World* was startled, "Some may see the publication of the Forest Service plans before those of the National Park Service as an example of unwanted conflict. . . ."

The Irate Birdwatcher commented in *The Wild Cascades*, "Leaders of conservation organizations, including the NCCC, had no prior notice and were not consulted . . . indeed, we only received details from a third party, which suggests the Forest Service has lost our address. The National Park Service apparently first heard about the plan from the newspapers."

Irate judged the plans for campgrounds, picnic areas, and visitor contact centers justified and necessary. He was delighted by the proposal for a trail along Lake Chelan from Twenty-Five Mile Creek to Stehekin. (Only later did he have a screaming fit when it was revealed the plan was not for a foot trail but a motorcycle runway.) The Around-Mount Baker Highway, to be completed by an Austin Pass–Swift Creek link, was rated, "Of all the crimes against humanity committed and contemplated in the North Cascades by the Forest Service, this obscenity ranks near the top." The notion of an aerial tram from Austin Pass to Table Mountain was judged good for a laugh. The laudable proposal for a "Visitor Center for Alpine Glaciation Interpretation" at Heather Meadows was considered an odd Forest Service invasion of Park Service function.

Happily, there is no need to dwell further on these plans drawn up during

Copies of The North Cascades National Park *(1969) by Harvey Manning and Bob and Ira Spring are presented to Congressmen Tom Pelly, Lloyd Meeds, and Tom Foley (left to right).*

the odd ebullience of "Guns and Butter," an early model of "Voodoo Economics"—the latter being George Bush the Elder's term for the absurdity of "Reaganomics" (which George Bush the Younger fully embraced). The tram plans and highways were defeated, if not by cool reason, by stark poverty.

Bystanders ignorant of the warm personal relationships that can coexist with fiery political relationships were surprised by the post-1968 "era of good feelings" between environmentalists and the Forest Service. What ranger could forgive the savagery of the Irate Birdwatcher? A stiff-necked few could not, but most took his attacks in good humor, knowing it was a case of, "Pardon me, pal, for sticking this knife in your ribs. Nothing personal. Just politics."

Even during the heat of the strife—when the Forest Service was mincing the facts very fine, conspiring with Barbecuers and breaking the law, and the NCCC was loudly denouncing the crimes—respect and friendship crossed the trenches. For example, in the 1960s two supervisors of Region Six national forests displayed such qualities of mind and spirit that had their sort held the top command during the 1950s there surely would not have been a dire need for a park until, perhaps, the 1980s. Yet a leopard may smile and smile and not change its spots. Conservationists were delighted to find rangers, good friends of the past, behaving as of old. Too soon they awoke from this second honeymoon to a realization that the New Ranger of Washington D.C. had selected staffers who could pass for "Old" and sent them into conservationist camps to strum guitars and sing Bob Marshall songs.

Typical of agents who very much enjoyed the duty was Richard Buscher, a middle-level staffer who as a matter of personal pleasure had been consorting with people on the Enemies List before 1968 and continued to do so well after the resumption of open hostilities. On an afternoon in November 1980, he stopped by Cougar Mountain to chat with the Irate Birdwatcher. In the course of exchanging tales of the Good and Bad Old Days, Irate removed the guard from the tip of his rapier and went after "Bush" about the boundaries of the North Cascades National Park:

> Who drew them? It certainly wasn't us—our park proposal was dumped in the garbage can. The Park Service's, too. It couldn't have been Jackson, though he is alleged to have gone camping a couple times when he was a little boy. It couldn't have been his staff—if any of them could tell the difference between a bird and a flower, I'd be surprised.

Irate proceeded to tick off the reasons he knew the boundaries were drawn by the Forest Service, and even nominated his candidate, Harold ("Chris") Chriswell, Supervisor of Mount Baker National Forest, and pointed to his fingerprints all over the map. Buscher squirmed in his chair a little and at last blurted, "*I* drew the boundaries!"

Jackson, without consulting or informing NCCC, had told the Forest Service, in effect, that it was going to have to stand still for a park, but it would get to say *which* park. Given the assignment, Buscher started from the Eldorado Peaks proposal, which carefully respected the personal desires of Mount Baker's Chriswell and Wenatchee's Blair and Wright. He omitted Heather Meadows from the park because Chriswell so loved the place he couldn't stand to hand it over to strangers. It was also crucial to his fond dream of an Around-Mount Baker Highway. Buscher omitted Ruth Creek and Hannegan Pass and the headwaters of the Chilliwack River because Chriswell (who in his heart properly belonged in the Mather–Albright Park Service) yearned to run a scenic highway up to Copper Ridge for a Pickets Picnic Overlook.

An uninformed critic might have pronounced the boundaries a little odd. But no, it was Chriswell—and Buscher, who, since everybody else was getting his personal druthers, felt he should be allowed some of his own. He drew the boundary on Ragged Ridge to allow hostels, for which he'd developed a passion during two years in Austria. His dream was a chain of backcountry Alps-like hotelettes at Fisher Pass, Ragged Ridge, and others at the start of every trail to wilderness. He "gave" us T-Bone Ridge, which had not been in the Eldorado Peaks proposal, because during resource studies for the Study Team Report little was found that the Forest Service could want and thus it could be freely employed as a makeweight.

On May 18, 1991, recently retired, Buscher elaborated in a postcard [slightly edited]:

As to drawing the boundaries of N. Cascades NP, Sen. Jackson authored them by deciding to adopt the boundary of the proposed NRA that I was writing a management plan for. At that point the Director [Hartzog] and Chief Cliff agreed that I knew the land as well as anyone since I had been tramping all over it, so I did the cadastral description for the act.

The Mountaineers, the Sierra Club, the NCCC, and allies had devoted a dozen-odd years to a detailed, thoughtful proposal. There is no evidence Senator Jackson ever gave it a look. Neither did George Hartzog, one of the two "friendly" members of the North Cascades Study Team, and soon thereafter, the director of the National Park Service. After the Jackson bill became law, Supervisor Chriswell told Patrick Goldsworthy that he "could not have believed it would ever have been possible for the Forest Service to have its lands converted into a North Cascades National Park." In a moment of candor, he agreed that "our mistake had been an inadequate Glacier Peak Wilderness."

NEWLY THERE: THE PARK SERVICE

George Hartzog, a former business booster and park superintendent working in the Ozarks, was promoted to the top spot upon Wirth's retirement in 1964. Hartzog stayed on when Nixon became president in 1969 and earned some notoriety that year when he closed down all the national parks in protest of Nixon's budget cuts. He assumed he would be fired, but wasn't—until 1972 when he booted a private houseboat from Biscayne National Monument in Florida. Said houseboat belonged to Nixon's friend Bebe Rebozo. A quarter-century after his expulsion from the directorship, a long-retired medium-higher-up in the Park Service judged Hartzog, along with the totality of his predecessors and successors during the first three-quarters of the twentieth century, as "second rate, at best." Certainly there were worse—Hartzog did support the Wilderness Act, helped bring a lot of small parks into the system, battled against budget cuts, and in 2004 criticized Bush II's efforts to trash the Land and Water Conservation Fund, saying, "The President knows the cost of everything and the value of nothing." In 1968, except for Phil Zalesky, Carsten Lien, and their companion seasonals who had been inside the bureaucracy, conservationists in Washington

State knew naught but good of the men and women in the broad-brimmed hats who had been their childhood idols at Mount Rainier and heroes of their youth on Olympic trails. The crimes committed in the Olympics were not yet widely known; the bad deeds at Rainier were attributed to a gone generation.

Alighting from The Lady of the Lake at Stehekin, veterans of the North Cascades campaign came not as thin-lipped Puritans alert for sins against nature, ready at any rumor to sound the tocsin, but as lost children who had found their way to a gingerbread house. As with Hansel and Gretel, they had lessons to learn. The NCCC's first teacher was Neil Butterfield, a staff member of the Study Team who subsequently was assigned to prepare a detailed plan for the North Cascades National Park "Complex," as the three units were called. Butterfield impressed the directors as honorable, intelligent, perceptive, and sensitive—and deeply, almost blindly, loyal to the Park Service. Yet through his dedication could be sensed a sadness or disappointment, maybe disillusion. Butterfield calmly hammered into the skulls of the naive that "the public has expectations of a national park." A new pin had been stuck in the Park-Lover's Map of America, and the fans would be thronging to collect their decals and souvenir pillows. They would expect to be treated in the manner to which they had been accustomed by Mather, Albright, and Company. They would demand a national-park-like experience.

Hartzog admits to having "deferred to Chairman Crafts leadership," admiring him for being "as cold and calculating as an Alaska grayling . . . a brilliant, skilled, career bureaucrat." Hartzog defined the new park's management as aiming "to preserve the scenic and scientific values while at the same time opening them to concentrated use."

The blood ran cold. There were to be permanent, "hardened" ski areas, the first within the national park system, a very different order of construction from the winter-only portable ski tows that had been permitted at Rainier and Yosemite. A car ferry from end to end on Ross Reservoir. "Aerial trams to transport visitors to within walking distance of ridge points offering superb views of the Cascades' most magnificent mountains, forested valleys, cirques, and glaciers." Said Hartzog, "Our plan is to develop most of these facilities within five years."

Hindsight helps the blood retroactively warm up. America was at a bad news–good news juncture. The bad news was that the nation had so wasted its substance bombing Southeast Asia that the infrastructure of the home civilization—schools, social services, even highway bridges, and most certainly parks—soon would begin to rust and dry-rot. The good news was that "Dandy Andy" Wright would not be able to complete his motorcycle trail system in Wenatchee National Forest because the guns were eating up all the butter. So, too, the Park Service was mouthing threats to the North Cascades that it never would be able to finance—such as the crowd-pleasing tramways high above Ross and Diablo Lakes.

During the Depression, the Forest Service's Old Ranger employed the cheap manpower of the Civilian Conservation Corps to build trails almost everywhere for the sheer joy of it. One climbed a steep four miles from the Skagit River to the high country above Big Beaver. The trail never was maintained, probably barely used except by wild animals, but it continued to be carried on the "Fireman's Map." In the 1960s a party of smokejumpers was dropped from the sky to extinguish a ridgetop blaze; afterward they consulted the map, and opted to take the short downhill path to Ross Reservoir, expecting a tramp of two hours or so. They were three hard *days* battling through the wilderness that was the special glory of the Picket Range. That the Park Service proposed to conduct tourists from an excursion boat onto a tramway up this creek was not good. Butterfield smiled, "Not to worry." It was window dressing, he explained, not real merchandise. Nevertheless, what mind could conceive such an idea even as a public relations ploy? The very act of putting the proposal on paper could exclude a wild valley from dedication in the wilderness core.

At Price Lake, tucked in a cirque in the side of Mount Shuksan, there was no trail, barely a boot track here and there. Except for the occasional climber, the lake was almost never visited; the trip required, for openers, a ford of the Nooksack River where it came brawling out of the Nooksack Cirque, aptly described as the "deepest, darkest hole in the North Cascades." But why a tram? The Forest Service in drawing the park boundary had retained the entire Heather Meadows–Austin Pass area and its world-famous roadside views of "the most beautiful mountain in America." Mount Shuksan was the park's most magnificent single peak. It belonged to the Park Service but was best viewed from Forest Service land. To provide its own Shuksan vista, the Park Service intended to sneak around the corner and violate a wild side of the mountain with a tram. So much for "inter-agency cooperation." Colonial Peak and Ruby Mountain were also eyed for trams that were reminiscent of the Swiss Alps and that even Jim Whittaker, the Everest climber, approved of.

In the spirit of Mather and Albright in their merry Oldsmobile, the Park Service gleefully embraced the proposed North Cross-State Highway. At Roland Point on Ross Reservoir, a spur road would be built from the new highway to a gigantic car campground and put-in for trailered reservoir-razzers. One can't be denied a spark of cynicism here. Did not the Park Service realize that every "Winnebugger" and "Silver Slug" in America, cumulatively towing a fleet of craft as daunting as that of the Allied invasion of Normandy, would take dead aim? That the summer gridlock would extend from Sedro Woolley to Twisp? That those campers who managed to get their seven tons of toys per family into Roland Point Campground never would be able to get them out?

None of the above was fated to happen, nor were the trams and hostels Hartzog was proposing here and in Mount Rainier, Olympic National Parks, and elsewhere around the country. However, in 1968–69 the possibility was appalling; more so was the knowledge that this was the bureaucracy to which the nation had entrusted its natural treasures.

June 3–4, 1970, the Park Service held public hearings in Mount Vernon on the General Development Plan (or Master Plan) and preliminary Wilderness Study for the North Cascades National Park Complex. On July 15 and 18, the Forest Service held public meetings in Wenatchee and Mount Vernon on its final recreation plan for Mount Baker, Okanogan, and Wenatchee National Forests. The latter plan was judged to be fairly good as far as it went, which of course was not far enough for those working to save wilderness.

The study team assigned to draft the Master Plan functioned under the direction of the first North Cascades National Park Superintendent, Roger Contor. NCCC President Patrick Goldsworthy was appointed by Hartzog to the team. The Master Plan was, by volume, 90 percent superb-to-excellent, stressing needs of land preservation, wildlife habitat, and visitor pleasing or controlling. Prominent in the opening sentences was the statement that "The Secretary shall not permit . . . any road . . . which would provide vehicular access, from the North Cross-State Highway to the Stehekin Road," which was something worth cheering about. But 10 percent of the plan amounted to a declaration of war on the wildness that remained in the North Cascades.

Patrick Goldsworthy orally delivered at the public hearing a point-by-point response to the Plan's proposed actions. As summarized in *The Wild Cascades*:

Plan: Backcountry trunk trails. Enclaves spaced one day-hike apart. Providing hostels, shelters, and camping facilities.
NCCC: No enclaves. No hostels.

Plan: Arctic Creek Tramway.
NCCC: No tram.

Plan: Plan for High Ross Dam.
NCCC: Plan for Low Ross Dam.

Plan: Roland Point. Spur road from North Cross-State Highway. Auto-oriented accommodations and services to serve water-related vacation and regional week-end use and casual use from highway. Base for boat access.
NCCC: No spur road.

Plan: Hozomeen–Ross Lake. Accommodations and services related to water-related activities. Scheduled scenic boat trips. Car ferry.
NCCC: No car ferry.

Plan: Price Lake Tramway.
NCCC: No tram.

Plan: Nooksack Cirque. Interpretation of glacier features. Accessible by short trail.
NCCC: Long trail.

Plan: Colonial Peak Tramway.
NCCC: No tram.

Plan: Ruby Mountain Tramway.
NCCC: Study impact before considering.

Plan: About Thunder Creek dam proposal, silence.
NCCC: No dam.

Plan: Cascade Pass. Day-use hiking, hike-in camping below and beyond pass. Major trunk trail and stock route.
NCCC: No horses.

The NCCC prevailed on all of the above items, while debate continued on the following:

Plan: Cascade River Road, Mineral Park. Possible shuttle vehicle terminal (if required) for controlled access to Cascade Pass trailhead.
NCCC: Silent approval (closing road at Mineral Park preferred).

Plan: Stehekin River Road. Vehicle access (public shuttlebus) to trailheads at High Bridge, Bridge Creek, Flat Creek, and Cottonwood (road-end).
NCCC: End road at Bridge Creek (High Bridge preferred).

Plan: Lower Stehekin Valley. Main focal point of development. Private development zone. Etc.
NCCC: Remove Stehekin Emergency Airfield.

If the Master Plan had flaws, the Wilderness Study was full of holes. That the three proposed wilderness cores (the Pickets, Desolation, and Eldorado) were too small was predictable; Forest Service, Park Service, Bureau of Public Lands, Department of Sanitation, Fire Department, every group of bureaucrats ever compelled by the public to set aside a wilderness is stingy. Eliciting more ire were exclusions for shelters, and the concept of a buffer zone, where the Park Service as a matter of policy, in the North Cascades and every other area under its jurisdiction, set back the wilderness boundary (in the North Cascades, one-eighth of a mile) from roads and from the outer park boundary. When hearings were held in Washington, D.C., on May 5, 1972, for fourteen proposals for additions to the National Wilderness System, Senator Frank Church of Idaho, chairing the Public Lands Subcommittee, vehemently insisted that the Wilderness Act did not contain a requirement for buffers, which had the effect of excluding the *critical edge* of the wilderness from full statutory protection, leaving it to management whim. The tender mercies of management whim were precisely the threat the Wilderness Act was adopted to forbid.

Even worse was the enclave concept, whereby dedicated wilderness would have interior holes excluded from wilderness status—a threat that was not limited to the North Cascades. They might be quite spacious to accommodate the eighteen backcountry hostels that Director Hartzog had in mind. A string of four was proposed in the high country northeast of the Stehekin River, from the Stehekin Landing to the Rainbow area; the entire valley wall from river to ridgeline and down the other side would thus be excluded from wilderness. For the other fourteen hostels—along Ruth Creek, Chilliwack, and Little Beaver, for example—holes would be excavated from the wilderness to permit any manner of mechanical-electrical-gasoline-diesel contrivance, including helicopter transport, limited only by the fatuity of whatever ranger came bounding down the pike to take command. In addition, there were numerous small circles, as if the map had been peppered by a shotgun, these to accommodate bureaucratic miscellany—generator-powered flush toilets? Soda pop machines? Saunas? No one knew.

Again Senator Church:

> Nothing in the Act or the legislative intent requires or forces the National Park Service . . . to carve out these kinds of non-wilderness enclaves—not for snow gauges and telemetering equipment, not for fire lookouts, not for ranger patrol cabins, not for pit toilets, not for helispots or shelters . . . the concept is undesirable, dangerous, inconsistent with the letter and intent of the Wilderness Act, and altogether unjustified.

Church said it for the Senate in 1972; Patrick Goldsworthy had already said it for the NCCC in 1970. The Council and companion organizations further asked for escrow clauses providing that if areas proposed for flooding by Seattle City Light were not flooded, if tram proposals were abandoned, and if private lands acquired, the exclusions involved automatically would be placed in wilderness without further governmental action.

Thanks to the Hartzog proposals, even Hansel and Gretel were wising up about the National Park Service and the perils it posed to the North Cascades. The same perils, they were learning, menaced all of America's crown jewels.

In 1972 the Conservation Foundation published "National Parks for the Future: An Appraisal of the National Parks As They Begin Their Second Century in a Changing America." The National Park Service was so shaken that it pressured the foundation into firing the man who edited the appraisal, which contained such judgments as:

> The American public and its political leaders must reject the notion that the parks can be all things to all people.

Automobiles can destroy our national park heritage just as surely as they have made our cities inhumane and dangerous to limb and lung and have desecrated much of the metropolitan countryside.

The National Park System can best meet the future needs of all Americans by reasserting its original mission—the preservation and interpretation of natural landscapes and ecosystems.

Any meaningful characterization of the National Park Service in those days must begin with a melancholy recognition of its lowly place in the nation's power structure, down there close to the absolute bottom of the pecking order. Within the Department of the Interior, it spoke very softly when the Bureau of Reclamation proposed, say, to flood the Grand Canyon. So accustomed it was to being pushed around by the lordly Forest Service that—except when there was an Ickes or Udall at Interior—it ran away and hid from confrontations.

The Service's mission was continually eroded as political forces from within and without, often in double-speak, volleyed innumerable threats against America's wilderness parks. Many Senators and Congressmen considered it their Constitutional right to supervise parks in their jurisdictions, dipping into the federal pork barrel for voter-pleasing roads, marinas, and tramways. These they might force upon the National Park Service and were generally accepted with a grateful smile. Local politicians might raise a storm if the Park Service took any action deemed to hinder the flow of dollars into cash registers of the tourist industry. In some parks, policy was often dictated by concessionaires closely tied to Chambers of Commerce and local and national politicos.

Many gainfully employed friends of wilderness lost faith and quit the Service. Decades of survivalism eroded idealism. A weakening of the agency's mission came, in part, from the dominance of "frontcountry" over "backcountry." The latter tends to nurture the preservers, intimately knowing and deeply loving the land. People-pleasing mostly takes place in the "frontcountry" where too many rangers, particularly the higher-ups, were either developers feeding their "edifice complex," or careerists seeking to preserve not the land but personal sanctuary from the storm and strife of the Real World outside, culminating in pensions. The route to promotion was, and still is, almost always via the frontcountry.

So it was in 1972, after a half a century of "second-raters, at best."

As these forces within the Park Service came to be understood, suspicion began to glimmer among conservation veterans of the long, long trail a-winding through the North Cascades leading to formation of a national park, that the journey to 1968 had been the easy part of the trip.

5

The U.S. Forest Service Revisited

Sources of lumber's what forests are for
Rend them asunder and plunder some more!
—If just like thunder the public should roar,
Just sing-g-g-g-g-g multiple-use!

        —Carmelita Lowry (NCCC Board Member), 1961

THE LAST DAYS OF THE PINCHOT CENTURY

GIFFORD PINCHOT WAS—according to Gifford Pinchot—America's first scientific forester. For little more than a year he studied in France, and one wonders what might have been had he stayed the full course and returned across the Atlantic as Dr. Pinchot. In truth he was not so much a scientific forester as he was a religious one, which is not a bad thing to be. Anyone given custody of ancient forests probably should be something of a priest. But care must be taken to be sure whom one is serving.

The science of forestry was born, or at least conceived, in the nineteenth century. Unlike chemistry, its laboratory experiments are not over in minutes or hours; the controlled manipulation of an individual tree requires decades; a community of trees and associated plants and animals—a forest—centuries. Through much of the twentieth century, foresters of scientific temper were intellectually able to employ multiple working hypotheses while cognizant that their discipline demanded a very long run to obtain useful data. Their frustration was that their compatriots in the colleges of forestry and the Society of American Foresters were mainly logging engineers with a minor in the theatrics of Smokey Bearism. Logging—not forestry—was the skill valued by industry, and since industry was the financial and political angel of forestry departments for generations, the curricula necessarily centered on building roads and laying out cutting circles. The science of trees and forests generally was well represented, but so intimately interwoven with pseudo-science that it was the rare student who was not indoctrinated by industry-friendly dogma. The pseudo-scientists were not so interested in good science as they were in providing respectable justification for their engineering.

One egregious case of professional refusal to be confused by the facts was the response to the Forest Soils Atlas series undertaken in the 1960s by the U.S. Forest Service Range and Experiment Station in Portland. The existence of this unit is a credit to the Forest Service and to Pinchot and the generation of Aldo Leopold. Autonomous from the operating arm and somewhat buffered from industry pressure, these stations scattered about the West have provided, over the years, a large share of America's uncontaminated forest ecology science. The first in the series of atlases, prepared for Olympic National Forest, documented in text and photographs road-building and logging activities so mindless that for every log taken to the mills a much larger volume of earth was washed down the rivers. Tree-growing soils were forever removed from the forest inventory. Fish-spawning grounds were destroyed. Even into the 1980s, industry generally shrugged off the cause and effect between logging and erosion. The second atlas scheduled for release was for Wenatchee National Forest. Supervisor Andrew Wright, having seen the Olympic atlas, raised a political uproar and similar work on his National Forest was suppressed.

The Forest Service resisted science, even that emanating from its own ranks. After the 1949 publication of Aldo Leopold's *Sand County Almanac*, genuine forest scientists began fleeing the term "forester," later preferring to call themselves "forest ecologists" as the study of ecosystems in Europe began to take root in the U.S. Forestry schools, by and large, improved their programs immensely beginning in the 1980s, offering a more holistic view of forest ecosystems that was by then achieving greater acceptance both publicly and institutionally.

The Forest Service also steadily narrowed its definition of the greater good. The "L" Regulations of 1929 that addressed "primitive areas" were replaced in 1939 by the "U" Regulations, drafted by Bob Marshall, which allowed the Forest Service to designate "roadless," "wild," and "wilderness" areas. In the 1950s–1960s the designation of such areas gave way to the notion of multiple-use (and abuse), which was formally legislated by Congress at the end of 1960. Oregon's Three Sisters was made the center of a 250,000-acre primitive area in 1938. In 1957 it was reclassified as a wilderness area of 200,000 "useless" highland acres that excluded 50,000 acres of low-elevation old growth. In 1961 the forests of Mount Jefferson and the Minam River in the Wallowa Mountains of northeastern Oregon, once off limits, were measured up for chainsaws. In 1963 Idaho's Selway-Bitterroot Wilderness was established—minus 500,000 acres of the preexisting primitive area. Many years earlier, Aldo Leopold's flagship Gila Wilderness Area in New Mexico was chopped in half by a road, and even the new boundaries would be further diminished.

The Forest Service, having recovered from its defeat at Kings Canyon in 1940, attained in the 1950s its apogee of power, independence, and a Pinchotian self-confidence that wore the face, predominantly, of arrogance. Then, as with Humpty Dumpty, circumstances changed. In 1964 Congress passed Howard Zahniser's Wilderness Act. It took most of a decade and sixty-six drafts to get it through, against the stubborn resistance of committee chair Wayne Aspinall. Even the Park Service opposed it. The bill was first introduced by Congressman John Saylor, the Republican conservationist from Pennsylvania. It languished for a time, but the national campaign led by the Wilderness Society was effective in forcing Congress to act. Predictably, opposition in the Northwest was considerable. One of its favored trumpets, the *Wenatchee Daily World*, on May 8, 1960, warned,

> If the wilderness advocates are successful, control of our forests will be taken away from the people who live in the Northwest and know its needs and potentials. It will be given to people in Iowa and Missouri and Kansas, and others who don't know a pine from a fir.

Senator Humphrey, in the July 1960 issue of *The Magazine of Family Camping and Outdoor Recreation*, wrote "it appears that 1960 may be the year of decision for the Wilderness Bill. Changes have been made to meet the objections of any reasonable and constructive critics." For those who preferred "scenic roads" over wilderness, Humphrey suggested we might "pave logging roads and build them enclosed hot dog stands for their vacation urges."

As noted in *American Forests* in 1961, forestry professionals were widely divided on wilderness preservation. When the American Forestry Association announced its opposition to the wilderness bill around 1960, more than one thousand members reportedly left the organization. Ultimately, the bill passed by a substantial margin.

The Wilderness Act of 1964 was also bitterly resisted by many in the Forest Service, not because it altered their functions, which already included—peripherally or accidentally, perhaps—wilderness preservation, but because it restricted bureaucratic freedom. For them, the North Cascades Act of 1968 was another stunner, reviving the dread that had haunted the heirs of Pinchot from the era of Muir to that of Ickes. Not since 1940 had the do-gooders defeated the exploiters, broken through the frontier, and won a province of the empire. Ironically, the defeat of the legions was not due to a lack of valor but rather a failure to reform their old religion: the worship of forestry-as-logging. While ritually paying lip service to the "greatest good of the greatest number in the long run," the timber rangers lost sight of the true long run, namely, the sustained health and integrity of ancient forest ecosystems.

The irruption of wilderness preservationists, or the eco-barbarians, as some might have perceived them, was not the rangers' most serious worry; viewed calmly, it was a danger only to pride. Though the eco-barbarians might speak a strange language and worship unfamiliar gods, an article of their faith was that if the Forest Service, somehow, was ever destroyed, the nation's first task would be to create, again, a Forest Service. No, the danger to the ranger was not the metaphorical Roman frontier but the anachronistic, yet real and thriving, American frontier. Thus the assault that by the 1980s would bring Pinchot's empire to the brink of ruin was not led by the barbarian environmentalist, but by the savage, money-grubbing Barbecuer.

THE BARBECUERS GO FOR BROKE

In late 1968 leaders of the forest industry and the professional forester (or logging engineer) societies gathered in Denver, Philadelphia, Seattle, and Washington, D.C., to organize the American Forest Institute, a reconstitution of American Forest Products Industries, which was an arm of the National Lumber Manufacturers Association. The first issue of its new publication, *National Timber Industry*, carried a "battle map" targeting 142 areas that were being considered for parks, wilderness, or other closures to logging. Three strategic objectives were adopted: first, to compensate for the creation of wilderness areas by designating matching logging areas; second, to authorize logging inside wilderness and parks under the guise of "salvage and improvement" cutting, which was coming to be a usual justification for a large proportion of Forest Service timber sales (and cuts inside Olympic National Park); and third, following the example of the environmentalists who through the Wilderness Act had restricted Forest Service freedom of action, to compel the Forest Service to substantially increase the annual cut, even to double it in the Northwest.

A National Timber Supply Bill was introduced in Congress, pushed hard by the industry, but was finally killed by the House of Representatives on February 26, 1971. Nevertheless, on June 19 of that year, President Nixon ordered a sharp increase in the cut on softwood forests. Congressman John Saylor of Pennsylvania called the order disastrous and condemned the industry for seeking to accomplish by executive fiat what could not be done legislatively. For their part, the timber-friendly rangers smugly recited the dictum: *Presidents come and go. The Forest Service is forever.* Because a timber sale takes time for the cruising, marking, surveying road access, advertising for bids, and awarding of sales, by dragging their feet, it was possible for the timber bureaucrats to string out a single sale for years; the hundreds of sales required by a massive increase in cut could easily outlast a two-term presidency. What the Forest Service could not foresee was that after Nixon would come Ford, then Carter, Reagan, Bush I, Clinton, and finally, Bush II, each of whom would stir the citizenry to new heights of aggravation.

A National Timber-Supply Policy?

In 1971 the Forest Service, caught between thunder on the right and thunder on the left, was compelled to begin a system-wide Roadless Area Review and Evaluation known as RARE. Candidate areas for wilderness designation were to be identified for individual consideration within each national forest. The balance of the system would be released, once and for all, to multiple-use. Conservationists, accepting the study as timely and reasonable, cooperated. The published results shocked them to their socks. Even as on-the-ground rangers and conservationists were teaming up in field studies, the desk rangers in Washington, D.C., had already given the game away by finding that only 17 percent of the national forests qualified for wilderness protection. The Sierra Club filed suit. The courts ruled that the Forest Service could do no logging, no road-building, or other activities that would compromise the wilderness character of the thirty-four million acres of roadless National Forest wilderness until it had complied with the National Environmental Policy Act of 1968.

Take two. The Forest Service revisited its work, resulting in the RARE II assessment, concluded in 1979. It was more of the same, only worse. One is reminded that "consistency," said Bernard Berenson, "requires you to be as ignorant today as you were a year ago."

The Barbecuers, settling in to their longest uninterrupted control of the White House since the Gilded Age, were getting steadily feistier. Conservationists responded to the growing controversy and the agency's reluctance to identify more lands for possible wilderness designation by forming local groups who would fight for the areas they knew best. The Mount Baker Wilderness Association, for example, was quickly formed and began attracting dozens of supporters, sometimes forty or more, to its meetings in the early 1980s. Its proposal for a two-hundred-forty thousand acre wilderness was ambitious, but the arguments favoring such protection were well documented by volunteer biologists and other professionals. A similar group formed to protect what would later become the Boulder River Wilderness. In Eastern Washington, the Kettle Range Conservation Group, formed prior to RARE II, intensified its efforts.

In Seattle, the Washington Wilderness Coalition, or WWC, helped to coordinate efforts statewide in response to the RARE I and II studies, and to ramp up public visibility of wilderness and threats to wilderness through the media and other venues.

In October 1982 the courts threw out the RARE II environmental impact statement. Assistant Secretary of Agriculture John Crowell was assigned to supervise the Forest Service—a job for which he was judged by Reagan to be splendidly qualified, having spent more than twenty-five years as general counsel for Louisiana Pacific, one of the major purchasers of national forest timber. Crowell simply gave up on the entire RARE process. On February 1, 1983, he announced that all roadless areas would be given another look in the normal course of forest planning, and that would be that.

This normal course of national forest planning was prescribed by the 1974 Forest and Rangeland Renewable Resources Planning Act (RPA), which stipulated periodic assessment of resources and programming of multiple-use goals, and its 1976 amendment by the National Forest Management Act (NFMA), which made provision for environmentally sound resolution of conflicts. Taken together, RPA and NFMA expressed a Congressional desire to reduce the dominance of timber production interests by paying greater attention to fish, wildlife, soils, water quality, recreation, and scenery. The law directed the development of a plan for each national forest. In keeping with the law, deadlines were set.

But deadlines were not met. On the one hand, Crowell and his deputy, Douglas MacCleery, who came to his federal post fresh from the industry-front National Forest Products Association, deliberately delayed completion of the plans in order to let the loggers hack away at the Nixon "harvest" rate as long as possible before a publicly induced reality check could cause a reduction in the allowable cut. At the same time, environmentalists were getting better at counting trees, and the Forest Service, using obsolete inventories, was regularly humiliated in public when taken to court. Forest economist Randall O'Toole sympathized, "Forest managers are walking a tightrope. If they don't log fast enough to meet their targets, they won't get promoted. If they get sued for breaking environmental laws, they won't get promoted either."

Perhaps not entirely by coincidence, 1968 was the year of both the North Cascades Act and the National Timber Supply Bill, industry's attempt to officially accelerate a virtual theft of the nation's forests. It was also the year of Nixon's election to the presidency, the beginning of a twenty-four year period, under five presidents in a row, that saw the Forest Service rangers at last stripped of their virtual autonomy and vestigial claims to the flawed but pure-hearted ideals of Pinchot. The rangers, now brought to the heel of the Barbecuers, mostly just wagged their tails. One might have expected more constructive resistance during the Carter Administration, but by 1977 the momentum toward massive cutting was already too much and, by and large, Carter opted not to intercede.

Not until 1990 did the Mount Baker–Snoqualmie, Wenatchee, and Okanogan National Forests topple, exhausted, from the far end of the tightrope and issue final forest management plans. Much of the work proved to be only marginally useful, based as it was on old inventories. The most egregious errors included clearcuts, young forests, and even talus fields in the count of 2.5 million acres of old-growth forest in the national forests of Washington and Oregon. Peter Morrison of The Wilderness Society, employing powerful new computer-mapping technology not available to Reagan-impoverished Forest Service scientists, found only 1.1 million acres.

For a century and more, Americans whose eyes were open to the future had seen that the virgin forests of the nation were exhaustible. John Osseward, who was active in the Olympics battle since the 1940s, recalled that when he was a boy he could see solid forest all the way from the shores of Puget Sound to the Cascades. By the 1980s, any citizen of Seattle could see that logging clearcuts had climbed to the crest of the front ridges of both the Olympics and Cascades. Tourists who came across America to enjoy the Golden Triangle of parks could view the damage close up, backdrops of scarred mountainsides behind signs that marked the entrance to a National Forest. The general public, the press, and elected officials could no longer ignore the impending end of the timber industry's and the Forest Service's outdated concept of the "long run."

The timber industry poured millions into television commercials and newspaper ads explaining in simple words and pretty pictures that, thanks to plantations, there were more trees, most of them vibrant little baby trees, growing now than ever dreamt of by Mother Nature. The story sounded convincing to folks who never left the city, even those watching the educational channel on television. But those who drove the highways of the Olympics and Cascades could tell at a glance the difference between Mother Nature's forests and man's second-growth, even-age, monoculture forests—the uninspired formula for an ecological time bomb. The forests of Europe, where tree farming began in the nineteenth century, were, by the end of the twentieth century, sharply declining, their ecosystem exhausted. Americans might not have been familiar with the end-product of the Prussian forestry so much admired by Gifford Pinchot. At a glance, however, they could see the difference between a Weyerhaeuser plantation of nursery-spawned Douglas firs, which would never be allowed to live beyond fifty years, and the forests of Mount Rainier and Olympic National Parks where the individual trees were five centuries or more old and the forest ecosystems were thousands of years old.

In the fall of 1988, a conference held in Portland to organize the Ancient Forest Alliance adopted "ancient" as a more useful and relevant term than "old growth." The alliance reiterated what everybody, even the industry, knew—that at the existing rate of cutting, none of the ancient forests outside of dedicated preserves would be left by the year 2000. Not merely birdwatchers and mountain climbers, but ordinary folks throughout the nation, were shocked by this revelation.

Congress awoke belatedly to discover that, by passing the National Environmental Policy Act and the Endangered Species Act, it had given citizens recourse to the third branch of government to seek justice denied by the other two. The Forest Service found its last shreds of freedom from public interference lost to the administrative appeals process prescribed by the NFMA and the subsequent litigation by citizens.

Caught between short-range demands of the forest industry and long-range needs of the planet, and flopped in the frying pan by the sweeping court injunctions placed on federal timber sales in 1989, Congress squirmed and in 1990 gasped out a compromise between ancient forest protection and logging in the forests of Region Six. It was a temporary expedient to give breathing space in which to devise legislation that belatedly would face up to the reality of a post-frontier forest economy. It was said that the forest industry had a past and will have a future, but did not have a present.

The good news was that Congress, except for its Northwest delegations, had entered a forest-preserving mood unequaled since the administrations of the two Roosevelts. Brock Evans, a leader in the October 1988 organizing of the Ancient Forest Alliance, subsequently exulted, "The Forest Service knew it was dead as soon as it heard that name." *Ancient forest.* Name magic. Americans on the street across the nation were instant converts. Industry-beholden owners of the press refused to allow their journalists to use the term. Newspapers, television stations, and public relations firms accepted millions of dollars of industry money to wave the shirts of groups like the Washington Citizens to Protect the Northwest Economy, but even in the Barbecuer heartland, those citizens whose living did not depend on a chainsaw shrugged. It was the same old guff Weyerhaeuser had been peddling since FDR's day, when it began tacking "Tree Farm" signs on stumps and making inflated claims about growing trees. To be fair, not all timber companies were waving their shirts, as Phil Zalesky observed in the *NCCC News* as far back as the late 1950s:

> Much of the forest industry manages timberland as if they still believe in the myth of inexhaustibility. A few . . . make a sincere attempt toward intensive integrated forestry. Part of the industry, however, still wallows in the timber-hog practices of the past. It is this latter group that is the most vociferous against national parks and other dedicated areas. One can only suspect that this is part of a propaganda offensive to camouflage their own failings.

NEW FORESTRY, NEW RANGERS

The literature of "New Forestry," intended to soften the impacts of large-scale timber cutting, began with a trickle of research papers in scientific journals, and grew to a freshet of articles in magazines that flooded over into books and newspapers. Very, very interesting. Promising. Exciting. However, to swallow it whole in oversimplified form would be to perpetuate the habit of forestry schools to hastily elevate hypotheses to laws and insert them into the susceptible heads of logging engineers. Indeed, the most attractive feature of New Forestry was the bent toward humility. The gonzo foresters seemed to recognize that forests are not corn fields and that no one now living truly knows enough to be a "tree farmer."

Pinchot was premature. So were his disciples of mid-century and later, the intensive managers. But so, too, were the public-relations-minded timber companies who jumped on the bandwagon wearing beatific smiles and false halos but kept right on sawing up the big old trees. Andy Kerr of the Oregon Natural Resources Council asserted that the Northwest was down to its last 10 percent of ancient forests and that none should be logged. "The New Forestry should be practiced only on new forests." For the ancient forests, the only proper forestry is preservation.

The *New York Times* of June 7, 1970, took note:

> A United States Forest Service investigative team has formally lodged some sweeping complaints about the service's own policies and practices. . . . Even more surprisingly, the allegations have been published, without comment, by the service itself in an apparent effort to ease alleged "pressures" from the Administration, Congress, and "outside groups" . . . The complaints include assertions that the service's operations lean too heavily in favor of exploitative interests, including mining and grazing, as opposed to conservation and recreation. . . .

Through the 1970s, an occasional disgruntled ranger resigned or took early retirement because he no longer could stomach his assigned duty. However, loyalty to the corps continued so strong that malcontents usually went away quietly.

In the 1980s the grumbling reached the top. In 1983 Forest Service Chief Max Peterson saw the handwriting on the wall: the cut had to come down, sharply. The same year, upper-level rangers confronted Douglas MacCleery at a conference and told him in no uncertain terms that they were fed up with the fabrication of phony numbers, with political interference. In 1986 Chief Peterson, after extended browbeating for his "reluctance" to over-cut, quit.

And then, the unthinkable—a public insurgency. In the summer of 1989, appeared Volume 1, Number 1, of *Inner Voice*, a publication of Forest Service Employees for Environmental Ethics (FSEEE), a group formed to hold the

228 • WILDERNESS ALPS

agency "accountable for responsible land stewardship." FSEEE declared its program to have five main goals: 1) *Responsibly manage American forests*: emphasize biological diversity by protecting whole ecosystems; 2) *Reform the budget*: the Forest Service should not be dependent on revenue from the sale of timber or grazing, oil, and mining rights. The budget should reflect equality among funding sources such as timber, watersheds, fisheries, and recreation; 3) *Get the Forest Service out of the Department of Agriculture*: The Forest goal should be conservation, not tree-farming. Forests are national treasures, not cash crops, and should be protected, not managed like corn or wheat; 4) *Increase citizen oversight*: The Forest Service should be accountable to the public, not timber companies; and 5) *Promote integrity, ethics, and competence*: The Forest Service needs to rescind the gag order barring employees from speaking out about forest policy, stop the harassment of whistleblowers, and hire the most qualified person for each job.

FSEEE's vision statement is also worth noting:

> To forge a socially responsible value system for the Forest Service based on a land ethic that ensures ecologically and economically sustainable resource managment. . . . FSEEE believes that the land is a public trust, to be passed with reverence from generation to generation. The Forest Service and other public agencies must follow the footsteps of Aldo Leopold, a pioneer of conservation, and become leaders in the quest for a new resource ethic. Together we must work toward an ecologically and economically sustainable future.

By the summer of 1990, FSEEE had over four thousand members, eighteen hundred of them current or former Forest Service employees—these being the only members permitted a vote. Though the mailing list was carefully guarded to protect anonymity, many employees wrote, anonymously, that fear of reprisal prevented them from joining. A good many of the non-voting associate memberships (*Inner Voice* subscribers) were taken out in the names of relatives or friends who were trusted to pass the publication along and not rat on the ranger. The organization could not be dismissed as the congenital gripers normal to any bureaucracy. Among the members fully out of the closet were district rangers on active duty and, surprisingly, retired forest supervisors.

Indeed, without joining FSEEE, the active supervisors of forests in Montana, Idaho, Utah, Alaska, California, Oregon, and Washington joined in demanding a reduction in timber sales. When John (Louisiana–Pacific) Crowell announced his goal to convert all the ancient forests of the Pacific Northwest to plantations in a single tree-growing cycle, the Region Six Regional Forester at the time, James Torrence, spoke out. "John has no idea what's out there on the ground," he said. "He's not in touch with reality and he never listens. He's living out there in fantasy land . . . even the new forest plans are not sustainable."

Among those who were out there on the ground were the wilderness rangers, a new group within the Forest Service that had been growing rapidly—an unforeseen consequence of the proliferation of national wilderness areas after 1964. Though in large part summer seasonals, they typically returned year after year and learned their lands and water, flora and fauna, as few logging engineers ever would, at least since the passing of the Old Ranger. They and their permanent supervisors have a mission entirely different from intensive management. Their counterparts in the Park Service are the backcountry rangers, similarly with a mission very different from that of the frontcountry. Presumably, more than a few subscribed to FSEEE's *Inner Voice*, and its successor, *Forest Magazine*, a quarterly journal that reached more than ten thousand members in 2003.

The Forest Service confronted by conservationists in the 1950s–1960s was a tightly cohesive group evidencing a dangerous tendency to become "unduly proud, aloof, and confident." But give this to the rangers of that period: whatever the deficiencies of their science, their esprit and morale were the highest. By the 1980s, many were feeling demoralized.

Among the magic tricks pulled off by the Reagan Administration was to succeed where predecessors had failed, to get the Forest Service under control. Having done so, Reagan's appointees humiliated it and squashed it out of shape. No esprit, no morale, no joyous faith in "the greatest good." In their places came despair, shame, fatalistic subservience, and cynicism. In 1989 Associate Chief Rex Resler took an early retirement. The next year, amid rumors that a high percentage of top-level rangers were on the verge of doing the same, Resler told the press that politics were destroying Forest Service morale. Political appointments were threatening to reach down to the level of regional foresters, and thus, in effect, to the supervisors of the national forests. Only now, in retirement, did he feel free to fully express his true feelings about the folly of another Barbecuer president.

The Forest Service of the 1990s would not be recognizable by Pinchot. Or Chief McArdle (1952–1962). However, a spark survived. Given a difference in the White House, it could be fanned into a firestorm. Indeed, even while the Barbecuers retained the White House, flames were breaking out. Ron Humphrey, supervisor of Tongass National Forest, protested that the sale target for his forest was too high; he was forced to transfer elsewhere. Well into Bush I's term, a September 25, 1991, story by the Associated Press reported that "Regional chiefs for the Forest Service and Park Service told Congress yesterday they were ordered transferred from their jobs after they resisted political pressure to disregard environmental laws." Regional Forester John Mumma, who oversaw fifteen national forests in Montana, northern Idaho, and portions of Washington and North and South Dakota, testified that "he was commanded to meet logging quotas on national forests in Montana and Idaho, even though he repeatedly told Forest Service Chief Dale Robertson that such excessive cutting would violate federal laws." In August, Mumma, age fifty-one, was forced to resign.

In the December 1991 issue of *Inner Voice*, Dan Heinz, who retired in 1983 as Range and Wildlife Staff Officer in Montana's Deerlodge National Forest and in 1991 was elected as a director of FSEEE, chronicled his personal "Loyalties: Old and New." He had this to say about the Forest Service, the agency that was his childhood ideal and that he served for twenty-five years, including two posts as a district ranger:

> Society will not forgive anyone who violates the public trust under the excuse that they were only following orders. . . . Pasternak said something to the effect that if you love your country enough you may well have to betray it. If you believe in a U.S. Forest Service which protects the land and serves the people then you will likely have to betray the current leadership.

Behaving ethically often comes at a price. "The history of land use reform," said Heinz, "is littered with the broken careers of reform-minded state fish and game biologists, Forest Service rangers, and BLM range conservationists."

WILDERNESS TO THE FORE

In 1976 one of the major lingering issues addressed by the North Cascades Study was dealt with, but only partially, when President Gerald Ford signed the Alpine Lakes Wilderness Act protecting 305,400 acres (another 57,400 acres would be added in 1984). However, the second major issue of the study, the Cougar Lakes Wilderness proposal, remained in limbo, as did other proposals being developed by an exhilarating proliferation of "spearhead" groups. The success of 1976 brought to a boil a seething frustration: in 1960 came the Glacier Peak Wilderness; in 1968, the North Cascades National Park and Pasayten Wilderness; in 1976, Alpine Lakes Wilderness—an apparent eight-year cycle. Would the turn of Cougar Lakes thereby come in 1984? Then perhaps Boulder River–Whitehorse Mountain in 1992? What in 2000? If the Forest Service and Congress were able to hold in their heads only one wild idea at a time, preservationists were facing an agenda of many, many decades, if any more wildness was even left by then.

Resorting to a strategy employed in other frustrated states, the Washington Wilderness Coalition drafted an omnibus Washington Wilderness Bill that delineated thirty units totaling some three million acres. An excited campaign developed, bills were introduced, modified, expanded to include areas like Mount Baker that many assumed would never make it into the final bill. June 2–3, 1983, Senator Jackson (presiding) and Senator Slade Gorton attended field hearings in Spokane and Seattle. Hundreds testified. The proceedings filled 2,313 pages, the testimony assuring them of what they already knew—that public

This aerial photo captures a portion of today's Alpine Lakes Wilderness; taken in 1963 for the North Cascades Study Team.

support for wilderness had reached a critical mass and was still growing.

Well into the Seattle hearing, Jim Whittaker stood and offered his full support. "Washington's wild heritage deserves support," he said, "because it is there." Next up was Patrick Goldsworthy, speaking for the NCCC:

> We are all here today to address a long delayed and still unfinished agenda. . . . It is our sincere hope that this final chapter will, henceforth, settle the differences between conservationists and the Forest Service so that we both can proceed in a spirit of mutual constructive cooperation, much as we have been able to do with the National Park Service.

Impassioned representatives of proposed wilderness areas around the state spoke at both hearings, as did the opposition—more than two hundred in total. Passage of the bill was almost inevitable at this point, the main uncertainty being which areas would be excluded.

Three months later, Senator Jackson, having carved an impressive, if incomplete, record for park and wilderness preservation in Washington, was dead of heart failure.

The Mountaineers supported the 1976 campaign by publishing a fine, Brower-like exhibit-format book, *The Alpine Lakes*. In 1984, they produced the less ambitious, yet handsome *Washington Wilderness: The Unfinished Work*. The myriad spearheads steadily stabbed away statewide, keeping members of Congress on the jump. The Washington delegation, Republicans and Democrats together, discussed and argued and wrangled another strenuous six months,

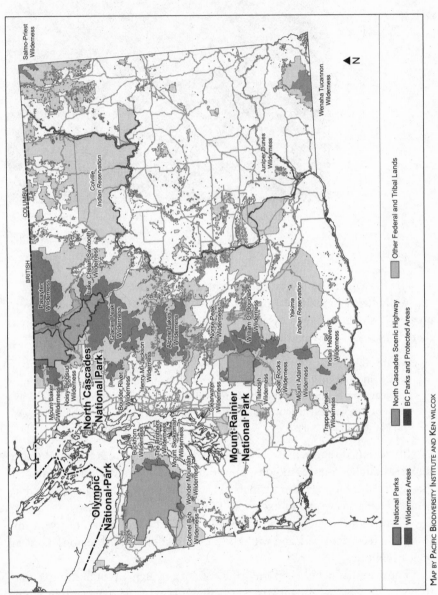

National parks and wilderness areas in Washington State through 1984.

the final wrestling match being to sit down upon a last holdout, Congressman Rod Chandler, the ideological son of former Congressman Jack Westland, and twist his arm.

President Reagan held no signing ceremony whatsoever—his administration had supported only 230,000 acres in total. The customary courtesy of notifying the state's Congressional delegation was delayed until after the fact. On July 3, 1984, Reagan quietly signed the Washington Wilderness Act, adding eighteen units—1,031,758 acres—to the state's share of the National Wilderness System. The same act also created a Mount Baker National Recreation Area of about 8,500 acres, and designated Highway 20 as the North Cascades Scenic Highway.

One out of three acres was surely better than Reagan's preferred one in ten. If the glass was still two-thirds empty in 1984, it was newly one-third full, and one-third of a glass makes a nice swill for a dry mouth. The Cougar Lakes area received its due, or much of it, in the 1984 act, with the designations of the William O. Douglas and Norse Peak Wildernesses. Others in the neighborhood of the North Cascades National Park Complex included:

Addition to the Glacier Peak Wilderness of 111,854 acres brought the total (which started with 458,500 in 1960 and was expanded by ten thousand in 1968) to 580,354 acres. The eleven units added were the Cascade River, Illabot, Big Creek, Buck Creek–Downey Creek, Box Mountain, Meadow Mountain, Pugh Mountain–White Chuck River, White River, Twin Lakes, Chiwawa River, and Entiat–Lake Chelan. Among the blessings, the Wenatchee National Forest scheme for a motorcycle raceway loop from Twenty-Five Mile Creek up Lake Chelan to Lucerne and over Milham Pass to the Entiat River was foreclosed.

A *Mount Baker Wilderness* of 117,528 acres had two units. The one north of the North Fork of the Nooksack River took in Tomyhoi and Silesia Creeks, draining north to Canada, and Ruth Creek and Hannegan Pass; that exorcised old notions of a scenic road to Copper Ridge, an entry road into Nooksack Cirque, and a tramway to Price Lake. The unit south of the North Fork of the Nooksack took in most of the roadless lands around Mount Baker and the northeast slopes of the Twin Sisters Range, giving the quietus to the Around-Mount Baker Highway. Once again, the rock and the ice were secure—or most of it anyway.

A *Mount Baker National Recreation Area* of about 8,600 acres was a serious compromise, a cynical hand-off to snowmobilers, who got free razzing from Schreiber's Meadows to Mazama Park to the deep crevasses of the Easton Glacier, and nearly to the summit crater of Mount Baker.

The *Henry M. Jackson Wilderness* of 102,024 acres covered the Cascade Crest and headwaters of valleys west and east of the crest from Stevens Pass to Glacier Peak; on the northwest edge it bounds the old mining community of Monte Cristo, where Jackson—honored by a renaming of this splendid area adjacent to the Glacier Peak Wilderness—was reputed to have camped out as a child.

The *Boulder River Wilderness* of 48,674 acres took in much of the roadless areas of Boulder River, Three Fingers, and Whitehorse Mountains, including a rare low-elevation stand of old-growth timber.

The *Noisy–Diobsud Wilderness* of 14,133 acres east of Baker Lake adjoined the west boundary of North Cascades National Park.

The *Pasayten Wilderness* east of Ross Lake gained 24,083 acres, protecting trails in the Chewack–Toats Coulee area.

The 1984 Act's largest single block in the North Cascades, at 152,835 acres, was the *Lake Chelan–Sawtooth Wilderness*, extending along the north shore of Lake Chelan and the divide separating it from the Methow-Twisp Rivers. Nevermore could Wenatchee Forest plot motorcycle raceways to Stehekin along the Chelan Lakeshore Trail and the Summit Trail. (An interesting footnote: the first boundary drawn by the Forest Service was far up the slope from the lakeshore, the rangers having explained to Congressman Morrison, chief proponent of this wilderness, that a powerline existed along the shore. Gary Paull of the Forest Service brought to the Congressman's attention that the powerline, built to serve the Holden Mine, had been gone for thirty years. Thanks to Paull, the wilderness was brought down to the water's edge.)

Not bad for 1984.

THE NORTHWEST FOREST PLAN, THE ROADLESS RULE, AND "HEALTHY FORESTS"

In 1992 Congress almost passed fairly decent, forest-friendly legislation, too decent for the industry, at whose behest Speaker Tom Foley, of Washington State, a protégé in 1964 of Senator Henry Jackson, wielded the power of his office to frustrate the manifest will of Congress and apparently the nation. As 1993 opened, Brock Evans, who had been in the front lines of the ancient forest campaign since 1968, had given the loggers a new epithet to replace "birdwatcher." The term of choice became "tree hugger." (He gave a rapturous description in *The Alpine Lakes* of the epiphany of embracing an ancient Ponderosa pine.) Evans ebulliently declared, "Foley and the rest will take another run at us, but we have beaten them four years in a row. The New Emperor [Clinton] seems determined to make a move."

In early April 1993, a new hope for old trees emerged with President Clinton's Northwest Forest Summit held in Portland, Oregon, the outcome of which would decide the fate of ancient forests and spotted owls from Washington to northern California. Vented there was a great deal of the usual nonsense and industrial bluster, but also much wisdom and righteous passion about ancient forests. In 1991 federal Judge William Dwyer had ruled the Forest Service logging plans were illegal, in violation of the Endangered Species Act. In July 1993 Clinton's Northwest Forest Plan for the federal forests was released, and among the alternative actions outlined, "Option Nine" was designed to be approved, it was hoped, by Judge Dwyer. In that hope, it proposed to drop logging levels on federal lands to about a quarter of the annual average of the Reagan–Bush years. But elephantine overcutting had gone so far that environmentalists retorted that the envisioned logging was still far too much of the little that was left. Moreover, what about state and private forests? Under the 1889 Statehood Act, land grants to the new state of Washington plus the Northern Pacific Land Grant and other coups of stolen public lands amounted to twice the extent of the remaining federal forests. Frances Hunt of the National Wildlife Federation said, "If the federal lands look like a mangy dog, a lot of the private lands look like a skinned chihuahua."

The Clinton Plan also relieved private landowners from making any significant contribution to habitat for the endangered spotted owl. Andy Kerr of the Oregon Natural Resources Council said that praising Weyerhaeuser, which fought against owl protections on much of its own land, as newspaper editorials and the White House were doing, was "like giving a slumlord credit for remodeling one building on an entire block of dilapidated structures." As it had since adoption of the tree-farm scam, the industry chose public relations fabrications over social responsibility.

The removal from office of Forest Service Chief F. Dale Robertson, a Reagan man, and Clinton's appointment of Jack Ward Thomas as the new Chief, the first biologist to hold the office, was worth cheering about. Yet Clinton's environmental initiatives in his first year in office were, on the whole, disappointing. Said the Washington Environmental Council, "Clinton is short-sighted and weak-kneed." Although the president hastily defended himself against charges that he was "unable to lead a line of ants to a picnic," an outbreak of bumper stickers read: "FREE AL GORE."

In 1994 the environmental impact statement for a new Northwest Forest Plan was released. Certainly there were some improvements over the old status quo, but Brock Evans, now vice president of the National Audubon Society, said of Clinton's revised plan, "The more you read it, the more your alarm bells go off. It's illegal over and over again." He predicted Judge Dwyer would void the plan as he did the Bush plan of 1991. Tim Hermack of the National Forest Council in Eugene, Oregon, also commented. "We've seen little change," he said, "lots of slicked up political rhetoric, but continuing forest destruction."

Washington's Senator Slade Gorton, a Republican expert on slick rhetoric who kept his finger in the dike to hold back a rising sea of ecological common sense, said of the issue, "I suspect it will be tied up in litigation for many more years." Indeed, six lawsuits were filed by industry and environmentalists, but in December 1994, Judge Dwyer rejected them all. The plan was upheld and remains in effect today, albeit weakened substantially by a throng of industry cronies and lobbyists appointed by Bush II to head up the federal agencies.

Clearly, things improved considerably in the Northwest during the Clinton years, including a major reduction in logging on national forests, though as before the moneyed interests frequently prevailed in their relentless national assault on public resources. In 1994, while working for American Wildlands on overgrazing issues, Dan Heinz, retired from the Forest Service in Montana, felt compelled to remind Clinton's Interior Secretary Bruce Babbitt that "the concept that persons with a direct financial interest in a decision must be excluded from the decision process is basic to our system of ethics." A few months later, Clinton signed into law the infamous "salvage logging rider," blocking citizen appeals and suspending environmental rules that protected old-growth forests. Clinton, Babbitt, and Vice President Al Gore all acknowledged later that the rider was a serious mistake, although a Republican Congress refused to undo it. The rider's principal author was none other than Mark Rey, a former lobbyist for the timber, pulp, and paper industries who, in 2001, was appointed Bush II's number-two man in the Department of Agriculture as Under Secretary for Natural Resources and Environment.

As the second term of the Clinton presidency waned, conservationists appealed for greater protections for the tens of millions of acres of roadless national forest across the U.S. that remained vulnerable to the big-tree barbecue. In October 1999, President Clinton issued a sweeping Executive Order creating a Roadless Initiative that could potentially prohibit commercial logging and road construction on 58.5 million acres of national forests. In his White House statement introducing the initiative, Clinton said,

> Too often, we have favored resource extraction over conservation, degrading our forests and the critical natural values they sustain. As the consequences of these actions have become more apparent, the American people have expressed growing concern and have called on us to restore balance to their forests. . . . I have determined that it is in the best interest of our Nation, and of future generations, to provide strong and lasting protection for these forests . . .

As the formal review process unfolded, the plan would generate more than 1.5 million public comments, the vast majority of them in favor of keeping these forests safe from those who would squander them. In January 2001, Clinton approved the Roadless Area Conservation Rule, which offered a substantial degree of protection for forests in many states, including over two million acres in Washington—half of it, incidentally, in the North Cascades (generally the same areas that were omitted from previously designated park and wilderness areas). Days later, however, the Clinton-Gore era was over, and predictably, the incoming Bush II administration would soon dedicate itself to overturning the roadless initiative. Several years of banter and legal skirmishing were followed in July 2004 with a new proposed rule squarely gutting the original intent of "strong and lasting protection" for roadless areas. The Bush proposal was met with another record-breaking 1.7 million public comments overwhelmingly opposed to the new rule. In May 2005 the administration gleefully ignored the public's input and formally repealed the roadless rule. The action was coupled with an invitation to state governors to kindly petition the Forest Service for any areas they believed should remain roadless—with no assurance that the petitions would accomplish anything at all. Numerous organizations, led by Earthjustice, immediately challenged the move. In August 2005, California, Oregon, and New Mexico filed suit in federal court to block the administration's petition process and called for reinstatement of the original roadless rule. The following February, Washington State joined the lawsuit and Montana and Maine soon added their support. On September 20, 2006, a federal court ruled in favor of the states and reinstated the roadless rule.

Anti-environmental meddling by the Bush II administration, as well as the Congress, was also illustrated well by the "Healthy Forests Initiative," a cleverly named program concocted after a particularly ferocious fire season in California and Oregon in 2002. Ostensibly, the initiative was about reducing the hazards of wildfire to people, communities, and ecosystems. The Sierra Club, among others, saw it for what it was. "The initiative is based on the false assumption that landscape-wide logging will decrease forest fires," they wrote, adding,

> The premise is contradicted by the general scientific consensus, which has found that logging can increase fire risk. This disconnect between what the administration says and what science says about logging and fire reveals the administration's true goal which is to use the forest fire issue to cut the public out of the public lands management decision-making process and to give logging companies virtually free access to our National Forests. . . . Real public protection requires honest fuel reduction a quarter-mile around communities and involving the public and community leaders in long-term education and planning. Instead, the President's plan would promote logging of large, commercially valuable trees miles from at-risk communities.

Timber interests funded a successful $2.9 million media campaign to push the initiative through Congress, and the media have continued to mischaracterize the core safety and environmental issues while fueling the hysteria over dangerous fires. The looming threat to old-growth posed by the Healthy (i.e. Stealthy) Forests Initiative received improved coverage, however, on June 8, 2006 in the *Washington Post*. The *Post* reported that bids were being accepted by the Forest Service for a precedent-setting 350-acre timber sale in an Oregon roadless area that had burned in the 2002 "Biscuit" fire. The sale pitted wilderness conservation against the worst of the Bush administration's forest management policies, including both Healthy Forests and the Bush administration's roadless rule, which Oregon Governor Ted Kulongoski actively opposed. This roadless area timber sale was a frightening development that threatened oldgrowth forests everywhere, including in the North Cascades.

The more things change, the more they stay the same—or so the saying goes.

6

The North Cascades Scenic Highway

To experience travel in the North Cascades wilderness is a realization that natural landscapes are where humans can reaffirm an innate awareness and appreciation for the ecological complexities of plant and animal communities in which we hold a lifelong membership. Traveling across North Cascades terrains dictates that we will adhere to the rules imposed on us by forest, slope, and glacier. There is a universality to the human living experience in this landscape, for it transcends time and culture.

—Bob Mierendorf, National Park Service archaeologist
From "Who Walks on the Ground," in
Impressions of the North Cascades (1996)

From Feet to Wheels

FOR MILLENNIA, FEET HAVE FOUND their way through the Cascades simply by placing one in front of the other, dodging glaciers, ramparts, impenetrable thickets, and chasms. Wheels, on the other hand, must have a route, a way through. But there must first be surveyors and maps.

The Northwest Boundary Survey teams of the 1860s drew maps that for a century were unsurpassed. Map details that lay some distance from the international boundary were seriously flawed, yet the work remains invaluable historically. A summary map of Washington Territory published in 1866 shows a "Reported Trail" up the "East Fork Skagit River" (Cascade River) that somehow got through a large area of white space to the Methow River east of the crest, yet missed the Stehekin River. A trail ran up the Methow to a dead end in a "Gold Mine Area" somewhat above the confluence with the Chewuch River. Farther south a trail crossed from the Twisp River to the Stehekin River, which was reached a bit up-valley from Lake Chelan. No names were given along the trail's route, but it fit the line of War Creek, Lake Juanita, and Boulder Creek. A "Reported Trail" also proceeded up the Stehekin and through another large white space where Glacier Peak was conspicuously absent, to the "Sauk River" (actually the Suiattle River). That seemed to represent, as there doubtless was, a Native American trail from Stehekin to the Suiattle via Agnes Creek and Sulphur Creek. In fact, archaeologists believe that Native American travel between the Stehekin and the Skagit River via Cascade Pass may have occurred as long ago as nine thousand years. There were other trails, of course, which did not appear on these maps. North Cascades National Park archaeologist Bob Mierendorf wrote recently that "indigenous bands or groups from north, west and east of the northern Cascades traveled through the . . . area, procuring tool stone and gathering some of the many subsistence resources along the way." Vast areas were also trailless. Thus the exploits of Henry Custer and his team of boundary surveyors, said Mierendorf, "must have mirrored the experiences of travel parties that for millennia penetrated the mountainous Cascade interior."

With a vision toward introducing the wheel to this rugged wilderness, the Washington Legislature in 1893 earmarked the new state's very first highway appropriation, $20,000 for a road across the North Cascades. Descriptions of two routes were published. The February–March 1973 issue of *The Wild Cascades* quoted one: the road was to extend "From the north fork of the Nooksack River and Glacier Creek, by the Pass north of Mount Baker . . . thence to Marcus, County of Stevens, on the Columbia." Never mind that there is no pass to eastern Washington anywhere near Mount Baker. The December 1962 issue of *The Wild Cascades* quoted the other route. The Cascade crossing was to consist of: (1) "a trail from the summit of the Cascade Mountains, connecting with the Methow road, and reaching to the Skagit River"; (2) "improvement of present trail up the Skagit River from Goodall to Ruby Creek"; and (3) "a wagon road from the present wagon road on the Methow [near Mazama], to the summit of the Cascades [Harts Pass], there connecting with a road leading to the Skagit." Those acquainted with the geography of the mountains today may find these descriptions amusing, yet it's pleasing to recall how wild and unknown the North Cascades were not much more than a century ago.

By 1895 the legislature had learned a little more about the country, but still envisioned a road "between Marble Mount, Skagit county, and the confluence of the Twitsp [sic] and Methow river, Okanogan county." The state road commissioners were directed to "examine the route up the Cascade river and over Skagit [Cascade] pass; the route via North Fork of Thunder Creek [that would be problematic] and the route via State Creek." A field party found the

"Twitsp pass, down Bridge Creek, up the Stehekin river, over Cascade pass" route to be "the shortest and most feasible and practicable." The road commissioners' report of 1896 is even more amusing. It says work proceeded from spring through fall, from a number of camps, on a forty-foot-wide roadway, though confessing that "only four feet of the road bed could be graded where heavy excavation was necessary." It also boasted that "The time between Cascade Pass and Marble Mount, after the road was constructed, was six hours; whereas, prior to construction, it required two days." From Cascade Pass to Marblemount in six hours! The horse that could do such a gallop would be quite a horse, considering the conditions of such a supposed road. Subsequent travelers detected little evidence of any work at all. A less dubitable construction project for 1896 was that of Merritt Field, the Stehekin settler and hotel-keeper who built a road "12 miles up the Stehekin River."

Well to the south, the construction of other cross-Cascade roads on more practical and useful lines stilled enthusiasm for the far-north route, but a rural-dominated legislature continued the fantasizing that is the soul of pioneering. In 1922 a reconnaissance was made through Cascade and Twisp Passes via the Stehekin Valley. The 1923 legislature ordered the building of a road to "connect Marblemount and Gilbert's Cabin on Cascade River and to make so much of the distance passable for light wagons or light auto travel." A 1932 survey recommended a route from Winthrop over Washington Pass, down to the Stehekin, and over Cascade Pass, but said Granite Creek was better in terms of cost and alignment.

The Cascade River road received particular attention. Funds from the federal Public Works Administration and Civilian Conservation Corps improved the ancient "wagon road" (actually, a trail) up the river as far as Sibley Creek, attained in the 1930's. In 1939 the state legislature adopted a Mine-to-Market Road Act, appropriating 50-percent matching funds to such counties as had been hornswoggled by "miners"; the money was allocated by a state commission. Between October 1, 1946, and September 30, 1948, the commission approved "extension Cascade River Road 7.652 miles, grading, surfacing, bridges." In 1950–52, funds were voted for "Cascade River Extension 1.245 miles, grade, surface, and four log bridges." Skagit County thereby extended a crude truck road to Mineral Park, and in 1947, up the steep step into the hanging trough of the North Fork Cascade River, and on to the Johnsburg mine in the side of Mount Johannesburg—so named because the North Cascades had been predicted to match the mineral output of South Africa. From this spot, a few yards short of one very old Gilbert's Cabin, the next push took the road steeply up and across the climax avalanche slopes of Forbidden Peak to the Valumine claims—a stock-selling vaudeville.

For those who must know, the crossing, in whole or in part, in this or that variant or alternative, was variously referred to over the years of its consideration as: the Skagit River Road from Marblemount to Barron near Harts Pass (in 1912); the Methow–Barron Road from Barron to Mazama, Twisp, and Pateros on the Columbia River (also in 1912); the Roosevelt Highway from Marblemount to Barron, Twisp, and Pateros (1922); the Methow Valley Highway from Pateros to Twisp and Barron (1924); the Cascade Wagon Road from Marblemount to Cascade and Twisp Passes and Twisp (also in 1924); the Cascade Pass Route from Marblemount to Cascade and Washington Passes and Mazama (1947); the Rainy Pass Route from Marblemount to Granite Creek, Washington Pass, and Mazama (again, 1947); and the Harts Pass Route from Marblemount to Harts Pass and Mazama (also in 1947).

The Cascade Wagon Road remained on maps into the 1960s and beyond, sometimes qualified as "under construction" or "proposed," but on many maps shown as wide-open to tourists. Early in the 1970s, on a fine day in May, this historian plugged steps in snow up the road to the foot of Johannesburg. On his return he met a couple in vacation togs, Easterners doing the West. As he jumped down from the snowbank onto the snowfree roadway where their car was stopped, they held up a gasoline-company road map and complained bitterly that they had motel reservations for the night in Chelan and were going to be late. "What do you mean, there's no road over Cascade Pass?" they chimed. "I suppose you're going to tell us there's no car ferry on Lake Chelan?"

In 1945 the legislature authorized another survey and in following years weighed the alternatives. In 1961 the route was officially designated North Cross-State Highway, Primary State Highway No. 20, and the choices narrowed on where to put it. Cascade Pass was at very long last judged infeasible for reasons self-evident to every realist who had walked there over the previous century. Harts Pass was also ruled out for its rough terrain, steepness, and high elevation. Rainy Pass was rated "the most desirable of any route considered. A connecting road from this route can be projected from a point between Rainy and Washington Passes to give access to the Stehekin Basin and the head of Lake Chelan."

Members of the State Highway Commission, who purportedly knew as much about the area as the dark side of the moon, were conducted by the engineers on a horseback inspection in 1956. By special invitation the party included a Methow rancher who had never left the shade of his apple trees on the valley floor but who often had wondered what was up there behind the ridges. Thus did George Zahn enter North Cascades history.

Farmerpower and Pork

Grant McConnell's delineation of the potential power of a small, cohesive, persistent group (such as was to become the NCCC, whose formation he urged so strenuously) derived from his research into how a handful of farmers had dictated policy to federal agencies, Congress, and the American nation. His respect for farmerpower is supported by the monument at Washington Pass:

> So that the passer-by may know of a friend who helped him
> on his way the Washington State Legislature
> directed that this monument be erected in honor of
> GEORGE D. ZAHN
> 1897–1971
> Whose lifelong career of public service in many capacities found its
> final role as a member and chairman of the Washington State
> Highway Commission and its fondest fulfillment in this North
> Cascades Highway for which he worked so hard and long.
> Dedicated at the opening of the NORTH CASCADES HIGHWAY
> September 2, 1972

An associate said of Zahn, "He was continually able to get appropriations from various public sources. . . . He pretty near became the Highway Commission."

In 1942 the cow-milkers of the west-side Skagit and the hay-rakers of the east-side Methow-Okanogan formed the Cascade Highway Association, reorganized in 1948 as the North Cross-State Highway Association. The name changed in 1972 to North Cascades Highway Association. Around the flag rallied the State Highway Department, ever eager to flex its bulldozers; the State Highway Commission, where engineers and the rural legislators who dominated state government met to scratch each others' backs; the Chambers of Commerce, ever eager to boost commerce; and the U.S. Forest Service, which sought more roads everywhere to extend intensive management. Senator Scoop Jackson was content to get out in front of this parade—at the same time he was waiting for the NCCC to get up a conflicting parade.

A Forest Highway Study completed in 1959 was the basis for determining that construction from the west side up to Washington Pass would be done by Forest Highway funds, the construction contracts awarded and supervised by the Bureau of Public Roads, Forest Highway Division (U.S. Forest Service). The location and construction on the east side from Mazama to Washington Pass would be by the state Department of Highways, using a combination of Motor Vehicle and Federal Aid funds. The total construction of the 63.5 roadless miles from Diablo Dam to Mazama would be split approximately equally between Forest Highway and State Highway funds, the latter largely federal in origin, the former entirely so. The swift and steady flow of tax money from

Washington City to Washington State, whether for weaponry, medical research, or just plain old-fashioned pork, was assured by the Jackson–Magnuson dynamic duo in the U.S. Senate. The final decision for the Rainy Pass route was agreed upon in December 1962 by the two agencies, and expenditures were authorized for twenty-two miles of construction. Ultimately thirty-five contracts were let, worth nearly $24 million.

The highway drums of the promoters began to beat in the late 1950s, getting louder each year:

> The continuing demand for the North Cross-State route is the result of the dreams of wealth that could be taken out of the vast primitive region. The road would open up . . . minerals . . . timber . . . bringing out the cattle and produce of the interior via a direct route. . . .
>
> —State Highway Department

> Such a highway would open up vast amounts of over-ripe timber resources which would yield an annual harvest of approximately forty million board feet of timber. Vast proven mineral resources could be economically mined.
>
> —Mount Vernon Chamber of Commerce

The NCCC commented in a 1957 resolution:

> It would be adverse to the long-range public interest to build trans-Cascade highways between Stevens and Harts Passes or between Harts Pass and the Canadian border . . . [we] request that data on engineering and economic feasibility of proposed trans-Cascade highways be reviewed by the state and the U.S. Forest Service with consideration given to comparative losses in intangible scientific and wilderness-recreation values and that these data be made available in public hearings.

Conservationists had expressed support for a Glacier Peak Wilderness that would include Granite Creek. Thus the Council requested that the highway project not proceed prior to preparation of what amounted to an "environmental impact statement"—a term that did not yet exist because the National Environmental Policy Act (ironically, another of Senator Jackson's parades) did not exist until 1969, becoming effective in 1970. Had that legislation been on the books in the early 1960s, the highway would still have been receiving the mature consideration it deserved until well after the great gob of national butter it required had sizzled away in the heat of Vietnam.

The NCCC preferred, as the least of evils, the Harts Pass Parkway proposed in 1959 by Congressman Thomas M. Pelly—not from a yearning to see machines in Canyon Creek, but because the Harts Pass route would intrude wheels through merely six miles of pristine wilderness rather than forty-one. In keeping with the principle of the as-yet-unborn concept of an impact statement, the Council wanted five routes besides Washington Pass and Harts Pass included in a study. The NCCC and its allies were brushed aside like so many

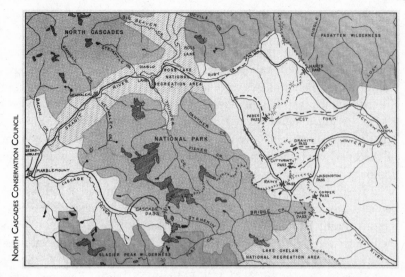

North Cascades Highway routing alternatives in 1968.

no-see-ums; in another decade they would be upsized to deerflies, even elk flies. But as the administration of Interstate Eisenhower was followed by that of Moonwalker Kennedy, objections to the enlarged dominion of wheels and exploding hydrocarbons went unheard. As had been so from the invention of the wheel, the Engineers were esteemed as the spearhead of civilization; the NCCC was considered the spearhead of the other thing.

In October 1964 bulldozers from the Methow crept up the hideous scar blasted in the magnificent rock wall of Liberty Bell to the summit of Washington Pass, separated by only thirty miles from the bulldozers churning through the wilderness from Ross Reservoir. The following June the ballroom of the Elks Club in Mount Vernon was filled for the annual meeting of the North Cross-State Highway Association. George Zahn was there, and a host of rural legislators, farmers, and small-town merchants. Engineer "Buzz" Matoon reported a pioneer road would be completed to Washington Pass on or about August 24. Governor Albert Rosellini commended the association for its determination to build what would be the "most scenic highway anywhere in this country." A *Seattle Times* reporter flew clear off the enthusiasm scale, calling the views "the most beautiful in the world."

In 1966 a new governor, Daniel J. Evans, hiked the route and remarked to companions, including NCCC's Polly Dyer, that the highway plainly lacked the economic importance claimed by ranchers, loggers, and miners, that it was purely a tourist attraction. Yet at the 1968 Congressional hearings, where he presented his plan for a Pickets National Park, Evans took a swipe at the competing proposal for a larger park which would encompass the highway by saying

"We have found in some other instances that there are some restrictions on highway use that have been somewhat troublesome." What instances, what restrictions, and how "troublesome" was unexplained. He and Senator Jackson yoked up to ensure that the highway would be kept free from interference by California and Pennsylvania troublemakers, and remain under firm control of the state, which is to say, the highway cabal. Some solace was provided by the 1967 Legislature, which passed a Scenic Highways Act that gave bureaucrats other than the engineers a voice—a very small voice, however, lost in the roar of the bulldozers, the orations of politicians, and the cheers of chambers of commerce.

In 1968 Governor Evans led his own parade, a caravan of four-wheel-drive vehicles, the length of the pilot road, culminating in "the historic meeting of the jeeps" at Rainy Pass, where he addressed a throng of three thousand onlookers, including two U.S. representatives and a senator. An NCCC director disguised in dark glasses and fake whiskers reported the largest massing of four-by-fours he'd ever seen, the most WALLACE FOR PRESIDENT bumper stickers, and so many Stars and Bars that he felt a patriotic urge to don the Union Blue and reopen the discussion adjourned at Appomattox Courthouse. Evans vowed that if re-elected he would guarantee opening of the highway by 1972. The

North Cascades Highway opening (1968), with ribbon-cutting Congressmen Tom Foley (left) and Lloyd Meeds (right), Senator Magnuson (center), and Governor Dan Evans looking on.

three thousand onlookers, save one, whooped and hollered, "Ya-hoo!"

On September 2, 1972, ceremonies were held at Winthrop, Newhalem, and Sedro Woolley. A man of the cloth prayed God to "grant that the wheels of commerce and avarice of man be kept within bounds to please Thee." Evans declaimed, "I can't believe that the National Park Service would allow the development of copper mining in this beautiful park," a statement that surprised those listeners who knew that no such mine had been proposed. The Camp Parsons Boy Scout was probably recalling the mining threat within the Glacier Peak Wilderness, which was outside the park.

In the summer of 1972, the Irate Birdwatcher spent a month in the Sierra Nevada. At Minaret Summit he missed by a day a press conference held there by the governor of California to affirm the state's unalterable opposition to the Mammoth Highway sought by farmers and ranchers as a cross-Sierra route from Owens Valley to the Central Valley. The governor forcefully declared that California took enormous pride in the 160-mile spine of alpine wilderness extending unbroken from Tioga Pass to Walker Pass. The wheelfree wilderness was, said governor Ronald Reagan, central to the state's character. The sentiments were not his, of course. As always, he was reading a script, in this case written by Ike Livermore, a High Sierra horsepacker, Sierra Clubber, Republican power, and Reagan's Secretary of Resources who worked to kill the proposal. Dan Evans could have used an Ike Livermore to wordsmith a little.

Words Never Swallowed

The state Highway Department magazine editorialized that traffic on the new highway "will enter a cathedral of quiet beauty. . . . It will pass beneath towering sentinels of granite which command awe. . . . It will ford rivers and creeks which are as pure and untamed as the virgin country through which the highway passes. . . ." A letter to the *Seattle Times* responded, "Highwaymen simply don't understand. They think 'traffic' can 'enter a cathedral of quiet beauty,' that a highway can pass through 'virgin country.'"

The National Society of Professional Engineers (possibly humankind's second oldest profession) listed the highway as one of the six greatest achievements of 1972. Richard E. Taylor of Aspen, Colorado, wrote to *Civil Engineer*, the society's official publication. His letter referred to the photograph published in the magazine and noted "the ugly scar eight times wider than the actual highway, and the excavation waste falling directly into what used to be a virgin mountain stream. . . . The North Cascades Highway," he said, "would easily make the list of this century's ill-conceived and poorly executed public works. . . ."

To glance back to the origins of the highway-to-be, the first projected use was by the military, who intended to gallop along it should the opportunity arise for another Sand Creek or Wounded Knee encounter. Then there was gold to be dug, except that there turned out not to be much to speak of. Never daunted, as the highway neared completion its boosters spoke of two thousand mining claims that would be able to truck ore to the Tacoma Smelter. Twenty years after completion, the only ore shipments made were in the rucksacks of rockhounds. The Tacoma Smelter was defunct. Granted, the highway surely has carried gold for entrepreneurs who peddle to the stock market. A 1971 issue of *Western Mining News* reported that

> Completion of the North Cross State Highway would afford year-around access to the property of Western Gold Mining, Inc., officials said this week. They said the firm's mining claims in the Slate Creek Mining District west of Harts Pass . . . have been accessible only during summer months. Western Gold Shares were accepted for trading on the Spokane Stock Exchange last week.

The stock purchasers, simple folks who signed their names on checks, apparently failed to ask how a highway over Washington Pass would melt the late-October through early-July snowpack from Harts Pass.

Another benefit of the route touted early on was to speed cattle drives from ranges of the Okanogan to butcher shops of Seattle, eliminating the detour south to Snoqualmie Pass; but the railroads put the drovers out of business. Another highway advantage: it would "encourage settlers to take up homes." White spaces on the map were described as ideal homesteads by city-bound newspapermen who were unaware that many of the projected homesites were as white on the ground as on the maps, some of them being glaciers.

The Forest Service trumpeted the existence of vast stands of over-ripe timber; but when the road was open and it was time to put up or shut up, the rangers lamely admitted that forests of the highway route were by species, elevation, and terrain mostly sub-economic. They continued to hunger for the scattered small groves of actually valuable trees and embarked on a program of "sanitation" sales, "danger" sales, and even "aesthetic" sales, as when in 1973 the messy, wasteful jackstraw left from an avalanche was proposed to be tidied up. Very quickly, though, the rangers were made to understand that tourists from Iowa never could be taught to appreciate the beauty of clearcuts and "sanitation," and were sure to return from vacation to vote "NO" on Pinchot and "YES" on Muir. Further, the valleys followed by the highway are too narrow to permit the Forest Service subterfuge of beauty strips—treed buffers that create the illusion that a forest is out there. So much for the "annual harvest of forty million board feet."

H.C. Chriswell, supervisor of Mount Baker National Forest and avid back-country skier, prepared a map showing a cross-mountain chain of world-class resorts. In 1992 just one of these (region-class only, the snow being sloppier than the powder of Colorado and Utah) remained a bare possibility. However, that site was not opened up by the highway, situated as it is on Sandy Butte, which has had road access via the Methow Valley Highway since the 1920s. In 1993 the developer took note of the economic reality of the situation, and the last of Chriswell's soap-bubble visions popped.

The highway was proclaimed a boon to agriculture, cutting travel time of hay trucks two hours from Winthrop to Sedro Woolley. The westside dairymen would save, said Zahn, "at least $5 a ton on hay." Skeptics asked if there were sufficient bales of hay in the Methow and Okanogan and cows in the Skagit to justify a $24 million construction cost. As things have turned out, hay trucks are seen on the highway so rarely that sightings cause as much excitement as among birders when a snowy owl is reported in Bellevue.

Much has been made of the time saved by lopping off one hundred miles of travel. But that saving applies only to those Winthropites with an uncontrollable itch to experience the bright lights of Sedro Woolley, and vice versa. From the center of "Puget Sound City," the Washington Pass route is only thirty-six miles shorter than the Stevens Pass route, measured from the same start to the same finish. Yet the saving of miles, and consequently time, is illusory. From Bellevue to Twisp (and thus to all the trails of that valley and the lower Methow), the Snoqualmie Pass–Swauk Pass route is quicker than Washington Pass by a half-hour. From Bellevue to Winthrop (and thus to the trails of the Chewuch and upper Methow), Washington Pass is quicker by a half-hour. Where travel time is concerned, the highway is much ado about very little.

Long before the highway was completed, every claim to economic benefits used to justify the $24 million spent had basically been thrown out of court. The boondoggle (as viewed by the NCCC) had to shift to a totally different defense: aesthetics. It was important because it was pretty.

How Beautiful Is It?

The *mentalité* that once hailed the North Cascades as the world's richest storehouse of minerals now extolled the North Cascades Highway as "the most beautiful mountain drive in North America—and probably the world." Was this the hyperbole of cupidity? A prominent expounder may sell tour guides to the route and also deal in real estate. Or is it the hyperbole of ignorance—of the damage done by the Going-to-the-Sun Highway in Glacier National Park; the Owens Valley highway beneath the Sierra's east scarp; the Jackson Hole highway of the Tetons; the Icefields Parkway in the Canadian Rockies; the Richardson Highway and the Anchorage–Denali Highway in Alaska?

In the state of Washington, the Mount Baker Highway isn't exactly chopped liver, and neither are the highways around Mount Rainier and at Hurricane Ridge in the Olympics. The Stevens Pass Highway sets the tourists to goggling when they pass beneath the Nordwand of Mount Index.

The North Cascades Highway surely has fine scenery. However, it does not reveal to motorists very many glories previously denied them. Most of the best scenery is from Marblemount to Ross Dam, which has been open to roadside (and before that, railroad) viewing, or Seattle City Light tour boat viewing, since the 1920s. The stretch from Rainy Pass over Washington Pass and down Early Winters Creek was newly opened to road-views, creating what many conservationists considered to be an obscene highway gouge in Early Winters Creek, a valley formerly as lovely as its name, and outright "vandalism" culminating on the scarface beneath Liberty Bell Mountain.

If wilderness were restored from near Thunder Arm on Diablo Reservoir, through Granite Creek to Rainy Pass, over Washington Pass and down Early Winters Creek to the Methow Valley, the rights, privileges, and pleasures of the motoring public would hardly be infringed. To the contrary, they would probably be augmented. Tourists do not invent their tours. They go where they are led. Many might enjoy an even fuller, richer, happier vacation if for the North Cascades Highway they substituted the following itinerary:

> Drive I-5 to Bellingham and turn east on the Mount Baker Highway. See North America's "iciest volcano, pound for pound," and Mount Shuksan, "the most beautiful mountain in America." Don't forget the camera.
>
> Backtrack south on I-5, turn east up the Skagit Valley to Marblemount, Newhalem, and the overlook above Diablo Reservoir. Glimpse the Pickets from the road. Take the tour boat up Diablo beneath the wall of Colonial Peak to Ross Dam and a walk along Ross Lake. All this was tourist-accessible before 1972.
>
> Backtrack to Marblemount and sidetrip east up the Cascade River to the stunning vista of the glaciers of Eldorado Peak and the high-walled valley leading to the pass (where certainly no road should be).
>
> Return to Marblemount, turn south to Darrington, where the glaciers of Whitehorse hang heavy over the large heads of cows grazing in pastures—very Alps-like. Drive the Mountain Loop Highway (expected to reopen after major flood damage but yet to be repaired by mid-2006) up the Sauk River to the avalanche-busy north wall of Big Four Mountain; proceed west to "Nanga Pilchuck," and a side-trip up that mountain's view road to panoramas of Three Fingers and much more.
>
> Turn south on I-5, then east on State Route 2 (the Stevens Pass Highway), close under the fearsome walls of Mount Index, Mount Baring, and Gunn Peak to Stevens Pass, and descend through the granite slot of Tumwater Canyon to the Columbia River.

Drive north along the river to Chelan, take a side-trip up the Chelan Butte road to enormous views of Lake Chelan and the Columbia River. Take a one or two-day carless break on the *Lady of the Lake* to Stehekin. Continue north along the Columbia and turn up the Methow Valley past Twisp and Winthrop to the head of the enormous glacial trough, ascend the spooky road around Dead Horse Point to Harts Pass and, in July, continue upward to the road-end on the side of Slate Peak and approximately a thousand times more scenery than is to be seen from the North Cascades Scenic Highway.

Return to Winthrop, turn up the Chewuch River, climb from the valley to a lonesome plateau of subalpine forest and meadow-marsh, then descend to the awesome trough of the Sinlahekin Valley, magnificently gouged by an enormous bulge of ice exported from the Pleistocene ice cap in Canada; cross the steppe ridges to the Okanogan Valley, and so home to Pittsburgh.

This itinerary would give a tourist a vision of the North Cascades so vast as to make the North Cascades Highway seem a peek through a keyhole. Further, to the satisfaction of Chambers of Commerce, our travelers will have poured into the Gross State Product as much or more for motels, gas, cheeseburgers, root beer, ice cream, postcards, and souvenir pillows. And, to the gratification of those who love the earth for what it is, not for what profit they can get from it, we will have helped reconstitute what was dissected by a needless highway, what was once, and in other ways still is, one of the grandest wildernesses in America.

North Cascades Highway scar below the pinnacles of Liberty Bell Mountain and Early Winter Spires (ca. 1967).

Joe Collins, North Cascades Conservation Council

NEAR-TERM REALISM

Until a future National Wilderness Restoration Act eliminates the North Cascades Scenic Highway altogether, a holding action could minimize additional damage. The more prominent highway corridor detractors are four in number: Seattle City Light (subject of another chapter), the National Park Service, the Forest Service, and the State Highway Department.

To take them in reverse order, the major threat posed by the highwaymen is their anxiety to keep the highway open all winter. When the route was completed, the State Highways director declared, "We most certainly did not spend $24 million to build a highway that is automatically closed because of winter." "Automatically" is the wrong word. The avalanche chutes are so many and so busy they would require dozens of snowsheds that could easily cost far more than the initial construction, and would not likely be built because they could not pass muster environmentally. The highway always will be shut down by normal winter conditions, notwithstanding that rascal, climate change. However, the worst that State Highways can do is bad enough, keeping the route open as late in the year and opening it as early in the year as is humanly and bureaucratically possible. The highway is the quintessential expression of engineering machismo. The NCCC has never been able to pry loose the data on the cost of keeping the highway open late and reopening it early. The state engineers have been known to churn out figures that seemingly could not stand an audit but never are audited and which the Legislature and the press willingly accept. Independent engineers estimated once that in an average snowfall year each and every car that crosses the highway after early November and before mid-June costs taxpayers at least $100. Perhaps a warmer climate will make keeping it open more affordable?

The 1984 Washington Wilderness Act inscribed on the map the words *North Cascades Scenic Highway* and a corridor of 87,810 acres, but it provided no protection of any kind to anything from anybody—except insofar as conservationists could employ the term "scenic" as a bat to beat on the heads of the State Highway Department, the Forest Service, and the Park Service. All three apparently possess either hard skulls or brains already jellied or both, as illustrated in 1991–1992 when four hundred thousand cubic yards of rock to resurface Highway 20 were mined from beside the "Scenic Highway" at the headwaters of Bridge Creek. Another example: several weeks after an epic rainstorm in October 2003, a massive rockslide let loose in the Skagit gorge just above Newhalem and buried the highway under two to three million cubic yards of rubble. The engineers would spend several years clearing the way and reshaping the mountainside, creating an enormous and vertical scar that ought not to have been allowed. At least one voice in the National Park Service quietly shook his head as the road-builders' dream unfolded. "Overkill," he said.

The Forest Service, having abandoned the attempt to teach the public the beauties of logging, took another path to the hearts of tourists. The interpretation center it built at Washington Pass, site of the famed "million dollar outhouse," did too much environmental damage to sensitive terrain for too little value to visitors who would probably be better served by a location at the edge of the Methow Valley, at Early Winters Creek Campground (as urged by the NCCC), where a museum already exists. For the ridges above the highway and the Cedar Creek Valley that properly belong in genuine wilderness, but were excluded from the Washington Wilderness Act by Congressman Morrison, the agency has encouraged helicopter-supported huts for the super-wealthy winter skier, the autumn goathead hunter, and the summertime collector of slide shows and videos.

The Park Service's June 1986 Development Concept Plan for the North Cascades Highway (and Cascade Pass) had one feature to which the NCCC took particular exception: a new visitor center in Newhalem. Marblemount, and not Sedro Woolley, Concrete, or Newhalem, said NCCC, should be the western gateway station. Located at the confluence of the Skagit and Cascade Rivers, Marblemount seemed an ideal location for the Park Service to interact with, even educate or inspire, those heading into the wilderness. As it happened, the North Cascades Visitor Center was built down a side road in Newhalem. Unlike the Sedro Woolley station, it is not shared with the Forest Service. That might have been acceptable, yet the very existence of the highway strengthens the position of the Park Service frontcountry rangers whose encouraged skills are principally people-pleasing, not land-protecting. Stehekin deserves and has a modest center of its own, although a park superintendent once frankly expressed his contempt for the importance of Stehekin Valley, saying "The highway, *that's* where the numbers are," as if speaking from the grave of Mather.

When the world supply of petroleum dwindles near exhaustion, as it is scheduled to do in the lifetimes of people now driving Winnebagos and SUVs, perhaps nobody will laugh when the suggestion is renewed to convert the North Cascades Highway to a bikeway, with separated lanes for boots and hooves. Well before that, the valleys of Early Winters Creek and Granite Creek should be formally designated as wilderness, if not transferred to the National Park Service. The wilderness boundary in these valleys should leave space beside the concrete for interpretive stations and trailhead facilities—that much and no more. Why so? For the very reason there was (and still is) need for a Wilderness Act: to prevent multiple-use managers from taking the first inch up the valley walls, realizing that inches inevitably grow to feet, then miles.

Until the ribbon of pavement that divides a wilderness is rolled up and put away, by all means, enjoy your drive.

North Cascades National Park Complex

7

The North Cascades National Park

Somewhere between Leatherstocking and Frankenstein, trees and timber, wilderness and bewilderment, Americans needed a moral compass to understand where they should go and what they could become without losing every vestige of who they once had been.

—Kim Heacox
An American Idea: The Making of the National Parks (2001)

THE COMPLEX

THE 1968 NORTH CASCADES ACT did not simply establish a park, but a "park complex"—the North Cascades National Park Complex—comprising two park units and two national recreation areas. The north and south units of the park proper are separated by the Skagit River—or what's left of it (Patrick Goldsworthy once called it a "ghost-river," its flow having been diverted through a tunnel en route to the Gorge Powerhouse). Both units are administered under provisions of the National Park Act of 1916. The two companion areas—the national recreation areas—are also looked after by the National Park Service under the same 1916 law, except for some very minor reservations specified by Congress in 1968. Yet in Stehekin, Chelan, Chelan County, and elsewhere, a few observers have labored under a mysterious delusion, stridently propagandized, that a national recreation area is much less rigorously protected by law than a national park. In the North Cascades, that is clearly not the case.

Some members of the public and the press, not fully clear in their minds on the difference between a national park, national recreation area, national forest, and Disneyland, may have been led down the garden path. Some within the National Park Service have stumbled down a similar path. The NCCC has always disagreed with the notion that national recreation areas administered by the park service are somehow less deserving of the protection that is bestowed on a park. It was at last officially joined in that judgment by the National Park Service itself. Once the official determination was made, there was no room left for serious argument to the contrary, which does not mean that all argument ceased. Photographs from space, we know, did not bring about the dissolution of the Flat Earth Society.

Of the two following chapters of this book, the first (Chapter 8) treats Ross Lake National Recreation Area (NRA), where the main struggle has been one of the NCCC, Run Out Skagit Spoilers (ROSS), and their allies versus Seattle City Light, the big city's publicly-owned municipal power company. The next, Chapter 9, concerns the Lake Chelan NRA where the conflict has been, and continues to be, between the national public interest, commonly represented by the NCCC and its allies, and the local private interests, often represented by the Chelan County Commissioners, the Sons of the Pioneers (more or less), the now-defunct Wise Use movement, and, all too often, the National Park Service.

The present chapter, however, considers the park proper, with a closer look at the stewards and administrators; the trammeling by anachronistic frontiering; the restoration to the public domain of lands preempted under ancient mining laws; various attempts by the National Park Service to plan for the future; and the return of parkland to wilderness. To better understand what the park once was—and was always meant to be—it helps to understand how conservation and conflict have shaped the complex as a whole.

We begin with leadership, and the lack thereof.

SMOKE AND MIRRORS

The little fish have big fish
Upon their backs to bite 'em.
Big fish have still bigger fish
And so *ad infinitum*.

It's no secret that many politicians blow smoke, then watch mirrors to see which way it's going. Bureaucrats watch politicians to be ready to jump, to avoid getting bit. Though it is true that the engine that propels the ship of state is the mass movement of people whose names never appear in the newspapers, the people navigating the ship, the big-wigs, are generally the only ones identified in books. We credit them with making history. The rule of thumb is that wherever the ship sails, by whatever means and for whatever reason, well, 'twas the captain's ship and that's the story.

Although this book is not animated by that view of history, a capsule history of the North Cascades must, by necessity, omit much naming of bureaucrats below the park superintendent level, as well as politicians of the executive branch of government below the Cabinet level (and those of the legislative branch altogether—a whole other empire). The good work of many is in no way meant to be minimized as we present the merest thumbnail sketches of the men who had the con of the ship since 1968 and, briefly, the directions in which they steered. It can be said up front that some were not particularly well suited, by background, to the idea of national parks as wilderness.

The North Cascades National Park Complex was signed into law just a month before the 1968 election. In his presidential campaign, *candidate* Richard M. Nixon hailed natural resources as "the growth stocks of America . . . the last place for Americans to be miserly." As president, Nixon appointed as his Interior Secretary a loose cannon from Alaska, Governor Walter Hickel, the quintessential Barbecuer. Terrifying though he was to conservationists, his actions often belied his threats. But that didn't matter. He was so unpredictably eccentric as to oppose the Southeast Asia War, and thereby infuriate Nixon, that in 1971 Hickel was replaced with Maryland Congressman and head of the national Republican Party, Rogers C.B. Morton, a designated fence-mender. That assignment was not easy, particularly with Nixon slashing appropriations from the Land and Water Conservation Fund. The Fund, established in 1965 as the repository for royalties from offshore oil and gas leases, was expected to be a perpetual and dependable source of funds for the ongoing acquisition of lands for federal, state, and local parks. Nixon as much as said, "No new parks while I'm in charge." By 1973 control of Interior had been stripped from Morton by the White House cabal, better known as the Watergate gang, and Morton opted to resign.

Nixon expressed further contempt for the Park Service by firing its Director since 1964, George Hartzog, a career ranger and self-taught lawyer from South Carolina, replacing him in March 1973 with Ronald H. Walker, a Pasadena insurance salesman. Ironically, the appointment ultimately would lead to perhaps Nixon's greatest contribution to wildland conservation. Hartzog, we should point out, earned some credit for the addition of sixty-eight new units to the National Park System, most of them small historic sites and recreation areas, during his nine-year tenure. The larger jewels of the time included Canyonlands (1964), the Guadalupe Mountains (1966), and of course, the Redwoods and North Cascades, all of which are more rightfully attributed to others. However, Hartzog's head had repeatedly been demanded by both the Sierra Club and Friends of the Earth for promoting tourism at the expense of wilderness. His 1988 apologia, *Battling for the National Parks*, in which he claimed to have supported the North Cascades National Park, was derided by those who were there twenty years before. Fiery denunciations by Senator Frank Church of Hartzog's wilderness plans finally made him too hot a potato and Walker was brought in, for the sake of change, if nothing else. Director Walker lacked experience in the field, which meant that the Assistant Secretary of the Interior, Nathaniel Reed, had to step into the daily fray of National Park politics, a role that Reed seemed to enjoy. Mike McCloskey visited Reed in his office several times finding him "on the phone with superintendents giving them directions." In the judgment of Patrick Goldsworthy, Reed's "agreement to correct weaknesses of Hartzog's proposals was one of the most significant and historic steps taken by any administration on behalf of the preservation of national park standards."

Prior to his appointment, Reed, who grew up on Jupiter Island in south Florida, had already established himself as a fighter who worked strenuously, and successfully, to protect the Everglades from a proposed airport outside Miami, as well as some misguided surface-water projects concocted by the Army Corps of Engineers. He later served prominently on the boards of the National Audubon Society and The Nature Conservancy, then founded 1000 Friends of Florida in 1986. In 2006, he was still serving as an honorary trustee with the Natural Resources Defense Council. In the 1970s, as Assistant Secretary of the Interior, Reed commented that

> [The American dream] has run aground on the natural limits of the earth. It has foundered on the shoals of the steadily emerging environmental crisis, a crisis broadly defined to include not only physical and biological factors, but the social consequences that flow from them. The American dream, so long an energizing force in our society, is withering. . . . The earth as a place to live has a limited amount of air, water, soil, minerals, space and other natural resources, and today we are pressing hard on our resource base. Man, rich or poor, is utterly dependent on his global life-support system.

Sardonic souls saw a serendipity in Nixon's dumping career ranger Hartzog, as if shaking up the bureaucracy with a Ron Walker might teach 'em a lesson. What Walker lacked in wherewithal, Reed made up for in political savvy, tenacity, and an honest conservation ethic.

Replacing Nixon, President Gerald Ford, who had once been a seasonal ranger at Yellowstone (in 1936), can be fondly remembered for a single half-hour of his more or less undistinguished later life. The bill for a new Alpine Lakes Wilderness between Mount Rainier and Glacier Peak received bipartisan support from the Washington Congressional delegation and easily passed both houses of Congress in 1976. The Forest Service, however, not content with having whittled the proposal to a size some 100,000 acres below a respectable minimum, successfully lobbied the Bureau of the Budget to recommend a veto. Governor Dan Evans, to his great credit, flew from his vacation spot in Europe to the White House carrying a complimentary copy of *The Alpine Lakes*, a full-color coffee-table book published by The Mountaineers. Obviously impressed by the images, Ford exclaimed, "It is such beautiful country! It must be saved!" In signing the bill to protect 305,400 acres of wilderness he gained absolution among conservationists for many of the sins of his pre-White House career in Congress. Governor Dan, meanwhile, also made quite an impression.

President Jimmy Carter, until near the end of his term, was not able to live up to the very high conservationist expectations that greeted him on inauguration day, at least not in the Lower Forty-Eight. He and his Interior Secretary, Cecil Andrus, oversaw the single most expansive day in the history of the National Park System on December 2, 1980, when lame-duck Carter—reminiscent of Teddy Roosevelt—signed the Alaska National Interest Lands Conservation Act (ANILCA), which put 104.3 million acres in national parks, wildlife refuges, and other protective units. The Wilderness Society called it "one of the most ambitious conservation initiatives ever enacted." It didn't come easily, of course. Decades of controversy over the fate of federal lands in Alaska eventually led to the 1978 withdrawal, by Andrus and Carter, of more than 100 million acres from multiple-use management. Of the total, 56 million acres were designated national monuments, an action the administration could take without the blessing of Congress. The *High Country News* called it "a classic Andrus power play." It turned the tables on Alaska Senator Ted Stevens and other wilderness opponents who "would need a bill to override Carter and Andrus' withdrawals." As a result, Congress was forced to take decisive action on the issue of wildland protections, native claims, and the development prospects for unprotected lands. Yet the ANILCA, so severely compromised on its way through Congress as to be less a victory than a promise, was described ten years later by The Wilderness Society as "the unfulfilled promise." In the 1990s the Society lamented that "many of the lands the law intended to protect remain under serious threats."

Still faltering since the start of the Nixon years, the National Park Service continued to drift downward. With the dramatic exception of ANILCA, additions to the park system were few under both Andrus and his National Parks Director, William J. Whalen, the former superintendent of Golden Gate National Recreation Area. Whalen was reportedly a principled manager, but after a tizzy with concessionaires in 1980, he too was outed. Had Carter been re-elected, perhaps he would have halted this downhill slide of the Park Service. We can at least speculate that, without Andrus, the story would have been far worse.

President Ronald Reagan, the master Barbecuer in the history of the nation, extinguished the fond belief that American political morality had risen above the greed of the Gilded Age. His first Interior Secretary, James Watt, did precisely what the boss wanted, but with such personal gusto that he served as a lightning rod, catching the hell that properly belonged to Reagan. Watt believed in a literal Second Coming and only wished Jesus would hurry up. By all appearances he *wanted* the Earth to be destroyed, and pending that Final Solution, did everything he could to ravage and waste the American environment, as well as the environmental movement, something he hated with a kind of passion that True Believers more commonly reserve for the Devil Himself.

After growing up on a Wyoming ranch, James Watt attended college, managed a law degree, and ultimately made his way to various political appointments in the Department of Interior under Nixon and Reagan. During the Carter years, he established and ran the Mountain States Legal Foundation in Colorado and worked to upend public land policies for the direct benefit of oil, gas, mining, logging, and ranching interests. As Reagan's fearless Interior Secretary, Watt fanned the flames of the emerging "Sagebrush Rebellion" against federal land protection in the early 1980s, while deeply slashing park and environmental programs within the agency. He made wholesale attempts to sell off public lands, proposed zero funding for new land acquisitions, and pursued long-term lease agreements for national park lands and wilderness areas for coal, oil, gas, and mineral development. Conservationists were infuriated and public resentment quickly rose to a rolling boil.

Watt had not been in office even a year when the Sierra Club and Friends of the Earth delivered 1.1 million petition signatures to Congress demanding his removal. But Watt kept at it, embarking on a massive coal-leasing program that offered companies dirt-cheap access to public lands in five western states, collecting public royalties of only a penny per ton on the coal extracted. While we can count our blessings that he did not directly harm the North Cascades in a significant way, he was certainly no inspiration to others in the agency who might have preferred to get something useful accomplished. Sufficiently disgusted, Congress finally halted his grand plan for coal leasing and pulled the funding in September 1983. The day after he lost the key Senate vote, Watt spoke to the U.S. Chamber of Commerce, at some point cracking a joke about the make up of his Coal Commission: "I have a black, a woman, two Jews and a cripple," he chirped. "And we have talent." With that, the camel's back was broken. Watt was forced to resign. Two weeks after he left, the U.S. invaded Grenada, and the *Washington Post* declared both Grenada and the Watt fiasco as two of the top ten news stories of the year.

Republicans unwilling to face the truth about Reagan's anti-environmental agenda shrugged off Watt as an aberration, a mistake that would quickly be corrected. Reagan's next Interior Secretary, William Patrick Clark, barely had time to review the files before leaving without much of a trace a year and two months later. In early 1985 Reagan's Energy Secretary, Donald Hodel, landed the job. Hodel, according to one observer, was "a Watt clone in a three-piece suit . . . ideologically identical but smoother." Environmentalists were skeptical. When NASA detected an ozone hole over Antarctica, Hodel advised hats and sunglasses. In the North Cascades, Hodel secured funding for a new visitor center with the idea that it would serve as a memorial to Senator Jackson, a favored mentor of the Secretary's, despite the party disparity. One of Hodel's more lasting legacies involved a policy developed in 1988 that allowed old and unmaintained footpaths, horse trails, and jeep trails to be viewed as "roads" in a scheme designed to prevent wildlands from being designated as wilderness. That policy, based on an obscure provision of the 1866 Mining Act, was undone by Secretary Bruce Babbitt in 1997 shortly after Clinton's declaration of the Grand Staircase–Escalante National Monument in Utah. Bush II's Interior Secretary, Gale Norton, a James Watt protégé from the Mountain States Legal Foundation, revived the old policy in a federal rule issued in January 2003, despite strong objections from both Congress and the public.

On another front, it remains a great mystery how or why Hodel would suggest, in August 1987, the removal of the notorious O'Shaughnessy Dam, thus restoring some of the wildness in the Hetch Hetchy Valley of Yosemite National Park. His term in office expired before he could take steps to get it done, which left unresolved whether he was serious or just making what passed in his circles as a joke. A relatively new group on the block, Restore Hetch-Hetchy, took Hodel at his word and still intends to "right one of the greatest wrongs ever done to the National Park system." With the nearly century-old dam and water delivery system in need of multi-billion dollar repairs, "Imagine," they say, "the opportunity we have to allow nature to recreate another Yosemite Valley." Hodel left his position in January 1989. Eight years later, he became president of Pat Robertson's Christian Coalition.

William Whalen's replacement as Director of National Parks, Russell E. Dickenson, deserves a special note because no other director of the Park Service has been as closely involved in the North Cascades. When, as deputy director, he was passed over for the top job, he voluntarily transferred to Seattle as Pacific Northwest Regional Director in January 1976. In 1980, under Carter–Andrus, he returned to Washington, D.C. It is reported that when James Watt went before the Senate for confirmation, Senator Jackson extorted from him the guarantee that Director Dickenson would be retained. The dark pit of Dickenson's career was the morning of July 1, 1982, when he appeared on NBC's *Today Show* with the head of The Wilderness Society who dispassionately cited dirty works of James Watt and looked on with evident pity as Director Dickenson endorsed them. He subsequently has been defended as a martyr-hero who accepted personal shame that he might continue to do what he could to hold Watt at bay—the task made steadily more difficult as Dickenson was increasingly surrounded in his own staff by appointments of Reaganite idealogues. Dickenson explained once to Patrick Goldsworthy that he was holding out as director to defend and preserve the good of the National Park Service. Polly Dyer once met with Dickenson in his office in Washington, D.C. and vividly recalls that "hovering just outside were some of Watts' people." Almost in a whisper, she asked him "if he wasn't taking a risk by expressing his pro-conservation views to me." But Dickenson carried on unabashed. "I concluded his office was not bugged," she said. Eased into retirement in 1985 (to Bellevue, where he maintained an active interest in Pacific Northwest parks), he was succeeded by William Penn Mott, who at the age of 77 emerged from retirement to carry on the defense. As director of California State Parks while Reagan was governor, and as a "peppery, silver-haired Republican," Mott had sufficient political juice to try to resist Hodel's meddlings in Park Service affairs and even to protest publicly the pro-development push of Interior and the White House.

The 1988 Republican candidate for president, George H. W. Bush, proclaimed that his would be the "environmental administration." Taking office, President Bush took up where Reagan left off. The close friend he appointed as Interior Secretary, Manuel Lujan, Jr., was cut from the same cloth as Watt, and though less dangerous, he also seemed less smart. He accomplished several good deeds, possibly because he didn't understand exactly what was happening. Conservationists did not react to his appointment as violently as they had those of Hickel and Watt. Numbed by eight years of Reagan and resigned to waiting it out, they felt Lujan was as good as could be expected in a 1980s Republican administration. To the directorship of the Park Service, Bush appointed James M. Ridenour, who as director of Indiana Natural Resources supported industrial development on the border of the Indiana Dunes National Seashore. He earned his appointment by serving as fundraiser for Vice President Dan Quayle—so dealing another bonk on the head for a Park Service that needed no further humbling.

As the 1992 election approached, the summary judgment of many political historians was that the "clowns had been running the circus" and it now was necessary for someone to clean up after the elephants. William J. Clinton was the great Arkansas hope, as Carter had been the great Georgia hope, and environmentalists waited with perfunctory applause for a sign that Clinton could truly feel their pain. That nearly 63 percent of the voters rejected Bush boded well, but that only 43 percent accepted Clinton did not (Bush received about 37 percent of the vote; reformer Ross Perot polled 19 percent). The new president's appointment of Arizona's green governor, Bruce Babbitt, as Secretary of the Interior was well-received, and of George Frampton, president of the Wilderness Society, as Assistant Secretary even more so. Both were soon outspoken in defense of Clinton's flawed forest plan. Of Roger Kennedy, appointed director of the National Park Service, little was expected beyond adequacy.

Completion of the Golden Triangle of Parks (Rainier, Olympic, and North Cascades) occasioned establishment of a Park Service base for the Pacific Northwest in Seattle, initially a district headquarters, but soon made regional. The style of the first regional director, John Rutter, was "do not kick sleeping dogs." He was succeeded in 1976 by Russell Dickenson, who is remembered with some fondness in the North Cascades for facing up to the necessity of personally acting as the *de facto* superintendent of the North Cascades National Park. Daniel J. Tobin, who went from the superintendency of Mount Rainier National Park (1972–77) to a high post for the Park Service in Washington, D.C., and hung tough there to combat Reagan idealogues as best he could, followed Dickenson in 1980 and served until his death in office in the summer of 1985. In January 1987 the post was filled by Charles H. Odegaard (not to be confused with Charles E. Odegaard, the deceased former president of the University of Washington). Odegaard was known locally as the director of Washington State Parks who logged ancient forests in the parks to obtain funds to develop facilities for Winnebagos, "Silver Slugs," and stinkpots, otherwise known as RVs and motorboats. In 1968, he was a member of Governor Evans' North Cascades advisory group, while also establishing himself in the minds of conservationists as another enemy of what became the North Cascades National Park. Before his appointment, and after, Odegaard was publicly criticized as a self-serving politician pursuing mysterious personal objectives. In 1990 Edward L. Davis, Associate Director of the Park Service, defended Odegaard by describing him as a "career employee with eleven years in National Park Service as of 1990 . . . Deputy Regional Director for five years . . . Regional Director, Midwest, three years . . . not a political appointee." The endorsement by Davis, himself a political appointee, was barely worth the paper it was written on. The worst news about Odegaard, aside from being generally distrusted in and out of the Park Service, was that while evading the spotlight he set himself up as the behind-the-scenes overlord of the North Cascades National Park, which he had opposed in 1968, siding with the Chelan County Commissioners and against the park superintendent. Among other deeds as regional honcho, Odegaard mandated that no consideration be given to the possibility of removing the blight known as the Stehekin airstrip.

In the real world of directorships, of course, there is no such animal as a non-political appointee. But there are politicians who make democracy possible by practicing the *art* of the possible. And there are politicians adroit in exploiting democracy for personal ends. This is known as the difference between good and evil. At a chance gathering of mid-level rangers of North

Cascades National Park, a director of NCCC regaled the group with anecdotes of Odegaard's career as director of Washington State Parks, and concluded by saying that "the only good thing ever done by Washington Governor Dixie Lee Ray was firing Odegaard." Obviously, neither were held in high regard by wilderness advocates.

Moving closer to the park, a fair judgment of the performances of all the superintendents of the North Cascades National Park Complex may be difficult to accomplish for years to come. A superintendent often is acting on orders from above and is often served by a top-notch staff.

The first superintendent, Roger Contor (1968 to 1970), who provided strong environmental direction to Neil Butterfield's Master Plan Study Team, held the post long enough to get started in a number of worthy directions, but not long enough to attain many of his goals, though his momentum continued to serve the park well. Contor, a respected wildlife biologist called up from Canyonlands in Utah, helped build the management structure of the park. He opted to locate park headquarters in the city of Sedro Woolley, where the mayor had been a vocal opponent of the park, and he hired locals to help smooth over strained relationships with nearby communities. Too quickly, perhaps, Contor moved on to higher office in the Midwest and Alaska, later pulling a shift as Olympic National Park superintendent from 1979 to 1983, and at last retiring to raise rattlesnakes in the rainshadow of the Cascades. What might have

Senator Jackson (left) and Congressman Lloyd Meeds with Roger Contor (center), first superintendent of North Cascades National Park, 1968-70.

PHOTO COURTESY OF THE SKAGIT VALLEY HERALD

become of the North Cascades had he stayed longer is a matter of conjecture; he remained too loyal to the ideals and the potential of the Park Service to comment specifically on where and how it went wrong.

Contor's successors, Lowell White (1970–78) and Keith Miller (1978–84), occupied the office a cumulative fourteen years. Superintendent White took on the issue of high-lakes fish stocking, concerned that lakes where fish were naturally absent should remain that way, and that non-native species should not be introduced into lakes with native fish populations. Fish stocking had been ongoing since the 1930s and anglers and state game officials maintained much pride and ownership of those efforts. They were not pleased with White's meddling, and his plans were defeated, at least for a time. In 1978 White swapped jobs with Miller, the superintendent at Acadia National Park in Maine. While Dickenson was in office in Seattle, conservationists found it useful to take problems directly to him as well, at times bypassing Miller and Park headquarters in Sedro Woolley.

John J. Reynolds, a landscape architect by training, came on in the spring of 1985 like a brisk cold wind sweeping into doldrums. If he was a young man in a hurry, frankly aspiring to glory in Washington, D.C., well, the nation could use a bit of glory there. If he was aiming to advance his career by cleaning up the already aging mess in the North Cascades, then what more could conservationists wish? The son of a Yellowstone park ranger, he gave promise of becoming the park's best superintendent ever, supporting a wilderness management approach for most of the complex, and even possible expansion of park boundaries to include Ross Lake and areas along the lower Cascade River and Bacon Creek. He was also supportive of the notion of an international park encompassing protected lands north of the border, perhaps leading to future designation as a world biosphere reserve. However, his record in the North Cascades suggested that securing the integrity of the ecoregion ranked somewhat lower in priority than his own Park Service career. To describe the judgment of his character that evolved among conservationists before his promotion in the fall of 1988 to a management postion with the Denver Service Center would be to risk intemperance. As one example of occasionally erratic behavior, he sought and gained support of the NCCC for siting the Western Visitor Center at Marblemount. Then, without so much as a courtesy call, he moved the site to Newhalem, in response to pressure from Mrs. Henry M. Jackson. His hasty planning efforts, never given the careful processing of an environmental impact analysis but only the shortcutting of perfunctory assessments, forced the NCCC to file a lawsuit, nominally against Odegaard, Ridenour, and Lujan, but actually against J. J. Reynolds (more about the lawsuit later).

Reynolds soon left the Denver center and was promoted to Regional Director of the Mid-Atlantic Region, making him one of the first baby-boomers to attain such heights. Disgruntled conservationists promptly cheered this increased distance from the North Cascades, though fearing he might go higher still. Indeed, this came to pass in 1993 when he was promoted to Deputy Director of the National Park Service by President Clinton. Reynolds closed the circle in 1997 when he returned west to San Francisco as Director of the Pacific West Region, finally retiring from the Park Service in 2002. To his credit, Reynolds interest in sustainable practices and conserving biodiversity seemed to increase later in his career. Despite a list of disappointments with Reynolds in the 1980s, the North Cascades might have fared far worse during those embattled years of the Reagan era.

John Earnst took office in January of 1989, just in time to be named in the lawsuit in place of Reynolds. With Odegaard forted up in Seattle and so tightly wired to political powers and Barbecuers as to be impregnable, and with the North Cascades in their most desperate circumstances since the summer of 1968, Earnst came to the plate with two strikes on him. He hung in there until mid-1992. Most significantly, indeed historically, under Earnst, the Lake Chelan NRA was officially recognized as being subject to the 1916 National Park Act. Despite the machinations of the Odegaard–Ridenour–Lujan–Bush–and–Senator Slade Gorton power structure, he adamantly refused to permit the Chelan County Commission to stage a *coup d'etat* in Stehekin. And though he was a pilot, Earnst did not object to removal of the Stehekin airstrip.

From the start, Earnst intended this to be his last post before retirement. Having won the appointment in a large field of strong applicants, and throughout his career having been consistently rated excellent, he appeared to have been brought on specifically to clean up the mess. But the bureaucrats who had been making the mess still were in charge in Seattle, Denver, and Washington, D.C. Principled decisions in Stehekin and Sedro Woolley infuriated the elite of Wenatchee, capital of the Confederacy of Chelan County. Its Copperhead allies joined local sympathizers to pull their behind-the-scenes wires. When Earnst came up for his annual performance evaluation, Odegaard gave him a grade of "Poor." Never having been so smeared in his Park Service career, and in the North Cascades having gained more respect and confidence than his three predecessors combined, Earnst retired on July 3, 1992. He had intended the North Cascades to be his final post before retirement, and had planned to remain until the task at hand was finished. Evidently he now saw the opposition so powerful and ruthless that he could best serve them by removing himself as their whipping boy. He went away quietly with no complaint, public or private, at least to NCCC ears.

The June 1992 issue of *The Wild Cascades* said, "Goodbye, John Earnst," and in reviewing his tenure, noted a long and distinguished career in the National Park Service. Perhaps his finest hours have come at the end of his service. John walked into a very difficult situation, a lawsuit by the N3C challenging virtually everything that had been done in planning for the Lake Chelan NRA in the previous five and more years. John leaves the Cascades for Colorado, having quietly and effectively settled the suit and gotten on with a major new planning process. He also has shown leadership in setting new directions for management of the North Cascades. John's work with Chelan county leaders should also be recognized. . . . N3C and the NPS have come to work very closely together on a variety of issues under John's tenure. . . .

The relationship which had begun so well under Superintendent Roger Contor, deteriorated under his three immediate successors to the door of the divorce court, then resumed its early warmth, and seemed likely to continue into the golden years. But there were, of course, the meddling in-laws.

Another national competition drew the largest number of applicants for a vacant directorship in the history of the Park Service. The North Cascades had gained a reputation as a challenge. The winner, announced in August 1992, was William Paleck, who made an excellent early impression. However, the NCCC no longer wore its heart on its sleeve, and chose to reserve judgment until he had been some years in office, or retirement. In 2006 Paleck still remained as superintendent, a respectable fourteen-year term—and twice as long as any of his predecessors. In late 2006, he announced he would retire in January 2007. Reflecting on those years, let it be said that ongoing conflict between Paleck and the NCCC concerning a number of park management issues, large and small, dominated an otherwise amicable relationship. As one board member put it, "Really, it's the political climate—he judged where the power lay and it wasn't with us." Others held out hope for a legacy or two on some of the key issues. Fortunately, there were several. But that comes later.

So much for the superstructure of the Park Service. The lower echelons may seem belittled by the few words given them here and that surely is not intended. The excuse is that the very best troops cannot win a war lacking good generalship. Let it be said there certainly are a great many superb troops. To be sure, as with any bureaucracy, the Park Service has its functionaries who slip into niches, erect barricades of protective paper, and snooze on to retirement. A disdain for wilderness activists—those who made their jobs possible, otherwise known as the "deep-breathers" (Seattle City Light engineers' endearing term for conservationists)—is characteristic of these timeservers, and those among them who rise to supervisory posts (and they do, they do), repeating the French admonition to workers in government, "*Surtout, pas de zele.*" Whatever you do, don't overdo it. When these appointees transfer to a new park they normally sniff out the neighborhood for The Founders, those sometimes sour-faced old men and women snooping in corners who are perpetually outraged, forever writing irate letters to Sedro Woolley, Seattle, Washington City Congressmen, and newspapers, and even publishing books, and then quaintly dismiss them.

For all that, many a child grows to a youth, an adult, gazing in hero and heroine worship at the rangers and desiring no higher fulfillment in life than service with that corps. In this lies the explanation for the good the Park Service has accomplished in the past, and here is the hope for its future. That so much dedication and idealism and selflessness (at such scandalously low pay and no benefits, or no job security in the case of seasonals, and sub-marginal housing) so often leads to disillusion and bitterness is a crime. If the Park Service is to survive, that crime needs to end. And to echo a previous reflection about the Forest Service, should the Park Service ever be destroyed, the first task of the nation would be to create a new Park Service more concerned with its mission than with its image.

PHOENIX REDIVIVUS

The North Cascades Act of 1968 was the victory of a coalition of citizen groups, most of whom were pumped up to a surge of exuberance. After a period of continued prominence, the spearhead of the victory, the NCCC, appeared to fade. The most visible evidence, leading to public invisibility, was that in the seventeen years following the October–November 1974 issue of *The Wild Cascades*, the NCCC's "journal of record" appeared a meager eleven times.

In the early 1960s, when activists were spread dangerously thin, burn-out at NCCC would have been a calamity. The example that comes to mind is the loss of Dave Simons, the consequent loss of his Oregon Cascades Conservation Council, and the loss of the Oregon Cascades Volcanic National Park that he might very well have won had he lived. But in the 1970s, citizens groups were proliferating ebulliently. A gap in the ranks might have been abundantly filled by formation of whole new regiments, divisions, and army groups. And hadn't the primary goal of the NCCC been obtained? What need for it now that the North Cascades National Park was a done deal? So it seemed to some within the conservation community, which entered the 1970s numerous and invigorated by a series of successes and eager to go a-tilting at every infidel and dragon infesting the earthly paradise. There was, of course, no shortage of adversaries.

One gap in the ranks was not filled, however. Newly arrived on the scene, the National Park Service had found the NCCC already in place and had accepted it as the North Cascades' voice of the preservation community. As the NCCC voice diminished in the mid-1970s, many rangers took this to mean the community was quietly content. Other rangers discerned what was happening, indeed had been predicting it, and snidely muttered that birdwatchers are good for a summer of battering fortress walls but never can settle down to a long winter's siege. Some pretended that the NCCC was the old council yet, thanking golly it was leaving them in peace, and taking care in public comment lest they stir up a new irruption of troublemakers. A conscious strategy or not, it worked. When stalwarts of the old campaign despaired of reviving the Council and sought help from other groups, they were turned away: "We respect and honor the NCCC too much to trespass on its terrain. Besides, our agenda is already overloaded."

The Park Service neglect of the North Cascades dates almost from the moment the citizens brought it into the North Cascades. Yet the pot must avoid taking a holier-than-thou attitude toward the kettle. A period that witnessed a great revival of the National Park idea, climaxing in Alaska in December 1980, saw in the North Cascades a frittering of fervor. The rangers, newly awakened from a long, institutional torpor, realized they hadn't dozed off by themselves. The activist leadership which should have kept shouting in their ears was resting a little and was not so audible as before. Most of the old soldiers did not retire or desert the ranks for other fields of battle. Patrick Goldsworthy and board member Dave Fluharty carried on the NCCC portfolio on the management plans of Mount Baker–Snoqualmie, Wenatchee, and Okanogan National Forests. It was not their fault that some of that effort was an exercise in futility, as the U.S. Forest Service and the timber industry drifted downstream toward the lip of a falls, denying that the loud sound meant anything. Distinctly and definitely not a waste of Goldsworthy's or Fluharty's time was the refusal to accept Seattle City Light's plans to raise Ross Dam (the consequences of that stubborn resistance are the subject of the next chapter). Meanwhile, by attending meetings and writing letters, they did not let the Park Service completely forget the NCCC. Yet those rangers who wished to do so managed to slip a

Park Superintendent Bill Paleck (served 1992-2007) at the ground-breaking for the Environmental Learning Center at Diablo Lake.

PHOTO COURTESY OF CITY OF SEATTLE

few fast ones past them. Not, however, past Grant McConnell. On visits to his former home in Stehekin, retained as a summer refuge, he came upon mischief in progress and tried to stir an old-style response from the NCCC. But the Park Service learned that he was headed back to Santa Cruz, that Seattle echoes of his anger would fade away, and they could essentially do as they wished.

What happened to end the Great Interregnum in Park Service–NCCC interaction? Credit the National Park Service. When Superintendent John J. Reynolds came onto the scene in 1984, he was, perhaps unwittingly, a flaming torch in a heap of long-accumulated tinder. The Sierra Club Legal Defense Fund (now Earthjustice) agreed to serve as legal counsel for the NCCC in filing suit against the National Park Service to compel it to obey the National Environmental Policy Act in the preparation of its General Management Plan. *The Wild Cascades* resumed regular publication. The membership of the ever-faithful began to be revitalized; the board of directors was reconstituted; and an early draft of this veritable history was undertaken, to the anguish of timeserving federal bureaucrats and Chelan County mythologizers. Thus from the ashes and a flickering flame rose the phoenix. The hiatus was over.

REPAIRING BATTERED LANDS

The stage set and the *dramatis personae* introduced, the curtain may now be raised on Act One of the Complex drama: the progress of the Park Proper since 1968. Scratch that. The play analogy doesn't fit. Acts Two and Three, Skagit and Stehekin, are simultaneous, not sequential, affairs. It may be better to call it a three-ring circus, with the park proper occupying the center ring, and livelier shows in the other two.

Of the National Park Service, having been roughly handled in previous pages and scheduled for more of the same in the following pages, a counterpoint of praise should be inserted, citing aspects of its performance that really do live up to the highest standards of a very high ideal. After all, it isn't *all* bad.

Roger Contor had spent two-and-a-half years on the North Cascades planning team before being appointed the first superintendent. Therefore, unlike his successors, he knew a good deal about what he was getting into. On his earliest examinations of the new wilderness park he was scandalized by the sprawling barrens of brown dirt where once had been lovely meadows. He was the first superintendent in the Northwest to do something about it. In 1969 he engaged Dr. Dale Thornburgh of Humboldt State University to survey Cascade Pass which, since extension of the "mine-to-market" road to the Johnsburg Mine in the late 1940s, and particularly since the Forest Service's 1960 extension of a recreation road and parking lot to the very foot of the pass, had been degraded to a subalpine slum by backpackers, horses, and, for a period in the early 1950s, mobs of prospectors.

The Thornburgh report described forty-two worn camping areas and numerous social trails in the Cascade Pass vicinity. Contor responded to the report by closing the pass and every other highland pass in the park to camping and campfires. On August 31, 1970, a traumatically memorable day for the frontcountry rangers, Contor summoned his entire deskbound staff to the backcountry, to Cascade Pass, to discuss the restoration of worn-out meadowland. As a result of that meeting, he gave Joe and Margaret Miller, directors of the NCCC, *carte blanche* permission to experiment with using native species to revegetate the partly denuded pass. There is a certain serendipity worth mentioning here. In March 1960, during a visit to Death Valley, the Millers happened on an old mining dump and curiously rummaged the spoils. A fading copy of *Cosmopolitan*, August 1917, emerged from the rubble, which Joe carried back to camp to ogle later. When he turned the pages, there were the words "Cascade Pass" next to splendid photos of the North Cascades. It was Mary Rineharts' story of her famous pack trip over the pass.

Margaret, the biologist, trained Joe to scientific respectability, and as a team they won national awards for pioneering a land-healing pattern now emulated in wildlands throughout the Northwest. A meadow can be destroyed by a single party of campers on a single weekend; its restoration demands years. Thus the Cascade Pass project was not officially completed until the summer of 1990. It could have been done faster had not the front-country Park Service vacillated at times between benign neglect and official indifference. In fact, Contor's successor as superintendent initially ordered the Millers to cease and desist. However, the arrival from Olympic National Park of backcountry ranger Bill Lester in 1978 inaugurated a new epoch. Aided by his wife, "Green Thumb" Kathy, Lester reconnoitered the Skagit District backcountry from the alpine to the forest zones and set about scrounging funds, recruiting volunteers, and nagging officials whose responses generally varied from apathy to hostility. Virtue had its reward in 1990, when Lester was appointed manager of the Wilderness District, a designation comprising about 93 percent of the Complex—the park and recreation areas together. Before his untimely death in May 1996, Lester exemplified the Park Service backcountry ranger who nourishes the Park Service flame even as frontcountry superiors and politicians at the nation's uppermost level work mindlessly to stomp it out.

The North Cascades were fortunate to be served by fourteen years of the sensitive professionalism of the Lesters. In 1992 a transfer took them to another post, but their work has been continued by worthy successors, as must be because many other highland meadows sorely need restoration. The range has been equally fortunate in its volunteering amateurs, crucially so in the first

Joe and Margaret Miller on Pumpkin Mountain above the Big Beaver Valley.

decade of the park. At the request of Contor in 1970, the Millers also carried out a pioneering survey of the ecosystems and cedar groves of the Big Beaver, Little Beaver, Baker, Chilliwack, and fire-scarred Silver Creek valleys. The scientific community praised the Millers' work. A competing study hired out to Professor Grant Sharpe of the University of Washington College of Forest Resources was less praised, appearing more tailored to the purposes of Seattle City Light. A small plaque at the park's Marblemount nursery commemorates the Millers' work.

RECLAIMING MINERAL CLAIMS

The 1872 Mining Laws were prevented from privatizing the entirety of the North Cascades only through the eventual lassitude of the normally indefatigable miners. As it was, the Park Service's 1986 *Historic Resources Study* determined that some six thousand claims had "blanketed the wilderness." Hodges' 1897 book, *Mining in the Pacific Northwest*, maps more than a hundred claims, many of them in clusters, from the Cascade River over Cascade Pass and down the Stehekin River; from Thunder Creek over Park Creek Pass and down Park Creek; from North Fork Bridge Creek up to Thunder Pass (a name lost to modern maps); and dozens more along upper Lake Chelan.

For the Park Service to rid the complex of unpatented claims was comparatively easy, because not even the ultra-permissive mining laws, at least technically, permitted the preemption of lands totally lacking in minerals of commercial value. This did not prevent the fools, thieves, and confidence men who were (and maybe still are) the majority of the prospecting population from driving stakes, filing papers at the courthouse, and selling stock. Most of the six thousand claims once filed had long been abandoned, but just to make sure, the three thousand that were inside the park proper were examined and invalidated by 1978.

Patented claims were tougher because once an agent of the government—corrupt, inept, or otherwise—accepted the solemn vow of a prospector that he'd found riches, the theft of public land was as legally impeccable as that which occurred under the Northern Pacific Land Grant. When the Park Service arrived in 1968, nearly two thousand acres of the Complex were in patent, most of it inside the park proper, the balance in the Ross Lake NRA and, strangely, almost none in the Lake Chelan NRA. Examination by qualified experts confirmed that none had commercial value and all appeared to be frauds by the prospector on gullible investors (or perhaps himself), although it was a little late—a couple of generations too late—to throw any of the crooks in jail. The patenting had converted to fully private, fee-simple property not only the rocks underground but the forests and summer-home sites above. With so much latitude for potential exploitation, there could be no wilderness. The 1968 Act provided $3.5 million for acquisition of these and other inholdings, and a subsequent appropriation brought the total, by October 1988, to more than $5.9 million for the entire complex.

The start was made in 1973 by purchase, for $290,000, of the 120-acre "Crescent Marble" property, a short distance up Marble Creek from the Cascade River. The next year thirty-eight acres in Horseshoe Basin—the Blue Devil and Black Warrior claims—were acquired through a gift from The Mountaineers Foundation, a memorial to Dwight Crowder, co-author of *Routes and Rocks: Hikers Guide to the North Cascades from Glacier Peak to Lake Chelan*, who was killed on a California freeway in 1970. An attempt by nationally respected conservationist Devereaux Butcher to employ the National Parks Foundation as conduit for another similar purchase was frustrated by the incomprehensible inability of the Park Service to find a way to use the gift.

The largest single mineral property in the complex lay in the heart of the park, at the junction of Skagit Queen Creek and Thunder Creek, immediately beneath the hanging front of the Boston Glacier and close to Park Creek Pass. Hodges' 1897 account extolled the riches at Skagit Queen, and stock was sold across America and in England. So much steel was horse-packed into the wilderness that, long after abandonment, the site was affectionately known as the "Stehekin Hardware Store." A realistic view of the mineral potential eventually replaced Hodges' credulous transcription of the prospectors' dreams, but the old fools were soon replaced by new charlatans whose sharp eyes spotted the potential blackmail value of national park inholdings.

In October 1975 Glenn A. Widing, a Portland trucking executive, and two partners filed an application to log more than two hundred acres on their thirty-six patented claims at Skagit Queen. This was preparatory, said Widing, to reopening the old silver mine. The Park Service examiners confirmed the judgment of the generations that the ore was not rich enough nor plentiful enough to justify mining. However, under existing law the Park Service could not deny operation of a mine nor access to the claim. But it did have the power to stipulate what manner of access would be allowed for the mining—and the logging.

Widing was perfectly willing to sell at *his* price, considered by many to be preposterously high. By 1977 he would have little chance gulling a court with the legend of a rich lode of silver ore. But there was another way. By exploiting an ancient law allowing one to legally steal from the public treasurehouse, he applied for a permit to build a logging road twelve miles up the wilderness valley of Thunder Creek. The road would slice through a majestic forest that had survived to a venerable age amid the thunder of avalanches on every side. The backpackers loved this place and would surely wail at the thought of its slaughter. Like the black-mustachioed villain holding a knife to the fair white throat of the bound-and-gagged heroine, Widing had made his demand. The Park Service denied the permit. Widing appealed. The Park Service filed a condemnation complaint action with the Department of Justice. On December 12, 1979, a "declaration of taking" and a court-determined payment of $284,137.41 acquired Widing's 645 acres. (Taken earlier, on October 5, for $169,860, were the fifteen and a half acres of the "Friedman" property, presumably part of the same deal.)

The big year for reclaiming claims was 1979. In addition to the takings, purchases were made of ten properties, totaling 516 acres, for about $200,000. The largest acquisition was the three "Brewster" claims (301 acres, $80,000), which ringed Doubtful Lake. Others were the two "Merz" claims (83 acres, $27,500), located in the Lake Chelan NRA on Meadow Creek; and, on the North Fork of the Cascade River, two of the "Wells" claims (37 acres, $45,500), the two "McLean" claims (53 acres, $25,000), and the "Soren" claim (41 acres, $16,500).

Another very good, though less busy year was 1981. The oldest of the area's mining fiascos dated all the way back to a private in the Indian-hunting U.S. Army who staked a claim at "Soldier Boy Creek," centered just west of Cascade Pass. During the Little Gold (or was it Uranium?) Rush of the early 1950s, a promoter assembled claims in the vicinity and began selling stock in

Valumines, Inc. A crude road was gouged up the Cascade River valley from the previous terminus at Gilbert's Cabin, construction was begun of a stamp mill, and acres of forest were mauled and trashed. If the Skagit Queen claims were a time bomb in the heart of the park, Valumines was a bombed crater in plain sight of every pilgrim visiting the park's most renowned scenic pass. In preliminary actions, the Park Service examined and extinguished the unpatented claims (including the site of the illegally built stamp mill) that Valumines had apparently been using to inflate the bubble of its prospectus. Details of the final ejection are somewhat obscured by the bareness of Park Service statistics. The sole purchase designated "Valumines" was for twenty acres ($22,000). However, a simultaneous 1981 purchase was a "Wells" claim of 56 acres ($76,000), perhaps a part of the same transaction.

In March 1978 the Park Service announced that by October 1 all patented claims in the park proper either would be acquired or condemnation proceedings instituted. October came, but it didn't happen. Nor by 1981, when acquisitions ceased for one or more of three reasons: Congressional appropriations were exhausted; available funds were shifted elsewhere; or the Park Service went dead in the water.

By December 1989, acquisitions in the park proper had been stalled for eight years at a total of 1,435 acres in twenty-one tracts purchased, and 660 acres in four tracts "taken" (with compensation). The Park Service listed seven tracts, or 226 acres, within the park proper that remained in private ownership. One of these, a twenty-one acre claim in Horseshoe Basin near Cascade Pass, was resolved amicably with the Courtney family in Stehekin Valley in the 1990s, though conservationists were not pleased with the terms. The others remained unresolved in 2006, including the worrisome Webster, or "Dorothy Lode" claims in upper Thunder Creek Basin. The owner recently threatened to log by helicopter or otherwise develop these claims—127 acres in total—unless paid well in excess of what the Park Service considered fair value for the property. Other claims still outstanding in 2006 (Johnson, Behrens, Clagstone, and Blackburn) comprise about eighty-four acres of uncertainty yet to be settled.

Private inholdings such as these amid the sea of North Cascades wilderness are a real threat and should be acquired, condemned if necessary. The days of heirs flaunting legal papers in the face of the Park Service belong to the past. While not entirely suppressing its irritation at the inability of the National Park Service to supply exact and current data on the status of transactions completed and properties still remaining in private hands, the NCCC recognizes that the Park's dedicated staff faced some enormous complexities. The records in county courthouses, in offices of the federal Bureau of Land Management in Spokane, and elsewhere have to be searched to find out who owns what and why. The hard nuts yet to be cracked in the North Cascades National Park are a handful compared to the basketsful plaguing the national forests of the region, where claims around La Bohn Gap, Monte Cristo, and Canyon and Granite Creeks have risen to some level of public consciousness. Many other claims on federal land also await the staff time and funding from Congress to get at them.

PLANS, PLANS, AND MORE PLANS

Nearly two decades after creation of the national park, NCCC director Dave Fluharty asked in *The Wild Cascades*, "Who would have thought that we would have to protect the Park from the National Park Service?" Management plans and the potentially destructive actitivies they might accommodate (overtly or not) had become the principal challenge for the park protectors.

George Hartzog's 1970 *General Management Plan for the North Cascades National Park Complex* was, to the NCCC, a potpourri of trivia. The more serious planning was left for his successors.

A 1974 brochure entitled *Joint Plan/National Park Service/U.S. Forest Service* presented the results of an effort mandated by Congress. Conservationists understood Congress to have intended a body of thoughtful recommendations on boundary issues, a joint policy on the closure of certain roads, and a "greater ecosystem" basis for continuing discussions among federal, state, and local levels of government and the public. The brochure, however, was mostly simple pictures and easy-to-read text. Lacking solid substance, it addressed agreements on trail signs, shared trail maintenance, and joint sponsorship of the Field's Point Landing on Lake Chelan, but little else.

As for the "spirit of interagency cooperation" promised in the brochure, differences of opinion elicited huffs and puffs from the Forest Service as the Park Service recoiled. A notable and rare instance in which the Park Service held its ground concerned the routing of the Pacific Crest National Scenic Trail (PCT), officially recognized in 1968 under the National Trails System Act, a law signed by President Johnson on the same day he signed the North Cascades Act. Unlike most trails maintained by the Park Service and Forest Service, the PCT exists independently under Congressional authority. In Washington State, the official supervisory board has been dominated by the tourist and timber industries and the Forest Service. When the Forest Service insisted that the route should climb from the valley at Rainy Pass to Maple Pass and return to Bridge Creek via Maple Creek, Park Superintendents Keith Miller and Lowell White each argued that the high country should be preserved as no-trail wilderness. The Forest Service went ahead anyway, blazing a trail up through the national forest to a dead end in fragile meadows at the Park boundary. The site soon became something of a ridgetop disaster area. While the Park Service was ada-

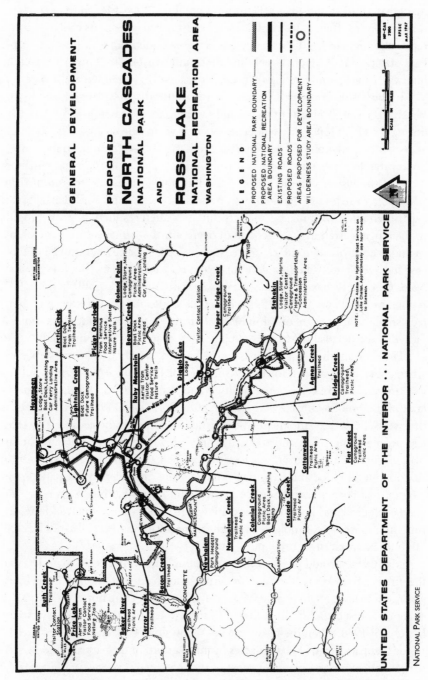

This early draft plan was prepared in 1967, shortly before the national park was created, and illustrates many of the NPS' ideas for new roads, trams, and other development.

mant that a trail would adversely impact a wildlife refuge, the "spirit of coopera-tion" was not sufficient to stimulate the Forest Service to put its trail to bed and repair the highland. (The agency has since extended the trail beyond Maple Pass, staying out of Maple Creek, and descending instead to Rainy Lake and the highway, thus forming a loop that doesn't leave hikers stranded at the pass.)

In the 1960s the North Cascades backcountry began to be deluged by the Backpacker Rush. Habits of travel and camping that ecosystems could tolerate during the era of lonesome wilderness were now anachronisms. The shocking and swift degradation of Cascade Pass emphasized the urgent need for protec-tion of fragile ecosystems from human overuse—and protection and enhance-ment of the visitor experience on the wildland's terms. The transition from *laissez faire* to strict management was traumatic, particularly since Park Service experimentation with management techniques often resulted in errors. Right-ly, the rangers erred in the direction of overcontrol—which is surely preferable to under-control when the resource, such as a patch of heather, can be obliter-ated in a weekend. The first good plan, the *Backcountry Management Plan for the North Cascades National Park Complex*, was drafted in 1974, published in 1977, revised in 1981, and on May 22, 1984, entered into the *Federal Register* in eigh-teen single-spaced pages of minutely specific do's and don'ts. Conservationists picked at the details but strongly supported its objectives and philosophy.

Fire was another can't-wait issue. The park hardly had been established when there came an extraordinary summer of lightning. Wilderness hikers, who for years had been at once amused and irritated by the Wagnerian stage-craft of the Smokey Bears, were delighted by horizons blooming with smokes that were allowed to smolder as they wished. Except for those caused by care-less people along roads and trails, the only fires fought were public relations blazes, which is to say, exercises to satisfy certain show-biz journalists ever on the lookout for blood and slaughter. The first superintendent of the park, Roger Contor, had been a Forest Service fireman and knew that Nature has fires for good ecological reasons, and that except when a blaze is very small and the sur-rounding tinder wet, Smokeys can fight a fire until their eyeballs are blistered, but only Nature can securely put it out.

Many years would pass before the public at large would begin to understand that fire is a friend of wildness, is wilderness incarnate, that Smokey is the inter-loper, and that we ought to accept the principle of "let nature burn." A fire policy, of course, must be politically realistic. Realism does not entail succumbing to the hysteria of 1988, when the press wailed "Yellowstone Park has been destroyed!" Inside that park, nearly 800,000-acres burned (a third of the park area), yet scien-tists overwhelmingly agree that most of the scorching was a natural, inevitable, and ecologically important event. An aid in educating the public is the recent rev-elation that what is killing forests of the inland Northwest is not fire, but the lack of periodic burns due to over-suppression of natural fires. It is the consequent build-up of unburned fuel that can lead to catastrophe.

The *Fire Management Plan for the North Cascades National Park Complex* first adopted on August 6, 1981, embodied a decade of detailed study of individual drainages. Maps delineated areas of discontinuous forest canopy and showed the location of lightning fires from 1970 through 1979; 108 fires burned 2,947 acres. Another 37 fires were human-caused. Studies recommended a total suppression zone along roads and trails and a modified suppression zone where nature would largely be left to do as it pleased—unless doing otherwise served as good public relations. Subunits of the complex were described in detail, treating forest cover, topography, and climate.

The plan's policy and objectives were endorsed by ecologists as exactly appropriate to a wildland (today, a let-it-burn approach to most wildland fires applies to about 90 percent of the park complex). The criticisms were two: first, the plan specified that for fires too big and complex and costly for local Park Service resources, a fire boss would be imported, usually from the Forest Service. The concern was that a career Smokey may have been trained in a College of Forestry whose faculty still abide by the Pinchot axiom: timber is a crop. It is fated to be houses. Houses must not be allowed to burn so neither should trees. The big-time fire boss can be a colorful figure on camera, and often has a charming country twang and a repertoire of archaisms—a show-biz delight. The press, being composed of less knowledgeable city dwellers, widely accepted the myth and quoted it with inflection to terrify the urban public. The pseudo-science of certain colleges of forestry and of Pinchot himself was perpetuated, though less so today. Fire-fighters lacking an understanding of natural fire could end up doing more damage to the ecosystem than the fire. More recently, the semi-retirement of Smokey Bear has made room for a new-style fire boss. While the TV talking-heads were mourning "the destruction of Yellowstone," certain bosses on the scene reportedly kept some of their crews on the sidelines, commenting off-camera that "the park has needed this burn for a long time."

The second criticism of the North Cascades' Fire Management Plan applied to the use of aircraft. When sensibly and sparingly used for ecological research and ecosystem repair, they enable efficient access in a very short high-country season by a small scientific staff. They also permit quick response to accidents and backcountry fires. However, whenever an agency has an air budget there seems to be a compulsion to use it up lest it go to waste. The record of the North Cascades National Park concerning flights has been excellent overall, as cannot always be said of the Forest Service Tactical Squads, for whom an impromptu training flight in a helicopter might be a welcome diversion on a boring afternoon. The conscientious behavior of North Cascades National Park is due to conscientious rangers, though not all of them have been. If the boss wants to fight a fire, a justification always can be cobbled up. In a conscientious world, fire management plans ought to stipulate that every agency overflight of wilderness for fire protection, or any other purpose, should have a written justification and authorization on the public record, subject to later examination and question.

A 1991 update of the 1981 fire plan refined the data. Through 1990 human-caused fires had increased to 106 and lightning fires to 194, with a total area burned of about 3,450 acres. According to the most recent assessment in 2004, another 150 fires burned from 1991 to 2003, charring about eight thousand acres, much of it in 2003 when two thousand acres burned above Big Beaver and another thousand acres went up in smoke at No Name Creek. In 2006, the Flick Creek Fire (in the Lake Chelan NRA) scorched nearly 8,000 acres near the head of Lake Chelan, giving a serious scare to the Stehekin community. None of these fires, however, were of the scale of several very large fires that have burned outside the park in recent years, mostly in the Pasayten Wilderness where a drier climate makes fire a more active force in the ecosystem. Nevertheless, very large fires are possible in the national park. In 1926 a lightning-caused, 40,000-acre burn spread across portions of the Big Beaver and Skagit River valleys (prior to the construction of Ross Dam). Since the 1970s, the occurrence of larger fires seems to be on the rise in the North Cascades, and one can only speculate whether we are beginning to see the effects of global warming.

There were other plans too. A 1984 summary listed nearly half a hundred plans, covering just about every conceivable aspect of park management for the whole or parts of the Complex. For two dozen plans the preparer was noted as park staff, two as Regional Office, a dozen-odd as Denver Service Center

2006 Flick Creek Fire above Lake Chelan (in the NRA).

PHOTO COURTESY OF CHELAN COUNTY SHERIFF'S OFFICE

(DSC), and two as Harpers Ferry Center. The relationship between park staff and the DSC was only less tense than that between DSC and environmentalists. The Center remains a swarming ground for ingenious and articulate technocrats who often see themselves as the brains of the Park Service. Field staff with the Park Service as well as environmentalists have often felt DSC may be strong on theory, but weak on knowing what's out there on the ground.

The bulk of the planning has sprung from mutual agreements, and conservationist criticisms have been confined to details, mostly minor. A June 1986 brochure presented the *Development Concept Plan for the North Cascades Highway and Cascade Pass* and praised the Cascade Pass trailhead as "the only place in the national park accessible by vehicle from the North Cascades Highway where visitors can view close at hand the spectacular mountain, glacier, and subalpine environments." There was no mention of Heather Meadows, located in the national forest adjacent to the park and accessible by another highway, but where the vaunted spirit of cooperation might have brought a joint Forest Service–Park Service sponsorship of a viewing area for all that scenery straddling the two jurisdictions.

This is not to say that Cascade Pass and the North Fork of the Cascade River should be instruments of interagency competition. They should be wilderness. The Forest Service cannot be blamed for the intruding vehicles above Mineral Park; the stock-sellers of the fraudulent mines and a prior government of Skagit County initiated that. But it was certainly boosting itself as a viable alternative to the Park Service in the scenery business when it extended the road, partly paved, to a new and unsightly parking lot just below Cascade Pass. The frontcountry rangers of the Park Service adopted the atrocity as their own, then constructed a concrete outhouse. The Denver designers doubtless pondered more, perhaps even a visitor center. The NCCC still proposes, as it did in 1968, shortening the road by about two miles so that visitors can have the satisfaction that comes from reaching this sublime scenery afoot—and without the scar of a parking lot messing up the view. The big floods in October 2003, November 2005, and December 2006 obliterated several portions of the road near Boston Creek more than a mile below the lot, which ought to convince the Park Service of the difficulty of maintaining the road.

Several other management plans for the park have been produced and updated over the years, including a Resource Management Plan that first appeared in August 1988, a Wilderness Management Plan of March 1989, and a Bear Management Plan dating back to 1975, updated in 1982. In May 1982 the Department of the Interior published a policy statement on use of the federal portion of the Land and Water Conservation Fund. In response, the National Park Service prepared Land Protection Plans for each unit of the park system that contained non-federal land. The purpose of the plans was to identify methods of assuring the protection of the natural, historic, scenic, cultural, recreational, educational, or other significant resources, and to provide for adequate visitor use. In February 1984 a Land Protection Plan for the North Cascades National Park (the park proper) was adopted. Updated in 1989, the plan had almost entirely to do with the unfinished work of reclaiming the mineral claims.

1988: THE GREAT BIG GENERAL MANAGEMENT PLAN

Having learned from the Hartzog North Cascades Complex Plan of 1970 what appeared to NCCC as techniques for orchestrating politically useful ecological disasters, the Denver Service Center in 1984 issued a *Statement for Management, North Cascades National Park Service Complex*. The fifty-four pages presented background on legislation, resources, land uses and trends, major issues, and an outline of management objectives for the park and the two national recreation areas. The NCCC promptly objected to the DSC's interpretation of the facts and its vision of the future.

On April 11, 1985, Superintendent John J. Reynolds, newly arrived, informed "Dear Friends of the North Cascades" that a long-range planning process was beginning for the three units of the complex, defining the management philosophy for the next fifteen to twenty years. A May 3 letter signed by NCCC President Dave Fluharty and Chairman of the Board Patrick Goldsworthy provided the Council's response.

The issues they addressed were many: impacts on the natural environment from past, present, and future human activity; visual impacts; the need for revegetation; air and water quality concerns; soil stability; fish and wildlife and their habitats; plants; forests; existing and proposed roads and tramways; trails; shelters; campsites; day-use areas; boating facilities; resorts; interpretive facilities; visitor centers; the *Lady of the Lake*; alterations to streams and rivers; proposed small-hydro development; clearing along the U.S.–Canadian border; backcountry use; party size limits; horse use; campfires; rafting; canoeing and kayaking; permits for commercial and non-commercial use; hunting; boating; airplane access and the Stehekin airstrip; motorized and mechanized access to roads and trails; fish stocking; wildfire; flooding; the acquisition of private inholdings; the Stehekin school; resource extraction (logging, mining, and aggregate removal); hazardous tree removal; compatible-use standards; private concessionaires; interagency coordination; wilderness management and legislation; and necessary park boundary adjustments.

A long year later, in June 1986, Superintendent Reynolds released a workbook called *North Cascades General Management Plan Alternatives*, an eighteen-page document, superseded by another one twice that size once all hell broke loose.

The Reynolds plan offered some odd choices among "Management Philosophies and Strategies" called No Action, Wild, Dramatic, and Subtle; to these was added (in August) the Stehekin Community Council Proposal, which was spun more from private interest than public. The Denver experts were too clever by half; "Dramatic" and "Subtle" had the sound of bright young bureaucrats brainstorming around a table with competing proposals scattered between these vague categories, seemingly determined by a roll of the dice. There was no recognition of the obvious fact—obvious to NCCC, at least—that the basic decision to be made in the North Cascades was between people-pleasing and land-protection, once again pitting the frontcountry needs against the backcountry. Addition of the Stehekin Community Council Proposal displayed an early wilting of the spine and possible grounds for a transplant. There was no addition of an alternative proposal from, say, the NCCC. (Several key issues raised during the resulting controversy were later resolved by the 1988 Washington Parks Wilderness Act.)

So much having been said as a general introduction to early planning for the Complex as a whole, it should be pointed out that the August 1986 document had three pages on the park, six on the Ross Lake NRA, and eleven on the Lake Chelan NRA, which was about the right emphasis. For all the artificiality of the prescribed alternatives, disagreements between the NCCC and the Park Service on the park proper were few. Along the Ross Reservoir, Park Service options were so limited there was not much latitude for blunders or disagreement. At Lake Chelan and Stehekin, however, there were, and remain today, a long list of major concerns.

Late the following year, in October 1987, the Park Service released its "preferred proposal," drawn from the August draft plan and environmental assessment (140 Denver pages, not counting a separate fourteen-page summary). The NCCC board of directors quickly reviewed the Park Service proposal, and with some trepidation. In The Wild Cascades, Dave Fluharty fired off his question, "Who would have thought . . ." that the North Cascades needed to be protected from the Park Service. Once more, "the National Park Service must be reminded of its duty," he said, "to protect the North Cascades from development." The NCCC's written review of the plan proceeded to "The Good, The Bad, and The Ugly."

Under "The Good," the NCCC commended the Park Service for proposing that "management of the entire NPS complex . . . be directed toward strengthening and enhancing the wilderness character," and that management be coordinated with the Forest Service, Seattle City Light, and the British Columbia parks ministry "to protect the natural values of the North Cascades ecosystem." Stated intentions to "study the establishment of an international park" and "determine the feasibility of designating the North Cascades as a world biosphere reserve" were magnanimous. The agency was also commended for recognizing that essentially all the park, most of the two national recreation areas, and lands down to 125 feet above the Ross Lake reservoir were "suitable for wilderness."

The NCCC applauded the finding that "the Ruby Mountain area, lower Thunder Creek, Big Beaver, and the area south of the Skagit River between Thunder Arm and Copper Creek, may more appropriately be included in the North Cascades National Park." It commended the proposal that "Ross Lake will continue to be managed as a roadless and primitive area without road access or major recreational facilities (except at Hozomeen)." The group supported the agency's determination to "exclude any new roads, tramways, other major visitor facilities . . . not expand the Stehekin docks to accommodate houseboat use [and] not grant permits there for houseboat rentals." NCCC endorsed the agency's intention to "oppose approval of licenses for small-scale hydroelectric projects within Ross Lake NRA that do not adequately mitigate . . . effects."

Proposals for new trails were generally supported, including an interpretive boardwalk at Happy Flat, a loop trail from Hozomeen to Desolation Peak, a complete trail system from Stehekin to Mount Baker, a new eleven-mile Stehekin Valley trail from Stehekin landing to High Bridge, and a three-mile trail from Cascade River Road to the historic Gilbert Cabin. (Most of these were never built.)

The NCCC endorsed plans for a "research project on the complete effects of stocking (with exotic fish) more than 240 natural lakes . . . all of which were originally barren of fish," as well as a plan to "survey the habitat and population of the northern spotted owl [and] assist in the interagency effort to determine habitat quality for the grizzly bear."

Finally, NCCC supported the Park Service in its "long-term objective to restore the shoreline between the Stehekin landing and the head of Lake Chelan to natural conditions" (this was reneged on later), as well as the preparation of a Land Protection Plan for Lake Chelan NRA.

Several proposals were specifically criticized under the banner of "The Bad," including plans to "maintain the twenty-three-mile Stehekin Valley Road at its current length, width, and character [and] retain the Cascade River Road to its existing terminus." The NCCC perspective, put simply, was (and is) that roads do not belong in wilderness. The agency was also strongly criticized for "considering private utilization of sand, gravel, and building stone by residents of Stehekin Valley to be an appropriate use of the Lake Chelan National Recreation Area." The impacts to a national treasure were simply too great to be compromised for convenience.

As for "The Ugly," the NCCC condemned most severely the "Stehekin Firewood Management Plan" and plans to retain the Stehekin airstrip.

Despite early good intentions, the Park Service also failed to defend its position adequately against high-lakes fish stocking. The High Lakes Compromise negotiated in 1988 allowed the state wildlife department to continue stocking lakes, in a flagrant violation of national park policy. The decline of amphibian populations in these ecosystems, among other impacts, has been widely attributed to the presence of alien fish.

In February 1988 Reynolds sent his "Dear Friends of the North Cascades" an analysis of public responses to the draft General Management Plan and Land Protection Plan for the Lake Chelan NRA. On September 16, 1988, the final General Management Plan for the three units was issued. It was acknowledged that "The process of arriving at this plan has been lengthy, intense, and at times controversial . . ." Nevertheless, said Reynolds, "the plan is a good one." For the park as a whole, the statements were generally correct, but for the more serious shortcomings in Stehekin and the Lake Chelan NRA that worked against the park and wilderness values the NCCC and others had tried to protect.

In the fall of 1988, Superintendent Reynolds was rewarded by promotion to head the Denver Service Center, and perhaps the man and the job had earned each other. John Earnst inherited Reynolds' troubles at Lake Chelan and almost immediately found himself named as a defendant in the unavoidable lawsuit filed by the Sierra Club Legal Defense Fund (Earthjustice) on behalf of the NCCC. The balance of that story and the gnawing difficulties at Stehekin and Lake Chelan will come later.

REDEDICATING THE WILDERNESS

Before taking an early retirement to treat his terminal disillusion, a Park Service ranger who rose high in the hierarchy once described Director George Hartzog's notion of wilderness as one of sitting on the veranda of a chalet, cold martini in hand, smoking his cigar, and watching the sun set behind a picture postcard. His "holey wilderness" of August 1970 was shot full of holes by Senator Frank Church, Idaho's staunch defender of true and meaningful wilderness legislation. Hartzog's proposal for wilderness in the North Cascades, some of 1968's unfinished business, encompassed 515,800 acres in the national park and national recreation areas—a sizeable area to be sure. The difficulties concerned what was left out. An amended version of the proposal was recommended to Congress sometime later but not acted upon, for two reasons. First, the Washington Wilderness Bill for the national forests had seized the stage in 1983, and the proposed omnibus bill for all three of Washington's national parks was somehow determined to be beyond the capacity of the legislative system. Second, the High Ross Dam issue remained to be resolved. In March 1984 the City of Seattle and the Province of British Columbia signed the Ross Dam treaty. Several months later the Washington Wilderness Act was passed by Congress. The path was clear. The NCCC, Olympic Park Associates, and Mount Rainier National Park Associates, backed by National Park Service regional headquarters, soon approached now *Senator* Dan Evans to inform him that the hour for the parks was at hand. Polly Dyer reminded Evans that he was likely the only member of the state's delegation who could get a bill through Congress designating wilderness within the three national parks.

Evans' re-entry into North Cascades wilderness politics deserves a brief explanation. A civil engineer by trade, Evans served ten years in the state legislature as a Republican from Seattle before winning the race for governor in 1965. He served an unprecedented three terms, finally stepping out of politics in 1977 to head Evergreen State College in Olympia. But a few years later, Evans found himself an unlikely appointee to the U.S. Senate upon the sudden death of Senator Jackson on September 1, 1983. Jackson, one of the most powerful senators in the country, and among the longest-serving public officials in the state, died at his home of a heart attack at 71. Fresh in everyone's mind were the hearings in Seattle and elsewhere that Senators Jackson and Gorton held on the bill that would become the 1984 Washington Wilderness Act. As a tribute, the legislation named a 102,673-acre addition south and west of Glacier Peak as the Henry M. Jackson Wilderness.

In the North Cascades, Scoop Jackson led the parade that brought us a park. But wilderness designation within this park and the park complex as a whole was another matter, and its success would now require Senator Evans' help. The Park Service had been administering the land in Hartzog's 1970 proposal by its own wilderness rules, and in August 1987 it assessed as "suitable for wilderness" essentially the entire park and most of the two national recreation areas. On March 15, 1988, Senator Evans introduced S. 2165, the Washington Parks Wilderness Bill, for himself and Senator Brock Adams, a kindly Democrat who had thwarted Gorton's reelection bid in 1986. (Gorton regained the seat in 1992 after Adams was stung by allegations of sexual harassment.) In the House, an identical bill, H.R. 4146, was introduced by Congressmen John Miller, Al Swift, and Rod Chandler. Both bills identified 634,614 acres of wilderness and 5,226 acres of "potential wilderness" in the North Cascades Complex, considerably more than Hartzog's 1970 proposal. Potential wilderness covered areas of nonconforming uses and private property; provision was made that when the uses were terminated or the lands acquired the areas could be added to wilderness without recourse to Congress. Of the park proper, 504,305 acres, or 99 percent, were to be designated as the Stephen Mather Wilderness.

The conservation community was pleased, mostly. Many of the items it had sought to no avail in the 1968 Act were to be granted by the 1988 Act, much to the credit of the 1988 Park Service. Locally, Superintendent Reynolds stayed on just long enough to see it through—perhaps his principal shining moment in the North Cascades. The archaic mining laws would be stricken for the entire complex, including both the park and national recreation areas. Jurisdiction by the Federal Energy Regulatory Commission to approve new power projects would be cancelled, halting expansion of an existing diversion of Company Creek in the Stehekin Valley, a Pelton wheel proposed for the Stehekin River, and any number of small-hydro schemes throughout the complex. Wilderness designation would not be confined to the park, and the boundaries drawn in the national recreation areas had such serendipities as to rule out small-hydro development of Thornton and Damnation Creeks.

Hearings on the Washington Parks Wilderness Bill, chaired by Senator Evans, were held June 27–28, 1988, in Washington, D.C., by the Public Lands, Public Parks, and Forests Subcommittee of the Senate Energy and Natural Resources Committee; NCCC Chairman Patrick Goldsworthy testified. The House Committee on Interior Affairs held hearings July 12; NCCC President Dave Fluharty testified. Many years before, Phil Zalesky must have seen it coming. In the August 1961 *NCCC News*, three years prior to passage of the Wilderness Act itself, he wrote, "We know that it is not within the province of this Wilderness Bill to create new dedicated areas. However, when this national park is created [in the North Cascades], much of the park should then fall within the direction of SB 1123, the Wilderness bill."

In the fall of 1988, Congress passed, without opposition, the Washington Parks Wilderness Act, embracing 1.7 million acres of wilderness in the three parks of the Golden Triangle. The Act was quietly signed by President Reagan on November 16, just eight days after the lopsided election of George H. W. Bush. At Mount Rainier, 228,480 acres were designated as the Mount Rainier Wilderness—about 97 percent of the park. The Olympic Wilderness covered 95 percent of that park, or 876,669 acres.

For the North Cascades National Park proper, the act of Congress was implemented by the June 1988 General Management Plan for the Complex, which put all federal land in the park proper in the Natural Zone, where "lands and waters are managed to ensure that natural resources and processes remain largely unaltered by human activity. Developments are generally absent or limited to dispersed recreational and management facilities." The plan also noted that "Research Natural Areas are a special subzone within this zone and are strictly protected for their scientific values."

Management was further guided by a Wilderness Management Plan approved March 1989. The Park Service was prohibited from using discretionary authority to allow roadbuilding, facility siting, and mechanized recreation. The final nail was driven in the coffins of the tramways and the proposed Roland Point Highway along Ruby Arm; other creative frills of the Hartzog–Mather–Albright era were finally dispensed with.

During the hearings, the NCCC sought improvement in the legislation to compensate for the "non-confrontational" stance of the Park Service. That 93 percent of the Complex was placed in wilderness was not to be excessively bragged about when, in the eyes of the NCCC, much of the remaining 7 percent should also have been included. The Act stipulated that boundaries adjacent to roads were to be drawn "as narrowly as practical to allow for maintenance," defined as one hundred feet on either side; the Council had argued that fifty feet were plenty. A provision to cease clearing a destructive and unnecessary fifty-foot swath along the international boundary with Canada was denied. The concept of "protective buffers" was only partly agreed to. A distinct success was the provision that when wilderness-surrounded mineral properties were purchased their placement in wilderness was to be automatic.

Elimination of mineral and hydro entry from the Ross Lake and Lake Chelan Recreation Areas was a bonanza beyond the hopes of earlier decades. Dedication of these two areas as wilderness in virtually every eligible sector had long been denied. Thus a good part of the work was done. But sticking out like a sore thumb in a measure designed to address wilderness was a clause that authorized the Park Service to continue disposal of "renewable" resources in the Stehekin Valley. Was this a juicy bone thrown by Evans to the Barbecuers, seemingly setting up a battle to be fought out later? Or something else? Polly Dyer revealed that Evans once told her that Senator McClure of Idaho, Chairman of the Senate Energy and Natural Resources Committee, "was insisting

Not everyone appreciated all the new rules in the national park (1970).

DOG WITH SIGN, NOCA 17097, IN THE COLLECTION OF THE NORTH CASCADES NATIONAL PARK COMPLEX, COURTESY OF THE NATIONAL PARK SERVICE.

on provisions for water projects in national park wilderness [and] Dan told me they came up with some innocuous language that finally was accepted by Mc-Clure" who then allowed the bill to move to a vote on the Senate floor.

Another deed was done in the House of Representatives, where Congressman Chandler, an airplane enthusiast, charged the Park Service to continue the Stehekin airstrip, which both NCCC and the rangers had been seeking to close since 1968.

The Council and others also sought unsuccessfully to have the 1988 Act provide for an ecosystem study of all three of Washington State's national parks, the resulting management recommendation to be the joint charge of the National Park Service and U.S. Forest Service. The Senate report directed by Senator Evans did instruct the National Park Service to examine the ecosystem study in the year following passage of the Act. The study was begun but never finished, someone in Washington, D.C., apparently having killed it. The circumstances are obscure, the assassin unknown.

Finally, the NCCC did object strenuously, but in good taste, to application of the name, "Stephen Mather Wilderness," in the North Cascades, Mather being the first Director of the National Park Service, but having virtually no connection to the park itself. A Mather Parkway already existed in Mount Rainier National Park, and the man very clearly could be associated with scenic highways in the parks much more so than with wilderness. However, at the behest of John J. Reynolds, acting on a request from the aging Albright, Senator Evans dropped the name into the legislation. Lose some, win some.

Confining the purview to the Complex and forgetting for the moment the other two million or so acres of the North Cascades left freely open to frontiering, it is gratifying indeed to compare the Hartzog proposal of 1970, the "wilderness suitability" findings of 1987, and the Stephen Mather Wilderness of 1988, and contemplate the growth of plausible wilderness in that period from 515,800 acres to 634,614, particularly because the added 118,814 acres are not in the interior but on the periphery, the most visible to visitors and the most vulnerable to de-wilding.

Nevertheless, the euphony of what had been accomplished for the park in those years could not drown the cacophony of concern for the future of the Stehekin Valley. Over the most vigorous protests by the NCCC, Congress provided for use of sand, rock, and gravel by Stehekin residents "as long as there were no adverse effects." It also authorized the "use or disposal of renewable natural resources" if "compatible with the purposes of this Act." The NCCC responded that it "smacked of political expediency instead of displaying backbone to properly protect the last vestiges of primitive America."

So while the scope of the controversies had narrowed considerably by late 1988, the seemingly endless game of protecting these lands was still far from over.

The Upper Skagit River valley (looking south) prior to the construction of Ross Dam. Big Beaver Valley lies between the two long ridges on the right that extend toward the river. Pumpkin Mountain (snow-free) rises at the end of the more northerly of the two ridges.

8

Ross Lake National Recreation Area

So farewell to the wilderness, the meadows and the forests,
Shining in the rain, blooming in the sun.
If we raise Ross Dam, we'll electrify a city
But we'll miss the lovely valley, when the wilderness is gone.

—Joan Reed
Farewell to the Wilderness
Sung into the official record of the Federal
Power Commission in Seattle, April 1974

THE SERENDIPITY THAT WAS NOT

ENTERING THE NORTHERN PICKETS via Little Beaver Creek, a few miles below Canada, four directors of the NCCC—Patrick Goldsworthy, Harvey Manning, Richard Brooks, and Ted Beck—ascended through forests as delightful as a wildlander could want. For the descent, they expected no greater pleasure in the valley of Big Beaver Creek and chose that as the way out purely for variety. What little praise of the Big Beaver had come to their ears was more than submerged by the grumbles of hikers who had come seeking a resounding panorama of the Picket Range, and in their disappointment offered accounts that were less than charitable. Big trees, it seemed, were blocking the views. However, in that summer of 1968, while waiting out the Congressional melodramatics of Senator Jackson and Congressman Aspinall, the pack-laden foursome felt they might as well enhance their geographical knowledge of the park-to-be by inspecting the unfamiliar valley. There was also a sizeable boundary indentation, perhaps insignificant, where the proposed Ross Lake

Ken Wilcox

Hiking among old-growth cedars in Big Beaver Valley.

NRA extended more than five miles up the Big Beaver, producing an odd deviation in the tentative outline of North Cascades National Park. After a week in glacial highlands, where every plant more than ankle-high seems a miracle, the descent into the woodlands below Beaver Pass was a joyous homecoming. The trail from the pass led downward into the valley through a textbook of forest zonation, a kaleidoscope of species, the trees steadily taller, trunks fatter—an ancient forest, if ever there was one.

That next-to-last day of the trip provided a fine, deep-forest complement to the time spent in the sky, rounding out a perfect North Cascades mini-expedition. The party awoke on the final morning, and since the prearranged pickup at the water's edge by Krazy Kat Dameron, operator of Ross Lake Resort, was not due until later in the day, they loitered over breakfast. The coffee-abstainers were first to pack up and leave. The three-cupper walked alone. During the final tramp to the Ross Lake reservoir, visions of cheeseburgers and milkshakes danced in their heads. Catching up with his companions at the reservoir, the three-cupper didn't say a word, just smiled. In fact, no one said a word. It was smiles all around, great big smiles.

What was there to say? Cumulatively, the four travelers could account for a century and a quarter of hiking in the North Cascades and a dozen-odd other mountain ranges. As experts in such matters, they were competent to adjudge, on the spot, with no further deliberation, that the Big Beaver was one of the supreme forest valleys of the Northwest, which, of course, meant the world.

By all indications, Congress would soon transfer the valley from multiple-use status under the Forest Service to assured preservation under the Park Service. Yet the four trekking directors scarcely had been aware that the Big Beaver Valley was there. To be sure, Brock Evans had returned from the valley in September 1966 in a giddy transport, but being fresh from the tall corn of the Midwest he hugged every big tree he met. The NCCC couldn't save the whole of the beautiful world and had to deliberately restrict its vision to the more immediately possible, which was improbable enough. "Save the Big Beaver" had not been among the NCCC's battle cries. Rather, it fell into their laps. A serendipity—a palpable serendipity.

Krazy Kat's catamaran carried them fast as a speeding bullet back down the reservoir. Nearing Ross Dam the group saw workers clambering on a cliff.

"What are *they* up to?" asked the wildlanders.

Said Krazy Kat, "Getting ready to raise Ross Dam."

Well, imagine that. *Sic transit* serendipity.

PUTTING WILD WATER TO WORK

To persuade ranchers to holster their six-guns in times of dispute, Congress adopted the common law of the frontier, under which water, among other things, belonged to whomever got to it first with the most firepower, at which point a use permit could be secured from the Department of Agriculture. The water rights so obtained were as absolute as those of a miner to an ore body and its appurtenant soil, trees, flowers, and birds. No conflicting claims were allowed to hinder an entrepreneur from digging into his ore, or putting wild water to useful work. If forests and wildlife habitat were drowned or annihilated as a result, the continent had an abundance of land suitable for that; if the fish were decimated, other rivers had more and the ocean was full of them.

Let us glance aside (and ahead) for a moment to the second of two great disasters caused by the frontier water law in the North Cascades. In 1893 the Chelan Water and Power Company dammed the outlet of Lake Chelan, raising the level several feet—until the flood of June 1894 removed the dam along with the houses at Prince Creek and elsewhere, endangering Moore's Hotel at Fish Creek and Field's Argonaut Hotel at Stehekin. During the flood, the lake rose eleven feet above its 1892 pre-dam, low-water level. The flood was a Noah-scale convulsion of nature. Yet this 1894 catastrophe paled beside that of 1927. The little power company had been content to install a run-of-river

294 • WILDERNESS ALPS

plant on the Chelan River in 1903, sufficient to power the local light bulbs. But in 1925 the Washington Water Power Company of Spokane heeded a request of the Great Northern Railroad to illuminate the tunnel under Stevens Pass, and by 1927 Chelan's new outlet dam was completed. The lake rose steadily through the summer, drowning the primeval beaches built up by a dozen millennia of wind-driven waves, as well as most of the deltas that derived their sediments from centuries of snowmelt torrents from the highlands. By the time the project was tidied up in 1929, the high-pool level had risen twenty-one feet, drowning thousands of acres, most tragically the five-hundred-acre delta of the Stehekin River. Its forest was logged and/or burned. Buildings were demolished or moved. The Field Hotel was dismantled, some of it salvaged for the Golden West Lodge; the rest was scavenged by residents or torched. The boat landing was shifted to Purple Point.

When the Chelan Public Utility District, which had taken over the license, went up for a fifty-year license renewal in the mid-1970s, the NCCC contributed to scoping the value of reestablishing a more natural lake, fixing the level permanently at low pool, and thereby limiting the operation to a run-of-river producer. This action would, of course, reduce power production. More importantly, the half-century accumulation of docks were unusable except near high pool, which by terms of the license was required to be attained on or near July 1 and maintained until about September 1. The Council recognized these political and economic realities but knew, too, that in another fifty years would come another application for relicensing, and felt that a precedent should be established on the record for possible future reference.

So it was that Lake Chelan was reservoirized, as were other lakes and many rivers on both sides of the Cascades. The deed done to Lake Chelan may sadden a visitor who arrives at Stehekin during low pool, gazes over the gray mudflats, perhaps visualizing the vanished groves of cottonwood and ancient cedars along the sloughs and oxbows, the wildlife once hidden away in that square mile of wildwoods and wild water. Yet there does still remain a veritable, if damaged, lake.

When the dams were built at Chelan, there was no Ross Lake. Today, from Newhalem to Canada—a stretch of more than thirty miles—there no longer is a Skagit River. After a Denver-financed local outfit went bankrupt mucking about Diablo Canyon from 1905 to 1908, contemplating the hydroelectric potentialities there, the water rights were secured by Stone & Webster, the Boston-based parent of Puget Sound Traction, Power and Light, which in 1913 obtained a fifty-year permit from the Department of Agriculture for its subsidiary, the Skagit Power Company. As it happened, a colossus was about to bestride the Skagit, and the firm would be forced to settle for dams on the much smaller Baker River (a Skagit tributary near Mount Baker).

James Delmage ("J.D.") Ross was born in Chatham, Ontario, in 1872, and by age 11 was emulating Benjamin Franklin by flying a kite in a thunderstorm. He came to the Northwest in 1898, first to dig gold, then was employed by Seattle City Light as an engineer shortly after the utility was founded in 1902. City Light was created by the voters to bust up the local electric power and streetcar monopoly run by Puget Sound Traction. The thirty-year-old Ross quickly convinced the boss to let him help design and oversee construction of the city's first power plant on the Cedar River, east of Seattle. Completed in 1905, it was the first municipally owned power-generation facility in the nation. However, the Cedar River project, by itself, would not be enough to power Seattle, and Ross quickly turned his attention to unused rivers. His first choices were the White River, just south of Seattle, the Skokomish River in the Olympic Mountains, and Sunset Falls on the Skykomish River east of Everett. For various reasons, including being beaten out by Puget Sound Traction, those sites were dropped from consideration. In any event, the really big sources of power were presumed to be in the North Cascades. By 1911, when Ross was appointed superintendent of Seattle City Light, he was already determined to develop the power potential of the upper Skagit River. The Skagit was, far and away, the region's largest river (second only to the Columbia River in Washington State), but the arch-enemy already had the federal permits. Ross filed claims on the Sauk and Suiattle but his drillers couldn't find any requisite bedrock beneath the sand and gravel. Then, glory be, the Boston magnates grew careless about their Skagit permits, neglected to start construction on time, and as quick as a blood-smelling shark, Ross made his move, cross-filing on Diablo Canyon and Ruby Creek. The Eastern interests, bogeymen of the Western populists, counterattacked with the forces of Harvard Law School. Ross then journeyed at his own expense to Washington, D.C., and there accused the Boston scoun-

Seattle City Light Superintendent J.D. Ross

PHOTO COURTESY OF SEATTLE CITY LIGHT

drels of unpatriotically failing to support the war effort by not putting the Skagit to work to defeat The Enemy. At the same time he so vigorously preached "power to the people" that he was able to persuade Secretary of Agriculture David Houston to take action. On December 22, 1917, Houston revoked the Skagit Power Company's permit and in less than a month, on January 18, 1918, issued the City of Seattle a preliminary permit to begin construction. Puget Sound Traction (a.k.a. Puget Power) was no quitter, however. Backed by Seattle newspapers and bankers, the rival continued machinating throughout the 1920s and into the 1930s, but ultimately Puget was outfoxed by Ross.

The first phase of the Ross gambit was the Gorge Powerhouse, built originally as a wooden dam. On September 17, 1924, President Calvin Coolidge pressed a gold key at the White House, which sent Skagit electricity south to ignite the bright lights of Seattle.

Second on the agenda was Diablo Canyon, but the Eastern Interests and their henchmen (some of them among Seattle's leading citizens) weren't about to throw in the towel to Ross's naked socialism. Bill Barich, in *The New Yorker*, later described the Ross combat strategy:

> In 1928 Ross escorted twenty-seven members of the Seattle City Women's Club on a tour of the project. This outing became the prototype of a more elaborate tour, which by the mid-thirties was capable of bringing nearly two thousand people a week to the Skagit during the warm summer months. The purpose was to sell them on the Rossian vision of power. "We lure 'em with a display of beautiful growing things they've always been taught couldn't thrive in regions this far north, and they come flocking—all we can handle," said Ross. "When they get here, they see the dam and the powerhouses—and that's what we want 'em to see." But it was the window dressing that made a lasting impression. Ross transformed the area around the project into an Arabian Nights fantasy. Exotic flowers and trees were planted by the riverside paths; in winter, the more perishable species, like orchids, were moved into the Gorge powerhouse to protect them against frost. There were trout and goldfish ponds along the paths, too. At Diablo, Ross collected a menagerie that included pheasants, peacocks, mountain sheep, cockatiels, African lovebirds, Mexican black squirrels, and an albino deer. His masterpiece was the waterfall at Ladder Creek, just behind the Gorge powerhouse. There, after dark, visitors gathered to watch colored floodlights illuminate the cataract while one of Ross's favorite songs—either "By the Waters of Minnetonka," or "Hark! Hark! My Soul"—soared from loudspeakers into the alpine atmosphere.

Upon completion in August 1930, Diablo Dam was the highest in the world—389 feet. It would take several more years to install the turbines, fill the basin, and begin producing power. In the meantime, tour boats on Diablo Reservoir cruised past islets where, upon approach of the vessel, music burst from the bushes. At night, colored lights on waterfalls played a visual symphony. The Eastern interests had their revenge in 1931 when their hireling, Seattle Mayor Frank Edwards, abruptly fired the ever-popular Ross. In response, public power advocates began a recall campaign, collecting 200,000 petition signatures, and within a couple of months the voters gave Mayor Edwards the boot. Federal antitrust laws took aim on overzealous private utility providers, and the Stone and Webster cartel was soon dissolved. Ross, the martyr triumphant, ascended to glory in the federal pantheon of Power to the People. In 1935 he was appointed by FDR to the new Securities and Exchange Commission (SEC), where he served with fellow commissioner William O. Douglas. In 1936, Diablo Dam, which had quickly become the world's second tallest—second to the just-completed Hoover Dam on the Colorado—finally came online, in an era that saw electric rates in Seattle plunge from twenty cents per kilowatt-hour for monopolized power in 1905 to less than a penny in the 1930s under City Light. The development of hydroelectric power in the Pacific Northwest advanced at full throttle as people gazed in disbelief at the Grand Coulee Dam rising out of the Columbia River. Bonneville Dam was next, with much more to come. With so much power for the people, President Roosevelt needed a capable manager—not to build the dams, but to manage all that power—and in November 1937 J.D. Ross was made the first administrator of the Bonneville Power Administration.

After 1937, tourists could begin to admire the start of Ross's most supreme erection, Ruby Dam. But The Colossus was no longer bestriding the Skagit. Nor did J.D. Ross live to see its completion. Upon his death in March 1939 (from a heart attack), he was buried at Newhalem in a crypt blasted from the rock of Goodell Mountain, renamed Ross Mountain. President Roosevelt sent Japanese cherry trees to grace the shrine. Ruby Dam was renamed Ross Dam, and this final Ross monument was brought to first-phase completion in 1940. By 1949 two lesser additions took the dam to a height of 540 feet from foundation rock to dam top—a towering mass, but almost two hundred feet shorter than Hoover Dam. At high pool, the new lake flooded twenty-four miles of valley all the way north to the Canadian border and a little beyond, the flat water averaging more than a mile in width from valley wall to wall.

Tens of thousands of Seattleites came for City Light's flowers and music, the tour boat on Diablo Reservoir, and the train ride on the city's railroad from Rockport to Reflector Bar in the town of Diablo, huddled near the base of the dam. The most famous attraction was not aesthetic but alimentary—the gut-buster meals served up at a fraction of the normal cost. In those hungry years of the Great Depression, the tens of thousands who returned to Seattle bulging at the belly became devout followers of Ross and Seattle City Light.

A price was paid, nevertheless, for those groaning bellies. Skagit historian Will D. Jenkins compared the before and after at Diablo:

> Only a remnant of the deep and narrow gorge once known as Diablo Canyon remains. It carries a trickle of water, or as much as the City sees fit to allow. . . . When I was a boy and before the City invaded the upper river, Diablo roared with the thunder of white water pouring from the snowfields of the high Cascades, spewing and boiling between vertical walls, that, at one point in the choke of the bore, were estimated to be less than eight feet apart.

The U.S. Geological Survey maps show the after and the before of Ross Lake reservoir. The long, wide strip of blue depicts the reservoir's high-pool elevation, which at the spillway is 1,603 feet (the dam top is 1,611 feet). Blue contour lines reach beneath the surface to trace the course of the drowned river that was—the meanders from one valley wall to the other, the meander-cutoff sloughs and oxbows, the marshes and swamps. Because the broad, flat valley of Big Beaver barely drops a hundred feet in the final six miles to the lake, all six miles would be flooded by a further raising of the dam. From the lake's 1968 high-water line, the Big Beaver's original stream course plunged three hundred feet in its last mile to the river. A hiker who knows Big Beaver Valley or the "Great Dismal Swamp" of Thunder Creek can visualize the lost Skagit, can see that J.D. Ross and his disciples, without exaggeration, wreaked more destruction of natural wonders in the North Cascades than all the other dammers, all the highwaymen, all the dirty miners, and half the loggers combined.

That damage was a foreword to what Glen Canyon Dam would wreak on 186 miles of the Colorado River and a hundred exquisite side canyons in the late 1950s and early 1960s. Engineers from the Bureau of Reclamation selected the site for that dam just as the Ross Dam neared completion. Finished in 1966 and still fresh in the minds of the NCCC foursome at Big Beaver, Glen Canyon Dam—a 710-foot-high monolith—was a tradeoff for convincing the Bureau not to build dams at Echo Park and Split Mountain in Dinosaur National Monument. The wildlands saved were David Brower's first big win as executive director of the Sierra Club, yet he always regretted what was lost. "I had never seen Glen Canyon," he wrote. "I sat on my duff. . . . I was uncharacteristically reasonable. I compromised." Once it was clear how costly that decision had been, Brower became convinced that he had underestimated the political clout of the conservation movement. "By being just a bit less reasonable," he said, "I could have stopped the construction of Glen Canyon Dam."

Photo courtesy of Patrick Goldsworthy

Artist's depiction of High Ross Dam, complete with roads, a large parking area, and boat launch. Powerhouse below, with North Cascades Highway in the upper right.

The dams on the Skagit—Diablo, Ross, and the new High Gorge Dam completed in 1961 near Newhalem—all slipped through before people had become sufficiently aware of what was about to be lost.

By 1968, however, the tide had turned. Thanks to the work of many, the public had become far more interested in saving what was left of the wild North Cascades. It became ever-apparent that Seattle City Light wasn't finished with the Skagit River. The utility was, in fact, finalizing its plans to raise its highest dam, Ross, by 125 feet, to which the four surveyors had been alerted at the end of that summer outing in 1968.

BACK-OF-THE-ENVELOPE ENGINEERING

The North Cascades Study Team recommended in 1965 that the Seattle City Light project area be placed in the national park. City Light requested otherwise, and thus we have now a Ross Lake NRA. The NCCC was not too upset, since the statutory protection given by Congress in 1968 was essentially identical to that of a park. Further, the Council was well aware of City Light's grander plans to raise Ross Dam and flood the Big Beaver; to flood Thunder Creek upstream to McAllister Creek and dry it up downstream by piping the water through a tunnel to Ross Reservoir; and to build a fourth dam on the Skagit River near Copper Creek, drowning an eight-mile stretch of the Skagit downstream from Newhalem. But the timing was thought to be so distant that years and years would be available for some polite reasoning.

Having learned otherwise from Krazy Kat on that serendipitous day at Ross Lake, the NCCC directors paid a friendly visit to the heir of J.D. Ross, City Light Superintendent John Nelson. They described their Big Beaver epiphany and suggested embarking on a joint and amicable cost-benefit analysis. For a start, they asked, "How much power will a higher Ross Dam generate?"

Nelson provided basic data: an increase in dam height of 125 feet and the additional water that would be impounded. Of the energy generated by water falling that many more feet, Nelson said, "You can figure it out yourself on the back of an envelope!"

NCCC engineers Richard Brooks and Ted Beck set out to do exactly that but quickly found that the math would require a fairly sizable envelope. What were construction costs and thus the per-kilowatt costs? Costs of alternative sources of power? Seattle's needs for more power? When was it needed? To what extent would the Skagit increments meet those needs? A further intricacy was the difference between firm power (which can be offered day in and day out, never ceasing) and peaking power (which, by opening wide the turbine intakes, can be a much higher figure, but only briefly, as during the daily supper-cooking hours in the cities).

Peaking power, declared by City Light to be the major contribution of their proposed High Ross Dam, is a slippery thing to get hold of. City Light's consulting firm said High Ross would provide 140,000 peaking kilowatts; Nelson told the Seattle City Council the figure was 204,000; he later told the press the figure was 240,000. Slippery indeed. More so when the Council engineers discovered mistakes in some basic arithmetic on the back of City Light's envelope. At one point City Light calculations counted the same water for firm power and peaking power—as in eating your cake and having it too. Nelson offhandedly estimated the High Ross cost at an attractive $44.6 million, but Brooks and Beck analyzed that sum item by item, plugged in overlooked necessaries (such as patching holes in the dam), factored in inflation (City Light estimates dated from an already ancient past), and arrived at a figure of $65 million. City Light issued a few groans but eventually confessed in the glare of public scrutiny to $208 million.

The NCCC had assumed City Light to be a soundly managed utility and was shocked, needless to say, to find high-paid, respected public officials proceeding in apparent reckless haste on a project of huge cost before performing any reliable engineering studies and calculations. Zero consideration had been given to environmental costs. The bureaucracy presumed to rest on Rock-of-Gibraltar science and engineering that was revealed to be as suspect as that of the Forest Service.

That was not, in itself, a bad thing. If Ross was the power angel of Seattle, history had made him so. For twenty-odd years he was the charismatic leader in a public ownership crusade against a free-enterprise devil, Stone & Webster's Puget Sound Traction, Power, and Light Company, that conspired in cabal with the Seattle Chamber of Commerce, as well as Seattle's largest newspapers, merchant chiefs, and thieves to extort excess profits from the citizens of Seattle. Officers of the NCCC were themselves fellow-travelers of the old-time religion of Ross, prophet of Progressive idealism. They were deeply disillusioned to find that Ross' successors in the high priesthood failed to notice that if the old ideals are not kept constantly renewed they can end up stinking like last week's fish.

For its part, City Light was deeply shaken by the revelation that there were people walking the same Earth once honored by the feet of J.D. Ross who did not venerate his monument. In 1968 Power to the People had not yet deteriorated into the Washington Public Power Supply System and its tragic misadventure in nuclear power generation. The WPPSS folly would be embalmed in history as "WHOOPS!" and Superintendent Nelson couldn't fathom what was happening to the world of his youth.

The well-publicized greed of Puget Sound Traction (later called Puget Sound Power and Light, or just Puget Power), and the recall of Mayor Edwards, had exalted City Light to a realm above politics. Its 1970 budget was expected to be, as always, reverently rubberstamped.

But on October 3, 1969, a year and a day after the park was established, came a shocker. The Seattle City Council chambers were jammed for the City Light hearing. Speaker after speaker delivered precise objections to City Light's proposals. Every local conservation organization was represented: The Mountaineers, Federation of Western Outdoor Clubs, North Cascades Conservation Council, Puget Sound Group of the Sierra Club, Seattle Audubon Society, Washington Environmental Council, Washington Roadside Council, and Friends of the Earth, as well as Allied Arts, Citizens Choose an Effective City Council, and many individuals. One concerned individual was an ecologist of the University of Washington College of Forest Resources who posed a formidable series of questions that had never occurred to City Light. (In 1990 Professor Samuel Epstein, from the University of Illinois, coined the term "indentured academics" in reference to fraudulent, industry-funded science in the debate over dioxins. Happily, there also are the unindentured.) The forestry professor offered his science for free, while two other U.W. professors were on hand to offer their testimony for a fee. One of them, Grant Sharpe, had helicoptered about the North Cascades looking for big, old western red cedars to help justify the City Light position that the Big Beaver's giant cedars would not be missed. Sharpe remained stoic when Philip A. Briegleb, chairman of the Forest Service Natural Areas Committee, and Dr. Jerry Franklin, liaison officer of the Society of American Foresters, testified that the Big Beaver was the sole site in the region that fit their needs for studies of valley-bottom cedar. Interest in designating the valley a Research Natural Area predated the park designation.

The City Light hearing was a good showing overall, and conservationists emerged jubilant—for a while. However, most City Councilors were of a generation that had come of age during the Ross crusade against Puget Power and took this to be yet another wrestling match between the angels and the devils of progress. Eyes clouded by the excitement of the 1930s failed to comprehend the new reality of 1969. On October 30 the Council met to hear Nelson's request to seek permission from the Federal Power Commission to raise Ross Dam. Patrick Goldsworthy warned that the conservation community considered the issue national and historic and would oppose every step of the lengthy legal procedures. He guaranteed a regional and national public information campaign, intervention before the Federal Power Commission (FPC), and court action after that.

The City Council voted five to four to give Nelson free rein.

DOUBLE, DOUBLE, TOIL AND TROUBLE

A five-to-four vote. The City Council was, after all, a bit confused and had been led to wonder whether it should trust engineers who seemed to struggle with grade-school arithmetic. A series of nine more City Council hearings brought some enlightenment, added to the confusion, and raised the temperature level.

City Light announced that it was deferring consideration of the Thunder Creek diversion pending further study. At Ross Dam, it was discovered that, without public notice, City Light already had raised high pool two-and-a-half feet, through spillway tinkering, which explained why reservoir-shore picnic tables installed by the Forest Service were awash in the waves and the reservoir had flooded a mile into Canada. The state Department of Game protested that raising the reservoir to 1,725 feet would destroy fish-spawning grounds for which there was no possible replacement. Professor Sharpe said he had found "whole valleys of western red cedar in other drainages" and opined that a loss of trees in the Big Beaver valley would be more than compensated by increased flat water for motorboats.

The late climber-industrialist Larry Penberthy spent a large sum on a series of Seattle ads addressed to Goldsworthy: "Dear Pat . . . You state that the animal life will be drowned. Pat, wake up! Beavers can swim!" The ads vilified the Big Beaver as "a vine-maple-filled, fly-and-mosquito-infested swamp." Penberthy continued: "I, and other mountaineers, would be delighted to pass quickly through this portion of the valley by boat. . . ." Penberthy, it should be added, was the founder of Mountain Safety Research (MSR) in Seattle and the inspiration behind a number of significant technological advances in mountaineering, from portable backpacking stoves and redesigned ice axes and ice screws to weather-resistant outerwear with the innovative ventilation systems generally known as pit zips. Yet he was not, as his own words testify, especially impressed with what others would revere as the largest stand of giant western red cedar in the United States. Nonetheless, Seattle City Light was happy to have him. Penberthy's advice, unlike Sharpe's, was free.

City Light claimed High Ross would bring $3 million per year in gross benefits. NCCC mathematicians took City Light's own figures and found a net annual *loss* in excess of $1 million.

On December 2, 1970, Mayor Wes Uhlman recognized that the world had changed and wrote the City Council opposing the application to the Federal Power Commission and ordering City Light not to proceed. On December 14 the City Council voted six to two to require City Light to make the application. On December 19 it was done. The NCCC immediately filed in opposition, engaged two attorneys, and set out to raise a $50,000 Skagit Defense Fund.

The "Kerosene Kid" (a.k.a. Joe Miller), lead pamphleteer of the High Ross years, offered a status report in *The Wild Cascades*:

> By their very nature, units of the National Park System are constantly vulnerable to those segments of our society which would exploit their resources. . . . To prevent Seattle City Light from implementing its destructive proposals in Ross Lake National Recreation Area will require as tough a fight as conservationists ever have waged. . . . The protracted battle through the Seattle City Council was a pretty foregone conclusion. It was a successful holding operation, however, gaining us 14 months. We have fallen back to prepared positions and are ready to take on Electric John's forces on a new field of battle. Surrender? *Merde!*

To the Federal Power Commission ·

On April 16 and 17, 1971, the Washington State Ecological Commission held its own hearings on High Ross Dam. Superintendent Nelson, grumping that previous hearings had been dominated by the conservation coalition, said, "Up until today we have not heard from the public. These hearings will correct that." City Light brought in forty of its friends, representatives of industry and labor and allied bureaucracies. The conservationists brought sixty-five speakers: ten experts—all serving *pro bono*—in ecology, economics, and engineering; eleven representatives of local citizen groups; five representatives of national and international organizations; eleven representatives of Canadian organizations; and four Canadian government officials.

John Nelson reacted predictably. "It was not a good hearing," he said. "It was just a soapbox on which people stood to make speeches."

On September 9 the Ecological Commission announced it was split, three to three, leaving it to the director, John Biggs, who previously, as state Game Department director, had opposed the project, to break the tie. The handwriting was on the wall, and on December 2 John Nelson resigned. Less than a week later, on December 8, 1971, John Biggs cast his vote: a resounding "No!" The next day Governor Dan Evans supported Biggs and suggested that Seattle take a closer look at the environmental impact of High Ross Dam.

The Seattle elections of November 1971 had already disheartened Nelson, converting what had become a six-to-three Council majority favoring High Ross into a five-to-four majority against. New hearings by the City Council were held on March 31, 1972. Mayor Uhlman reiterated his opposition. A large Canadian delegation suggested the city adopt a good-neighbor policy, given that the raised dam would flood more than six thousand acres of land north of the

The deforested bed of the Ross Lake reservoir near the border with Canada.

THE WILD CASCADES
April 1970

NORTH CASCADES CONSERVATION COUNCIL

border. High Ross would have been doomed had not the five-member majority included three unique individuals, one perhaps a shade too clever, one a shade too erratic, and one a shade too invisible to the naked eye. All three were suspected by conservationists of being secret agents for the enemy. These well-scrubbed reformers managed to craft three separate, different, and ingenious compromises that made little sense. On April 10, City Light emerged trembling and sweating but triumphant from a close, confused vote that no one really understood.

The Kerosene Kid summed up, perhaps too generously: "We shall not criticize our friends on the Council too strongly, but . . . We're back where we started eighteen months ago."

To January 29, 1973. City Light submitted its wheelbarrow full of testimony to the FPC. The Kerosene Kid, now metamorphosed by the national oil shortage into the "Kaopectate Kid," reviewed the submittal: "The direct testimony and exhibits consisted of four Sears-catalog-sized books [including that of] Professor Grant Sharpe [and] 194 half-page photographs reproduced from his famous slide show. The most artistically composed shots were four pictures of outdoor latrines."

On October 25 the FPC released its draft Environmental Impact Statement, based chiefly on City Light data. Then on February 1, 1974, the state Department of Ecology published its Environmental Assessment, a 197-page analysis of environmental data submitted by both advocates and opponents. The thoughtful document concluded, "The loss of Big Beaver Valley has not been justified." Further, "the environmental implications in Canada . . . remain critical and unsolved." Finally, "prior to any approval to raise Ross Dam, approval also must be assured for the designation of pristine and wilderness areas, including Big Beaver Valley, within the National Recreation Area."

In a rare concession to public opinion, the FPC held hearings on April 23, 25, and 26 in Bellingham and Seattle. Testimony in Bellingham was two for High Ross, and forty against, all but five of them Canadians. In Seattle the testimony was two-to-one against. So many people had no opportunity to speak that Hearing Judge Lande graciously acceded to Patrick Goldsworthy's request for a Saturday session; the vote there was thirty-five-to-zero against. Monday, April 29, was the first of five days of formal evidentiary hearings in Seattle. On May 20 the hearings resumed in Washington, D.C. and continued intermittently into November. At the end of fifty-three days, cross-examination began of twenty-two witnesses for City Light, eleven for the FPC, four for the state of Washington Departments of Game and Fisheries, and nine for Canadian intervenors; the transcript of this first stage ran to 7,826 pages and was evaluated by the Kerosene Kid as being "deadly dull, boring, nit-picking, and repetitious."

In January 1975 Judge Lande returned to Seattle for rebuttal testimony, shuttling to Washington, D.C. for more in late February. On June 18 the FPC testimony was completed, and final briefs were submitted by August 15. The ensuing months passed quietly.

Then on May 27, 1977, recently elected Governor Dixy Lee Ray and her new ecology director, Wilbur Hallauer, reversed the state's position on High Ross to one of support, but hardly anyone noticed. The matter had gone beyond the state's influence, which was purely advisory, carrying no weight either in city or federal affairs. On July 5, after sixty-eight days of hearings over six years, generating some ten thousand pages of testimony, the FPC issued its decision: Seattle City Light's application was approved. NCCC attorneys J. Richard Aramburu and Thomas H.S. Brucker were not surprised; the FPC had never deviated from a straight-out nineteenth-century utilitarianism. The agency never had met a dam it didn't like. Historically, the agency had routinely approved projects that caused the destruction of enormously valuable economic and recreation resources.

On September 16 the NCCC, Run Out Skagit Spoilers (ROSS) from Canada, David Brousson of the British Columbia Legislative Assembly, the U.S. Department of the Interior, and a coalition of affected Indian tribes (Swinomish Tribal Community, Sauk–Suiattle Tribe, and Upper Skagit Tribe) filed for rehearing, which the newly renamed and reorganized Federal Energy Regulatory Commission (FERC) granted.

On August 4, 1978, FERC issued final approval of High Ross Dam. Seattle City Light Superintendent Gordon Vickery (who replaced Nelson in 1972), declared construction would start in December. But on September 27, the conservationist coalition filed a Petition for Review in the District of Columbia Circuit Court of Appeals. The appeal was denied in 1980. The next logical step would have been the U.S. Supreme Court, but the NCCC's attorneys advised that nothing further was likely to be gained. So the Ross circus moved to another tent—to the north.

From 1968 to 1978, the NCCC spent $60,000 on the High Ross debate, an enormous sum for a citizen group lacking funding from tax-supported agencies and businesses expecting a profit from their contributions. Over the same period, City Light spent $4 million. Up to 1972, $12,000 had gone to Dr. Sharpe alone and at least $700,000 to other "forestry and recreation" consultants who generally provided whatever "science" the client ordered.

It was all for naught, or so it seemed. All the hearings in Seattle, all the posturing in Olympia, all the FPC's and FERC's slow grinding, for naught. But the effort, really, was not for nothing. Victory was seen at the outset to be improbable at best, but the holding action gained time, years, keeping in check the seemingly invincible City Light steamroller, poking holes in the boiler which let out so much steam that it was no longer beyond citizen control. Meanwhile, new forces in the north were mobilizing. The final whip, in fact, was held by a ringmaster north of the international boundary.

Had any functionary of City Light listened to the NCCC with a more open mind, its back-of-the-envelope engineers could have offered the City Council an easy, rational, and mutually profitable way out of the High Ross standoff, the one that eventually was adopted: don't build High Ross Dam. Instead, sign long-term contracts with British Columbia to purchase power, of which its own dam-crazed government had a huge surplus and little market. Granted, the problem of reservoirizing would be exported to Canada, to be confronted there later, but meanwhile the Big Beaver, the Canadian Skagit, and tributary valleys would be preserved.

CANADA, O CANADA!

The opening scene in the High Ross drama was the threatened destruction of Big Beaver's cedar groves and marshes. Also to be drowned were the lower stretches of Ruby Creek, Little Beaver, Lightning Creek, and every other tributary south of the international boundary. What was to be the final act began with a public appearance of Run Out Skagit Spoilers, or ROSS, at the 1971 and 1972 Seattle City Council hearings. ROSS, founded December 9, 1969, was the spearhead for the British Columbia Wildlife Federation, Lower Mainland Wildlife Association, Alpine Club of Canada, Varsity Outdoor Club, Society for Pollution and Environmental Control (SPEC), British Columbia Mountaineering Club, and Sierra Club of British Columbia. Among its leaders were Ken Farquharson, a consulting engineer experienced on three continents, who became a director of the NCCC in order to serve as liaison, and David Brousson, Liberal Member of the British Columbia Legislative Assembly for North Vancouver. Although much of the drama unfolded south of the border, the decisive power lay to the north.

At those early hearings ROSS described the losses in British Columbia: High Ross would flood 6,300 acres, or roughly ten square miles, of public lands in the Canadian Skagit, the only major valley in the Lower Mainland with a spacious bottomland that had not been drowned by British Columbian reservoirs. It had the best fly-fishing near Vancouver, a large wildlife population, and a huge potential for camping and hiking in easy range of the bulk of the province's population. The agreement signed with City Light in 1967 would run 99 years. For the inundation, British Columbia would receive $36,000 a year, or $5.50 per flooded acre. Many Canadians would have loved to obtain vacation-camp acreage at rent this low.

Until the High Ross affair mounted to a scandal, few Canadians and fewer

Americans knew that the International Joint Commission (IJC), which had been established by the 1909 Boundary Waters Treaty between the United States and Great Britain and given authority to approve or disapprove various kinds of proposals affecting waters crossing the border, had assembled in a veritable closet in Vancouver in 1942. Representatives of the British Columbia provincial government and the City of Seattle authorized City Light to flood British Columbia. In 1942, as a frightening war raged across Europe, the press on both sides of the border had more urgent matters to report than hypothetical constructions in a remote wilderness. In 1969 the constructions no longer were hypothetical, highways had brought the wilderness close to the metropolis of the Canadian West, and the archaic agreement was flushed out of the closet into the public press.

The fourteen years from the formation of ROSS to the Skagit River Agreement of 1983 are told in some fourteen thousand words by John Gibson in the Fall 1985 through Spring 1987 issues of *The Wild Cascades*. Candidly, though the essay is masterful, it is so minutely definitive that no reader who was not a veteran of the combat could get through it without nodding off. It was like a chronicle of the Thirty Years War for a person who didn't care a fig about seventeenth-century Germany. As the battle dragged on, the Seattle environmental community (not to mention the general public) grew weary of the skirmishes, one after another, year after year, on the same fields of battle. Had it not been for a handful of activists south of the border whose patience and fortitude were inexhaustible, and the bursting energy of the growing host of activists to the north, City Light would have won the fight by the weight of sheer boredom. Years later, Ken Farquharson commented, "We were naive enough to think that the deal that Seattle had made with the province was so one-sided and so bad, that we could turn this thing over in twelve months. . . . Yes. We were naive."

On the Seattle front, City Light continued to plod doggedly in the footsteps of J.D. Ross. Mayor Charles Royer, elected in 1977, was aware that this cow no longer was sacred, and his sentiments were openly environmental. However, circumstances forced him to play a deep game. His opposition to nuclear power, another City Light enthusiasm, compelled him to look favorably on hydropower. There was also the boodle. Granted, Seattle had negotiated a steal from British Columbia in 1942, but were Seattle ratepayers so upright they would make voluntary restitution?

On the British Columbia front, the government alternated between the Socred (Social Credit) premier, W.A.C. Bennett, darling of Seattle City Light and the corporate exploiters of a dozen nations, and the New Democrat (Socialist-lite) premier, Dave Barrett, foe of exploiters of every nation, including the Empire of Seattle. Later came the son of W.A.C., W.R. ("Bill") Bennett, subscribing fully to his father's principles (or lack of same). But thanks to the chastening effect of an electoral defeat at the hands of Barrett, this Bennett was more pragmatic. ROSS and its partners had done their work. All eighteen members of the province's delegation to the federal Parliament stood in opposition to High Ross Dam; two of these were in the federal cabinet.

The press made things a bit hot for the City Light-loving Socreds. The *Vancouver Sun* editorialized: "Ottawa has saved BC from itself before when it passed the International Rivers Improvement Act to prevent Mr. Bennett from striking a sweetheart hydro power deal with the American Kaiser interests. Once again, it must fall on Ottawa to keep us from mutilating ourselves."

Chapter followed chapter. To recap, non-chronologically: In 1974 Mayor Uhlman conducted secret correspondence with British Columbia. In 1979 Deputy Mayor Bob Royer engaged in *tête-à-tête* behind closed doors also up north, the first meeting of political leaders on the two sides since 1967. Governor Evans opposed the dam awhile before reverting to a more comfortable stance that bordered on mugwumping. Governess Dixy's stentorian shout was "Dam! Dam! Dam them all!" (A conservative Democrat and leading advocate of nuclear power, Ray lost her bid for reelection in the September 1980 primary to State Senator, and now Congressman, Jim McDermott.) In November 1981, outraged by the WHOOPS! nuclear power fiasco, including billions of dollars in cost overruns, Washington State voters handily approved Initiative 394, requiring voter approval of bonds to finance any energy project of more than 250 megawatts. The unthinking approval of public power *per se*, simply because it was not private power, had obviously cooled, and a major pre-WHOOPS! catalyst for that reversal of sentiment was High Ross.

At the end of 1981, City Light was scrambling to begin construction by spring in order to meet the FERC deadline. Mayor Royer kept up his deep game, repeating that he couldn't see giving away a valid contract without value received. But such value was being discussed, and Canadians who had been militant in their rhetoric were softening toward a willingness to accept a compromise. Construction was delayed. Victory was nearly at hand.

On March 30, 1983, having computed the dollar costs and benefits to each nation of not raising the dam, of inundated lands, and the rest, an agreement was signed whereby Seattle would make payments to an endowment fund of $1 million a year for four years plus an annual payment based on power sold. British Columbia would maintain a similar obligation at $250,000 for four years. The eighty-year term of the agreement factored in the amount of power High Ross would have generated. Seattle would allow British Columbia to raise the level of its Seven-Mile Reservoir on the Pend Oreille River, backing up water about a mile onto American land owned by City Light. The agreement was ratified as an international treaty (U.S. Treaty #11088) on April 2, 1984. High Ross Dam was not to be.

Over the next century the High Ross affair may expand in recognized significance as historians review the way the times were a-changing, from the Woody Guthrie songs in praise of FDR's New Deal dams to the comedy-tragedy of WHOOPS! and the end of an era of nuclear power plants and large new dams in the Pacific Northwest. In 1983, however, the Seattle public was far more enthralled, and understandably so, by hurricanes in Florida and violence in New Jersey. The Skagit River story had gone on too long, the action was mainly behind closed doors, and though there was a lot of it, a single newsworthy multi-vehicle accident on the freeway splashed more blood across the blue-lit screen.

In the rare moments of visible drama, public officials jostled their way in front of the cameras. The NCCC shrugged, "That's show business." The Big Beaver epiphany of 1968 had been the beginning of a road that Seattle—and the nation—henceforth would travel. By 1984 the NCCC had spent $76,000, a huge amount for a small volunteer organization, but a tiny fraction of the Seattle outlay. As the Kerosene Kid commented, "We got a lot more miles per dollar out of our lawyers." North of the border, ROSS's Farquharson reflected, "It was totally volunteer. . . . Many of us were sort of seeing things that David Brower had done in the Colorado Canyon, and [we] took heart that indeed it was possible to stand up to government and to make a point."

In early 2003, NCCC attorney and board member Tom Brucker recalled things this way:

> People believed City Light was proceeding recklessly to build a project which had been proposed simply because it had been proposed, when there were alternatives. . . . You didn't need to do it. . . . If we had not intervened, [Seattle City Light] would have had their license, oh, four years after they applied, and the dam would have been built. But . . . the American interveners, the Canadian interveners, the State to some extent, really fought tooth and nail. It was apparent that there really would have been some significant environmental damage: wildlife, land, fisheries. I mean wildlife was going to lose a lot of winter range. We got the point across. Even though City Light got its license, we won the war. And I feel pretty good about that.

Brucker's comments were part of an interview for an oral history project of the Skagit Environmental Endowment Commission on which he presently serves. A graduate of Columbia Law School, he added a personal note on his interest in environmental law. In the 1960s, he said, "many, many people felt, as I did, that we have to have a different way of looking at things. . . . You don't get into environmental practice because of the money. You get into it because it's important."

In an era when Seattle City Light still was honored as among the noblest exhibits of Progressive populism, a small band had cried out, "The clothes have no Emperor!" And in an era when British Columbia was being so shamelessly sacrificed to a nineteenth-century-scale Great Barbecue that the United Nations denounced it in the same breath as Brazil, an even smaller band defied the province's brazenly corrupt and seemingly omnipotent Socred Machine and the bullying by its Big American Brother.

Kerosene Kid summarized in *The Wild Cascades*:

> The history of the fourteen-year-long High Ross struggle . . . stands out as a shining example of cooperation between environmental organizations of two adjoining nations. . . . The resentment ROSS was able to whip up over this blatant example of Yankee imperialism led to a new ecological awareness in B.C.

The two groups, ROSS and the NCCC, formed an alliance that shook governments from Seattle to Olympia to Washington, D.C., Vancouver to Victoria to Ottawa, and boldly emplaced the foundation for international recognition of the Greater North Cascades Ecosystem.

RELICENSING AND MITIGATING

As it happened, there was another critical layer to the Ross Reservoir saga.

To sum up Round One: In 1977 City Light's fifty-year license to exploit public waters of the Skagit River expired. A license amendment to permit High Ross was granted, effective in 1980, but construction was delayed by the NCCC/ROSS appeals to the courts, the British Columbia appeal to the International Joint Commission, asking for revocation of its 1942 decision to allow flooding of the Canadian Skagit, and at last the bartering negotiations between B.C. Hydro Authority and Seattle City Light.

In 1984 the U.S.–Canada Treaty implemented the agreement between Seattle City Light and British Columbia for a long-term transfer of electricity from Canada, payment by City Light of the equivalent capital cost of constructing increased generating capacity, and putting High Ross on hold until 2064. More importantly, the agreement established an environmental endowment fund of $5 million (plus annual contributions tied to power production) to be administered by a joint Canada–U.S. commission whose charge would be (verbatim):

a) To conserve and protect wilderness and wildlife habitat;

b) To enhance recreational opportunities in the Skagit Valley;

c) To acquire mineral or timber rights consistent with conservation and recreational purposes;

d) To conduct studies of need and feasibility of projects;

e) To plan for and construct hiking trails, foot bridges, interpretive displays and the like;

f) To cause the removal of stumps and snags in Ross Lake and on the shoreline as deemed appropriate, and the grooming and contouring of the shoreline, consistent with wildlife habitat protections; and

g) To connect, if feasible, Manning Provincial Park and the North Cascades National Park by a trail system.

The first appointments to the Skagit Enviromental Endowment Commission (SEEC) were NCCC Board Chairman Patrick Goldsworthy and ROSS's Ken Farquharson. Since its founding, SEEC has underwritten a host of projects in the upper Skagit basin with the funding supplied by Seattle City Light and the B.C. government under provisions of the treaty. The Commission continues to invest in conservation and recreation needs and remains a strong advocate for the protection and management of the upper Skagit watershed as a single cross-border ecosystem.

Round One, the long, bitter and at last successful fight to defeat High Ross, had taken the combined resources of the NCCC, ROSS, the tribes, state and federal resource managers (all of these as formal intervenors in the FERC deliberations), and myriad environmental organizations cheering them on from the sidelines. The fundamental issue had been the conversion of a wild river to a reservoir. In the 1920s, when exploitation of natural resources was defined as progress, society had rejoiced in the benefits of dams and ignored the costs. What mattered a few fish and trees alongside electric lights and trolley cars? Fifty years later, society reluctantly faced up to the "external" costs of the lost fish and forests.

While the High Ross Dam controversy was finally settled, Seattle City Light's federal license for the *existing* Skagit Project expired in 1977. The license would need to be renewed in order for the existing dams to keep operating. FERC granted the utility annual extensions, until the treaty of 1984, which removed any valid reason for delay. But delays continued, trying the patience even of the utility-friendly FERC, which in 1988 informed City Light that it must conduct studies to complete its application for relicensing and must do so in a timely manner. Thus began Round Two: the Skagit relicensing saga.

In the 1920s the chief function of the Federal Power Commission was allocating hydroelectric sites among fiercely competing applicants, private and public. By the late 1980s, a river was recognized by the nation as having many other things to do than make kilowatts. The FERC decision would need to take into account not only such legislation as the Fish and Wildlife Coordination Act of 1934 (and amendments thereto in 1958), the National Historic Preservation Act of 1966, and the Endangered Species Act of 1972, but also the National Environmental Protection Act of 1969, which required FERC's decision on relicensing to divulge the impacts, to consider alternative actions, and to propose mitigations that would at least partially compensate the nation for the fish, the forests, and the rest of the ecosystem to be sacrificed.

Other regulatory and land management changes also had to be factored in by FERC. In 1968 Congress had established Ross Lake NRA, a huge chunk of park-worthy scenic splendor split from the rest of the North Cascades National Park by Senator Jackson at the behest of City Light, but by no means cut from the nation's treasure house, administered as it was by the National Park Service. The importance of wildlife habitat was well established. Free-running Skagit waters not impounded behind the dams are protected under both the Wild and Scenic River Act designation for much of the upper Skagit and the Skagit Bald Eagle Reserve at Rockport.

Probably more significant to Round Two was the internal evolution of Seattle City Light. The top leadership of old was so set in its ways that there had to be a lot of retiring and dying off before the utility could enter modern times. In 1974 City Light was required by terms of the settlement of the NCCC lawsuit to set up an Environmental Affairs Department (EAD), although it functioned as a meek and mild little band among the engineers. As the older gorillas struggled to understand the increasingly complex technical environmental regulatory maze, they were grudgingly forced to accept EAD guidance. Conservationists, though ever suspicious of possible co-opters, also came to respect the EAD, set up by Superintendent Gordon Vickery, as an honest broker.

When Randy Hardy arrived at the City Light superintendent's desk in 1984, he understood the changes that had occurred since the era of Saint Ross. He saw that rear-guarding had made Round One of the relicensing an exercise in frustration, and perceived the inability of the Departments of Power Supply, Planning, and Engineering to envision alternatives other than those they had been trained to live by. He further saw the benefits of new ways of doings things, things of the sort that might be suggested by the EAD. When the FERC order came down from above, Hardy ordered his departments to shape up. Get to work, he said, and by that he didn't mean get to work stalling and frustrating, snooping for loopholes, evasions, or means of defeating the intent of new legislation and regulation, but getting together with all parties who had an interest in the relicensing, including the NCCC, to assemble a mitigation package to which all would agree before submitting it to FERC.

The NCCC did not contemplate full restoration of the Skagit River and tributaries, instant replacement of thousand-year-old cedars, ripping out dams, powerhouses, roads, and the bones of J.D. Ross from his crypt. However, neither did it come to the table hat in hand, thankful for whatever crumbs might be brushed its way. The High Ross victory was as frightening to City Light as the North Cascades National Park was to the Forest Service. To argue with a mule, the saying goes, first take a two-by-four and clout the critter on the head to get its attention. Conservationists had City Light's attention.

As a legal intervenor in the High Ross hearings, the NCCC was the only conservation organization to have official standing in the negotiations, but it by no means had to stand alone. Exercising its rights to enlist expert advisors, the NCCC drew on the Nature Conservancy for assistance on wildlife habitat and on the North Cascades Institute for environmental education plans and the concept for an Environmental Learning Center. Other intervenors spoke to the same or similar concerns: the Upper Skagit Tribe, the Swinomish Indian Tribal Community, the Sauk–Suiattle Tribe, the Bureau of Indian Affairs, the U.S. Fish and Wildlife Service, the Washington Departments of Wildlife, Ecology, and Fisheries, the National Marine Fisheries Service, and the National Park Service. The U.S. Forest Service said it could not afford to have a staff member participate in this process because of its other more important obligations. When NCCC President Dave Fluharty wrote back explaining the opportunity to advance river recreation and management objectives and said that the Council would be pleased to represent the Forest Service in these matters, the agency promptly sent a representative to the next meeting, and he served with distinction.

A note for the files of historians wishing to be truthful in assigning credit: the initiative in these proceedings was not taken by City Light or Seattle city government, even if at the conclusion their public relations people issued a prideful statement of self-congratulation. The press dutifully gulped the release, not seeking a second opinion, while singling out Superintendent Hardy for fulsome praise. The press failed to mention the names of the citizens who spent eleven years getting the mule's attention, most vigorously and persistently Patrick Goldsworthy, Dave Fluharty, Tom Brucker, Rick Aramburu, Lynn Weir, and most courteously Joe and Margaret Miller.

Seattle City Light and the NCCC-led coalition came to terms on the relicensing and signed a precedent-setting Settlement Agreement on April 26, 1991. The mitigation provided by the settlement agreements (there were several) included the following:

Flow modifications to protect anadromous fisheries, to make habitat improvements, and to do fish propagation and research.

$17 million to purchase more than four thousand acres of wildlife habitat and payments of $90,000 a year to monitor and research wildlife and ecosystems.

Construction of a greenhouse facility to raise thirty thousand plants a year for a North Cascades native plant propagation program.

$6 million to purchase the Diablo Lake Resort concession for the construction and support there, for thirty years, of an Environmental Learning Center.

Construction, rehabilitation, and maintenance of trails, campgrounds, and boat launches.

Landscaping in the towns of Newhalem and Diablo and along the powerline corridor and reservoir shore.

Steps to control erosion.

Documenting and mitigating impacts on archaeological resources, funding an inventory of traditional tribal cultural properties, and making payments to the tribes to support cultural activities.

This landmark agreement was not at all routine and must have shocked a few higher-ups at FERC. River exploiters do not generally express a desire to spend something on the order of $40 million (City Light claimed $100 million) mitigating their projects. Even with this price tag, many items that had been discussed for mitigation remained unmitigated, such as the visual impact of the power lines and transmission towers. This would have been a big expense had NCCC and other intervenors not settled for changes in management of the transmission corridor and decided to spend scarce mitigation dollars on land acquisition in the upper skagit ecosystem and establishing and equipping an environmental learning center where the environmental benefits seemed more important. At the NCCC's insistence the pact did not bar any party from fighting High Ross in the future, should the need arise. Should that construction ever be re-contemplated, it would require separate mitigation, and if $100 million was the price of mitigating City Light's ongoing operations, how much more would it have to pay to mitigate impacts to the Big Beaver valley? Or to Canada?

Five days after it was signed, Seattle City Light submitted the settlement agreements for all the licensing intervenors to FERC. In March 1994 FERC issued a draft environmental assessment for the Skagit River Project that cherry-picked certain provisions of the settlement agreements that it considered relevant to the license, and ignored the rest. In 1995 City Light and the intervenors petitioned FERC to reconsider its position, but FERC simply issued the license without incorporating all the terms of the settlement agreements. In *Contested Terrain*, David Louter's excellent administrative history of North Cascades National Park (published in 1998), he notes that the City of Seattle asked FERC to explain "why certain parts of each of the settlement agreements were included as license conditions and others were not." As Louter explains, "The most detailed explanation they received, for example, was when the commission excluded elk habitat from the wildlife mitigation plan. The commission chair stated tersely that FERC was not 'in the business of managing elk habitat.'" After another year of haggling over the fine print, FERC relented and the license was issued on June 27, 1996, with the settlement agreements intact. The mitigation could begin. A hugely expensive and endlessly protracted legal battle was avoided. Seattle City Light saved a ton of money. FERC had to remodel its applecart. The precedent set the stage for hundreds of upcoming FERC relicensing cases nationwide, and the agency grudgingly accepted the fact that settlement agreements worked far better than litigation.

THERE AIN'T NUTHIN' EVER EASY

Some distance into the twenty-first century the call will be raised, "Once more unto the breach, dear friends." Nothing is ever over until it's over. Thanks to the Skagit Wars of 1968–1991, there is and will be a breach to go unto. To pronounce High Ross dead and buried would be exaggerating the victory. Highways and dams never die; the engineers just slip them into the file to await the next opportunity. Someday, around 2064 to be precise, the Seattle–British Columbia treaty will expire and disciples of J.D. Ross will roll the rock from the entrance to his crypt. Albeit any new threats that might emerge are certain to face a formidable resistance.

A side-benefit of the High Ross resolution was that the arithmetic there had proved so wanting that the Thunder Creek flooding and diversion project, dubious even by City Light standards, was quietly shelved, thus preserving from inundation the mysteries hidden there in what's been called the Great

Members of the Skagit Environmental Endowment Commission tour the North Cascades Institute's Environmental Learning Center at Diablo Lake in 2006. The facility incorporated sustainable design and opened in the summer of 2005.

KEN WILCOX

Dismal Swamp of the Northwest.

In the pre-settlement era, one other project remained on the want list: a fourth Skagit River dam in the vicinity of Copper Creek. In 1979 the Seattle City Council voted seven to one to continue planning the $137 million dam, in which $1.3 million already was invested. The November 1980 hearings drew attention to the Straight Creek Fault, the Skagit River Bald Eagle Natural Area, the ten-mile stretch of free-running river that would be ponded, and the Boldt II court decision, which had given both fish and Native Americans legal standing in the courts. Seattle Mayor Charles Royer took a look at the little bit of compensating power, and listened to conservationists who pointed out that a like amount could, in effect, be generated by turning out the all-night lights in one or two of Seattle's downtown office towers. In January 1981 the mayor kiboshed the Copper Creek dam.

As Mehitabel the alley cat complained, "Sometimes it seems life is just one damn kitten after another." So it wasn't much of a shock when City Light joined the Nuclear Rush—that is, until the state of that non-art and the good sense of Mayor Royer forced the utility to drop out. In the early 1980s came the Geothermal Rush, and City Light eagerly filed on nearly 100,000 acres of Mount Baker. That fad faded as well. Then came "small hydro," which even Seattle City Light opposed.

In 1978 Congress passed the Public Utility Regulatory Policy Act (PURPA), strengthened by the Energy Security Act of 1980. The laudable intent was to encourage what Amory Lovins called the "soft path" toward energy sufficiency by providing economic incentives to explore alternatives to "hard path" nuclear power. The result in the North Cascades was something else: a Small Hydro Rush that by 1983 brought fifty-eight applications in portions of Mount Baker–Snoqualmie National Forest that were proposed for wilderness, as well as applications in existing wilderness, including Agnes Creek and Railroad Creek, where the Lutherans at Holden Village filed.

FERC preserved the tradition of the FPC by disregarding environmental consequences. These were few to none on low-head, high-volume projects utilizing irrigation canals, water-supply conduits, and storm-sewer outlets. However, the high-head version better suited to the mountains, relying more on the fall of water than its volume, could not avoid radical disruption of stream, forest, soils, and views by the required dam or weir, the diversion intake leading to the high-pressure penstock and powerhouse, and the transmission lines and switchyard to connect to an existing power-distribution system.

In the Ross Lake NRA, schemes were floated for Damnation Creek, Sky Creek, Thornton Creek, Birch Creek, Thunder Creek (three sites), Panther Creek, and Ruby Creek. Others outside the NRA on the North Cascades Scenic Highway were Ruby Creek, Granite Creek (three sites), and Canyon Creek (three sites). Among the applicants for these and other North Cascades sites were Puget Power, Mountain Rhythum [sic] Resources, Mountain Water Resources, Watersong Resources, Scott Paper Company, Tacoma City Light, High Country Resources, Glacier Energy Company, Cascade Group, Cascade River Hydro, and Bear Creek Water Power. Who were these people? Sons and grandsons, perhaps, of the mine promoters, timber claimers, and road agents of old, opportunists with a sharp eye for a belated slab of ribs from the Great Barbecue.

The Northwest Rivers Council, Native Americans, and environmental organizations generally support the intent of the law, but not the FERC-encouraged, hell-for-leather, devil-may-care environmental consequences of the rush to riches.

What of the Park Service? The NCCC met with the Pacific Northwest Regional Director in 1984 and was told "the Park Service has no authority to deny small-scale hydro." The Council's attorneys submitted a brief showing that the Park Service did indeed have authority. The Park Service responded that, anyhow, it had no plans to seek denial. For the Thornton and Damnation Creek proposals, it issued findings of "no significant impact," a reminder of a similar Park Service evaluation of what a dam would do to Glen Canyon on the Colorado, leading one to wonder what makes certain authorities in the National Park Service dislike trees, predators, unpaved nature, and wild rivers.

In 1991 the Oregon Rivers Council convened sixteen of the nation's leading aquatics experts to assess the status of the nation's rivers. The group agreed that the United States should stop building dams, because the hydroelectric power wasn't worth the ecological devastation. In the Northwest in particular, more dams would cause even further loss of critical salmon and spawning habitat. The experts even recommended that existing dams that cause the most damage should be breached or removed. As for small hydro, the conclusion was that though the projects are very small they do considerable damage, and that if every project possible were carried out, the nation's hydroelectric power production would be increased, at great environmental cost, a mere one or two percent of the six percent of the nation's electricity currently supplied by falling water.

Now, for a change, something in the way of a fairly happy ending: The Washington Parks Wilderness Act of 1988 removed FERC's authority to permit new hydro claims anywhere in the Ross Lake NRA. Further, the Act placed the wilderness boundary downstream from the proposed diversion intakes on Thornton and Damnation Creeks. This occurred at a time when the applications for those projects had lapsed for lack of work. The action subsequently was appealed but, strangely, FERC was unsympathetic.

Oh Yes, the Park Service

The Park Service, which has little to do with the impounding of the Skagit River, was a sideliner in the contest between reservoirizers and wild water preservers. The agency thought its sympathies were obvious enough and what could be done without getting mud on its britches mostly was done—with one notable exception. At one point the Park Service offered tentative support for High Ross as a way to get a road built to the lakeshore, perhaps to Roland Point, as a condition of approval. (The only public road that leads to the lake is the one from Canada at Hozomeen, and it barely reaches the north end.) Fortunately, that position was reversed as the responsible authorities quickly realized that supporting the dam did not make for good public relations for an agency whose prime public purpose was to safeguard the nation's parklands, including the Ross Lake NRA.

And it is, indubitably, a land worth safeguarding, its unspoiled parts (the bulk of it) being of the same caliber as the park and wilderness areas it adjoins. When it was created by Congress in 1968, the Ross Lake NRA embraced 115,857 acres of federal ownership, 80 percent of it pristine. Subsurface mineral rights were held on 746 of these acres by Sound Timber and Great Northern, and limited rights on 19,267 acres by Seattle City Light; 481 acres were state land (the bed of the Skagit River); 1,129 acres belonged to the City of Seattle; and 108 acres were in four private ownerships: two patented mining claims, a gravel stockpile, and a bit of old road.

The 1990 Land Protection Plan for the Ross Lake NRA summarized $566,400 spent for purchase of ten tracts, or 913 acres. To protect the visual character of the river/highway corridor, historic and other cultural values, and critical bald eagle habitat, as well as to provide access easement for a kayaker's take-out on the river, the Park Service identified eighteen surface and five subsurface tracts, totaling 1,619 acres that remained to be protected by cooperative agreements. These agreements would limit development by the owner (City Light and others) to uses compatible with Park Service values. The 746 subsurface and 108 surface acres would be purchased.

Not surprisingly, in view of the shortage of money and the abundance of critical needs elsewhere in the National Park Complex, the Park Service has not addressed all of these land protection needs, the principal exception being the acquisition of bald eagle winter feeding grounds along the Skagit River in 1988. Conservationists have not blamed the agency too harshly for the inaction, nor for much of anything else it does or doesn't do in the Ross Lake NRA, recognizing that the difficulties lie near the bottom of the Interior Department's totem pole. (The Park Service is expected to revisit these issues beginning in the fall of 2006 as it updates its Ross Lake NRA General Management Plan.) Conservationists do blame the Park Service for siting its west-side visitor center within the Ross Lake NRA at Newhalem rather than Marblemount, where the wilderness values eastward to Cascade Pass and Lake Chelan could share emphasis with the highway corridor.

Let this section conclude with yet another happy ending. Regional Park Service Director Charles H. Odegaard was the official who forced that choice of Newhalem for the new visitor center (it was completed and open in May 1993). The North Cascades National Park superintendent and the NCCC wanted to buy the Diablo Lake Resort's concession to serve as the Environmental Learning Center (ELC) to be developed under the relicensing Settlement Agreement. But Odegaard refused to buy the resort and insisted on using the Newhalem facility instead. In May 1992 Seattle City Light bought the resort as site for the learning center as part of a larger package to fund and equip the ELC.

Keep punching and you won't lose 'em all.

As an aside, the North Cascades Act of 1968 included several provisions to govern activities in the Ross Lake NRA that are not within the traditional scope of the Park Service. Exploitation of renewable resources (a euphemism for logging), was permitted. Thus clearcuts from Forest Service days were inherited in Newhalem Creek and Goodell Creek. The authority of the FPA or FERC to charter continued existence of the Ross, Diablo, Newhalem, and Gorge Dams was confirmed. The Act allowed planning for High Ross and new dams in Thunder Creek and at Copper Creek. Mineral leasing was accepted; small quarries long had dug the occasional truckload of talc or dolomite. Hunting was to continue along the Skagit and its reservoirs.

When Scoop Jackson's S. 1321 was amended in 1968 to set up the Lake Chelan NRA, through whatever mysterious backstage machinations (as yet undiscovered), the new unit was given little attention, the only major change in the legislation being to amend "National Recreation Area" (the Ross Lake unit, that is) to "Areas." Provisions written expressly and solely for Ross Lake and the Skagit were extended by reference to the Stehekin. Was it intentional?

Thanks probably less to malice than myopia, much of that mischief was undone in the Skagit by the 1988 Washington Parks Wilderness Act, but it was reinforced in the Lake Chelan NRA where, once again, a great swath of superb North Cascades wildlands was at risk. And because the politics there were heating up, the worries were significantly compounded. At Ross NRA, the prime issues centered on the dams—quite unlike its sibling, the Lake Chelan NRA, where nearly everything but the dam was in contention, and mostly still is.

Onward, then, to Lake Chelan.

9

Lake Chelan National Recreation Area

Until very recently most conservationists thought that the battle
to protect the Stehekin Valley had been won. . . . Those who knew
and loved the place breathed a sigh of relief. We should never have
been so complacent.

—Ann McConnell
In *The Wild Cascades*, Fall 1984

From Naysayers to Deerslayers

IN 1892 WHEN THE *Chelan Falls Leader* carried the story of a great national
park proposed for most of Lake Chelan and the wilderness that enclosed it,
the Barbecuers were quick to condemn the idea, killing what could have,
should have, become an American legacy—and the new state of Washington's
first national park. As noted earlier, such a park would have extended from
Twenty-Five Mile Creek on Lake Chelan to Stehekin and from the Chiwawa
to Methow Rivers. When the Mazamas mountaineering club from Portland
gathered in Chelan in 1906 once again to endorse "a national park and perpetual game preserve," they were countered five days later by a similar group
of naysayers.

The NCCC rekindled the flame a half century later. Throughout the
North Cascades campaign, the NCCC proposed that Stehekin Valley and
upper Lake Chelan—the "Yosemite of the North" and one of North America's
most magnificent inland fjords—be put where they belonged, and still belong:
in a national park. It also proposed, as a complement to the national park, the
creation of a Chelan National Mountain Recreation Area located well down-

lake from Stehekin and including much of the 1892 proposal. The recreation area was retained in the 1968 act under a modified name, but in an entirely different place, within what the NCCC and the original bill in Congress had proposed as park.

Something funny happened to the North Cascades bill on its way through the U.S. Senate. Explaining his amendment to exclude the lower Stehekin Valley from the park, Senator Jackson remarked, "The most important result of this change will be continuation of the historic use of this area for hunting." Senator Magnuson said the recreation area status would "preserve for the hunters of the country an area which has been traditionally open to hunting." The report of the Senate Interior Committee also affirmed, "The establishment of the Lake Chelan National Recreation Area will perpetuate the traditional back-country hunt in the Stehekin Valley, Rainbow Creek valley, and Rainbow Ridge areas." Of other reasons mentioned in the report as explanations for recreation area status, hunting is the *only* one legislatively prohibited in a national park, and would most definitely have been a deciding factor in the committee's decision.

The House Interior Committee repeated the language of the Senate. Congressman Lloyd Meeds said, "Deer hunting in this area has always been popular, and it would continue under our bill." Neal Butterfield, a National Park Service planner closely involved with the North Cascades, explained his understanding, "The Lake Chelan NRA was established almost solely for hunting." Roger Contor, first superintendent of the park, said, "There is no question in my mind that enough political pressure was exerted to keep the Stehekin Valley open to hunting."

Statewide, hunting activity was on the rise. In late 1958, the state game director had predicted a record fall hunt of "seventeen million pounds" of wildlife statewide. As many as 400,000 hunting licenses would be sold for about $24 million. The numbers increased in the 1960s when a quarter of the state's "big game harvest" occurred within some parts of the North Cascades, something on the order of 15,800 deer, 2,400 elk, 1,300 bear, and 300 mountain goats, according to the Washington Department of Game.

Presumably, the Game Department, which had opposed any park at all, brought to Senator Jackson the pleas of, among others, a dozen wealthy and politically potent Chelan County orchardist-hunters who annually came uplake to bag their deer, and the Senator gave them what they asked for. Perhaps in Jackson's view the parade for a national park could proceed even though the band was now lacking its trumpet section; after all, it had survived the loss of its oompahs and kettle drums—Glacier Peak, that is.

Hunting. That is how the public record reads. But certain powers in Chelan County and Wenatchee had something in mind beyond the sport of its deerslayers. It's what the powers usually have in mind (besides their bank accounts), and it drives the underlying strategy of the powers and the puppets in government, as well as the press and the public they manipulate. That strategy, described in a medieval manual on rhetoric as *argumentum ad misericordium*, elicits a sympathetic response to a false premise. Stehekin's detractors used the tactic *ad nauseum* by insisting that the intent of Congress was not about hunting *per se*, but "to preserve the Stehekin community." The record states otherwise. So while the national recreation area designation was most directly about hunting, there were those who, overtly or surreptitiously, wanted it to be about something else.

So what about this "something else," this lovely place of contention known as Stehekin?

Once Upon a Time in Stehekin

Located within the boundaries of the Lake Chelan NRA and enclosed by wilderness on three sides, this small mountain village lies at the head of the 55-mile long lake and is commonly known as a primary jumping-off place for smiling backpackers headed into the Lake Chelan NRA, portions of the Glacier Peak Wilderness, as well as the national park proper (beginning near High Bridge). But the valley itself inspires adoration, especially among those who have called Stehekin home for more than a summer or two. Grant McConnell describes it in his 1988 memoir, *Stehekin: A Valley in Time*:

> There was a time and there wasn't a time—so runs the folk tale beginning. It's proper here, for there was a time, the end of World War II, and there wasn't a time, just the American past. But there was a place—one unique and beautiful, as perhaps most places of the earth once were, but known to only a few.

> No road reached it from outside. This was enough in the middle of the twentieth century to render it remote and little touched by the currents of American life racing past the mountain barriers around it. And this was ironic, for its name, Stehekin, means "the way through." It is an Indian name, and maybe it tells the whole of an epoch—that the bands that came were mere travelers, outriders of a nomadic people whose true life lay on the rolling plains to the east. . . .

> There is a lake here that drains down through a series of falls into the Columbia six hundred feet below. . . . Lake Chelan is a dramatic piece of water. It lies in a trench dug by a prehistoric glacier seventy-five miles long. The glacier receded after it had cut its hole in the range; water filled the bottom of the hole, covering the deepest part fifteen hundred feet. Peaks alongside the upper end of the lake rise more than six thousand feet above the water. The distance from shore to shore is about a mile and sometimes less than that. . . . After the glacier retreated and the lake formed, the plug at the lower end wore down and some of the water

went out. This shortened the lake by ten miles and at the upper end added a level valley to the gorge. . . .

It is, indeed, a unique setting with tremendous vertical relief. The highest point of land in the vicinity of the glacier-carved trough of Lake Chelan is the summit of Bonanza Peak, rising 9,511 feet above sea level. (Bonanza is also the highest non-volcanic summit in the Cascades Range.) The lowest point of land in the basin is, of course, the bottom of the lake, at 386 feet below sea level—104 feet below the lowest point in Death Valley (the lake elevation is approximately 1,100 feet). Since great relief typically means great scenery, it's no wonder the backpackers are smiling.

The pleasure from a first reading of McConnell's book is as purely independent of the wide world beyond the Valley as a summer afternoon sitting by a mountain stream. Now and then, the corner of the mind's eye catches sight of a small cloud. An accomplished social scientist, McConnell continued:

> In one way or another everyone in the valley had a streak of fierce independence. Houses were scattered with so much distance between them that self-reliance was a necessity, but there was probably an element of choice in this distribution. The one place where several households lived in close proximity was at the dock, and it was a notable fact that, although there were some changes in the inhabitants, friction was its persistent condition. It seemed to follow from all this that organized community activities were impossible. . . . And yet there were community activities. . . . How [they] came about was a mystery.
>
> The roots of change must have got their start during World War II, although it wasn't apparent until quite a bit later. You wouldn't think the war would affect Stehekin, but it did—in several ways. In the first place, the government, which in a technical sense owned most of the area, more or less moved out. There had been a Forest Service ranger station and a couple of guard stations at Stehekin, occupied by a succession of men working for that bureau. But with the war, the Forest Service got short-handed, so they abandoned the area and moved downlake to Chelan, where things were more comfortable. Anyhow, Stehekin was too worthless to bother with. . . .
>
> The other change was a lot more serious. Ray and Curt [Courtney] got drafted. . . . Curt got upset about it, partly because he hated the thought of being asked to do any killing, but also because he didn't see how his folks, who were aging, could get along without help from him and his brothers. So he went down to Wenatchee where the draft board lived and told them he was needed at home. The draft board asked him how much cash the family needed to live on for a year and Curt told them a few hundred dollars. At that they replied Curt would be sending home an allotment from his pay for a lot more than that, and he was in the army.

Thus the cash economy of downlake stuck its nose under the tent of the subsistence society of Old Stehekin. In time, electricity followed. Soon they began improving the road.

> People began buying refrigerators and toasters. Then there were vacuum clean-
> ers and electric ranges. The list was enormous, and before long Stehekin was
> engaged in the biggest buying spree there ever had been. . . . The little strip of
> green between the wheel tracks was the first thing to go. Then in one place after
> another, the road got wider.

A bit of Eden had survived long past its proper time, at last to succumb to the Serpent. Again at first reading, the author seemed content to ramble anec-
dotally about his own Valley and tales of times past. In the second reading the cloud darkens. In the third, night engulfs Arcadia:

> Looking back on those later years, it was as though an invisible and poisonous
> cloud had crept up the twisting canyon of Lake Chelan. A considerable time
> passed before we were conscious of it. There were portents, of course, and we
> should have paid them more attention. But their meaning was as obscure as the
> clicking of a Geiger counter to the inhabitants of a Pacific atoll.

> The passage of time continued to be measured by the seasons—the first red flare
> of vine maple, the first valley snow, and the rise and fall of waters. It was mea-
> sured, too, in the span of human life. Olive Buckner, Mamie and Hugh Court-
> ney, Jack Blankenship, the Leshes, the Wilsons, Dad Imus, Daisy, one by one lived
> out their lives and were gone from the valley. . . .

> It had seemed that here were two worlds separated by the outer ranges of the
> Cascade uplift and only tenuously connected by the canyon of Lake Chelan. The
> contrast between the two outlooks was at times as sharp as if they had been two
> distinct cultures. The distance between them, however, was one of time. The
> cultures were the same. Had the lake's canyon been less twisting, it might have
> been possible to imagine it as a window for the nation to look upon its own
> past. So looking, it might have seen itself in the last moment before the crossing
> of a shadow line. The issue before human life in Stehekin, the one transcend-
> ing all others, was the same as that prevailing downlake; but just as there, it was
> hidden by its very transparency. It was recognition of the terms of the covenant
> by which human existence could go on without destruction of the other things
> of the earth.

> In the history of Stehekin—or America—it would be hard to say that such a cov-
> enant had ever been recognized. Instead, there was the myth of a virgin land: a
> place—a continent—without history, waiting for the arrival of its master to enter
> into its possession.

THE LAST YEARS OF OLD STEHEKIN

From July to November of 1979, Stehekin was the nearly full-time home of Susan E. Georgette and Ann H. Harvey, researchers in the Environmental Field Program of the University of California, Santa Cruz. Their 130-page report, "A Case Study of Ten Years of National Park Service Administration in the Stehekin Valley, Washington," was published in 1980 under the title, *Local Influence and the National Interest*. Their work never received the attention it deserved nationally, in the offices of the bureaucracy, in the halls of Congress, or even in the environmental community. Nowhere else had so thorough a job been done of pinning a unit of the National Park System under a microscope and meticulously dissecting it. Neither was their work absorbed through the thick skins of many politicos, the press, or some residents who didn't wish to confuse their thinking with facts. Nowhere else had such an objective analysis been made of the final days of a frontier community (or "lifestyle") and the hitching-up to modern times—in this instance, "downlake"—as the shift from Old Stehekin to New.

Homesteads, found Georgette and Harvey, accounted for most private ownership in the Valley, though some derived from the Great Northern Railroad which purchased the Stehekin delta in order to drown it (with a dam at the other end of the lake). One Stehekin family is said to have owned most of the Valley, one piece at a time, plus Moore Point a few miles downlake. Disappointing as it would have been to Thomas Jefferson with his vision of the honest yeoman, the typical pattern of homesteaders was not to establish a lasting home but to prove up, sell out, and homestead again for profit, although prior to 1968, land speculation in the remote Stehekin Valley would not have been the most lucrative means of earning a buck.

The solid citizens downlake who prospered in agriculture and business looked on their pioneer neighbors and predecessors as shiftless. But homesteading—which is to say, wheeling and dealing in real estate—has always been as American as football and was Stehekin's earliest and most dependable means of capital formation. At the turn of the twentieth century and briefly after World War II, selling stock in imaginary mines spurred an infusion of outside capital. Other than that, the economy was mainly one of subsistence and barter. Kitchen gardens and wild meat figured heavily in the diet. Government money dribbled in via stipends of the postmaster and schoolteacher. Others obtained meager, irregular cash money working trails and fighting fires for the Forest Service, logging a little on private (homesteaded) land, trapping, horse-packing, and serving tourists at several lodges. The sole enterprise recognized by downlake folk as being respectably civilized was the Buckner orchard.

Georgette and Harvey found:

The characteristics of life in Stehekin from the early 1900s to the mid-1950s were strongly reminiscent of those in small communities in nineteenth century America. . . . As a remote area virtually unknown to the outside world, Stehekin was protected from the tremendous changes that occurred in the United States. . . . life in Stehekin continued to be slow, oriented to the seasons, and relatively free from technological change. . . .

Year by year from the mid-1950s, Old Stehekin withered.   The Serpent offered riches for the age-old price of submission.   Early in the 1960s residents held a community meeting to complain about the hardships of life lacking electricity.   Ray Courtney stood up to say, "You can get all these good things you want for the price of a boat ticket to Chelan." Yet his service in World War II had also accustomed him to more cash in a year than he'd known in his whole pre-war life.   In the 1960s he and his children might read at night by kerosene light; their favorite reading material was mail-order catalogs.   To support a catalog lifestyle, for most of two postwar decades he went downlake every winter to work at ski areas where he spliced steel cable.   Thus the transition from Old Stehekin to New was also characterized then by the annual post-tourist-season exodus of the town's wage-earners.   Ray Courtney wistfully hoped to build his Stehekin income from horse packing so that he could, as in childhood, winter over.

Georgette and Harvey:

The old Field's Hotel at the head of Lake Chelan in 1911, dismantled in the late 1920s.

From the 1920s to the early 1970s, the population of Stehekin usually comprised 30 to 50 year-round residents with occasional fluctuations to less than 25 or more than 60 inhabitants. At the time the North Cascades Park Complex was established in 1968, the permanent population was approximately 35. By 1973, 50 lived year-round in Stehekin; 5 years later that figure had doubled to nearly 100 individuals wintering in the valley.

So when did Old Stehekin turn up its toes? By the time the 1968 Act was passed and the National Park Service arrived, it was already moldering in the grave. But its afterlife, The Myth, is thriving still in New Stehekin.

THE PANIC OF 1968

When the park was created in 1968, these thirty-five individuals living year-round in Stehekin were not unanimously opposed to a change in management. Of the Courtney family, Ray was a director of the NCCC (since 1957) and an outspoken supporter of a park. Others were less bold in public, perhaps fearing retaliation by anti-park neighbors. Photographer Paul Bergman, a Valley visitor since the 1930s and full-time resident since 1947, wrote "Deep Throat" letters warning conservationists of foul deeds afoot.

Not all, but most pre-1968 residents were anti-Park Service. Due credit for some of that sentiment must be ceded to the Forest Service, perhaps the most visible opponent of all. During the tourist season a ranger was posted on the *Lady of the Lake* to provide a running loudspeaker commentary on beneficent past management, stopping just short of implying that the Forest Service had uplifted these mountains, watered this lake, and planted these forests. No mention was made of the intended Stehekin "cutting circle." This propagandizing of tourists was fair enough, no real harm done, since most of the really dirty business was done locally and generally out of sight from visitors. In a 1967 letter to Senator Jackson, a Stehekin resident wrote:

> In early May, 1967, the Wenatchee District Supervisor came to a meeting at Stehekin, showed colored slides, narrated and passed out colored pamphlets, all from Outdoors Unlimited. . . . All of the local opposition is based on what the Forest Service people have told them, always using the term, 'Your land will be condemned,' never 'acquired.'

The panic stirred by the Forest Service did not save the Valley for the Forest Service, but it did lead Congress to speak to the fears of the government confiscating private lands. During the final hearings on the park, Park Service Director George Hartzog testified:

The National Park Service will not seek to acquire private inholdings within the Stehekin Valley . . . without the consent of the owner, so long as the lands continue to be devoted to present compatible uses now being made of them—such as for modest home sites, ranches, limited eating establishments, lodges, etc. This applies to the present owners and to any future owners of the property. The present owners are at liberty to dispose of their property. . . . Subsequent owners may be assured the National Park Service will take no action with regard to acquiring the property without their consent so long as the properties continue to be used for these same compatible purposes as at the time of the authorization of the park.

Hartzog further made it clear that in the case of incompatible uses, the Park Service would attempt to negotiate with the owner for acquisition. If that failed and the incompatible use persisted, the power of eminent domain would be exercised. The 1968 Act of Congress embodied Hartzog's promise.

The 1968 Act has been accused of demolishing at a single stroke a thriving Old Stehekin. Letters written by one faction of residents complained that the Park Service "came in here with a program of coercion," that people were "driven out of the valley." Other residents have recalled it differently:

More people moved out afraid of what the Park Service would do than what it actually did. Residents were told by the [Forest Service] rangers their land would be confiscated. We didn't understand. We subdivided and sold before 1968. The damage was done before the Park Service ever got here.

Whatever was demolished in the Stehekin Valley was by the inexorable steamroller of national history; it clearly wasn't done in 1968, nor was the Stehekin community steamrolled by a national park. Though it may accurately be said that the demolishee was the last surviving relic of Old Stehekin, the demolisher was not the Park Service but principally a few Forest Service people and their unfortunate stirring up of pre-park hysteria and paranoia.

Congress authorized appropriations for land acquisition, the budget ceiling originally set at $3.5 million. By December 1968, just weeks after the park's creation, the Park Service had a long list of property owners wanting to sell. Many feared there wasn't enough money to go around, triggering a panic. It must be kept in mind that some of these folks truly had little experience in a cash economy. The federal funds may have loomed as a pot at the end of the rainbow. As Superintendent Contor recalled, "There was no need to pressure residents." The most vehement park opponents were first in line to offer their lands for sale. Certain of those who were quick to grab a sack of greenbacks and scurry downlake toward cheap electricity came to rue their rashness and returned years later, after property values had risen, alleging the Park Service had swindled them.

By 1973 the Park Service had bought forty "improvements" and eighty tracts totaling 986 acres, leaving about 648 acres in private ownership. Dozens of offers by willing sellers were received, but a 1976 appropriation of $1 million was used mostly to acquire patented mining claims in the park proper. By 1979 the funds were exhausted.

The federal money (the Park Service acquisition program) and eager sellers combined to prevent the swift disaster that would have been inevitable under continued Forest Service management. All three of the lodges at the Landing were acquired and consolidated, which ended an amusing, pre-park circus in which the *Lady of the Lake*, as it neared the Landing, was bombarded by competing loudspeakers, shouting the splendors of their lunches. The Buckner Ranch had been surveyed into thirty-seven lots, but only several were sold before the Park Service acquired the rest. Most of the holdings of Chelan Box, which had thrown in its jackknife and gone out of business, were purchased prior to 1968; a group of Valley landowners bought eighty-seven of those acres near the Buckner Ranch and held them in protective custody until the Park Service had funds to buy them in 1973. Some twenty-three smaller parcels were obtained, the owners retaining right of use and occupancy for a set period of years or life. Had it not been for these acquisitions, the Stehekin of 1980 might have resembled West Yellowstone or the tourist-trapping towns encircling Great Smoky Mountains National Park—with the enormous difference being that land development would have been not on the edge, but in the heart of wilderness.

Weaver Brothers Taxidermists, Stehekin, 1907.

The Birth of New Stehekin

In Old Stehekin residents went their own ways, now and then helped out by neighbors, returning the favor when called upon. Pick-up volleyball games on spring evenings; pie and coffee at the Landing lunch counter while waiting for the boat to bring the mail; a potluck supper at summer's end. The rare crisis might occasion an impromptu town meeting, but not often. Old Stehekin didn't like to speak up in public; saying what you had on your mind might bring conflict out in the open. These were your neighbors. You had to live with them. So Old Stehekin was also tolerant. To choose to live there was, by definition, to be an individualist. Since everybody had personal quirks, the rule was, "Respect my quirks and I'll respect yours."

New Stehekin could not afford the nigh-universal peace existing when each human will is buffered from every other by a power vacuum, wherein flourishes the condition we call anarchy, which in reality is the purely rational order of Nature. There was now cash in the Valley, and into the power vacuum flowed the opportunists. Whether motivated by avarice or the egotistic pugnacity of the congenital rebel, their jousting against the Park Service and "those damn Yankees from Seattle" jangled the old harmony. This quiet state of anarchy, if it existed, died in the 1950s with the fight over wilderness protection. The silence was broken by ripping letters from some who were against the park, and by the NCCC, which quite unintentionally began to fill part of the power vacuum.

From the 1950s, artists, poets, craftsmen, Utopian commune-ists, practitioners of new and old religions and philosophies flowed as if by osmosis from the mediocre places of the nation to the good and the great, including Stehekin. The flow included youths and the young at heart who sought a lifestyle intimate with Nature. Few members of this inflow could survive on income from their creative imaginations or had the skills needed for the lifestyle of Old Stehekin. They needed cash-paying jobs, and after 1968 most Valley jobs would be with the Park Service. ·

If the American counterculture brought new residents, so did mainstream American wealth. Though the nation as a whole was grossly poorer in the 1950s than it once had been, an increasing number of citizens were egregiously richer, able to retire early in life, perhaps to maintain a second (or third) home in Stehekin. The growing wealth of Chelan County was especially startling. Wenatchee denizens who once had not been too proud to work alongside the Dust Bowl Okies picking fruit in season now could afford vacation homes; they came to look upon Stehekin as their private summering place and made very sure their elected officials—county, state, and national—looked after their property interests.

Also flitting into the vacuum of Stehekin was a kind of fundamentalist Christianity, and not just any old Christianity, but a full-on, speaking-in-tongues Pentecostalism. In the old days, many people came to Stehekin, in part, to get away from organized religion, and it could be said that most were downright hostile to evangelism or proselytizing. Live and let live, each to his own conscience and quirkiness, was the dominant sentiment, and religious dogma grated against this grain. This hostility was shared by, among others, Hugh Courtney, who settled with wife Mamie and five kids on a fifty-three-acre claim in 1918. Years later, a series of Courtney family tragedies (Ray's death off a cliff, a Courtney child's death by drowning, Esther's death from cancer), for which no doubt great comfort was needed, seemed to coincide with a strange national turn to religious fervor amounting to a third Great Awakening. Following a national trend, when the lack of any great political ideology to speak to the experience of working-class Americans left a national void, religion rushed into the Stehekin void. Whatever the cause, the result was a sad diminishment in Old Stehekin's live-and-let-live-ism, even if it did fit tidily with anti-governmentalism, though less tidily with private property-ism.

Grant McConnell's memoir portrays Old Stehekin in its late prime, a community whose members shared a place and a time and therefore shared certain characteristics, though they were, above all, individuals. The New Stehekin that began to crystallize after 1968 is perhaps somewhat less individualistic, certain patterns of behavior becoming more common, and the social framework reducing the freedom of individualism in Stehekin as in the whole of America, if not the world. Yet as before there is not a single simple community, as described in the usual expertise of the Sunday travel section columnist who may have visited the place for a day or in the self-serving rabble-rousing of politicians.

A sociologist's eye examining the Stehekin community of the immediately post-1968 years would distinguish two basic groups, the *winterers* and the *summerers*. The winterers ("permanents") who by 1973 numbered fifty, and by 1978 nearly twice that, are obviously different from the summerers. They are not, however, so very different in their feelings for the Stehekin Valley. Every one of them loves the Valley; those who know the Valley and don't love it are not there anymore. However, some winterers and summerers seem to love their property rights even more than the Valley. If they lived in Eden they might be hankering after apples, scuffling with their brothers. Some love the Valley, period, and don't want to get involved in matters that belong downlake.

Love is the beginning. Then comes economics. The winterers of Old Stehekin loved the Valley so well they wanted it to stay as it was, bringing them a little cash so they could stay on at home. Usually they had to go downlake for spells to earn enough money to keep their families at home. New Stehekin had an increasing number of winterers whose income arrived regularly in the mail, fruits of a former life in the world beyond Chelan County, perhaps of a parent's life there in the Valley. But among the winterers of New Stehekin are also people who would like to eat their cake and have it too. They want the

Stehekin life, but with cash in downlake quantities.

The summerers might support their Stehekin life with money earned working for the Park Service or the concessionaire or other tourist-servers and thus have to go downlake when summer ends. Or they might spend their Stehekin days or weeks or months on vacation from life downlake in Wenatchee, Seattle, Los Angeles, or Boston. Among summerers are people (mostly from Chelan and Wenatchee) who enjoy the Valley because of its convenience as a weekend and vacation getaway. Some confidently expect their land investment there to provide them, upon retirement, the comforts of golf courses and swimming pools in January, which of course are not in abundance in Stehekin.

The majority of winterers and summerers is peace-loving and quiet, aware that the times they are a-changin' and wishing they wouldn't, but as resentful of the fussing by defenders of the scene (the Park Service and environmentalists), as by that of the would-be exploiters. The strident and combative exploiters insist it is their scene to do with as they please. This minority has been so persistent, so unsleeping, so steadily pressuring neighbors, that it has chagrined the Valley lovers (who wish the world would go away and leave them alone) into accepting, as gospel, that way back in the olden days of 1968 the American Congress erected a protective umbrella over the Valley environment to guard the interests of the thirty-five year-round residents and every other person who would join them in the coming years, and to do so forever and ever.

What was this Umbrella of 1968? Existing owners could stay on their land if they used it more or less traditionally. And willing sellers could sell. That was the whole of it. The Park Service was neither required to buy property nor prohibited from doing so. It could condemn property only if its current use was incompatible with the qualities that give the scene national importance. The umbrella is amply commodious for the national interest, while it generally protects the private interests of those who place Stehekin-as-is above Stehekin-as-boodle. It does not satisfy those who want The Government to go away and let them dig for gold while providing cops to defend their property rights.

By itself the National Park Service presence would have created a New Stehekin, simply due to the need for a workforce and the housing it would require. Until 1968, the federal government was represented by a single Forest Service ranger, and for many years in summer only. The 1979 Park Service had nine full-time employees and one part-time, plus twenty-five seasonals.

The Georgette-Harvey study documented this radical and dramatically rapid transition to a very different community than that of the pre-park era:

> The Stehekin population has not only been characterized by growth but also by a noticeable turnover. Of the current [1980] year-round residents, 57% did not live in Stehekin 5 years ago and 75% did not live in the valley in 1968. . . . Only 12 percent of the current [1980] year-round residents lived in Stehekin 20 years ago

[1960] and only 5 percent lived in the valley in 1948. . . . The common portrayal of Stehekin as a . . . community of . . . pioneering families is simply inaccurate.

The character of the Stehekin community has also been altered by a change in the livelihood. . . . In place of the old subsistence economy that had essentially disappeared by the 1970s, a new economy developed that is almost entirely dependent on the National Park Service and on outside sources of income. Of the 38 permanent households in Stehekin in 1979, only 13 were independent of the National Park Service for finances; 10 of these received retirement income, leaving 3 valley households employed independently of the National Park Service . . . clearly the economic base of Stehekin. . . . Without the employment it provides, many residents would not be able to remain in the valley.

A 1991 count found eleven year-round Park Service-dependent households and fifteen non-dependent households, for a total year-round population of about fifty residents. A catch-all category of "ultra-transients," park and non-park affiliated, brought the total year-round population to some eighty-two. Thirty-five percent of these were Park "permanents" who occupied 42 percent of the year-round housing units. The seasonal (summer only) Park Service population in 1991 was at least twenty-nine. To house permanents and seasonals, the Park Service had to buy or build a number of units. Three of these, the mobile homes in the "Maintenance Area," were easily the most offensive structures in the Valley, save only the house of the District Ranger, which squatted on the lakeshore in front of Purple Point Campground. Built in 1940 and known as the Miller house, it remained rangerless for a time when the position was eliminated. Later, it was converted to park housing. A small victory was achieved in the fall of 1994 when the mobile homes were finally removed by the Park Service, which auctioned off the monstrosities.

Despite purchases by the National Park Service, enough private land remained to support a building boom in the 1970s. Fewer than one-fifth of the houses in the Valley in 1979 were there before 1960. By 1979, the Valley contained 101 dwellings plus seven small house-trailers with seven more under construction. Of the 101, fifty-seven were built prior to 1968, forty-four after. With dwellings under construction, the increase by late 1979 was 85 percent. On the lakeshore below the Valley were five more dwellings, three built before 1968 and two after. Of the post-1968 houses, 41 percent were built in the three years ending in 1979. The small size of the valley floor and the growing number of Valley lovers drove property prices steadily higher. This alone would have been the death blow to Old Stehekin had it not long since withered on the cold ground. By 1994 the dwelling units had increased from 1979's 101 to 137.

The dollar value of Valley real estate shot up accordingly—something that Georgette and Harvey also commented on:

The implications of the high cost of property in Stehekin are great. A community where a substantial amount of money is required to purchase land and pay property taxes cannot be described as pioneering and self-sufficient. . . . Stehekin will be more and more transformed into an exclusive haven for seasonal use by the financially secure.

The cash nature of the heritage of New Stehekin was exhibited nicely by a booklet called *The Stehekin Guidebook*. The 1990 issue, "proudly published" since 1985 by Stehekin Heritage, was supported by a list of advertisers that would surprise even Rip Van Winkle awaking in Stehekin after a quarter-century nap: North Cascades Lodge; McGregor Mountain Outdoor Supply; Silver Bay Inn and Cabins (operated by a couple who advertised themselves as "permanent residents since 1979"); The House That Jack Built; Crafts by Caity; Discovery Bikes; Chelan Airways; Fishing Stehekin Waters; Stehekin Potluck Collection; Stehekin Discovery Camp; Stehekin Mountain Cabin; Flick Creek House; Stehekin Air Service; and chiefly, Stehekin Valley Ranch and the Courtney family's subsidiaries, Stehekin Pastry Company and Stehekin Log Cabin.

New Stehekin was, more than anything else, new people who, along with the Park Service, helped accelerate the emergence of a new cash economy. With the growth in post-1968 tourism, comparatively little diligence was required to achieve Ray Courtney's ambition to winter over. Money was to be had serving the backpackers and sightseers, as well as working for the nation and wheeling and dealing in real estate. The Stehekin of the 1980s truly did maintain at least this latter tradition of the homesteading era. The expansion of households *not* dependent on government jobs said a lot about the change that had taken place.

THE PEOPLE OF THE MYTH

Whether reached by voyage up the lake or a journey over the mountains, Stehekin has the magical ability to transform itself before the visitor's eyes from mundane geography to a vision of the Happy Valley. Leaving aside prospectors and homesteaders, who had their own reasons for doing what they did and who rarely composed poems, the earliest visiting literates went home to publish their hallelujahs. In the eyes of these beholders the natural scene resonated through the persons of the Valley inhabitants whose interesting qualities (and a person who would choose to live in Old Stehekin was, by definition, interesting in some respect) were enhanced by the surroundings. City folk returned home to dream of summer visits to the lake and the river, the forests and alpine meadows, and their dreams were peopled by heroes and heroines of legends, sagas, epics, and picaresques.

Old Stehekinites tended to be embarrassed, even offended, by the attention of downlakers, a species that did not figure prominently in their winter dreams except for fantasies of income that the summer would bring. At what point did Stehekinites become aware of the commodity value of their status in the eyes of the downlake beholders? Likely before 1968 for those residents who had extensive commercial contacts with visitors. However, one does not recall Ray Courtney ever striking a conscious pose; if he wore the picturesque garb of a horseman, well, that, after all, is what he was: the cowboy boots and hat and wide leather belt with silver buckle maintained a sense of purpose, identity, and continuity with father and forebears. Glamorous perhaps, but not pretentious. The Myth was the creation of New Stehekin, the post-1968 arrivals who sat around the hot stove in winter spinning visions of summer gold, perhaps anticipating the summer hours strutting on stage with the Stehekin Community Players, performing pageants, skits, and tableaux. Downlake journalists flew in for a day or two; having been told by preceding downlake journalists what they were going to see, they saw that life was "frontier simple, basic survival, family close." They read in a 1987 publication (*Beyond Words Writers*) that:

> Due to remoteness we must rely on what is immediately around us for basic survival rudiments [sic]. This is the difference and this is the beauty and this is the pioneer's life. . . . To live Stehekin's lifestyle of self-reliance keeps alive a respect for ourselves and our abilities. . . . Stehekin is important to the rest of the world as a reminder of values from the past. . . . Yes, experiencing Stehekin is like stepping back in time. . . .

Lovely thoughts, pure myth.

Experiences too deep for words truly do occur in Stehekin. Visitors for as short a spell as a week or two can appreciate the book's sentiment, because even they will board the *Lady* for the downlake voyage feeling ennobled by their stay—taller than before, probably more handsome or beautiful, certainly purer of soul and clearer of head, an experience distinctly superior to that of the jittering, gaping, dwarfish daytrippers, cameras a-whir, faces full of overpriced hot dogs.

To visit Stehekin is a surpassing joy; to live there can be a religious experience. A person is, on the average, a better person for possessing religious instincts, and Stehekin may without hyperbole be described as a temple; indeed, that is why it was put into the National Park System. But to describe it as a pioneer community is something of a stretch, equipped as it is with microwave ovens and satellite dishes; relying for survival far less on what is immediately around than on expeditiously filling a Safeway shopping list downlake; reached via transport service of the *Lady*; served by more bureaucrats per capita than Seattle or Wenatchee; enjoying the mobility of a plethora of motor vehicles and boats, plus seaplane service that brings the fleshpots of Chelan within minutes of the frontier.

Old Stehekin.

New Stehekin hangs onto some of the Old.

BULLDOZERS, NOCA 26970U, 26970Z, FROM THE COLLECTION OF NORTH CASCADES NATIONAL PARK COMPLEX, NATIONAL PARK SERVICE. ALL OTHERS COURTESY OF SEATTLE CITY LIGHT

Clockwise from top: Seattle City Light tour boat on Diablo Lake; J.D. Ross with tourists; Bulldozers clearing the bed of Ross Lake; Curly Chittenden (who later opposed the raising of Ross Dam); the Toonerville rail coach carried tourists from Rockport to Newhlem; Diablo Dam.

KEN WILCOX

Ross Lake from Desolation Peak Trail; Ross Lake National Recreation Area.

*Left: Ross Dam and powerhouse.
Right: Clouds over Ross Lake with
Hozomeen Mountain at Sunrise;
Ross Lake National Recreation Area.*

KEN WILCOX

DAVE SCHIEFELBEIN

Fisher Creek drainage; North Cascades National Park.

DAVE SCHIEFELBEIN

Napeekqua River wends beneath the summits of Dakobed Range; Glacier Peak Wilderness.

PAT O'HARA

TOM HAMMOND

*Lupine, bistort, and many other species of wildflowers exist in close proximity to glaciers through-
out the North Cascades, as here along Ptarmigan Ridge; Mount Baker Wilderness.*

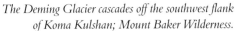

*The Deming Glacier cascades off the southwest flank
of Koma Kulshan; Mount Baker Wilderness.*

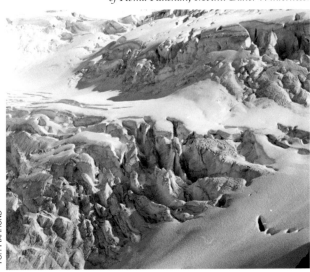

TOM HAMMOND

TOM HAMMOND

Glacier Peak is a frequent sight for climbers in the North Cascades; Glacier Peak Wilderness.

*Venus and Spade Lakes; Alpine
Lakes Wilderness Area.*

TOM HAMMOND

KEN WILCOX

*A small flock of always-friendly ptarmi-
gans on Goat Mountain; Mount Baker
Wilderness.*

PETER MCBRIDE

Above: Shadows of climbers ascending Bonanza Peak, Washington's tallest non-volcanic mountain. The 9,511-foot summit rises 8,213 feet above Lake Chelan. Right: On the summit, with Glacier Peak in the background; Glacier Peak Wilderness.

PETER MCBRIDE

PAT O'HARA

Wild country from High Pass; Glacier Peak Wilderness.

Nooksack Falls near Mount Baker; unprotected area.

KEN WILCOX

PAT O'HARA

From near Lake Ann, the Upper and Lower Curtis Glaciers and
the west face of Mount Shuksan; North Cascades National Park.

KEN WILCOX

Old-growth forest at Ashland Lakes, a rare, but outstanding example of forest protection on lands managed by the Washington Department of Natural Resources; Mount Pilchuck Natural Resource Conservation Area.

Ken Wilcox

Tiger lilies at Welcome Pass; Mount Baker Wilderness.

Ken Wilcox

"Feature Show Falls" empties into the Boulder River; Boulder River Wilderness.

KEN WILCOX

Mount Redoubt (left) and Depot Glacier; Mount Shuksan (right-center); and Mount Baker beyond; North Cascades National Park.

The Border Peaks (left: Canadian, center: American) and Larrabee (right). The international boundary passes between the two Border Peaks; Mount Baker Wilderness.

TOM HAMMOND

TOM HAMMOND

A climate research team measures the Columbia Glacier below the high crags of Columbia Peak in the Monte Cristo Range. This glacier has lost 134 meters in length and thinned fourteen meters in twenty years. It is considered to be in "disequilibrium" and will likely be gone in a few decades. Henry M. Jackson Wilderness.

Above: A protected species, grizzlies in the North Cascades are extremely rare. Below: A typical hiker's view of the more common black bear, often seen in high meadows feeding on berries later in summer (this encounter was near White Pass).

GARY KRAMER, U.S. FISH & WILDLIFE SERVICE

Rarely seen or heard, only a few gray wolves are known to survive in the North Cascades.

Austin Pass in winter, near Mount Baker Wilderness.

KEN WILCOX

DAVE SCHIEFELBEIN

Lake Chelan from above Stehekin; Lake Chelan National Recreation Area.

Stehekin River, its bank damaged by development; Lake Chelan National Recreation Area.

DAVE SCHIEFELBEIN

No harm is done acting out a self-designed role as acolyte in a rite that expresses a love of God or Nature, a respect for the past of the nation and mankind, and entertains paying customers. But there is harm in using The Myth to demand entitlements, as some have been prone to do. Grant McConnell observed:

> From the earliest days of the American nation, something approximating a natural right to the untrammeled occupation and exploitation of land and its resources has been asserted by people living near the areas where publicly owned resources are located. Simple proximity has been offered as sufficient ground for appropriation, the claims often being made good against counterclaims on behalf of government or the national community.

In this regard the New Stehekin really does exhibit a kind of frontier spirit.

ENTITLEMENTS AND SOVEREIGNTY: THE STEHEKIN VALLEY ROAD

In 1828 and again in 1832, the sovereign state of South Carolina, under the generalship of Senator John C. Calhoun, fired the first shots in the Civil War, issuing manifestos nullifying the federal Constitution. Fire in his belly and in his eyes, Calhoun was, until his death in 1850, the prophet of Nullification, the doctrine that a state could accept or reject at its pleasure the law promulgated in Washington, D.C. Fifteen years later the argument was lost at Appomatox Courthouse, though only temporarily. It was predicted that "The South shall rise again," and eventually it did, as in Northern Idaho, in the secessionist fever of the western Cascade foothills (which sought liberation from Seattle's King County), and in Chelan County, where country folk sought freedom from the growth-control laws forced upon them by the state legislature in Olympia. The county's impact on development issues in Stehekin was not insubstantial. The county refused for six years to adopt countywide development restrictions ordered by the Growth Management Act. In the spring of 1996, the county challenged the act in court. The county attorney cried, "Nonsense!" to the challenge. So the county commissioners threatened to sue him instead. To pursue their case (or non-case, as it were), they hired a private attorney from the far horizons of the right wing.

The pundits of urban politics stand agape that so considerable a social unit as Wenatchee should be the tail on the kite of little ol' Stehekin. But as will be noted later, grander pols than those of the Chelan County courthouse would grasp the symbolism of the scene: "Stehekin is . . . what America was." As Mark Twain or somebody like him said, "Nobody ever went broke betting on the gullibility of the voter." Thus the Stehekin Myth would charm the American voter into reopening the gates to the Barbecuers of the nineteenth-century

Gilded Age, that they might expand on their monkey business in the Glitz Age of the late twentieth century.

Among the restless and confused, the need for an issue, a rallying cry, was met by the Stehekin Valley Road, a dusty track originally built to serve a bustle of small-time prospecting from Bridge Creek to Horseshoe Basin that had begun in the late 1800s. In 1970 the Chelan County Commission deeded to the federal government "all right, title, and interest in and to the Stehekin Valley Road." This was an obviously rational course for a valley that was a lake-length in distance from the rest of the county. Maintaining the road for the few residents was a disproportionately heavy burden on taxpayers of the county. Stehekin residents accepted the transfer without complaint.

The overwhelming majority of Stehekin residents still don't care much about the road, or at least its upper reaches. They may debate how good and how fast a road it should be, and they may have disagreed with the NCCC that it should have been terminated well short of its official and former end at Cottonwood Camp (sporadic flooding, particularly in 1995 and 2003, shortened it considerably). And its ownership is of no concern to most.

In 1971 the Stehekin River Resort convinced twenty-nine property owners to join in a suit against Chelan County to nullify the conveyance. The reasons seemed petty and mysterious, unless one invokes the memory of John C. Calhoun, a chief architect of the Confederacy. The suit was settled in 1973 on stipulation that the Park Service would maintain the road, which, of course, it was already doing. For twenty-one years thereafter, the county did no maintenance on the road, and did not assert any interest. Then, on July 9, 1991, on the motion of Commissioner John Wall, the County voted to rescind the quit-claim deed. The surface motive for this extraordinary action was that various profit-making enterprises by the Stehekin community's "Heritager" faction were denied certain freedoms of road use. (Lest there be any doubt, the Heritagers were not tree-huggers.) For example, the bus trip from the Landing to Rainbow Falls, a favorite tourist attraction, and a quick and easy cash cow, had been exclusively the right of the Landing concession, an enterprise thin on profitability and needing every edge given by its contract with the Park Service. After some years the Heritagers sought a cut of the Rainbow action and were given it in a compromise satisfactory to the concessionaire and the Park Service.

There then became visible a deeper motive hidden by the surface dust. The road was less a geographic or economic fact than a political symbol. A battleground was desired. Enough with the bushwhacking and guerrilla raids. Yes, the hour had come for champions of the Calhoun faith to fix bayonets and fight. John Wall, from a family that once had dreamed of rafting the ancient forests of Agnes Creek to its apple-box factory downlake, and others adopted a battle plan. County machinery was barged uplake to patch chuckholes and

*Old Harlequin Bridge,
Stehekin Valley Road,
washed out in a flood
in 1948.*

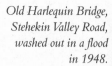

remove snow, even as Park Service crews were on the way to do so. A police patrol car was shipped uplake for road patrol, which nearly triggered a counter-revolution when the officer began snooping around for minor offenses.

The county's action was as aggravating, perhaps, as children yelling at adults. However, the adults kept their cool until the county, without consulting the Park Service, undertook reconstruction of the road at "Eight Mile," where the river had washed it out and the Park Service had made temporary repairs. The county issued itself a shoreline permit for eight hundred feet of riverside roadway, without seeking a Park Service permit, and authorized the contractor to take twelve hundred cubic yards of riprap from the talus slope at Harlequin Bridge, a feature of the natural scene admired by travelers for generations.

On August 31, 1992, the Park Service filed suit (on September 18, 1992, the NCCC joined the suit). On September 3 the federal district court entered a temporary restraining order, prohibiting excavation from the Harlequin talus and the riprapping at Eight Mile.

It should be noted that the Stehekin Valley Road, formerly two wheeltracks separated by a green median of grass and flowers and properly fated to dwindle in its upper reaches to a trail, had been taken as a responsibility and challenge by the Park Service, which undertook to reopen the road to the fullest possible extent each year. The lower stretch of the road was inch-by-inch widened to a two-lane highway and paved, ostensibly to solve the dust problem, though it brought a doubling or tripling of the average speed of vehicles using it. A resident commented, "The road was rebuilt here under supervision of engineers from outside the local staff, and plainly their technology required them to build as roads are built elsewhere—for the benefit of machines, not the country." The Park Service had somehow missed the inspiration of naturalist Joseph Wood Krutch who spoke of "the good that bad roads do."

On June 4, 1993, the court granted the motion for summary judgment (a legal procedure to avoid a trial made unnecessary because the facts are not in dispute) brought by the Sierra Club Legal Defense Fund (SCLDF—later renamed Earthjustice, a completely separate entity from the Sierra Club) on the grounds that the natural character of the river would be altered, endangering its opportunity to be included in a Wild and Scenic River System. The Park Service's authority was affirmed. A sidelight of interest to Chelan County taxpayers and voters: the county prosecutor refused to take the case, and the County Commission had to pay a private law firm $32,817 to preside over their bullish blunderings.

Observers from a distance wondered what was going on in Chelan County, or rather, what was *not* going on. The new park superintendent, Bill Paleck, contented himself with a mild comment that the road dispute was making the "development of a cooperative rapport with the county more difficult than necessary." Stephan Volker of the SCLDF told the press, "Chelan County officials and Stehekin residents no longer will be able to use the road to kick sand in the face of the National Park Service. Hopefully, this decision will give the Park Service much-needed backbone to protect the fragile environmental resources of the Stehekin Valley as the law requires."

Could it be true? A happy ending? In the June 1993 *The Wild Cascades* President Fluharty reported,

> The continual gamesmanship over management of the road has finally been resolved . . . now that the ownership of the road is clear, the possibilities for a sensible approach to commercial access and development can prevail . . . the NPS is now in a better position to deal with . . . matters that have made relationships with private property owners uncertain. Judge McDonald's decision is a valuable cornerstone in the construction of a stable resource management environment in Lake Chelan NRA.

Ten years later, in the fall of 2003, another major flood occurred. Calculated to be a 500-year event, it not only destroyed previously repaired road sections, but eliminated a narrow section at Carwash Falls that was deemed impossible to fix without rerouting the road through designated wilderness. Heritagers wanted it reopened, while the Park Service wisely took the position that the wilderness gods must have intended the road to end below Carwash Falls, as it was going to keep costing the taxpayers millions upon millions of dollars to keep fixing what could never truly be fixed. The NCCC maintained that the economic and environmental benefits of permanently closing the upper few miles of road above the falls far outweighed any conceivable benefit of rebuilding it for the convenience of a handful of cars. Above the falls, the road was of very little utility to the Stehekin community and was quite plainly an unnecessary intrusion into the wild heart of the North Cascades. In late 2006, Paleck issued his decision to permanently close the road at Car Wash Falls and to decommission the abandoned portion, some of which could become a trail.

ENTITLEMENTS AND EXPROPRIATIONS: FIREWOOD

Citizens of American cities, suburbs, and farms do not expect the federal government to provide their family fuel free of charge. New Stehekin did because that is how it was in Old Stehekin.

But Old Stehekin was history, like a foreign country in another time. The handful of firewood-gathering winterers of that era had no great impact on the Valley forest, considerably less than the intermittent logging operations of the period. Yet that same manner of firewood scavenging, multiplied by the relatively larger population of New Stehekin, threatened to burn up far more trees than the loggers ever hauled away to the mill. To be sure, the locally preferred firewood came from toppled and dead-standing trees. However, these quite

Firewood cutting in the Stehekin Valley.

DAVE SCHIEFELBEIN

obviously were a vanishing species. By 1978 the annual wood usage on public land, under a 1971 Interim Firewood Management Plan, had doubled in several years to 245 cords—the equivalent of about five hundred sizeable pick-up loads. Nearly all available dead trees within sight of the Valley road had been cut as well as "danger" trees (dead and alive) in campgrounds. The unceasing demand for firewood was threatening to exceed what natural mortality was providing. A proliferation of *ad hoc* woodcutting roads was built by ramming trucks from private property into the public forest. From each of these sprouted spur roads, until the public lands in the Valley were well on the way to being seriously roaded. The effect on the wild character of these sites was profound. Additionally, the woodcutting ignored the after-death role of a slowly rotting tree, providing nutrients for plants, nests for birds and small mammals, food for little creatures in the great Web of Life that feeds the bigger creatures. Without snags and fallen logs a forest ecosystem is functionally incomplete, as the Park Service would know.

Certain firewood cutters, who were known by name, routinely were caught committing eco-crimes and allowed by the Park Service to continue. In one example, hikers following a woodcutting road came upon a fresh stump which was, as a count of rings revealed, seven hundred years old. Slash fires, which had sought to destroy the evidence and failed, revealed that the tree still had green branches. To be sure, it was "dying," but this ancient Douglas fir would have been an important component of the system for many more centuries, first as a standing snag and then as a fallen log, providing diverse habitats, supporting the food web, storing carbon, returning nutrients to the system. The hikers found the wood neatly stacked at a nearby dwelling. A 700-year-old tree would be burned up by spring to heat a single home.

In 1979 the Park Service engaged Professor Chad Oliver from the College of Forest Resources of the University of Washington to carry out a study of Valley timber. The fieldwork was performed not by the professor, who lent the prestige of his academic rank to the project, but by a graduate student generally unfamiliar with forest ecology. In 1985 the resulting Oliver–Larson Report was used as the basis of a Draft Firewood Management Plan that led to the September 2, 1987, Decision Notice by Superintendent Reynolds to adopt one of the four alternatives offered, even though it was endorsed by only six comment letters of the 153 received. The NCCC adjudged only one of the alternatives barely palatable, and 80 percent of those commenting agreed. Conservationists were dismayed. Rumor had it that so were Oliver and Larson. The chosen alternative apparently was not written by them, nor based on their research, but was added by the Park Service to suit its preconceived management desires.

As a result of Reynolds' decision, the Lake Chelan NRA became, and might very well remain, the only area in the entire National Park System where a woodlot with green timber has been so designated. Whether the wood came from selective removal of dead and down or dying trees or from clearcut woodlots of green and healthy trees, the scale of firewood removal amounted to logging—precisely what had caused the ejection of the Forest Service in 1968. Some worried that the Park Service of the 1980s intended to out-log the Forest Service of the 1950s.

The NCCC complained that nothing in the 1968 Act required the Park Service to provide firewood to anyone; public fuel was not provided to private homes in Bellevue, Omaha, or San Diego, and no rationale could be adduced to keep Stehekin on the dole. The firewood plan made no attempt to give criteria for need, made no provision for closing logging access roads, did not forbid taking downed trees from the river, provided no supervision for cutting, and was wholly lacking in inducement to reduce fuel use. It would not contribute to "the conservation of scenic, scientific, historic, and other values." It seemed no less than a welfare scheme benefiting a small group of residents, an irresponsible proposal that would guarantee a creeping destruction of a jewel of the National Park System, setting a terrible precedent for the entire system.

The NCCC argued that, in an age when wood fires were being eliminated both from backcountry trails and city suburbs, federal forests should not be burnt up by Stehekin residents as an entitlement. Their fuel, whether wood, propane, or whatever, would have to come to the Valley from outside the North Cascades National Park Complex and would have to be paid for by the users. The Park Service, said NCCC, should also encourage energy conservation in its own and other residences.

When Superintendent Reynolds chose his course and the NCCC's subsequent appeal to the Regional Office was denied, the Council saw that administrative recourse had been exhausted. On September 20, 1987, the directors voted to engage the SCLDF to prevent implementation of the Firewood Plan. The challenge was later deferred, to be incorporated into a more comprehensive action to follow.

Entitlements and Expropriations: The Stehekin Emergency Airstrip

The Forest Service fire-lookout cabins, including Boulder Butte and McGregor Mountain near Stehekin, were replaced after World War II by patrol aircraft. Their glide angle was so low that they generally could dead-stick to airports on the periphery of the mountains. However, the spaciousness of the North Cascades occasioned the construction in the interior of several emergency landing strips. Such a strip in Stehekin was urged by Art Peterson, who envisioned a plush resort immediately adjacent, and gave 12.3 acres of his land to further the project. In 1957 the Forest Service engaged a logger to clearcut the needed space in the Stehekin Valley. The area was graded and sown with fieldgrass; a windsock was hung on a pole. Upon departure of the Forest Service, sponsorship was assumed by the Washington State Division of Aeronautics through a special-use permit for forty-five acres from the Park Service, which retains ownership of the land and absolute control of use.

Conservationists long have sought closure of the strip, which has never been used for its intended purpose. A significant factor in its abandonment by the Forest Service was that as an emergency airstrip it actually created emergencies: to date, five deaths and several fires have resulted from its use.

The strip is a gross blemish on the Stehekin Valley scene. It is so vast within its wild surroundings that every other work of man in the Valley, buildings and roads together, could be accommodated in a fraction of the space. Further, the airstrip has infected the Valley with knapweed and rush skeleton weed, noxious exotics whose eradication is very costly. Early on the Park Service set its paperwork mill grinding toward closure of the airstrip. Reforestation done then could by now have mostly healed the scar that jolts the hiker who views it from heights of the Purple Creek and Rainbow Creek trails and distresses the humble hiker who passes by the edge on the otherwise sylvan path down the Stehekin River to Weaver Point. Admittedly, the view of McGregor Mountain is impressive from the airstrip, but certainly not worth such an enormous scar.

Another mystery for a future scholar to solve by digging into the archives is this: why after a quarter century of Park Service administration is the airstrip still open? And why is the peace of the Valley repeatedly disturbed by low-level overflights? Since 1968 there has been a continuing thread of Park Service intention to rid the scene of the nuisance. But also since 1968 there has been a thread of indecision—and wrong decisions. At one time or another, this or that park superintendent has been responsible for the failings; at other times, the director of the National Park Service Pacific Northwest Region. The more devout scholar might want to examine closely the political alliances and personal connections of Regional Director Charles Odegaard. A word from him and the strip would have ceased to exist years ago. He did not give that word. Indeed, his underlings were explicitly directed to give the contrary word. One explanation heard is that Congressman–pilot Rod Chandler heeded the alarm call of the Washington Pilots Association and put the fear in Odegaard. After Chandler, someone else was apparently doing the same.

The number of fliers who have used the strip in recent years has remained small. But some among them evidently have been well connected in county, state, and federal bureaucracies. Their creature was the State Aeronautical Board, which in 1984 had requested permission to clear the native vegetation encroaching on the strip. The Park Service answered in a letter of October 15:

"It is our judgment the minimal clearing . . . will not result in any irreversible or long-term impacts that would preclude eventual restoration of the airstrip should the General Management Plan review result in that decision." To interpret, "Go ahead and cut brush—this time—but don't settle in."

In June 1986 a pro-airstrip faction, knowing the Park Service draft of the new Land Protection Plan was considering several alternatives for the airstrip, including closure, solicited a letter from the State of Washington, pronouncing that the "Stehekin Emergency Air Strip" did not exist. It had been replaced by the "Stehekin State Airport," a public airport "open to all without discrimination." The airport was essential, the state's bureaucrat opined. For one, it is the primary means of protecting the Lake Chelan National Recreation Area, he said. Protecting it from what, no one knows. Secondly, it is needed to save the lives of fliers in trouble. Nobody can remember such a use, though many clearly remember the five fliers who were killed, perhaps believing that the state's sponsorship meant it was safe. Thirdly, this is a recreation area and flying is recreation. On a single summer day in 1986, over fifty landings and takeoffs provided recreation for an inconsiderate few, noise for the entire Valley, and disruption of the qualities the National Park Service exists to protect.

Where did this desk-pilot in Olympia find these ideas? One can make a shrewd guess from the fact that the Parks' own Stehekin District Ranger addressed a pithy critique of the strip to Superintendent Reynolds, who warmly sat on it. Odegaard, one may infer, had given the orders.

Stehekin Emergency Airstrip.

DAVE SCHIEFELBEIN

On August 20, 1987, a group of twenty fliers rumored to be from Hayden Lake, Idaho, descended on the airstrip and "cleared brush." They removed the sign reading "Stehekin Emergency Airstrip," and replaced it with "Stehekin Airport." In 1989 the continuing insistence of conservationists was rebuffed by Odegaard's claim that the state Department of Natural Resources demanded perpetuation of the strip. In two letters, dated May 19 and June 21, the head of that department, State Land Commissioner Brian Boyle, emphatically declared, "We have no interest or need in the Stehekin airport. It isn't required for any Department of Natural Resources service. It would not affect us in any way if the airport were eliminated." Copies were sent to Odegaard, but still nothing was done.

In the summer of 1989, aircraft began flying tourists on schedule from Chelan to the airstrip. One large plane brought a number of passengers from Seattle, and thankfully, the Park Service quickly put a stop to that. In 1991 a commercial pilot was congratulated by some in the Stehekin community for personally mowing the lawn as a public service. He was, himself, a substantial portion of the public so served. For a time, a campground at the strip accommodated fliers' emergency vacation trips. During an annual maintenance outing, the flyers channelized and damaged a wetland at one end of the strip.

The developing pattern of the downlake wealthies is to have a vacation home in Stehekin, a razzer-boat at the Landing for churning up the lake water, a four-wheeler for racing along the Valley roads—and for some, an airplane to put all these pleasuring devices within handy reach.

The airstrip was acknowledged by the Park Service early on to be an anomaly, but later was accepted as part of the heritage. In 2003 the Park hired a new chief of law enforcement for Stehekin who happened to be an avid flier, leaving some to wonder about the prospects for stringent enforcement of "emergency" use and limits on maintenance of the airstrip.

The Washington Department of Transportation's Aviation Division has taken over responsibilities for its so-called state airport at Stehekin, acknowledging that it is "definitely a strip for an experienced mountain pilot." The agency boasts that it "provides access to some of the most awesome scenery in Washington. . . . a favorite of campers, fishers and hunters," despite the fact that "conditions are primitive . . . the runway is extremely rough . . . frost-heaved rocks are common . . . approaches are difficult . . . [there is] a large mountain [in the way] . . . the runway slopes significantly . . . tall trees surround the airport . . . terrain rises rapidly . . . the valley narrows quickly . . . strong gusty winds are common . . . [and] animals are frequently present." It is, they add, "the most interesting of our airports."

ENTITLEMENT NOT: THE STEHEKIN RIVER

The twelve miles of the Stehekin River in the Lake Chelan National Recreation Area are the finale of a chorale of tributaries reaching south nearly to Glacier Peak, north halfway to Canada, to Park Creek Pass, Thunder Pass, and Rainy Pass, and west to Cascade Pass and the Ptarmigan Traverse (a famed mountaineering route). The river miles in the lower portion of the National Recreation Area are the central artery of Stehekin's human community, as well as its riparian plant and wildlife communities. Because the Stehekin Valley road parallels the river so closely, it is not eligible under the law for designation as a Wild River. But it qualifies abundantly for Scenic River, a classification that accepts a degree of human presence but only the most minor human tinkering.

"Wild" and "scenic" were not much in the Stehekin vocabulary before 1968. Float logs were salvaged from the banks for firewood or construction, log decks were placed to armor against swift waters, gravel was mined from the bed. Over those years the riverbank owners felt free to do as they pleased. What harm they did to the flow was minor and temporary; the wounds were healed by the next spring flood. But tampering with a river at one point does have consequences upstream and down. If no one lives there, who would notice? That was Old Stehekin.

In New Stehekin the frequency and scale of riverbank manipulation increased. As always, the river exerted its will. After a flood in 1973 several Stehekinites, backed by Chelan County, summoned the Army Corps of Engineers. The Park Service rangers in Stehekin at that time tended less to whistle-blowing, yet Superintendent White in faraway Sedro Woolley eventually did hear a whistle and wrote the Army Corps asking them not to do it again—at least not without permission. In 1986 the same resort that had instigated the road suit illegally rip-rapped the river banks on federal lands. The resort was located near the river mouth on floodway and floodplain, areas that should belong to the river, but legal title was held by a friend of Regional Director Odegaard. The penalty was a light slap on the wrist. Time and again, year after year, Heritagers dumped rocks here, moved a log there, pushing, pushing to see how far they might go, effectively taunting a Park Service that was doing more but still had Heritagers among its Valley rangers and still had mixed-motive superiors in Sedro Woolley and Seattle. Thus the pot was kept a-simmering.

In a special NCCC "Action Alert" mailed in early November 1992, Kevin Herrick, NCCC's only paid staff, addressed "Dear friend of the Stehekin Valley":

Ride your bike up the road, past the head of the lake, and over gurgling Boulder Creek. Enjoy your coast down the hill. Glance ahead . . . a small (as they go) logging truck. Logging truck! Watzatfor? . . . . Stunned, you take a look . . . The trees are gone along the river bank. A dirt road leads down to a big flat area of dirt, rock, and gravel on the bank above the river. It looks like a dock of some sort has been built at the edge of the river. 'But I thought this river was to be protected!' . . . a friend takes you rafting in the afternoon. After rounding the bend below the Buckner Orchard, you take a look up Rainbow Creek but something up ahead wrenches your attention away. There it is. That dock-looking thing you saw this morning . . . A wall of wood and rock squats where once was the river bank . . . The flat area fronted by the bulkhead is being expanded back toward the road by the removal of the earth that naturally slopes down to the sharp bank of the river . . .

The Mike Sherer family . . . plans to build a destination resort Bible Camp that will host up to 130 people a day . . . the largest single development in Stehekin . . . By increasing the number of overnight visitors in the lower valley by 130 people, this resort will obviously have an impact on the quiet quality of the lower Stehekin Valley . . .

For comparison, in 1994 the entire Valley had approximately 150 beds to rent for the night. Sherer's camp would easily double the number of overnight visitors to Stehekin.

Embarrassing questions arise. Why did the NCCC fail to discover the project until the summer of 1992, when the bulkhead was already one hundred feet long, extending fifteen feet out into the river, walling off forty feet of formerly pristine riverbank, supplemented downstream by seventy-five feet of rip-rap? Why had the Park Service failed to mention the construction to anyone who might possibly object, like the NCCC? Why did neighbors upstream and down fail to lodge complaints about the inevitable effects of this massive disturbance of the river's balance on their own stretches of riverbank? Perhaps if the project proceeded, the Heritagers could establish a precedent: an ability to play with the river as if in a sandbox.

The developer, a retired submarine officer, was a recent arrival in the Valley and his religious entrepreneurship mingled with an enthusiasm for moving dirt reminiscent of Old Stehekin's Curt Courtney, a passion only exceeded by his drive to joust with the federal government. Perhaps a few Heritagers saw some potential here to help topple the Federals and the birdwatchers and make Stehekin the Yorktown of the United States of Chelan.

Sherer had begun the bank-hardening preliminaries in 1988, before his retirement from the Navy. Not until the summer of 1992 did the NCCC learn this was preliminary to the Bible Camp. Presumably, the Park Service already knew about it. In 1992 Chelan County issued a permit for essentially a lemonade stand beside the Stehekin Valley road that divided the 26.2-acre property. The bulkhead and site preparation were done under an October 1991 single-family-residence exemption granted by the county, though the residence in question was more than two hundred feet from the river and on the opposite side of the Stehekin road. In a Chelan County notice published September 4,

1992, in the *Wenatchee World*, application was noted for a Substantial Development Permit to construct "two bunk rooms designed to serve thirty people, a lodge structure to serve an additional thirty people, and nine cabins to serve six persons each . . . Notice is also given that on August 31, 1992, the Chelan County Planning Department did issue a Determination of Non-Significance . . ." that alleged no significant environmental impact.

The Board of Adjustment of Chelan County was first up. Hearings on the bible camp scheduled for November were postponed to December 14. The NCCC's Dave Fluharty and Kevin Herrick crossed the Cascades from Seattle in harrowing snow and ice, joined by representatives of the Washington Environmental Council (WEC), the Park Service, and the Bowles family, downstream neighbors whose stretch of riverbank was bound to pay the price for the upstream defiance of the laws of hydraulics. But the Board of Adjustment failed to show up in quorum strength. The hearing finally was held January 4, 1993, the Board attending but not the Seattle interests, who due to weather and traffic got no closer to Wenatchee than Issaquah. By telephone the NCCC and allies learned that their motives were questioned by the Board, which voted unanimously to grant the permit for the first phase of the project—the first phase, that is, beyond the bulkhead and rip-rap.

From here the NCCC turned to the Eastern Washington Growth Management Hearings Board, where the NCCC argued that Chelan County had failed to comply with the state's 1990 Growth Management Act by failing to complete its critical area planning for Stehekin, which would almost certainly preclude a bible camp or any other development of this scale beside the river. On May 14 the Hearings Board denied Chelan County's motion to dismiss the NCCC appeal filed by the SCLDF. On June 9, the Board noted that the county was not in compliance with rules for designation of Critical Areas, that it had been given an extension of 180 days to March 1, 1992, and a year later still had failed to act. The upshot of all this was that NCCC and SCLDF had exhausted the administrative remedies under the Growth Management Act and were free to pursue the issues in superior court.

Based on the design of the bible camp shown in the application for a Substantial Development Permit, the NCCC challenged the bulkhead as violating the Washington State Shorelines Management Act. Chelan County had approved a major plan without adequate environmental review. Further, said the NCCC, issuance of the exemption to build the bulkhead for a single family residence was clearly in error—it was for the bible camp. Beyond the state-level issues were the federal ones. This time the Army Corps of Engineers was in the permit seat for any filling of wetlands or obstruction of navigation. The bible camp did not have a Corps permit and apparently refused to seek one.

The matter occupied two weeks, the first in Chelan, during which the entire Washington Shorelines Hearings Board flew to Stehekin to view the site of the proposed bible camp; the second was spent in Lacey, near the state capital. Stephan Volker named twenty-eight witnesses he intended to call: six, including Superintendent Paleck, from the National Park Service; a geomorphologist from the University of Califormia, Santa Cruz; personnel of the state Shorelines Management Program at the Washington Department of Ecology, the U.S. Environmental Protection Agency, the U.S. Army Corps of Engineers, and the U.S. Fish and Wildlife Service; the WEC; the NCCC; and ten Stehekin property owners. Bible camp proponents began to grasp how formidable a devil they had conjured up from the deeps.

On January 28, 1994, the NCCC and WEC agreed to a settlement with Chelan County and Mr. Sherer. Chelan County agreed to pay for removal of the bulkhead and agreed to amend its Shorelines Master Plan to reduce the likelihood of similar episodes. Sherer agreed to make no efforts to harden the banks to prevent erosion. He would explore the sale of a conservation easement to the Park Service. NCCC and WEC agreed to drop their suits before the Chelan County Superior Court and Shorelines Hearings Board. The decision in NCCC's action before the Eastern Washington Growth Management Hearings Board required Chelan County to move forward on its Critical Areas Plan. Perhaps the most significant aspect of this was the building of an alliance between defenders of Stehekin and the taxpaying citizens of Chelan County. All parties agreed to a much smaller and more environmentally sensitive bible camp. The enforcement action taken by the U.S. Army Corps of Engineers and the Environmental Protection Agency for bulkhead construction without a permit would probably, as a result of this settlement, be adjusted. As a footnote, the U.S. Army Corps of Engineers, at the request of several property owners and the Chelan Chamber of Commerce, and without consulting the Park Service, had brought in bulldozers to clear logjams from the Stehekin River, placing a foot in the door that would ultimately, according to the Corps manual, lead to channelizing and diking. The Park Service, strangely, did not object.

Not long after the bible camp episode was resolved, the river bank collapsed, eroding all the way to the road. The Park Service was forced to intervene by recontouring the bank and placing a rock "barb" in the river to reduce further erosion.

Entitlements and Exploitations:

Gravel, Sand, Critters, Cars, What-Have-You

Were a Seattle resident to run his pickup truck into that city's Discovery Park and load up on sand and gravel, or a San Francisco resident were to carry home topsoil from Golden Gate Park, or a New York City resident to quarry rock from Central Park, the denouement would be a wagon ride to the pokey and a bill for damages, if not an extended lockup in a hospital for the criminally insane. Not in Stehekin.

Among the entitlements claimed as part of the "heritage" is all the gravel desired from public land. Until 1979, this use was not regulated; riverbed, valley floor, and alluvial fans are still pockmarked with borrow pits. Topsoil is a limited commodity in a mountain valley where the terrain is so frequently shifted by nature that accumulation is the exception, and it was routinely scooped from a fairway of a once-fantasized golf course. The Park Service eventually regulated the practice but chose not to stop it.

In January 1986 a park employee found a number of unmarked traps in the Valley, traced them to a prominent resident and caught him skinning a marten; his possession further included six other marten skins, two of bobcat and one of coyote. The employee assumed the trapping, contrary as it was to the presence of the Park Service in the Valley, was illegal. However, the trapper, whose

Stehekin quarry.

DAVE SCHIEFELBEIN

father and grandfather had also been trappers, considered the legislation ambiguous. The sheriff came uplake and cited the park employee for tampering with a trapline. Rather than defend his employee and Park Service principle, Superintendent Reynolds settled the matter by looking the other way. Later, a failed National Rifle Association lawsuit (*NRA v. Potter*) removed the last shred of imagined ambiguity. The court agreed that trapping (unlike hunting) in the National Recreation Area is as illegal there as it is in the National Park.

In 1987 some familiar faces were cited for snitching wood and bulldozing in Rainbow Creek; the citation was defied, no penalty assessed. One also built the sole house that exists beside the Chelan Lakeshore Trail. The Park Service did not object to construction of what was advertised as a "boat-in hotel." But rather than go to court to establish adverse possession of a trail used by the public for more than a century, the Park Service relocated the trail.

Some hell broke loose when a ranger began checking vehicles for registration. Few old pick-up trucks in the Valley were registered annually, and at least a few certificates of title may have become inadvertently non-locatable. For most, the harmless disobedience of a little state law, now and again, would be of near-zero consequence. At the same time, the Park Service seemed slow at enforcing the most rudimentary parking regulations at the landing, directly in view of the District Ranger's office, which is not of particular concern here either, other than to remind one of the term "National Parking Lot," coined by the late Edward Abbey who was jaundiced by his own experience working for the Park Service in the Southwest. There were, of course, much more serious things to be concerned about. However, the Park Service seemed to have adopted a policy of issuing citations for violations on a willing-recipient basis only. A ranger who flatly refused to ticket friends caught in the act of burgling timber from public land was not eagerly disciplined. An Associated Press story dated February 22, 1987, quoted the Stehekin postmaster: "We're just tired of the federal government trying to run our lives."

While sanctimoniously declaring an intent to preserve the character of the Stehekin Valley, the Park Service has often seemed content to let it be nibbled to death, a morsel here, a chunk there. But the cumulative impact of this kind of nibbling over time threatens to devastate the Valley, foot by foot, mile by mile.

LOCAL VERSUS NATIONAL INTERESTS

After 1968, to deal with the new federal presence, a local group was formed, the Stehekin Property Owners and Residents Association (SPORA), apparently with some encouragement from the Park Service, which hoped to find a single voice for calm conversation. Once the park was established and the NCCC stepped back from the forefront, SPORA filled the vacuum with more cred-ible local talent. However, since SPORA proved to have too many voices who spoke for people rather than property and it was not deemed exclusive enough for those who found the pro-preservationists disruptive. SPORA was replaced in 1970 by the Stehekin Property Owners Association (SPOA). Only two of the board members elected at the organizational meeting on October 15, 1970, were longtime residents. Most were not residents at all, though they were indeed property owners. The headquarters of the association was in Manson, which is about as downlake as a person can get without moving to Seattle. Paul Bergman reported that the leaders

> think they have the Park Service over a barrel. Several residents have not joined—I am one of these. Even (Blank) agrees the (Blonks) will never be satisfied and will keep on making new demands. I agree with him, think the (Blonks) will be a big pain in the neck. For a party who resides here only a short part of the year, they sure act big.

But again, the SPOA wasn't exclusive enough to keep out those property owners who spoke for the nation and the future. The group was in turn super-seded by the Stehekin Community Council, its membership limited to voters registered in the Stehekin Precinct of Chelan County. The Park Service recog-nized this group as representative of local opinion until local opinion crystal-lized into two distinct groups: one was vociferous and resolute in its determina-tion to turn back the clock for a renewal of Barbecuing unrestrained by a federal presence or national opinion; the other was so dismayed by the rant and bluster of self-appointed leaders it ceased attending meetings, and went on about its business and pleasure in peacefully anarchistic fashion to the extent the ensuing greed plague would allow.

Trying to be an Old-Stehekin-style anarchist—in the midst of a war that soon spread beyond the confines of the Valley to the courthouse of Chelan County and to the statehouse in Olympia, and even to Washington, D.C.—was not easy. A ranger, after transfer elsewhere, reported to the Park Service on "seething hatreds in the Valley." Visitors who had cherished warm friendships found themselves given the cold shoulder, or at best a frosty nod, at the Land-ing. To live in or visit the Valley as a voice for the nation's future was something to be avoided if one did not want to face ostracism by the leaders of the vocifer-ous group. People attracted to the Valley by the peace of Nature who found themselves within a tornado had essentially two choices: move on or shut up.

Not happy with these limited choices, the Stehekin Valley Protection Committee (SVPC) was formed in 1984 to try to control the juggernaut of de-velopment and resource exploitation. It struggled along fitfully for a few years, motivated to defend Stehekin because, as Ann McConnell (daughter of Jane and Grant) wrote, "It is out of the way and not on the road from anywhere to anywhere else. It is unique and special, one of the most beautiful places in the world. It is also uniquely vulnerable." Members going to the Landing to pick up mail felt as if they had stenciled on their foreheads, "SVPC. Unclean." It took more gumption than most peace-lovers were willing to invest. The quiet many left the podium to the braver few.

The vulnerability was demonstrated in 1984 by formation of the Stehekin Heritage Defense Committee (SHDC), which started by filing an unsuccessful lawsuit against the Park Service, in essence asking the courts to make it go away. It also published a paper, *Stehekin Heritage*, plucking the strings of the Myth harp and stating as credo an *argumentum ad* straw man: "We believe people do belong in this world of trees, mountains, and streams. That to exclude people is to contrive an unnatural scenario." What made this a straw-man argument was that no known group disagreed. The context implied that conservationists did. But the NCCC, for example, maintained then, as it does now, that the "unnatural scenario" for Stehekin is too many people doing the wrong things, like overdeveloping and plundering the wilderness.

An annual publication issued by Cascade Corral–Stehekin Valley Ranch cataloged the Courtney family enterprises. The 1991 issue contained an editorial that defined the problem and the Heritage platform: "a group of outside extremists . . . have combined with the National Park Service to both destroy the rich heritage of our mountain community and its ability to serve the public [sic] by taking away our land base. . . . We only desire . . . to retain [it]."

Land base. Even today, that is essentially what the "heritage" is about. The test question of the Heritagers remains, "Are you for or against my land base?" New Stehekin has many, though far from limitless, opportunities to make a living, even a decent living, providing necessary and useful visitor services, as the Courtney family has done since the 1950s. But nobody ever got rich working for a living, in Stehekin or anywhere else. When a Stehekinite cries "land base!" the audience might assume they are being driven off their land, or at least accept that they need more land to grow on and without it will shrivel and die. However, if Stehekin already exists as a viable community—"America as it used to be"—why must it grow? If the existing land base is insufficient, then perhaps Stehekin is not and never was a viable community. The presumption that growth and development are necessary for a community to become or remain reasonably prosperous and sustainable is itself one of the great American myths.

Strangely (or not), Heritagers often have friends on the Chelan County Commission. The credence given the "Heritagers" by them, the media, and the less informed seems to increase geometrically with distance from Stehekin. Newspapers and magazines from afar, for example, may offer sympathetic treatment and absolute acceptance of The Myth, and travelers who know nothing of the place are easily entertained by a good story or two. A concessionaire was once accused by a reporter of serving "weak coffee, Wenatchee-baked pie," but when given a chance to respond to his accuser, said: "A lot is perceived that isn't real. It all boils down to greed. There's lots of rhetoric but it boils down to this—who's going to get the buck?" The other name for Stehekin Heritage, the embattled concessionaire implied, was greed. Whether or not that is true, the various Valley groups and individuals cited herein speak well enough for the local interest. Even the late SVPC, though it addressed national values, did so from a local perspective. But Stehekin lies within the National Park System. North Cascades National Park and Lake Chelan NRA belong to everyone. Thus it is not indisputable that an individual or a family residing in the Valley can claim a larger share of ownership of the Stehekin Valley than, say, the combined populations of California, Massachusetts, and Illinois.

Having a choice in Stehekin between the national interest and the local, how did the National Park Service of the 1970s to 1980s go wrong? Superintendent Lowell White provided part of the answer at a 1976 meeting with conservationists and Stehekin property owners. He pointed out that of the 800,000 annual visits to the North Cascades National Park Complex, a comparative handful were to Stehekin; the North Cascades Highway was the hot spot. Taking a page from the Mather–Albright book, which had some validity when the Park Service was fighting for its life, he equated a half-day drive-through by a Winnebago with a hiker's week in the backcountry. Frontcountry was where careers were built. Stehekin was a sort of front-country, but it was remote front-country, a semi-backcountry.

Through the early years of the North Cascades National Park Complex, upwardly mobile rangers sought postings to the highway sector over an assignment to the isolated little valley where in winter the sun rarely shines, a Siberia for troublemakers, which is to say an apparent dumping ground for third-raters who might be an embarrassment in Sedro Woolley or Marblemount. But always, and increasingly, there have been first-raters who prized Stehekin, not only because they fell in love with the Valley, but because the occasional ineptitude of predecessors provided a challenging career opportunity. However, as the caliber of rangers has risen, the Valley has suffered from another Park Service flaw, the ritual of the "triennial wipe-out," in which management-level staff are often transferred just as they are getting a grasp of things.

Hiring local residents seemed an excellent way not only to support the local economy, but to bring the Park Service and the Stehekin community to share a common interest. That indeed is what happened, though sometimes to the detriment of the national interest. Of the eight permanent positions based in Stehekin in 1979, five were held by people who already were residents before being offered Park Service jobs. Five of the permanent employees and three of the seasonals were property owners, actual or potential subdividers, or at the very least, parents of children who added to the population of the Valley. Some locals are devout conservationists, superb stewards of a land they love. Others are not. The danger arises that the Park Service may be co-opted. Charged to defend the natural and scenic qualities to fulfill their national responsibilities, the conflict of interest tends to evolve their attitudes to a union with self-aggrandizing localists. When the park reorganized and the Stehekin ranger position was eliminated, park staff remaining in Stehekin were left powerless to defend the park's interest.

Some seasonals were locally oriented when hired and remained so. Thus the bewilderment of visitors who are true believers in the sanctity of the national park system at hearing men and women in Park Service uniforms attacking the Park Service—for the wrong reasons.

Seasonals and permanents alike frequently fail to understand the principles of the National Park Service. In the past their superiors failed to educate them and by osmosis they learned that the timidity of political neutrality is safer than the boldness of advocacy and ignorance safest of all. Nobody gets fired for talking up The Myth.

Even when politically neutral, the typical seasonals scarcely sense where they are. The interpretive staff may have only the most rudimentary knowledge of their subject, despite the wealth of published material available. The ignorance by no means has been confined to the lower levels; when J.J. Reynolds arrived as superintendent, he took an airplane ride, raved about the scenery, and exclaimed, "We ought to have a book showing all this!" He was unaware that three large-format photo books already had been published—but never had been for sale by the Park Service in Stehekin because they advocated National Park values that were objectionable to some of the more dominant voices in the Stehekin community.

The Park Service bookshelf and display at the Stehekin Visitors Center have eliminated many of the more ridiculous errors for which it was notorious in early years. Yet decades later it did little to educate the public about what distinguishes the place from just another amusement area. Visitors gain little sense of the Park Service mission in the Valley, nor why the nation's conservationists labored so long and strenuously to bring the Park Service here. At many national parks, citizen advocates—the park founders—are warmly recognized for their dedicated efforts leading to the parks having been established. Not so in Stehekin. Perhaps that will change one day with a suitable memorial to the proud work of Jane and Grant McConnell—kudos that are long overdue.

10

Once More Unto Stehekin

Stehekin, yes, it is in great danger and it is up to us [citizens] . . .
to do the saving. The soul of the National Park Service, yes, it is
walking in the valley of the shadow and it is up to us to help the
good people in the NPS wrestle with the devil and win through to
glory.

—Irate Birdwatcher, from "Fear and Loathing on Lake Chelan"
Winter 1991, *The Wild Cascades*

DRIFT ON, O RUDDERLESS SHIP OF STATE

I N 1976 SUPERINTENDENT WHITE, responding to demands that he halt Stehekin sprawl, acknowledged that he'd sort of been thinking about meeting
with Chelan County officials to talk about zoning. He repeated the Park
Service party line at the time that the nation had no control over subdivision
and construction by property owners. And he felt Chelan County folks were a
decent sort who could be trusted to do the right thing.

Regional Director Russell Dickenson put White on notice he had better
clean up the Stehekin mess, but White seemed to wring his hands. Dickenson despaired of White's reluctance and, as the only other choice he thought
he had, summoned a planning team from Denver Service Center. National
Park Service staff from San Francisco, Denver, Harpers Ferry, and other offices
regularly tripped in to various parks to solve problems the local staff was afraid
to address. The solutions often were worse than the problems. The Denver
Service Center became an epithet for the textbook-trained technician who had
seen hundreds of sites in maps, photographs, and helicopter glimpses and never

yet broken in a pair of boots, and who was so slick at blueprints and brochures it would demean him to seek the counsel of on-trail rangers, much less the on-trail public. Newton Drury, as National Park Service Director (from 1940–1951), calmed Congressional fears of over-development by the Park Service, saying, "We have no money. We can do no harm." Later, critics added, "If only this were true of the Denver Construction Center."

Once again, in Stehekin, the NPS solution became the problem. The team held workshops in Stehekin, Chelan, and Wenatchee, home of the People of the Myth and Chelan County wealthies for whom a vacation home in Stehekin and a fast boat had become regional status symbols. Only in response to a vigorous protest by the NCCC did it add a workshop in Seattle. The team apologized, saying it never had heard of the NCCC. This evidenced total ignorance of the campaign for a park and details of the consideration by Congress. The team publicly stated that the purpose of the recreation area was wholly unclear, and then asked the People of the Myth what *they* wanted the valley to be! The workshops encouraged locals to reopen controversies that had been definitively settled by Congress. Challenge of the very values of the National Park System was invited. Fortuitously, the Denver team was prevented from doing further damage by a new nationwide policy on Park Service land acquisition. Their project was suspended in September 1978.

That same month Lowell White ran out his string in the North Cascades and was transferred to Acadia National Park on the Maine coast, whose superintendent, Keith Miller, had run out his string there and was transferred to the North Cascades.

As early as 1969, the Park Service had sought to involve Chelan County in Stehekin planning as a means to slow subdivision; the county began work and went so far as to declare a moratorium on building in the valley, but the effort languished and the Park Service gave no indication that it noticed. If the Park Service didn't care, why should the county?

In June 1978 Chelan County officials were stirred to a renewal of action. Commissioners and a member of the Planning Department voyaged uplake to meet a five-person committee of SPORA (the Stehekin Property Owners and Residents Association), this being the core group designated to help the planner—somewhat akin to the blind leading the blind. In September Dickenson told the commissioners that the Park Service would release a Development Concept Plan in several weeks. The county planner said he wouldn't be ready to address the issues until spring. The Park Service agreed to suspend its own planning, and then forgot about it altogether.

Superintendent Miller attended the meetings between the Chelan planner and the Stehekin core, taking no position on any issue raised; from this came the name by which certain conservationists remembered him, "Zero." As one resident put it, "We feel like we are operating in a vacuum, and it is difficult to focus attention on the issues, because no one knows what the outside constraints are."

Why, NCCC asked the Park Service, is the Stehekin parkland subject to the jurisdiction of Chelan County? "Why don't you flat-out tell those apple-knockers to mind their own apples and leave national business to the nation?"

The Chelan County draft plan submitted to public comment in April 1979 was, as the apologetic planner confessed, "very permissive." The entry by Chelan County, which claimed it had been invited in by the Park Service, was gasoline on a smoldering fire. Miller expressed an opinion, but it was the wrong one. The county plan would be accepted by the Park Service, he predicted, and be the basis for whatever happened in Stehekin. The Park Service, he said, was powerless to control private land. Some parts of Stehekin simply were going to have to suffer.

A workshop was scheduled in Seattle for September 5, 1979, against a background of preceding weeks in which Chelan County granted a variance for a building on a postage-stamp-sized lakeshore lot; a resident began drilling test holes on the slope above Logger's Point, intending to pump sewage uphill from a planned waterside restaurant. Heavy equipment started digging beside the river, permitted by a County-granted floodway variance; five new foundations were on order, in addition to twelve new houses already completed since January. The county planner was telling folks that sixty-eight building sites were available without any further subdivision.

The Seattle workshop was attended by ten National Park Service officials, led by Regional Director Dickenson, Superintendent Miller, and the Denver planner; by two Chelan County planners; and by public members representing half a dozen local, state, and national organizations. The Denver chap was just clearing his throat in preparation for a description of Chelan County's plans when a citizen broke in to ask innocently, "Pardon me, but why are we talking about Chelan County plans for a National Recreation Area?" The Denverite went numb and Dickenson responded (just a bit of steam issuing from his nostrils) that after eight-and-a-half years of stewing the Park Service hadn't produced a plan and was just getting started when local residents (not the park) invited the county in. (Note the denial that the Park Service had extended the invitation. It is credible that Miller did, in fact, invite the county, but without a clearance from Dickenson.) Each person around the circle was asked to express their concerns. The Park Service heard a dozen variations on the theme, "No more subdivision!" and Dickenson admitted he'd received a number of letters along those lines.

Dickenson announced that the Chelan County planners would hold an October 6 hearing in Stehekin and the Park Service would comment on their plan at that time. He also declared that, at the right time, the Park Service would come forward with its own land-use plan. The 1968 Act, he said, did not have specific language saying that any local-agency planning had to be approved by the Secretary of Interior, and that in the opinion of National Park Service attorneys, local planners had to be heard out or risk challenge, probably successful, in court. Asked what the Park Service intended to do about this serious flaw in the 1968 Act, he said they were looking to "fix the Act." How? When? That depended on the local Congressional delegation.

The Park Service comment was delivered as promised, but not by Dickenson, who was absent. Miller read it, sweating heavily. Dickenson's treatment of the county was "just short of brutal." He notified the planners they could adopt the points enumerated in his statement or go fish. The points, framed after the September 5 Seattle hearing, were reasonably responsive to the concerns expressed there. They also were framed after letters had been received from the SCLDF (now Earthjustice), which had been drawn in by the question, "Where would we rather fight the battle for Park Service principle—Stehekin or Anchorage?" Dickenson's position amounted to an acceptance of the SCLDF's assessment of Park Service powers within the NRA, an assessment at opposite poles from that of Miller.

Some Stehekin property owners didn't hear what Dickenson said, or didn't believe what they heard, and why should they? Miller, mopping his brow,

Lady of the Lake at Stehekin.

DAVE SCHIEFELBEIN

told them that Dickenson didn't really mean it: "The statement would not be strictly applied at this time." He repeated that the Park Service was powerless.

The building boom in Stehekin continued unabated, as much to the dismay of Stehekin-protective Stehekinites as to the Seattle–California–Boston axis of environmentalists. A petition was circulated in the Valley asking that a moratorium be declared on building until adoption of a zoning plan. The petition was signed by many, killed by a few. In December, Dickenson and Miller met with the Chelan County Commissioners, asking them to revise their zoning to Park Service specifications and to declare a moratorium on new plats. If there was no moratorium and if an attempt was made at a large new development, the Park Service would test its powers in court via condemnation. A bill was being drafted to give the Park Service any powers it needed that it might lack. The message to Chelan County was, play your games as you wish but if the Park Service doesn't like the outcome, it's no contest.

A distinction must be made here between the citizens of Chelan County and their government. Citizens harbored diverse views and generally tried to get along. Their government, on the other hand, pressed on with its good-ol'-boy agenda. People west of the Cascades, the "wet-siders," joke about how too much sun east of the mountains desiccates the brains. People east of the Cascades, the "drysiders," joke about how too much rain makes the brains go moldy. It's all friendly joking. The government of Chelan County, on the other hand, was no joke.

In that final year of the Carter administration, the Park Service, through Dickenson, was showing at least a fractured interest in mitigating some of Chelan County's planning initiatives. What position it would take in the Reagan–Bush era about to commence was anyone's guess.

THE INMATES TAKE COMMAND

The second-most corrupt administration in the history of America, and the second looniest of any modern nation since that of King Ludwig of Bavaria (the other hailing from Crawford, Texas), was ushered in by a January 22, 1981, report by the Comptroller General entitled "Lands in the Lake Chelan National Recreation Area Should Be Returned to Private Ownership."

The genesis of this oddity has never been explained. The hypothesizer is free to connect the dots between Stehekin speculators, political powers in Chelan County, and apparatchiks in Washington, D.C. The heirs of the late Robert Byrd, a Courtney cousin and sometime wanna-be entrepreneur in Stehekin, were later to claim credit for his successful lobbying. A team of auditors spent weeks in Stehekin, Wenatchee, and Seattle. Looking like the seventeenth-century fly-fishing poet, Charles Cotton, in his $500 kangaroo-leather boots, with a sleek associate in her Italian fashions, the pair lacked only scented hand-kerchiefs at their nostrils, as they giggled and half-listened to a series of presentations by NCCC directors. They did not read the Georgette–Harvey report, though a copy had been placed in their hands, and they ignored the brief prepared by the SCLDF. Their minds apparently had been made up (with some obvious coaching) before they left Washington, D.C. The question remains for scholars to ferret out: Who sent 'em?

First-hand testimony is available from Valley residents that Byrd met the U.S. General Accounting Office (GAO) team in Wenatchee and conducted them uplake, on the way telling them what they would see and hear. After explaining their purpose to a community meeting, they agreed to meet with individuals. At one of these homes "Cotton" repeated his statement made at the community gathering. "I've never met a willing seller," he said. His host of the evening responded, "You have now," adding, "In '73 we approached the Park, asking if they wanted to buy. They couldn't approach us. We sold, taking a twenty-year lease." But Cotton was not programmed to hear the facts. The GAO report declared that this family, too, was forced to sell.

The report drifted off, half-sinking, though never quite to the bottom of the sea. It gave early warning that the Reagan era was not going to be land-friendly. A decade later, some Stehekin property owners were solemnly citing Cotton as if he were Moses, and Washington's Senator Slade Gorton, having gone along with the Myth, was publicly vowing to punish the Park Service rascals who dared not to abide.

The immediate consequences (clues now for that ferreting scholar) were that the owner of thirty acres on the Stehekin River filed with the county to subdivide into nine lots. The son of Oscar Getty, a Stehekin old-timer, brought in a boatload of men in business suits and women in high heels and presented a plan for forty condominiums on his 153.6 acres, to be priced at around $100,000 each. The rumor spread that the Park Service shortly would be handing out deeds, free of charge, to all the property it had acquired.

In October 1981 the Park Service distributed a thick and ploddy Denver Service Center hodge-podge, "Environmental Assessment—Compatibility Standards—Lake Chelan–Stehekin–National Recreation Area," and asked for comment on two questions. First, should lands be returned to private ownership as recommended by the GAO, that is, by Kangaroo-Boots Cotton; and second, who should control use of the Stehekin Valley?

Semi-coherent *Denverese* offered three alternatives: (A) primary authority for development issues would be Chelan County; (B) a sliding-scale formula would protect against large-scale subdivision of properties while allowing flexibility in utilization of private parcels (the flexibility would result in an estimated 137 additional residences—this was the alternative preferred by the Park Service); and (C) a more restrictive formula would provide greater protection to the traditional character of the Valley. This final option was the one alternative considered by the NCCC to be worth discussing, but solely as a starting point for tightening up the restrictions because even it, the best the Park Service had to offer, would allow 108 new homes.

A workshop was held in Stehekin February 5, 1982, to hear the localists. A second was held in Seattle February 9 to hear the nationalists. But they weren't heard. A bus was hired to bring fifty-odd Stehekin–Manson–Chelan–Wenatchee folks across the Cascades to fill the speakers' sign-up sheet and the fifty-odd seats in the tiny hearing room. Jammed into standing-room-only, the "outside interests" shrugged and went home, leaving Miller surrounded by the People of the Myth. Letters, excerpted below, ensured his career would not end in much glory:

> With a very few exceptions, there no longer are Stehekin residents who have "historic" rights. If those who came in after 1968 claim special rights to Stehekin, what about those of us who were there before 1968 as visitors? I feel the visitor, not the resident, is the one who has historic rights to Stehekin.
>
> I vigorously and bitterly protest your giving any countenance to a Stehekin Community Council, another name for the speculators and inholders and poor damn fools, unless you give equal and full recognition to a Stehekin National Council, representing the people of the nation, the ideals of the National Park Act, and your better selves.

The Park Service heard two things loud and clear: shut off the land speculators and you're going to get sued; fail to shut off the speculators and you're also going to get sued.

The February 9 packing of the Seattle hearing was tactically clever, strategically tragic. Denied a fair chance to speak, the "outside interests" standing in sardine mass sought eye contact with friends in the fifty chairs, and failed. The accepted procedure when war is wanted is to deliberately polarize, squeezing out the middle ground where peace might be negotiated. Many of those who attended the meeting in the good faith of the middle ground began to wonder if there ever could be peace until localism was eradicated.

Things might still have been made right. Five months later, in July 1982, a chance meeting at Twin Springs Camp on the Chelan Summit Trail broke through the new ice to reaffirm the old friendship uniting a spokesman for outside interests (Manning) and Ray Courtney. In a burst of mutual emotion it was vowed not to let politics wreck a twenty-year family relationship. A date was set to meet at the Courtney Ranch in October, after tourist season, to sit by the hot stove and haggle out a new middle ground. Several weeks after the

Twin Springs encounter Ray fell to his death from the Hilgard Pass trail.

Had Ray lived . . . Driven though he was by the economic imperative of a large family and its revolution of expectations, his inside and outside interests had been as one from the 1950s, when he began a long service as a director of the NCCC, until well into the troubles of the 1970s. His love of the country never dimmed. Neither did that of his family, but lacking the last Courtney of Old Stehekin, the economic pressures of trying to be year-rounders without outside money-earning spells, and perhaps a little social pressure from neighbors, inevitably drove part of the family toward becoming New Stehekin Heritagers. That is not to deny, however, that there is also a well deserved pride among the Courtneys for their substantial contributions to the rich history of the Stehekin Valley, as well as the great wilderness that embraces it.

The People of the Myth needed Ray to help validate their claims to be heirs of the Pioneers. After his passing, the uneasy community recognition that Old Stehekin was dead and gone, that the Myth was becoming an outright fraud, made it ever more difficult for a middle-ground Valley resident to risk association with outsiders.

A 1980s piece in *The Wild Cascades* reminded readers that the intent in the 1960s had been for Stehekin to be in the national park and suggested that this remain an option. One or more Stehekinites stripped the details from the historical fact in retelling the story, thus triggering a valley-wide panic. Few residents subscribed to *The Wild Cascades*, and the offending article was not shown around but only described. The Paul Reveres failed to inform listeners that the subject was the 1960s, and reported the proposal as news that was hot off the griddle. "The N3C is coming! The N3C is coming!" Cavalry was reported galloping. Hessians were marching. Tanks were massing on the frontiers. The widowed Esther Courtney mailed a tearful appeal to customers of the Courtney Family Enterprises for help in "saving the Courtney Ranch." No known person or agency has ever expressed a desire to take away the ranch, which is acknowledged by virtually everyone, including NCCC, to provide valuable visitor services. However, hundreds of Courtney customers across America whose sole information about Stehekin was based on incomplete communications reacted as though the family's ruin were plotted. They sent cash to "save the ranch." They wrote letters to Congressmen across America, effectively spreading the myth.

The local spokesman for the philosophy once expounded by the John Birch Society was quoted in the press calling for a revolution—a *violent* revolution. Cooler heads who understood that verbal craziness can be a prelude to physical violence were appalled and frightened to have such a neighbor in the midst.

In January 1985 the SHDC (Stehekin Heritage Defense Committee) filed suit against the Park Service, citing as grievances the limitations on the size of guided tours, trapping, use of roads, restrictions on other commercial activities, and "a host of additional matters" not spelled out. The NCCC intervened, engaging as counsel the SCLDF. The Sierra Club and the newly-formed SVPC (Stehekin Valley Protection Committee) joined the intervention. In October the SCLDF moved for summary judgment, establishing in detail that the suit was in all respects frivolous. The Heritagers, having discovered that even silliness can cost a lot of money, offered to settle, made especially eager to do so because the SCLDF motion correctly pointed out that claims challenging Park Service acquisitions were barred by the six-year statute of limitations governing judicial review of civil actions against the United States, a fact their attorney might have warned them about before he took their money. The SCLDF motion also showed that the Park Service possessed ample authority to adopt compatibility standards to guide its acquisition of private lands (by condemnation, if necessary); that the plaintiffs had no constitutional right to conduct unregulated hunting and trapping on federal land; and that the Park Service had plenary authority to regulate public use of all lands and waters within the Lake Chelan National Recreation Area. A hearing was held January 2, 1985, at which Judge McNichols was persuaded on these points and accordingly entered judgment for the NCCC and the National Park Service, dismissing the Heritagers' suit on August 6, 1985.

The Heritagers had pulled their cash from the mattresses and got whupped and were furious with the outside interests. That anger might have been better spent questioning the ethics of the attorneys who took their money and rethinking the irresponsible rhetoric that was wedging apart ancient friendships.

THE MYTH LIVES ON

The evolution of Park Service administration has followed a pattern familiar to students of various government regulatory commissions. The life cycle is characterized first by a period of aggressive regulation in the public interest; second, by a period of rather routine administration; third, by a period of inactivity; and finally, by a stage in which the regulatory body identifies its objectives with protection and promotion of the industry it was set up to regulate. What took something like a half-century for the Interstate Commerce Commission, as one example, occurred in Stehekin in the remarkably short period of a decade.

According to an economic theory of administration, which looks for what is being maximized in administrative behavior, it is the growth of administrative personnel that is maximized, along with appropriations, since these determine economic return to administrators. The theory is too simple for full application to Stehekin, yet something was indeed being maximized there and it had economic roots. Certainly there was a proliferation of personnel, permanent and seasonal, making more and loftier supervisory positions for career staff.

It must be remembered that opposition to the installation of the Park Service in Stehekin was primarily local, that is, it came from Chelan County, the Valley itself, and the downlakers who owned land there. The Park Service, arriving on the scene, sought to placate the continuing opposition, hired some locals, and even turned a blind eye to illegal actions by others. The commendable sensitivity to people whose lives might otherwise have been seriously disrupted was fully supported by the NCCC. Some of its directors frequently sat in hot-stove seminars with Ray Courtney and family to discuss how Park Service policies might be modified in ways that would not threaten the national interest while meeting reasonable needs of the local interest.

An unavoidable side-effect of the North Cascades Act was to publicize the Valley and thus attract new residents not only from downlake, but across America, including some individuals who adopted the ideology of localism. The Park Service in Stehekin generated a new constituency for itself: a local group of concessionaires, contractors, and those Park Service personnel who, to one degree or another, renounced national loyalties. The welfare of this group has come to be seen as that of the Stehekin community. The nation-serving Park Service rangers and the summer visitors were not viewed as part of the community but as outsiders.

The accelerated planning efforts, in themselves necessary and desirable, increased the dominance of localism because, in a laudable desire to behave democratically by consulting the public, the planners implicitly defined the public as the *local* public (as also happened in other parks in other states). Only after protest was there an effort to consult as far away as Seattle. Further, the frame of consultation was such that this peculiarly defined public was invited to reconsider the purposes defined by Congress—purposes which had been opposed by precisely the groups now being consulted in Stehekin, Manson, and Chelan. The Park Service seemingly mobilized opposition to its own purposes as set forth in the fundamental Act of 1916 and the instructions given by Congress in the Act of 1968.

The national park idea expressed in 1865 by Frederick Law Olmsted, whose other famous idea was New York's Central Park, demands protection of the national interest. The first requirement, he said, is to *preserve the natural scenery*. The necessary accommodation of visitors must be restricted within the narrowest limits. Structures should not detract from the dignity of the scene. "In permitting the sacrifice of anything that would be of the slightest value to future visitors," he wrote, "to the convenience, bad taste, playfulness, carelessness, or wanton destructiveness of present visitors, we probably yield in each case the interest of uncounted millions to the selfishness of a few." Parks pro-

Bonanza Peak and the Mary Green Glacier (ca. 1907). The glacier, mislabeled Isella on the photo, has receded considerably over the past century.

tected *for* people must be protected *from* them as well.

Through the 1970s and 1980s, the years witnessed a growing debilitation of Park Service administration in the North Cascades, with both a steady reduction in the national commitment and a strengthening of The Myth. As the memory of subsistence-and-barter Old Stehekin was fading, the New Stehekin was portrayed in the press and the commercial brochures and by the utterances of residents as the perpetuation of that old-time model. However, nobody who spent more than a few hours in Stehekin could imagine it to be so. The person who tried to buy a piece of property quickly learned Stehekin had become a Myth-exploiting, cash-oriented suburb of Chelan, or Wenatchee.

The Myth had two bases. One was historical. Stehekin lay just outside the boundary of congressionally designated National Wilderness; *ergo*, it was the frontier; those who live on the frontier have traditional entitlements, they are entitled to eat the animals, to burn the wood, to dig gravel and sand and topsoil and mine rock for riprap, to dike and channelize the river, to park cars and dump junk wherever they please on public land. There is an even darker side to entitlements. The Park Service at one time alleged that in the Stehekin Valley there was "an 80 percent noncompliance rate" with Park regulations by locals—illegal roads, poaching wildlife, stealing firewood. Was this so central to the unique lifestyle that the Park Service should look the other way? The violations usually were not committed out of any need or for any real profit, but seemed more in the spirit of a child determined to assert independence from adult authority. In the Fall 1984 issue of *The Wild Cascades*, NCCC President Dave Fluharty wrote, "Given the small size of the Stehekin community in 1968, the demands were not exorbitant. . . . With growth in population and visitation in the area, the demands for all these resources have been increasing."

The other basis for The Myth was a kind of show business: when a property-owning summerer who had been a half-century in the Valley complained about junkyards along the road, a Valley schoolteacher who had plans to open a summer camp and whose chosen role was that of Heritager Poet Laureate, thought of them more as a tourist attraction. Junk, he said, held a lesson for visitors, it exhibited frontier thrift and ingenuity. "Beauty," said he, "is in the eye of the beholder." It was explained that people came to see people. Of course some do and some don't. A newspaper piece told how a visitor "sips the camp coffee that brews in a two-gallon stoneware pot on a grate at the back of the fireplace. 'Isn't this wonderful! If it weren't for the Ranch and the Courtneys, Stehekin wouldn't be Stehekin anymore. I wouldn't come!'"

A non-Heritager testified otherwise:

I am proud of the fact that I attended a one-room log-cabin school, spent part of my childhood without electricity, and grew up listening to the tales of prospectors, trappers, homesteaders, and an endless flow of other dreamers who came to the Valley. The Stehekin Mystique is as compelling as it is enduring. . . . The Frontier Myth is a powerful one. It is now, however, only a myth.

Much of the pro-development agitation from locals is couched in frontier terms, as in the claim that the Park Service 'is destroying the old-time Stehekin Community and traditional ways of life.'. . . . most disturbingly, and this cannot be overstated, the Park Service itself has fallen prey to the myth that some frontier community still exists, and that it has some God-given right to exploit the wilds for its private use. . . .

The Park Service should expunge the 'unique Stehekin lifestyle' argument from its policy debates once and for all. The pioneer days of the Valley are gone forever; I know of no true subsistence living in Stehekin today. As a member of the Stehekin community, I resent the Park Service's view that the way I live is in some ways enriching to visitors; this is ultimately paternalistic and makes me feel that, when in Stehekin, I live in some human zoo operated by the Park Service. . . .

One could be charitable and acknowledge that the Park Service found itself squeezed between so many rocks and hard places, people making demands from all sides, not all of them particularly motivated by the national interest in our parks and wildlands. The Park Service's general reluctance to stand up to the county and the Heritagers only intensified many of the disputes that might otherwise have been avoided. It nurtured, directly and indirectly, the myth of a Stehekin that never existed, one that ought not to be the story of historians.

WISE GUYS IN COONSKIN HATS

The Stehekin Myth recited by the Heritagers is a chapter in a larger myth as old in America as the Whiskey Rebellion, which the moonshiners of western Massachusetts considered a continuation of the American Revolution. A bit of the larger myth was revealed when the campaign to preserve the Columbia Gorge was at its climax in the 1980s, and two leaders of Stehekin Heritage journeyed downlake to regale with a Congressional committee of the heinous crimes of the Park Service. The Sagebrush Rebellion in the 1980s inflamed the passions of Barbecuers of the West who interpreted the Declaration of Independence to mean freedom to do as they please with the public domain. President Reagan elevated the Rattlesnake Flag and its motto, "Don't Tread on Me," to official status with his appointment of James Watt as Secretary of the Interior. Watt had founded the Mountain States Legal Foundation to ensure fat landowners a fair day in court should they become unpleasantly harassed by a cloud of conservationist mosquitoes.

Cutting a remarkable figure on the vaudeville circuit in those days was Charles ("Chuck") Cushman, an insurance salesman who in 1977 gave that up to lead the crusade to free property owners from oppression by the Park Service, among others. In 1978, Cushman put on a show at Manson and a number of Stehekinites attended to learn about the horrid policies of the Park Service, which dared to encourage land uses in the Valley that were compatible with the park. Later, in 1994, the name of Cushman's group was enlarged from the National Inholders and Multiple-Use Association to the American Land Rights Association, which could draw upon a larger reservoir of potential dues-payers. The headquarters was moved to Battleground, Washington, which gave Cushman an irresistible postmark convenient to the Columbia River, Lake Quinault, Stehekin, and Northern Idaho, and their masses waiting to be inflamed.

Cushman's strategy was to rouse the rabble of one area by telling lurid tales of Park Service persecution in another. The rabble, of course, seldom checks its facts. Once, he persuaded a national television network of the pitiful plight of an elderly couple supposedly evicted from their homestead by the rangers. The network failed to offer an on-air correction when print journalists discovered the couple was happily at home, living comfortably on the funds from a voluntary sale of their home on a life-tenancy basis. Cushman's portrait of the "guvment"-persecuted couple was accepted as gospel by the Heritagers, and in exchange they dampened eyes and unzipped purses in Tennessee. His expertly crafted film, "Big Park!," infuriated his followers, but amused them, too, when he had a pair of porcine rangers in Smokey hats throw an aging couple out of their rocking chairs and then go into a dance, singing "Big Park!" Environmentalists roared with laughter that there were people who believed the film portrayed the way things are, but then went quiet when they read the papers and learned that there are Americans who deny that the Holocaust ever happened. Apparently there is nothing so absurd not to be believed by people who have reasons to want to believe. Nicknamed "Rent-a-Riot," Cushman was a figure of fun among conservationists until President Reagan appointed Watt to his cabinet who, in turn, instantly added Cushman to the federal payroll.

In 1988 the Watt agenda, rough edges smoothed for easier consumption, was submitted to a gathering in Reno, Nevada, of three hundred defenders of the sanctity of private property: enemies of the socialist conspiracy to advance the public trust, doing their duty to God and the country as ranchers, loggers, miners, developers, riflemen, and off-road-vehicle cowboys. This "Wise Use" coalition was organized by two friends who shared a cubbyhole office in Bellevue, near Seattle. One was a convicted tax felon who founded the Citizen Committee for the Right to Keep and Bear Arms. The other, James Watt's biographer, Ron Arnold, headed the Center for the Defense of Free Enterprise. Arnold's unabashed goal was "to destroy environmentalism once and for all." Cushman was, of course, a Wise User. In *War Against the Greens* (1994), David Helvarg explained that "the movement has developed its own social base, idiomatic language, ideological alliances on the Right, and support network, which reaches from unemployed loggers, off-road motorcyclists, and rural county commissioners to the top levels of industry and government." People of the West!, twelve of whose thirteen directors were mining industry executives, was allied. The Unification Church of the Reverend Moon, whom many faithful believe represents the Second Coming (which Moon tends not to deny) also supported the work of the Center for the Defense of Free Enterprise, another Ron Arnold stage.

Wise Use was brazenly pro-industry, a stance that, oddly, failed to alienate contemporary populists, who welcomed Big Business as an ally against Big Government, mindlessly ignoring how their great-granddaddies fought oppression by the railroads, the timber barons, Eastern bankers, and the trusts. Another oddity of alliances was that between Wise Guys who were outspoken atheists and Wattites who trusted in God to call us all to Heaven in the very near future, save those of us ticketed for Hell. Presumably today's fundamentalists, even in Stehekin, consider the Devil their ally against the do-good meddlers. Washington Senator Slade Gorton remained a revered champion of the Wise Users until the voters removed him from Congress in 2000.

A false impression is that Wise Use may have run its course after a decade or so. In reality, the sentiments are still strong, with some fine friends in high places in the administration of Bush II. Writing for *Sierra* just prior to the 2004 election, Helvarg warned "the movement no longer needs its blowhards and bullies as it quietly and effectively implements its radical agenda."

One more slice of history is in order here. In 1989 still another battle-ground in the Civil War erupted when four ranchers from New Mexico, Utah, and Nevada founded the National Federal Lands Conference "to protect local custom, culture, and economic stability" by giving local governments "co-equal authority in management of federal lands." Catron County, New Mexico, ad-opted the appropriate ordinances. By 1995 the Catron ordinances had been adopted by forty counties throughout the West; several hundred more were mulling.

In 1993 Chelan County Commissioners John Wall (of the Chelan Box Company family) and Ron Meyers directed their Public Works Engineer to write down the county's "traditional customs and culture." In 1994 a "secret group" of citizens drafted "Catron County" articles, intended by Wall to be tacked onto the county's Growth Management Plan, whenever that might come to pass. Made public in the fall of 1995, the document included enforcement provisions under which the National Park Service and the NCCC would be thrown in jail. However, not to rudely overstep and be judged certifiable, the commissioners unanimously voted that, yes, the Constitution of the United States was okay by them.

Great Winds Blow in Cloud-Cuckoo Land

This historian's (Manning's) grandmother, born in Nova Scotia in 1876, having immigrated to Boston as a serving girl and married a meat-cutter from New Brunswick, presided over a Maritimes–New England kitchen. The New England boiled dinner was a perennial favorite—thick soups, barley and whole pea, with rutabagas and turnips, parsnips and soup bone, Boston baked beans and homemade piccalilli. These were all generic. One standby was branded: Gorton's codfish balls. The Gorton firm was respected, as well, for its halibut cheeks. The balls, though, were the Gorton guidon.

From the Gorton family came a little boy who took a vow to become a United States senator, a dream that would also carry him westward. Upon graduating from Columbia Law School in 1953, Slade Gorton chose Washing-ton as the state of a size and temper to present him a seat when he was ready. To get ready, he attached himself to the coming man of the Republican Party, Dan Evans. He moved upward with Evans through the legislature, espousing a progressive yet pragmatic environmentalism, then a trademark of Northwest Republicanism. In 1964 Evans was elected governor and served three terms, while Gorton moved to the post of state attorney general where he helped form the state's new Department of Ecology. In 1980 that U.S. Senate opportunity came knocking. By now Senator Magnuson was 74, and Gorton was still jogging and biking at age 52. That was all the platform he needed. Gorton ousted Maggie and seemed set in his new seat for life. With the passing of Senator Jackson in 1983, Evans was appointed to the seat, then won a special election to finish Jackson's term. Thus with some irony, Evans and Gorton remained on a parallel course for several years more. Evans, however, was no longer the coming man but the going, and had it not been for "Democrats for Evans" would likely have gone quicker. Still, Evans was a home boy who generally believed what he said, and the voters liked that. Gorton, the Eastern Patrician, was up to the eyeballs in *noblesse oblige*. To many rustic Northwesterners, the lanky Senator came across as Ivy-haughty, his intelligence a bit smarty-pants. His electoral victories were always nail-biters; for Gorton, a two-percent spread was a landslide.

With Reagan in the White House, the Republican Party was changing. At both the caucus level and nationally, strangers were rising through the ranks, bursting with anti-government rhetoric, radicalizing the party in multiple ways, and of course, dismissing more traditional Republican concern for the environment. Gorton liked what he saw and eagerly joined the revolution. Perhaps out of decorum, he went along with Evans on such worthy causes as the Washington Wilderness Act of 1984, although it was clear that his interest had become much more about keeping the public timber *out* of wilderness and in the hands of the timber industry. But the times caught up with him; in 1986 the worst happened. Gorton was ejected from his Senate seat with no parachute, losing to Democrat Brock Adams, alas, by two percentage points. Two years later, Evans announced he was retiring from politics, taking his tattered coattails with him. Gorton would run again for the open seat but he would have to go it alone. He smartly realized he could no longer make it as the Old Gorton. But rather than reclaim the old moderation of Northwest politics that had served so many so well, he reinvented himself through an adjustment of his moral compass, swinging it around nearly 180 degrees and aligning with the Sagebrushers and the Wise Users. The strategy worked where it needed to—in Washington's agitated ruraldom—and Gorton was back, with another two-percent victory. In the 1994 race for re-election, the New Gorton, far-right and now bitterly anti-environmental, was seen perpetually dashing about the D.C. Beltway in running garb, in quest of press photographers and TV cameras. Following another "landslide" victory, he firmly established himself among conservationists as one of the most serious threats to environmental progress the

Northwest had ever known. Most notably, he opposed meaningful protection of pristine old-growth forests and lobbied instead for the "timber salvage rider," which allowed those forests to be decimated. He proudly served the backward-looking initiatives of the Wise Use movement, and tripped up Native American strides toward self determination, while also making failed attempts to gut the Endangered Species Act.

What drew Gorton to tiny Stehekin? Probably the same thing that brought Speaker of the House Newt Gingrich to the area in the late 1990s. Not its handful of voters. Not the special interests fishing those troubled waters— strictly bush league. The Myth, now there was the thing!— the Heritagers of Stehekin, the poor but honest yeomen, heirs of Davy Crockett and Dan'l Boone, suffering under the merciless contumely of city folk and their arrogant government officials. Gorton's (and by extension, Newt's) poster children wrung the hearts of the little people all over Eastern Washington.

National park historian David Louter summarized Gorton's actions well in *Contested Terrain* in 1998. The Park Service signed a consent degree with the NCCC and SCLDF in April 1991 to settle the groups' lawsuit over misman-agement of the Lake Chelan NRA. Louter acknowledged this as "a benchmark in the history of land protection in Stehekin." In order to protect both natural and cultural values in the Valley, "sound land acquisition policies" would be required. In March 1992, "while planning efforts and environmental studies went forward, Washington's Senator Slade Gorton threatened the new accord," wrote Louter. "He lashed out at the Park Service for its land acquisitions in Stehekin," which Gorton alleged "ran counter to the intent of Congress as set down in the 1981 GAO report." Gorton, in his own words, scowled, "I will not stand for that." The senator, said Louter, "was responding to the views of his local constituents." And he meant it. "Unless the Park Service took steps to reform its activities in Stehekin, Gorton vowed to amend the Interior appro-priation bill to halt it himself. Two months later, on May 15, Senator Gorton followed through with his warning."

But Gorton had galloped headlong into a trap. The best and brightest set to work to "lay to rest many of the misconceptions" about land-protection poli-cies and to "finally bury the GAO report." On May 13, 1992 came *A Discussion of Laws Affecting the Administration of Lake Chelan National Recreation Area.* After a decade and more of confusion and debate, the National Park Service's own legal scholars agreed that the principles of the 1916 National Park Act are in full force in national recreation areas administered by the Park Service, *except* for activities that are specifically called out in the legislation creating any given recreation area. The agency thereby confirmed that the Lake Chelan National Recreation Area, despite Gorton's contorted view, required the protections of a national park. The NCCC had been right all along.

NCCC and others fought against the Senator's meddling and ultimately a compromise was struck in which the Park Service agreed to suspend further land purchases, hunker down, and write another report.

When Gorton cited the Kangaroo Cotton Report in 1992 as grounds for bringing the Park Service to heel, his Senate compatriots chuckled, but his Wenatchee fans lapped it up. In the June 1992 *The Wild Cascades*, NCCC President Dave Fluharty wrote,

> We long have tried to explain in great detail the Stehekin situation to Senator Gorton. Gorton has ignored our information. Friends, please do one thing for the North Cascades this summer. Write the Senator and tell him to stop interfering with the National Park Service and the intent of Congress.

In the spring of 1995, at the Seattle hearings on the Environmental Impact Statement for the General Management Plan for the Lake Chelan National Recreation Area, an aide read a letter from Gorton, the burden of it being that "the Senator believes local interests should carry much greater weight than long-term national interests supporting protection of the valley." He couldn't say it any plainer than that.

Why, one might ask, was the Park Service so attentive to the senator who so obviously held it in contempt? There are, perhaps, two lines of explanation.

That "two-percent landslide," for one. Gorton relied on the big boys with the big bucks for the bulk of his vote, but it was the dab of votes here and there that put him over the top. The environmental movement as a whole had long since got him dead to rights, whereas there were sentimental Republicans who needed no more than the occasional chicken bone to sustain their loyalty. Importantly, however, for the duration of his final term in office, Slade Gorton chaired the Senate Interior Appropriations Subcommittee. Knowing this, Superintendent Paleck held onto a half-promise that Gorton would somehow get him some money for the North Cascades, a half-promise that would also help build that two percent. Park Service Director Roger Kennedy, too, was not stupid.

The second, weaker explanation is upward mobility. The rumor had it that if George H. W. Bush had been re-elected to the presidency in 1992, John J. Reynolds would have been in line for Director of the National Park Service. It was similarly rumored that if Gorton had won the election in 2000, he would have had the naming rights on the new Director.

As Gorton prepared to run again in 2000, he knew he would need to sell himself as a young 72—as contrasted to the old 74 of the late Senator Magnuson. "It's time for a change," Gorton, at 52, had said in the 1980 campaign. His young Democratic opponent and wealthy computer geek, Maria Cantwell, borrowed the phrase in 2000. After weeks of waiting, counting, and recounting,

Cantwell emerged the winner by a hair's breadth. Gorton's two-percent magic streak was over. He lost by less than one-tenth of one percent. Cantwell's dramatic victory split the U.S. Senate fifty-fifty, setting the stage the following spring for Vermont Senator Jim Jeffords' heroic departure from a now fully radicalized, anti-environmental Republican Party. Always an advocate for the environment, Jeffords, unlike Gorton, never doubted his compass.

Congressional Intent

Gorton, Cushman, Chelan County government, the Heritagers, and others were prone to impute the "intent of Congress" as something other than what it was. The 1968 North Cascades Act provided the following as the fundamental basis for administering the Lake Chelan National Recreation Area:

> Section 202. In order to provide for the public outdoor recreation use and enjoyment of portions of the Stehekin River and Lake Chelan, together with the surrounding lands, and for the conservation of the scenic, scientific, historic, and other values contributing to public enjoyment of such lands and waters, there is hereby established, subject to valid existing rights, the Lake Chelan National Recreation Area. . . .

> Section 301. Within the boundaries of the park and recreation areas, the Secretary of the Interior . . . may acquire lands, waters, and interests therein by donation, purchase with donated or appropriated funds, or exchange, except that he may not acquire any such interests within the recreation areas without the consent of the owner, so long as the lands are devoted to uses compatible with the purposes of this Act.

> Section 402(a). The Secretary shall administer the recreation areas in a manner which in his judgment will best provide for (1) public outdoor recreation benefits; (2) conservation of scenic, scientific, historic, and other values contributing to public enjoyment; and (3) such management, utilization, and disposal of renewable natural resources and the continuation of such existing uses and developments as will promote or are compatible with, or do not significantly impair, public recreation and conservation of the scenic, scientific, historic, or other values contributing to public enjoyment. In administering the recreation areas, the Secretary may utilize such statutory authorities pertaining to the administration of the national park system, and such statutory authorities otherwise available to him for the conservation and management of natural resources as he deems appropriate for recreation and preservation purposes and for resource development compatible therewith.

The words of the 1968 Act might strike the cursory reader as clear enough; the critical reader, though, could ask, "What do the words *really* mean?" Explicators refer repeatedly to "Congressional intent." The term "compatible" in Section 301, for example, was not explicitly defined in the Act, but the legislative record speaks eloquently to the intent: Congress intended that the character of the Stehekin community not be changed appreciably. The community was not to be abolished by a forced outflow but neither was it to undergo a "natural growth" to, as George Hartzog put it in the Senate hearings, "a high-density subdivision." Congress did not set aside the Stehekin Valley to become a vacation-home community peopled from downlake. The park's original superintendent, Roger Contor, said, "Congress, the National Park Service, and conservationists all agreed that subdivision should not occur in the Stehekin Valley. Those who had bought land before the NPS came could build single-family residences in keeping with the area but it was not the intention of Congress to allow people to build who came in after the park."

Congressional intent, when applied to practical living, became something of a mystery in the storybook village of Stehekin. Some of this two-decade-old uncertainty was dusted off by Senator Dan Evans in a 1988 wilderness bill.

One take on the story is that Senator Evans, an incorrigibly nice guy, may have blotted his copybook and allied with the Wise Guys, the Professional Inholders, and the rural county commissioners of southern Washington in the mid-1980s who were hoping to skewer legislation intended to preserve the Columbia River Gorge. Evan's mug and wump having been placed on opposite sides of the fence, old friends were biting in their criticism. Thinking to placate them, he agreed to sponsor what they long had sought, wilderness protection for the national parks of Washington. However, an alternate view is that Evans was only trying to encourage cooperation among Columbia Gorge antagonists in order to secure as much protection there as possible. As NCCC's Polly Dyer explained, the two acts really had nothing to do with each other. "The proposal for designating wilderness in the national parks came from conservationists." She recalls sharing the idea with Evans personally. "He was enthusiastic." In any case, the Columbia Gorge was ultimately designated a national scenic area, and most of Washington's three national parks were designated wilderness, for which Evans deserves considerable credit.

The 1988 Washington Parks Wilderness Act also corrected for the Ross Lake National Recreation Area several anomalies of the 1968 North Cascades Act, tidying up discrepancies between the Hartzog fantasy and the North Cascades reality. For the Lake Chelan National Recreation Area, 1988 also saw small improvements. However, Evans' bill stepped outside the subject of the legislation—wilderness—in order to specifically authorize the continued exploitation of "renewable" resources, such as cutting trees, in the six thousand acres of the Stehekin Valley floor. The language seemed to be telling rangers that they could relax when cowed by Heritagers into agreeing that these activities "are compatible with, or do not significantly impair public recreation and conservation of the scenic, scientific, historic, or other values contributing to the public enjoyment. . . ." In other words, go ahead and destroy the place, just be pleasant about it.

Evans' bill would have an almost immediate effect as the Park Service developed its management plans for the Lake Chelan NRA. The original plan of 1968 had defined three zones in Stehekin Valley: Zone 1, Public Use and Development, included lands needed by government and concessionaire for public-use facilities; Zone 2, Preservation and Conservation, included lands necessary for environmental preservation; and Zone 3, Private Use and Development, included private lands not required for public use but that served a public purpose that would be permitted as long as the uses were compatible with the purpose of the recreation area. Park Service officials were so confused by the distinctions that by 1980 they no longer acknowledged existence of the zones.

The new land-acquisition policy promulgated nationally in 1977 contained a rather strict definition of incompatible acts that triggered an uproar among landowners in Olympic, Grand Teton, and Yosemite National Parks, coincidentally bringing Chuck Cushman's National Park Inholders Association a financial bonanza. The Park Service responded in 1978 with a slightly amended version. However, the Denver Service Center concluded that the policy did not apply in Lake Chelan National Recreation Area; the private-use zone there was judged to be exempt from compatibility standards. This interpretation was never endorsed higher up but Superintendent Lowell White took it as gospel and preached it around Stehekin and Chelan County. Conservationists and bewildered residents wondered which side of the Park Service's mouth they were supposed to believe.

In August 1985 word came that an appropriations bill in the House of Representatives included an item (pushed by Congressman Mike Lowry, of Seattle) of $1 million for land protection in the North Cascades National Park Complex. When the funds became available, Reynolds noodled the notion of buying merely an easement on the large Getty property, allowing the land to be sold to build 13 houses, while putting the bulk of the appropriation elsewhere. He was soon talked out of that blunder, and in July 1986 the money was used to purchase the 153.6-acre Getty property. This was the largest land acquisition since the 247-acre purchase from Chelan Box in 1970, and one of the most important actions yet taken by the National Park Service to protect the Stehekin valley from over-development.

In October Reynolds informed conservationists that the Park Service had "lots of money for land acquisition but wouldn't spend any until the Land Protection Plan was complete." Heritagers alternated between spreading scare stories that the government was going to take it all and crowing that the Park Service was planning a big land auction. People actually flew to Stehekin and came to the ranger station to submit bids.

Independence Day, 1987, brought a new-old player into the game. Emulating the Emergency Conservation Committee, which in the 1930s played so crucial a role in pamphleteering for Olympic National Park, the Stehekin Emergency Committee (SEC), organized one summer day on the banks of the Stehekin River, mailed its first flier to more than half-a-thousand "organizations and individuals concerned for the Lake Chelan National Recreation Area . . . and the precedents being set there for the entire National Park System."

Signed by the likes of David Brower, Grant McConnell, Jim McConnell, and Harvey Manning, the newsletter authored by the two McConnells caught the attention of Reynolds, who checked around in some panic to learn if the SEC was after his career. It was, of course, but only incidentally. Reynolds reportedly went to Odegaard, who told him to batten down the hatches and ride out the storm.

The draft Land Protection Plan was issued in September 1987, the final signed by Reynolds March 8, 1988, and by Odegaard on April 5. As was to become significant later, the plan was not subjected to a full environmental impact statement, only the hastiest of an environmental assessment, and was proclaimed by Reynolds to be invulnerable to administrative appeal.

The data summary in the plan stated that 60,154 acres of the Lake Chelan National Recreation Area had been transferred from the Forest Service. Subsequent acquisitions—all by purchase, none by condemnation—were 1,134 acres in eighty tracts. No acknowledgment was made of assistance by conservationists. For example, Stuart and Abigail Avery, who earlier had financed Brower's film, *Wilderness Alps of the Stehekin*, joined with Oliver Webb and others to buy eighty-seven acres on Rainbow Flat and on the opposite side of the Stehekin River, holding them until the Park Service had funds, then selling them for their own cost plus six percent to partly defray expenses in the transaction.

The summary also showed 61,285 acres in federal ownership, 99 acres in Chelan County ownership, 3.2 acres owned by the Stehekin School District, and 502 private acres, in 179 tracts (not counting those underwater during high pool). Over the years, $5.9 million had been supplied by Congress for the entire Complex. In the Lake Chelan NRA, $2.8 million was "obligated to date" (as good as spent). For the Complex as a whole, there was an "unobligated" balance of $1.1 million (budgeted, but not spent). Subsequent to the Land Protection Plan of 1988, through 1994 the Park Service purchased fourteen tracts totalling 38 acres, bringing the total acquisitions of non-federal land to

1,173 acres.

By November 1989 when John Earnst, the park's fifth superintendent, took over the reins, the land-acquisition program was moving at a somewhat less sluggish pace. Some $500,000 was left from the Getty pot; Harlan Hobbs, Regional Chief, Division of Lands, was negotiating eight to ten properties. Two of the owners refused to sell to the Park Service; residents who dealt with the government felt ostracized by Heritagers and sensed their game was getting meaner. Hobbs did not pursue a parcel on Weaver's Point, which due to his neglect was sold to a developer who intended recreational rentals. The Park Service later acquired the land from the developer. In October Hobbs was urged to acquire Loggers Point, the sole sizable flat along the lake beyond the Landing, making it one of the Valley's premier viewpoints. In a letter of November 15, 1989, he wrote:

> We simply cannot buy everything that might be a problem. I do believe that a selective acquisition program that includes land exchanges coupled with good planning and zoning ordinances and strict enforcement of county regulations would go a long way in protecting the valley. . . . I also believe that we have had an aggressive program to acquire inholdings at Stehekin. Over the past year we have successfully negotiated the purchase of nine properties containing approximately 25 acres. This represents five percent of the private property in the valley.

Staying the Course

Developed simultaneously with the Land Protection Plan was the General Development Plan, which was released for discussion in the summer of 1986, recommended by Reynolds on June 24, 1988, and signed by Odegaard. Again, there was no environmental impact statement, merely a scaled-down environmental assessment, a stunning omission for a document purporting to guide the area's course well into the next century. (At the end of 1988, Reynolds hied himself away to the next rung of his career ladder, the directorship of the NPS Denver Service Center.) Both plans contained similar faults that may be summed up in composite:

> 1. The Frontier Myth was swallowed hook, line, and sinker. Repeated references were made to a "unique lifestyle," as if the summer homes of downlake wealthies were unique and their lifestyle deserving of federal protection.

> 2. The Valley population, which from 1968 to 1980 had tripled, was expected to grow more. A large "community development subzone" in a highly sensitive ecosystem was selected for the purpose because it was located where tourists wouldn't see it. A major portion of the Valley was frankly designated a sacrificial

area. The Park Service refused to admit that its plan inevitably entailed at least a further doubling, and more likely, a quadrupling of the Valley population.

3. The worst fault of the plans was the failure to apply its own criteria for placement of Valley lands into various categories. The categories were defensible and the criteria were good, but so haphazardly applied as to add up to so much ecological nonsense and administrative chaos.

4. The air strip was to continue indefinitely.

5. Wild and Scenic status for the Stehekin River was to be deferred for study "in ten to fifteen years." Illegal manipulations by residents, incursions by the Army Corps of Engineers, and meddling by Chelan County were as much as invited.

6. Pious sentiments were expressed about wetlands, but specifics of protection were inconsistent.

7. Plans for acquisition embodied the concept of lands of "No Interest." This flew in the face of the customary readiness to buy any land willingly offered for sale. Publicly distinguishing between high priority and low priority was a retreat from the recognition that all lands were important. Some of the "no-interest" parcels were on the lakeshore and the riverbank, the sites most vulnerable to disruption of shorelines and riparian zones, illegal filling and riprapping and log removal. Many of the most sensitive ecosystems of the Valley were written off as being of no interest. Some sixty-two parcels, totalling sixty-five acres, or 14 percent of the private lands, did not interest the Park Service. Even when funds were available and willing sellers at hand, the Park Service would consider only noncontroversial parcels, like on the Moon.

8. A policy of land exchange was instituted to acquire wanted parcels for which funds were not immediately available. Though the Park Service is required by law to consider exchanges, it is not compelled to make them, and conservationists universally agree the Park Service should never alienate any of its protected lands. The immediate consequence in Stehekin was that the lands proposed for exchange all rated "high" in terms of criteria for acquisition; the program thus shot itself in the foot. Obtaining sensitive, wanted, but unbuildable lands by giving up in exchange buildable lots leads directly to more construction. In 1988 Cliff Courtney acquired mining claims in Horseshoe Basin that the Park Service had neglected to buy. The area has very high wilderness value and is reasonably accessible from Cascade Pass. The claims likely had near-zero mineral value but the land was patented, thus fully private. One proposal was to set up a pack-in camp, cabins and satellite dish, all in the middle of dedicated wilderness. The Park Service possessed regulatory powers that could have blocked such development and rendered the property worthless for any non-park purpose. Rather than purchase the property outright, it acquired the parcel in exchange for an eminently buildable parcel in the Valley adjoining the Stehekin Valley Ranch.

9. The Park Service (that is, the Denver Service Center, Reynolds, and Odegaard) perceived an "historic pattern of development" that it believed should be permitted to continue, supporting the Heritager plea for more growth.

10. The Park Service was silent about crucial details of recent Stehekin history. When specifics were requested the response was that they didn't exist. For example, no data were available on the number of parcels subdivided in Stehekin since 1968, but "Chelan County might know." Records were incomplete or lacking on removal of topsoil, rock, gravel, and sand from public land; only partial records had been kept of removal of "hazard" trees by private parties. A December 1988 communication from the Park Service responded to a request that a program be started to inventory historical data by calling such information irrelevant to the management of the area.

Having concluded that the Park Service was unwilling to admit that Reynolds, Odegaard, and the Denver Service Center had fouled the national nest, the NCCC again called in the SCLDF. The chief goal of the Council in filing suit was to settle, once and for all, the management authority and future cause of the Park Service in Stehekin. It was forced instead to settle for a lawsuit under the National Environmental Policy Act.

It was not a step taken lightly. Frustration had mounted steadily during the scoping process and public hearings. Comments on the plans fell on deaf ears. The appeals to Odegaard were denied.

When in Doubt, Sue the Blank-Blanks

In the Lake Chelan National Recreation Area, the Council's most pressing concern was the cumulative impact of development over time in the Stehekin Valley—and the failure of the Park Service's plans to recognize that fourth dimension.

The Stehekin Emergency Committee kept up a drumbeat with Letters No. 2, 3, 4, and 5 through the summer of 1990. In January 1989 the SEC noted:

> The Superintendent now departed has left a cobbled collection of plans for the area that presume to blaze the administrative course well into the 21st Century. Some of these schemes are final, others are still pending but are apparently certain of adoption. Despite several years and great resources devoted to these plans, they are confused, ineptly coordinated, and project a destructive future. Despite their degrading character and prospectively sweeping impact, they are supported by no Environmental Impact Statements.

In July 1989 the SEC greeted Reynolds' successor, John Earnst, with frustration:

The neglect and febrile administration of past superintendents have gone far to convert this part of the National Park System, one of its finest naturally, to a private enclave with materials and services to a select few.

His [Earnst's] arrival comes on the heels of a series of low-octane previous superintendents, administrative invertebrates, men whose vision is self-promotion, politicization of Park operations (including moves to pit conservationists against local inholders), with fundamental inclination towards development, appeasement of monied interests, and, perhaps, an underlying distaste for wilderness. We welcome Superintendent Earnst, and wish him well in the large and difficult job ahead.

Mailings of the NCCC were only slightly less contemptuous of Reynolds and even more cordial to Earnst. When the Sedro Woolley brass visited Stehekin and were told by conservationists that the Park Service needed a change in attitude, Superintendent Earnst quietly observed, "The suit is about the fact you mistrust us."

Right. The lawsuit.

On March 14, 1989, Stephan C. Volker, on behalf of the Council, invoked the Freedom of Information Act to request from Superintendent Earnst records of decision on the Firewood Management Plan, Land Protection Plan, General Management Plan, Draft Backcountry Plan, Draft Wilderness Management Plan, Draft Sand and Gravel Plan, Draft Development Concept Plan, Draft Stehekin River Management Plan. All of these plans had been approved by former superintendents without an environmental impact statement or meaningful public participation.

On September 7, Volker and Lynn D. Weir, attorneys for the plaintiff (Weir also joined the NCCC board), entered a complaint in the United States District Court for the Western District of Washington at Seattle for declaratory and injunctive relief from the defendants, namely:

MANUEL LUJAN, Secretary of the UNITED STATES DEPARTMENT OF THE INTERIOR; JAMES M. RIDENOUR, Director of the UNITED STATES NATIONAL PARK SERVICE; CHARLES H. ODEGAARD, Regional Director of the UNITED STATES NATIONAL PARK SERVICE, PACIFIC NORTH-WEST REGION; JOHN R. EARNST, Superintendent of the NORTH CAS-CADES NATIONAL PARK COMPLEX

On December 20, Volker responded to an approach by Kenton W. Fulton, Attorney, General Litigation Section, Land and Natural Resources Division, U.S. Department of Justice, Washington, D.C., stating that the Council was willing to discuss possible settlement. "Although we have no doubt that the National Park Service has violated the National Environmental Policy Act and that we would prevail in this litigation, we are certainly willing to secure the

Park Service's compliance with the law. . . ."

The Council's terms were these:

The Park Service must prepare a comprehensive environmental impact statement (EIS), and implementation of existing plans must be stayed pending the EIS. The EIS must address in detail resources of the Lake Chelan NRA. On a specific time schedule, it would need to review and document effects of past growth and expanding visitor use, and inventory 'Historic and projected changes in population, number of structures, property ownership, commercial, residential, and visitor uses'—the information the Park Service had said was inconsequential, expensive, and low priority. 'Because adequate EIS will require at least 2 years, it is essential the interim management actions be modified.'

In the Land Protection Plan: 'Purchase all property offered. . . . Make no land exchanges. . . . Pursue acquisition, including condemnation . . . encourage compatibility standards as local and County ordinances.' In the Firewood Plan: 'Phase out firewood cutting from public lands over the next year. Close all informal logging roads. Build no new roads to access the woodlot area.' For Transportation: 'Defer action on renewing the permit for the airstrip. Prepare a transportation plan.' Others: 'Defer adoption of all plans and management activities including sand and gravel removal. Prohibit development of wetlands and riprapping, etc. Prohibit further expansion of commercial and residential uses.'

On January 12, 1990, the opposing attorneys met. The government response was, "Trust us!" The answer: "No, thanks." On January 26, Fulton made a counter-offer, asking the Council to file dismissal with prejudice, to confer in good faith with the Regional Director, and agree to a time frame "no later than 3 years after funding approval." Two items, he said, were not negotiable: the Land Protection Plan was to be renewed without change in April 1990; the Park Service would continue to acquire properties by purchase or exchange pursuant to the existing plan.

On February 15, Volker responded: "[We] cannot agree to a settlement which is not embodied in a Consent Decree. A settlement which is not directly judicially enforceable defeats the purpose of this litigation, which is to compel the Park Service to obey the law. . . . We have no objection to conferring with the Regional Director . . . provided the Park Service would likewise agree to confer promptly and in good faith upon request from NCCC. We agree to limit the EIS to Lake Chelan NRA and Stehekin River watershed, reluctantly."

In February the news broke nationally that the SCLDF had won a consent settlement against a huge oil company, Unocal, for its ten-year poisoning of San Francisco Bay. In addition to an array of constraints, the defendants paid $5.5 million. The winning attorney was Stephan Volker.

In August 1990 the NCCC and legal counsel developed a bottom-line strategy, deferring most substantive issues to the environmental impact statement. In November the Park Service agreed in principle to settle out of court. However, as the haggling dragged on through the winter, the good faith of the federals was not confirmed until April 22, 1991. A news release of May 6 spread the good tidings:

> The North Cascades Conservation Council today announced it has secured a Consent Decree from federal district court in Seattle approving settlement of its lawsuit against the National Park Service concerning management of the Lake Chelan National Recreation Area. To settle the case the Park Service agreed to conduct a thorough, detailed, wide-ranging examination of public and private land uses and management practices in a comprehensive Environmental Impact Statement for the area. The EIS will evaluate Park Service plans for cutting live trees for firewood, mining sand and gravel, and providing transportation services. It will address the need for Park Service acquisition of private land to protect the natural and scenic environment from incompatible development, and to allow visitor access and enjoyment. The Park Service agreed to defer management decisions which would irrevocably alter the area's natural resources until the EIS process is completed.

> 'This is a great victory for the people of the Pacific Northwest and indeed all the people of the United States,' said staff attorney Stephan Volker of the San Francisco-based SCLDF, who filed suit on behalf of the NCCC in late 1989. 'Heretofore, the Park Service has rarely conducted EIS reviews of its plans for management of the nation's parks. By this settlement, it has finally recognized its duty to do so.'

"Lake Chelan NRA is a national jewel of alpine peaks and fjord-like waters," Volker explained. "The Park Service was presiding over the destruction of the recreation area by private and public development, and refusing to do the environmental studies that would have revealed what was being lost."

"This settlement forces the Park Service to look before it leaps," announced NCCC President Dave Fluharty. "The Park Service will now prepare the environmental studies we need to determine on a rational basis how to preserve the scenic grandeur and ecologic values of this spectacular area." The environmental impact statement was to be completed by late 1993.

The suit was prompted by a series of Park Service plans and programs that members of the NCCC felt would continue the destruction of the little community of Stehekin and do serious damage to the environment of both the Lake Chelan National Recreation Area and the surrounding North Cascades National Park.

Particularly galling to the conservationists was a decision by the Park Service to allow the clearcutting of old-growth trees from public lands within the recreation area for use as firewood. Some of the best specimens of the Stehekin Valley's primeval forest have been cut down to satisfy the burgeoning demand for firewood from the Valley's growing population. The Consent Decree asked that live trees be taken only as a last resort.

The NCCC also objected to the Park Service's failure to assess the environmental impact on public lands of continued development on private lands, particularly those in ecologically fragile and scenically sensitive areas at the head of Lake Chelan. The once pristine Stehekin River Valley and spectacular head of Lake Chelan have been cluttered with satellite dishes, lake-front land fills, and dense pockets of urban development. The stream banks and wetlands of the Stehekin River have been fouled by the placement of rock "rip-rap" and the removal of trees. Since the Recreation Area's creation in 1968, the number of buildings in the Stehekin Valley has more than doubled. The Park Service's plans challenged in the lawsuit would have allowed a further doubling of development in the Valley. The Consent Decree held those plans in abeyance.

In March 1992 the Denver Service Center issued a Planning Newsletter for the General Management Plan EIS that was so wildly off course that NCCC President Dave Fluharty responded with a warning that such bizarre behavior would imperil the Consent Decree of April 22, 1991, and force a return to the courts. "NPS does not appear to be making a good faith effort to carry out the Consent Decree," wrote Fluharty.

It must be kept in mind that when Stephan Volker negotiated the Consent Decree, he specifically refused to forego further resort to the courts. The SCLDF was not out of the game. Wily Washington, D.C. had wanted the NCCC to renounce this option in writing; Steve Volker backed up his refusal by a threat to walk out on the negotiations.

In a May 3, 1992, letter to the Park Service, Fluharty began by noting that this first response to the public meetings and comment period was long overdue, a delay which in itself "does not inspire confidence. Specific concepts iterated in the Consent Decree and in the NCCC letter to Superintendent Earnst on July 21, 1991, are conspicuously missing." Organization of the Planning Newsletter was "strange," lumping apples and oranges and baseballs, omitting key elements specifically required by the Consent Decree, incoherently hop-skipping from subject to subject. It got facts wrong. It ignored issues strenuously emphasized by the NCCC in the scoping process. It failed to define the terms under which the EIS was supposed to be prepared. It made patently false statements about the nature and role of the NCCC, and it demonstrated a lack of comprehension of—or disagreement with—the intent of Congress.

Fluharty said in conclusion,

N3C strongly argues that many of the issues and concerns that it has expressed in response to the request for EIS scoping are not represented in the document. . . . A full report of all positions stated by all parties is prerequisite for an adequate scoping process. . . . the agency carrying out the scoping has responsibility to respond to the statements and explain which lie within its competence and which do not. Artificially constraining the input to the process for any reason sets the process up for challenge by any or all parties. The worst consequence of biased reporting of scoping comments is a loss of professionalism and credibility. This must be addressed before the process can go forward.

The year's delay already had ruled out any chance that the Denver Center could meet the scheduled EIS release date of late 1993. Poor performance in the spring of 1992 raised the question whether it ever could do the job. One wondered if Dave Fluharty's letter led to a few rolled heads in Denver.

The Park Service Gets Itself a Reprieve

Fortunately, there were better and brighter bulbs outside Denver. Whenever park officials visited Stehekin, a stop not to be omitted was a cabin up the river, at the foot of Si Si Ridge, especially if Grant McConnell was in residence. A conversation there set the visitors to careful analysis of the 1968 North Cascades Act, subsequent amendments to the 1916 National Park Service Organic Act, and precedent-setting rulings of federal courts. In August 1991 John Earnst, cut the ground from under the "Stehekin Constitution" by delivering the verdict that should have been rendered by his predecessors. He released a Park Service summary of relevant legislative history, from the National Park Act of 1916 to the North Cascades Act of 1968, the General Authorities Act of 1970, the 1978 Redwoods Act, and the 1988 Washington Parks Wilderness Act. The summary also stressed the judicial history, in which the courts have consistently affirmed an overriding preservation mandate throughout Park service lands.

The Stehekin reaction to the Earnst announcement was predictable—a storm of denial.

May 13, 1992, brought the culmination of these studies, an historic document, *A Discussion of Laws Affecting the Administration of Lake Chelan National Recreation Area*, recommended reading for members of Congress, Chelan County electeds, anyone who aspires to definitive expertise on the legalities of Stehekin Valley, and the writers of newspaper editorials from Seattle to New York City.

Many Park Service employees had a strong hunch all along about what was right concerning the Lake Chelan NRA, and their diligence helped bring about the "Discussion." Prominent in this group were Superintendent John Earnst, Chief Ranger David Spirtes (who authored the document), Chief of Resource Management John Jarvis, the Regional Solicitor's Office, and a host of reviewers. Prominent in the opposing Park Service faction was Regional Director Odegaard, whose ultimate objectives were mysterious, but whose political alliances and machinations were all too clear.

The publication of the Discussion document earned the Park Service a reprieve, which was confirmed and extended upon John Earnst's departure by the interval of suspended judgment owed by laws of courtesy to Superintendent Number Six.

William F. Paleck arrived in the North Cascades on August 23, 1992. In twenty-five Park Service years he had served at Sequoia-Kings Canyon, Hyde Park (FDR's estate in New York state), Wupatki and Sunset Craters, the Alaska Regional Office, Wrangell–Saint Elias, the Southern Arizona Group of eleven parklets, and Saguaro National Monument, the last two as superintendent. As before, Paleck's appointment was from a large number of applicants for what appeared to be the most sought-after superintendency in the National Park System. Given the quality of this super-jewel of the national treasure house, the unique troubles of the Stehekin Community, the rebel yells from the Confederates of Chelan County, the perseverance of the NCCC, and the formidable incisiveness of the SCLDF, the combination totaled to the sort of challenge that could be both stimulating in itself and if successfully met, a career-maker.

The Lake Chelan National Recreation Area (LCNRA), like nowhere else in the park, is the litmus test for North Cascades Park supers. The LCNRA is where National Park Service ideals and professionalism are placed in direct conflict with development. These pages have given assessments of five superintendents, two good men who left records as good as circumstances allowed, two who were lesser achievers, and one who was an alleged disaster. The early judgment of Number Six was as sensitive, intelligent, promising. Paleck made it clear that he was not throwing himself into the bosom of the NCCC, yet the NCCC felt neither was he lollygagging down the garden path arm in arm with the People of the Myth. At least not initially. The situation called for an honest broker, and that seemed to be Paleck's chosen role.

A reminder to readers who might have lost their way in all of this: the General Management Plan of 1988 (GMP)—the Reynolds–Odegaard masterwork—necessitated the NCCC suit of 1989 demanding the preparation of an environmental impact statement, which would inevitably require a revised GMP. The lawsuit's result was the Consent Decree of 1991, whose first fruit from the Denver Center was the March 1992 Lake Chelan NRA Planning Newsletter, belatedly plucked from the vine and best consigned to the compost heap. Newsletter Number One was followed in December 1992 by Number Two, which at least recognized the issues as land protection and development; transportation; energy use; sand, rock and gravel; wilderness management; provision of services; and natural and cultural resources protection. For each of these, Denver dug a deep hole and pulled itself underground.

In March 1993 the Park Service issued a booklet that summarized research

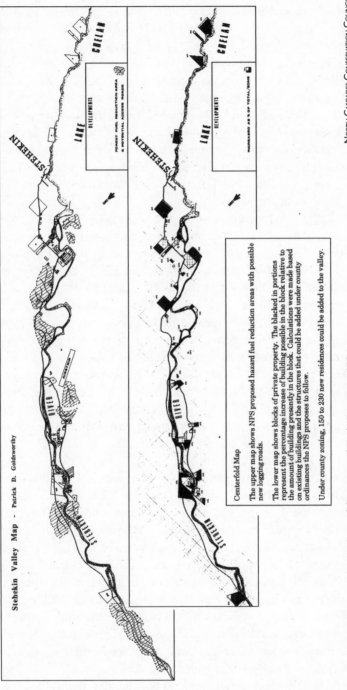

Stehekin Valley Map - Patrick D. Goldsworthy

Centerfold Map

The upper map shows NPS proposed hazard fuel reduction areas with possible new logging roads.

The lower map shows blocks of private property. The blacked in portions represent the percentage increase of building possible in the block relative to the amount of building presently in the block. Calculations were made based on existing buildings and the structures that could be added under county ordinances the NPS proposes to follow.

Under county zoning, 150 to 230 new residences could be added to the valley.

NORTH CASCADES CONSERVATION COUNCIL

This map illustrates the thinking of the National Park Service in 1994 on firewood gathering and land development in the lower Stehekin Valley.

completed for the EIS and held public meetings in Seattle, Chelan, and Stehekin. *The Wild Cascades* treated the research respectfully:

> Studies show that Stehekin Valley is a rich but fragile place. . . . Because of its
> small size and increasing tourism rate, which is now approximately 50,000 visi-
> tors a year, the Stehekin Valley has the potential to be more heavily impacted than
> many larger parks. Most of the human activity is directly reflected by the growing
> numbers of cleared developed land parcels . . . and by less obvious effects such as
> structural alterations to the Valley's old growth forests.

The NCCC responded, "This may be the most important plan the NPS
will ever write for the Stehekin Valley. The decisions the NPS makes will set
the long-term course for the management of this beautiful valley."

In June 1993 Denver issued "Alternatives Newsletter for the GMP and EIS
for LCNRA." On July 1 the NCCC responded at length, reiterating positions
it had elaborated again and again over the years, repeating, albeit in a tone of
extraordinary courtesy, that the Denver Center was blind, ignorant, confused,
and incompetent. More or less. In private correspondence, a NCCC director
summarized,

> Every new plan from Denver emerges as stupid and unreadable. So what we have
> from the Park Service now likely will have little in common with the final ver-
> sion. A Park Service friend says that the final version likely will have to be written
> not in Denver, but in Sedro Woolley, and not by the Servicers but by Paleck.

Other NCCC directors were amused by a change in Park Service (Denver)
strategy. Whereas earlier in the planning process their best and brightest had
presented three options, the middle one being their obvious choice and in their
minds so positioned to be the one approved, they now offered four. The reader
thus was meant to pay attention only to the two in the middle. Neither bore
more than a faint family resemblance to anything the NCCC ever had sponsored or could ever accept. Features were so jumbled together one could say,
"Well, it has Cousin Charlie's ears, and Aunt Matilda's feet, and the milkman's
hair. But the only one with a nose like that is Rover."

LET THE CONDOS BEGIN

Long before the park was established, the Chelan Box Company filled shallows
at the head of Lake Chelan to provide a turnaround space for trucks dumping logs to be rafted to their mill. After Mr. Wall was expelled in 1960 from
the Agnes Creek Valley by designation of the Glacier Peak Wilderness, the fill
remained and became known as "Loggers Point." In 1990 the property was

snapped up by a Spokane physician-developer who set about trying to subdivide into three building lots upon which to construct thirteen cabin-condos, a big house, and a twenty-slip boat dock—the largest condominium development yet proposed for Stehekin. The house would occupy the lakeside flat, which many felt should be a picnic and habitat area. The cabins would be built upslope, served by an electric tramway. An elaborate pumping system would handle sewage disposal. In the 1980s the property was appraised at around $120,000. It was purchased in 1990 for $150,000. In February 1991 environmentalists had recommended that Congress appropriate $2 million to acquire 250 acres in Stehekin, including Loggers Point, as well as mineral properties in the Park Proper. Nothing was appropriated. As the condo project advanced, Paleck informed Chelan County that he failed to see how the project could be compatible with the Lake Chelan National Recreation Area—but added that the National Park Service had never, anywhere, used its power to bar incompatible uses.

In the fall of 1995, a lawsuit was filed by the NCCC, naming as defendants the landowners and Chelan County. In March 1996 Chelan Superior Court ruled the Planning Department had granted a conditional-use permit too vague to be meaningful and noted that issues must be fully aired *before* a permit, not after. "Your honor, this is how things work in Chelan County." The judge was not swayed. On August 11, 1997, the Chelan Board of Adjustment granted its approval. Within weeks, Valley residents formed Stehekin Alert to stop the project. Their petition was signed by 800 people, of whom forty-five were residents. They represented a major portion of what had been trumpeted by the Heritagers as a "Stehekin community" as rock-solid as the Confederacy. The rest of the 800 were merely Americans come to worship at a national shrine of nature. Significantly, a founder of the group and circulator of the petition was Myra Bergman Ramos, daughter of Paul Bergman, who had known Stehekin since the 1920's and was a full-time resident since the 1930's. He was as "Old Stehekin" as his daughter is vigorously "New–Old Stehekin." Paleck expressed surprise at the intensity of the local opposition.

In the spring of 1998, the NCCC, preparing to appeal violations of the Shorelines Management Act, agreed to delay while the Park Service negotiated with the developer. As it had been doing previously, the Park Service deemed the negotiations "proprietary," meaning the public could not be involved in the details. At the beginning of 1999, Chelan County having approved the development, the land was suddenly worth over a million, thus the Park Service issued an Environmental Assessment on a land exchange. Three alternatives were presented, none of which was acceptable to the NCCC. The Park Service preference was for the owner to retain the Loggers Point flat for construction of a personal residence. The Park Service would place covenants on the buildings, this being the device that had emerged as one of Paleck's preferred substitutes for "no." That reluctance to say no to proposed development, combined with Paleck's strong support for land exchanges, was perceived by NCCC to be potentially disastrous. To ensure the public isn't swindled, the law requires that properties exchanged by the federal government with private landowners match in value within a few percentage points. If the deal did not pencil out well for the public's interest, Superintendent Paleck would reduce the value of the NPS parcel by imposing covenants on its future development, creating a burden of enforcement over the long run. The whole business, then, is rum, as the Western Lands Project has found through its many investigations of shady federal land exchanges.

The twenty-five mountainside acres would be exchanged for buildable, park-owned property in Little Boulder Creek and a site near Rainbow Falls, the deal based on an inflated value of $1.25 million. The mountainside acres had no real-world value except that given by the Chelan County permits, thus the NCCC saw no choice but to challenge those permits. Once revoked by the courts, the value of those twenty acres would be reduced considerably. The Park Service then could have proceeded, as preferred by the NCCC and Stehekin Alert, to a fee-simple acquisition of Loggers' Point. As it happened, the land exchange was sunk by public outcry in response to a spotted owl nest discovered on the gorgeous public land the NPS planned to let go in exchange for the Logger's Point condo property. In the end, the NPS purchased outright all but the point—a happy ending, despite an exorbitant price paid by the public.

The acreage of the national recreation area as a whole is substantial, but the Valley floor downstream from the Stehekin River-Agnes Creek junction is small. Yet this acreage is crucial to both people and wildlife. It is one of the more beautiful places imaginable. It is also the portion of the recreation area that is most visible to visitors and serves as their gateway into the wilderness. It is ecologically vital and unique, a still largely intact lowland valley, where eastern and western Cascades ecosystems meet and mingle. Yet in the 1990s, a major portion of the Valley floor—460 acres—was potentially subject to catastrophic commercialization and residentialization. The NCC and others continued to advocate for acquiring key parcels to slow the speculation mill to a tolerable level. Today, land acquisition by the park and a clear policy on private land use remain key to the preservation of Stehekin.

DEUS EX MACHINA

A veteran park ranger who rose so high and so fast in the National Park Service (on merit rather than smooth manners) that he was thought a good bet to be appointed director, wasn't. So Midwest Regional Director Don Castleberry chose an early retirement out of disillusion with the mentalite of the upper levels, though he declined to join a full corps of disillusioned rangers within the Forest Service Employees for Environmental Ethics (FSEEE). However, he did say privately, emphatically, that in all its years the Park Service had never had a director "better than second- or third-rate." In April 1995, Castleberry told the *High Country News* that "Top leadership in the National Park Service has been fragmented and lacking vision pretty much for fifteen years." Conservationists, of course, would have welcomed a new director who might alter that trend.

On the afternoon of August 16, 1995, the board of the NCCC and friends gathered in extraordinary session beside the Stehekin River at the foot of Si Si Ridge to host a casual meeting with the Director of the National Park Service, Roger Kennedy. Appointed by President Bill Clinton in 1993, Kennedy was the fourteenth director of the National Park Service. A question in the minds of the NCCC board was how to rate the man. They knew the story on him: a professor of something or other, of some reputed distinction, a former NBC news producer, a student of Burr, Hamilton, and Jefferson, and later, Director of the Smithsonian Museum of American History. Kennedy had also worked as an outside consultant to see what could be done to straighten up a collapsing Park Service, before eventually becoming its director. Reducing the Park Service budget by eliminating jobs, reorganizing the agency, and closing four of ten regional offices, including Seattle's, became his primary mission. Presumably, he came to Stehekin for a first-hand inspection of the fuss. Perhaps the director's brief encounter with the North Cascades, its splendor towering directly above him, would present an avenue toward understanding the urgency of the Stehekin challenge. The NCCC directors also knew that at afternoon's end he would be feted at a Heritager potluck, with Senator Gorton's aide ever at one ear, Superintendent Paleck at the other.

It had been another Year of Decision, with the public release in July of the "final" Lake Chelan National Recreation Area General Management Plan and the supporting Environmental Impact Statement, portions of which reflected NCCC's legal victory of 1991 and fulfillment of the promises made by the federal government in the Consent Decree.

There was much ground to cover. When Director Kennedy joined the gathering, the NCCC would have its last good chance in a while to be heard by someone of such authority within the Park Service. Kennedy had been supplied with words, photos, and maps that informed him precisely where he was, that let him know he was in the presence of the little people who had brought the National Park Service into the valley and were now, as an organization, in their fortieth year of striving to protect the North Cascades from all depredators, including the National Park Service.

Kennedy arrived, with Paleck, quite naturally, carrying his train. The man took the seat of honor and smiled graciously down upon the attentive circle. The sun was shining, the forest shadowing, the river sounding. Kennedy began. He complimented the NCCC for its grass-roots labors. He highly esteemed such little groups of little people, so much more useful than "traditional, national organizations." He then launched into a primer on what we should be doing that we weren't. To paraphrase: "If you folks want to do some *real* good, get your asses to Washington, D.C. Kiss the hands of Congressmen. Then get your asses back home and elect friendlies *who are not extremists.*" Kennedy would not have said it, but the board knew well enough that Slade Gorton, for one, would have to go (and in 2000 he did).

Kennedy was not the first professor known to the NCCC. One of its founders had lived some years at this spot at the foot of Si Si Ridge, and it was in the field at the front door of his home that this session was being held. Grant McConnell moved in the most respected circles of academia, and he knew professors, knew them well, for good and ill. But Grant had passed on two years earlier. It could have been wished that he was here, at the birthplace of the vision of a North Cascades National Park. Professor Kennedy would have felt the pin pricking his balloon. Several directors swore they heard the Stehekin River snort.

As his page carried the papers away, Kennedy was respectfully thanked for his wise counsel on how the NCCC could do some real good. He was petitioned to pay closer attention to rangers appointed to regional and local offices, so that grass-roots loyalists would not find their efforts frustrated by—to mention names, and the NCCC did—Charles Odegaard and John J. Reynolds. Kennedy snarled (in effect) that he hadn't come so far and spent so much of his valuable time to suffer *lese majesty* at the hands of a rabble of rubes in the woods. By not submitting to the rabble, he could more easily avoid a confrontation with Senator Gorton.

That autumn the National Park Service was reshuffled. The position of Northwest Regional Director was abolished (there went Odegaard), replaced by a Deputy Field Director based in Seattle at the rank of a park superintendent. Responsibilities formerly belonging to the Regional Director were largely assigned to a Columbia–Cascades Cluster of national parks. The executive committee was chaired by William Paleck. Charles Odegaard became Assistant to Park Service Director Kennedy. The Northwest was subsumed under the Western Region whose director, based in San Francisco, was John J. Reynolds. The shells had moved, but the beans were the same.

The Fall 1995 *The Wild Cascades* had carried Dave Fluharty's point-by-point analysis of the Lake Chelan NRA General Management Plan and EIS. Following is a sampling, comparing NCCC objectives and National Park Service decisions:

NCCC: Continue the policy of fee-simple purchase from willing sellers based on eight factors: ecological value, visitor use, avoiding non-conforming uses, Park Service administrative needs, presence of endangered or threatened species, lakeshore/riverbank location, cultural values, needs and desires of sellers.
NPS: Continue some fee-simple acquisition and easement purchases.

NCCC: No exchange of lands having any of the eight above characteristics.
NPS: Exchange of lands.

NCCC: Effective compatibility standards.
NPS: No compatibility standards.

NCCC: Encourage Chelan County to collaborate with Park Service.
NPS: Encourage county planning; county takes all responsibility for private property.

NCCC: Halt or minimize Park Service production of firewood from public lands.
NPS: Phase out wood lots but provide wood from "selective thinning of fuel-reduction areas" (a new policy to prevent major fires by tidy management which would result in a forest ecosystem entirely man-made, non-natural).

NCCC: Adopt a "let-it-burn" policy except for man-caused fires threatening human life and allow a prescribed fire regime to restore the role of fire in a natural valley ecosystem.
NPS: Human and lightning-caused fires to be suppressed to protect life and property; selective logging to create "firebreaks".

NCCC: Eventually close Stehekin Road above High Bridge; in the interim, above Bridge Creek.
NPS: Maintain Stehekin Road to Cottonwood Camp.

NCCC: Close Stehekin airstrip as a non-conforming, dangerous, and annoying nuisance.
NPS: Keep airstrip open.

Fluharty summarized, "This is an agonizing article to write. After so much time and effort. After long hours of discussion. How could we have been so hornswoggled?"

In the early months of 1998 the NCCC prepared a group of white papers on many of the same Stehekin issues. On June 6th, nearing the end of his fifth year in the North Cascades, Superintendent Paleck met with eight members of the NCCC board of directors for an afternoon's discussion of the papers. Directors recalled Paleck's description of his negotiation strategy as something like: "I don't play to win, I play to not lose," which sounded uncomfortably like compromise right from the start. Paleck seemed to view the principal challenge in Stehekin as "not to prevent growth but rather to manage it." Yet he did not say what his management objectives were, or what they might mean for the natural world in and around Stehekin. It was felt that the Park Service lacked "a vision of the uniqueness of the Stehekin Valley," and that the real aim was only peaceful coexistence among residents, bureaucrats, politicians, and perhaps conservation groups, NCCC being the group most actively opposed to Stehekin development.

One NCCC director noted the inevitable result of Paleck's and the agency's compromise-based management strategy. "What they are trying to manage is being lost by the gradual peneplanations of their decisions." Under Paleck's watch, the landscape of possibilities was getting flatter. The critique continued:

> We used to have the Park Service playing the middle between NCCC and the right wing in the Valley. They blamed us for forcing decisions the right wing didn't like and vice versa. Now, instead of playing conflict manager, Paleck wants to push at least part of the conflict-resolution role out of the Park Service consensus process. When this process brings recommendations he likes, he can implement them and defend against naysayers by saying it isn't his decision, it's the consensus group. If the public is presented with a democratic-looking process (the consensus group), dissenters can be ignored as extremists who don't know how to participate in the give-and-take of democracy. Compromise and consensus do not protect the land, they give it away. . . . I realize now what we are up against.

After reading the recollections of those present, one director admitted he was glad to have missed the meeting. "My only alternative to bleak despair would have been immediate defenestration."

That director may have been tempted to throw himself out a window so he wouldn't have to witness the state of frustration into which the superintendent's strategies and, to be fair, the national context have taken Stehekin. In recent years, the Park Service has engaged in a building spree of its own to create new and better housing for its employees—even as staff has been cut. Yet land exchanges remain the darker cloud over Stehekin. In another deal negotiated by Paleck, an untouched tract of maple forest was to be traded for a small lot in a developed area. The lots were of uneven size. The larger maple property to be lost was part of a wildlife corridor and scenic backdrop where the road diverges from the lake. The spot frames the visitor's entry into Stehekin Valley and approach to wilderness. Equity would ostensibly be achieved through covenants, none of which would prevent most of the property from being logged off, save for a "beauty screen" of trees along the road, which most landowners would maintain anyway as a buffer for privacy. The NCCC prepared to sue yet again and Stephan Volker was retained. Just before filing the suit, however, Volker lost a similar land exchange lawsuit in the Ninth Circuit Court, which also governs Stehekin, The cause appeared lost and the suit was not filed. The deeds were signed over. By the time you read this, it will be likely that the land has now been cleared and developed.

Newcomers to the valley see these dealings and assume they can finagle the same, and all too often they can. As this book went to press, the Park Service was in negotiation with at least one new property owner who wanted to exchange their new lot on the river for another lovely parcel close to the aforementioned maple property. Buildable lots in Stehekin, once more limited in number, seem less scarce as the Park Service has morphed into a local land office.

Curiously, another kind of development threat to Stehekin reared its head in the new millennium: telephones. Most residents say they don't want them. Residents and visitors stay generally connected with cell phones and satellite phones, and an unsolicited proposal for landlines by a company called WeavTel was widely viewed as an affront to the Stehekin identity. While blame for this fiasco could also be laid at the feet of the Park Service, it is actually derived from a well-meaning provision of the 1996 Telecommunications Act. The act established a universal access fee on all phone users to provide affordable phone service to poor or remote communities that lack such service. Stehekin may be remote, but it surely isn't poor anymore, and people come there precisely for its remoteness. Sometime in the late 1990s, a father-son team from Chelan spotted the opportunity to make millions by providing phone service in Stehekin, regardless of whether the community wanted it or not. The law makes no provision for asking a community whether it wants the service. Thus it is obvious to many that a business interest is what's being served here, not the public interest. WeavTel, for a time, did the unthinkable: it united Heritagers, NCCC, and quiet middle-of-the-roaders alike in opposition to the proposal. Heritagers didn't like the idea of this kind of corporate welfare and big government spending any more than NCCC did, and nobody wanted Stehekin to lose its unique freedom from rings, beeps, and buzzes. Superintendent Paleck issued an Environmental Assessment, sniffed the wind, read a tall pile of letters against the project, then denied a permit to run the phone lines on park land. He may have been warned by his lawyers later that the Park Service might get sued for denying the permit, thus a new strategy emerged. Paleck reversed himself and granted the permit, contingent on WeavTel gaining easements from property owners. Senator Maria Cantwell strangely intervened, though it's likely she was not well informed of the community's take on WeavTel. A further irony was a lawsuit against the Park Service by WeavTel which insisted that the former had no right to make its approval contingent upon easements. At the time of

PHOTOGRAPHER UNKNOWN (POSSIBLY GRANT MCCONNELL)

Buckner cabin; Lake Chelan National Recreation Area.

this writing, the NCCC was preparing to enter the suit in support of the park. A greater irony, perhaps, was Chelan County's role. Though normally a champion of development, the County twice rejected permit requests from WeavTel. How times change! In late 2006, the project appeared unlikely to wither given the millions of dollars at stake. Ideally, Senator Cantwell will introduce legislation to revise the 1996 Telecommunications Act so that it does not work against the collective will of any community.

Unless the national political context changes significantly, Stehekin faces increasing degradation in the coming years. More and more new homes have been built, several along the lakeshore visible on arrival, some on swampland or formerly public paradise, and some of them extraordinarily bulbous, obtrusive, and at odds with the Stehekin that everybody else loves. "Grant McConnell," says his granddaughter Carolyn, "is rolling in his grave."

Nevertheless, Mother Nature takes care of herself. Thanks to several catastrophic floods, the Stehekin River has claimed large chunks of the upper Stehekin Road, most notably in the October 2003 storm. As a result, the road was permanently closed not far from where the NCCC had for years called for its closure—just above High Bridge. The road closure will surely rank as one of Superintendent Paleck's legacies in the North Cascades. Instead of the drone and dust of sporadic car traffic impacting the ambience, hikers will have a newly wilded, gently sloping trail on which to approach the Cascades Crest, hearing only waterfalls, the wind, birdcalls, and the rushing Stehekin River.

STEHEKIN: FIFTY YEARS INTO THE FUTURE

—By Kevin Herrick

[Ed. note: Kevin was a National Park Service ranger in Stehekin six seasons, then two years a student of the Valley community while serving as NCCC Special Projects Coordinator, before joining the NCCC board and eventually acquiring a home in the Valley. He remained a board member until his untimely death in 2006. His essay, originally published in The Wild Cascades, *summarizes well the challenges that NCCC and the non-Heritager community were confronted with year after year in Stehekin.]*

No matter the state of the weather—driving rain, blustery wind, or calm morning fog, my daily commute never caused me to regret my job location. The four-mile bike ride down the Stehekin Valley to the Landing in Lake Chelan National Recreation Area proved to be a gift rather than a chore. The tenor of Rainbow Falls told the tale of the region's recent precipitation. A sharp eye was often rewarded with the sight of a bear pawing for ants and grubs. Does and their fawns bounding across the road were the only cause to apply the brakes unless particularly good morning light necessitated a picture stop of mountains reflected in the lake. Once down at the landing the view back upvalley took in the towering ridges converging into glaciated peaks of Buckner, Booker, Boston, and Sahale.

From the perspective of the early morning commuter, the Stehekin Valley appears quite tranquil and well taken care of. Thus, I reacted with a little annoyance when I first read the late Grant McConnell's book, *Stehekin: A Valley in Time.* Grant likened the growing pressures of development to a "poisonous fog" that "had crept up the twisting canyon of Lake Chelan." Compared to the rate that most Americans are accustomed to development—miles of wheat fields turned into cement and chem-lawn suburbs in a half-decade—Stehekin has not been heavily assaulted. However, a look about the valley with some historical perspective bears out Grant's words.

Stehekin's first "building boom" arrived in the 1880s in the form of homesteaders, miners, and associated tourism developers. Parts of the valley were logged to supply timber for mines, homes, and to power steamboats plying Lake Chelan. In 1927 construction of a small dam at the outlet of the lake flooded the wetlands at the head of the lake at Stehekin. By the end of that decade, homesteading and tourism had played out and the valley's small mining boom had gone bust. Stehekin's population settled into an average of twenty-five to fifty residents, and the valley began to recover.

Unfortunately, the recovery has been interrupted. The last thirty years have proven that Stehekin is not immune to civilizing pressures despite being shielded by lack of a connecting road to any other roads. Wetlands have been filled and houses built on the delicate Stehekin River delta. Forty acres of forest have been clearcut to provide a landing strip for a few private pilots. The homesteaded lands have been subdivided into tiny parcels. Chainsaws cutting firewood for an expanding local population continue to punch holes in the valley's forest. National Park Service gravel pits have left scars upon the valley floor. Development has restricted public access from most of the head of the lake and the mouth of the Stehekin River. The number of private homes has more than doubled and will double again if no action is taken.

But what about the National Park Service? Did not designation of the Lake Chelan National Recreation Area bring greater protection to this region? Well, yes and no. The National Park Service has preempted some development via purchase of approximately 1,200 acres of land. . . . Some have used Stehekin as an ideological chest-beating ground to promote their own agendas at the expense of Stehekin's nationally recognized natural resources. Even the county, in the 1980s and 1990s, seemed to flout its own regulations that could protect the valley. Recently, it permitted the building of a home and septic system on a tiny piece of property that is regularly flooded by the Stehekin River. In another location, the county ignored state regulations when it allowed a property owner to install a bulkhead wall and rip-rap in the otherwise pristine river. In the latter case, the NCCC was forced to go to court to protect the Stehekin River.

Unfortunately, the forces that have degraded the valley over the past thirty years appear to be increasing rather than abating. The 1988 Park Service General Management Plan estimated that two hundred to two hundred fifty more residential units could be built in the valley under existing laws. The chance of this happening is very real. Across the nation, rural areas are being bought up and developed. Just around the corner from Lake Chelan, the once sleepy Entiat Valley has been struck by development fever. Land has been subdivided. First and second homes and cabins are being built for city-dwelling folks trying to buy a piece of the American West. In Stehekin itself, a new resident who happens to have a successful history as a realtor claims that "The easiest part of my job is the demand for property exceeds the supply. The market is brisk for property that is available" (*Stehekin Choice*, December 1993).

National Park Service research shows what many people have felt for some time—that Stehekin Valley is a valuable and fragile place. The valley supports 138 terrestrial vertebrate species, including osprey, spotted owl, black bear, and marten. The great range of species in such a small valley is largely due to the terrific variation of habitat types (37) spread across the valley floor. Since animal populations are already small due to the size of the rich lower valley (less than eight square miles), habitat reductions can push populations to unsustainable levels. The 460 acres of private land, NPS developed areas, the airfield, gravel pits, roads, and public infrastructure facilities in total displace or severely degrade over one square mile of valley habitat.

The degradation of critical habitat is not only a loss for the valley, it is a loss that affects the entire region. With its mix of cottonwood, alder, Douglas fir, ponderosa pine, yellow cedar, and western red cedar, Stehekin is a rare low-elevation eastside valley caught in the jumble of North Cascades peaks, ridges, and hanging valleys. No eastside valley with the richness of Stehekin's penetrates as deeply into the heart of the North Cascades ecosystem. To allow the Stehekin Valley to continue to be fragmented by development, private or NPS, is to allow the loss of one of the North Cascades' most valuable and scarce resources. There are plenty of pristine high peaks. There are very few pristine valleys.

In my commutes up and down the valley, I often wondered whether I will see the Stehekin Valley sustained and its sensitive parts restored. Or will the opposite occur? Will the NPS fail to purchase critical private lands and will it fail to limit its own development? Will development continue to fragment habitat and drive the wildlife out as it has in countless places across the United States? Will the National Park Service continue to allow the forest to be logged for firewood? Will aircraft continue to land on a gash in the valley floor that ought to be carpeted with towering trees? Will two hundred new residents and a camp or lodging facility permanently turn the valley into an urban enclave with a wilderness backyard? In fifty years will we wring our hands and wonder, "Why didn't someone do something back in the early 1990s?" Just as we today wring our hands and wonder why someone didn't do something fifty years ago to save Yosemite Valley and Lake Tahoe.

THE ONCE AND FUTURE STEHEKIN SPEAKS

"If there is no truth today, there will be myths tomorrow," said Yuli Khariton, a Soviet scientist, reflecting on differing official histories of the "Evil Empire." And certainly, the historians of the North Cascades have been sorting myth from the truth over the century and a half in which written records have been kept.

The Wild Cascades, in issues from October 1992 to June 1993, examined some of the Stehekin myths that the Heritagers were pressing upon visiting journalists and politicians, and by ceaseless repetition were convincing even themselves of. Then, at the invitation of Valley residents, a half-dozen members of the NCCC board came to Stehekin and spent several hours discussing, with some thirty Valley people, the relationship between NCCC and "Heritage."

Honest disagreements were aired, and hearty agreements found. The Irate Birdwatcher accepted admonishment for his "Moral Tale for Young Birdwatchers" published June 1992. The tale, said Irate, had told the "true and veritable facts" about the Stehekin Valley, judged by some to be rude, mean, and downright nasty. Apologies were made, along with a promise that Irate would be ordered to mind his manners. Yet it was not possible to avoid suggesting what made him irate. In polite terms, it was his view that though private property rights are indeed expressly affirmed in the U.S. Constitution, and "an Englishman's home is his castle," what is not spelled out in the Constitution, because it is the foundation on which the Constitution is built, is the common law. Common law dates at least to Runnymede and the Magna Carta, as well as to the Code of Justinian, and a central tenet is the Public Trust Doctrine, which declares that in much "private" property there is a public interest, and it is a solemn duty of government to preserve that trust, to prevent private abuse. To bring that down to specifics, the true "Stehekin community" is the entire American nation, the entire human community of Earth, and it is the sworn responsibility of the National Park Service to serve this broader community, not a chance and transitory minute fraction of residents in the Valley at some particular time. In the long view of the Stehekin River, "private property" is as short as a human life.

It was a good meeting, face to face, there within sound of the Stehekin River—for those who could hear the waters. But a meeting changes nothing. Time does. History is "of time and the river." It also helps, as happened that day, to "let the mountains talk, and rivers run," an effective therapy often prescribed by David Brower.

The post-1968 Heritagers may brag up their personal credentials to the visiting press ("resident since 1975") and cite as their imprimatur the words and works of Ray Courtney, the son of an early settler, longtime director of the NCCC, and longer-than-that listener to the river. Near the untimely end of his life, he seemed to be facing up to the growing conflict between his love of the land, the river, and his love of family. Ray Courtney also would have understood the observation by the French historian, Fernand Braudel, who in *The Mediterranean World in the Age of Phillip II* noted that the salubrious air of the mountains tends to bring about high fertility and low infant mortality. Thus:

> Mountains are frequently overpopulated . . . in relation to their resources. The optimum level of population is quickly reached and exceeded; periodically the overflow has to be sent down to the plains.

Increasing numbers in the valley were (and are) an obvious threat to the future of Stehekin, yet the most vociferous of Heritager complaints revolved around the restriction on their free enterprise, their "commercial purposes," more specifically, the services provided to visitors by a handful of residents, most prominently the Courtneys. These services are of inestimable value in giving visitors from the outside world a comfortable welcome to temporary membership in the Stehekin community. What the complainers often failed to acknowledge was the obvious future of "commercial purposes" if not kept in check. Proposals like Sherer's and Stifter's foreshadowed the commerce to come if the Park Service failed to keep the public trust.

The population of the United States has nearly doubled in the past 50 years, and is predicted in the next 50 years to increase by another half. The country is filling up. Moreover, as this millennium ends, a single solitary person, a resident of Puget Sound City, has personal wealth greater than the entire bottom half of the nation's people. That bottom half is crowding into the New Tenements of megalopolis. The upper-upper fraction of the top half is buying up all the good places in the world: Montana, the San Juan Islands, the Methow Valley.

How long can the Secret of Stehekin be kept? When will a billionaire decide to buy it for himself and friends? Not the Heritage Community, not the County of Chelan, not the United States Senate, not the NCCC, and not all the king's horses and all the king's men can prevent it.

But the nation can, if it becomes aware of the threat to the national heritage. The National Park Service, under its current leadership, is vaguely aware. However, the "planning skills" of Reynolds and the "people skills" of Paleck have been less concerned with the Public Trust than with "getting along" with a "Heritage Community," the Chelan County Commissioners, and United States senators.

"There was a time. . . . There was a place. . . ." There can be again, if not an Old Stehekin, a New–Old. There is still—and can continue to be "a place."

Listen to the voices of Stehekin, not the "New" Stehekin of post-1968, but the New–Old that is speaking steadily louder in order to make itself heard above the babble and shrill that the show-biz press loves. When a newspaper lamented the failing health and near death of Stehekin, a longtime resident wrote a letter to the editor: "Give me a break! Stehekin continues to be a wonderfully wild, undeveloped, laid-back special place to live. We just want to keep it that way."

GETTING TO STEHEKIN

—By Carolyn McConnell

[Ed. note: The following originally appeared in 1994 in The Wild Cascades. Carolyn is the granddaughter of Grant and Jane McConnell, daughter of Ann McConnell.]

Getting to Stehekin is always an act of faith. Faith that no matter how fraught with peril and frustration the trip is it is possible to get there, and faith that the destination is worth all that trouble. The journey has always seemed like a pilgrimage, whose length and difficulty purifies for the entry into paradise. The difficulty in getting to Stehekin and the demands of the outside world kept me from Stehekin for close to eight years. It took the horror of a summer and a winter in Hoboken, New Jersey, to let me know it was time to return to Stehekin. As my grandfather always said, "We McConnells come to Stehekin to heal." So I came to Stehekin this spring carrying an immense baggage of wounds and nostalgia. Would Stehekin still carry enough magic to cure?

It did and does, and I carry away from this summer enough joy, enough memories of the river's polyphonic chuckle, the fingers of dawn on McGregor, and the lake's resident great blue herons to carry me through an entire winter in Baltimore. Though Stehekin is not "What America Was," it holds fragments of what America has lost, along with enough grandeur and peculiar beauty that even in an unspoiled world it would be unique. The wonderful combination of a spectacularly deep valley, towering crags, sparkling river, a natural community awesome in its richness and diversity, and a human community that for all its flaws is still human-sized and gentle, is a matchless treasure.

Yet the magic is more threatened than ever.

The demise of Stehekin is not something that will suddenly happen tomorrow or the day after or the day after in a howl of chainsaws and bulldozers. There will be no event we will point to and say, "That is the end." But if things continue as they are, in twenty years we will suddenly look up and notice that Stehekin is no more though no one saw at just what moment it took its last breath.

The tragedy of Stehekin is unfolding with the agonizing slowness and invisibility of the movement of the hands of a clock, only to be seen by watching for a long time. But almost no one has been watching long enough to notice that forty years ago there were hardly any houses defacing the lakefront, no suburban ghetto behind the bakery, no double-lane paved road, no gravel pit, no knapweed, and no airstrip. Certainly not the wealthy Seattle computer execs who have built homes in the valley recently, certainly not the Park Service seasonals who come into the summer and are gone, and not the Park Service power structure itself.

I have been watching for all my young life, still short yet long enough to see an impressive tally of destruction. What I saw with infinite pain this summer were: cars that have proliferated wildly in the time I was absent, in part because the Park Service has all but given up on shuttle buses; dozens of new houses, especially behind the bakery where the lucky residents can look into each other's windows just as if they were home in Manhattan, and where Chelan County only recently gave a permit for a home built on a raised foundation in what is obviously a floodway; so many new summerers that I no longer can recognize every car and driver who passes me on the road; and a Valley resident who took a dog up to the dedicated wilderness of Cascade Pass under the noses of rangers but whom the Park Service hadn't the nerve to ticket.

If anyone does notice the changes, they are told the destruction is inevitable as the movement of the hands of a clock, no one's fault, as blameless and inexorable as time.

That is a lie. The destruction of the matchless Stehekin Valley is not inevitable and it is someone's fault. It is the fault of the agency entrusted with its preservation unimpaired for my children's children's children—the Park Service. The Park Service has a unique opportunity right now to remedy its past sins and stop the slow march of devastation.

A haven from the inhuman mechanization of urban America is essential not only for those lucky enough to visit Stehekin. Its mere existence reminds us of what we have lost getting where we are and that where we are is not the only place to be. For me, the simple knowledge that Stehekin *is* will sustain me through many cold East Coast winters. But Stehekin itself must also be sustained.

THE PATH NOT TAKEN

A favorite device of science fictioners is to change a single crucial historic fact and then follow out the logic of an alternative time track. Let it be imagined that the Forest Service had won the ice-and-rocks Glacier Peak Wilderness it proposed, and that it had retained jurisdiction of Stehekin. What then?

Intensive multiple-use management would have established a Stehekin cutting circle comprising the Valley floor, the Valley walls, and the tributaries. Chelan Box Company would have thrust a road up Agnes Creek to the upper limit of big trees; the road inevitably would be connected west across Suiattle Pass to the logging road up the Suiattle River to the limit of its big trees; a spur would have led to picnic tables on the shores of Image Lake. A road would have been built from Stehekin six miles downlake to Fish Creek to add that drainage to the cutting circle; the survey stakes were, in fact, on site in the early 1960s. Later would have come the helicopters to extend the circle up the slopes, plucking fat trees off cliffs.

Upon completion of the North Cascades Highway, a spur would have descended Bridge Creek a dozen miles to the Stehekin Valley Road, which would have been widened to Winnebago dimensions and paved all the way to an RV campground on Weaver Point—a campground the Forest Service denied was ever planned. The contrary testimony by Ray Courtney is important; he saw the blueprints. Asking how those RVs would get into the valley, he was told by a ranger, "Down Bridge Creek."

The maps of the American West that advertised every expanse of road-accessible flat water would have added the access via the upper end of Lake

Chelan, and by 1994 plenty of Winnebuggers happily would have come, most likely towing razzer-boats. Those that didn't would have rented "personal watercraft," a.k.a. "jet-skis," or "lake lice," to snarl over the lake and up the river. Credit the National Park Service with banning these machines on Ross Lake and the northern portion of Lake Chelan in the late 1990s.

Had there been no national park, tourist services and facilities would seem likely, under Forest Service management, to have proliferated uncontrolled from the Landing upvalley as far as McGregor Mountain. The ancient lakebed which forms the Stehekin Valley from Lake Chelan to the base of McGregor is nearly identical in length, width, and total floor area to the ancient lakebed that forms Yosemite Valley in California.

Speaking of which, Yosemite Valley, visited now by four million people a year, has become less degraded—and thus more beautiful—than it was a half-century ago when visitation was hardly a tenth of the present. Still, the Park Service record has not been without fault there, most notoriously by failure to curb egregious molestations by the concessionaire–politician–Chamber-of-Commerce machine. Yet for all the mortal sins committed by the national-parks-as-amusement-parks mindset and all the Yosemite-bashing by journalists, no place in America continues to impress so many millions with such minimum relative impact.

Under the utilitarian, *laissez faire*, multiple-use management (or non-management) of the Forest Service, Stehekin would surely have been condominiumized—possibly Yosemitized with direct road access and hordes of automobiles—by 1980. There would likely have been no Georgette–Harvey study in 1979 because there would have been nothing left worth their attention. A similar sort of disaster has struck countless beauty spots throughout the West.

Yes, the continued presence of the Forest Service would have amounted to something else altogether. The 1968 Act was worth the effort.

Among those who have kept us on the right path: Patrick Goldsworthy, Dave Fluharty, Dick Brooks, and Dave Brower (left to right).

Clouds lift over Mount Shuksan; North Cascades National Park.

TOM HAMMOND

11

The Perfect Wild

Make no little plans
They have no magic to stir men's blood

—Daniel Hudson Burnham (1846-1912)
Quoted by David Brower in *For Earth's Sake*

America's Wilderness Alps

WRITING FOR THE *NCCC NEWS* in May of 1961, John Warth asked "Do the North Cascades really exist?" He pointed to several tourism and economic development promotional pieces and their crude depictions of the range: Mount Rainier and Mount Baker rising high above the horizon, but nothing else between them. A classic photo of Mount Baker from Baker Lake was still in use long after the scenic lake was buried sixty feet under the reservoir behind Upper Baker Dam. Lake Chelan was shown as if it was "a reservoir in the sand hills of Kansas—surely not a lake occupying the deepest chasm in the United States." A magazine article on the North Cascades was illustrated by "a lovely panorama of the Olympics." Wrote Warth, "It would almost appear the Cascades have been deliberately hidden from the public." That, despite being "one of the world's great mountain complexes, extensive as the Swiss Alps and fully as scenic," yet in these depictions, "all but lost."

In the years since—thanks to the good fight to protect the region's wilderness—the North Cascades have become far more familiar to millions of Americans, especially those of us in the Pacific Northwest. "With knowledge comes appreciation," Warth observed, "and with appreciation comes a desire to protect." The North Cascades range was eventually reunited in the public mind with its landmark volcanoes—Mount Baker and Glacier Peak—but a small irony remains. North Cascades National Park emerged missing both volcanos—the region's two tallest mountains. In 1968, the most obvious oversight was Mount Baker. Its exclusion was an aching disappointment. A national park in the North Cascades that lacked its highest mountain was like a Venus de Milo without a head. A national park lacking the entirety of "the magnificent pair," Glacier Peak *and* Mount Baker, sculpted a very incomplete Venus. East of Baker's snowy flanks, the national park boundary follows a severe rectangular jog meant to encompass "the most photographed mountain in the world," Mount Shuksan—an oddity of compromise in Scoop Jackson's final 1968 bill before the Senate. With all three mountains now mostly protected, the irony has turned out to be a happy one. Splendid Mount Shuksan, after all, is in the park, and the two lurking volcanoes are now included within Congressionally designated wilderness. Glacier preceded the park by four years (1964); Baker came sixteen years later (1984).

In the span of two decades, legislated park and wilderness protection in Washington's North Cascades went from virtually nothing to nearly 2.2 million contiguous acres, including the park complex itself, and the Glacier Peak, Mount Baker, Noisy Diobsud, Pasayten, Lake Chelan–Sawtooth, and Henry M. Jackson Wilderness Areas. Two nearby areas add another 0.4 million acres to the total, though they are somewhat detached from the others: the Boulder River Wilderness west of the Sauk River, separated from the rest by seven miles; and the Alpine Lakes Wilderness south of Stevens Pass, separated by a similar distance. Also worth noting are 25,000 acres of protected lands within the Loomis State Forest (adjacent to and east of the Pasayten Wilderness), and several protected areas immediately north of the international boundary, all of which add nearly a half-million acres to this contiguous core of protected wildlands. British Columbia's contribution to the total includes four provincial parks—Chilliwack Lake, Skagit Valley, Manning, and Cathedral—plus the Cascade Recreation Area and Snowy Protected Area. "Snowy" lies along the border north of the Loomis Forest and immediately east of Cathedral Lakes and was established by British Columbia in 2001. In total, eighteen parks and protected areas encompass 2.7 million acres of international paradise—which speaks to the tremendous grassroots efforts that ensued over many years on both sides of the border.

Yes, it's a lot, but is it enough? Too much? Too little? Loaded questions.

It is very clear to those who know these mountains intimately that there are still too many spectacular and pristine areas deserving of protection that remain vulnerable to the winds and whims of short-sighted politics and scheming depravity.

The North Cascades Act, passed in 1968 with boundaries drawn up by the Forest Service, did not adhere much to nature, thus the natural boundaries of

PROTECTED AREAS IN THE NORTH CASCADES (2006)

AREA	ACREAGE
North Cascades National Park	504,781
Ross Lake National Recreation Area	117,574
Lake Chelan National Recreation Area	61,947
Stephen Mather Wilderness (acreage included above)	--
Total North Cascades National Park Complex	*684,302*
Lake Chelan-Sawtooth Wilderness	151,435
Pasayten Wilderness	529,477
Mount Baker Wilderness	117,528
Noisy-Diobsud Wilderness	14,133
Boulder River Wilderness	48,674
Glacier Peak Wilderness	570,573
Henry M. Jackson Wilderness	100,356
Total National Wilderness	*1,532,176*
Loomis State Forest	24,677
Total area protected (U.S.)	*2,241,145*
Chilliwack Lake Provincial Park	22,877
Skagit Valley Provincial Park	69,061
E. C. Manning Provincial Park	175,059
Cascade Recreation Area	29,302
Cathedral Provincial Park	82,217
Snowy Protected Area	63,973
Total British Columbia area protected	*442,489*
All North Cascades protected areas	*2,683,634*

the park complex are deficient on every side. To help remedy that, Congressman John Saylor of Pennsylvania, in 1969, introduced a second park bill—the original NCCC bill that Senator Jackson, *et al.*, quietly dismissed. It came hard on the heels of the first, but its time was not yet. When the hour does come, and new protections are carved into bills before Congress, a number of questions will need to be answered about what belongs to the park and what belongs to wilderness. For example, will the boundaries of the Ross Lake NRA be adjust-

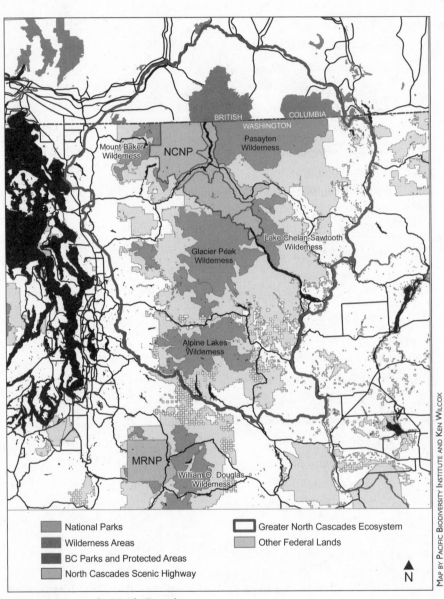

Protected Areas in the North Cascades.

ed to exclude any pretense for a revived High Ross Dam once the eighty-year hiatus expires? Will the considerable wilderness lands around Sauk Mountain, Golden Horn, and Washington Pass achieve the status they deserve?

There are some issues to sort out, to be sure, but they are nothing like the scene in 1968 or 1984 when hungry eyes and gnashing teeth threatened these wildlands on all sides. The threats are still there, but some are less obvious. And it isn't solely about chainsaws. The November 1995 issue of *Alaska Airlines Magazine* contained this promotional bit on the winter recreation potential of an unprotected corner of the North Cascades: "Heli-skiing puts untracked snow in remote, pristine mountains within easy reach." Come to "the biggest ski area in the Northwest—and the wildest, since there are scant signs of human intrusion in any of the 300,000 acres over which the helicopters are permitted to roam." Permitted by the Okanogan National Forest, it is "rugged alpine terrain as breathtaking as any in the French Alps." The NCCC would assert that this area, too, properly belongs in wilderness, not multiple-use. The cost to the consumers of commercial recreation might hold down the crowds: two days and a night in a yurt at 6,000 feet on the edge of the Pasayten Wilderness near Harts Pass went in 1997 for $515. But for that kind of money a person could have heli-skied the Canadian Bugaboos, on real glaciers, on genuine powder snow. Still, the current bumper crop of billionaires can indulge whims that could be called insane if entertained by people not rich beyond reason. Will one of them take a fancy to building an Alpine-style *balcon* on the summit of Silver Star or Kangaroo Ridge?

Urban sprawl and the increasing number of recreationists demanding access to wildlands pose growing threats that may have seemed less imminent not so long ago. With that in mind, should the Stehekin Valley at last, as originally intended, come home to the park? There may *seem* to be less urgency here since May 13, 1992, when it was formally recognized that the Lake Chelan National Recreation Area was in every important respect part of the park, yet it does remain unfinished business. The airstrip, the firewood cutting, the road, the river, the condos . . .

Above Marblemount, the Cascade River certainly belongs to the park, the whole of it, as a grand west-side entry into America's Wilderness Alps. The Cascade River became the most popular west-side access to the Glacier Peak area when the mine-to-market road of the 1950s gave vehicles quick entry to the high valley just below Cascade Pass. Two major feeders of the river flow from the national park (Marble Creek and the North Fork of the Cascade River) and five from the Glacier Peak Wilderness (Sonny Boy Creek, Kindy Creek, Found Creek, and the South and Middle Forks of the Cascade River). The Forest Service intended to log the portions of these valleys under its control. The effect of Clinton's Northwest Forest Plan has been to minimize the damage, without giving permanent protection. In the lower Cascade River valley, the Washington Department of Natural Resources must manage its lands as if it recognizes the economic value of the area to state and local tourism. The NCCC continues to insist, as it has for more than forty years, that the twelve-mile entrance corridor to the park provided by the Cascade River valley—along the mainstem and all tributaries—must be removed from the hypothetical cutting circle. Concurrently, the National Park Service and U.S. Forest Service must jointly develop dispersed recreational alternatives in the valley corridor, opening more of its wonders to more people of varied abilities and interests, enhancing the greatest good of the greatest number at sites of scenic splendor other than Cascade Pass. The NCCC would argue further that the Forest Service, Park Service, and Skagit County must agree to cut back the valley road to a point well short of its present end, where the massed vehicles of the parking lot are a shocking intrusion into the wildness viewed from Cascade Pass. Together with the shortening of the Stehekin River road, Cascade Pass would thus be rescued from over-used shallow wilderness—an amenity for Puget Sound area day-hikers—and returned to the deep, nationally significant wilderness of the pre-1950s.

Heather Meadows, too, could be considered for park status because it is a proper place for the frontcountry rangers of the National Park Service to exert their interpretive skills. And what of Glacier Peak, where the idea began? Which Service, Park or Forest, is most likely to steward such a grand place most effectively over the long term? How can we help the Canadians further secure that portion of the range that floods northward across the boundary?

There are several missing pieces in the upper Skagit River watershed, a few thousand acres worth, that clearly belong to Manning Provincial Park, some of which is at risk of being logged or mined in the very near future. Fully a third of the upper Skagit watershed in British Columbia, much of it pristine, remains unprotected, most notably the "donut hole," a large area adjacent to Manning Provincial Park and virtually surrounded by protected wildlands, but where recent logging across some portions has already taken a toll. The Skagit Environmental Endowment Commission considers its protection a priority. The U.S. portion of the Pasayten River watershed, a very wild place east of the Cascade Crest, is well protected, yet the Pasayten on the British Columbia side is not at all secured, partly due to substantial logging in the recent past. Occupying the gap between Manning and Cathedral Provincial Parks, it is a serious candidate for wilderness recovery.

South of the border, private inholdings must be cleaned up, finally and permanently. In December 1989 the Park Service listed seven tracts totalling 226 acres in private ownership, claims patented by prospectors of the ancient past. Those in Thunder Creek, Cascade River, Boston Basin, Bridge Creek,

KARL FORSGAARD

Hikers enjoy a stroll through Whistling Pig Meadow in the Entiat Mountains above Mad River. A large, unprotected roadless area here, southeast of Glacier Peak, has been the site of increasing conflict with off-road vehicles.

and Lake Anne are small, if not worthless, yet very little space is needed to dig a hole or set up a hot-dog stand on one of these quasi-private plots. Held as hostage, or in effect ransomed, even a few acres can get the speculators' heads dancing to visions of sugar plums.

The largest inholding, more than half the total, is the Dorothy Lode, 126.76 acres in Thunder Creek two miles west of Park Creek Pass. The Thunder Creek Mining Company was issued patents in 1921. Serious thought of mining had long ceased by the time the Webster family began making offers to sell out, the asking price ranging from $2 million to $50 million. Park Service appraisals by qualified geologists and mining engineers ranged from $38,000 down to $6,500. In 1990 the Park Service offered $56,000. (For comparison, condemnation proceedings in another Thunder Creek property concluded in 1981 when the courts awarded the Skagit Queen owners $277,000 for 645 acres.) In 1987 the Park Service, losing patience, informed Webster that "your efforts to rationalize some substantial mineral values have been a waste of time and money." Kidnappers may threaten to murder or maim the victim if the loved ones don't pay up. Webster might try to log ancient forest to elicit a payment, or maybe develop a helicopter-served backcountry camp, or even airlift ore to Canada or Idaho for smelting. In September 1991, Webster countered with an offer to sell to the Park Service for $3.4 million, then cut that offer in half a few months later, a figure well above the claim's value as determined by the agency. (For the full story, see the book, *Contested Terrain*). In the meantime, in 1998 a Boy Scout troop from the Midwest was helicoptered into the Dorothy, couldn't find the trail out, and had to be rescued.

· The claimholders mouths may be excused for watering. The Golden Gate Lode, 20.66 acres at an elevation of 4,200 feet in Horseshoe Basin, had been acquired by Ray Courtney's son Cliff. He conducted a blustering campaign that is standard nowadays all over the West—and it worked. In 1999 the Park Service relented. As mentioned above, for twenty acres of seemingly worthless rock staked out in 1889, Courtney got five acres of prime Stehekin Valley floor adjoining his Stehekin Valley Ranch, where he could pour some great coffee for the tourists. A few other claims should also be acquired by the Park Service or, in the interim, by the Forest Service for areas adjacent to the park that are not yet protected.

While most of the wild North Cascades is federal land, there are opportunities, albeit limited, for conservation on nearby state lands as well. Once severely threatened by logging, the Loomis Forest is a good example. This 25,000-acre state-administered Natural Resource Conservation Area was protected in 2000 only because a citizen campaign, led by Northwest Ecosystem Alliance (now Conservation Northwest), was able to raise $16.5 million to essentially pay the state *not* to log the public's forest. Mostly roadless, the Loomis is home to the healthiest population of the imperiled Canadian lynx in the Lower Forty-Eight. We can hope for more successes like Loomis, perhaps in the western foothills. However antiquated laws, a perennially distracted legislature, and stump-friendly attitudes within the Washington Department of Natural Resources make it nearly impossible for the public to protect its own lands, even when the sentiment favoring conservation is overwhelming, as it is at Blanchard Mountain south of Bellingham—the westernmost reach of the North Cascades' foothills.

Nevertheless, the vast majority of what could be saved lies on federal lands within Washington's North Cascades. They are the same wildlands that Bob Marshall and others recognized in the 1930s as being "the second-largest potential forest wilderness in the United States" (second only to the Selway-Salmon River wilderness region in Idaho)—as it was so described by the Wilderness Society in its first issue of *The Living Wilderness* in September 1935.

These are America's Wilderness Alps, yet far too much is still at risk. We should finish the work.

A Change in the Weather

As we stare into our collective crystal ball and imagine a future where all the wild places that remain in the North Cascades are protected as park or wilderness or some other kind of ecological reserve, we will also be contemplating something that wasn't on our radar fifty years ago: the adverse effects of climate change on the natural landscape, from valley-bottom forests to the highest alpine meadows, and every place in between. It is now apparent that strategies for protecting and restoring wilderness need to seriously consider and address these effects as best we can.

With the political minions of the oil and gas industries continuing to deny the science of global warming and working feverishly to exacerbate climate change and its damaging effects on humanity and the planet, many in the Pacific Northwest are taking note of the regional consequences of this grotesque national failure. Among the areas where changes may be most dramatic—and where major changes are already occurring—is in the North Cascades.

The *Seattle Post-Intelligencer* offered a lengthy heads-up for its readers in a feature story on the subject in November 2003. "From the crest of the Cascades to the bottom of Puget Sound," they wrote, "this region stands in coming decades to be transformed: shorter ski seasons. More winter flooding. Reduced summer water supplies. Increased destructive wildfires. Further stressed salmon runs. . . . Only a handful of scientists who have seriously studied the matter doubt that significant and potentially destructive warming is coming."

Scientists at the Climate Impacts Group at the University of Washington and elsewhere tell us that, in winter, more precipitation at higher elevations will fall as rain instead of snow, substantially reducing the snowpack that historically has melted quite gradually over the spring and summer months to provide much of the water used by lowland cities, farms, fish, and hydroelectric dams. Winter storms that used to bring heavy snow to the Cascades' high country will instead dump rain, triggering increased flooding and erosion. With less total snowpack melting more quickly, the forests will become drier earlier in the summer, making them much more vulnerable to massive wildfires—including areas of old-growth forest that haven't burned in hundreds of years. Changing climate conditions will favor some plant and insect species and impede others, significantly altering habitat conditions, food webs, and subsequently entire ecosystems. Familiar, rare, and endangered wildlife species will be squeezed from existence when there is nowhere else to go. The carbon balance—in the biosphere and the atmosphere—is getting worse, not better. Shrinking glaciers mean less meltwater and warmer temperatures in streams and rivers that salmon and other fish depend on for their survival. This, too, is already happening.

More than seven hundred glaciers—over half of all the glaciers in the contiguous U.S.—are contained within the North Cascades. Called "rivers of ice"

PHOTOGRAPHER UNKNOWN (POSSIBLY GRANT McCONNELL)

This arm of the Chickamin Glacier below Sinister Peak has receded significantly since this photo was taken (ca. 1960s).

by geologists, glaciers form where more snow accumulates than melts in a typical year. As the snow piles up, it turns to ice under its own weight and slowly begins to slide downward in response to gravity, literally carving out the mountainsides in the process. In the North Cascades, glaciers large and small have produced some of North America's most dramatic scenery and inspired, perhaps more than anything else, the nickname "American Alps." Most of them have been in existence for thousands of years. Since regular scientific measurements started in 1984, these glaciers have lost, in total, as much as a third or more of their total mass. Some at lower elevations are disappearing altogether.

Led by Dr. Mauri Pelto at Nichols College in Massachussets, scientists have been conducting the longest-running study to date on North Cascades glaciers. After observing the Lewis Glacier near Rainy Pass for two decades beginning in 1978 (when it was ninety acres in size), Pelto returned in 1989 to find that it had totally disappeared. Indeed, at least eight glaciers have ceased to exist in the twenty-plus years of the study. From 1984 to 2005, glaciers on the flanks of Mount Baker receded upslope by more than three hundred meters. With a warming of only two-degrees Celsius, it is expected that another third or more of our glaciers will disappear within the next several decades.

The natural process we humans are interfering with is about basic equilibrium. Glaciers advance and retreat in response to a positive or negative "mass balance" which is determined by how much snow is falling up high (the accumulation zone), and how much is melting or breaking up at the lower elevations or along the margins (the ablation zone). As a direct result of global warming, even the accumulation zone may slip below the mean elevation of snowfall, resulting in a state of "disequilibrium." During retreat (a negative mass balance), a glacier that wants a future must be able to recede to a point where equilibrium can be reestablished, otherwise it is condemned to disappear.

Pelto's studies suggest that some glaciers in the North Cascades are already in a state of disequilibrium, and many others have an equilibrium point that will eventually render them irrelevant as a summer-season water resource. NCCC board member and climber Tom Hammond joined Pelto's field teams several years in a row, and warned that "Implications for fish, farmers, Tulip Festivals, and burgeoning growth in a region that demands water resources should not be underestimated."

Human-induced climate change is an unprecedented threat in the North Cascades and we are only beginning to understand what it might mean for the future. But regardless of how severe the effects on the greater ecosystem ultimately are, NCCC believes it is imperative that we do everything we can now to keep wild places wild—as we also strive to enlighten the public and a few select politicians about the severity of the threat.

Where It All—or at Least Half of It—Began: Glacier Peak

The Forest Service refusal early on to set aside an adequate Glacier Peak Wilderness, combined with its opposition to protecting the Stehekin Valley, were critical factors in the creation of the national park. The original proposal by the NCCC to enclose the Glacier Peak Wilderness within the national park remains on the table, though at a comparatively low priority. As urgent as ever, however, are the dangers to certain areas that were excluded from the wilderness by the boundaries set in 1960 and also by the 1968 and 1984 enlargements.

The White Chuck River is the classically respectful deep-forest approach to the wilderness volcano. In 1960 the Forest Service gave respectful protection to the uppermost four miles of the valley, mainly above the limit of big trees. In 1968 three-and-a-half more down-valley miles were added, and in 1984 another mile. In the mid-1990s the Forest Service was moving toward logging the ancient forest on the alluvial terrace south of the river and, on the north side of the valley, the mid-elevation slopes of Meadow Mountain. This intrusion into wilderness was not very respectful. The storm of October 2003 knocked out the road as well as much of the trail leading into Kennedy Hot Springs, and destroyed the tepid, murky springs. The Forest Service is determined to rebuild the road. The NCCC, however, believes this is a time for the Forest Service to rethink the need (and long-term cost) for a road that penetrates so far into wilderness. The group proposes that instead of rebuilding an expensive and environmentally destructive road that serves very little need, the Forst Service convert it to a multi-use trail for hikers, climbers, horses, and mountain bikers (the old road only, not in the wilderness). It may be one of the easiest valleys to re-wild in the North Cascades, and the recreational, ecological, and economic benefits of doing so should be seriously considered.

Another crucial west-side wilderness access is the road along the Suiattle River, one range north of the White Chuck. The Forest Service should be forbidden to carry out previous plans to log its Buck, Downey, and Sulphur Creek tributaries, all of which are only partly in wilderness and should be totally so. As evidenced by the same storm and flood in October 2003, the Suiattle River has proven very hard to tame. Perhaps it should be left to do its own thing, automobiles be damned. The same could be said for a portion of the Mountain Loop Highway, a popular, unpaved, scenic drive through the mountains between the historic logging towns of Darrington and Granite Falls. It, too, was heavily damaged in the 2003 storm. The Forest Service presented its plans for reconstruction in 2006 and repairs were begun late that summer. The river flooded again in December 2006, taking another big bite out of the repairs that were underway. The NCCC proposed that repeated impacts to this important salmon river that result from road construction might be offset somewhat by decommissioning unnecessary logging spurs south of the Suiattle and elsewhere, but as of 2006 the Forest Service would provide no assurance those roads would be closed.

Southeast of Glacier Peak, the roadless gems of the Mad River watershed

The first of two major washouts along the White Chuck River Road, a result of the October 2003 storm. Note the vehicle on the left.

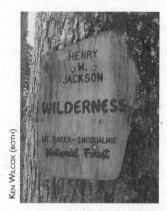

Ken Wilcox (both)

The Henry M. Jackson Wilderness adjoins the Glacier Peak Wilderness to its southwest and includes Sloan Peak and the Monte Cristo Range.

are logical candidates for wilderness additions. Instead, conservationists have had to battle the Forest Service, in court and out, to keep motorized users from destroying the place. When the Forest Service attempted to expand and develop in piecemeal fashion a "world-class" trail system for motorcycles in a roadless area that the agency had already identified as potential wilderness, the NCCC, Sierra Club, The Mountaineers, and Washington Wilderness Coalition sued in federal court. Conservationists argued that cumulative impacts must be considered for the entire project. In June 2006 the judge agreed, ruling that an environmental impact statement must be prepared that gives adequate consideration to adverse impacts on wildlife and wilderness. The Forest Service has since backed off on its pursuit of "motorhead" trails in the area.

The Wild Sky Wilderness in the wild Skykomish River watershed has been on the brink of wilderness designation for several years, hamstrung by a zealous Congressman from California. The Wild Sky will be the first new wilderness in Washington since 1988. The largest unprotected roadless areas within the Mount Baker-Snoqualmie National Forest are located within the Wild Sky—and at Sauk Mountain north of the Skagit River where volunteers with Mount Baker Wild! are working to win protection for this equally spectacular area of alpine peaks and old-growth forest.

These are examples of the opportunities and the status review that is needed around the entire periphery of the North Cascades National Park Complex and the Glacier Peak Wilderness. A number of extensions of existing park and wilderness boundaries are surely warranted. Furthermore, some sort of management classification must be devised to give road corridors, which are ineligible for wilderness, the protection they would have received had they been placed in the national park in 1968. The roadside forests of the Cascade, White Chuck,

Suiattle, and North Fork Sauk valleys on the west, and the Little Wenatchee, White, Chiwawa, and Entiat valleys on the east simply cannot best serve the nation under multiple-use as currently defined by the Forest Service. Pockets of forest that may have been logged, but which are otherwise surrounded by pristine lands should also be considered for some kind of "wilderness recovery" status so that they are not denied the protection they deserve.

Beyond the boundaries of the North Cascades National Park Complex are the Pasayten Wilderness (1968), Alpine Lakes Wilderness (1976), and the 1984 bushel basket of new wilderness: the Henry M. Jackson, Boulder River, Mount Baker, Noisy-Diobsud, and Lake Chelan-Sawtooth Wilderness Areas, of which none has attained its optimum boundaries; most of these glasses are still two-thirds empty. Neither Congress nor the White House (even under Clinton) has moved in a progressive direction, nor are they visibly moving now to gather the remaining pieces. The third branch of the federal government— the courts—and the will of the citizenry have been tested to somewhere near their limits. Yet they almost always agree that given what has been lost, the best of the North Cascades' remaining wildness must always be protected.

BACKWARD INTO THE FUTURE: A LAKE CHELAN NATIONAL PARK

Sequoia National Park was set aside in the beginning era of the national park concept and served well to display its Big Trees. However, it did not encompass the Big Canyon, the most awesome gash in the Sierra, and in 1940 Sequoia was complemented by Kings Canyon National Park.

The very first national park proposal in the Cascades in 1892 was not thought of as a showcase for volcanoes, nor forests, nor glaciers, but for Lake Chelan. Never in the following century has the traveler's eye failed to perceive this very special and absolutely unique marvel of the American earth. In the 1960s the NCCC proposed that the entire lake northward from Safety Harbor Creek be transferred from Forest Service and other jurisdictions to the National Park Service. The 1968 Act did not go anywhere near that far.

In 1994 a passenger on the *Lady of the Lake* was lulled by the omnipresence of lakeshore wilderness and enchanted by the few occupied niches—small, homestead-like, frontier-like. However, the historically aware passenger, upon arriving in Stehekin Valley and witnessing that scene, envisioned a downlake extension of that Barbecuing and began to sweat. Along the lakeshore within three miles of Stehekin, residential and lodging structures appeared, displacing the scenery and the century-old tread of the Chelan Lakeshore Trail. In 1998 there came to Hazard Creek (a half-mile from the Stehekin Landing) on the Lakeshore Trail, a favorite spot for walkers to come for a picnic, a subdivision approved by Chelan County for three large structures.

A Forest Service map of Lake Chelan delineates the size and location of private ownership along the shore. According to the Chelan District Ranger several years ago, about half the private lands are patented mining claims, the other half acquired under the Timber and Stone Act, though some very likely were taken under the Homestead Act. The rangers say the largest of these ownerships is the 160-acre patented claim (homestead or mining) at Meadow Creek, but the Railroad Creek property at Lucerne is also sizable, as are the privately owned alluvial fans of Four-Mile Creek and Canoe Creek. The bulk, but not all, of the homestead on the Fish Creek delta (Moore Point) was acquired by the Forest Service in the 1960s. The Chelan ranger noted the existence of six lease permits for summer homes on the shore, totaling about six acres. These leases were for twenty-six years and were renewable. This lease program, once prevalent in the national forests, has been terminated; no new permits are given, but existing ones were grandfathered in. As the new millennium unfolds, the Stehekin barbecue can be predicted to proceed farther downlake, and when it does, the Chelan County government will have an opportunity to weigh in.

While voyaging on the *Lady of the Lake*, a person inspecting the shores with an ownership map in hand can foresee a future of tumult and destruction—a future that can be prevented if action is taken soon enough. On the alluvial fan of Canoe Creek, envision Canoe Creek Condos. Spot Meadow Creek Lodge, nostalgic relic of the century's earlier decades, sitting duck for a hotshot great-grandson or roving entrepreneur who would have all those 160 acres to develop. See the cute chalet on a bluff above the lake, where until his death, a picturesque solitary received his mail from the boat; now that he is gone, envision on that bluff a not-so-cute row of picture windows. On the broad alluvial fan of Fish Creek, only part of it in public hands, imagine Moore Point Retirement Village. Attend to Lucerne, on the alluvial fan of Railroad Creek, where a little resort once catering to the public was privatized by the Chelan Yacht Club. The spacious delta ought to be used as a visitor center for the upper lake, a supplement or substitute or alternative to Stehekin. Nearing Stehekin, pass the alluvial fan of Four-Mile Creek and in mind's eye see the Hollywood mega-star or Wall Street super-thief or television evangelist building a private Xanadu and fencing off the Lakeshore Trail. On the outskirts of Stehekin, see Adams Point, subject of Chelan County Short Plat Number 2016. Note on the shore and on the map other properties, some unoccupied, others with a modest cabin or two; their turns, too, will come once entrepreneurial opportunities are exhausted in the Stehekin Valley.

And therefore, *Lake Chelan National Park.*

On the one shore, Twenty-Five Mile Creek is a reasonable boundary, because there the road and residences and orchards give way to steep, wild steppe and lichen-encrusted cliffs, distinctly Eastern Washington. On the opposite shore, the earlier proposal began at Safety Harbor Creek because uplake from there the shore is cliff-walled and impassable afoot. However, the grand long stretch of downlake steppe is rarely hospitable to boat landings and is remote from roads, for the most part cleanly pristine. Such an example of a sagebrush steppe that merges without human interruption into pine-grass forest of the lower (dry) timberline is so typically east-slope Cascades it would form an invaluable component of a complete display of the region's ecosystems.

Why a national park? Because the lakeshore (as perhaps distinguished from the wilderness backcountry) is not suitable business for the Forest Service. Because, despite its shortcomings, the Park Service has precisely the frontcountry experience and enthusiasm to exhibit and interpret the scene to America. Because not the Chelan County Commission nor the downlake wealthies, nor the United States Coast Guard, nor the state Department of Inland Navigation, nor the Washington State Aviation Division, not nobody, separately or cumulatively, has the firm will or full authority to regulate traffic on and above the lake and its shores. A single national authority is the one recourse for defense of the national interest. The place worth protecting in the 1890s has certainly been battered around the edges, but much is intact and remains a great American treasure, easily deserving of a noble recognition.

Lake Chelan National Park. It's high time—and a hundred years late.

THE GREATER NORTH CASCADES ECOSYSTEM: AN INTERNATIONAL PARK?

In the 1930s the Powers That Be (or Had Been) fought off an Ice Peaks National Park by issuing maps showing the entirety of the National Forests in the Cascades and telling the gullible press and public this was the preserve proposed by Secretary of the Interior Harold Ickes and the National Park Service. In the 1950s the U.S. Forest Service littered the state with copies of a Sierra Club map identifying the entirety of the North Cascades as an area meriting intensive study, and brayed that this whole thing was the preserve sought by "them city folks" from California and Seattle. In the 1990s the Wise Use chorus chanted the old lie again, warning loggers, fishermen, hikers, and picnickers that they were about to be fenced off and excluded from an entity some were calling the Greater North Cascades Ecosystem. The Prophet from Battleground orated as the enraged audiences shook their fists at the screen.

But there is no plan for such a big park—an international park—at present. There should be. A credible study should be conducted to help form a variety of proposals: some parks, some wilderness, some recreation areas, indeed, even some commodity-extraction and residential areas on the periphery.

DAVE SCHIEFELBEIN

★★*Lake Chelan aerial view.*

No ecosystem smaller than the planet is adequate for healthy nature. Though the greater ecosystem of the Washington Cascades extends at least to the Columbia River, that of the North Cascades may expediently be considered to have as its southern boundary Interstate 90 over Snoqualmie Pass, and as a northern boundary the Fraser River not far beyond the international border and the 49th Parallel. The western boundary is the saltwater into which empty the Snohomish (Skykomish plus Snoqualmie), Stillaguamish, Skagit, Nooksack, and Fraser Rivers, and the wall of Chuckanut and Elephant (Blanchard) Mountains rising more than two thousand feet sheer from the beaches. On the northeast, Chopaka Mountain's eastern slope may be considered the terminus of the range, the scarp plummeting to the Similkameen River and the trough of an ancient Pleistocene glacier. South of that, the boundary is the Columbia River.

The effective beginning of the proposal for an international park, ideally encompassing all or most of these areas, was the coming together of the NCCC south of the 49th parallel with Run Out Skagit Spoilers (ROSS) north, each the spearhead for a host of other organizations. With that effort, the international "conspiracy" to let the land stay wild had begun. Year One was 1968.

On May 11, 1993, the Bellingham branch of the Mountaineers and the NCCC sponsored a forum in Bellingham attended by officials of the National Park Service, the U.S. Forest Service, British Columbia Parks, and representatives of citizen groups from both sides of the border. The concept is too large to be treated adequately in a book that must also cope with Lake Chelan and other challenges. However, among the subjects on the agenda of the NCCC are:

Wildlife: Protect and recover populations of grizzly bears, wolves, wolverines, badger, lynx, goshawks, spotted owls, and associates.

Fish: Restore anadromous species to the rivers; rid high lakes of introduced species that cause destructive predation and over-use of fragile ecosystems.

No-trail areas and no-people areas: Keep them that way, for critters that don't like people all that well.

Ancient forests: Communities of life. Gene pools.

Endangered plants: Identify populations and guard them. They are the perfect survivors of undisturbed nature.

Rivers, Wild and Scenic and Recreational: From the glaciers to the salt (west) and the Columbia (east).

While we're at it, let's stop making wars. If that is too much to ask, maybe we can at least forbid military jets from scrambling the brains of hikers and climbers with their thundering, low-flight, terrain-following exercises along North Cascadian glaciers and ridges.

Unprotected areas in the North Cascades are largely comprised of "inventoried roadless areas." The Clinton Roadless Rule helps to keep these places wild, despite efforts by the Bush Administration to undo that work. Other uninventoried roadless areas also exist.

Ban close overflights by civilians, as well. Rid the wilderness sky of air taxis carrying the kin of Croesus to high trails and picnic tables, ski slopes and huts, and goat heads to be chopped off and taken home to mount on the wall above the wet bar.

Trail wheels: motorized or plain mechanized—not in the wilderness.

On December 10, 1992, citizens of the two nations met in Leavenworth under the auspices of the National Parks Conservation Association. In March 1994 the Nature Has No Borders conference was held at the University of Washington, attended by 200 representatives of organizations north and south, including the NCCC, to form the Cascades International Alliance (CIA) and officially announce the Cascades International Park campaign. A book, *Cascadia Wild*, published in 1993 by the Greater Ecosystem Alliance (now Conservation Northwest), suggested such a park might include the North Cascades National Park, Ross Lake National Recreation Area, the Skagit Valley, Chilliwack, E.C. Manning, and Cathedral Lakes Provincial Parks, the Cascades Provincial Recreation Area, and intervening lands and habitat linkages that were (and for the most part still are) unprotected.

George Frampton, Assistant Secretary of the Interior, addressed the conference, stressing that this was a study area, "not a lockup," and never would be. However, in a region where black helicopters hover everywhere overhead according to some, and United Nations troops notoriously stage secret maneuvers, the bottom-feeding Chuck Cushman and his National Parks and Inholders Association surrounded the conference with 200 troopers (by Cushman's count) and revealed that a plot was afoot to confiscate nine million acres of private lands. Perhaps the Cascades International Alliance slipped up on its acronym.

However, under cover of *green* helicopters, a Canada–United States treaty provided for a Skagit Environmental Endowment Commission (SEEC), itself concerned primarily with the upper Skagit, and there the NCCC continues to tend the crops sown by the settlement over High Ross Dam. The commission also believes that cooperation among land managers is crucial to the future of this cross-border ecosystem.

As SEEC and other organizations work to establish cross-border ecosystem-based management strategies, a measure of success will be the eventual —and hopeful—recovery of sustainable populations of grizzly bear, wolf, lynx, and a host of other wildlife species whose demise was so effectively engineered over the past 150 years. We can bring them back and we can share the landscape with them. For anyone who doubts that possibility, consider the recent results of random household surveys conducted in 2003 and 2005 by the Grizzly Bear Outreach Project, or GBOP. In rural areas of eastern Whatcom and Skagit Counties, where one might expect residents to be most fearful of an increased grizzly bear population, 76 percent favored grizzly recovery in the North Cascades. It is estimated that as few as five bears may presently roam there; sightings are extremely rare. A few obstructionists in the state legislature and a lack of follow-through on bear recovery efforts by the U.S. Fish and Wildlife Service under Bush II have so far blocked plans to relocate a handful of bears from Canada to the North Cascades in order to slowly increase and stabilize this tiny population. Fortunately, a few wolves have returned to the range in recent years, but they too remain virtually invisible to the hundreds of thousands of recreationists who frequent these mountains each year.

An international park, perhaps even a world biosphere reserve (formal recognition by the U.N. Education, Scientific, and Cultural Organization), might be an exciting, even achievable, goal. But there's more. As a viable future for this greater ecosystem becomes more assured in the coming years (are we being too optimistic?), we may also begin to reap the benefits of even larger networks and linkages of giant-sized corridors and continental landscapes, from the Cascades to the Kettle Range, and to the Colville and the Rockies—a daunting cause otherwise known as the "Rainforest to Rockies Conservation Initiative." Further, in the Central Cascades, the Cascades Conservation Partnership has worked to acquire old-growth forest and other habitat corridors linking the Alpine Lakes Wilderness to Mount Rainier National Park. The effort to date has resulted in sixty square miles of newly protected lands. West of Mount Baker, a string of almost continuous foothills leads to the Chuckanut Mountains, Blanchard Mountain, and the marine coast at Samish Bay south of Bellingham—the only place in the entire Cascades Range where the Cascade foothills touch the sea. It won't all become wilderness, but there are certainly abundant opportunities to recover some of what's been lost, to move ourselves a little closer to that perfect wild.

While certainly ecological interests are the prime drivers behind the need to protect this great wilderness, no one can deny the outstanding scenic and recreational values that exist here and that will also be conserved for the enjoyment of generations. In his film *Wilderness Alps of Stehekin*, David Brower called it an "alpine wilderness that belongs to our national gallery . . . rugged alps built in grand scale, unique, unsurpassed anywhere in the United States." Hundreds of miles of hiking trails are woven through landscapes of forest and stream, meadow and wildflower, rock and ice—where one can gaze up, said Brower, at "the old contest between the crags and the mists." Mountaineers who have traveled the world's mountain ranges call the North Cascades one of the most sublime. In fact, mountaineers like the Browers, the Dyers, the McConnells, the Zaleskys, the Goldsworthys, the Mannings, and scores of others had a direct role in bringing to the attention of the world the superlative wildness that is this range.

★ ★ ★

And so this book ends, but the story does not. The need for conservation action continues, and it is hoped that those who have read this book will share the message with friends, family, and especially younger generations. It is, after all, the future generations of our planet that have the most to gain by the forward-thinking, and more importantly, the forward-acting people of our day. Taking action is not easy, but it is essential and it is worthy. The NCCC invites all to participate in this cause. As with all difficult journeys, the first steps are always the hardest: the pack weighs the most at the trailhead, the strain is greatest on the steep switchbacks of the approach. But ultimately the toil, pain, and exertion are rewarded with the satisfaction that washes over us as we gain perspective to see beyond our immediate surroundings to the infinite possibilities of wilderness and a healthy planet.

In America's Wilderness Alps—these splendid North Cascades—it is the wildness of the place, its integrity as a regional ecosystem, threatened as it is, that inspires its preservation. So let us carry our packs up the trail knowing that once the missing pieces are secured, the largest intact wilderness ecosystem anywhere along the U.S.–Canadian border will have been preserved.

Harvey Manning (left) pauses for a photo with fellow mountaineers Dick Brooks and Lou Crittenden somewhere in the wilderness (ca. 1960s).

Photo courtesy of Betty Manning

The 'lunatic fringe,' that subspecies of conservationist that dares to defy government bureaucracies, industrial interests, and commercializers of outdoor recreation, wins a battle now and then. Its members are identified by this name of derision because they are so simple as to refuse to swap a clear-running stream, a National Monument, public rights, or a wilderness area for a fast and slippery buck. . . . Man's urge to dominate and destroy must be checked unless 'civilized' man desires his own destruction. . . . Americans will find that only by joining the 'lunatics' will they be able, as a nation, to avoid genuine, total and permanent insanity.

—Phil Zalesky, *NCCC News,* June 1961

The unique virtue we claim for this history is that it comes straight from the horses' mouths. Maybe we'd better say hikers' mouths—the wilderness hikers who are proud to say the North Cascades National Park was their idea and they got it done. The conservationists who have since re-formed ranks to finish the job also provided invaluable input to this book.

When a representative of NCCC showed the manuscript to a publisher and told him it was the real scoop on the how and why of the park's conception, birth, and (to a sorry extent) unhappy childhood, the aghast response after a quick flip of the pages was, "But where are the footnotes? You don't get no respect, you don't got no footnotes!"

Now, with all due deference to academic ornamentals (Betty and I fondly address our son as "Herr Doktor Professor Manning"), the principal function of footnotes is to testify that the historian at his desk has at least some tenuous connection to the real world. An "apparatus" demarcates history from myth. We are, of course, as wary of myth as any doctor of philosophy. But, simply, we carry our apparatus around in our heads. We were there.

If footnotes are desired, we refer you to the nearly magisterial 1998 publication of the National Park Service, *Contested Terrain: North Cascades National Park Service Complex, An Administrative History* by David Louter. This 338-page volume has footnotes enough for the both of us, and we appreciated the reasonably polite treatment of the NCCC. We may be excused for suspecting its publication was stimulated by our 1992 publication of the preliminary edition of this book.

The primary target for our 1992 publication was the Park Service itself. We had found that many superb rangers (in our experience, most rangers we have met are superb, or tend in that direction) have had their minds clouded by myths deliberately spun by those few rangers (mainly in the topmost echelons) at the other end of the scale. It is our prayer that rangers learning about the history of the North Cascades in order to perform their duties in the present, complement their reading of the very useful *Contested Terrain* with a reading of our *Conservation and Conflict*. Let me cite one example, reflecting my personal experience as a writer of "official history" for certain governmental and quasi-governmental agencies. There was the case of this football coach, you see, who had spent public funds in a manner that would have triggered headlines had that (illegal) manner become public knowledge. It was my assigned task, having been made privy to the "eyes only" file, to write a story that was not exactly a lie, but would avoid risking our team's chances at another Rose Bowl.

Accustomed as I became to my drafts being "vetted" by higher powers, I have a certain sixth sense about these things. When author David Louter says (on page 163), "Reynolds' proposals thrust North Cascades forward to meet its new challenges, though many of his ideas would remain in the planning stages for some time," I feel an aura of Reynolds hovering over Louter.

Definitive history must await scholars who enjoy the security of the cloister and its timeless, measured pace. We, here, write from the turmoil of the trenches and the barricades, in the rockets' red glare, bombs bursting in air—history as pamphlet, wall poster, manifesto, ultimatum. The central body of our source materials is the memories and writings and archives of the veterans of the war. Whatever primary research is embodied in this work has been done by listening to friends talk, reading their letters, and submitting rough drafts to them for detailed critiques.

However, our sources go back well before the start of the war. The letters of Anna Stevens, with whom I corresponded regularly in the last years of her life, tell charming tales of that past which is "a foreign country, they do things differently there." Growing up in Winthrop, the town her stepfather founded, she listened in her bed at night to the wolves howling in the sagebrush steppe of the Methow Valley. Bands of Original Inhabitants came from afar on pilgrimage to gaze in awe at her flaming red hair and, with her permission, to reverently touch the strands hanging down to her shoulders. She knew "The Virginian" and "Trampas" personally. She accompanied Owen Wister and his bride on their packtrain honeymoon journey over "the Methow Pass" and on to catch the steamboat at Marblemount. She voyaged down the Columbia River to Chelan to attend the balls sponsored at swank hotels by the Inland Empire gentry.

When I worked for Rinehart and Company in New York, I talked to and corresponded with Stan, who as a child accompanied his mother, Mary Roberts, on her Great Northern-sponsored packtrain trip from Lake Chelan over Cascade Pass. I knew her traveling companion, "Silent Lawrie," a member of The Mountaineers famed for his lantern-slide shows.

I remember listening raptly to Leo Gallagher recalling his introduction to the North Cascades on a Summer Outing of The Mountaineers in the early 1920s—the railroad trip from Seattle to Darrington, the pack-train journey up the White Chuck River, and at last, from a "fly camp," the ascent of the "last wild volcano," Glacier Peak.

Still need footnotes? I was personally (almost) there. In actual physical flesh, except for a few fishing trips with my folks, I didn't set boot in the North Cascades until Boy Scout years just before WWII, and climbing years just after. But NCCC people—that is, the people who would become NCCC when it was founded—were there. Grant and Jane McConnell climbed in Old Stehekin on the eve of the war and resided there in the trauma-recovering aftertime. Ray Courtney was a son of Hugh who was there almost before the Old began. Well into the years of New Stehekin, as fellow directors of the North Cascades Conservation Council, Ray and I talked about the Valley, the Lake, the peaks, the past, the future. We talked in the meadows, at his ranch, at Betty's and my 200-meter hut on Cougar Mountain, at the Landing lunch counter. Paul Bergman, who first visited Stehekin in the 1920s and lived there from the 1930s, always came out of his photo shop to meet us as the Lady docked. Harry Buckner, postmaster at the Landing, wrote recollections for The Mountaineer of his arrival at Stehekin in 1911, joining his uncle who had been there since the 1890s.

But enough bragging ("My father knew Lloyd George, Lloyd George knew my father"). The portion of this history that is not yet finished had its jump-start in the mid-1950s, in the Conservation Committee of The Mountaineers and then, after 1957, in the North Cascades Conservation Council.

Directors of the NCCC have reviewed the manuscript, adding and subtracting, confirming and correcting. Several have gone at it line by line and deserve specific thanks. The reader will gain the impression that on any occasion since 1953 when two or more conservationists gathered to discuss the North Cascades, Polly Dyer was one of them. It's very nearly true, and this book embodies innumerable contributions only she was in a position to offer. Grant and Jane McConnell brought a unique perspective from having been visitors to the head of Lake Chelan in the 1930s, fulltime residents of Old Stehekin for a period after World War II, and, from the part-time home they maintained in the Valley until Grant's death in 1993, close students of New Stehekin. Grant was the head of our departments of philosophy and political strategy, and, with Dave Brower, was grand marshal in the decisive move to take the campaign national. A third close reading was by Phil and Laura Zalesky. Phil was the founding president of the NCCC and during the crucial period of the 1950s-1960s was preeminent among "the natives"—those Northwesterners who did not begin their conservation careers with David Brower in the San Francisco Bay chapter of the Sierra Club, as did John and Polly Dyer, Grant and Jane McConnell, and Pat and Jane Goldsworthy. Pat, incidentally, also made a close reading and much of the text derives from his writings in *The Wild Cascades* as NCCC president. The third president (until 1994), Dave Fluharty, participated while a student in the mass excitement of the 1960s. Since the 1980s he has led both the relicensing-mitigation negotiations on Seattle City Light's Skagit River dams and the challenge to the National Park Service by the lawsuit over the Lake Chelan National Recreation Area. He also instigated this book. The historian was not bullied into it, but when Dave said, "We got to have a book," he was looking straight at nobody else. In the spring of 1992 he arranged for the invaluable research services of Kevin Herrick, who excavated from the archives innumerable facts and figures essential to fill gaps in the history. Drawing on six seasons as a Park Service ranger in Stehekin before becoming NCCC Special Projects Coordinator, Herrick provided valuable corrections and refinements in our portrait of that community as it exists today. Stephan Volker of Earthjustice, who knows plenty about the North Cascades, on the ground and in the courts of federal judges, provided a legal review. Jim McConnell, conceived in Stehekin, and for a time a student at the Stehekin School, and a property owner in the Valley, gave a critique embodying the Old Stehekin perspective and his own close observations of New Stehekin. The fourth, and incumbent, president, Marc Bardsley, got his basic training in the Conservation Division of the Mountaineers during the wild and whirling 1960s and help fire up the completion of the present edition of our history.

Books and periodicals have chanced our way during a fifty-year involvement. However, not a step has been taken nor a finger lifted to systematically prepare a bibliography that could stand muster before the tribunal of a doctoral inquisition. Indeed, this appendix is offered less for the benefit of scholars than to assure the lay reader it's not all made up out of whole cloth. (Scholars are referred to the North Cascades Collection at the University of Washington Library, established for their benefit and maintained by Karyl Winn when much of this book was being written.)

The method by which the history could be inserted into the stream of American consciousness was a puzzle for which no solution was readily seen, until Betty Manning volunteered to (1) accept into the Manning house an electronic device purchased by the NCCC; (2) learn how to use the infernal machine; and (3) take the cuneiform and runes produced by the historian's manual typewriter and Number 2 lead pencil and translate them into computer English.

Here, then, are some additional sources and further reading:

BOOKS

Adams, Nigel B. *The Holden Mine: Discovery to Production 1896-1938.* Tacoma: Washington State Historical Society, 1981.

Bartholomew, Mary Ellen. *Legislative History for North Cascades National Park Service Complex: 97th Congress through 100th Congress.* Seattle: Pacific Northwest Regional Office, NPS, 1990.

Bates, Malcom S. *Three Fingers: The Mountain, the Man, and a Lookout.* Seattle: Cloudcap Press, 1987.

Beckey, Fred. *Cascade Alpine Guide: Rainy Pass to Fraser River.* Seattle: The Mountaineers, 1981. CAG: Stevens Pass to Rainy Pass, 1977.

Beckey, Fred. *Challenge of the North Cascades.* The Mountaineers, 1969.

Beckey, Fred. *Range of Glaciers: The Exploration and Survey of the Northern Cascade Range.* Portland: Oregon Historical Society Press, 2003.

Berner, Richard C. *Seattle 1900-1920: From Boomtown, Urban Turbulence, to Restoration.* Seattle: Charles Press, 1991.

Beyond Words Writers. *Stehekin Community, Beyond Words, a collection of writings.* Stehekin: Beyond Words Writers, 1987.

Billington, Ray Allen. *Westward Expansion: A History of the American Frontier.* New York: Macmillan, second edition 1960.

Brant, Irving. *Adventures in Conservation with Franklin D. Roosevelt.* Flagstaff: Northland Publishing, 1988.

Brower, David. *For Earth's Sake: The Life and Times of David Brower.* Salt Lake City: Peregrine Smith Books, 1990.

Byrd, Robert. *Lake Chelan in the 1890s.* Wenatchee: World Publishing, 1972.

Collins, Janet R. "Jurisdictional and Boundary Changes of the North Cascades National Park Complex, 1891-1968." In *Pacific Northwest: Essays in Honor of James W. Scott.* Bellingham: Western Washington University, 1993.

Committee on Interior and Insular Affairs. *Compilation of Selected Acts Concerning National parks and Recreation and Related Matters.* Washington, D.C.: Committee on Interior and Insular Affairs, 99th Congress, First Session. 1985.

Cooley, Robert A. Wandesford-Smith, Geoffrey, editors. *Congress and the Environment.* Seattle: University of Washington Press, 1970. (Essays by Grant McConnell and Allan Sommarstrom)

Council on Environmental Quality. *The Taking Issue: A study of the constitutional limits of governmental authority to regulate the use of privately owned land without paying compensation to the owners.* Washington City, U.S. Government Printing Office, 1973.

Crowder, Dwight and Tabor, Rowland. *Routes and Rocks: Hikers Guide to the North Cascades from Glacier Peak to Lake Chelan.* Seattle: The Mountaineers, 1965.

Crowder, Dwight. *Hiker's Map to the Mount Challenger Quadrangle.* Seattle: The Mountaineers, 1969.

Dennis, Robert T., coordinator. *National Parks for the Future.* Washington D.C.: The Conservation Foundation, 1972.

De Voto, Bernard. *The Year of Decision 1846.* Boston: Houghton Mifflin, 1942.

Dilsaver, Lary M., and Tweed, William C. *Challenge of the Big Trees: A Resource History of Sequoia and King's Canyon National Parks.* Three Rivers: Sequoia Natural History Association, 1990?

Evans, Brock. *The Alpine Lakes*. Seattle: The Mountaineers, 1974.

Ervin, Keith. *Fragile Majesty: The Battle for North America's Last Great Forest*. Seattle: The Mountaineers, 1989.

Everhart, William C. *The National Park Service*. New York: Praeger, 1972.

Frank, Kathleen and Linda Rhines. *Legislative History for North Cascades National Park Service Complex: 86th through 96th Congress*. Seattle: Pacific Northwest Region Library, 1986.

Friedman, Mitch, editor. *Forever Wild: Conserving the Greater North Cascades Ecosystem*. Bellingham: Greater Ecosystem Alliance, 1988.

Friedman, Mitch and Lindhardt, Paul, editors. *Cascadia Wild: Protecting an International Ecosystem*. Bellingham: Greater Ecosystem Alliance, 1993.

Frome, Michael. *The Forest Service*. Boulder, Colorado: Westview Press, second edition 1984.

Frome, Michael. *Regreening the National Parks*. Tucson: University of Arizona Press, 1992.

Georgette, Susan E., and Harvey, Ann H. *Local Influence and the National Interest: Ten Years of National Park Service Administration in the Stehekin Valley, Washington, A Case Study. Publication No. 4, Environmental Field Program*. Santa Cruz: University of California, 1980.

Hartzog, George. *Battling for the National Parks*. Moyer-Bell Limited, 1988.

Harvey, Mark W. T. *Wilderness Forever: Howard Zahniser and the Path to the Wilderness Act*. Seattle: University of Washington Press, 2005.

Helvarg, David. *War Against the Greens: The "Wise Use" Movement, The New Right, and Anti-Environmental Violence*. San Francisco: Sierra Club Books, 1996.

Hibbard, Benjamin H. *A History of the Public Land Policies*. Madison and Milwaukee: The University of Wisconsin Press, 1965.

Hines, Rev. H.K. *An Illustrated History of the State of Washington*. Chicago: Lewis Publishing Co., 1983.

Hodges, Lawrence K. *Mining in the Pacific Northwest*. Seattle: Seattle Post-Intelligencer 1897. (Facsimile edition, Shorey's Bookstore, Seattle)

Jenkins, Will D. *Last Frontier in the North Cascades: Tales of the Wild Upper Skagit*. Mt Vernon: Skagit County Historical Society, 1984.

Jensen, Derrick, George Draffan and John Osborn. *Railroads and Clearcuts: Legacy of Congress's 1864 Northern Pacific Railroad Land Grant*. Spokane: Inland Empire Public Lands Council, 1995.

Kresek, Ray. *Fire Lookouts of the Northwest*. Fairfield, Washington: Ye Galleon Press, 1984.

Lien, Carsten. *Olympic Battleground*. San Francisco: Sierra Club, 1991; revised edition, Seattle: The Mountaineers, 2000.

Louter, David. *Contested Terrain: North Cascades National Park Complex, An Adminstrative History*. Seattle: National Park Service, 1998.

Louter, David. *Windshield Wilderness: Cars, Roads, and Nature in Washington's National Parks*. Seattle: University of Washington Press, 2006.

Luxenburg, Gretchen A. *Historic Resources Study: North Cascades National Park Complex, Washington*. Seattle: Pacific Northwest Region, National Park Service, Department of the Interior, 1986.

Manning, Harvey. *The Wild Cascades: Forgotten Parkland*. San Francisco: Sierra Club, 1965. Sierra Club-Ballantine edition, 1969.

Manning, Harvey, Tom Miller, photographer. *The North Cascades*. Seattle: The Mountaineers, 1964.

Manning, Harvey, Ira Spring, photographer. *The North Cascades National Park*. Seattle: Superior, 1969.

Manning, Harvey, Ira Spring, photographer. *The National Parks of the Northwest*. Seattle: Superior, 1976.

Manning, Harvey, Pat O'Hara, photographer. *Washington Wilderness: The Unfinished Work*. Seattle: The Mountaineers, 1984.

Mantell, Michael A., editor. *Managing National Park System Resources: A Handbook on Legal Duties, Opportunities and Tools*. Washington, D.C.: The Conservation Foundation, 1990.

Majors, Harry M. *North Cascades Archival Resources in Washington State Repositories*. Seattle: University of Washington Library, 1974.

McConnell, Grant. *Private Power and American Democracy*. New York: Alfred A. Knopf, 1966. Vintage edition, 1970.

McConnell, Grant. *Stehekin: A Valley in Time*. Seattle: The Mountaineers, 1988.

McConnell, Grant. *Conservation and Politics in the North Cascades*. Sierra Club Oral History Project. Sierra Club History Committee. San Francisco, 1983.

McCloskey, J. Michael, *In the Thick of It: My Life in the Sierra Club*. Washington, D.C.: Shearwater Books, 2005.

McCloskey, J. Michael, editor. *Prospectus for a North Cascades National Park*. Seattle: North Cascades Conservation Council, 1963.

McKee, Bates, *Cascadia: The Geologic Evolution of the Pacific Northwest*. New York: McGraw-Hill, 1972.

McPhee, John. *Encounters with the Archdruid*. New York: Farrar, Strauss, and Giroux, 1971.

Meany, Edmund. *Mount Rainier: A Record of Exploration*. New York: Macmillan Company, 1916.

Mierendorf, Robert R. *People of the North Cascades*. Seattle: North Cascades National Park Service Complex, Cultural Resources Division, Pacific Northwest Region, 1986.

Mierendorf, Robert, David Harry and Gregg Sullivan. *An Archeological Site Survey and Evaluatin in the Upper Skagit River Valley, Whatcom County, Washington. Technical Report NPS/CCCNOCA/CRTR-98/01*. Sedro Woolley, Washingon, National Park Service, 1998.

Miles, John C. *Impressions of the North Cascades: Essays About a Northwest Landscape*. Seattle: The Mountaineers, 1996.

Molenaar, Dee. *The Challenge of Rainier*. Seattle: The Mountaineers, 1971.

National Geographic Society. *The New America's Wonderlands: Our National Parks*. Washington, D.C.: National Geographic Society, 1980.

National Geographic Society. *Wilderness USA*. Washington,D.C.: National Geographic Society, 1973. (Essays by Harvey Manning)

National Geographic Society. *A Guide to Our Federal Lands*. Washington, D.C.: National Geographic Society, 1984.

National Park Service. *Management Policies*. Washington, D.C.: National Park Service, 2001.

Northwest Underground Explorations. *Discovering Washington's Historic Mines, Volume 12, West Central Cascade Mountains*. Arlington: Oso Publishing, 1999.

USGS? "On Batholiths and Vulcanism," *U.S. Geological Paper No. 604*. Washington D.C. 1969.

Peattie, Roderick, editor. *The Cascades: Mountains of the Pacific Northwest*. New York: Vanguard Press, 1949. (Essays by Charles D. Hessey, Grant McConnell, etc.)

Pitzer, Paul C. *Building the Skagit: A Century of Upper Skagit Valley History, 1870-1970*. Portland: The Galley Press, 1978.

Poehlman, Elizabeth S. *Darrington: Mining Town/Timber Town*. Kent: Gold Hill Press, 1979.

Roe, JoAnn, *The North Cascadians*. Seattle: Madrona Publishers, 1980.

Ruby, Robert H. and John A. Brown. *A Guide to the Indian Tribes of the Pacific Northwest*. Norman: University of Oklahoma Press, 1986.

Ruby, Robert H. and John A. Brown. *Half-Sun on the Columbia; A Biography of Chief Moses*. Norman: University of Oklahoma Press, 1963.

Runte, Alfred. *Yosemite: The Embattled Wilderness*. Lincoln: University of Nebraska Press, 1990.

Scherrer, Wendy. *Teaching for Wilderness*. Sedro Woolley: North Cascades Institute, 1991.

Schmoe, Floyd. *Our Greatest Mountain: A handbook for Mount Rainier National Park*. New York: G.B. Putnam's Sons, 1925.

Scott, Doug. *The Enduring Wilderness: Protecting Our National Heritage Through the Wilderness Act*. Golden: Fulcrum Publishing, 2004.

Simons, David R. *The Need for Scenic Resource Conservation in the Northern Cascades of Washington*. Sierra Club Conservation Committee, Northern Cascades Subcommittee. San Francisco: 1958.

Spring, Ira and Harvey Manning. *One Hundred Classic Hikes in Washington*. Seattle: The Mountaineers, 1998.

Spring, Ira and Harvey Manning. *One Hundred Hikes in the North Cascades National Park Region*. Seattle: The Mountaineers, third edition, 2000.

Spring, Ira and Harvey Manning. *One Hundred Hikes in Washington's North Cascades: Glacier Peak Region*. Seattle: The Mountaineers, fourth edition, 1994.

Stevens, Anna Greene. *My Life in the West*. La Jolla: 1960.

Stone, Carol M. *Stehekin, Glimpses of the Past*. Friday Harbor, WA: Long House, 1983.

Sunset Books. *National Parks of the West*. Menlo Park: Lane, 1965.

Tabor, Rowland and Ralph Haugerud. *Geology of the North Cascades: A Mountain Mosaic*. Seattle: The Mountaineers, 1999.

Thompson, Erwin N. *North Cascades National Park, Ross Lake N.R.A., and Lake Chelan N.R.A., History Basic Data*. Washington, D.C.: U.S. Department of the Interior, National Park Service, 1970.

Udall, Stewart L. *The National Parks of America*. New York: G.P Putnam's Sons, 1966.

Udall, Stewart L. *The Quiet Crisis*. New York: Holt Rinehart Winston, 1963.

U.S. Government. *North Cascades Study Team Report*. Washington, D.C.: 1965.

U.S. Government. *Senate and House Interior Committee Hearing Records, North Cascades-Olympic National Park, 1966-1968*.

Verne, Jules. *The Begum's Fortune, the Fitzroy edition*, edited by I.O. Evans. London: An Ace Book from Arco Publications, 1958.

Washington State Planning Council. *Cascade Mountains Study*. Olympia: Washington State Planning Council 1940.

Weisberg, Saul and Rindel, John. *From the Mountains to the Sea: A Guide to the Skagit River Watershed*. Sedro Woolley: North Cascades Institute, 1991.

Whitesell, Edward A., editor. *Defending Wild Washington: A Citizen's Action Guide*. Seattle: The Mountaineers, 2004.

Williams, John. *The Mountain That Was God*. Tacoma: Author Published, 1910.

Winthrop, Theodore. *The Canoe and the Saddle, Adventures Among the Northwestern Rivers and Forests and Isthmiana*. Boston: Ticknor and Fields, 1865.

Wollcott, Ernest. *Lakes of Washington, Vol I,II, 3rd. ed.* Olympia: Washington Department of Ecology, 1973.

Wood, Robert L. *Trail Country: Olympic National Park*. Seattle: The Mountaineers, 1968.

PERIODICALS

Amicus Journal. Hennelly, Robert, "Getting Wise to the Wise Use Guys." Fall 1992.

Backpacker Magazine. Manning, Harvey, "Elders of the Tribe: Dave Simons." New York: Spring 1975.

Conservation Biology. Noss, Reed F., "Sustainability and Wilderness." March, 1991.

Forest Watch. Fluharty, David, "The North Cascades — Has Park Service Management Met Preservationist Goals?" January-February, 1988

Harper's Magazine. Dillard, Annie, "A Trip to the Mountains." New York: August, 1991.

Inner Voice. Eugene, OR: Association of Forest Service Employees for Environmental Ethics (AFSEEE). Published since 1989.

The Mountaineer. Monthly Bulletin (consulted) 1947-1991. Seattle: The Mountaineers.

The Mountaineers Annual, a number of articles used, including:

Osseward, John. "Land Laws and Land Usage in Washington State." Vol. 54, No. 4, March 1, 1961.

Coleman, Winifred S. "Exploratory Expeditions Through North Cascades." Volume 57, No. 4, March 15, 1964.

Chriswell, H.C. "Historical Sketch — Mt. Baker National Forest." same

Manning, Harvey. "Stehekin Mines of Olden Days." same

Goldsworthy, Patrick D. "Washington's Golden Triangle of National Parks." Vol. 59, No. 4, March 15, 1966.

Manning, Harvey. "This Land Is Your Land." same

Long, William G. Jr. "Conservation Minutes." same

National Geographic. Edwards, Paul, "Washington Wilderness, the North Cascades." Washington, D.C.: March 1961.

Northwest Conservation. Bellingham: Greater North Cascades Ecosystem Alliance.

Northwest Discovery. Majors, Harry, editor. Seattle: Northwest Press.

Custer, Henry. "First Crossing of the Picket Range, 1859." Vol. 5, No. 22, May, 1984.

Custer, Henry. "Discovery of Mount Shuksan and the Upper Nooksack River, June, 1859." Vol. 5, No. 21, February, 1984.

Hodges, Lawrence K. "How a Prospector Lives." Vol. 1, No. 4, October, 1980.

Lindsley, D.C. "Railroad Survey of the Sauk and Wenatchee Rivers in 1870." Vol. 2, No. 4, April, 1981.

Pierce, Henry H. "An Army Expedition Across the North Cascades in August 1882." Vol. 3, No. 1, May, 1982.

Seattle Times, January 14, 1906, March 16, 1969. Julian Itter in the North Cascades.

Sierra Club Bulletin. Monthly and annual. San Francisco: Sierra Club.

Largely overlapping The Mountaineer of the time and therefore not exhaustively consulted but a number of articles used, including:

Albright, Horace M. "Highest Use VS Multiple Use." April-May, 1960.

Brower, David R. "Golden Triangle of National Parks Proposal." January, 1966.

McCloskey, J. Michael. "A North Cascades National Park." October, 1963.

Ulrichs, Herman F. "The Cascades Range in Northern Washington." February, 1937.

Sunset Magazine. "Our Wilderness Alps." Menlo Park: Lane, June, 1965.

Stehekin Choice. Stehekin: published irregularly since 1991.

Transitions. Osborn, John, coordinator, "Reportage In Search of Sustainable Forests and Diversified Economies in America's Northwest." Spokane: Inland Empire Public Lands Council, published 12 times a year since 1983. The definitive on-going reprinting of newspaper and magazine and book coverage of Northwest forests.

Unattributed: "A Profile of Burlington Northern, Burlington Resources, and the Plum Creek Timber Company." June, 1990.

Washington Earth First! Published sporadically, usually with no return address.

Washington Wildfire. Seattle: Washington Wilderness Coalition. Published some six times a year.

The Wild Cascades (N3C News). Seattle: The North Cascades Conservation Council. Published since 1957, first monthly, then bimonthly, then quarterly, then very occasionally until regular publication resumed in the summer of 1991. Now published three or four times a year.

OTHER

Newspapers: Seattle, Portland, Wenatchee, Chelan, Bellingham, San Francisco, New York City; masses of clippings.

Private and public correspondence; stacks and stacks and stacks.

National Park Service and U.S. Forest Service publications; many.

North Cascades Glacier Climate Project. Dr. Mauri S. Pelto, Director, Nichols College, Dudley, MA.

FILMS

Glacier Peak Holiday, 1960. Charles Hessey Jr. North Cascades Conservation Council.

Lassie Come Home, 1943. A North Cascades Conservation Council member (as she later became) was summering at Stehekin when the movie was made. Roddy McDowall was, in person as well as on screen, a very nice little boy. Elizabeth Taylor was a beautiful little girl on screen, a pain in the neck off. A number of Stehekin-area scenes are mingled confusingly with scenes in California. The high point of the film is Lassie swimming the Stehekin River, apparently in the vicinity of the old "Swayback Bridge." No stunt double, that's the actual star herself (actually, himself) dog-paddling through the white water.

Monumental: David Brower's Fight for Wild America, 2004. Loteria Films

Wilderness Alps of the Stehekin, 1958. Sierra Club, by David Brower.

Wind in the Wilderness, 1965. KING-TV, Seattle.

454 • WILDERNESS ALPS

CASELAW

Treaty with Canada relating to the Skagit River and Ross Lake in the State of Washington, and the Seven Mile Reservoir on the Pend D'Oreille River in the Province of British Columbia, and creating the Skagit Environmental Endowment Commission. Treaty Document 98-26 (1984).

North Cascades Conservation Council v. Manuel Lujan, Secretary of the U.S. Department of the Interior, et al., U.S. District Court (W.D. Wash.) No. C-89-1342D. Consent Decree requiring National Park Service to prepare an Environmental Impact Statement for the Lake Chelan NRA General Management Plan and to address specific concerns relating to land exchanges, firewood collection, sand and gravel extraction, transportation, wilderness protection, and other matters (1991).

Northwest Motorcycle Association v. USDA, 18 F.3d 1468 (9th Cir. 1994), upholding exclusion of off-road vehicles (ORVs) from Pyramid Mountain and North Fork Entiat area of proposed addition to Glacier Peak Wilderness, Wenatchee National Forest; also provides judicial guidance on use conflict caused by ORVs.

Washington Trails Association v. U.S. Forest Service, 935 F. Supp. 1117 (W.D. Wash. 1996), enjoining ORV construction project on Juniper Ridge and Langille Ridge in proposed Dark Divide Wilderness, Gifford Pinchot National Forest.

North Cascades Conservation Council v. U.S. Forest Service, 98 F. Supp. 2d 1193 (W.D. Wash. 1999), enjoining Goose-Maverick ORV construction project in Mad River area of proposed addition to Glacier Peak Wilderness, Wenatchee National Forest.

Northwest Motorcycle Association v. State of Washington, 127 Wn. App. 408 (2005), upholding constitutionality of recreation funding program (NOVA) administered by the State's Interagency Committee for Outdoor Recreation (IAC).

The Mountaineers v. U.S. Forest Service, 445 F.Supp. 2d 1235 (W.D. Wash. 2006), enjoining Mad River ORV construction project in proposed addition to Glacier Peak Wilderness, Wenatchee National Forest.

WEBSITES

www.northcascades.org - North Cascades Conservation Council (NCCC)

www.wildwashington.org - Wild Washington Campaign

www.wilderness.net - Wilderness Net (research)

www.nps.gov/noca - North Cascades National Park Complex (NOCA)

www.fs.fed.us/r6/mbs - Mount Baker-Snoqualmie National Forest (MBS)

www.ncascades.org - North Cascades Institute (NCI)

www.mountaineers.org - The Mountaineers

www.federationofwesternoutdoorclubs.org - Federation of Western Outdoor Clubs (FWOC)

www.cascade.sierraclub.org - Cascade Chapter Sierra Club

www.wildernesswatch.org - Wilderness Watch

www.wilderness.org - The Wilderness Society (TWS)

www.npca.org - National Parks Conservation Association (NPCA)

www.bearinfo.org - Grizly Bear Outreach Project (GBOP)

www.skagiteec.org - Skagit Environmental Endowment Commission

CHRONOLOGY OF EVENTS IN THE NORTH CASCADES

9,000+ years ago - Archaeological evidence of Native American presence in the North Cascades dates back more than 9,000 years, and continues today.

1790 - During an official Spanish expedition with Manuel Quimper, Spanish pilot López de Haro sketches a chart in which the North Cascades are labeled "Sierra Nevadas de S. Antonio." Mount Baker is called "La Gran Montaña del Carmelo."

1792 - Captain George Vancouver and his flagship Discovery sail into the Gulf of Georgia, naming dozens of islands and waterways, as well as the highest summit in the North Cascades, Mount Baker, for the ship's officer who sighted it.

1814 - Fur-trader Alexander Ross and his "Project of Discovery" make the first recorded crossing of the range, from Fort Okanogan to the Skagit River.

1826 - The name "Cascades" is credited to British botanist David Douglas, referring either to the cascading streams found throughout these mountains, or to a steep drop in the Columbia River also known as The Cascades.

1853 - Captain George McClellan leads a Northern Pacific Survey team in search of a railroad route through the Cascades. They explore mountain passes from the Columbia River to Canada and skirt the south shore of Lake Chelan.

1858–62 - American and Canadian teams conduct the Northwest Boundary Survey, erecting monuments along the border. The leader of the U.S. team, Henry Custer, is the first European to travel the interior of the North Cascades. The survey is repeated in 1901-08.

1864 - Congress establishes Yosemite Park, transferring Yosemite Valley and the Mariposa Grove of Big Trees (giant sequoias) to the state of California. The area becomes a national park in 1890.

August 17, 1868 - Edmund T. Coleman and three others achieve the first recorded ascent of Mount Baker.

July 14, 1870 - Exploring for the Northern Pacific, D.C. Linsley and John A. Tennant ascend the Suiattle River and Sulphur Creek to the Cascade Crest near Glacier Peak, and are the first Europeans to reach the head of Lake Chelan from the west.

March 1, 1872 - Congress establishes Yellowstone National Park, the nation's first.

1872 - The General Mining Law of 1872 is passed by Congress. Many of its obsolete provisions remain in effect today.

1880s - Millions of acres of what would soon become Washington State are handed over to the railroads.

1889 - The Rouses and Gilbert Landre stake claims at Horseshoe Basin and Doubtful Lake. The *Belle of Chelan* begins passenger steamboat service on Lake Chelan to Stehekin.

September 25, 1890 - In California, Sequoia is named America's second national park.

October 1, 1890 - The nation's third and fourth national parks, Yosemite and General Grant, are established (the latter would be incorporated into Kings Canyon National Park in 1940).

March 3, 1891 - The Forest Reserve Act, passed by Congress as a rider to another bill, is signed by President Harrison.

1892 - The *Chelan Falls Leader* reports on the first proposal for a Lake Chelan National Park.

May 28, 1892 - John Muir forms the Sierra Club "to make the mountains glad."

1893 - President Grover Cleveland sets aside the Pacific Forest Reserve centered on Mount Rainier.

1893 - The Washington Legislature approves the new state's first highway appropriation: $20,000 for a road across the North Cascades.

1893 - The Chelan Water and Power Company dams the outlet of Lake Chelan, raising the level several feet, but a flood the next year destroys the dam.

February 22, 1897 - President Cleveland proclaims forest reserves in seven states totaling 21,174,960 acres, the largest single set-aside in the nation's history. Three are in Washington: the Olympic, Rainier (encompassing the former Pacific Reserve), and the 3.6 million acre Washington Forest Reserve (in the North Cascades).

1897 - Gifford Pinchot visits the North Cascades, becoming one of the first to climb Columbia Peak near the mining town of Monte Cristo.

1897 - The Lone Jack claim near Twin Lakes triggers a brief Mount Baker gold rush.

1890s - President William McKinley adds only seven million acres of forest reserves, while removing 750,000 acres from the Olympic Reserve to accommodate logging.

March 2, 1899 - Mount Rainier National Park, the nation's fifth, is established.

1902 - The General Land Office inventories Stehekin and finds a hotel, post office, schoolhouse, three residences, and two barns.

May 22, 1902 - Oregon's Crater Lake National Park is created, encompassing 180,000 acres.

July 1, 1905 - The Interior Department's Division of Forestry (under Pinchot) is moved to Agriculture. Pinchot renames it the United States Forest Service and appoints himself Chief Forester.

March 10, 1906 - Mazamas of Portland (founded in 1894) visit Stehekin. In Chelan, the club adopts a resolution calling for "a national park and perpetual game preserve." Five days later, opponents meet to adopt their own resolution condemning the Mazama proposal.

June 1906 - Congress passes the Antiquities Act which allows the president to proclaim "objects of historic and scientific interest" on federal lands as "national monuments." Three months later, President Theodore Roosevelt proclaims Devils Tower in Wyoming as the nation's first national monument.

March 1907 - The forest reserves are renamed "national forests."

1908 - President Theodore Roosevelt designates 800,000 acres of the Grand Canyon as a national monument. It becomes a national park in 1919.

1908 - The first timber sales are held in the North Cascades region, mainly in response to local requests for fence posts and shake and shingle bolts.

March 2, 1909 - Two days before the end of his term, President Theodore Roosevelt proclaims a 615,000-acre Mount Olympus National Monument.

1909 - A railroad is completed to the town of Glacier near Mount Baker and large-scale logging begins in the upper North Fork Nooksack valley.

May 11, 1910 - Glacier National Park in Montana is established.

January 26, 1915 - Rocky Mountain National Park in Colorado is established.

1915 - Mount Baker Club in Bellingham gets a bill introduced in Congress for a national park centered on Mount Baker. They are confident the bill will pass.

August 9, 1916 - Lassen National Park in California is established.

August 25, 1916 - Congress passes the National Park Act, creating the National Park Service with Stephen Mather as Director.

February 26, 1917 - Mount McKinley National Park in Alaska is established.

1917 - A fire lookout cabin replaces a tent atop Sourdough Mountain and is thought to be the first in the nation. By the 1930s Mount Baker National Forest will have forty-three lookouts.

August 1917 - Mary Rineharts' story of her famous pack trip over Cascade Pass appears in *Cosmopolitan*.

February 26, 1919 - Grand Canyon National Park in Arizona is established.

November 19, 1919 - Zion National Park in Utah is established.

1922 - A twenty-year contract on 5,800 acres of the Sauk and White Chuck valleys near Glacier Peak is awarded to the Sauk River Lumber Company.

1923 - National Park Service Director Stephen Mather flatly opposes parks centered on Mount Baker, Mount Adams, and Mount Olympus, arguing that Mount Rainier is enough.

January 1924 - Although large portions of Washington National Forest have been spun off into other national forests (Chelan, Okanagan, Wenatchee, Snoqualmie, and Rainier), the remainder is renamed Mount Baker National Forest.

September 1924 - The Skagit River's first dam and powerhouse are completed. Gorge Dam is originally built from wood by Seattle City Light, later replaced by a concrete structure.

1926 - Secretary of Agriculture William M. Jardine designates 74,859 acres around Mount Baker for recreational use (logging and mining are also allowed). The area is first referred to as the Mount Baker Park Division, later changed to Mount Baker Recreation Area.

1926 - The Forest Service establishes a Mount Baker Game Preserve of 188,000 acres and an Upper Skagit Game Preserve of 74,000 acres.

1926 - The impressive new Mount Baker Lodge is dedicated, but burns to the ground five years later.

1926 - The Glacier Peak Association is formed to advocate for the area's protection.

1927 - The Mount Baker Highway is completed to Heather Meadows, mirroring the Park Service highway to Mount Rainier's Paradise Meadows.

1927 - Construction of a new dam raises Lake Chelan twenty-one feet, inundating thousands of acres, including the broad delta of the Stehekin River.

1929 - At the urging of Aldo Leopold and others, the Forest Service issues Regulation L-20, providing for the designation of "primitive areas" that are "to be kept in as near a natural and primitive condition as is physically and economically possible." L-20 offers a form of administrative wilderness protection where roads are prohibited and other interests of the public are served, including education, research, and recreation.

August 1930 - Seattle City Light's Diablo Dam is completed on the Skagit River just upstream of Gorge Dam. At 389 feet, it is for a short time the highest in the world.

1931 - Forest Service establishes a Glacier Peak–Cascades Recreation Unit of 233,600 acres, but it does not preclude logging, mining, or grazing.

1931 - A 172,800-acre Whatcom Primitive Area is established, the eighth such tract in the national forests.

1935 - The Wilderness Society is founded by Bob Marshall and others.

1935 - The Whatcom Primitive Area is expanded to 800,000 acres and renamed the North Cascade Primitive Area.

1936 - A Glacier Peak "Wilderness Area" is announced by the Regional Forester, but a month later it is mysteriously withdrawn.

August 18–September 11, 1937 - National Park Service field teams scout 250 miles of Washington's Cascades from Mount Saint Helens to the Canadian border, resulting in a proposal for Ice Peaks National Park (which is soon forgotten).

June 29, 1938 - President Franklin Roosevelt approves the creation of Olympic National Park, replacing the 1909 monument.

1939 - Bob Marshall proposes a 795,000-acre Glacier Peak Wilderness Area reaching from Lake Wenatchee to Ruby Creek.

1939 - The "L" Regulations of 1929 that addressed "primitive areas" are replaced by the "U" Regulations, drafted by Bob Marshall, which allow the Forest Service to designate "roadless," "wild," and "wilderness" areas. In the 1950s–1960s the designation of such areas give way to the notion of multiple-use (and abuse) which is formally legislated by Congress at the end of 1960.

1940 - The Forest Service designates a Glacier Peak Limited Area of 352,000 acres, of which 233,600 acres had comprised the old Glacier Peak–Cascades Recreation Unit.

1940 - Seattle City Light completes the first phase of Ross Dam, the largest on the Skagit River. After a phase three addition in 1949, the dam reaches its current height of 540 feet. The 24-mile inundation reaches into Canada.

March 4, 1940 - A 454,000-acre Kings Canyon National Park is established.

1942 - Olympic National Park is quietly opened to commercial "salvage" logging. The cutting continues for more than a decade as thousands of truckloads of old-growth timber are removed from the park.

June 12, 1944 - A 700,000-acre Big Bend National Park is established.

1945 - Jane McConnell acquires a cabin at the foot of SiSi Ridge for herself and husband Grant.

December 6, 1947 - A 460,000-acre Everglades National Park is established. The park is significantly expanded in 1950, 1958, and 1989 to its current 1.5 million acres.

1948 - Olympic Park Associates (OPA) is formed to "save the park from the Park Service."

September 14, 1950 - President Truman approves a new 310,000-acre Grand Teton National Park that incorporates a smaller preexisting park and national monument.

April 1951 - The Sierra Club's First Biennial Wilderness Conference is held in Portland.

1952 - Dave Brower is appointed first executive director of the Sierra Club.

1952–53 - Gary Snyder serves as a fire lookout atop Crater and Sourdough Mountains. He introduces the area to fellow poet Philip Whalen who is hired to man the cabin on the summit of Sauk Mountain in 1953, then Sourdough in 1954–55. Their friend, Jack Kerouac, also applies and is stationed at Desolation Peak in 1956.

1953 - The annual timber cut from Olympic National Park reaches 14.6 million board feet.

1954 - The Pacific Northwest Chapter of the Sierra Club is formed in Seattle by Patrick and Jane Goldsworthy, John and Polly Dyer, Dave Brower, and others.

April 7–8, 1956 - The First Biennial *Northwest* Wilderness Conference is held in Portland, chaired by Leo Gallagher. The Wilderness Society's Howard Zahniser unveils his draft legislation for a Wilderness Act.

Fall 1956 - Grant McConnell introduces the Stehekin area, via slides, to Dave Brower in Berkeley.

March 23, 1957 - The North Cascades Conservation Council is created at the Mazama clubroom in Portland to "protect and preserve the North Cascades' scenic, scientific, recreational, educational, wildlife and wilderness values."

1957 - NCCC begins a major effort to establish a Glacier Peak Wilderness.

Summer 1957 - Volume 1, Number 1 of the North Cascades Conservation Council's *NCCC News* is published.

July 1, 1957 - The Holden Mine above Lake Chelan closes.

1957 - A large swath of public forest at Stehekin is bulldozed for an "emergency airstrip."

March 1958 - David Brower's film, *Wilderness Alps of Stehekin*, premiers at the second biennial Northwest Wilderness Conference in Seattle.

June 4, 1958 - Dave Simons' "The Need for Scenic Resource Conservation in the Northern Cascades of Washington" is published.

Summer 1958 - U.S. Supreme Court Justice William O. Douglas leads a famous hike along the Olympic Coast beach to protest plans for a new highway. The hike is organized by Polly Dyer and Howard Zahniser.

August 1958 - *Sunset Magazine* publishes a major article on the North Cascades.

August 23-26, 1958 - The Council of The Wilderness Society gathers in Stehekin for their 30th annual meeting. The four-day conference is attended by 92 representatives of regional and national conservation organizations.

February 1959 - The Region Six office of the Forest Service releases its proposal for a Glacier Peak wilderness area encompassing 422,925 acres, far less than Bob Marshall had proposed twenty years before; public testimony at hearings is highly critical.

June 4, 1959 - The Mountaineers endorse a national park in the North Cascades.

October 1959 - The *Sierra Club Bulletin* publishes Dave Simons' essay, "These Are the Shining Mountains," a proposal for a Cascade Volcanic National Park in Oregon.

January 3, 1960 - The *New York Times* carries a column by John Oakes, editorial page editor, in support of conservationists' proposal for a Glacier Peak Wilderness.

January 6, 1960 - Congressman Tom Pelly (R) introduces H.R. 9360, and Congressman Don Magnuson (D) introduces H.R. 9342 in the House of Representatives calling for the Secretary of the Interior "to investigate and report to Congress on the advisability of establishing a national park or other unit of the national park system in the central and North Cascades."

February 4, 1960 - Senator Warren G. Magnuson (D) introduces S. 2980 in the Senate, essentially restating the Pelly-Magnuson bills.

1960 - The King County Republican convention passes a resolution to "commend and heartily support the proposal by Congressman Pelly for a study of the Northern Cascade Mountains by the National Park Service."

1960 - NCCC proposes to the U.S. Forest Service that the northeastern portion of the North Cascades be designated as wilderness. Under the 1968 North Cascades Act, the area is designated as the Pasayten Wilderness.

September 1960 - Agriculture Secretary Ezra Taft Benson overrules the Region Six Forester and the Chief of the Forest Service, adding 35,580 acres in the designation of a 458,505-acre Glacier Peak Wilderness Area.

December 1960 - Congress passes the Multiple-Use Sustained-Yield Act. Its provisions are similar to the 1897 Organic Act that created the forest reserves.

1961 - High Gorge Dam is completed, replacing the old dam near Newhalem.

1961 - J. Michael McCloskey is recruited by Dave Brower to serve as the first Northwest Representative of the Sierra Club in Seattle, primarily reporting to the NCCC.

May 1961 - The *NCCC News* is renamed *The Wild Cascades*.

1961 - Washington State officially designates North Cross-State Highway No. 20. Rainy Pass is rated "the most desirable" route. Construction is authorized in December 1962. NCCC had preferred a less damaging route over Harts Pass where, due to the existing mine road to Chancellor, it would intrude on only six miles of pristine wilderness rather than forty-one.

1961 - On a visit to Mount Rainier, Stuart Udall confides to Patrick Goldsworthy that there will be a North Cascades National Park.

1962 - NCCC launches its wilderness campaign for Cougar Lakes, which under the 1984 Washington Wilderness Act would become the William O. Douglas and Norse Peak Wilderness Areas.

March 5, 1963 - The Bureau of Outdoor Recreation announces a North Cascades Study Team to be comprised of the rival Departments of Interior and Agriculture.

Spring 1963 - A *North Cascades National Park Prospectus* is drafted by Mike McCloskey for NCCC detailing a proposed national park in the North Cascades.

1963 - Conservationists develop a proposal to establish an Alpine Lakes Wilderness Area.

October 7, 1963 - Field hearings are held by the North Cascades Study Team in Wenatchee, Mount Vernon, and Seattle. Most public comment strongly favors a park.

1964 - A new exhibit-format book, *The North Cascades*, is published by The Mountaineers.

1964 - *The Wind in the Wilderness* is aired on local television stations in Seattle, Portland, and Spokane. Produced by Bob Schulman for King-TV (company president, Stimson Bullitt, was an NCCC member), the film highlighted Glacier Peak Wilderness.

1964 - A disappointing 258,000-acre Canyonlands National Park is established in a remote area of southern Utah where a much larger park was warranted.

September 3, 1964 - The Wilderness Act of 1964 is signed into law by President Johnson, permanently designating 54 wilderness areas, including Glacier Peak, Bob Marshall, Selway-Bitterroot, Boundary Waters, Gila, and John Muir Wilderness Areas, among others.

February 1965 - The Forest Service designates a 533,460-acre Eldorado Peaks High Country Recreation Area, an administrative maneuver offering little protection.

Spring 1965 - Walt Woodward, roving columnist for the *Seattle Times*, writes a series of seventeen articles in twenty-three days on the North Cascades national park debate.

June 1965 - The Sierra Club publishes a new exhibit-format book, *The Wild Cascades: Forgotten Parkland*, the 11th in a series. Much of Brower's narrative from the film, *Wilderness Alps of Stehekin*, is included.

June 1965 - *Sunset Magazine* publishes a 14-page cover story, "Our Wilderness Alps," suggesting that the North Cascades may become America's next national park.

1965 - The Mountaineers publishes *Routes and Rocks: Hikers Guide to the North Cascades from Glacier Peak to Lake Chelan.*

January 6, 1966 - Senators Jackson (D) and Magnuson (D) and Edward C. Crafts, Study Team Chairman, host the release of *The North Cascades Study Report.*

February 11–12, 1966 - Hearings are held in Seattle before the Senate Committee on Interior and Insular Affairs, with Senator Jackson presiding. The published record bore the title, *North Cascades–Olympic National Park,* reflecting Jackson's continuing interest in joining potential creation of a North Cascades National Park with the removal of old-growth forest acreage from Olympic National Park.

March 4, 1966 - Governor Dan Evans (R) convenes a 16-member committee to prepare a Governor's Plan for the North Cascades.

1966 - Kennecott Copper Company announces plans to develop an open-pit copper mine near Image Lake within the Glacier Peak Wilderness Area. A concentrator is planned for the upper Suiattle River valley. NCCC spearheads the opposition and Brock Evans organizes a major protest near the site in 1967. Supreme Court Justice William O. Douglas addresses the crowd in support of the protest. The company ultimately cancels its plans.

January 30, 1967 - President Lyndon Johnson asks Congress to establish four new national parks, including one in the North Cascades.

March 20, 1967 - S. 1321 is introduced in the 90th Congress by Jackson and Magnuson at the request of the White House. Lloyd Meeds (D) introduces in the House an identical H.B. 8970. The park is only half the size of that proposed by NCCC.

April 24–25, 1967 - Hearings on the North Cascades Senate bill are held in Washington, D.C.

May 25–29, 1967 - Field hearings on the North Cascades bill are held in Seattle, Mount Vernon, and Wenatchee.

October 25, 1967 - Amended S. 1321 is reported by the Interior Committee to the floor of the Senate and is easily passed on November 2nd.

August 7 1967 - Congressman Pelly introduces H.R. 12139, mirroring the 1963 NCCC proposal.

1967 - Congresswoman Catherine Mays (R) introduces on behalf of Governor Evans H.R. 16252, the State of Washington's official national park proposal, drawn up by John Biggs.

1967 - Brock Evans is named the Sierra Club's Northwest Representative.

April 19–20, 1968 - A hearing on H.B. 8970 and related bills is held in Seattle by the sub-committee on National Parks and Recreation of the Committee on Interior and Insular Affairs of the House of Representatives. Similar hearings are also held in Wenatchee (July 13) and Washington D.C. (July 25–26).

1968 - Seattle City Light conducts its field survey work for High Ross Dam; NCCC takes note and begins a vigorous campaign against the utility's proposal to raise the existing dam by 125 feet.

1968 - Governor Evans leads a caravan of four-wheel-drive vehicles along the length of the North Cascades pilot road, culminating in "the historic meeting of the jeeps" at Rainy Pass. Evans addresses a throng of three thousand onlookers.

September 16, 1968 - The U.S. House passes the North Cascades National Park bill.

September 19, 1968 - The U.S. Senate passes the House's amended bill and sends it to the White House.

October 2, 1968 - The North Cascades Act of 1968 is signed into law by President Johnson. The Act designates lands in two national wilderness areas, two national recreation areas, and a national park, encompassing a total of 1,660,000 acres.

October 2, 1968 - The Wild and Scenic Rivers Act and the National Scenic Trails Act are signed by President Johnson on the same day that new parks are created in the North Cascades and the Redwoods.

October 26, 1968 - The NCCC and friends (250 people) assemble in Seattle to celebrate the new park.

February 25, 1969 - Conservative Congressman John Saylor of Pennsylvania introduces in Congress H.R. 7616, a bill to add Mount Baker and Granite Creek to North Cascades National Park.

1969 - Mike McCloskey succeeds Dave Brower as Executive Director of Sierra Club.

1969 - Senator Jackson receives the Sierra Club's John Muir award.

October 30, 1969 - The Seattle City Council narrowly approves City Light's request to seek a license from the Federal Power Commission for High Ross Dam. The raised dam would destroy the magnificent cedar grove in Big Beaver Valley and flood more than 6,000 acres of land north of the border.

December 9, 1969 - Run Out Skagit Spoilers (ROSS), a coalition of groups opposed to High Ross Dam, is founded in British Columbia.

June 3–4, 1970 - The Park Service holds public hearings in Mount Vernon on the General Development Plan (or Master Plan) and preliminary Wilderness Study for the North Cascades National Park Complex. On July 15th and 18th, the Forest Service holds public meetings in Wenatchee and Mount Vernon on its final recreation plan for Mount Baker, Okanogan, and Wenatchee National Forests.

1970 - NCCC's Joe and Margaret Miller carry out a pioneering survey of the ecosystems and cedar groves of the Big Beaver, Little Beaver, Baker, Chilliwack, and Silver Creek valleys.

1970 - The Stehekin Valley Road is deeded to the federal government by Chelan County.

December 2, 1970 - Seattle Mayor Wes Uhlman writes the City Council opposing High Ross Dam. Twelve days later, the council rebukes the mayor and requires City Light to move forward with the project. NCCC steps up its opposition and establishes the Skagit Defense Fund.

1971 - The Forest Service begins a system-wide Roadless Area Review and Evaluation known as RARE. The results are strongly biased against wilderness protection and the Sierra Club files suit. The courts rule that the Forest Service can do no logging, road-building, or other activity that compromises the wilderness character of roadless areas until it complies with the National Environmental Policy Act.

December 1971 - The Washington State Ecological Commission votes to oppose High Ross Dam, a position supported by Governor Evans. Several years later Governor Dixie Lee Ray (D) abruptly reverses the state's position, but the move lacks credibility.

1972 - NCCC joins Canadian groups to begin the push for an international park to help protect adjoining wildlands within British Columbia.

September 2, 1972 - The North Cross-State Highway (SR 20) officially opens, with ceremonies held at Winthrop, Newhalem, and Sedro Woolley.

1976 - Congress passes the National Forest Management Act (NFMA) amending the 1974

Forest and Rangeland Renewable Resources Planning Act (RPA). The new law requires periodic assessment of resources, programs, and multiple-use goals.

1976 - The Mountaineers publishes a new exhibit-format book, *The Alpine Lakes*.

1976 - The Alpine Lakes Wilderness Area is established by Congress.

July 5, 1977 - The Federal Power Commission approves High Ross Dam. NCCC and ROSS file an appeal in federal court, which is denied in 1980. The battle turns to the province of British Columbia where a backroom deal that was struck with City Light in 1967 is publicly challenged.

July 12, 1976 - President Gerald Ford signs the Alpine Lakes Wilderness Act protecting 305,400 acres (another 57,400 acres would be added in 1984).

1978 - The year-round population of Stehekin is approximately 100, nearly twice the number five years earlier, and almost triple the number wintering over when the park was created in 1968. Later the number of permanent residents would fluctuate considerably as the number of seasonal residents trended upward. By 1978, annual firewood consumption from public lands had increased dramatically to 245 cords.

1979 - Following the first failed RARE study, the RARE II assessment is concluded. After a challenge by conservationists, the RARE II environmental impact statement is rejected in federal court in October 1982.

December 2, 1980 - President Jimmy Carter signs the Alaska National Interest Lands Conservation Act (ANILCA), which places 104.3 million acres in national parks, wildlife refuges, and other protective units.

August 27, 1982 - Mount Saint Helens National Volcanic Monument is established. NCCC had proposed protection of the area in 1963.

February 1, 1983 - Assistant Secretary of Agriculture John Crowell, who for more than twenty-five years was general counsel for Louisiana Pacific (one of the major purchasers of national forest timber), simply gives up on the entire RARE process and announces that all roadless areas will be given another look in the normal course of forest planning.

September 1983 - Former governor Dan Evans is appointed to the U.S. Senate upon the sudden death of Senator Jackson.

March 30, 1983 - The 14-year battle against High Ross Dam ends when the City of Seattle and the Province of British Columbia sign an agreement leading to the Ross Dam treaty between the U.S. and Canada, ratified on April 2, 1984. The Treaty also establishes the Skagit Environmental Endowment Commission which is directed to fund conservation, recreation and education projects in the upper Skagit watershed for 80 years.

1984 - To showcase the statewide wilderness campaign (underway since the RARE II), The Mountaineers publishes *Washington Wilderness: The Unfinished Work*.

July 3, 1984 - President Ronald Reagan quietly signs the Washington Wilderness Act, adding eighteen units (1,031,758 acres) to the state's share of the National Wilderness System. The same act also creates a Mount Baker National Recreation Area (to accommodate snowmobiles), and designates State Route 20 as the North Cascades Scenic Highway.

1986 - North Cascades National Park archaeologist Bob Mierendorf finds a series of subalpine obsidian quarries and related campsites; prior to this, intensive use of subalpine resources, particularly tool stone, was unknown. The surprising finds reshape old assumptions about the presence of Native Americans in the North Cascades during prehistoric times.

1987 - The first of a series of indigenous chert quarries, used for at least 8,500 years, is discovered. Prior to this, the chronology of Native American use of the North Cascades was based on the 1,500 year-old Newhalem Rockshelter.

October 1987 - The Park Service releases a draft of its "preferred proposal" for a General Management Plan and environmental assessment for the North Cascades National Park Complex.

March 15, 1988 - Senator Evans introduces S. 2165, the Washington Parks Wilderness Bill, for himself and Senator Brock Adams. In the House, an identical bill, H.R. 4146, is introduced by Congressmen John Miller, Al Swift, and Rod Chandler. Both bills identified 634,614 acres of wilderness and 5,226 acres of "potential wilderness" in the North Cascades Complex.

1988 - Grant McConnell's memoir, *Stehekin: A Valley in Time*, is published.

November 16, 1988 - The Washington Parks Wilderness Act is signed by President Reagan. The Act declares 95 percent of Olympic National Park, 97 percent of Mount Rainier National Park, and 93 percent of North Cascades National Park Complex as wilderness.

April 22, 1991 - NCCC secures a Consent Decree from federal district court in Seattle approving settlement of its lawsuit against the Park Service concerning management of the Lake Chelan National Recreation Area. The NPS agrees to prepare an environmental impact statement for its plans.

April 26, 1991 - Seattle City Light and the NCCC-led coalition sign a precedent-setting Settlement Agreement on relicensing of the existing Skagit River dams which requires extensive mitigation of the dams' environmental impacts.

May 13, 1992 - The Park Service releases its *Discussion of Laws Affecting the Administration of Lake Chelan National Recreation Area*. The agency's own legal scholars determine that the principles of the 1916 National Park Act are in full force in national recreation areas administered by the Park Service, *except* for activities that are specifically called out in the legislation creating any given recreation area.

May 1992 - As provided in the 1991 Settlement Agreement, Seattle City Light purchases the former Diablo Lake Resort as the future home for the North Cascade Institute's Environmental Learning Center (completed in 2005).

1993 - President Clinton convenes a Northwest Forest Summit in Portland, Oregon, the outcome of which will decide the fate of ancient forests and spotted owls from Washington to northern California.

1994 - Following a controversial first draft, the environmental impact statement for a revised Northwest Forest Plan is released. Considered by conservationists to be improved but inadequate, parties on both sides of the debate sue in federal court. In December 1994, Judge William Dwyer rejects the lawsuits and the plan is upheld. It remains in effect today, but has been weakened substantially by former timber lobbyists and other Bush II appointees within the federal agencies.

September 1996 - President Clinton proclaims 1.9 million acres of Bureau of Land Management lands in southern Utah as the Grand Staircase–Escalante National Monument.

January 1998 - Mardy Murie, at 95, receives the Presidential Medal of Freedom from President Clinton.

1998 - An administrative history of the North Cascades, *Contested Terrain*, by David Louter, is published by the National Park Service.

1998 - A Wild Washington Campaign embarks on the cause for new wilderness areas in Washington, including many of the areas that were omitted from the 1984 Washington Wilderness Act. Local working groups are, or soon become, active within each national forest.

August 1999 - Edgar Wayburn, at 92, receives the Presidential Medal of Freedom from President Clinton.

October 1999 - President Clinton issues an Executive Order that creates the Roadless Initiative intended to prohibit commercial logging and roadbuilding on most of 58.5 million acres of national forests in the U.S. The plan generates 1.5 million public comments, vastly favoring protection.

January 2001 - President Clinton approves the Roadless Area Conservation Rule. The Bush II administration would soon dedicate itself to overturning it.

November 2002 - A bill for a new Wild Sky Wilderness south of Glacier Peak wins broad bipartisan support in Washington State and is passed in the U.S. Senate. The Wild Sky would be the first new wilderness in Washington in 14 years and is supported by the state's Congressional delegation, former governors, and the mayors of 66 communities in Western Washington. Nevertheless, notoriously anti-environmental Congressman Richard Pombo (R) of California chairs the House committee that oversees the legislation and blatantly obstructs movement on the bill. Pombo also works aggressively for corporate interests to gut the Endangered Species Act and allow oil drilling in the Arctic National Wildlife Refuge.

October 2003 - A major flood eliminates portions of the upper Stehekin Valley Road and the Park Service proposes its permanent closure at Carwash Falls. NCCC supports this position which would not only help reclaim the wilderness character of the valley, but potentially save taxpayers millions of dollars in current and future repairs.

April 23–24, 2004 - The Northwest Wilderness Conference in Seattle celebrates the 40-year anniversary of the Wilderness Act.

May 2005 - Predictably, the Bush II administration repeals the Roadless Rule and invites state governors to petition for areas they believe should remain roadless, but with no assurance those areas will be protected. Many organizations, led by Earthjustice, challenge the move.

2005 - Evidence of Native American presence in the North Cascades (in the vicinity of Cascade Pass) is dated at 9,000 years (the oldest yet discovered) and provides a record of indigenous travel across the spine of the range, as well as the use of tool stone and other resources along the crest.

August 2005 - California, Oregon, and New Mexico file suit to block the Bush II administration's roadless area petition process and call for reinstatement of the Clinton Roadless Rule.

February 2, 2006 - Washington State joins the lawsuit to reinstate roadless area protections. Montana and Maine also add their support to the effort.

August 17, 2006 - Park Superintendent Bill Palleck announces a final decision to close the upper 9.9 miles of the Stehekin Valley Road from Car Wash Falls to Cottonwood Camp, a major victory for wilderness recovery in this beautiful remote valley.

September 20, 2006 - A federal district court rules in favor of the states and reinstates the Roadless Rule.

1968 NORTH CASCADES ACT

Signed into law by President Lyndon Baines Johnson
October 2, 1968

NORTH CASCADES COMPLEX

An Act to establish the North Cascades National Park and Ross Lake and Lake Chelan National Recreation Areas, to designate the Pasayten Wilderness and to modify the Glacier Peak Wilderness, in the State of Washington, and for other purposes. (82 Stat. 926)

Be it enacted by the Senate and House of Representatives of the United States of America in Congress assembled,

TITLE I – NORTH CASCADES NATIONAL PARK

SEC. 101. In order to preserve for the benefit, use, and inspiration of present and future generations certain majestic mountain scenery, snowfields, glaciers, alpine meadows, and other unique natural features in the North Cascade Mountains of the State of Washington, there is hereby established, subject to valid existing rights, the North Cascades National Park (hereinafter referred to in this Act as the "park"). The park shall consist of the lands, waters, and interests therein within the area designated "national park" on the map entitled "Proposed Management Units, North Cascades, Washington," numbered NP-CAS-7002, and dated October 1967. The map shall be on file and available for public inspection in the office of the Director, National Park Service, Department of the Interior, and in the office of the Chief, Forest Service, Department of Agriculture.

TITLE II – ROSS LAKE AND LAKE CHELAN NATIONAL RECREATION AREAS

Sec. 201. In order to provide for the public outdoor recreation use and enjoyment of portions of the Skagit River and Ross, Diablo, and Gorge Lakes, together with the surrounding lands, and for the conservation of the scenic, scientific, historic, and other values contributing to public enjoyment of such lands and waters, there is hereby established, subject to valid existing rights, the Ross Lake National Recreation Area (hereinafter referred to in this Act as the "recreation area") . The recreation area shall consist of the lands and waters within the area designated "Ross Lake National Recreation Area" on the map referred to in section 101 of this Act.

SEC. 202. In order to provide for the public outdoor recreation use and enjoyment of portions of the Stehekin River and Lake Chelan, together with the surrounding lands, and for time conservation of the scenic, scientific, historic, and other values contributing to public enjoyment of such lands and waters, there is hereby established, subject to valid existing rights, the Lake Chelan National Recreation Area (hereinafter referred to in this Act as the "recreation area"). The recreation area shall consist of the lands and waters within the area designated "Lake Chelan National Recreation Area" on the map referred to in section 101 of this Act.

TITLE III – LAND ACQUISITION

SEC. 301. Within the boundaries of the park and recreation areas, the Secretary of the Interior (hereinafter referred to in this Act as the "Secretary") may acquire lands, waters, and interests therein by donation, purchase with donated or appropriated funds, or exchange, except that he may not acquire any such interests within the recreation areas without the consent of the owner, so long as the lands are devoted to uses compatible with the purposes of this Act. Lands owned by the State of Washington or any political subdivision thereof may be acquired only by donation. Federal property within the boundaries of the park and recreation areas is hereby transferred to the administrative jurisdiction of the Secretary for administration by him as part of the park and recreation areas. The national forest land within such boundaries is hereby eliminated from the national forests within which it was heretofore located.

SEC. 302. In exercising his authority to acquire property by exchange, the Secretary may accept title to any non-Federal property within the boundaries of the park and recreation areas and in exchange therefor he may convey to the grantor of such property any federally owned property under his jurisdiction in the State of Washington which he classifies as suitable for exchange or other disposal. The values of the properties so exchanged either shall be approximately equal, or if they are not approximately equal the values shall be equalized by the payment of cash to the grantor or to the Secretary as the circumstances require.

SEC. 303. Any owner of property acquired by the Secretary which on the date of acquisition is used for agricultural or single-family residential purposes, or for commercial purposes which he finds are compatible with the use and development of the park or the recreation areas, may, as a condition of such acquisition, retain the right of use and occupancy of the property for the same purposes for which it was used on such date, for a period ending at the death of the owner or the death of his spouse, whichever occurs later, or for a fixed term of not to exceed twenty-five years, whichever the owner may elect. Any right so retained may during its existence be transferred or assigned. Any right so retained may be terminated by the Secretary at any time after the date upon which any use of the property occurs which he finds is a use other than one which existed on the date of acquisition. In the event the Secretary terminates a right of use and occupancy under this section, he shall pay to the owner of the right the fair market value of the portion of said right which remains unexpired on the date of termination.

TITLE IV – ADMINISTRATIVE PROVISIONS

SEC. 401. The Secretary shall administer the park in accordance with the Act, of August 25, 1916 (39 Stat. 535; 16 U.S.C. 1-4), as amended and supplemented.

Sec. 402. (a) The Secretary shall administer the recreation areas in a manner which in his judgment will best provide for (1) public outdoor recreation benefits; (2) conservation of scenic, scientific, historic, and other values contributing to public enjoyment: and (3) such management, utilization, and disposal of renewable natural resources and the continuation of such existing uses and developments as will promote or are compatible with, or do not significantly impair, public recreation and conservation of the scenic, scientific, historic. or other values contributing to public enjoyment. In administering the recreation areas, the Secretary may utilize such statutory authorities pertaining to the administration of the national park system, and such statutory authorities otherwise available to him for the conservation and management of natural resources as he deems appropriate for recreation and preservation purposes and for resource development compatible therewith.

(b) The lands within the recreation areas, subject to valid existing rights, are hereby withdrawn from location. entry, and patent under the United States mining laws. The Secretary, under such reasonable regulations as he deems appropriate, may permit the removal of the nonleasable minerals from lands or interest in lands within the recreation areas in the manner prescribed by section 10 of the Act of August 4, 1939, as amended (53 Stat. 1196; 43 U.S.C. 387), and he may permit the removal of leasable minerals from lands or interests in lands within the recreation areas in accordance with the Mineral Leasing Act of February 25, 1920, as amended (30 U.S.C. 181 et seq.). or the Acquired Lands Mineral Leasing Act of August 7,1947 (30 U.S.C. 351 et seq.), if he finds that such disposition would not have significant adverse effects on the administration of the recreation areas.

(c) All receipts derived from permits and leases issued on lands or interests in lands within the recreation areas under the Mineral Leasing Act of February 25, 1920, as amended, or the Acquired Lands Mineral Leasing Act of August 7, 1947, shall be disposed of as provided in the applicable Act; and receipts from the disposition of non leasable minerals within the recreation areas shall be disposed of in the same manner as moneys received from the sale of public lands

(d) The Secretary shall permit hunting and fishing on lands and waters under his jurisdiction within the boundaries of the recreation areas in accordance with applicable laws of the United States and of the State of Washington, except that the Secretary may designate zones where, and establish periods when, no hunting or fishing shall be permitted for reasons of public safety, administration, fish and wildlife management, or public use and enjoyment. Except in emergencies, any regulations of the Secretary pursuant to this section shall be put into effect only after consultation with the Department of Game of the State of Washington.

(e) The Secretary shall not permit the construction or use of any road within the park which would provide vehicular access from the North Cross State Highway to the Stehekin Road. Neither shall he permit the construction or use of any permanent road which would provide vehicular access between May Creek and Hozomeen along the east side of Ross Lake.

TITLE V – SPECIAL PROVISIONS

SEC. 501. The distributive shares of the respective counties of receipts from the national forests from which the national park and recreation areas are created, as paid under the provisions of the Act of May 23, 1908 (35 Stat. 260), as amended (16 U.S.C. 500), shall not be effected by the elimination of lands from such national forests by the enactment of this Act.

SEC. 502. Where any Federal lands included in the park or recreation areas are legally occupied or utilized on the effective date of this Act for any purpose, pursuant to a contract, lease, permit, or license issued or authorized by any department establishment, or agency of the United States, the Secretary shall permit the persons holding such privileges to continue in the exercise thereof, subject to the terms and conditions thereof, for the remainder of the term of the contract, lease, permit, or license or for such longer period of time as the Secretary deems appropriate.

SEC. 503. Nothing in this Act shall be construed to affect adversely or to authorize any Federal agency to take any action that would affect adversely any rights or privileges of the State of Washington in property within the Ross Lake National Recreation Area which is being utilized for the North Cross State Highway.

SEC. 504. Within two years from the date of enactment of this Act, the Secretary of the Interior and the Secretary of Agriculture shall agree on the designation of areas within the park or recreation areas or within national forests adjacent to the park and recreation areas needed for public use facilities and for administrative purposes by the Secretary of Agriculture or the Secretary of the Interior, respectively. The are as so designated shall be administered in a manner that is mutually agreeable to the two Secretaries, and such public use facilities, including interpretive centers, visitor contact stations, lodges, campsites, and ski lifts, shall be constructed according to a plan agreed upon by the two Secretaries.

SEC. 505. Nothing in this Act shall be construed to supersede, repeal, modify, or impair the jurisdiction of the Federal Power Commission under the Federal Power Act (41 Stat. 1063), as amended (16 U.S.C. 791a et seq.), in the recreation areas.

SEC. 506. There are hereby authorized to be appropriated such sums as may be necessary to carry out the purposes of this Act, but not more than $3,500,000 shall be appropriated for the acquisition of lands or interest in lands.

TITLE VI – WILDERNESS

SEC. 601. (a) In order to further the purposes of the Wilderness Act, there is hereby designated, subject to valid existing rights, the Pasayten Wilderness within and as a part of the Okanogan National Forest and the Mount Baker National Forest, comprising an area of about five hundred thousand acres lying east of Ross Lake, as generally depicted in the area designated as "Pasayten Wilderness" on the map referred to in section 101 of this Act.

(b) The previous classification of the North Cascades Primitive Area is hereby abolished.

SEC. 602. The boundaries of the Glacier Peak Wilderness, an area classified as such more than thirty days before the effective date of the Wilderness Act and being within and a part of the Wenatchee National Forest and the Mount Baker National Forest, subject to valid existing rights, are hereby extended to include portions of the Suiattle River corridor and the White Chuck River corridor on the western side thereof, comprising areas totaling about ten thousand acres, as depicted in the area designated as "Additions to Glacier Peak Wilderness" on the map referred to in section 101 of this Act.

SEC. 603. (a) As soon as practicable after this Act takes effect, the Secretary of Agriculture shall file a map and legal description of the Pasayten Wilderness and of the Glacier Peak Wilderness, as hereby modified, with the Interior and Insular Affairs Committees of the United States Senate and House of Representatives, and such descriptions shall have the same force and effect as if included in this Act : Provided, however, That correction of clerical or typographical errors in such legal descriptions and maps may be made.

(b) Upon the filing of the legal descriptions and maps as provided for in subsection (a) of this section the Pasayten Wilderness and the additions to the Glacier Peak Wilderness shall be administered by the Secretary of Agriculture in accordance with the provisions of the Wilderness Act and thereafter shall be subject to the provisions of the Wilderness Act governing areas designated by that Act as wilderness areas, except that any reference in such provisions to the effective date of the Wilderness Act shall be deemed to be a reference to the effective date of this Act.

SEC. 604. Within two years from the date of enactment of this Act, the Secretary of the Interior shall review the area within the North Cascades National Park, including the Picket Range area and the Eldorado Peaks area and shall report to the president, in accordance with subsections 3(c) and 3(d) of the Wilderness Act (78 Stat. 890; 16 U.S.C. 1132 (c) and (d)), his recommendation as to the suitability or nonsuitability of any area within the park for preservation as wilderness, and any designation of any such area as a wilderness area shall be accomplished in accordance with said subsections of the Wilderness Act.

1988 Washington Parks Wilderness Act

Signed into law by President Ronald Reagan
November 16, 1988

(EXCERPT) To designate wilderness within Olympic National Park, Mount Rainier National Park, and North Cascades National Park Service Complex in the State of Washington, and for other purposes.

TITLE II—NORTH CASCADES NATIONAL PARK SERVICE COMPLEX WILDERNESS

SEC. 201. DESIGNATION

(a) WILDERNESS.—In furtherance of the purposes of the Wilderness Act, certain lands in the North Cascades National Park, Ross Lake National Recreation Area, and Lake Chelan National Recreation Area, Washington, which—

(1) comprise approximately six hundred and thirty-four thousand six hundred and fourteen acres of wilderness, and approximately five thousand two hundred and twenty-six acres of potential wilderness additions, and

(2) are depicted on a map entitled "Wilderness Boundary, North Cascades National Park Service Complex, Washington," numbered 168-60-186 and dated August 1988, are hereby designated as wilderness and therefore as components of the National Wilderness Preservation System. Such lands shall be known as the Stephen Mather Wilderness.

SEC. 206. MINERAL RESOURCE USE IN RECREATION AREAS.

Section 402(b) of the [North Cascades] Act of October 2, 1968 is hereby amended to read as follows:

"The lands within the recreation areas, subject to valid existing rights, are hereby withdrawn from all forms of appropriation or disposal under the public land laws, including location, entry, and patent under the United States mining laws, and disposition under the United States mineral leasing laws: *Provided, however,* That within that portion of the Lake Chelan National Recreation Area which is not designated as wilderness, sand, rock and gravel may be made available for sale to the residents of Stehekin for local use so long as such sale and disposal does not have significant adverse effects on the administration of the Lake Chelan National Recreation Area."

"A Discussion of Laws Affecting the Administration of
the Lake Chelan National Recreation Area"
National Park Service, May 13, 1992

IV. THE NPS ORGANIC ACT

By 1970, the national park system had grown to encompass a diverse collection of "superlative natural, historic, and recreation areas in every major region of the United States, its territories and island possessions." That year, Congress, in the NPS General Authorities Act declared:

> That these areas, though distinct in character, are united through their interrelated purposes and resources into one national park system as cumulative expressions of a single national heritage; that, individually and collectively, these areas derive increased national dignity and recognition of their superb environmental quality through their inclusion jointly with each other in one national park system preserved and managed for the benefit and inspiration of all the people of the United States; and that it is the purpose of this Act to include all such areas in the System and to clarify the authorities applicable to the system.

This Act is significant to Lake Chelan NRA because Congress made it clear that all units of the system are equally protected by law without regard to their various titles. It further emphasized that while each unit of the System is to be managed according to its specific enabling statute, each unit is also subject to the purposes and mandates established by the [National Parks] Organic Act to the extent that those mandates do not conflict with the provisions of the units enabling legislation.

Congress further amended the Organic Act on March 27, 1978 (the act expanding Redwoods National Park):

> The authorization of activities shall be construed in light of the high public value and integrity of the National Park System and shall not be exercised in derogation of the values and purposes for which these various areas have been established, except as may have been or shall be directly and specifically provided by Congress.

This amendment makes it clear that the NPS does not have the discretion to authorize activities that are incompatible with, or significantly impair the recreational, scenic, scientific, historic, and other values of Lake Chelan NRA.

The NPS and Management Policies state: "park managers should ascertain park-specific purposes and management direction by reading the park's enabling legislation or proclamation and determine general management direction, not inconsistent with the enabling legislation from the Organic Act. . . . Absent such specific legislative exceptions, general NPS legal mandates and policies apply."

VII. NATIONAL PARK SERVICE AUTHORITY

The applicability of some laws and regulations is dependent on the type of jurisdiction that the Federal government has. . . . The NPS has jurisdiction over certain Federal offenses, such as the Endangered Species Act, which are offenses wherever they are committed. The NPS also has authority to regulate activities on privately owned land that threaten the resources or values of Lake Chelan NRA.

VIII. CONCLUSION

Recreational activity and development is permitted in such manner and by such means as will leave the resources and values unimpaired for the enjoyment of future generations.

NORTH CASCADES CONSERVATION COUNCIL
BOARD OF DIRECTORS, 1957-2007

To right is the year the term ends or was vacated.
★ Denotes current board members in 2007

Elected in 1957

Polly Dyer, *Seattle*	2007★
Patrick Goldsworthy, *Seattle*	2007★
Phil Zalesky, *Everett*	2007★
Dave Brower, *Berkeley*	2000
Grant McConnell, *CA*	1993
Emily Haig, *Seattle*	1976
Charles Hessey, *Naches*	1974
Joseph Collins, *Spokane*	1970
John Warth, *Seattle*	1968
Una Davies, *OR*	1967
Jack Stevens, *Manson, Seattle*	1967
Chester Powell, *Seattle*	1964
Yvonne Prater, *Ellensburg*	1963
Dave Simons, *OR*	1963
Ray Courtney, *Stehekin*	1962
Rod O'Connor, *Bellingham*	1961
Rick Mack, *Sunnyside*	1960
Jack Wilson, *Cashmere*	1960
Art Winder, *Seattle*	1960
Leo Gallagher, *Tacoma*	1959
Ned Graves, *CA*	1959
Phil Hyde, *CA*	1959
Neva Kerrick, *Seattle*	1959
Paul Gerhardt	1958

Elected in 1958

Edith English, *Seattle*	1964
Burr Singleton, *Manson*	1964
Ruth Lampert, *Spokane*	1961
Jess Peck, *Manson*	1961

Elected in 1959

Irving Clark, Jr., *Seattle*	1980
John Anderson, *Seattle*	1970
Byron Fish, *Seattle*	1962
John Osseward, *Seattle*	1962

Elected in 1960

Don Fager, *Wenatchee*	1969
Bill Halliday, *Seattle*	1968
Bill Obeteufer, *OR*	1963

Elected in 1962

Harvey Manning, *Issaquah*	2006
Joe Miller, *Bellevue*	1994
Duke Watson, *Seattle*	1983
Mike McCloskey, *OR, CA*	1978
Hal Foss, *Yakima, Olympia*	1974
Eileen Ryan, *Seattle*	1974
Jesse Epstein, *Seattle*	1970
Fred Darvill, *Mount Vernon*	1967
Art Kruckeberg, *Seattle*	1967
Marion Marts, *Seattle*	1967
Bob Wood, *Bremerton, Seattle*	1967

Elected in 1963

Bob Albrecht, *Seattle*	1965
Henry Kral, *Everett*	1965

Elected in 1965

Louis Huber, *Seattle*	1968
Frank Richardson, *Seattle*	1968

Elected in 1966

Brock Evans, *Seattle*	1974

Elected in 1967

Jim Hodge, *Bellingham*	1967
Vern Morgus, *Shelton*	1967

Elected in 1968

Tom Brucker, *Mercer Island*	2008★
Jim Henriot, *Tacoma*	1974
Rev. Robert Burger, *Port Townsend*	1970
Robert Cole, *Olympia*	1970
Rod Pegues, *Edmonds*	1970

Elected in 1969

Dick Brooks, *Seattle*	1997
Dale Jones, *Seattle*	1990

Elected in 1970

Frank Fickeisen, *Bellevue*	1984
Bill Asplund, *Wenatchee*	1981
Larry Williams, *OR*	1974

Elected in 1971

Dave Fluharty, *Bothell, Seattle*	2007★
Margaret Miller, *Bellevue*	1995
Ken Farquharson, *Vancouver, B.C.*	1985
Walt Halperin, *Seattle*	1979
Bill Nordstrom, *OR*	1978
Ben Shaine, *CA*	1974

Elected in 1976

Charles Ehlert, *Mercer Island, Seattle*	2007★
Rand Jack, *Bellingham*	1990
Susan Marsh, *Bellingham*	1990
Karyl Winn, *Seattle*	1985
Hal Lindstrom, *Bellingham*	1984
Karen Fant, *Seattle*	1983

Elected in 1977

Marc Bardsley, *Snohomish*	2007★
Dick Fiddler, *Seattle*	1981
Eliza Anderson, *Seattle*	1980

Elected in 1980

Rick McGuire, *Seattle*	2007★
Cindy Reid, *Seattle*	1990
Ruth Ittner, *Seattle*	1981
Dave Keyes, *Seattle*	1981

Elected in 1984

Ken Wilcox, *Bellingham*	2007★
Laura Zalesky, *Everett*	2007★
Jim McConnell, *Seattle*	1999
Steve Ralph, *Seattle*	1999
Lyn Fenton, *Seattle*	1990
Al Friedman, *Snohomish*	1990
Lynn Weir, *Seattle*	1990
Willa Halperin, *Seattle*	1988

Keith Kurko, *Seattle*	1988
Kathleen Learned, *Seattle*	1988

Elected in 1988

Oliver Webb, *Stehekin*	1990

Elected in 1989

Mitch Friedman, *Bellingham*	1999

Elected in 1992

Bruce Barnbaum, *Granite Falls*	2007★
Conway Leovy, *Seattle, Kenmore*	2007★
Betty Manning, *Bellevue*	2007★
Leonard Flanagan, *Bellevue*	2000
Peter Hurley, *Seattle*	1999

Elected in 1994

Carolyn McConnell, *Seattle*	2007★
Hazel Wolf, *Seattle*	2000

Elected in 1995

Kevin Herrick, *Seattle*	2006

Elected in 1998

John S. Edwards, *Seattle*	2007★

Elected in 1999

Katy Sauter, *Seattle*	2000
Sharon Stroble, *Seattle*	2000
Dave Ward, *Monroe*	2000

Elected in 2000

Martha Hall, *Anacortes*	2001

Elected in 2001

Karl Forsgaard, *Mercer Island*	2007★
Thom Peters, *Snohomish*	2008★

Elected in 2002

Kevin Geraghty, *Seattle*	2008★

Elected in 2004

Tom Hammond, *Seattle*	2008★

Elected in 2006

Phil Leatherman, *Bainbridge Island*	2009★

Elected in 2007

Jim Davis, *Bellingham*	2011★

NATIONAL PARK DIRECTORS AND SUPERINTENDENTS, 1968-2007

Year	President	Secretary of Interior	NPS Director	PNW Regional Director	NCNP Superintendent
1968	Lyndon Johnson	Stewart Udall	George B. Hartzog, Jr.		Roger Contor
1969	Richard Nixon	Walter J. Hickel			Lowell White
1970				John A Rutter	
1971		Rogers C. B. Morton			
1972					
1973			Ronald H. Walker		
1974	Gerald Ford				
1975		Thomas J. Kleppe	Gary E. Everhardt		
1976				Russell E. Dickenson	
1977	Jimmy Carter	Cecil D. Andrus	William J. Whalen		
1978					Keith Miller
1979					
1980			Russell E. Dickenson	Daniel J. Tobin	
1981	Ronald Reagan	James D. Watt			
1982					
1983					
1984		William P Clark			John J. Reynolds
1985		Donald P. Hodel	William Penn Mott, Jr.	William J. Briggle (Acting)	
1986					
1987				Charles J. Odegaard	
1988					John R. Earnst
1989	George H. W. Bush	Manuel Lujan, Jr.	James M. Ridenour		
1990					
1991					
1992					William F. Paleck
1993	Bill Clinton	Bruce Babbit	Roger G. Kennedy		
1994					
1995					
1996				John J. Reynolds	
1997			Robert Stanton		
1998					
1999					
2000					
2001	George Bush	Gale Norton	Fran P. Mainella		
2002				Jon Jarvis	
2003					
2004					
2005					
2006		Dirk Kempthorne	Mary Bomar		
2007					

INDEX